Cases
in
Strategic Management

Cases
in
Strategic Management

JOHN M. STOPFORD
London Business School

DEREK F. CHANNON
Manchester Business School

JOHN CONSTABLE
Cranfield Institute of Technology
Cranfield School of Management

A Wiley–Interscience Publication

JOHN WILEY & SONS
Chichester · New York · Brisbane · Toronto

Copyright © 1980 by J. M. Stopford, D. F. Channon, and C. J. Constable

Reprinted February 1982

British Library Cataloguing in Publication Data:

Cases in strategic management.
  1. Corporate planning—Great Britain—Case
studies
  I. Stopford, John Morton II. Channon, Derek
French III. Constable, John, *b.1939*
  658.4'01'0722   HD30.28   79-41492

ISBN 0 471 27705 3 (Cloth)
ISBN 0 471 27707 X (Paper)

Typeset by Preface Ltd, Salisbury, Wilts
and printed by Page Bros. (Norwich) Ltd., Norwich

Acknowledgements

Producing a casebook is a collective effort involving many people and wholly dependent upon the goodwill of those whose firms are being described. We acknowledge with gratitude the willingness of all the managers involved to share their experience so that others might learn. We are also grateful for the active support of our colleagues. We acknowledge particularly those who helped in writing the cases or who contributed their own cases: Professor Ram Charan for Bancil and the original version of Solent; Professor Dean Berry for the Lex (D) Case; Dr. Thomas and Professor E. P. Learned for Crown; Mr. Stuart Slatter for Anglian Canners and NSS Newsagents; Mr. Chris Voss for the note on case reports; and our research assistants and students, A. Benedict, D. Brewin, P. Cooper, B. Crowe, P. Edmonds, M. Flash, I. Jones, M. Laner, K. Mayeda, S. Pipe, D. Robinson, W. M. B. Steele, and R. Wagstaff. The Anglian Canners Case was made possible by the generous assistance of Multinational Management Group (MMG) Ltd.

We are also grateful to the following for permission to reproduce copyright material: Extel Statistical Services Ltd., 37/45 Paul Street, London EC2A 3PB; The *Financial Times*; *The Observer; The Guardian*; Moodies Services Ltd; North Western University; Cranfield Institute of Technology; IMEDE; London Business School; and Manchester Business School.

Contents

Preface

This new casebook on strategy and general management has been produced in response to demands for up-to-date materials dealing with European problems that are likely to be of predominant importance to industry in the 1980's. The emphasis in the selection of cases is on British firms, most of which have important European or international activities and competitors. To allow comparisons to be made among strategic issues in different international settings, over a quarter of the cases deal with conditions facing American, Japanese and Continental European firms. A few 'classic' cases have been retained from the authors' earlier casebook. These are cases which have proved particularly successful over several years and in which the problems are as relevant today as they were when the cases were first written.

With a single exception, all the cases were written or adapted at the institutions where the authors are or were teaching Business Policy: Cranfield, IMEDE, London and Manchester. These four business schools all firmly believe that Strategy and Business Policy can only be taught effectively if detailed consideration is given to actual problems and decisions. Thus there is a need for timely and challenging case studies. All the cases in this book have been tested and have proved to be effective means of stimulating the types of analysis and discussion necessary for learning about the complexities of general management and for forming judgments about appropriate actions to be taken.

Strategy or Business Policy is usually one of the central integrative courses in postgraduate and executive general management programmes. The purpose of the course is to study the organisation as a whole so that perspective may be gained on skills developed in functional and technique oriented courses. We teach Business Policy, not because we believe that all participants on courses should immediately become Chief Executives and General Managers, but because all managers will be better managers if they understand the process of strategy and strategic management. Managers in functional areas frequently find it difficult fully to understand why particular decisions are made higher in the organisation which are not optimal from their functional viewpoint. Equally when making decisions in their own areas they may fail to perceive the strategic significance such decisions can have for other parts of the organisation. A clear understanding of policy and strategy should improve the decision making of functional managers. Also, in time, a proportion of students will become general managers and some eventually Chief Executives. On executive programmes some participants have already reached these levels. Whether the time lapse is short or long between the course and the assumption of a general management role, experience shows that the ideas and concepts gained in the classroom will be of great value in the practical context.

The successful general manager needs to be sensitive to the changes taking place in the many faceted environment in which his organisation operates. He must understand how his organisation reached its current competitive position and how its capabilities match the future threats and opportunities posed by the operating environment. He must have imagination to conceive potential new strategies. He must have the skills required to assemble resources, to design and shape new organisational structures and to create a corporate purpose amongst the organisation's employees. Above all, he must have the ability to lead and persistence to ensure that strategies are pursued consistently over time.

It has of course been argued that the skills and attributes of the general manager can only be learned through the hard experience of the real world. We do not accept that argument. We believe that much knowledge and concepts of strategy can be formulated and tested by individuals in the classroom. For this to happen, the teaching material must involve real and significant strategic problems. Teachers must be skilled in extracting the issues from the case studies and in requiring students clearly to articulate and support their points of view. Participants will only gain maximum benefit from the case study method if they prepare the material thoroughly before the class and become fully involved in the classroom discussion. Such discussions simulates and complements 'real world' experience. By the end of the course, participants should have improved their ability to think strategically; that is the main benefit to be gained. Such ability, of course, must eventually be applied and tested in practice before it becomes of real worth.

The case studies in this book cover a wide variety of both strategic problems and issues, and types of organisations. We do not expect that all the cases will appeal equally to a particular teacher. Our aim has been to assemble cases of sufficient number and variety that each teacher will be able to construct a course that fulfils both his own and his students' interests.

For convenience of presentation we have grouped the cases under seven headings:

1. Introduction to Strategic Life Cycles.
2. Industry Structure and Strategy.
3. Managing the External Environment.

4. Planning Systems.
5. Styles of Management.
6. Decision Making and Leadership.
7. Managing Complexity.

These headings suggest the importance in course design of choosing cases that taken together consider concepts and problems of change, of adjustment to external forces, of styles of management, and, above all in a world where firms are becoming increasingly diverse in their spread of activities, of managing complexity. The challenge of the 1980's is for managers to retain control and a coherence of approach during what seems likely to be a turbulent decade.

It must be emphasised that the essence of the issues and problems raised in each case is such as to defy neat categorisation under a single heading. The heading for each case merely indicates a major topic for discussion, not an exclusive one. Thus, for example. *Texas Instruments*, though placed under the heading of Managing Complexity, also provides data and raises issues of planning, of change in the industry structures and of styles of leadership. To a degree, the choice of emphasis in the case discussion is a matter of taste and in the instructor's control.

No successful course that aims to teach concepts and ways of thinking can rely solely on case studies for its material. Other materials, drawn from journals and books, and, when appropriate and possible, visits from practising managers are needed. The assembly of a comprehensive course design is a demanding task. Moreover the preparation of new case material before leading a class discussion can be most time consuming. To assist bona fide teachers, the authors have prepared a Teachers Manual. The Manual includes alternative course outlines, suggestions for supplementary readings and class assignments as well as analytical notes on the teaching content of the cases themselves. In addition, follow-on cases or notes on subsequent events have been included for some of the cases. Follow-on cases have not been published in this book so as to preserve the suspense of decision making without the benefit of hindsight. Enquiries about the Manual should be directed to the Case Clearing House of Great Britain and Ireland, Cranfield Institute of Technology, Cranfield Bedforshire, U.K.

August, 1979

JOHN STOPFORD
DEREK CHANNON
JOHN CONSTABLE

To the Student—Case Preparation

All students, but particularly those of you who have had limited experience of the case study method of teaching, should find the following comments helpful in your efforts to obtain maximum benefit from the use of these case studies. By far the most important point which should always be remembered is that the greater the effort put into preparation and classroom participation, the greater will be the individual benefit. You are seeking to develop your skills of analysis and powers of reasoning and persuasion. You will not do this by relying on others to do the preparation and talking.

You must not expect correct and tidy solutions to the case studies. Generally several solutions are possible. Whether one turns out to be better than the others may depend on future events, speed of implementation, personal conviction and behaviour, etc. What the managers of the organisation actually did is not necessarily the best answer. You should not press your class teacher for his 'solution' because that is not the answer either. Indeed it is not his role to provide a solution to the case. His role is to make you think about the situation, formulate your solution and argue for that solution possibly against the opposition of your class colleagues.

In preparing a case you should try and specify:

1. The nature of the problem or problems.
2. The alternative courses of action which are possible.
3. Which course of action you think most appropriate.
4. How you would implement this chosen course of action.

Sometimes the writing of the case emphasises some problems and issues but obscures the most important ones. Here diagnostic skill is essential; the manager often sees the symptoms not the disease. You should be prepared to question all the information given in the case. What is the source of this data or opinion? How reliable is it likely to be? Is the analysis correct? Only by delving below the surface will you discover many of the most important points.

Intuition, imagination and creative thought are as much a part of your preparation as is quantitative analysis of the data available. However, wherever it is possible to support your judgement and intuition with quantitative analysis, you should do so. Failure to use the available information properly weakens your argument.

As a practical guide to the preparation of cases the student will probably find that the best plan is to begin by reading fairly quickly through the whole case, next study the type and form of any data available, and then go back to examine the material in detail. The best method of assessing whether or not you have any firm conclusions is to try to write down, on one side of paper, your views and supporting evidence. If you cannot do this then you are not really ready to discuss the case with other students. The time taken to reach this stage will, of course, depend on your experience of case analysis and the scope of the case. As a rough guide it will usually be a minimum of two hours, on average about three hours. You will then be ready, if necessary, to write up a full case report along the lines indicated in the Appendix.

Introduction to Strategic
Life Cycles

1

Kitchen Queen Group Limited

On November 10, 1978 the Kitchen Queen Group made a public offer for sale of 6.81 million ordinary shares of 10p each at a price of 29p per share payable in full on application. The offer represented a milestone in the career of Neville Johnson, Kitchen Queen's 35 year old Chairman and Chief Executive, who had started the company in 1965 while working as a sales representative from a rented garage in North Manchester. For fiscal year 1978, the Kitchen Queen Group had sales of over £15 million and a profit after tax of £1.46 million. Details of recent financial performance are given in Exhibits 1 and 2. In the intervening 13 years Mr. Johnson had developed the group to include one of the largest specialist kitchen furniture stores in the North of England and had integrated backward into the production of D.I.Y. kitchen furniture.

THE KITCHEN FURNITURE MARKET

The kitchen furniture market had been transformed by aggressive marketing and promotion. In 1963, sales of kitchen furniture were under £3 million at manufacturers' selling prices, and only 6 per cent of all furniture sales. Then, in the early 1970's as the whole furniture industry grew and increased its share of consumer expenditure kitchen unit sales soared far above the industry norm. By 1975 kitchen storage sales exceeded £122 million and accounted for 25 per cent of total furniture sales.

One company, Hygena, initiated the change. It launched and heavily promoted a moderately priced self-assembly range of kitchen units in the 1970s and thereby brought attractive fitted kitchens within the price range and capability of any-one who could use a screwdriver. The acceptance of the 'fitted kitchen' became widespread as consumers were stimulated by the introduction of new product ranges which transformed the kitchen into an exciting and glamorous room rather than just a work area. At the same time many electrical appliance manufacturers became interested in

EXHIBIT 1

Kitchen Queen Group Profit and Loss Accounts (£'000)

	16 months ended 31st August, 1974	Years ended 31st August			
		1975	1976	1977	1978
Sales	3,043	5,211	10,572	14,829	15,085
Cost of Sales	2,675	4,663	9,430	13,866	13,621
Profit before taxation and extraordinary items	368	548	1,142	963	1,464
Taxation	39	29	56	50	125
Profit after taxation, before extraordinary items	329	519	1,086	913	1,339
Goodwill, written off	140	6	145	158	18
Minority interests	26	16	71	—	—
Extraordinary items	15	25	—	—	—
Dividends	—	—	10	79	82
Retained profit	148	472	860	676	1,239
Adjusted earnings per share	1.3p	2.1p	4.3p	3.6p	5.3p

ANALYSIS OF SALES AND PROFITS

	16 months ended 31st August, 1974	Years ended 31st August			
		1975	1976	1977	1978
Sales					
Retailing	2,026	2,712	4,286	5,087	5,097
Manufacturing	1,017	2,499	6,286	9,742	9,988
	3,043	5,211	10,572	14,829	15,085
Profit					
Retailing	265	320	311	162	391
Manufacturing	103	228	831	801	1,073
	368	548	1,142	963	1,464

EXHIBIT 2
Kitchen Queen Group Balance Sheets and Cash Flow Statements (£'000)

BALANCE SHEETS

	31st August				
	1974	1975	1976	1977	1978
Fixed assets					
Freehold properties	—	—	411	656	925
Long leasehold properties	106	143	160	238	251
Short leasehold properties	2	2	2	2	9
Plant, equipment and motor vehicles	224	350	682	1,585	1,666
	332	495	1,255	2,481	2,851
Hire purchase liabilities	(15)	(43)	(101)	(291)	(275)
Secured loan	—	—	(144)	(119)	(94)
	317	452	1,010	2,071	2,482
Current assets					
Stock and work in progress	483	1,057	1,791	2,759	4,839
Debtors	310	609	592	1,022	1,343
Quoted investment	—	—	—	—	177
Bank and cash balance	257	291	470	146	115
	1,050	1,957	2,853	3,927	6,474
Current liabilities					
Creditors	704	1,371	1,931	2,589	3,088
Taxation	52	17	28	22	80
Bank overdrafts (secured)	256	212	—	788	1,980
Proposed dividends	—	—	—	—	2
	1,012	1,600	1,959	3,399	5,150
Net current assets	38	357	894	528	1,324
	355	809	1,904	2,599	3,806
Deferred liabilities					
Taxation	21	48	70	89	98
Unsecured loan	102	41	41	41	—
Minority interests	29	45	—	—	—
Net tangible assets	203	675	1,793	2,469	3,708
Representing					
Share capital	16	17	417	417	835
Share premium	—	—	201	201	—
Reserves	187	658	1,175	1,851	2,873
	203	675	1,793	2,469	3,708

stimulating replacement demand for products approaching maturity by the introduction of split-level stoves, dishwashers and the like.

It was estimated that 1977 UK production of both factory assembled and self-assembly kitchen units was approximately £175 million with imports accounting for a further £13 million.[1] Since 1971 self-assembly units aimed largely at the DIY market had substantially gained share over factory assembled units and by 1978 accounted for about half the market in money terms and somewhat more in volume. The proportion of households purchasing complete fitted units in 1975 was around 3–5 per cent, representing half to one million purchases. Of the 19 million households in the UK probably only 6 million had completely fitted appliance integrated or partially fitted kitchens by 1976. Most of the others used free standing units. Then from 1976 to 1978 the market underwent a considerable recession, especially in the contract market as the building industry declined.

The market could be subdivided into two sectors: the contract market and retail. Within these sectors, however, the potential purchasers varied greatly. There were large local authorities, individual architects and quantity surveyors, large and small private builders and, finally, individual consumers. Local authority purchasers bought fitted furniture virtually as a commodity with a very low average cost per kitchen. A recent survey estimated that the local authority and other institutional markets represented around 13 per cent of the total market in money terms and around 17 per cent of unit volume sales.[2]

Private houses represented about half the house completions in the UK and were built by nearly 20,000 registered builders. The kitchens provided varied from basic to luxury. Larger builders tended to centralise their purchasing, usually buying direct from manufacturers. Rapidly changing delivery schedules made it increasingly common for large builders to buy units, usually self-assembly, from local builders merchants. On luxury developments it was common to allow house purchasers to specify the type of units. Similarly most units for housing modernisation were specified by the consumer. Overall, builders accounted for around 19 per cent of the market by both value and volume.

The retail and consumer-specified sector accounted for the bulk of the market at around 68 per cent by value and 64 per cent by volume. At the lower end of the market there were many ranges which were almost indistinguishable from one another, while at the top end kitchen units were a fashion-oriented luxury purchase representing probably the most expensive consumer durable after a car. The products were distributed through a wide range of outlets including builders merchants, department stores and specialist retailers. Although the modern kitchen was marketed

---

[1] Sales at manufacturers prices, source, *Business Monitor*.
[2] EIU Retail Business, September 1976

as an idyllic environment it remained basically functional. Thus, despite substantial product differentiation, units were still broadly similar in size and construction.

The total number of outlets was around 7000 while a few manufacturers sold their products direct. Details of sales by different types of distribution outlet are shown in Exhibit 3.

A few manufacturers sold direct to the public through their own showrooms of displays. They tended to have high promotional costs especially for literature, and stressed planning expertise and personal service. The leading direct sales company, Multyflex had sales of less than £1 million in 1975 in a total direct retail sales market of about £4 million.

Builders merchants represented the main outlet for kitchen furniture. These organisations which traditionally sold to the building trade had become increasingly involved in retail selling. It was estimated that some third of their sales were for contract application. A number of large multiple groups were developing, some of which were owned by major corporations such as Thomas Tilling and Marley. Multiples included Sasco/Magnet, Louis G. Ford (part of Thomas Tilling), Marley Building, and, most important, United Builders Merchants (UBM). Sasco/Magnet had over 200 outlets offering only their own brand kitchen units. Sasco sold mainly to the trade while Magnet was retail oriented. UBM had over 100 outlets selling kitchen furniture and some 80 stores with display kitchens. In toto, UBM was thought to sell nearly 10 per cent of total kitchen unit sales, about 60 per cent of which were UBM's own brand units.[1]

Furniture retailers, despite their numbers, held only a small share of the kitchen furniture market. They had traditionally stocked free-standing kitchen cabinets but with the exception of a few groups such as MFI and Queensway most had missed the swing toward fitted kitchens.

Department stores were important both in relation to their number and their potential. John Lewis and Debenhams both offered own brands. However the department stores had not maximised their potential for integrated sales of furniture and appliances and their market share remained low.

Variety, household and DIY stores were a broad category of distribution outlet and in some cases overlapped with builders merchants which had expanded their retail activities. Five larger multiple DIY discount retailers accounted for about half the sales of this channel. These five – Status Discount, Timberland, Texas Discount, Marley Retail and Woolworths – had kitchen unit sales of around £11 million in 1973 while other multiples such as Dodge City, LCP, Big K and Calypso were also expanding fast. In 1978, W. H. Smith, the stationery retailers moved into the DIY superstore market with a bid for LCP. Status, Timberland, Texas

EXHIBIT 3

Kitchen Furniture[1] Distribution Characteristics

Type of Outlet	No. of Outlets	Percentage Stocking Kitchen Units	Percent of Total Sales By Value	Percent of Total Sales By Volume
Manufacturers selling direct[2]	200	100	21	24
Builders merchants	1200	70–85	47	50
Domestic furniture shops	9800	15–25	7	6
Department stores	800	70–85	7	6
Variety and general household stores, wallpaper, paint and DIY stores	3000	40–70	10	9
Specialist kitchen outlets	200–300	50–75	5	3
Electricity and Gas Board showrooms and others	2300	N.A.	3	2

Source: EIU, October 1976

1. Includes sales of kitchen seating and free standing kitchen cabinets.
2. Includes contract as well as retail sales, these accounted for almost 85 per cent of direct sales.

and Marley all offered an own-brand range of kitchen furniture which together with Hygena QA and Di Lusso made up the bulk of sales.

Kitchen centres were a new idea. They tended to feature a high standard of display and to offer a total design service including wall and floor coverings. Imports which tended to be at the top of the market were largely sold through kitchen centres. Kitchen Queen was one of the pioneers of the kitchen centre concept and had one of the largest display areas for kitchens in its Manchester store.

Recently both the Gas and Electricity Boards had introduced 'own brand' kitchen units, both made by Be Modern. However, these showrooms had very low sales levels as their principal objective was the sale of appliances and, in particular split-level cooking units. Few consumers knew that kitchen units were stocked. An uneven stocking policy which meant supplies varied substantially from region to region compounded the problem. Even so, the strength of Boards made it likely that matters would improve.

Trade margins and discounts varied between manufacturers with 40 per cent discount being common. Other manufacturers offered a lower basic discount of around 33–35 per cent with volume steps. In addition a further discount was often offered to display stockists. Discounts were calculated on the basis of recommended retail prices. However this was rarely paid due to intense price competition which also led manufacturers to give special deals. Own brands were not always cheaper than heavily promoted manufacturers brands since they tended not to be discounted whereas manufacturers products were frequently discounted by up to 30 per cent.

Official statistics placed the number of kitchen furniture manufacturers at 235. For simple production the basic machinery required was unsophisticated, a few thousand pounds being adequate to equip a small factory. As a result there were many small manufacturers although on large contracts and increasingly for high volume consumer markets, margins were extremely low and there were advantages in volume production. It was still possible for small and medium-size manufacturers to compete with large ones. A typical cost structure was production labour 20–25 per cent, materials 40–45 per cent, profits and overheads 35–40 per cent. Raw material costs climbed steeply in the mid 1970s due to the high component of imported board and cabinet fittings.

Most fitted furniture was produced in standard modules. Usually units were laminated throughout with white carcases and either colour, woodgrain laminate or timber on doors and drawers. Most manufacturers also offered a range of ancillaries and internal fittings such as vegetable racks and rubbish bins.

Worktops were thicker and used a heavy duty laminate. Self-assembly ranges tended to feature only standard sized worktops while other manufacturers offered worktops which were custom built to fit the precise shape of a kitchen. Recently there had been a further trend to post-formed laminate worktops which were in 1978 available in many self-assembly ranges. The move to increased product differentiation had led to a proliferation of product ranges and increased ranges of features such as textured surfaces, planked wood, metallic and high gloss finishes. The country kitchen had also become popular with natural wood doors and drawer fronts. Some manufacturers offered different drawer and door finishes based upon the same basic frame.

Given the increased popularity of split-level appliances, by 1978 most manufacturers offered hob, oven and refrigerator units designed to fit leading appliance brands. Meanwhile leading unit producers had linked with appliance suppliers for promotional purposes.

Major Competitors

The leading kitchen furniture manufacturer was Hygena, a subsidiary of Norcros. The company had grown rapidly in the early 1970s and had substantially influenced the development of the market by its heavy use of TV advertising and by introducing the QA range, one of the first self-assembly systems in 1969.

In 1974 Hygena's growth was sharply checked by increased competition. Hygena was forced to cut prices in order to try and hold market share and became increasingly dependent upon high discount multiple outlets such as Marley and Woolworth. Further its product line was becoming dated and in need of a facelift. Two-thirds of sales were accounted for by its QA range introduced in 1969 and its System 70 range introduced in 1963. Over the next three years these ranges were replaced by Contour and New QA. At the top of the market Hygena introduced two new ranges, Oakland and Sovereign and led the luxury segment although continental imports were gaining ground. Despite its apparant dominance Hygena lost share sharply from its peak of 21 per cent in 1973 and in 1977 was forced to rationalise its production capacity with factory closures and redundancies. By 1978, Hygena's market share was down to about 9 per cent and the company was struggling back to profitability. However, the company no longer dominated the mass distribution outlets, was no longer the leader in advertising expenditure and had lost its dominance.

Details of other leading manufacturers are shown in Exhibit 4. Grovewood had been increasing its market share as a result of a modern and well balanced product range including a post-form top option to rival Hygena's Contour and a self-assembly range offering good design features. Wrighton had a solid middle/up market position but its failure to produce a self-assembly range had cost the company market position and its profitability had declined. Eastham produced its own self-assembly and medium-priced ranges but was also a major own label producer for Sankey and UBM. Gower had been losing share in the self-assembly market as a

Leading Manufacturers, Selling Through Builders' Merchants

Company (subsidiary brand)	Approx. Kitchen Unit Turnover, 1975 (£ million)	Ranges		Sample price (£)	Distribution
Grovewood	9.0	Six 5 (Contract) Impact Impact de Luxe Daintymaid Grovewood S.L.	SA SA SA FAU FAU	29.93 56.37 56.37 75.56 92.67	Strength in builders' merchants. No direct contract.
Wrighton	7.5	Californian Pageant Waltham	FAU FAU FAU	51.33 61.08 76.20	Over three-quarters through builders' merchants & kitchen specialists. 1150 display stockists. Some direct contract.
Eastham	6.5	SA E-line 'Own brands' Sankeys Sunline, & U.B.M.		33.37 57.57	900 display stockists. Subsidiary distribution for S.A.
DiLusso	4.5	U.K. Forestar	SA SA	42.02	Supplies only through wholesale distributors. Claims 1800 retail stockists.
Gower	4.0	Module 21 L.A.	SA SA	39.10 56.08	'Up to 1,000'. No direct contract.
Program Meredew	2.8	KF 900 (Contract) Caravelle Mistrale Ultima	FAU SA/FAU SA/FAU FAU	45.15 79.90	(i) Contract, direct (30%+ of turnover) (ii) 200 display outlets, plus wholesaler distribution to smaller outlets.
English Rose	2.8				Builders' merchants & kitchen specialists. No discount, 450 display stockists. No direct contract.
Elizabeth Ann	2.8				As English Rose.

Note: F.A.U. = Factory Assembled, S.A. = Self Assembled
Source: E.I.U., October 1976, p. 64

result of the rise of newcomers especially Di Lusso. The Kitchen Queen subsidiary Di Lusso was the fastest growing self-assembly producer largely as the result of its policy of stocking a wide range of attractive colours and finishes. Schreiber, which was linked with GEC, concentrated on selling a range of self-assembly units through furniture retailers rather than builders merchants or DIY retailers. In addition Schreiber had gained penetration in some electricity showrooms. Own brands were also a growing force in the market and in 1975 were estimated to account for 12–15 per cent of sales. Imports, too, accounted for a growing share of the market especially in the high price segment. German manufacturers notably Poggenpohl and Siematic were the leading importers, the former offering a standard range throughout Europe with an average retail price per kitchen of over £2000, while the latter offered a wider price choice over 9 ranges.

Advertising was mainly devoted to stressing product features and price promotions were extensively used in local press media. In 1976, total advertising on kitchen furniture amounted to £2.4 million mainly devoted to press. Media expenditure was heavily concentrated amongst the major producers and despite cutbacks, Hygena maintained its position as the industry's leading advertiser accounting for 33 per cent of the total. In 1977 and 1978 the dominant position of Hygena was increasingly eroded and in 1978 several firms spent about the same including Schreiber and Di Lusso. Indeed by the end of 1978 Di Lusso claimed to be the major supplier of self-assembly furniture. Advertising expenditures by major spenders are shown in Exhibit 5.

EXHIBIT 5
Advertising Expenditure of Principal Manufacturers
(£'000)

	1976	1978 (3 Quarters)
Hygena	796.1	343.8
Gower	51.7	175.7
Grovewood	189.2	237.3
Moben Continental	—	180.3
Poggenpohl	43.7	103.2
Schreiber	270.5	381.4
Siematic	74.8	135.8
Wrighton	309.8	299.0
Be Modern	—	130.0
Di Lusso	94.5	328.4
Eastham	225.5	150.6
TOTAL:	2381.0	2874.5

Source: MEAL

HISTORY AND BUSINESS OF KITCHEN QUEEN

Mr. Johnson, in recommending the company to prospective shareholders described the development of Kitchen Queen as follows[1]:

'In 1965 I started Kitchen Queen whilst still working as a representative for a plastic laminate company. I rented a garage in North Manchester, bought several kitchen units and, keeping prices to a minimum, began advertising in the classified columns of the *Manchester Evening News*.

'Choice of merchandise was influenced by the problems I had experienced in fitting my own kitchen on getting married. There was simply no one specialising in kitchen furniture and I felt this presented an opportunity of which I could take advantage. At this time the only people who would supply me were the small non-branded jobbing manufacturers to whom I was supplying plastic sheeting. The business made a successful start and very shortly I was forced to look for larger premises. This move took me to a shop in Salford which, once again, the business quickly outgrew. My next move was to a larger shop in the centre of Manchester. The first major move, and probably the most significant took place in 1969 when I moved into 15,000 sq. ft. multi-storey premises in Rochdale Road, Manchester. Until this time I had continued my job with the plastics company, whilst employing full-time staff in my own business. With this move I decided to enter the business full-time and Kitchen Queen Limited was formed.

'During this period it was virtually impossible to see displays of fully fitted kitchens and to compare the products of different manufacturers side by side. With the setting up of the Rochdale Road store we installed our first five kitchen displays. This in itself was no easy matter as at the time none of the major manufacturers would supply us. Plumbers and builders merchants had a vested monopoly over the retail kitchen business and certainly there were no kitchen specialists on the scale we envisaged. We also believed that it was not enough in itself to offer displays. We considered that customers should be offered a complete design, planning and installation service, not confined to kitchen units, design, planning and installation service, not confined to kitchen units, but extending to built in electrical appliances and ceramic wall and floor tiles.

'The formula was successful and, shortly after this, fitted bedroom ranges were introduced again with a complete design, planning and installation service. The major fitted furniture manufacturers, seeing the success of Kitchen Queen, then became interested in supplying the company.

'Early in 1972 we made a decision which was to have a profound and

[1]Letter to Halliday Simpson & Co. reproduced in Offer for Sale document Nov. 10, 1978.

significant effect on the future of the business. As a company we had always used extensive newspaper advertising, yet we had never used the medium of television. We decided to mount an intensive television campaign presenting the displays and the services offered by Kitchen Queen. The advertising was so successful that business escalated to a level even greater than we had envisaged and, as a result, we were supplying fitted kitchens and bedrooms throughout the North-West. In the process we became one of the best known retailers in the Granada television area.

'On planning this campaign we realised that the Rochdale Road premises would not live up to the image portrayed on television, nor be big enough for this expansion. Accordingly, in November 1972 Kitchen Queen moved to its present Manchester retail store in Stocks Street, a modern building, now having a selling area of 32,000 sq. ft.

'At this time deliveries from manufacturers regularly took up to 26 weeks from date of order. Within eighteen months of the move to Stocks Street we acquired warehouses in the immediate vicinity of the store which gave us a warehousing area of 42,000 sq. ft. We began to build up large stocks of furniture, which enabled us to offer our customers very fast or even immediate delivery on a wide range of merchandise which our competitors were offering on extended delivery.

'By late 1972 we had extended our display into self-assembly kitchens, living rooms, and dining rooms, from manufacturers whose names were well known to the public. In the trade the showroom displays were regarded as the finest and most outstanding in the UK. The combination of the extended furniture range, the fast delivery, competitive prices, and heavy advertising maintained the continued high rate of growth.

'I think it is worth pointing out that each of our moves to bigger and better premises had been financed from our own resources.

'In May 1973 I entered into a contract to sell 50 per cent of my holding in Kitchen Queen to Cranleigh Group Limited (Cranleigh) at a total price of £525,000. 25.1 per cent was sold immediately, and the sale of the remaining 24.9 per cent was conditional upon achievement of a profit forecast which was duly met. It was felt that the involvement of a quoted public company would enhance the financial status of the company and enable us to progress with our expansion with a view to ultimate flotation.

'In early 1975, due to the collapse of the stock market and adverse economic conditions the Board of Cranleigh decided to close down their investment division and concentrate upon their manufacturing interests. With my confidence in the record and future of the company, I took this opportunity of re-acquiring these shares at the price of £350,000 sought by Cranleigh. . . .

'In May 1976 Industrial and Commercial Finance Corporation

(ICFC) and its associated company Estate Duties Investment Trust Limited (EDITH) together acquired 10.78 per cent of the share capital of Kitchen Queen Limited from my wife at a price of £300,000.

'Earlier this year we acquired a business called The Room Set Limited, trading from a 33,000 sq. ft. store next to Yorkshire Television Studios in Leeds. We changed the name to Kitchen Queen and introduced the proven Kitchen Queen retailing formula. The store was relaunched in September backed by heavy advertising, both in the press and on television.

'Each of the three main outlets in Manchester, Leeds and Coventry contains the ranges of most major UK and the top EEC kitchen furniture manufacturers, and our own Di Lusso self-assembly kitchen settings and over 25 displays of fitted and self-assembled bedroom furniture. Personal loan facilities are available for customers at all stores by arrangement with leading finance houses.

'The Manchester store also has an extensive DIY department covering many of the needs of the home handyman.

'A further venture has been a move into small shop units in town centres, selling mainly Di Lusso products. The trading name is Kitchens Today and the first unit opened in Hanley in April of this year. The shop has about 20 Di Lusso kitchen displays, a Di Lusso bedroom display, a range of bedroom chests, and wall and sink units. Early trading results are encouraging and as a result of this we are now active in our search for additional sites.'

Di Lusso

Mr. Johnson had also integrated backwards into the production of kitchen furniture. In some ways this venture had been more successful than his retail activities. Describing the purchase of Di Lusso, Mr. Johnson went on

'I think it important to explain why it was decided to acquire a 50 per cent interest in Scala and De Blasio Limited in August 1973. The management at Kitchen Queen were constantly studying the retail market both in this country and the USA, watching trends and developments. It came to the conclusion that the largest potential growth area in Great Britain was in DIY retailing. This was going to result in a very real need for merchandise which could be supplied in quantity, and in a wide range of qualities. Thus it seemed to us that self-assembly furniture was the ideal vehicle through which we could move into the DIY sector as a supplier.

'In September 1974 a further 25.1 per cent of Scala and De Blasio was acquired and in 1975 its name was changed to Di Lusso Kitchens Ltd. In May 1976 Di Lusso became a wholly owned subsidiary of Kitchen Queen Ltd.

'Following the acquisition of Di Lusso, we immediately moved the business from small back street premises into a 170,000 sq. ft. factory just outside Oldham. We purchased modern machinery and were then able to cope with the increasing demand for Di Lusso self-assembly kitchens which subsequently took place. The growth in the market for self-assembly kitchens resulted in very large sales through the DIY outlets. We were helped in this by our own experience in the retail business, and a very effective network of distributors which was quickly set up across the country and equipped to handle Di Lusso furniture.

'The factory was soon in full production with our customers taking as many kitchen units as we could produce. So great was the demand that for a period we were forced to have furniture made by sub-contractors to help us meet orders. Eventually in July 1976 we bought a second factory just outside Rochdale with a further 210,000 sq. ft. and substantially increased the production capacity.

'There has now been a slight change in emphasis as far as distribution is concerned. Whereas initially we were selling solely through distributors, Di Lusso is now also supplying a number of major retailers directly.

'To assist in delivery to such retailers, for whom delivery times are vital, we have now leased a modern warehouse at Horwich (adjacent to the M61) of 170,000 sq. ft. This additional warehousing for finished goods will allow Di Lusso to maintain even levels of production throughout the year and thus to expand its overall capacity by using these stocks to supplement supplies at peak periods of demand.[1]

'The UK market for DIY products has been expanding rapidly for a number of years. We are consequently manufacturing goods with the specific needs of DIY customers in mind. Di Lusso produces several ranges of self-assembly furniture which between them cover the whole spectrum of the market, from the basic self-assembly kitchens to the highest quality furniture. The range is continually being increased both by the addition of new lines and by the extension of existing lines.'

The Di Lusso model line at the end of 1978 consisted of 4 main ranges which were described as follows:

Avanti   — Basic range of kitchen furniture with limited group of

[1]Casewriter's note: In November 1978, Kitchen Queen's property was as follows:

	Sales	Office	(thousand sq. ft.) Warehouse	Manufacturing
Freehold	32	21	15	181
Leasehold	39	17	323	182

A further 33,000 sq. ft. was under construction.

Manufacturing was done in old textile mills, one of which was owned Freehold and the other leased at an annual rent of £177.61.

facing laminates. Worktops in Italian Elm or Classic Onyx Marble. Cost of 300 mm base unit £31.80 at K.Q. discount price.

Roma — Luxury range of self-assembly with postformed contoured worktops in four finishes, Orange Damask, Vellum, Classic Onyx Marble, Classic Traveline Stone and a range of four front laminates including two hessian textured. RRP of a 300 mm base unit £64.84 discounted to £42.15 at K.Q.

Domani — Intermediate range of kitchen furniture with postformed contoured worktops with a choice of six worktop finishes including, Maple, Sunteak and Elm in addition to others in the Roma range and a choice of 5 cupboard front laminates. RRP of a 300 mm base unit £54.09 discounted at K.Q. to £43.30.

Foresta — De luxe self-assembly range of kitchen furniture with cupboard fronts veneered in real oak or mahogany and the same worktop finishes as with Roma plus another marble variant. RRP of a 300 mm base unit £60.32 discounted at K.Q. to £48.25.

Mr. Johnson added,

'Di Lusso displays can now be seen in some 1100 outlets throughout the UK, all planned and installed with the help of our strong technical planning and sales team.

'In the past twelve months we have also exported goods to Scandinavia and the Middle East.

'Di Lusso enjoys very good working relationships with its principal suppliers. It has sufficient warehouse capacity to enable it to buy in quantity and stockpile raw materials, thus obtaining the advantages of bulk purchase and ensuring continuity of supply.

'In the year ended 31 August 1978 one leading manufacturer will have supplied approximately 25 per cent of Di Lusso raw material purchases. Nevertheless, there are a large number of alternative sources of supply open to it.

'Di Lusso products are sold by Kitchen Queen in its retail outlets and in the year ended 31 August 1978 this accounted for approximately 9 per cent of total sales of Di Lusso; Di Lusso in turn accounted for approximately 23 per cent of Kitchen Queen sales.

'We advertise Di Lusso kitchens through the national dailies, home interest magazines and colour supplements. We also occasionally advertise on television. In addition we make large advertising allocations to major customers to be expended in joint advertising in which our products are prominently featured.'

ORGANISATION

Kitchen Queen was subdivided into a series of separate subsidiaries each responsible to the group holding company. Each of the major retail outlets was a separate subsidiary while the Manchester operation was further split into a bedroom subsidiary and kitchen and other furniture.

Mr. Johnson described the key executives in the organisation and their roles as follows:

'I am the Chairman and Chief Executive of the Company and am 35 years old. My responsibility is determination of overall group strategy and the direction of retailing.

'Antonio De Blasio is 37 and one of the founders of Di Lusso. He is managing director of the manufacturing division. Aniello De Blasio is 35, another of the founders of Di Lusso and is now its purchasing and production director.

'Malcolm Roussak, a chartered accountant, is 33 and joined the Group 6 years ago. He is responsible for the overall financial control of the Group. Eric Powell is 58 and joined Kitchen Queen ten years ago as general manager of the retailing division. He is now responsible for coordination of the various activities of the Group.

'Nicola De Blasio is 42 and another of the founders of Di Lusso. He is the works director of the manufacturing division. Harvey Wilson is 27 and joined Kitchen Queen eleven years ago. He is sales director of the retail division.

'On the retail side, there is a general manager, and a manager for each store. They are all trained in the Kitchen Queen methods and carry out the marketing and selling philosophies of the Board.

'At Di Lusso the Chief Accountant heads the accounting department, and a distribution manager has responsibility for transport and warehousing. There are two works managers in charge, respectively, of factory administration and production. The Sales Manager has overall responsibility for sales with individual managers below him for each of domestic sales, export sales, marketing and technical services.'

The Group operated a very extensive staff training policy. Retail staff spend time with the various manufacturers and attend their training courses both in the UK and on the Continent. The Group had 551 employees and the labour relations record was extremely good; staff were considered to be highly motivated. Company policy was to promote from within.

2

Anglian Canners

Anglian Canners Limited manufactured and sold a range of canned food products. In 1976, Anglian's sales were £14.3 million and profit before tax and interest was £815,000. The company was one of the two UK subsidiaries of Amalgamated Food Products Inc., a large US multinational corporation with sales in excess of $US 2 billion. Amalgamated's other UK subsidiary was a large bakery company with sales of over £60 million. These two subsidiaries operated quite independently of each other.

During 1976, losses for the second year in succession were announced and a new management team arrived at Amalgamated. A thorough strategic appraisal by a leading firm of management consultants led to Amalgamated's being re-organised into three major divisions: bakery products, meat products, and diversified products. Anglian Canners was placed in the Diversified Products Group as it was Amalgamated's only canning operation anywhere in the world. At the time of re-organisation, a new President of the Diversified Products Group was appointed from outside the food industry. He was Mr Charles Hodges, aged 45, who had previously been Vice President of a major US conglomerate. He had a reputation for being a tough, no-nonsense manager who was never satisfied with current levels of performance.

Mr Hodges immediately imposed strict financial reporting requirements on all the subsidiaries for which he was responsible. Previously, each company had operated its own control system and had only reported back to Amalgamated on an annual basis. Then Mr Hodges and his team began to appraise the performance and future potential of each of the subsidiary companies under their control. In April 1977 they turned their attention to Anglian Canners.

PRODUCT LINE

Anglian's principal product lines were canned vegetables and fruit, pet food, mushrooms, Irish stew, preserves and certain provision such as

19

EXHIBIT 1
Sales Summary 1972 to 1976

	1972	1973	1974	1975	1976	Gross Margin (as % sales) in 1976
Canned Vegetables						
Processed peas—blues	681	755	976	1,213	1,515	
Processed peas—marrowfats	47	70	164	513	733	
Beans in tomato sauce	773	878	1,333	1,552	1,824	
Garden peas	440	466	558	820	958	16.5
Mixed vegetables	214	269	390	535	656	
Other	339	442	564	755	745	
	2,494	2,880	3,985	5,388	6,431	
Catering Vegetables	325	382	499	763	674	
Canned Fruit	147	156	143	248	270	20.3
Preserves	NIL	1,052	1,462	1,314	1,221	19.2
Other Canned Products						
Irish stew	248	332	339	355	500	13.0
Mushrooms	527	633	730	761	679	14.6
Dog Food	601	881	1,233	1,635	2,137	19.7
Lard	954	1,218	1,770	1,732	1,541	11.3
All Other	717	794	682	692	853	11.5
	£6,013	£8,328	£10,843	£12,888	£14,306	16.1 (average)
Percentage sales increase over previous year	+16%	+38%	+30%	+19%	+11%	

Source: Company Records

imported meats. Exhibit 1 summarises the major product lines and their sales growth from 1972–76.

Over 60% of the total company turnover was sold under one or other of Anglian's brand names and another 10% under the 'Fruity' brand name. The 'Anglian' brand name was used primarily for canned fruit and vegetables, mushrooms, some lard and imported provisions. The 'Fruity' brand name was used primarily for preserves, marmalade, and jam products. Three separate brand names were used for dog food. Private label sales accounted for 24% or £3.4 million, of total company sales. They were heavily concentrated in canned vegetables where they accounted for 46% of total canned vegetables sales, or £3.2 million. Gross margins (sales less cost of goods sold) of the major Anglian product groups varied as Exhibit 1 also shows. Within each product group there were wide differences in margin among product lines, from 6% for some imported provisions to 35% for Anglian canned potatoes.

THE MARKET FOR ANGLIAN'S PRODUCTS

Anglian competed in a number of different segments of the processed food market in the United Kingdom. Exhibit 2 shows the estimated size and historical growth of the market.

Canned Fruit and Vegetables

The total market had been growing at 2% to 3% per year. Certain segments such as carrots and canned new potatoes continued to show sound growth in both the retail and catering markets, while other segments grew only slowly (beans in tomato sauce, mixed vegetables) or even declined (processed peas). Industry production figures fluctuated more than consumption figures, but available data (see Exhibit 2) clearly indicated that whereas overall canned vegetable production continued to expand, albeit slowly, canned fruit showed long term declines. Some items not previously canned (e.g. cauliflower) might develop but over the next three years a fairly static market seemed more likely.

Mushrooms

The UK canned mushroom market doubled between 1970–74 but became static or declining as the UK economy traded down. The market was still considered to have good long term growth potential because per capita mushroom consumption in the UK was still well below that of Europe (33 oz per year versus 42 oz in France and 58 oz in Germany) and canned mushrooms accounted for a relatively low 12% of total mushroom sales in the UK.

EXHIBIT 2

Canned Vegetable and Fruit Production 1967–1975

(Net can content—in 000 tons)	1967	1968	1969	1970	1971	1972	1973	1974	1975
Canned Vegetable									
Garden Peas	90.5	68.3	84.7	104.5	86.1	78.1	69.8	92.3	82.8
Broad Beans	10.7	3.9	7.3	11.3	17.4	15.3	9.2	6.9	6.7
Carrots	77.9	66.2	102.0	99.8	82.1	70.6	74.8	75.1	98.6
Macedoine (mixed vegetables)	16.9	12.5	13.8	21.8	12.1	11.4	14.0	18.2	18.7
Processed peas	174.0	175.2	192.4	182.5	158.6	176.5	178.2	165.1	172.7
Beans in Tomato Sauce	258.2	270.0	260.1	257.8	261.5	296.6	292.6	316.5	331.1
Potatoes	16.5	26.3	24.3	23.5	35.6	33.1	23.3	31.4	24.4
	644.7	622.4	684.6	701.2	663.4	681.6	661.9	705.5	735.0
Canned Fruit									
Strawberries	18.4	15.2	15.7	14.6	19.2	16.4	11.3	18.0	12.6
Other berries & currants	6.4	6.9	6.0	10.1	7.2	5.6	5.2	9.3	5.1
Rhubarb	17.5	20.0	21.6	14.4	12.4	11.6	21.5	20.0	17.8
	42.3	42.1	43.3	39.1	38.8	33.6	38.0	47.3	35.5

Source: Food News
N.B. Care should be taken in interpreting the above data as crop yields fluctuate from year to year.

Dog Food

The canned dog food market had not changed during the previous three years after growing at more than 10% a year from the mid-1960's. Total dog food sales (£120 million) were still rising slowly, but dried and semi-dried products (£35 million) were expanding their market share at the expense of 'wet' meat products (£85 million).

Preserves

The preserve market included jams, conserves, marmalades, fruit curd and honey. The estimated market size in 1976 was about £51 million of which £31 million was jam and £20 million marmalade. In addition, marmalade products for home preparation had an estimated made-up value of about £5 million. The market was relatively static.

Lard

This was also a static market.

COMPETITION

There were 23 canning companies competing in the UK market. This number had declined in recent years as the least efficient firms had found themselves unable to compete effectively. Anglian's competitors tended to be large (often multinational) companies with dominant brands in one or more market segments. Exhibit 3 indicates Anglian's estimated market share and that of the leading companies in each market segment in 1975.

Price and consumer service were the major elements of competition. Branded products usually obtained slightly higher margins over private label products, but price was of over-riding importance in both cases. Only in the markets for dog food and beans in tomato sauce was consumer advertising a major competitive factor. The preserve market in which Anglian competed with its 'Fruity' product range was less of a commodity market and provided manufacturers with greater opportunities for product differentiation. Apart from regular marmalade, most of these products tended to be relatively high margin specialty products competing on the basis of quality and brand image rather than price.

MARKETING POLICIES

Anglian sold its products to over 1,900 accounts throughout the United Kingdom. Twenty five of these represented 51% of total sales (see Exhibit 4).

Anglian's distribution was strongest in the North East, Yorkshire and the

EXHIBIT 3
Estimated 1975 % Market Shares

Brand	Parent Company	Processed Peas	Garden Peas	Carrots	Broad Beans	Potatoes	Beans in Sauce	Mixed Vegetables	Canned Strawberries	Canned Rhubarb	Mushrooms	Irish Stew	Marmalades	'Home-made' Preserves	Canned Dog Foods
Private Label	—	50	45	35	30	8	30	45							9
(Anglian's Private Label included above)															
Anglian	Amal. Foods	3	2	1	1	5	2	10	2	6	16	17			2
Fruity	Amal. Foods	4	4	1				12					1	35	
Batchelors	Unilever	32													
Mortons	Beecham	5	5												
Hartleys	Cadbury/Schweppes		15	8		10									
Chivers & Roses	Cadbury/Schweppes														
Smedleys	Imperial Tobacco		12	12	14	10		8				} 34			
HP	Imperial Tobacco						10								
Lockwoods	Lockwoods Foods			10											
Lincan	Del Monte				25	10									
Yeomans	Mars Ltd														
5 Brands	Pet Foods (Mars)														60
Heinz	Heinz						49								
Crosse & Blackwell	Nestle						11								
Chesswood	RHM Foods										72				
New Forge	Fitch Lovell											33			
Robertsons	Robertsons Foods												42		
Chunky	Quaker														9
Others	—	9	19	31	30	57	—	35	98	94	12	16	33	65	20

Total percentage of all market shares = 100%

Source: Company Records

EXHIBIT 4

Sales by Size of Customer

	Own Brands			Private Label			Total*		
	Sales Value (£'000)	% of Total	No. of Accts.	Sales Value (£'000)	% of Total	No. of Accts.	Sales Value (£'000)	% of Total	No. of Accts.
Annual Purchases									
£100,000 and over	£ 3,910	37%	19	£3,348	93%	6	£ 7,258	51%	25**
£ 50,000– 99,000	1,736	16%	24	128	3%	2	1,864	13%	26
£ 20,000–£49,000	1,650	15%	52	93	3%	3	1,743	12%	55
Up to £19,000	3,411	32%	1,837	29	1%	2	3,441	24%	1,839
	£10,707	100%	1,932	£3,598	100%	13	£14,306	100%	1,915

*Total Number of Accounts does not represent number of buying-points. Some accounts require branch calling.
**Three 'brands' accounts are also private label accounts.
Source: Company Records

North West and weakest in the London–South East area. (See Exhibit 5). In addition, Anglian's distribution was strongest in independent stores throughout the country and in multiples in Scotland and the North East. These strengths were the result of a conscious management policy to select customers where possible who were:

—Not so large that Anglian was unable to meet their requirements
—Located in the North of England thus minimising distribution costs from the Norfolk warehouse
—Less likely to demand large quantity discounts

Anglian's retail prices were generally in line with its competitors, except that:

—Anglian was able to obtain slightly higher prices for mixed vegetables because of its position as a brand leader in this segment.

EXHIBIT 5
Anglian Sales by Area and by Channel of Distribution

Area	Percentage Share of Total Grocery Sales*	Percentage Share of Anglian Sales**
Scotland	9	4
Newcastle (Tyne-Tees)	5	11
Yorkshire	8	18
North West	13	21
Midlands	14	15
South Wales	—	4
South West	9	5
London and South	34	14
Rest	8	8
	100%	100%

Area	Multiples		Co-operatives		Independents		Total A + N
	Anglian	Nielsen	Anglian	Nielsen	Anglian	Nielsen	
Newcastle	53%	46%	1%	21%	46%	33%	100%
Leeds	42%	34%	2%	17%	56%	49%	100%
North West	27%	36%	2%	15%	71%	49%	100%
Notts.	16%	38%	3%	20%	81%	42%	100%
South Wales	10%	31%	3%	15%	87%	54%	100%
South West	11%	42%	3%	11%	86%	47%	100%
London	43%	63%	7%	9%	50%	28%	100%
Scotland	45%	35%	10%	22%	45%	43%	100%

*Nielsen Food Index.
**Anglian's head office sales have been re-allocated to regions based on Nielsen data.
Source: Company Records.

—Anglian branded lard generally sold at a premium over private label and other branded lards.

—In the dog food market, Anglian had positioned its products as good quality low-priced brands.

Anglian emphasised special product promotions with retailers and wholesalers, not consumer advertising. Among competitors' products only beans in tomato sauce, mushrooms, preserves and pet food were heavily advertised by the market leaders. The company relied on private label manufacturing in the beans in tomato sauce market, while it competed on price rather than advertising in the dog food market.

The company had a field sales force of 21 sales representatives and 5 regional Managers who, in addition to their management responsibilities, took responsibility for selected accounts. The 14 private label accounts were however handled direct from Head Office. Only 4 of the 26 managers and representatives were located south of the Midlands. Little in-store merchandising was undertaken, except some 'one-off' displays in individual stores. Some checking of customers' stocks was done in certain outlets.

Anglian's management recognised delivery as a key competitive factor. For this reason, the company had developed a reliable and efficient system of physical distribution.

MANAGEMENT AND ORGANISATION

The Board of Directors of Anglian was comprised entirely of operational executives each with considerable experience in the canning industry. Brief biographical details of the six directors are given in Exhibit 6. That there were no representatives of Amalgamated Foods on the board indicated the freedom which UK management had enjoyed prior to Amalgamated's re-organisation.

All the key decisions are taken by the Chairman and Chief Executive, Mr Moore, although he frequently communicated with and consulted the other directors. Asked to describe his style of management, Mr Moore commented

'I suppose you might say I'm rather paternalistic although I do like people to pull their weight.'

The company employed a total of 576 people of whom 286 were production employees.

MANUFACTURING OPERATIONS

The company had two plants located about 25 miles apart at Kings Lynn and Fakenham. These produced almost all the canned products Anglian

EXHIBIT 6
Composition of Board of Directors

Chairman and Managing Director (Charles Moore)
Prior to joining Anglian and Financial Director in 1963, Mr Moore had been a Manager for an international firm of chartered accountants. He became the Chief Executive of Anglian in 1965. He was a Chartered Accountant.

Marketing Director (Frederick Hubert)
Mr. Hubert had spent eight years in the marketing function and had been Marketing Director for the past two years. He began his career as a sales trainee for Anglian.

Sales Director (Peter Bonner)
Prior to becoming Sales Director in 1976, he was the Director responsible for all contract sales and exports—a responsibility he kept in his new position. Mr. Bonner began his career as a sales representative for Anglian, later becoming Regional Manager in the Midlands area.

Purchasing Director (Ray Forbes)
Prior to taking his present position in 1965, Mr. Forbes had worked his way through the Anglian organisation from sales representative to Regional Manager to Pet Food Products Manager.

Controller (Jack Lebetkin)
A Chartered Secretary, Mr. Lebetkin had been the company's Chief Accountant prior to joining the Board.

Production Director (John Phillips)
Mr. Phillips joined Anglian as Production Manager and soon became Production Director. Immediately prior to joining Anglian he had been manager of the Campbell Soup plant at King's Lynn.

Age and Length of Service

Executive	Age	Length of Service
Moore	51	14 years
Hubert	44	22 years
Bonner	50	34 years
Forbes	59	38 years
Lebetkin	48	9 years
Phillips	52	8 years

sold. Only mushrooms, raspberries and some carrots were bought in from outside suppliers. Of these three, mushrooms were the most important and were purchased from two growers who also were canners.

The Kings Lynn plant had more modern equipment than Fakenham. Three of Kings Lynn's five canning lines were high speed, each capable of producing 400 cans of processed peas per minute and as fast as any in the industry. Fakenham had only medium and low speed lines. Management recognised that the Fakenham plant in particular would benefit from new plant and equipment to increase line speed and improve productivity, and paid considerable attention to plant maintenance, especially to the old equipment.

Both plants operated close to one-shift capacity. Using the 1976 product mix as a guide capacity levels were as follows:

Plant	Capacity (cases per year)
Kings Lynn	3.5 million
Fakenham	1.2 million
Total 1976 Annual Production Capacity	4.7 million cases

Drought had affected 1976 conditions considerably. In more normal years, management considered that existing annual production capacity was about 4.9 million cases. Overtime rather than a partial second shift was used to gain flexibility and greater control over labour costs. A second shift was possible but at Kings Lynn plant effluent regulations would have posed problems. With one shift, the greatest constraint from the point of view of plant equipment was retort (cooking) capacity. To overcome shortages of production capacity particularly for carrots at peak loading periods, Anglian sub-contracted production to other canners. Generally speaking, however, increased demand for Anglian products in recent years had been matched by an increase in plant productivity.

Anglian maintained good relationships with all its suppliers and tended to keep the same ones from year to year. The company made annual contracts ahead of the season with farmers for 80% to 90% of its fruit and vegetable requirements. These contracts usually included a fixed price per ton. For garden peas however, Anglian bought a fixed number based on weight and tenderness. Additional quantities were bought from farmers on the open market when shortages occurred.

Most supplies were obtained from the Lincolnshire–Cambridge–Norfolk area. Those products such as potatoes and rhubarb most easily transported could be purchased at greater distances from the plants. While the bulk of fruit and vegetables were purchased in the UK, some such as beans and processed peas were purchased abroad. In 1976 total foreign purchases of raw materials amounted to £1.75 million.[1]

The company bought almost all its metal cans from Metal Box Limited, the dominant UK supplier of cans. Terms were negotiated every two years and competitive quotations obtained.

---

[1]Includes lard and imported provisions. Only £40,000 of this amount was bought from Amalgamated companies.

EXHIBIT 7

Anglian Canners Limited Consolidated Profit and Loss Statement

	1972	1973	1974	1975	1976
Sales—Factory Products	3,816,195	5,584,368	7,710,809	9,759,310	11,232,256
—Bought-in	2,196,463	2,643,831	3,131,994	3,129,209	3,073,343
	6,012,658	8,328,199	10,842,803	12,888,519	14,305,599
Cost of Sales					
Factory Materials	1,274,820	2,015,485	3,392,950	3,556,071	3,907,041
Factory Cans/Ends	1,074,637	1,546,435	1,639,110	2,391,575	3,027,381
Factory Others (Misc. Packing and					
Fuel and Power	256,073	367,190	408,904	673,654	835,788
Factory Labour (Direct)	182,226	316,491	371,782	456,622	625,388
Factory Overheads	312,045	456,048	542,125	878,187	899,795
Total Factory Products	3,099,801	4,701,649	6,354,871	7,956,109	9,295,393
Brought-in Goods	1,957,229	2,211,235	2,702,537	2,778,920	2,707,679
Total Cost-of-Sales	5,057,030	6,912,884	9,057,408	10,735,029	12,003,072

Distribution Costs	657,261	599,372	498,323	440,678	330,167
Advertising and Promotion	250,580	190,852	119,132	88,713	93,461
Selling and Marketing Expenses	265,609	250,746	225,959	209,604	170,659
Administration—Salaries	164,449	147,882	119,071	112,166	85,765
—Others	150,009	147,746	106,537	104,559	56,163
Trading Profit	814,619	816,892	716,372	459,595	219,413
Interest Expense—U.K.	335,146	349,425	390,864	201,320	78,063
Interest Expense—New York	52,428	42,290	5,200	5,200	Nil
Currency Loss (Gain)	84,637	54,908	(2,303)	558	21,275
Chicago Administration Cost	15,605	14,851	Nil	Nil	Nil
Additional Pension Premium	Nil	40,000	30,000	Nil	Nil
Profit Retained in New York	Nil	Nil	Nil	23,841	Nil
Other	22,000	Nil	Nil	Nil	Nil
Pre-tax Profit	304,803	315,418	292,611	228,676	120,075
Tax	124,005	137,475	143,750	75,052	37,500
After Tax Profit	180,793	177,943	148,861	153,624	82,575
Profit on Compulsory Disposal of Freehold and Leasehold Properties	—	—	—	48,166*	—
Net Income After Taxes	£180,798	£117,943	£148,861	£201,790	£82,575
Depreciation Charged (included in above figures)	£117,132	£113,245	£90,435	£77,131	£52,668

*Resulting from the compulsory sale to the Greater London Council of leased administration and freehold warehouse.

PAST FINANCIAL PERFORMANCE

Anglian had achieved an impressive rate of growth in the period 1971–1976. As Exhibit 7 shows sales had increased from £5.2 million to £14.3 million and trading profit increased from £177,000 to £815,000.

After-tax profits were not considered to be a good measure of the company's profitability, because interest payments on loans from Amalgamated Foods Inc were not always on an arm's-length basis. Interest on the dollar-denominated loans were neither accrued nor paid for many years, although interest on the sterling loan from Amalgamated's other UK subsidiary had always been paid on an arm's-length basis. Had Anglian's borrowings been entirely denominated in Sterling and had arm's-length interest been paid, profit before tax would have been as follows:

			£'000			
	1971	1972	1973	1974	1975	1976
Trading Profit	171	219	460	460	817	815
Interest of £ loan and Overdraft	(102)	(78)	(201)	(391)	(349)	(335)
Interest on $ loans	(23)	(19)	(36)	(48)	(42)	(52)
Profit before Tax	52	122	233	277	426	428

Anglian paid no taxes in the period 1971 to 1976 as a result of accelerated depreciation, the introduction of stock appreciation relief provisions in the UK, and the tax losses acquired when it purchased Fruity Products Limited in 1972. As of year-end 1976, Anglian had a tax loss carry forward of £540,000. Of this amount, £125,000 was the balance of Fruity Products' losses and £415,000 result from the stock appreciation relief provisions. Exhibit 8 shows Anglian's consolidated balance sheet for the past three years.

FUTURE PLANS

In preparation for his appraisal of Anglian, Mr Hodges requested that Anglian prepare a five year sales profit forecast, (Exhibit 9). Management saw a large part of the company's sales growth coming from the consumer vegetable market. Apart from the introduction of one new product, mushy peas, the projections assumed no other new product introductions and no major changes in marketing strategy. Mushy peas had already been test marketed and the company planned to 'go national' during 1977. They were to be sold under the Anglian brand name and were considered to match

EXHIBIT 8
Consolidated Balance Sheets (£'000)

	Dec. 28, 1974	Dec. 27, 1975	Dec. 31, 1976
Current Assets			
Cash	10	1	3
Debtors and Prepayments	1,630	1,700	1,717
Inventories	3,625	3,326	3,848
Total Current Assets	5,265	5,027	5,568
Current Liabilities			
Amalgated Foods Inc.			
$ Short-term financing	212	328	390
Amalgated Foods Ltd.			
£ Short-term financing	300	302	303
Bank Overdraft	2,756	1,890	1,957
Creditors and accrued			
expenses	1,308	1,447	1,515
	4,576	3,967	4,165
Net Current Assets	689	1,060	1,403
Fixed Assets (Net)	621	596	586
Deferred Assets	26	19	12
Total Net Assets Employed	£1,336	£1,675	£2,001
Financed by			
Amalgated Foods Inc.			
$ Term Loan	130	153	182
Deferred Taxation	257	395	511
Equity (Capital stock,			
reserves, P & L account)	949	1,127	1,308
	£1,336	£1,675	£2,001

Source: Company Records.

'Bird's Eye' frozen mushy peas in taste. Sales of this product were expected to reach £700,000 in 1979 and also to reduce sales of processed peas by about £250,000. However, the gross margin on mushy peas was 23% compared to only 10% on processed peas.

The sales projections assumed that production capacity would increase by an additional 150,000 cases per year as a result of equipment replacements and additions that management planned. The following table summarises

EXHIBIT 9

Forecasted Profit and Loss Statements at 1977 Prices (£'000)

	1977*	1978	1979	1980	1981
Net Sales	17,104	19,154	19,649	20,198	20,492
Cost of goods sold	14,336	15,971	16,299	16,729	16,974
Gross Margin	2,768 (16.2%)	3,183 (16.6%)	3,350 (17.0%)	3,469 (17.2%)	3,518 (17.2%)
Overheads					
Warehousing & Distribution	695	771	778	789	793
Advertising & Promotion	330	372	380	387	390
Operating Overheads	593	593	604	604	604
Total Overheads	1,618	1,736	1,762	1,780	1,787
Profit Before Tax, Interest, and Depreciation	1,150	1,447	1,588	1,689	1,731
Total Depreciation	89	165	214	251	263
Profit Before Tax and Interest	£1,061	£1,282	£1,374	£1,438	£1,468
Profit before tax and interest as percentages of Sales	6.2%	6.7%	6.8%	7.1%	7.1%

*Budget figures: including depreciation of £4000 on assets sold during the year.
Source: Company Records.

the planned net capital additions from 1977 to 1981:

Capital Additions (1977–1981)
(1977 prices; £'000)

	1977	1978	1979	1980	1981
Plant and Equipment					
King's Lynn	116	210	213	152	95
Fakenham	219	215	130	90	90
Motor Vehicles (net of disposals)	16	23	23	23	23
Other	10	—	—	—	—
	361	448	366	265	208

Anticipating Mr Hodge's visit, Mr Moore, Anglian's chief executive asked Jack Lebetkin, the company's controller, to project the company's financial requirements up to the end of 1981. Exhibits 10 and 11 show Anglian's projected financial requirements together with the assumptions used.

EXHIBIT 10
Projected Earnings 1977–1981 (at current prices) (£'000)

	1977	1978	1979	1980	1981
Profit before Interest, Tax, and Depreciation	1150	1558	1933	2251	2538
Depreciation	(89)	(168)	(225)	(274)	(299)
Profit before Interest and Tax	1061	1390	1708	1977	2239
Interest	(326)	(615)	(646)	(590)	(450)
Profit before Tax	735	775	1062	1387	1789
Tax	(323)	(402)	(552)	(721)	(930)
Profit after Tax	412	372	510	666	859

Major Assumptions:
1977 figures based on actual monthly costs and prices. For 1978–81 the annual rates of inflation used are 15.4% for 1978 and 10% thereafter.
Budgeted 1977 interest payments assume current financing arrangements between Anglian and parent company. Post 1978 interest payments assume 15% p.a. payable on total borrowings.
Source: Company Records

EXHIBIT 11
Projected Balance Sheet (at December 31st) 1977–1981 (£'000)

	1977	1978	1979	1980	1981
Net Assets Employed					
Net Fixed Assets	862	1198	1444	1552	1588
Inventory	4687	5775	6696	7540	8412
Receivables	2052	2475	2870	3231	3605
Other Current Assets	105	118	140	160	183
Payables	(1796)	(2166)	(2511)	(2827)	(3155)
Net Assets Employed	5910	7400	8639	9656	10633
Capital Employed					
Shareholders' Funds	1720	2092	2602	3268	4127
Deferred Tax	834	1237	1789	2510	3440
Total Borrowings	3356	4071	4248	3878	3066
	5910	7400	8639	9656	10633

Assumptions
1. Inflation assumptions as in Exhibit 10.
2. Current legislation concerning deferred taxation will continue to the end of 1979 and no tax will be payable during the period due to the tax loss carry forward position. Tax is budgeted at 52% except for 1977 when the tax liability is estimated to average only 44%.
3. Receivables, inventories and payables have been estimated as a per cent of sales: receivables (12%); finished goods inventories (22%); raw materials inventories (6%); payables (10.5%).

3

Lesney Products & Company Limited (A)

In 1947 two ex-Servicemen, John W. Odell and Leslie C. Smith put their war gratuities together and started to produce pressure die castings for industry in an old pub in Tottenham, North London.

Odell and Smith built up a steady business with commercial die castings, and in 1949 they made a few die cast toys, more or less as a side line, in order to keep some sections of their small factory fully operating. In 1950 they produced a large model, sixteen inches long, of a state processional coach with a team of horses. Few of these were made however, because with the outbreak of the Korean War there was a ban on the use of zinc for the manufacture of toys.

In 1952 Queen Elizabeth II came to the throne, and with the approaching coronation the Company decided to make the same coach, only in miniature. The coach, containing a mass of detail with a team of horses, was little more than five inches long. It was priced at just 15p, and in the coronation year 1953 over one million of these models were sold. This made the Company realise the potential of producing miniature vehicles, and three more, namely a road-roller, a dumper truck and a cement mixer were put into production. These models were introduced to the British toy trade packed in an imitation matchbox. Thus the MATCHBOX series was born.

The models were priced at 7½p including purchase tax, and this resulted in many people in the toy trade refusing to regard them seriously, and dismissing them as Christmas cracker trinkets. However, there was a rapid growth in demand for MATCHBOX models throughout the United Kingdom by the public.

The demand for the product resulted in the Company moving to larger premises in 1955. It was in this year that the range 'Models of Yesteryear' was introduced. These models appealed not only to children but also to collectors and model enthusiasts throughout the world. In 1957 because of further expansion another move was made to yet larger premises in Hackney Wick in East London. In September 1960, Lesney Products offered 400,000 25p shares to the public at one pound each. The offer was over-subscribed fifteen times.

In 1962 construction began on a purpose-built 200,000 square foot factory in Hackney Wick to augment existing plant. This building was completed at the beginning of 1964, and was entirely equipped with machinery designed, built and installed by Lesney engineers. It was also in this year that Lesney Products purchased the Fred Bonner Corporation in the U.S.A. The Fred Bonner Corporation had been acting as the distributor for Lesney Products throughout the United States.

After 1968 further manufacturing capacity was added in Hackney and Rochford in Essex. The total amount of factory space available by 1970 was expected to exceed one million feet. Anticipated output from these facilities was approximately five and a half million MATCHBOX models per week. Additionally, more than one million commercial die castings were manufactured weekly for companies in the automobile, electrical, textile, radio and television industries, both at home and abroad. Altogether over 6,500 people were employed.

In 1969 wholly owned subsidiaries were formed in Australia and in Canada. These companies were essentially concerned with the distribution of the product, but were also equipped with packaging facilities.

MARKETS

As of 1969, the Company sold its products in the United Kingdom and 130 countries around the world. Approximately 80% of the products were exported and the Company received the Queen's Award to Industry for Exports for the trading years 1965, 1967, 1968 and 1969. 1969 sales represented an increase of 42% over the previous year. The United States represented by far the largest export market, accounting in 1969 for approximately 35% of the Company's total sales. Other major export markets included old 'Commonwealth' countries such as Canada, Australia and South Africa, and European countries, particularly Germany, France and Italy. During 1969 Japan became a major export market. The lesser export markets ranged from countries behind the Iron Curtain to the South American Republics and tiny islands like the Canary Islands, which had one of the highest sales per capita throughout the world.

THE MANUFACTURING PROCESS

By 1969 more than six hundred million MATCHBOX models had been made since the series was first introduced in 1953. The output rate of over five million models per week, involving many tens of millions of parts, had resulted in an extremely sophisticated manufacturing process being developed.

There were three quite separate basic processes in the production of a MATCHBOX model. The first could broadly be described as the design, research and development, tool and pattern making process. The second involved the mass production of the die castings and plastic components, and the painting and plating of the components. The third stage involved the assembly, packaging and shipping of the finished models. The following paragraphs consider each stage in more detail.

Once a vehicle had been selected for introduction into the MATCHBOX range, work commenced from full size drawings supplied by the actual vehicle manufacturer. The first stage was the manufacture of a model carved out of resin blocks. This model, generally called a 'pattern' was usually four times larger than the eventual mass-produced model. This was done to permit any errors in the shape or measurements to be easily detected at this stage, rather than when it was reduced to the smaller size in the tool and die-cutting stage. The pattern was split into two halves, from each of which a resin mould was obtained. This mould was baked to provide a hard reverse impression known as a cataform, which was the basic shape from which the miniatures were eventually die-cast. Skilled tool-makers, using pantograph machines produced a die which was usually one quarter the size of the cataform, with a fine needle cutter similar to a dentist's high-speed drill. Dies were made out of the highest grade of chrome vanadium steel. When the die was cut, it was fitted into a complete mould able to convey cold water, hot metal and hot compressed air in various directions simultaneously.

The second stage involved the use of automatic die-casting machines to produce zinc-based pressure die castings. In 1969, the Company had over 150 such machines all designed, built and installed by the Company's own engineers. Each machine was capable of producing up to 20,000 parts in a day. The rough castings were automatically ejected from the moulds and an endless conveyor system took them to operations known as rumbling and fettling. The rumbling process removed unwanted metal known as sprews runners and risers. The castings, sorted from the unwanted material, which was sent back to the foundry for re-melting, were degreased before paint spraying took place.

Once again the paint spraying machines were unique, having been built to Lesney specifications. The most common type of machine was the rotary spray machine, where models were loaded onto spindle work holders which revolved at high speeds, while multiple spray heads completely covered the models with paint from many directions. The models received up to three coats of paint and three baking processes. A further method of spraying was known as traverse spraying. In this process multiple jets sprayed as they moved slowly backwards and forwards across a moving belt of models, covering them with a fine coat of lead-free paint. The models then passed through ovens which stove-enamelled the paint. After passing through the first oven the models were turned over, allowing a similar operation for the under side. Up to four million components could be stove-enamelled in a single day.

Components were stored between the component manufacturing stage and the assembly stage. 350,000 cubic feet of storage space was used, containing the equivalent of seven million MATCHBOX models.

The third and final stage involved the assembly of the various components. This took place on 60 separate assembly lines. Operations such as the automatic riveting of miniature car chassis to the bodies, the riveting of plastic windows, axle positioning and wheel and tyre attachment took place on each side of the conveyor lines.

After assembly the models were placed in trays which were carried by over head conveyors to the packing section. Female operatives were able to pick up as many as six models at a time from specially constructed trays and place them accurately into boxes. This was done after the packing machine had picked up the flat box, shaped it and sealed the bottom. When the model was placed in the box, the machine sealed the top. Finally, the models moved in box batches to the transit store where electronic selection equipment routed each package to a specific shipping point.

PRODUCT DEVELOPMENT AND INNOVATION

As mentioned previously, the MATCHBOX range was first introduced in 1953. By 1969 there were 75 models in the range. Two new models were introduced every month, whilst two of the older models were withdrawn. The price of a MATCHBOX car had increased from $7\frac{1}{2}$p in 1953 to $12\frac{1}{2}$p in 1969. The real 'price' of a MATCHBOX model had, therefore, remained about stationary, while the 'value' had increase considerably since the models of 1969 were much more complex and sophisticated than the models of 1953. Also mentioned previously were the 'Models of Yesteryear', first introduced in 1955. There were 16 models in this range, retailing at between 30p and 36p. The final model range consisted of the MATCHBOX King-Size. These larger, more complex models retailed at between 31p and 82p. Peripheral products to the model ranges included such items as collectors' cases which held 48 MATCHBOX models (retained at 86p), cardboard layouts (retailed at 15p), and a service station to go with such layouts (retailed at 68p). Combinations of models, packed as gift sets, and retailed between £1.05 and £1.32½ were also available. Finally, veteran car gift sets, such as ash-trays, book-ends and pen-holders, were sold for adults, retailing at from 85p.

In 1968 MATCHBOX Motorways were introduced; these sets, retailed at between £2.15p and £5.15p consisted of track layouts on which ordinary MATCHBOX models could be driven electrically with the use of a small attachment using either battery power or mains power.

1968 was also the year when Mattel Inc., of America, entered the die cast model cars field with the trade name of 'Hotwheels'. Mattel, owned and managed by a husband and wife team, Ruth and Elliott Handler, became a well-known company in 1959 with the introduction of the Barbie doll. The Barbie doll introduced a new concept into children's toys by giving the child a basic toy to which it could add items over a period of time. Until the introduction of Hotwheels Mattel had not been a serious contender in the die cast toy market. Hotwheels, however, contained a basic product innovation in that it had 'friction free' wheels. These wheels, running on a plastic bearing, resulted in a car running many times further for a given 'push', and allowed such things as looping-the-loop and leaping across gaps to be performed. These cars were introduced into the United States market in 1968 and into the British and other markets in 1969. In Britain they retailed at 30p. In response to this product innovation, Lesney Products introduced the Superfast Car. While the first Superfast Cars were introduced towards the end of 1968, problems were experienced throughout 1969 in converting the whole range of MATCHBOX cars to the Superfast type. It was decided that all the basic MATCHBOX models should be manufactured with Superfast type wheels, and retailed at the previous MATCHBOX price, namely 12½p. Plastic track containing loops, jumps and banked curves was introduced with the Superfast along with many other accessories.

INDUSTRIAL PRODUCTS

As described earlier, Lesney was originally established to manufacture pressure die castings for industry. This business was highly competitive and the purchasing power of large customers, e.g. car and appliance manufacturers, limited the die cast manufacturer's profitability to modest levels. Although the industrial die casting business has continued to grow steadily over the years, as a proportion of sales, this side of the business had steadily declined. In 1969 it represented approximately 5% of the Company's activities.

COMPANY ORGANISATION

In 1968 Leslie Smith and Jack Odell still ran and controlled Lesney Products. Between them, as individuals and through family holdings they controlled approximately 55% of the ordinary share capital. They held the positions of joint managing directors. Mr. Smith was responsible for sales, marketing and all financial matters, while Mr. Odell was responsible for the research and development of new products, the tool rooms required to make the dies and for the design and manufacture of special machinery used in the various production processes.

There were only three other directors of the Company. The Chairman, Mr. Tapscott, was a partner in the stock broking firm which had made the offer of Lesney shares to the public in 1960. He had become Chairman at this time. The remaining two directors, Mr. Evans and Mr. Floyd were both full time employees of the Company. Mr. Evans joined the Company in the 1950's and was responsible for the Industrial Products Division and for personnel matters and service functions throughout the Company. Mr. Floyd joined the Company in 1966, after undertaking an assignment as a consultant to reorganise the manufacturing procedures. In 1968 he was responsible for the manufacture of all toy products within the Company.

During 1968 four 'Divisional' directors were also appointed. These posts involved taking responsibility for functional activities rather than Divisions within the Company in the sense that the term 'Division' would normally be used. The four divisional directors were responsible for home sales, export sales, tooling & research and management services. All the personnel appointed were long serving members of the Company.

EXHIBIT 1

Consolidated Profit and Loss Account

	52 Weeks Ended 26th January 1969 (£'000)	52 Weeks Ended 28th January 1968 (£'000)
GROUP TURNOVER	£19,301	£13,024
TRADING PROFIT BEFORE TAXATION	5,558	3,708
Add: Profit on Devaluation of Sterling		71
		3,779
TAXATION	2,767	1,742
PROFIT AFTER TAXATION	2,790	2,036
Deduct: Expenses of Capitalisation of Reserves	—	4
		2,032
Add: Unappropriated Balance from previous year	—	865
	£2,790	£2,897
APPROPRIATIONS Dividends (Gross): On 7½ per cent. Cumulative Preference Shares for the year ended 31st December 1968	53	53
On Ordinary Shares and Restricted Voting Ordinary Shares: Interim of 10½ per cent paid 9th December, 1968 (1968—10 per cent.)	116	110
Recommended Final of 11.49 per cent (1968 11.735 per cent)	126	129
	294	291
Deduct: Waived	53	57
	241	235
TRANSFER TO RESERVE—From Previous Year	—	865
Current Year	2,549	1,797
	£2,790	£2,897

FINANCIAL PERFORMANCE

The financial results of Lesney throughout the 1950's and 1960's were remarkable by any standards. In the trading year ending January 26th 1969, the Company made a profit of £5.56 million on a turnover of £19.30 million. Profit growth for the past seven years had averaged 45% compound per annum. These results placed the Company third in the business growth league published in *Management Today* for the second year running. In June 1968 Lesney shares were being traded at £5.50 giving a price earnings ratio in excess of 50 times and placing a stock market valuation of £120 million on the Company. At the time, this exceeded the stock market valuation of the British Motor Corporation (prior to the merger with Leyland). With bonus issues and the increase in the share price, a Lesney share purchased for £1 in 1960 was worth the equivalent of £110 when the

EXHIBIT 2

Consolidated Balance Sheet

	26th January 1969 (£'000)	28th January 1968 (£'000)
CURRENT ASSETS		
Stocks & Work in Progress	2,089	1,452
Debtors	3,395	3,278
Short Term Deposits	2,364	500
Bank and Cash Balances	91	66
	7,939	5,296
CURRENT LIABILITIES		
Creditors	1,486	1,023
Bank Overdraft	196	364
Current Taxation	1,665	974
Corporation Tax payable 1st January, 1970	1,347	997
Recommended Final Dividend (Gross) less waived	102	101
	4,796	3,459
NET CURRENT ASSETS	3,143	1,837
SUBSIDIARY COMPANIES	—	—
FIXED ASSETS	5,028	3,616
	£8,171	£5,452
CAPITAL AND RESERVE		
Share Capital	1,900	1,900
Reserve	6,271	3,552
	£8,171	£5,452

EXHIBIT 3

Record of Financial Progress as a Public Company

	1969	1968	1967	1966	1965 (54 weeks)	1964	1963	1962	1961
SUMMARY OF BALANCE SHEETS (£'000)									
Fixed Assets	5,028	3,616	2,001	1,838	1,764	1,229	680	575	497
Net Current Assets	3,143	1,837	1,366	422	70	337	469	284	184
TOTAL CAPITAL EMPLOYED	8,171	5,453	3,367	2,260	1,834	1,566	1,149	859	681
Financed as follows:									
Ordinary capital	1,200	1,200	840	840	700	600	450	400	400
Reserves	6,271	3,553	1,827	1,370	863	689	480	308	154
TOTAL FUNDS APPLICABLE TO ORDINARY CAPITAL	7,471	4,753	2,667	2,210	1,563	1,289	930	708	554
Preference capital	700	700	700	—	—	—	—	—	—
Provisions	—	—	—	50	271	277	219	151	127
	8,171	5,453	3,367	2,260	1,834	1,566	1,149	859	681

EARNED FOR SHAREHOLDERS (£'000)								
Before tax	5,558	3,779	2,262	1,359	853	797	558	385	332
After Tax	2,790	2,036	1,271	774	463	425	268	190	166
EARNED ON CAPITAL EMPLOYED (%)								
Before Tax	68	69	67	60	46	51	49	45	49
After Tax	34	37	38	34	25	27	23	22	24
SHARE STATISTICS (adjusted to basis of present ordinary share capital)								
Net asset value per Ordinary Share (5p)	31.25	20.0	11.25	9.17	7.50	6.67	4.58	3.75	2.92
Gross earnings per Ordinary Share (5p)	11.41	8.27	5.19	3.23(a)	3.16	2.90	1.83	1.30	1.13
Gross dividend per Ordinary Share (5p)	1.10	1.09	1.05(b)	1.09	0.88	0.75	0.61	0.50	0.46
Dividends covered by earnings—times	10.4	7.6	4.9	3.0	3.6	3.9	3.0	2.6	2.5

(a) Change to Corporation Tax.
(b) Excludes preference dividend from capitalisation issue to which Ordinary Shareholders also entitled.

shares reached their peak value. Details of the financial results for 1968/69, comparative figures over a ten year period and extracts from the 1969 Chairman's Annual Statement are given in Exhibits 1 to 4.

EXHIBIT 4

EXTRACTS FROM THE 1969 CHAIRMAN'S SPEECH

THE FUTURE

Our sales force has again outsold our capacity to produce. However, very large building projects are now maturing and the second half of the current year should see increasing benefits from new factory, warehouse and office accommodation to provide a floor area ultimately some 50% greater than last year. Additions to premises are stated in the Director's report: particularly, mention should be made of the factory at Rochford, Essex, which has begun the build-up of operations six months ahead of the time envisaged in my statement last year. We should thus be benefiting fully from this important new factory by early in 1970. Accordingly, we have been able to budget for a further very substantial increase in group sales and pre-tax profit, and it should be possible to maintain the company's record of rapid growth.

Our products continue to receive the closest scrutiny and this year we shall be introducing 30 new models in the 'Matchbox' range. Many of these new releases will include 'Superfast', the friction free wheel models which have been well received throughout the world. Due to our rapidly rising volume of output, we have in the main held prices to the trade which is enabling purchasers to receive even better value. Costs, however, continue to rise.

The export market continues to offer the greatest opportunities: during the year we have surveyed the Japanese market, where we believe our sales could be greatly expanded. I would wish that the urgency of the fight for exports could receive greater sympathy in the planning departments of national and local bodies: the daily production of 15,000,000 components in the correct quantities and their integration at the right rate, time and place is a very exacting task. It is made far more difficult and costly if factories have to be widely dispersed, and planning applications are not treated with both an appreciation of the economic facts as well as with urgency.

We are now at the stage where much greater overseas investment is likely to be necessary in order to consolidate fully our leadership in our class of toys throughout the world.

CONCLUSION

At our rate of growth an obvious problem is the obtaining, retention and reward of a rapidly increasing executive. In the United States we are experiencing the greatest difficulty in obtaining top executives of the calibre we demand without some form of equity participation scheme. In the United Kingdom, also, we believe that such a scheme would be most beneficial, not only in attracting suitable executives but also in synchronising the attitudes of professional managers with those of the Company's shareholders.

To support the management we continue to be most anxious to foster a loyal and enthusiastic team. To this end on 18th January we introduced a Company Pension Scheme to cover all male personnel. We are also encouraging attendance at educational establishments and a number have participated in business and other courses.

Finally, I must again express a personal word of thanks and appreciation to all those who have helped to make this past year another of outstanding success.

We have an ambitious budget but one within our means, despite growing competition and the adverse effects of inflation. Our thoughts beyond the current year continue to be optimistic and the Board remains confident that the regulated growth of the company should continue.

P. M. TAPSCOTT

4

NSS Newsagents Limited

NSS had become a national chain retail newsagents by mid 1976. The company had grown rapidly in both sales and profitability. In 1963, NSS had 55 branches with a turnover of £1.6 million. These had increased to 349 in 1976 with an expected turnover of £36.3 million by the end of the year. This case reviews the company's development from 1963 to date and discusses some of its current management problems.

HISTORY AND BUSINESS

NSS was incorporated 1904 as a private company. For nearly 60 years it had remained more or less the same, adding a few new branches from time to time. In 1963, the company's legal advisor, Mr Byam-Cook (senior partner in a firm of City solicitors), acquired a large interest in NSS from Mr George Holmden and his family, the then owners of the company. Sales and profitability continued to grow throughout the 1960's and in 1971 a successful public offering of 1.35 million NSS ordinary (10p) shares was made at a price of 62p per share. The company's financial statements from 1965 and 1975 are summarised in Exhibits 1 and 2.

The company's principal business was the sale from retail shops of newspapers, periodicals, cigarettes, tobacco and confectionery. The range of goods sold included books, toys, greeting cards, fancy goods and records. The relative importance of each of the principal classes of goods sold in 1975 together with the percentage gross margins obtained was as follows:

	Percent of Total Sales	Percent of Total Gross Profit	Percent Gross Margin
Newspaper and periodicals	33%	46%	$27\frac{1}{2}$%
Cigarettes and tobacco	40	22	10
Confectionery	16	15	24
Greeting cards	3		35
Stationery	2	17	30
Books	2		30
Sundries (incl. records)	4		various
	100%	100%	

EXHIBIT 1
NSS Newsagents Limited
Income Statements 1965–1975 (£'000)

	1965	1966	1967	1968	1969	1970	1971	1972	1973	1974	1975
Sales	£3511	£4063	£4124	£5074	£5939	£6931	£8730	£11,213	£14,431	£20,206	£29,272
Gross Profit	687	759	827	1047	1237	1452	1872	2,464	3,138	4,007	5,465
Branch Expenses	459	556	568	684	837	956	1145	1,391	1,747	2,379	3,326
NET BRANCH PROFIT	228	203	258	363	403	496	727	1,073	1,391	1,628	2,139
Head Office Income	25	35	41	50	67	74	100	154	241	322	441
Wholesale Contribution	–	–	–	–	–	–	–	–	–	–	39
Mail Order Contribution	–	–	–	–	–	–	–	–	–	–	(12)
sub-total	253	238	299	413	470	570	827	1,227	1,632	1,950	2,607
Head Office Expenses	113	143	122	146	178	190	261	339	388	504	630
Interest Payable	38	40	36	34	46	44	34	25	23	31	35
PRE-TAX PROFIT	102	55	141	233	246	336	530	863	1,203	1,418	1,942
Tax	39	20	65	10	126	138	205	343	555	742	1,016
NET PROFIT AFTER TAX	63	35	76	126	120	198	325	520	648	676	926
Depreciation included in branch and head office expenses	20	26	27	31	38	42	50	58	76	95	120

c

EXHIBIT 2
NSS Newsagents Limited
Consolidated Balance Sheets (£'000)

	1965	1966	1967	1968	1969	1970	1971	1972	1973	1974	1975
FIXED ASSETS											
Freehold and leasehold properties	£152	£196	£187	£184	£219	£151	£181	£N/A	£386	£504	£616
Retail outlets	783	813	844	1295	1503	1699	1880	N/A	2702	3319	4068
Furniture, fittings and motor vehicles	122	144	154	184	204	228	265	N/A	426	586	767
CURRENT ASSETS											
Stock	291	317	352	484	556	584	731	816	972	1664	2282
Debtors	76	82	98	142	142	181	172	240	293	435	872
Staff loans	16	10	2	10	2	2	20	18	36	54	74
Cash	2	1	10	2	3	4	4	5	120	80	1143
	385	410	462	638	703	771	927	1079	1421	2233	4371

CURRENT LIABILITIES										
Creditors	333	358	385	524	544	726	999	1143	1406	2099	3235
Bank overdraft	303	341	347	313	384	237	135	83	–	121	1
Taxation	40	84	53	65	105	109	136	197	382	544	464
Dividend	–	–	10	34	34	39	76	76	81	91	201
	678	783	795	936	1067	1111	1346	1499	1869	2855	3901
NET CURRENT ASSETS	(291)	(373)	(333)	(298)	(364)	(340)	(419)	(429)	(448)	(622)	470
less deferred taxation	53	34	79	125	151	187	244	390	586	789	1398
NET TANGIBLE ASSETS	713	746	772	1240	1414	1551	1663	2017	2481	2997	4523
CAPITAL EMPLOYED										
Issued share capital	82	82	82	146	146	147	618	618	894	894	1715
Reserves	301	338	360	779	828	965	795	1149	1336	1858	2532
TOTAL SHAREHOLDERS FUNDS	383	420	442	925	974	1112	1413	1767	2231	2753	4283
Debentures	330	330	330	315	440	440	250	250	250	245	240
TOTAL CAPITAL EMPLOYED	713	746	772	1240	1414	1551	1663	2017	2481	2997	4523

The only change in the sales mix over the past ten years had been a slight reduction in sales of cigarettes and tobacco (down from 47% in 1968) and slight increase in sales of newspapers and confectionery (up from 28% and 12% respectively in 1968).

Most branches operated delivery rounds of newspapers and periodicals according to standing orders on weekly or monthly credit terms. The 349 branches, all trading under the name 'NSS', were spread throughout England and Wales but not in Scotland. Branches were situated in or near areas of dense population, and were generally in a parade of local shops. Fifty five of the branches incorporated sub-Post Offices. NSS' principal suppliers included cigarette manufacturers, wholesalers of newspaper and periodicals and confectionery manufacturers. The two largest suppliers accounted for approximately 25% and 6% respectively of total company purchases. Goods sold by the branches were purchased on terms agreed at Head Office so as to obtain advantages of scale for better prices, quality and delivery. Supplies were ordered by and delivered direct to branches.

THE CTN INDUSTRY

There were an estimated 30,000 confectionery, tobacco and newsagent (CTN) retail outlets in the United Kingdom in 1976. Between 2500 and 3000 of these were owned by multiple chains, although not all chains presented the same face to the public. In particular W H Smith and John Menzies had a different product mix from the rest of the industry. The number of retail outlets owned by the major chains together with their product mix are summarised on page 53.

The multiples had been growing faster than the industry and although they accounted for about 10% of all outlets, they owned a much higher percentage of profitable outlets. Industry leaders expected about 5000 of the smaller retail outlets (those with under 700 sq ft of floor space) to disappear over the next ten years as it became increasingly uneconomic to operate these shops. There had been a move in recent years among the multiples towards larger units and prime site locations in shopping centres, although this had not been a complete success. Consequently many multiples were becoming less eager to take large units at expensive rents and were expanding by acquiring independent retailers.

CTN shops competed with grocers, pubs and other outlets for consumer spending. They accounted for about 85% of all newspaper sales and had maintained this share of the market for many years. For confectionery, however, their share had slipped from 47% in 1967 to 41% by 1975. Even more serious was the slippage in tobacco and cigarette sales from 42% in 1968 down to 33% in 1975. Grocers had increased their share to 31% from 24% during the same period, whereas pubs had held a reasonably steady

	Number of retail outlets	1975 Turnover (£ million)	1975 Return on Net Assets (%)	Product Mix
W. H. Smith	371	266	8.0	Newspapers, books, stationery, records
Menzies	260	128	9.2	As Smiths, all tobacco & con-fectionery
Martins	450	45	13.0	Confectionery, tobacco & CTN
Forbuoys (sub. of Gallaher)	400	N/A	N/A	CTN
NSS	360	29	20.5	CTN
Cavenham (Cavenham Ltd sub.)	200	N/A	N/A	CTN
Preedy	150	40	7.2	CTN
Lavells (sub. of Guiness)	120	N/A	N/A	CTN
Balfour	80	N/A	N/A	CTN
Knight	30	N/A	N/A	CTN
Bristol & W England Kiosks	20	N/A	N/A	CTN

Source: Company Annual Reports and NSS Estimates

share of about 14%. Continued pressure on the CTN share for all products was expected as shopping habits changed.

Within the CTN sector, the proportion of sales in each category varied considerably. Smaller outlets relied more heavily on newspaper sales than did the larger ones. Overall, according to *THE CTN STORY* (published by MGN Limited, 1976) the income (roughly equivalent to NSS's gross profit figures) distribution was as follows:

	1971(%)	1976(%)
Tobacco and cigarettes	34	28
Newspapers	28	33
Confectionery	20	18
Other Products	18	21

GROWTH POLICY

NSS had operated a policy of steady expansion for the past twenty years by purchasing established retail newsagent businesses for cash and opening new shops. The table below shows the growth in the number of units over the past six years.

Growth in Number and Type of Retail Outlets

	1971	1972	1973	1974	1975	mid-1976
Traditional Newsagents	167	201	237	262	295	328
Town Centre Units	10	10	11	17	21	21
Branches at year end	177	211	248	279	316	349

Most of the additional branches were acquired. In 1975, a typical year, 32 of the 37 new branches were the result of acquisition. Most of the acquisitions had been single units, though NSS had bought a few regional groups of retail newsagents. During 1974 and 1975, small groups had been acquired in the South West (10 shops), Sheffield (10 shops) and in the home counties (8 shops).

The implementation of the company's expansion plans was the responsibility of Mr Glen Kelway-Bamber, aged 55, director in charge of property expansion and personnel. He had joined NSS in 1966 as Personnel Manager after a career as an army officer. He described the group's criteria and procedures for selecting and assessing existing businesses as follows:

'When buying an existing business we have certain minimum sales and profitability targets. We won't look at any business with sales of less than £1800 per week. We reckon that a small 600 sq.ft. shop requires a turnover of at least £1800–£2000 per week to be profitable for us.

'Potential acquisitions are brought to us by proprietors wanting to sell out, by sales agents and by our regional managers who always keep a look out for possible new branches. However, we only look seriously at about one in six of all opportunities since most are too small or poorly located. As an initial screening exercise we usually send an area manager in to buy a packet of cigarettes. It's amazing what he can tell . . .

'In appraising a business we obtain the average weekly takings from cash register receipts, bank statements and other documents and analyse the purchases of tobacco, cigarettes and newspapers. These two product groups usually account for 70% to 75% of most newsagent's sales and we then make an estimate of confectionery and other sales. Since we know from experience what gross profit we can obtain on each product group, we can build up a fairly accurate gross profit and hence net profit figure for the business. After deducting from the net profit figure any future expenditure thought to be necessary we then value the goodwill at between 3 and $3\frac{1}{2}$ times the resulting profit figure. Besides potential profitability we have two other important criteria. Firstly we try to avoid freeholds since we don't want our capital tied up in property. Where attractive businesses have freeholds we attempt to sell and lease back the property. Secondly, geography is important. We tend to buy businesses in regions where we are already established, since there are costs of going into new areas in terms of the area manager's time. As we have expanded we have concentrated up the motorways or bought a group of shops as we did in the South-West last year.

'Opening new branches has generally been more difficult. We have tried going into empty shells in the high streets, but there are very few situations where this could be successful as there is often another newsagent already well established. Prior to 1974 the largest new shops we had opened were only 1000 sq.ft., usually on new housing estates. However, we have now opened six larger branches (between 3000 sq.ft. and 12000 sq.ft.) in prime locations. In the future we hope to open three larger shops per year in prime locations, providing suitable sites are available.'

1974 saw two other significant divergences from previous management policy: the company acquired a wholesale confectioner/tobacconist in Manchester; and entered the mail order business. Commenting on these diversification moves, Mr Tagliavini, NSS's Managing Director said:

'The initial impetus for moving into both of these areas was government control over our gross profit margins. These encouraged us to go for large volume sales at a low gross profit rate. Warehousing, however, is not essential to our business as we are able to get almost the same terms for direct delivery to our branches as for bulk delivery to a warehouse. Consequently double handling costs and stock losses make warehousing uneconomical. Nevertheless, we do have a concentration of branches around our Manchester wholesaler which seem to benefit from its presence.

'Our venture into the mail order business was unfortunately a failure. We were attempting to sell poor quality, electrical products. They just didn't sell and we discontinued the business after making a small loss.'

ORGANISATION AND CONTROL

The organisational structure of NSS is shown in Exhibit 3. The Board consisted of six executive directors and two non-executive directors both of whom were substantial shareholders in the company. The top management team and organisational structure had remained essentially the same over the previous ten years since Mr Vic Tagliavini had been appointed Managing Director in 1966. Mr Tagliavini, then aged 54, had joined the company three years earlier as an accountant after having found himself out of work when the small electronics firm for which he was Chief Accountant was closed down.

The only major change in the management structure had been in the area of branch management. Growth in the number of branches had led in 1974 to the splitting of branch control on a geographical basis, and the addition of a Branch Services Administrator.

In 1974 branch control in the south of England was put under the control of Mr R Hanna. Mr Hanna, aged 47, had joined the company in 1961 as an area manager and prior to his present position had been the company's Director of Merchandising and Purchasing. He described the process of branch management as follows:

'I have an assistant divisional controller reporting to me as well as five area managers, each of who is responsible for between16 and 22 shops. The area managers are the key managers of the organisaion. They make the profit and train the branch managers. They look at the layout, the merchandise, and the allocation of space to different products. The management problem at the branch level is basically to get people to buy something more. With the help of our Merchandising Manager we have moved to new layouts with more self-selection to promote sales even more. While layout helps, good branch management affects sales even more. For this reason we operate our own training scheme. I reckon that

EXHIBIT 3
NSS Newsagents Limited
Management Organisation Chart 1976

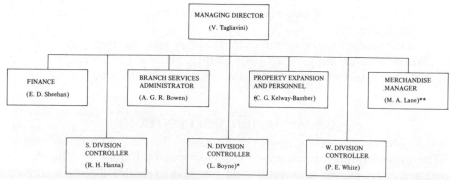

* Joined NSS in 1975; formerly Area Manager with Unigate and Oakeshott; age 34
** Joined NSS in 1974; formerly with Marks & Spencer; age 34. Not a board member

if you put a good manager into what was a bad shop, you can increase sales by up to a third. A good manager who makes people welcome and gets his staff to sparkle is probably the most important factor in deciding whether to refit or extend a branch.'

The new Branch Services Administrator, Mr Alan Bowen, aged 34, had been brought into the company in 1971 as Personal Assistant to Mr Tagliavini. A graduate who had previously had administrative jobs with Unilever and British Shoe Corporation before joining NSS, Mr Bowen described his position as follows:

'My job is at the in-between stage between the accounts and the control function. It is my job to change the information produced by the accounts department into a form that is useful for the branches. Before I came the Branch Controller had an impossible position. He was bogged down all day long in administration and not really able to devote sufficient time to effective control.'

The evolution of the company's management control system was described by Mr Tagliavini:

'When I started with NSS in 1963 the company had expanded to about 50 branches but had not built an organisation to cope with this growth. All that we received were half yearly accounts from the auditors six months late. The company had no financial manager and stock-taking was undertaken semi-annually by the branch managers.

'My first job was to organise stock taking teams. We paid stocktakers on the basis of the amount of stock they handled. In this way we could control stock-taking for each branch. Today each branch is subject to a complete physical stock take at least every three months and additional stock takes are made as necessary. For example, on the appointment of a new manager a stock take is made within six weeks of the appointment.

'Probably the biggest thing we did in the early years was to work out incentives for the branch managers. Current incentives are geared to the achievement of a net profit figure by each branch.* Budgeting is undertaken at head office and area managers are sent weekly sales figures, results of stock checks and quarterly P & L accounts for each branch under their control. They then discuss this with the individual branch managers, and take corrective action where necessary. In this way we are able to keep a close watch on each branch manager's performance. On an annual basis each branch is graded according to its weekly gross profit, permitting us to identify any 'dead branches' in the organisation. Last year we sold or closed three branches.

*Exhibit 4 shows a budgeted profit and loss statement for a typical branch.

'On a company-wide basis our financial department produces monthly P & L statements. The true gross profit is calculated from a continuous programme of stock takes. As far as annual budgeting is concerned, I normally provide branch administration with a percentage factor to be applied to sales revenues to take account of inflation, and they estimate the increases that can be expected from individual shops based on refits and management changes. The system works pretty well, really.'

EXHIBIT 4
NSS Newsagents Limited
Branch Trading and Profit & Loss Account

MIDLANDS ....AREA   ....BRANCH

	MODEL ACCOUNTS												
	%	£	£	%	£	%	£	%	£	%	£	%	£
SALES		94900											
GROSS PROFIT	2150	20403											
Delivery Profit		50											
Post Office Income													
Sundry Income		350											
TOTAL INCOME	2192	20803											
Fixed Establishment Expenses	372	3530											
Wages	695	6500											
Light & heat		240											
Vehicle & cycle		–											
Post & phone		90											
Carriage		60											
Stocktaking		220											
Wastage		200											
Bad debts		–											
Miscellaneous		260											
TOTAL SELLING EXPENSES	798	7570											
TOTAL ALL EXPENSES	1170	11100											
NET PROFIT BEFORE BONUS	1022	9703 9550											
Managers Bonus		250											
NET PROFIT													

STOCKCHECKS

*Rents, Insurance, Depreciation, Rates, Repairs

FUTURE PROSPECTS

The company undertakes no formal planning apart from the annual budgeting exercise. Commenting on the company's future prospects Mr Derrick Sheehan, aged 41, the Finance Director who had worked for Mr Tagliavini prior to joining NSS in 1964 said:

'We have no formally stated financial objectives but I suppose our principal objective is to maintain our historical growth rate. As long as Mr Tagliavini is chief executive we will buy about 40 retail branches per year and will only develop wholesaling as it benefits the retail side of the business. In short, we'll continue pretty much as we are but everything depends on who takes over when Vic retires. He makes all the major decisions and so a new Managing Director could go off in a completely new direction.

'In the longer term, I would like to see us diversify into other areas of retailing since the number of newsagents available for acquisition will eventually dry up. However, there are other constraints on growth, namely the availability of suitable branch management and our ability to digest more than 40 new branches each year from a control point of view. Unlike many companies finance is not a constraint. We have little debt and we have just had a rights issue which raised an additional £850,000.'

When asked about the future, Mr Tagliavini said:

'I've always tried to practise open communications within the company but when it comes to talking about the company's corporate strategy I suppose I'm the only person who actually gets involved in those issues. I suppose you'd call me a "back-of-the-envelope" planner.

'Right now there seems to be an increase in the number of independent newsagents selling their businesses, and so I am expecting the rate of expansion to increase in the near future. We have sufficient resources to take advantage of this situation and, whilst it may be difficult for us to maintain a growth rate in net profit of 20% or more, I am confident that we can get somewhere near to this figure. Our long term prospects continue to hinge on the acquisition of existing businesses and opening of new shops in similar proportions as in the past year. Apart from some possibilities of bulk purchasing of confectionery, we have no intentions of increasing our wholesaling activity or diversifying in other ways. There are still, however, one or two issues we need to sort out as far as the future is concerned.

'Government controls over profit margins are a continuing problem for us since they restrict our opportunities to improve our sales mix. Under these conditions the only way to increase profits is by a substantial increase in turnover even if some of this is obtained at a relatively low margin.

'The big new stores that we have opened present us with a bit of a dilemma. Each costs about £100,000 and it normally takes about three years to show a reasonable return whereas acquiring existing businesses shows an immediate ROI of 30%. Experience in the US has shown that the catchment area of major shopping centres grows over time, so for long term growth we cannot ignore the trend in this direction.

'Perhaps our biggest problem in the future is management succession. I was to have retired in 1977 but have now agreed to stay on for another three years. The problem is that there is nobody in the company to replace me. I must admit I have failed to delegate sufficient authority but you know how it is when you've been there from the beginning and built up the business from a small family-owned company to a successful public company. I've discussed this with the Chairman at our monthly luncheons but he says not to worry as we can afford to pay a lot for the right man when the need arises.'

5

Tizer Limited (A)

In the spring of 1972 Mr P. Quinn described to the casewriter his move from Polyfoil Ltd, an aluminium foil manufacturer, to Tizer Ltd, the soft drinks manufacturer. Mr Quinn had been the general manager of Polyfoil Ltd, a subsidiary of Alcan Ltd, until February 1970, when he assumed the position of managing director of Tizer Ltd. Mr Quinn was reviewing both his evaluation of Tizer prior to joining the company, and his subsequent approach to the task of returning the company to a position of profitability.

THE SOFT DRINKS INDUSTRY

In 1970 the total value of the British soft drinks market was in excess of £200 millions. From 1963 through to 1969, the value of this soft drinks market had been increasing at a rate of 9.1 per cent per annum. Within the soft drinks business, there were three major product areas,

1. Concentrated soft drinks—squashes—need to be diluted· before drinking
2. Mixers—soft drinks and fruit juices—generally to be added to spirits and alcoholic drinks
3. Carbonated soft drinks—e.g. lemonade, Coca-Cola.

By 1968 concentrated soft drinks represented 54 per cent of the total market, and unconcentrated soft drinks 46 per cent. The market for concentrated soft drinks had grown faster than that for unconcentrated soft drinks (from 1963 production of unconcentrated soft drinks had grown at 4 per cent per annum).

There were two main types of carbonated soft drinks.

1. Branded products—e.g. Schweppes, Coca-Cola, Pepsi, etc. Products being sold under a manufacturer's or brand name.
2. Commodity products—e.g. lemonade, limeade, dandelion and burdock, etc. These products were not sold under a brand name, and this had resulted in fierce price competition between local drink manufacturers, with resultant narrow profit margins.

Immediately after the war, there were some 2000 companies manufacturing soft drinks. By 1969 this number had been reduced to between 500 and 600, due to intense competition. Many of the companies that went out of business were small regional companies serving local markets who had not the resources to withstand competition from the major manufacturers. Within the concentrated soft drinks market in 1968, there were four major companies controlling 55 per cent of the market: Schweppes, Beechams, Reckitt and Colman, and Unilever. For the unconcentrated soft drinks market, the major market shareholders were Corona (20 per cent), Schweppes (10 per cent), Coca-Cola (8 per cent), Pepsi-Cola (7 per cent), CWS (6 per cent), Whites (5 per cent) and Tizer (3–4 per.cent). Most of the major companies retailed their products on a national basis. With their large financial resources, they were in a position to invest in the latest high-speed bottling plants, as well as in advertising and promotion. In the retail chains and supermarkets, this gave them a significant advantage against the local manufacturers in competing for shelf space.

Sales of soft drinks had traditionally been made through local 'corner shop' retail outlets. However, during the 1960s the pattern of demand had significantly changed with the advent of supermarkets, chain and self-service stores. National chain stores and supermarkets were able to buy in bulk from the major soft drinks manufacturers to the disadvantage of the small local manufacturers. The small local manufacturer had difficulty in serving the national chains, and also in competing on price with the major soft drinks manufacturers on bulk ordering. Off-licences had also been a traditional retail outlet for the soft drinks manufacturers. Acquisition by brewing companies of soft drinks manufacturers had, however, resulted in many of the off-licences being tied to the brewers' products. Thus the opportunities for small manufacturers to gain access to the high volume retail outlets (with the consequent lowering of distribution costs) had been limited.

Immediately prior to 1970 there had also been significant changes in the type of packaging used for the products. Supermarkets and chain stores did not want returnable bottle sales. The result was an expansion in the use of cans, plastic cup drinks, and one-trip bottles: can production of soft drinks increased from 300 million units in 1967 to 450 million units in 1970; and sales of soft drinks in one-trip bottles increased from 180 million units in 1968 to 363 million units in 1970. Furthermore, the use of newer materials in packaging led to changes in the package design and in the advertising carried on the packages.

TIZER LIMITED (PRE-1970)

Tizer Ltd was founded in 1933 as a manufacturer of soft drinks. Over the years the company grew and established itself as a major manufacturer of carbonated soft drinks sold in returnable bottles. By the early 1960s Tizer was operating twenty-one depots spread across the country. These regional depots combined both production and regional sales departments in all but one of the depots.

In 1969 Tizer's major products were still the carbonated soft drinks sold under the trade names of Tizer and Jusoda. These products were sold in three different sizes of returnable bottle, i.e. 6 oz., 25 oz., and 40 oz. The company also manufactured a line of concentrated cordials under the trade name of Nectose, in order to enter the fast-expanding concentrated soft drinks market. A franchise agreement had recently been made with the American Royal Crown Cola Company to permit Tizer to enter the cola market, which represented over 20 per cent of the UK carbonated soft drinks market. Tizer did not produce soft drinks in cans or paper cups and nearly all sales of carbonated drinks were in returnable bottles. The company had invested approximately £1 million in bottles and boxes.

Exhibit 1 (see end of case study) identifies the organisational structure of the company as of 1969. The company operated on a regional basis. Each depot/branch operated within an assigned geographic territory. Each branch manager was in charge of a production facility, a storage facility, a group of van drivers/salesmen, a fleet of vehicles and an administrative staff. Most of the managers were men who had originally been van drivers/salesmen, and had risen through the ranks to assume their current positions.

Because no single branch manufactured a full product line, it was necessary to 'trunk' products by lorry from one branch to another to try to maintain adequate supplies at each branch. Trunking became very critical each summer at the height of the seasonal demand, to prevent stockouts and loss of sales. The production equipment at the branches was, in many cases, quite old and of a design incompatible with modern bottling equipment. Therefore the branches were dependent on the head office engineering department for parts and major servicing overhauls.

The company as a whole owned a fleet of 560 vehicles in varying states of repair and these were assigned to particular branches. The vehicles were used for trunking as well as for the supplying of retail outlets. Selling was undertaken at each branch by a team of van drivers/salesmen who sold direct to retail outlets. Tizer had traditionally sold to the small retail outlets and each driver had his own route and accounts to which he sold. Sales were made to the retailers either on a direct cash transaction or a credit sale basis, by the van driver/salesman. The tasks of the salesman included loading the vehicle, making rounds, cashing in his takings at the branch on completion of the rounds, checking the remaining stocks on the lorry as well as off-loading empties collected on the round. The van drivers/salesman were paid commission on sales; different products had different commission rates which could be adjusted depending on whether any particular product was being promoted.

The operating performance of the company deteriorated through the 1960s. Whilst sales turnover had remained nearly constant at £3 million per annum since 1961, profitability fell from 1963 onwards. In 1969 profit after tax fell drastically from £133,355 to £29,986 (see Exhibit 2). At this stage, representatives of an institutional shareholder intervened and insisted that a new managing director bc found from outside the company. The services of a management selection consultant were engaged, and in February 1970 Mr P Quinn became managing director of Tizer Ltd.

QUINN'S EVALUATION OF TIZER LIMITED

Many people ask what makes a person leave the security and prospects of a well-paid job with one of the world's biggest industrial groups to take on such a hot seat. The answer is simple: I saw in Tizer a very challenging situation; a situation with some good assets that could provide the foundation of a long-term recovery. When I was at Alcan, I had already successfully turned round a subsidiary in a similar position.

Prior to my applying for the position, I had made a detailed study of available (1968) financial reports so that I could make up my mind whether the company could be turned around. People who fail in such turnaround situations are liable to carry the tag with them through their careers.

My accounting qualification helped me to analyse some of the more fundamental problems. I felt that a staff of 1375 people should be producing more than £3 million sales. Sundry debts had been allowed to increase from £212,206 in 1967 to £288,933 in 1968 in a period of declining sales. The company also had a very high level of liquid assets, which could have been invested elsewhere to reduce the operating costs. The level of depreciation of the fixed assets at approximately 66 per cent suggested that much of the equipment was fairly old; even without knowing Tizer's method of depreciation. Why were some of the liquid assets not being invested in equipment to spur sales? In the reserves and surplus, six reserves were being held, as against the three one would expect to find, i.e. capital, revenue, profit and loss. The number of reserves suggested either little financial faith in the business or a lack of planning. Dividend and sales promotion expenses should be deducted out of current profitability not past profit. (Exhibits 3 and 4 provide financial details for 1967 and 1968.)

Looking at the fixed assets, there were no indications of the true value of the assets; however, I assumed that if the plant and equipment was not worth as much as stated, then the property was worth more. Hence the net worth of the company was probably reasonably represented. Even so half the net worth of the company was in property and the return on assets was down to 4 per cent. The company was making no use of debt and all these factors indicated that the company's assets were lying 'fallow' whilst the plant was running down. The money should have been in working capital, transport and bottling equipment. There was, moreover, no shortage of assets with which to turn the company around.

Some of the comments in the Chairman's Report (Exhibit 5) raised serious questions in my mind, for example: 'I am reluctant to forecast trading prospects for 1969, because the soft drinks industry is so susceptible to variations in the weather.... The company experienced difficult personnel relations in distribution.'

I looked at the problems in general management terms, because I felt that my general management experience with Alcan would be relevant. There were similarities between Polyfoil and Tizer; the biggest common point was in marketing. Foil is sold to the consumer through the grocery trade, which has its own methods of buying. You sell it with consumer advertising and consumer promotional support. Tizer products are largely sold through the grocery and food trades to the same buyers with a similar marketing approach. Tizer products are, of course, also sold through other retail outlets.

In both cases, the products are being sold in literally millions of units at very low prices; this demands a certain frame of mind. A man who is used to selling huge capital items valued at hundreds of thousands of pounds cannot think in terms of the other end of the scale where you are selling millions of items at pennies a time. The total over the year may be the same, but it demands a different approach to business.

From an external analysis, I considered Tizer to have a major strength in the market awareness of the Tizer name; however, from a marketing angle, I was aware that the real growth areas were in non-returnable bottles, cans, squashes, and the multiple stores. Tizer was not pursuing any of these areas.

I feel that managers often make mistakes in changing companies. They move to companies involved in an unfamiliar business and then they find that, although the general management skills and responsibilities are the same, they cannot be applied in quite the same way. You have got to know something about the business you are in before dealing with the general management responsibilities of creating policies, creating a management structure, setting up budgets, and controlling performance against those budgets.

Parts of the job were, of course, new to me. Tizer as a public company had 4,000 shareholders, and this clearly meant involvement in financial public relations work with the shareholders. There was an obvious need to convince the shareholders that Tizer was worth sticking with. The public relations work would also have to be designed to have a secondary appeal to the trade. There was undoubtedly a lot of thought in the trade two years ago that Tizer was a dead company, and that there wasn't any point in continuing to buy from Tizer because it was going out of existence. It would be necessary to create more confidence in the company so that buyers would feel the company was going to stay in business, and that it would be worth supporting.

Another new area was in terms of labour relations. Almost 100 per cent of Tizer employees were members of unions and the unions were fairly militant. Tizer, in the year before I joined, had had a very sorry record of strikes and industrial strife, particularly within the sales organisation. My involvement in Alcan in labour relations had been at second hand.

IMMEDIATE ACTIONS

On arrival at Tizer, I felt as chief executive that I had four priority tasks to be discharged. They were

(a) to define the true nature of the company's business
(b) to create a company strategy and plan
(c) to build a strong team of people
(d) to set up and measure performance of objectives to achieve that plan.

Ideally these tasks are sequential. However, in practice, you have to deal with them concurrently at times.

To define the true nature of the company's business for a marketing orientated company like Tizer really means starting at the marketing end. What are your markets, who are your customers, and what are they buying from you? If you assume that they are buying satisfactions from you rather than physical products, what are these satisfactions? Although it sounds good to say that one starts off with the market and the consumer, I think basically that you are trying to compare and so you initially require a basis for comparison. Very often one must contrast the most and the least successful firms in your business. What are the successful firms doing that is giving them success, and what are the unsuccessful firms doing that is causing problems? What is successful about Coke or Corona on the one hand, and unsuccessful about our small local competitors?

Tizer as a company lined up much more with the local competitors. It was, in effect, a series of twenty or so branches, all of which were small local operators rather than a cohesive national company operating in a similar manner to Coke or Corona. Coke seemed to have identified with the satisfaction area of soft drinks; what sells Coke is not that it is a better soft drink, but the whole aura around the product. Corona, in contrast, does not have the same image, but its strength lies in a much greater national identity, an efficient network, central objectives and standard operating methods—in other words, a rational, national approach to the business.

Having made these external comparisons, one can identify why people are buying your product and which people should be buying your product. Then it is possible to define the type of sales and marketing organisation required to reach this market, and the people required to manage that organisation. When making such comparisons and evaluations, it is impossible to be totally objective; you are bound to apply your own personal standards to some extent. The differences between success and lack of success is presumably whether your personal standards happen to be successful standards. There's a lot of timing and luck involved in business success—being in the right place at the right time—and if you are in tune with current market needs, you are far more likely to be successful than if you are out of tune. Tizer's method of doing business through regional production plants selling to small local retail outlets was very much out of tune with the needs of the seventies.

When determining the true nature of the company's business, it is important to evaluate your own management team. If you are to be successful you have to have the right team as soon as possible. This process of evaluation is in many ways judgemental. There are, of course, practical aspects like the setting of objectives and assessing performance against those objectives. If you agree an objective with a manager and it is not attained then there is cause for anxiety. If the pattern is repeated then you have to replace him. However, an evaluation of this nature presents two problems.

1. Information systems tend to be based on accounting, and not all operations can be transplanted into accounting terms.
2. The higher the management level, the longer the time span required to evaluate a manager against objectives.

The major measure to me was a man's ability to get results, to get things done. If they failed to achieve results due to an inability to cope with elementary techniques of management, they had to be suspect. Clearly another point to consider is the ability of the management to function as a team. If, as was certainly the case with Tizer, there is obvious evidence of conflict among the board members, then changes have to be made.

My evaluation of the existing management team included branch managers. One of my first priorities was to visit all the branches and branch managers and see them personally two or three times so that I would have some personal knowledge of some fifty or sixty people in the company. My personal evaluation only went as far as branch managers, because beyond that level there would be just too many people to know, and also because there is a very strong case for saying that the branch manager is the critical level of management. Our first real line manager ought to be the supervisor, but they have not, in the past, been given a lot of management responsibilities. In fact, they can only basically influence sales level, which, although very important, is not necessarily a management function.

Whilst evaluating the branch managers, I also had the opportunity to appraise the physical assets of the company. There were obviously some very fundamental changes needed in the physical assets, but it would have been a waste of effort to try to do too much internally until we were satisfied that we had a position in the market. Relocation of the physical assets of the company could not be considered until we had determined where our market was.

The evaluation of the company's financial position was another major area. Again you cannot accurately evaluate whether your financial resources are adequate for the job until you know, at least, in outline, what your commitments are going to be. However, one has got to have some criteria for assessment before looking at the details. If you are in a heavy industrial situation, you may require £1 of capital for £1 of sales. Now, the lighter your business becomes, the less capital you need per £1 of sales, so that when you finally get down to retailing, you can do your turnover with a minus capital. Companies like Tesco realised years ago that they could do turnover with a minus capital, and therefore the more branches they opened the more money came in.

Looked at in this way, Tizer's turnover of £3 million was not enough from a company that had a net worth of £2½ million. On general principles, in this business, £2½ million net worth of company should support at least £5 million, and possibly as much as £10 million turnover. When I realised that 50 per cent of Tizer's net worth was in property, I felt immediately that for a trading company far too much of the company's net worth was in property. However, this did not mean that if the company were to run short of cash for trading, there would be property available for conversion into cash.

Having made these evaluations of the company, marketing emerged as the one critical area to the development of a strategy. As a consumer product manufacturer, it was essential to have a lot of market information and a strong marketing team. I brought in a consulting group to provide me with the market information which I did not have the time, nor the company the skills, to obtain. If you know what the market is for each product, you can then determine how to sell it, how to produce it, and how to finance that production.

The determination of the objectives for the company inevitably, I suppose, comes back to financial terms. One definition I had was 'Profit is not the name of the game, but it is the score'. Thus we were not in business to make a profit, but it was merely telling us how well we were doing in our business. The influence of shareholders in determining a financial objective is clearly that, in order to keep them happy, you have to provide dividend income and sheer capital growth. To do so, you have to ensure that the objectives established are adequate for them. However, the financial objective set to meet shareholders' needs must also be a realistic target for the company to reach.

Clearly, when I came to the company, they were in a situation that did not satisfy the shareholders, and it was also clear that it was going to take some time. My initial assessment was that it would take three years, not necessarily to satisfy our shareholders, but at least to make them feel that we would substantiate a promise.

To determine the shareholders' opinion in Tizer's case, I spoke to half a dozen major shareholders who held 35–40 per cent of the total shareholding. From these people I got a reading of what the opinion of that major body was, although obviously I could not solicit the opinion of 4,000 individual shareholders.

Having identified their expectations, there was then the question of determining how far one could meet their needs without it proving detrimental to the ongoing business. With a known difficult position to be negotiated over the next two or three years, the more money that could be available internally the better. However, the responsibility to the shareholders, the need to keep them and try to give them confidence in the company's future, all pointed to payment of a dividend. If we had not had to worry about shareholders, we could have made investments with long-term paybacks: instead we had to think of short-term returns. We might have spent £3–400,000 on advertising as an investment for the future. It would, however, have been a risk investment, and one can only assume that, had the shareholders been asked to choose, they would not have chosen that sort of risk. The same approach applies in terms of fixed assets. With our very dilapidated vehicle fleet, we had to adopt a policy of replacing it progressively over a 3–4 year period, even though we had the cash to do it straight away.

All the shareholder and business constraints are finally accommodated in the routine function of budgeting, in order to arrive at one financial objective. The budgetary system should be flexible enough for the budgets to be adjusted to the various activities that are going on which were not originally allowed for, and at the same time still produce an acceptable end result, bearing in mind the total work to be done. The final figure came about by massaging the figures from a 'top-down' and 'bottom-up' budgetary process until they finally agreed. Basically, the function of budgeting is an allocation of resources, and you allocate resources to achieve what you feel is the optimum result within the external circumstances. The allocation of resources has to be fitted in to a time framework, and in my view the chronic sickness of the company meant taking a fairly long view of this. Really we had to say what we wanted to achieve in 3–5 years' time. How do we set about it? What is the shortest time period in which we can achieve a satisfactory result? How do we achieve it? Within this sort of framework, you can start setting up short term objectives. Even if you do know what your end objectives are going to be in detail, you still tend to come back to the fact that in the early stages you have got to have a budget of some sort. Part of the art of management is stretching people to do more than they think they can produce, and a budgetary system allows you to state objectives that are going to stretch them.

The above outlines much of the process by which I set about returning Tizer to a position of profitability.

EXHIBIT 1

Tizer Limited. Organisational Chart

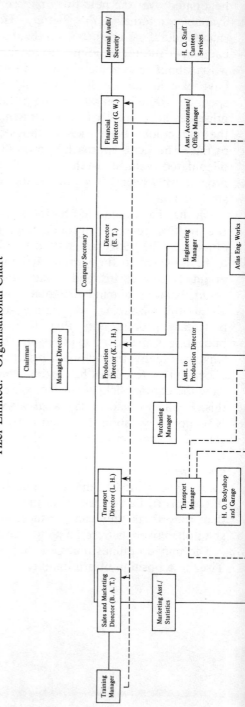

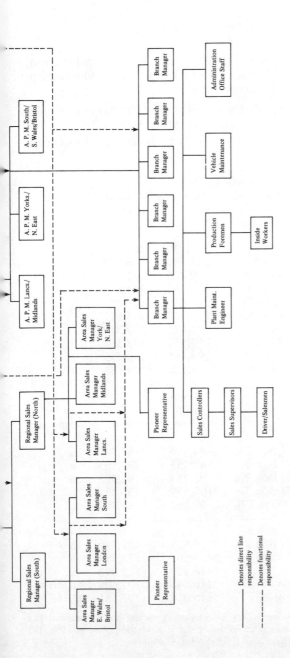

Branch Manager

Branch Manager

Branch Manager

Branch Manager

Branch Manager

Branch Manager

Administration Office Staff

Vehicle Maintenance

Production Foremen

Inside Workers

Plant Maint. Engineer

A. P. M. South/ S. Wales/Bristol

A. P. M. Yorks./ N. East

A. P. M. Lancs./ Midlands

Area Sales Manager York/ N. East

Area Sales Manager Midlands

Area Sales Manager Lancs.

Regional Sales Manager (North)

Pioneer Representative

Sales Controllers

Sales Supervisors

Driver/Salesmen

Area Sales Manager South

Area Sales Manager London

Regional Sales Manager (South)

Area Sales Manager E. Wales/ Bristol

Pioneer Representative

——— Denotes direct line responsibility

- - - - Denotes functional responsibility

EXHIBIT 2

Tizer Limited.

Excerpts from Extel card (up-dated to 26.5.70)

MINERAL WATER AND CORDIAL MANUFACTURERS

Co. was formed to acquire following businesses engaged in manufacture and distribution of mineral waters, botanic beers, cordials, non-alcoholic wines and vinegar. Co. has an agreement with Royal Crown Cola Co. of Columbus Georgia, to bottle and sell Royal Crown Cola in Great Britain.

SUB. COS: Hampshire Mineral Water Co. Ltd (Mineral Water Manufacturers); Our Boys Mineral Water Co. Ltd, and Rider Wilsons Table Waters Ltd (ceased to trade during 1969); Hills Chapman Ltd (property Co.).

DIRECTORS: F Hindle (Chairman); P. Quinn (Managing Director); L. Hilton, E. Taylor, B. A. Taylor, G. Wilkinson, K. J. Hammer, MBE, E.D.

DIRECTORS' INTERESTS in Ord. shares of Co. at 31.12.69: Beneficial 15,941; as trustees 850,000.

CONSOLIDATED PROFIT AND LOSS ACCOUNT

Year ended 31 Dec	Turnover* £000	Divs & Int. recd £	Net profit before tax £	Total tax £	Net profit after tax £
1960	a	27,065	494,542	231,139	263,403
1961	a	33,104	619,571	303,381	316,190
1962	a	30,048	480,596	219,405	261,191
1963	a	31,853	598,160	293,561	304,599
1964	a	36,727	567,471	246,646	320,825
1965	a	47,047	438,588	134,967	303,621
1966	s	45,194	443,760	171,421	272,339
1967	a	41,682	361,112	157,551	203,561
1968	2,984	41,810	231,840	98,485	133,355
1969	2,949	47,657	60,111	30,125	29,986

Year ended 31 Dec	% on ordinary, less tax		Retained profit for year £	Depn £	Av. no employees
	Earned	Paid			
1960	43.0	Int 7½ Fin 17½ Bon 2½	94,966	87,747	a
1961	51.6	Int 7½ Fin 17½ Bon 2½	147,753	92,585	a
1962	42.6	Int 7½ Fin 17½ Bon 2½	92,753	98,398	a
1963	49.7	Int 7½ Fin 17½ Bon 7½	105,537	136,135	a
1964	54.3	Int 7½ Fin 17½ Bon 17½	69,262	131,304	a
1964	j39.5				
1965	30.4	Int 7½ Fin 17½ Bon 2½	.e 28,621	131,746	a
1966	30.4	Int 7½ Fin 17½ Bon 2½	M 2,661	133,304	a
1967	20.4	Int 7½ Fin 17½	M46,439	122,093	a
1968	13.3	Int 7½ Fin 7½	M16,645	102,609	kl,360
1969	3.0	Int Nil Fin 7½	M45,014	92,181	kl,360

*Excluding purchase tax. (a) Not disclosed. (e) Dividends deducted gross (Income Tax retained £30,937). (j) Estimated earnings after allowing for Corporation Tax at 40%. (k) Remuneration £1,038,000 in 1968, and £1,126,000 in 1969. (M) Minus

LONDON PRICES OF 5/- ORDINARY SHARES

Cal. Year	1961	1962	1963	1964	1965	1966	1967	1968	1969	*1970
Highest	26/6	25/6	29/9	27/9	27/9	24/10	26/7	24/3	21/9	11/9
Lowest	20/4	20/-	20/3	21/4	22/-	14/3	16/1	17/1	6/9	8/3

*To 18 May

NET ASSET VALUE (BOOK VALUE), excluding intangibles, at B/s. date per 5/- Ord. share: 1969 11/-

FINANCE ACT, 1965. So far as is known Co. is not a close company within provisions of Act.

LAND AND BUILDINGS. Value of land and Building is substantially in excess of book value and valuations made since 31.12.69 indicate that this excess could be in region of £500,000 in open market, but as major part is used for trading Co. it is opinion of Directors that current open market value is not of great significance in context of these accounts.

CHAIRMAN'S STATEMENT. Trading results are disappointing as Directors had hoped to achieve an increased turnover. Failure of this, and a fall in Group's total gross sales value by £35,000 can be specifically attributed to a number of factors among which were (a) a policy of rationalisation of manufacturing, by closure or reduction to distribution points of certain units, particularly closure of their branch in Glasgow due to an increasing non-profitability which had applied for some years in spite of changes in management, whilst certain smaller branches in the North East and in South Wales were closed or consolidated for same reason; (b) inability during exceptional weather in June and July (when they were able to trade at full production for first time for some years) to recoup general fall during poor winter months at beginning of year, and (c) a price increase granted by Ministry in August last which for a time met sales resistance in certain areas. In addition, account must be taken of increasing encroachment into family soft drink market of American brands of Cola products.

Fall in profit however overtook amount lost in turnover due to persistent rises in labour, materials and in operating and marketing costs during year which had to be absorbed by Co. Both turnover and profit suffered from labour unrest whilst changed regulations in SET alone cost Co. £20,000. An additional charge for packaging costs was sustained despite reduction in volume, although to a minor extent this was offset by increased deposit charge on 40 oz. size bottle. An outstanding item of expense was substantial increase in cost of transport aggravated by new regulations imposed by Road Transport Act, 1968. Return to profitability depends upon ability to contain or pass on these extra costs.

Board have given continual attention to product innovations and, in view of reduction of number of trips of returnable bottle, to extension of marketing operations including that of use of non-returnable bottle. During latter part of 1969 a pilot operation in this type of outlet was started and in present year sales into multiple stores and supermarkets are being extended. It is as yet too early to forecast success and profitability of these operations in a highly competitive market.

As American branded Cola accounts for approx. 25% of carbonated drinks sold in UK decision was taken during latter part of 1969 to enter competition in this field. Co. subsequently negotiated franchise agreement to bottle and market in Great Britain Royal Crown Cola, and Co. has now commenced to produce this Cola. Last year, he referred to a proposed development of a new major production unit. In view of large capital commitment required by this project Co. is now considering this matter again before proceeding.

N.B. At the time of Quinn's taking over, liquidation of the company would have realised 13s.6d. per share. (Casewriter's notes.)

Source: Extel Statistical Services Ltd

EXHIBIT 3
Consolidated Balance Sheet as at 31 December 1968

1967 £		£	£
	SHARE CAPITAL OF TIZER LIMITED		
	Authorised 6,000,000 Ordinary shares		
£1,500,000	of 5/- each	£1,500,000	
	Issued 4,000,000 Ordinary Shares		
£1,000,000	of 5/- each, fully paid		£1,000,000
	RESERVES		
12,201	Capital	26,652	
1,000,000	Revenue	1,000,000	
75,000	Dividend equalisation	75,000	
40,000	Sales promotion	25,000	
60,000	Taxation equalisation	60,000	
167,325	Profit and loss account	170,673	
1,354,526			1,357,325
£2,354,526	TOTAL CAPITAL AND RESERVES		£2,357,325

1967 £		£	£
	FIXED ASSETS (See note)		
886,580	Land and Buildings		823,153
547,828	Plant, machinery and motor vehicles		530,849
1,434,408			1,354,002
	CURRENT ASSETS		
409,711	Stock in Trade	361,631	
240,309	Sundry debtors & amounts prepaid	323,481	
	British Government and other securities (Market value £228,894–		
232,174	1967 £221,552)	232,174	
475,000	Municipal and other deposits	475,000	
241,446	Cash at Bankers and in hand	179,832	
1,598,640		1,572,118	
	Deduct: CURRENT LIABILITIES		
247,048	Sundry creditors and amounts accrued	293,583	
157,894	Current taxation	155,592	
175,000	Provision for final dividend (Gross) now recommended	75,000	
579,942		524,175	
1,018,698	NET CURRENT ASSETS		1,047,943
2,453,106			2,401,945

	Deduct: DEFERRED LIABILITY	
157,170	Corporation Tax due 1st January 1970	103,210
2,295,936		2,298,735
	Add: GOODWILL at cost less amounts written off including net premiums on	
58,590	shares acquired in subsidiary companies	58,590
£2,354,526	TOTAL NET ASSETS	£2,357,325

NOTE ON ACCOUNTS

1. FIXED ASSETS	1968	1967
LAND AND BUILDINGS	£	£
At Cost 1 January 1968	684,020	650,370
At Valuation	369,418	369,418
	1,053,438	1,019,788
Additions during the year at cost	13,424	44,059
Less: Disposal during the year	69,195	10,409
	997,667	1,053,438
Cumulative depreciation	174,514	166,858
At net book value 31 December 1968	£823,153	£886,580
Freehold	740,003	800,338
Leasehold	83,150	86,242
	£823,153	£886,580
PLANT, MACHINERY AND MOTOR VEHICLES	1,613,937	1,607,275
Additions during the year at cost	92,672	61,820
Less: Disposal during the year	167,150	55,156
	1,539,459	1,613,939
Cumulative depreciation	1,008,610	1,066,111
At net book value 31 December 1968	£530,849	£547,828

Source: Annual Report

EXHIBIT 4
Consolidated Profit and Loss Account
Year ended 31 December 1968

1967 £		£	£
468,549	Trading Profit of the year		308,249
–	Add: Profit arising on change of stocktaking basis		18,291
1,966	Profit on sale of properties		8,433
470,515			334,973
	Add: Investment income		
9,540	Investments	10,067	
32,142	Cash on deposit	31,743	
41,682			41,810
512,197			376,783
	Deduct:		
122,093	Depreciation of Fixed assets	102,609	
2,818	Losses on sales of fixed assets	5,139	
25,520	Directors' remuneration	27,790	
1,506	Other miscellaneous charges	6,111	
151,937			141,649
360,260	Profit of the year subject to taxation		235,134
152,443	Deduct: Taxation on profit of year		96,786
207,817	Profit of the year after taxation		138,348
174,508	Add: Balance brought forward from previous year		167,325
35,000	Add: Transfer from sales promotion reserve		15,000
417,325			320,673
	Deduct: Share dividends:		
75,000	Interim 7½% (Gross) already paid	75,000	
175,000	Final 7½% (Gross) now recommended	75,000	
250,000			150,000
£167,325	Balance carried forward to next year		£170,673

Source: Annual Report

EXHIBIT 5

Chairman's Review

To the Shareholders.

Dear Sir or Madam,

I beg to submit this Review with the Accounts and Directors' Report of your Company for the year ending 31st December, 1968. Following on the Companies Act 1967 the published Accounts for the year with the accompanying notes and Directors' Report are set out to give more information than in previous years.

First I wish to refer to the death in December of Mr. Pickup, the founder of the business and until 1962 Chairman of the Company, since when he remained on the Board and maintained an active interest in its affairs until just before he died. He combined a long experience of every aspect of the mineral water trade with a shrewd appraisal of its commercial and manufacturing problems which enabled him to enlarge a small business into its present-day position. I personally regret the passing of a respected colleague and life-long friend.

The trading results of the year have proved most disappointing, particularly as the general price increase introduced last May was expected to absorb a greater part of the ever rising costs than had been the case in the previous year, but this was dependent on volume turnover being at the least maintained. In the event this volume was not achieved and a substantial fall in the trading profit has resulted.

The fall in business can be attributed to several factors. The main reason being the weather conditions prevailing in a summer reported to be the wettest since 1931, particularly in the South. Two increases in purchase tax during the year together with a general increase in price necessitated by increased costs caused our selling prices to be uplifted by 15% which resulted in resistance to sales. In addition the Company experienced difficult personnel relations in distribution. These factors collectively diminished the impact of an increased marketing effort mounted by our sales organisation during the year.

As mentioned briefly in the Directors' Report the trading profit was further depleted by a higher level of replacement bottles necessitated by a very severe fall in the average number of journeys per bottle. This may have been affected by a slowing down in replacements by the same number of consumers, such as happens in cold or wet summer weather, leading to both slow turnover and increased wastage. Your Directors have taken steps to mitigate this problem which is causing concern to the carbonate soft drinks industry at large who rely upon the returnable bottle to keep down packaging costs, but these measures are not expected to become effective until 1970.

I am reluctant to forecast the trading prospects for 1969 because experience has shown how susceptible the soft drinks industry is to variations in weather, especially in the peak summer months, whilst the particularly bad weather in the early months of this year has resulted in a reduction of sales against target.

Your Board are naturally continuing their policy of strengthening the sales organisation. The Company's main product still remains a firm favourite and, commencing in 1969, the use of our nationally known registered trade mark 'Tizer' is to be developed so that advantage is gained from a more extensive consumer exposure to this name. Consideration is particularly being given to product innovation in order to strengthen the Company's competitiveness in a changing market situation, whilst a feasibility study is also being carried out into an alternative method of selling by pre-ordering.

Your Directors are pursuing a policy of concentrating production into fewer manufacturing plants in the future with a view to reducing overall production costs and a new major unit is already in the process of being developed.

Resulting from these activities the Board are confident that long-term development of sales and profitability will materialise.

Your Directors have decided to recommend the payment of a Final Dividend of 7½% less tax making 15% less tax for the year.

Following the resignation of Mr. Williams and the death of Mr. Pickup, Mr. G. Wilkinson and Mr. K. J. Hanmer, M.B.E., E.D., have been appointed to the Board of the Company and the Annual General Meeting will be asked to confirm these appointments. Mr. Wilkinson joined the Company early in 1968 as Financial Controller to implement the Touche, Ross, Bailey, Smart & Co. report and has taken full charge of the accounting and financial matters of the Company. Mr. Hanmer joined the Company in May 1968 having previously managed a major Soft Drinks manufactory abroad.

I regret to have to report the death earlier this year of our Secretary, Mr. W. E. Speake, who had held the position for some 19 years.

Source: Annual Report.

FRANK HINDLE
Chairman

6

Tizer Limited (B)

This case reviews the developments in Tizer Ltd between the time when Mr Quinn became Managing Director in 1970 and the sale of the company to A. G. Barr of Glasgow on 7 December 1972.

MR QUINN'S ADMINISTRATION

Once he had assumed office, Mr Quinn moved quickly to cure the problems he had identified in his prelimary audit of the company (described in Tizer Limited (A)).

His overall goal was to establish Tizer as a strong national soft drinks manufacturer and distributor. He believed that a growth target of 20 per cent per annum for sales was achievable. He also believed that within four years Tizer ought to be making at least 15 per cent pre-tax return on investment.

As a first step towards realising these goals, Mr Quinn assembled a new younger team of top managers. New directors of finance and sales were appointed by the summer of 1970, as were new managers of marketing and transport. Together with existing personnel in operations, engineering, personnel and administration, they constituted what Mr Quinn considered a well-balanced group with the skills and experience necessary to create the desired growth.

The changes instituted on the marketing side were described by Mr Sproat, the new sales manager, as follows.[1]

> Everything we have done in the last eighteen months has been aimed at getting Tizer firmly positioned in the branded section of the market and out of the commodity area where local bottlers are still cutting each other to pieces in trade price wars without making any serious attempt at expanding the total market.
>
> We aim to restore Tizer to its rightful position as one of the leading

[1]Presentation to the Northern Stock Exchange, October 1971.

branded soft drinks, and then to do likewise with our Jusoda range and with Royal Crown Cola.

So we had taken the first step. We knew where we wanted to go. But how to get there? We identified our major weaknesses as:

—an old-fashioned image
—a declining market share
—inadequate channels of distribution through which we sold our products.

These problems are closely interrelated but they also need specific attention and remedies.

Firstly, we tackled the old-fashioned image. We commissioned depth research to find out what the consumer really thought of Tizer. Most of them—and Tizer is as well known by soft drink consumers as Coca-Cola—thought of Tizer with affection but as rather dull. So we commissioned Conran Design to prepare for us a completely new corporate identity which shows Tizer's public face to the consumer. Conran have done a superb job, and we now have an image which is vivid, contemporary and alive, but which still suggests a product with a long and honourable history.

And this is not just to be seen on our products. The new identity covers vehicles, stationery, factory signs, salesmen's uniforms—every area in which the consumer or trade customers come into contact with us.

We were also faced with a very serious decline in market share, much of which can be traced to our failure to keep abreast of changes in packaging and containers. Many of us—and particularly in recent months those of us who claim to be socially aware—are fulsome in their praise of returnable bottles. Unfortunately, consumers at large do not seem to share this enthusiasm and are buying their drinks increasingly in non-returnable bottles and cans.

In the middle of last year we introduced a range of non-returnable bottles, including Tizer itself. Sales of these are increasing steadily. In April of this year, we brought out Tizer in ring-pull cans. Sales of Tizer cans have been sufficiently encouraging to allow us to consider an early introduction of other canned drinks.

Our third major problem was our failure to keep pace with the changing pattern of retail distribution. Here in the north we have a sentimental attachment to the corner shop, immortalised in Coronation Street. Corner shops still exist and in large numbers. My belief is that they always will. But self-service stores, supermarkets and even hypermarkets are each year taking an increasing share of total food and confectionery purchasing, and Tizer has simply not been sufficiently aware of these changes. Such outlets require non-returnable containers, as previously stated, and these have recently been added to our range.

But really curing these problems is a long term task: a task which must be carried through by managers with professional marketing and selling skills and a broad and vigorous outlook. Frankly there were not sufficient people of this style in the company when Peter Quinn arrived. But today we now have a compact, but effective marketing department, including a marketing manager and two brand managers. Their role is simply defined: development and implementation of effective marketing policies to achieve our objective sales and profit.

The particular concerns are brand and product marketing strategies which include such items as advertising and promotion—both above and below the line—market research and evaluation, packaging design and product innovation. In short they are concerned with the use of resources and the coordination of policies and activities which are aimed at satisfying the needs of our customers—but at a profit.

While the marketing department was and is working so hard to get our product range right in every way, we also had to begin the job of ensuring that Tizer products are available in all those outlets and places where the consumer now shops or enjoys his leisure.

So I recruited a team of key account salesmen, all men experienced in negotiating at top level with major multiple organisations. They have been presenting Tizer to such organisations for some time now and you can now see Tizer products on the shelves of renowned retailers like Sainsbury and Tesco, or you can buy Tizer from new-style discounters like Kwik-Save and Woolco.

We are well represented in multiple off-licence groups and the confectionery/news chains which are rapidly gaining strength throughout the country. And in the vital 'on-premise' area we are at this time conducting a major sales campaign to have our products available in all types of catering and leisure outlets—licensed or unlicensed.

Also, we have created a mobile sales development team whose job is to go into districts where we have sales problems or to open up areas where we hope eventually to establish branches. This is the sort of organisation which is common in the field of fast-moving consumer goods, but which did not exist in Tizer until only a few months ago.

We are also working hard to improve the sales effectiveness of our 300-strong driver sales force by better on-job training, more attractive promotional activity and better merchandising aids.

Our aim in 1971 has been to reinforce our traditional business in terms of products, whilst developing new products and getting into new channels of distribution.

In relation to reinforcing our traditional business we initiated substantial media campaigns this year. We ran a major TV campaign throughout the north of England from May to September.[1] We used

[1]Tizer did not advertise during the period when the new image was being developed.

children's comics for a campaign aimed specifically at our younger customers. We redesigned the labels on our entire range. We engaged in promotional activity specifically aimed at our corner-shop customers. And we undertook special below the line activity to strengthen our grip on multiple retailing. This package has served to increase the awareness of trade and consumers alike of the new Tizer.

We have also done much in the new product area, particularly in terms of products suited for modern distributive channels. As previously stated we introduced NRBs and cans. We supported the can introduction in the south of England with cinema commercials shown throughout the south and the south-west. We also brought to the market, Quencher—a range of still drinks in four flavours, in cartons—which have been a great success.

And of course we have obtained the franchise for Royal Crown Cola, an American cola of international repute, which will greatly help us in our drive on catering outlets.

For the future, we have plans to attack the huge squash market much more vigorously. I have mentioned other flavours of cans. There are other products under detailed consideration. We are moving into the export field.

In distributive terms, we must consolidate our position as a leading supplier of carbonated drinks to multiple organisations. We have detailed plans aimed at achieving this. We are currently examining the possibility of private label packing of carbonates. And we are alert to all developments in competitive products packaging and labelling.

The production and distribution functions were put under the control of Mr Hanmer, assistant managing director. Mr Hanmer had joined Tizer in 1968 after twenty years in the Far East and was the oldest of the executive directors. He described the changes instituted as follows:[1]

At the beginning of 1970 the company operated twenty-one factories throughout the country from Newcastle in the north to Southampton in the south and Swansea in the west.

From each one of these factories sales were achieved through a total of approximately 350 van salesmen selling in the main to retail outlets. The sales vehicles had open bodies which exposed the products to the elements and many of the vehicles would very shortly have commanded a high price in the vintage car market.

Each factory had its own bottling line or lines supplying its own sales needs, and production was carried out very much on a make-today, sell tomorrow basis, which resulted in very poor productivity figures, underutilization of labour, wastage of raw materials and poor quality

[1]Northern Stock Exchange presentation, October 1971.

control. Also because of the intermingling of sales and production functions, we had poor stock control.

The bottling equipment in use was to a large extent designed and fabricated in Tizer's own engineering workshops, and although probably very adequate in the 1930s, had been out of date for more than a decade. As this equipment grew older, so the expenditure on maintenance and replacement of worn parts made ever-increasing drains on company profits.

Managers of undoubted and unquestionable loyalty to the company had, in the main, been promoted from their original jobs as van salesmen and, not having had adequate training in production techniques or budgetary control, were unable to run their factories so as to produce the best financial results.

The management structure was such that factory managers found themselves in a split command situation: they were responsible to a sales director and a production director simultaneously. This frequently resulted in a confused situation ultimately leading to inefficiency in both functions, and a top-heavy and disgruntled workforce.

In summary, we had to deal with low productivity, over capacity, out-of-date equipment and poor organisation. Therefore we set out to rationalise the total operation to increase productivity, and create an effective sales organisation in order to increase sales, and achieve an increased turnover with a smaller total workforce.

To achieve the objectives, the following actions have been, or are being, taken. Production has ceased at ten production units and is being concentrated still further so that we shall enter 1972 with six production units for carbonated products and one production unit for squashes, supplying twenty-three depots throughout the country.

All production units have been or will be equipped with plant and machinery which will not require the services of the previous central engineering workshop, which has been disbanded. In fact, one of the production units will be fitted with high speed machinery of continental manufacture, which will make use of the very latest production and mechanical handling techniques. The remaining production units will operate against centrally-planned production programmes in order to achieve maximum rationalisation and productivity. The closure of production units has brought, and will bring about, further reductions in the total workforce.

The transport fleet will be supplemented with a primary distribution fleet of heavy-load carrying vehicles with trailers to supply goods from production units to sales depots, and the retail sales vans replaced with up-to-date covered vehicles so that non-returnable cardboard containers can readily be carried.

Our management structure has been reorganised so that managers are directly responsible to regional managers, who in turn are directly responsible to the operations director. We are also setting up a central laboratory for routine quality control and flavour research and development.

With an eye to the future, we have this year recruited graduates as management trainees, some of whom are currently doing a six-month stint as driver/salesmen.

We believe that our van selling force will be our primary means of increasing sales turnover for some time to come—and this is the reason why we are re-equipping our sales force with new vehicles, new uniforms, a planned programme of sales promotions, ranging from incentives for the individual salesman to retailer and consumer promotion schemes. But we are nevertheless investigating other means of supplying retailers and have already two tele-sales depots operating in the south of England on a pilot scheme basis.

By the end of 1970 the start of these activities had produced a small loss, and had had no appreciable effect on turnover. By the end of 1971 a large loss had been recorded, but turnover had increased by almost 20 per cent. Exhibits 1 and 2 provide the relevant financial information.

Time, however, had run out for Mr Quinn. On 6 December Armour Trust Ltd offered for the whole of Tizer equity at an underwritten value of £2,300,000. The offer was satisfied by an issue of ordinary shares and partly convertible unsecured loan stock, which provided the Tizer shareholders with an offer equivalent to 55 pence/share, at the date of issue. Tizer's institutional shareholders, including Slater Walker, accepted the offer immediately. Only a small group of shareholders considered that Tizer would be better off as an independent company, but they were unable to muster enough votes.

ARMOUR TRUST'S ADMINISTRATION

Armour Trust was a financial holding company with close links to the Slater Walker empire. At the time Tizer was purchased, Armour was active in the fields of property development, consumer finance, and television retailing.

In the offer document Mr Quinn and his board, after consultation with their advisers, forecast a pre-tax loss for the year to 31 December 1971, of about £90,000, before charging extraordinary losses of £27,000. In the event the disclosed losses totalled £244,000, before charging extraordinary losses of £140,000.

The management of Armour attempted to stem these losses mainly by selling off property and closing sales branches. They were, in effect, reversing Quinn's policies of national expansion and instituting policies designed to make Tizer once more a collection of regional bottlers.

The Armour Trust administration lasted only for one year and one day. Under an agreement dated 7 December 1972, A. G. Barr & Company

Limited acquired the whole of the issued capital of Tizer with effect from 3 December 1972. The transaction was for cash. Armour Trust received £2,000,000 on 8 December and £500,000 on 12 April 1973.

In the statement to shareholders, Armour Trust attributed the problems of Tizer to a lack of effective control systems. They stated

Your Board instituted new financial and operational controls with Tizer, which inevitably required a number of months to produce tangible improvements. In the opinion of your Board these new controls were proving effective and Tizer was on the recovery path but, due to the poor summer of 1972, the results of Tizer for the period to 2 December 1972 were disappointing.

In November 1972 your Board was approached by Barr who wished to purchase Tizer and thereby create the largest group exclusively engaged in .the soft drinks trade in the United Kingdom. Your Board considered that such a merger would be likely to lead to the faster development of Tizer and the better safeguard of the future of its employees. Furthermore, your Board considered that although the rationalisation programme which was being implemented would have led Tizer in due course to good level of profitability, the proceeds of sale could be more profitably utilised in other directions. The offer from Barr was, therefore, accepted.

EXHIBIT 1
Tizer Limited (B) Income Statement (£'000s)

	1969	1970	1971	1972 (to 2 Dec)
Turnover	2,949	2,978	3,551	3,266
Trading profit (loss)	143	68	(104)(est)	(13)
Add				
Surplus on sale of branches	9	13	See Note 2	See Note 3
Investment income	48	46	20 (est)	–
	200	127	(84)(est)	(13)
Deduct				
Depreciation	92	105	110	116
Other	39	49	50	68
	— 131	— 154	— 160	— 184
Profit/(loss) before tax and extraordinary items	69	(27)	(244)	(197)
Extraordinary items	–	–	(340)	111

1. At 31 December 1970, the value of plant, machinery and motor vehicles was reduced by £165,551 to allow for items which, in the opinion of the directors and in view of the plans for rationalisation of production in 1971, had little or no further useful life. This amount, together with a terminal loss on reorganisation of £95, 160, was charged to reserves in the 1970 accounts.

2. Extraordinary expenditure (less income) charged in the consolidated profit and loss account in the year ended 31 December 1971, but not charged above, was as follows:

Costs incurred on closure of branches and withdrawal of certain production facilities	£97,912
Stock written off on cessation of Royal Crown Cola franchise	23,700
Expenses in connection with the acquisition of Tizer by Armour	15,250
Surplus arising from sales of investments and properties (net)	(13,217)
Costs of redesigning Tizer's 'logo'	16,992
	140,637
Provision for Tizer redevelopment costs	199,000
	£339,637

3. Extraordinary income (less expenditure) charged in the consolidated profit and loss account in the year ended 2 December 1972 but not charged above, was as follows:

Surpluses on sale of properties	£149,000
Costs incurred in closure of branches and withdrawal of production facilities.	(50,491)
Other income (being £28,388 less expenditure of £15,791)	12,597
	£111,330

Sources: For 1969 and 1970, Tizer Limited Annual Reports
For 1971 and 1972, Armour Trust Records

EXHIBIT 2

Tizer Limited (B) Consolidated balance sheets (£'000s)

	1969	1970	1971	1972 (2 Dec)
FIXED ASSETS				
Land and buildings	805	1,321	1,242	1,043
Plant, machinery and motor vehicles	551	419	505	618
Goodwill	59	–	–	–
	1,415	1,740	1,747	1,661
CURRENT ASSETS				
Stocks	406	495	575	797
Debtors	300	336	315	417
Investments	677	422	221	–
Cash	36	12	10	4
Amount owing by Armour	–	–	–	271
	1,420	1,265	1,122	1,489
CURRENT LIABILITIES				
Creditors	302	350	684	608
Bank Overdraft	–	57	–	477
Taxation	99	5	3	–
Dividend (Gross)	75	25	–	–
Amount owing to fellow subsidiary	–	–	–	10
Provision for branch closures	– –	–	–	159
	477	436	687	1,253
NET CURRENT ASSETS	943	829	435	236
Deferred taxation	94	–	–	–
NET TANGIBLE ASSETS	2,264	2,569'	2,182	1,897

Notes:
1. Totals do not match because of rounding errors.
2. Buildings stated (except for 1969) at 1970 open market valuation.
3. Stocks have been valued at the lower of cost and net realisable value or, for certain returnable cases, at cost less provision for deterioration. The value of manufactured stocks includes an appropriate addition for production overheads.
4. At 31 December 1971, following the acquistion of Tizer by Armour, provision of £199,000 was made to meet expected future expenditure and losses expected to be incurred over the following two years arising from the closure and relocation of certain of Tizer's branches. The amount of £159,083 shown above represents the balance of this provision after charging expenditure in the period to 2 December 1972.
5. Capital expenditure authorised at 2 December 1972, but not provided for above amounted to £45,000, of which £39,000 had been contracted for.
6. At 2 December 1972, there were unrealised surpluses of £390,863 arising from the revaluation of properties in 1970. No provision has been made for the potential liability to tax on the chargable gains which may arise is such surpluses were realised by the sale of the freehold and leasehold properties at the values stated above.

88

7. There are losses for taxation purposes amounting to approximately £900,000, which are available for set-off against taxable trading profits arising in future to relieve the liability to taxation thereon.

Sources: 1969 figures from Annual Report
1970 and 1972 figures from Shareholder Offer Documents
1971 figures from Armour Trust

Industry Structure
and Strategy

7

Background Note on the Hotel Industry

In the mid-summer of 1977, the management of hotel groups throughout the world found their industry at a crossroads. The most important influence on the industry during recent years had been the rapid inflation of costs which had not only squeezed profits at existing properties but had made future developments less attractive. The rapid rise of construction costs had created a situation where 'new' hotels were at a considerable economic disadvantage to hotels built before recent cost increases. As the Annual Report of the American Society of Travel Agents (ASTA) said in 1976:

> '... it can cost as much as $80,000 per room to build a modern hotel complete with convention facilities. This would mean that rooms would have to be priced at a daily rate of about $80. Clearly the hotels that were built only a few years ago when construction cost was about $30,000 per room will have a competitive advantage over new properties'.

This period of cost inflation was accompanied by a general economic depression which caused sluggishness in some demand growth trends for hotel accommodation. Hotel managements in 1977 were, however, more confident about future demand trends and were evaluating their approach to the future.

INDUSTRY CHARACTERISTICS

The hotel industry although in the 'service' sector has many similarities to heavy industries. For example, new capacity is usually added in large discrete units, expansion of existing capacity often being restricted by built up areas.

It is not possible to increase supply in response to a gradual increase in demand with the inevitable result that periods of temporary excess capacity arise especially when several industry members react to the same demand

EXHIBIT 1
Pattern of Hotel Openings at London (Heathrow) Airport

Hotel	Opening Year	Capacity (Rooms)	Percentage Increase in Total Capacity
Ariel	1961	184	
Skyways	1962	490	266
Excelsior	1964	660	98
Centre	1968	360	27
Skyline	1971	365	21
Holiday Inn	1973	300 ⎫	
Holiday Inn	1973	300 ⎪	
Post House	1973	600 ⎬	113
Heathrow	1973	680 ⎪	
Sheraton	1973	440 ⎭	

trends. This type of situation is typified by the pattern of hotel openings at London's Heathrow Airport 1961–1973, as shown in Exhibit 1.

The hotel industry operates in a variety of markets both industrial and consumer and often on an international basis. There is a wide range of potential markets, e.g. business, holiday, leisure, conference, training and contractual, each with their own characteristics of seasonality, service standard requirements and price sensitivity. Many hotel chains adopt similar market stances at all their properties whilst others attempt to 'tailor make' individual hotels to local conditions. Many properties are specifically designed to exploit particular market segments through design features such as conference facilities or training syndicate rooms.

The hotel industry basically comprises two businesses; firstly, rooms and secondly, food and beverage. Most hotel organisations reflect this split of operation, especially at unit level. These two businesses are, of course, complementary and the market segmentation strategy adopted for the rooms operation will affect the food and beverage facilities required and vice versa. For example, the exploitation of the contractual accommodation segment (e.g. aircrew contracts) generally produces lower food and beverage revenues per room than exploitation of the conference or business segment.

These two businesses also have different economic characteristics with differing levels of fixed cost and contribution. These different characteristics are demonstrated in Exhibit 2 where the Pannell, Kerr and Forster Company (consultants specialising in the hotel trade) have aggregated the results of several U.K. hotels' rooms and food/beverage operations. Also in Exhibit 2, PKF analyse the aggregated source and use of funds in 354 international hotels throughout the world.

Leading worldwide hotel chains have accumulated considerable experience and often adopt an approach to their operations based on centrally laid down standards and objectives. Management at the hotel unit level in large chains often tend to be implementors of standard operating procedures and service levels. Management control is implemented through exception principles. Where performance is not in line with central standards, action to rectify the situation is introduced.

These standard operating procedures have been developed to exploit profitably the particular market segment(s) chosen by the chain. Their experience gained in the operation of many similar properties is especially invaluable when new properties are opened, as systems can be readily 'plugged-in'. The large hotel groups can also manage the allocation of their management resources and match managerial skills to the life cycle stages of their properties. The chain operators have managers with direct experience of opening new properties, who can be allocated accordingly.

Some chain operators have gained considerable reputations in particular market segments. For example, in the U.S.A. the luxury segment market leaders are probably Loew's and Western International. These reputations,

---

EXHIBIT 2

(A) Sources and Use of the Hotel Income Dollar (1975)

Source

Room Sales (including public room rentals)	47.4c	
Food Sales (including sundries)	29.0	
Beverage Sales (including sundries)	15.0	
Telephone Sales	3.5	
Casino—net profit	1.7	
Other department profits	0.8	
Store Rentals	0.9	
Other Income	1.7	
Total Hotel Income		100.0c

Use

Employees:		
Salaries and wages	25.5c	
Employees meals	1.9	
Employees Benefits	5.5	32.9c
Other Operating Costs:		
Cost of Food Sold	10.2c	
Cost of Beverages sold	3.9	
Management fees	2.9	
Operating Supplies + Expenses	26.4	43.4c
Balance available for Insurance, Taxes, Rent, Interest, Depreciation and Income Taxes		23.7c
Total Hotel Income		100.0c

Source: Pannel, Kerr, Forster and Company
Trends in the Hotel Business 1976

EXHIBIT 2 (continued)

(B) *Hotel Operation Cost and Revenue Structure (1976)Cost as % of Revenue (U.K.)*

Rooms Operation

Rooms Sales	100.0%

Expenses

Salaries	9.9
Employees Meals	1.2
Employees Benefits	2.4
Total employee related	13.5
Laundry	2.7
Linen etc.	0.8
Commissions	1.6
Other expenses	5.2
Total rooms related	23.8

ROOMS GROSS PROFIT (before Fixed Costs) 76.2%

Food and Beverage Operation

Food Sales	67.6
Beverage Sales	32.4
Food and Beverage Sales	100.0%

Expenses

Cost of food sold	24.9
Cost of beverages sold	10.7
Total cost of sales	35.6
Salaries	28.7
Employees Meals	2.6
Employees Benefits	5.5
Total Employee Related	36.8
Laundry	0.9
Linen, crockery, etc.	2.0
Music and Entertainment	0.9
Menus and drink list	0.4
Kitchen fuel	0.6
Other expenses	5.6
Total Food/Bev. related	10.4
Incidental income	(3.1)
Total Expenses	79.7

FOOD AND BEVERAGE GROSS PROFIT
(before Fixed Costs) 20.3%

gained over some years, have considerable marketing benefits as customers are assured of acceptable standards wherever their business (or pleasure) takes them. The chain concept is also seen in world-wide reservation systems often linked to airline and travel agent networks.

RECENT INDUSTRY TRENDS

Exhibit 3 shows the world league table of hotel and motel chains showing the clear leadership of the Holiday Inns Inc. chain with almost 300,000 rooms linked in a world-wide chain. Holiday Inns has three times as many rooms as its closest competitor, Ramada Inns.

During 1976, the Holiday Inns announced a five year plan that included an operating philosophy distinctly different from that previously followed. The chain would in the future concentrate on quality rather than quantity – no more plans to build a new inn every 3 days! In fact there would probably be a reduction in the total number of units. Future developments would be more selective and increasingly directed towards airports, downtown areas and convention/conference properties much less dependent on automobile traffic. A much more professional market approach would be adopted. Expansion in Europe, where a more 'up-market' stance had been adopted, would also be more controlled.

Hilton Hotels, the world's fifth chain, suffered an overall decline in room occupancy in 1975, 63% as opposed to 66% in 1974. The chain decided to move away from ownership and to seek more contracts to operate properties owned by outside investors. During 1975, the group sold a 50% interest in six of its largest properties to the Prudential Insurance Company for $83 million. From Hilton's viewpoint this made them less vulnerable to cyclical swings. For the Prudential, hotel ownership was a better protection against inflation than commercial properties. Room rates can be adjusted quickly while commercial properties generally operate under long-term leases.

A further development in the hotel industry has been the entry of airline operators seeking both diversification and integrated marketing capabilities. In 1975 both Pan Am and TWA had heavy airline losses but made profits on their hotel subsidiaries, Inter Continental and Hilton International. These chains were neck and neck for the position of 12th largest world-wide hotel chain.

In the U.K. the Government grant scheme of £1,000 per new room added over 40,000 new hotel rooms in the U.K. in the 1973/75 period. Half of these were in London even though the scheme was originally conceived to assist out of London developments. Overall hotel occupancy in London throughout 1976 was 57%, a significant advance on the 1975 rate of 51%. At the luxury end of the market hotels like the Carlton Towers and the Inn on the Park reported occupancy rates above 90% for 1976. However, hotel owners were not uniformly successful. Lyons was obliged

EXHIBIT 3
World's Largest Hotel/Motel Chains 1974

Rank	Name of Chain	Number of Rooms	Number of Hotels/Motels
1	Holiday Inns, Inc.	267,032	1,688
2	Ramada Inns, Inc.	91,621	669
3	The Sheraton Corporation	90,218	352
4	Howard Johnson Company	58,078	527
5	Hilton Hotels Corp.	56,679	141
6	Trust Houses Forte, Ltd.	56,600	724
7	Balkantourist	50,000	300
8	Days Inns of America, Inc.	35,378	222
9	Quality Inns Int'l., Inc.	33,741	337
10	TraveLodge Int'l., Inc.	30,500	468
11	Red Carpet Inns of America	30,050	236
12	Intercontinental Hotels Corp.	26,646	70
13	Hilton International	22,644	60
14	Motel 6, Inc.	20,627	213
15	Intourist	19,846	60
16	Western Int'l. Hotels, Inc.	19,648	43
17	Club Mediterranee	19,592	70
18	Rodeway Inns of America	18,950	160
19	Hyatt Corporation	17,300	40
20	Marriott Corporation	14,270	40
21	Pontin's, Ltd.	14,189	33
22	Commonwealth Holiday Inns	12,457	61
23	Topeka Inn Mgmt., Inc.	12,023	76
24	CEDOK	11,550	–
25	Grand Metropolitan Ltd.	10,272	66
26	Americana Hotels	10,000	19
27	Downtowner/Rowntowner	9,000	60
28	Hospitality Mgmt. Corp.	8,200	32
29	Chaine Novotel	8,019	88
30	American Motor Inns	8,000	59
31	United Inns. Inc.	7,892	36
32	Interhotel G.D.R.	7,704	27
33	Canadian Pacific Hotels, Ltd.	7,652	19
34	J. Lyons & Co., Ltd.	7,551	34
35	Hyatt International Corp.	7,517	16
36	TraveLodge Australia, Ltd.	6,841	78
37	Crest Hotels Europe	6,613	86
38	LQ Motor Inns, Inc.	6,212	56
39	S.E.M.I.-S.P.A.	6,250	63
40	Tokyu Hotel Chain	5,726	27
41	Melia Hotels	5,632	21
42	Econo-Travel Motor Hotels	5,602	110
43	Loews Hotels	5,589	11
44	Orbis	5,589	28
45	Plava Laguna Hotel & Tourist Enterprise	5,471	21
46	Dunley Family Corp.	5,400	22

47	Southern Sun	5,218	34
48	Hungarhotels	5,200	37
49	EHC Hotel Services, Ltd.	4,804	10
50	Centre Hotels	4,728	24

Note: Lex, in 1976, operated six hotels with 2130 rooms
Source: American Society of Travel Agents (A.S.T.A.) Annual Report 1976.

to sell off their hotel interests. Trust House Forte acquired the major part, 35 hotels for £27.5 million, at the end of 1976. At £5,000 per room, this seemed very cheap compared with building new high rise hotels at £30,000 per room. In mid 1977 the only major new hotel development in London, the 705 room Melia on the South bank of the Thames, still remained only half finished with the receiver Price Waterhouse looking for new investors. In the long term, the success of the U.K. hotel industry, particularly in London, was heavily dependent on foreign visitors. It was important, therefore, that increases in capacity should closely match the rise in tourism.

OWNERSHIP TRENDS

The ASTA Annual Report on World Travel Trends and Markets (1976) reported:

> 'Most hotel chains are now beginning to de-emphasize ownership and are concentrating on acquiring management contracts to operate hotels owned by outside investors or government agencies. Although this reduced the opportunity for large profits in boom years, it helps to produce a steadier, more even flow of profits in a business that can be affected by both economic cycles and foreign political upheavals.'

A survey of ten major U.S. hotel chains showed that between 1970 and 1977 the proportion of company owned or leased hotels fell from 33% to 20% while franchised hotels rose from 68% to 72% and hotels with management contracts rose from 1% to 8%.

These ownership trends reflect both a supply and demand situation. The supply of suitable hotel properties had been enhanced by the notorious 'property booms' of the 1960's and early 1970's. Property developers with no experience of hotel operation have consequently been seeking reliable and competent hotel operators to manage their property. On the other hand, hotel operators, faced with rapidly escalating development costs, have been attracted towards alternative methods of operation.

THE MANAGEMENT CONTRACT

In the typical management contract, the most fundamental provisions can be summarised as follows:

(i) That the management contract assigns to the operator all responsibilities for thc 'operation' of the hotel

(ii) That the contract assigns to the owner all financial and legal responsibilities.

Exhibit 4 is a summary of the main areas of responsibility under an hotel management contract.

However, a developing trend in the hotel management contracting field is towards a greater sharing of financial responsibility between the owner and operator. As a result, there is also considerable variation in the management fee structure with greater emphasis on the incentive component rather than the 'basic fee'. The bargaining power of the major hotel chain operators who are able to offer well known brand names, worldwide booking systems and standard operating systems and procedures has meant that they have negotiated larger incentive components. Four main types of contract where the operator makes an 'equity contribution' can be identified.

(i) *Joint venture or partnership*: Legal partnership where operator contributes equity and jointly 'owns' the property.

(ii) *Furniture, fixtures and fittings*: The operator purchases the lease of fittings, etc.

(iii) *Pre-opening expenses*: The operator contributes his expertise pre-opening and bears the pre-opening expenses.

(iv) *Working Capital*: Operator contributes initial working capital but is not responsible for maintaining balances.

EXHIBIT 4

Main Areas of Responsibility under Hotel Management Contracts

The *operator* is responsible for:

(a) The management of all matters affecting the hotel personnel; hiring, firing pay and conditions.

(b) The determination and implementation of pricing policies and the collection of all revenues.

(c) The installation and operation of suitable accounting systems and the payment, in the name of the owner, of all expenses incurred.

(d) Purchasing all materials and supplies for the hotel operation.

(e) Advertising, promoting and selling the hotel.

(f) Obtaining all necessary licences, the leasing of equipment (where appropriate) and the management of any service sub-contracts.

(g) Planning and budgeting the hotel operation, obtaining the owner's approval for the budget and any other capital expenditure programmes.

(h) The repair and improvement of the hotel property, again usually subject to owner's approval.

The *owner* agrees to:

(a) Provide all fixed and working capital requirements, usually with provisions that increased injections of working capital will be provided if working capital falls below a pre-arranged level.

(b) Grant the operator sole and exclusive rights to operate the hotel on behalf of the owner, in his name and for the owners account.

(c) Not to interfere in the general operation of the hotel, but to retain rights of approval of budgets, capital expenditure, plans, etc.

(d) Permit the management contract to survive the sale of the hotel (usually).

(e) Carry fully fire, general and employer's liability.

(f) To compensate the operator through:

    (i) a basic management fee (usually a fixed percentage of gross revenue)

or

    (ii) An incentive management fee (usually a percentage, perhaps on a sliding scale, of operating profits).

8

The Lex Hotel Strategy

The Lex company was founded in 1928 and initially operated a few garages in the London area. Under the management of the Chinn brothers, Norman and Rosser, the group, after 1945, greatly expanded its garage, forecourt, servicing and parking activities. The company went public in 1960 and in 1962 slightly diversified its activities by buying Albany Travel and Albany Freight. The company also extended its influence in the motor distribution market by dealing in a variety of British, European and American marques and also through geographical expansion in the South, South West and Northern England. However, by the end of the 1960's Lex had concentrated on the Volvo, British Leyland and Rolls Royce ranges. In 1970, 92% of Lex turnover came from vehicle distribution and leasing.

DIVERSIFICATION STRATEGY

Trevor Chinn, Rosser's son, became the managing director in 1968 and soon announced the group's intention to enter new business areas. It was believed that the Lex position in the vehicle distribution industry had been achieved through the exercise of management skills. It was his intention to apply these skills in other service industries, especially in upper market segments. An objective to generate more than 50% of profits from non-auto operations by 1972 was set in 1968. In 1970, Trevor Chinn specified the new business strategy for Lex:

'It is our intention to become a diversified company, operating in a number of major service industries. Each target industry will be selected on certain criteria:

(a) It must be large enough totally to allow Lex to establish a business entity complete in line and staff management of the highest calibre.

(b) It must have a growth potential in the coming decade which will enable us to maintain a rate of profit growth equal to that or our existing businesses.

(c) Lex must be able to establish itself among the market leaders of the industry.

(d) Lex must expect that within a reasonable time, it will draw an important contribution to company profits from that service industry.

(e) We will select industries that require a high level of service to customers, that preferably are fragmented and operate on a decentralised basis and where accordingly profit improvement can be achieved through the exercise of planning, financial control, marketing and personnel management.'

DIVERSIFICATION MOTIVES

Trevor Chinn appreciated that Lex was in 1968 heavily involved in the vehicle distribution industry. This meant that Lex was largely dependent on the success of the vehicle producers. If they produced uncompetitive and unreliable products Lex suffered. Therefore Lex sought greater autonomy in order to meet their growth aspirations by entering other markets. Various sectors of the economy were studied and eventually the service sector was chosen as the one offering greatest growth prospects.

At first Lex diversified into service sectors close to motor retailing, leasing, accessories, tyres, batteries, etc. but subsequently a broader spectrum of service activities was considered including transportation, plant-hire, freight-forwarding and hotels.

In the 1972 Report and Accounts, Trevor Chinn commented on the choice of the hotel industry:

'We believe the hotel industry ideally fits the shape of the business activity for which we are searching. The difference in the hotel industry is the actual level of capital intensity. Vehicle distribution has a high level of operational gearing but hotels have an even higher level. Otherwise the business structure is very similar.'

Trevor Chinn was also keenly interested in international expansion and viewed the developing interests in hotels, travel and freight-forwarding as the basis for overseas expansion.

IMPLEMENTING THE HOTEL STRATEGY

In June 1970, the first move into the hotel industry was made with the purchase of Pondust Ltd. involving Lex in the construction of a Hilton Hotel in Stratford-on-Avon. In December of that year, a ten year management agreement was signed between Lex and the Hyatt International Corporation for the construction by Lex of an hotel at Heathrow Airport that would be managed by Hyatt.

October 1971 saw the purchase of the The Carlton Tower Hotel from the Sonesta Corporation for £4.6 million. This well established luxury grade hotel was operated by Lex. In January 1972, Lex initiated the building of a hotel at London Gatwick Airport for operation by Lex.

In 1972 and 1973, Lex acquired three already operating hotels in the USA. Firstly, the Friendship International at Baltimore Airport and subsequently two further Sonesta properties, the Royal Orleans in New Orleans and Sonesta in Houston (renamed The Whitehall). The Royal Orleans was a well established luxury hotel, while the Whitehall Houston was a newer hotel which had never established itself in the community. Shortly after its takeover, Lex embarked on a refurbishing and upgrading programme at the Whitehall Houston.

By March 1973 when the Heathrow Hotel was opened, Lex had decided to buy out Hyatt and operate the 680 room hotel, by far the largest at the airport, as owner-operators. In the final stages of construction at The Heathrow, Lex incorporated a highly sophisticated custom built conference facility (The York Theatre). This facility was to be the basis of Lex's entry into the conference market at The Heathrow. Also during 1973, the Stratford property owned by Lex was opened under the operation of Hilton International under a long-term management contract.

EXHIBIT 1
Lex Involvement in Hotels (August 1977)

Hotels	Location	No of Rooms	Grading*	Ownership/ Operation
U.K.				
Carlton Tower	London City Centre	300	5 star	Ownership sold July 1977. Lex operate under management contract
Heathrow Hotel	London Airport	680	4 star	Owner/operator
Gatwick Park Hotel	London Gatwick Airport	155	4 star	Owner/operator (due to open 1978)
Stratford Hilton	City Centre	N/A	4 star	Owned by Lex and operated by Hilton International under management contract.
U.S.A.				
Royal Orleans	New Orleans City Centre	400	4 star	Owner/operator
Whitehall Chicago	City Centre	227	4 star	Owner/operator
Whitehall Houston	City Centre	325	4 star	Owner/operator
Friendship International	Baltimore Airport	200	3 star	Owner/operator

Source: U.K. Hotels AA Guide
  U.S. Hotels Mobil Travel Guide. (4 star is top grade in this ranking)

Lex had been involved in the renovation of a private club and residential hotel in Chicago, in conjunction with the landlord, since 1972. In June 1974, the property opened as The Whitehall Hotel Chicago, now designed to be a premier grade hotel in Chicago city centre.

Having successfully owned and operated The Carlton Tower Hotel for nearly six years, Lex sold the property in July 1977 for £14 million but as part of the sales agreement, were retained as operators under a long term management contract. Exhibit 1 shows the portfolio of Lex hotels in August 1977.

RESULTS OF THE HOTEL STRATEGY

The Lex Service Group first earned revenue from its hotel operations in 1971. By 1976, 9% of total group turnover came from hotel activities. Exhibit 2 shows the distribution of sales revenue and profits between the main activity groupings of Lex for 1971–1976. Prior to 1974, the hotel and travel activities were grouped together in Lex accounts.

Exhibit 3 contains the 1974–76 operating results of the individual hotels in the Lex portfolio excluding the Stratford Hilton and the Gatwick property (which remained unopened even in 1977). The results are analysed by the traditional split of hotel activities, i.e. Rooms and Food/Beverage Operations. Exhibit 4 shows the cost and revenue structure of the Lex Hotel portfolio using 1975 as a sample year. The split of revenue between Room and Food/Beverage operations at each hotel is shown as well as the direct costs attributable to these separate operations.

During the diversification phase, the Lex Service Group financial structure underwent considerable change as new sources of capital.were utilised in order to finance the expansion into transportation, plant hire, personnel services and hotels. Exhibit 5 shows trends of profits and capital structure over the 1968–1977 period.

MANAGING THE HOTEL PORTFOLIO

The Lex management approach to the hotel industry was largely governed by the factors that lead to the choice of the industry in the first instance. Amongst the most important influences were:

– susceptibility to decentralised management
– need for high quality service standards
– the ability to position the properties in the upper market segments
– the achievement of results through the application of modern management techniques.

Therefore Lex did not seek to create a chain of hotels but rather to create individual units suited to the needs of the local markets. It was felt that

EXHIBIT 2

LEX Service Group Revenue and Profit by Main Activities 1971–1976 (£'000)

	1971		1972		1973		1974		1975		1976	
	Sales Rev (% Tot)	PBT (% Tot)	Sales Rev (% Tot)	PBT (% Tot)	Sales Rev (% Tot)	PBT (% Tot)	Sales Rev (% Tot)	PBT (% Tot)	Sales Rev (% Tot)	PBT (% Tot)	Sales Rev (% Tot)	PBT (% Tot)
Passenger car distribn and servicing	101980 (92)	4574 (92)	89226 (69)	6173 (78)	101184 (62)	6784 (74)	93244 (56)	5293 (53)	119408 (63)	6295 (62)	159446 (63)	8552 (58)
Comm'cl V'hcle Plant Distbn & Servicing			26339 (20)	216 (3)	35668 (22)	847 (9)	35254 (21)	1684 (17)	28652 (15)	681 (7)	39019 (16)	724 (5)
Transpn, freight handling & veh. leasing	3041 (3)	99 (2)	4214 (4)	505 (6)	7901 (5)	454 (5)	8716 (5)	591 (6)	11049 (6)	1023 (10)	14239 (6)	1647 (11)
Plant Hire	–	–	–	–	2849 (2)	779 (8)	8812 (5)	2368 (24)	9327 (5)	1925 (19)	9862 (4)	1990 (13)

*Hotels UK	3470 (3)	(13) loss	6957 (5)	750 (9)	8157 (5)	(144) (2)	5543 (3)	(464) (5)	7536 (4)	524 (5)	9084 (4)	1746 (12)
*Hotels USA	⎱ (combined)	⎱ (combined)	864 (1)	22	4842 (3)	(196) (2)	7251 (4)	61 (1)	10032 (5)	(484) (loss)	13441 (5)	46
Personnel Services	2834 (3)	293 (6)	1832 (1)	287 (4)	3593 (2)	673 (7)	3702 (2)	570 (6)	2682 (1)	245 (2)	2071 (1)	120
Others	–	–	–	–	–	–	5608 (3)	(48)	218; (1)	(40)	4305 (2)	(10)
TOTAL	111325 (100)	4953 (100)	129432 (100)	7953 (100)	164194 (100)	9198 (100)	165400 (100)	10052 (100)	190866 (100)	10169 (100)	251467 (100)	14815 (100)
Property	–	300	–	275	–	472	–	452	–	185	–	124
Interest payable less receivable	–	(917)	–	(882)	–	(3436)	–	(6658)	–	(6099)	–	(6417)
Group overhd less mgt charges	–	46	–	6	–	(223)	–	(144)	–	(169)	–	(687)
PROFIT BEFORE TAX	–	4382	–	7352	–	6011	–	3702	–	4086	–	7835

*Before 1974 Hotels include Travel

Source: Company Accounts

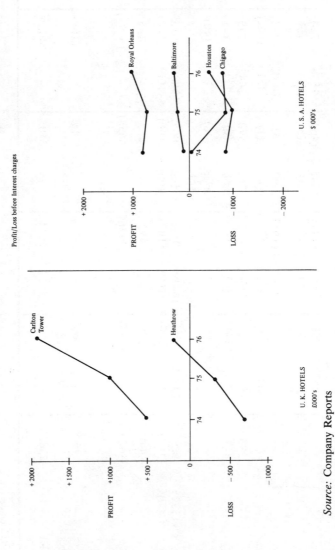

106

EXHIBIT 3
Profit Record Lex Hotels 1974–76

Profit/Loss before Interest charges

Royal Orleans

Baltimore

76

Houston
Chigago

75

74

+ 2000
PROFIT   + 1000

0

LOSS   – 1000

– 2000

U. S. A. HOTELS
$ 000's

Carlton
Tower

Heathrow

76

75

74

+ 2000

+ 1500

+ 1000

PROFIT   + 500

0

LOSS   – 500

– 1000

U. K. HOTELS
£000's

Source: Company Reports

Financial Results Lex Hotels 1974-76 (£'000's/$'000's as appropriate)

— £ 000's — / — $ 000's —

	Heathrow			Carlton Tower			Royal Orleans			Houston			Chicago			Baltimore		
Year	74	75	76	74	75	76	74	75	76	74	75	76	74	75	76	74	75	76
Rooms turnover	1178	1647	2250	1513	2181	2904	4952	5457	5955	1752	1841	2261	408	2032	2459	1365	1411	1584
Food & beverage turnover	1212	1445	1779	1505	1701	2160	3391	3852	4086	1820	1774	2153	1346	1998	2577	1574	1563	1770
Other turnover (A)	33	66	80	–	–	–	–	–	–	–	–	–	284	338	–	–	–	–
Total Turnover	2423	3158	4109	3018	3882	5064	8343	9309	10041	3572	3615	4414	2038	4368	5036	2939	2974	3354
Rooms Profit	507	950	1393	1221	1774	2417	3347	3684	4075	958	1015	1360	188	1164	1456	851	923	1055
F & B Profit	171	316	536	276	316	533	648	745	807	204	223	434	38	98	571	339	448	512
Other Profit	4	32	53	–	–	–	–	–	–	–	–	–	284	338	–	–	–	–
Total Profit (Depts)	682	1298	1982	1497	2090	2950	3995	4429	4882	1162	1238	1794	510	1600	2027	1190	1371	1567
'Discretionary' Fixed Costs (B)	792	816	879	514	548	736	1605	1784	1949	1174	1236	1284	471	1128	1406	617	625	716
Gross Operating Profit	(110)	482	1103	983	1542	2214	2390	2645	2933	(12)	2	510	39	472	621	573	746	851
Fixed Costs (C)	703	826	840	424	500	308	1427	1807	1787	749	877	929	56	1250	1320	489	540	596
Profit (Loss) Before Interest	(813)	(344)	263	559	1042	1906	963	838	1146	(761)	(875)	(419)	(17)	(778)	(699)	84	206	255
Occupancy %	62	61	68	72	79	81	78	78	77	51	46	53	41	48	54	75	67	67
Average Room Rate	£6.6	9.1	10.9	15.8	20.2	26.3	$41.0	45.6	48.8	26.7	31.4	33.8	48.9	47.6	51.3	23.7	27.0	30.2

(A) – Includes conference, training and syndicate rooms revenue
(B) – Includes Admin., Advertising, Promotion, Utilities, Repairs & Maintenance – Net of income from shop rentals, etc.
(C) – Includes Rent, Rates, Depreciation

107

EXHIBIT 4
Lex Hotels Cost Structure – 1975 (Percentages)

	Heathrow	Carlton Tower	Baltimore	Chicago	Royal Orleans	Houston
Revenue						
Room Sales	52	56	47	50	59	51
Food and Beverages Sales	48	44	53	50	41	49
Total	100	100	100	100	100	100
distributed as follows:						
Direct Costs						
Room operations	22	10	16	21	19	23
F & B operations	36	35	37	47	33	43
Total Direct	58	45	53	68	52	66
Indirect Costs						
Overheads	27	15	22	28	20	34
Fixed	26	13	18	31	19	24
Total Indirect	53	28	40	59	39	58
Profit before interest	(11)	27	7	(27)	9	(24)

Source: Company Reports

EXHIBIT 5
Profits and Capital Structure Lex Service Group (1968 – 1976) (£000's)

	Profit Before Interest and Tax	Capital Employed	Long and Medium Term Debt	Long/Medium Interest Charges
1968	1169	6587	2316	116
1969	1479	10620	3429	229
1970	2922	21575	9500	467
1971	5120	36795	8719	738
1972	8059	54938	22049	707
1973	8261	76161	34858	2250
1974	8244	80724	38081	4542
1975	8325	83330	40344	4239
1976	12752	95380	48349	4917

Source: Reports and Accounts

there were negative connotations associated with the 'chain hotel image' that were not suited to the chosen upper market segments: each individual hotel unit was managed as a profit centre with a self contained organisation structure.

Lex chose to operate its hotels in two main market segments, i.e. first class airport hotels and luxury city centre hotels. The up-market posture adopted meant that Lex was involved in refurbishings at the newly acquired hotels in order to reposition them in the market place. This repositioning process also created higher staffing levels in order to produce high standards of personal service. On the revenue side, large increases in room rates and restaurant prices were also introduced.

The repositioning of some Lex hotels was an evolutionary process. For example, at the Heathrow Hotel, the initial market strategy was to achieve high volume and high occupancy ratios in the middle market price range. This strategy did not produce profitable results and thus the fourth General Manager of the hotel appointed in October 1975 increased room rates markedly and concentrated on the upper market segments with greater financial success. The marketing strategy at the Heathrow also directed considerable effort into the exploitation of the conference and training/seminar markets utilising the dedicated resources.

It was felt that the management skills acquired by Lex in its garage operations would be transferable to hotel management. However, Lex acquired hotel management resources along with the established hotels taken over. Even at the Heathrow the first two years were managed by professional 'hotelier management' brought in by Lex. It was gradually appreciated that different management styles, and consequently different managers, were required at the various stages of hotel operation. For example, a project controller was needed during the 'opening and start-up' phase, whereas perhaps a more market oriented approach was required during normal operations or repositioning.

Although the geographically dispersed hotels were managed on a decentralised basis, a three tier management structure was evolved (see Exhibit 6). The tiers are:

Group management
Divisonal management (UK and USA)
Hotel (Unit) management.

In each tier, functional management was responsible to its own General Manager but also had a 'dotted line' relationship with functional management in the next tier.

Over the 1971–76 period group and divisional management concerned itself largely with the control of the hotels in the portfolio and the creation of central policies. It was soon discovered that the day to day demands of running a hotel did not enable much strategic and tactical thinking at unit

EXHIBIT 6
Lex Hotels Organisation Framework

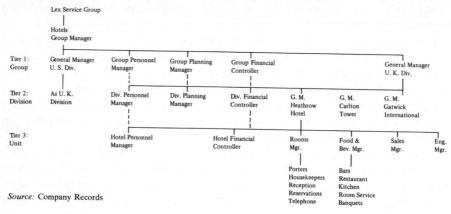

Source: Company Records

level. By mid 1977, it was believed that viable operating and marketing policies had been created and that group and divisional management attention could turn to the possible expansion of the group.

FUTURE HOTELS STRATEGY

Senior management in the Hotels group began to consider some of the aspects of the Lex hotel business that could determine its future shape. They also examined the world wide hotel industry and its developments in order to identify potential opportunities for Lex.

A future hotel strategy would have to be in line with corporate needs and objectives. Specifically, the strategy would need to satisfy the specifications of the diversification strategy established by Trevor Chinn in 1970. The starting position for any strategic development within Lex was their appraisal of their main strengths as summarised by Trevor Chinn in 1973.

> 'We have developed skills in the management of decentralised service businesses; businesses that were fairly large, with a high service content where the necessary strength was high quality management in the unit itself rather than the centre.'

Mr. Chinn had observed that Lex's corporate strength lay in businesses characterised by:

- high service levels
- reasonable degree of technical skill
- large number of employees where clear benefits can be derived from training
- opportunities for planning, information and control systems.

The problem for the management of Lex Hotels was carefully to prescribe a viable future development strategy. The main areas requiring specification were:

(a) Ownership. In 1977, the Lex Hotel portfolio incorporated a variety of styles. Management needed to decide whether a specific pattern should emerge.

(b) Market segments. Again the present portfolio sought to satisfy a range of markets although all properties were in the upper segments.

(c) Geographical considerations. In 1977, Lex Hotels had properties in the UK and USA with only London having more than one Lex property. This geographical split was reflected in the divisional organisation.

(d) Size. Lex had 8 hotels ranging from 180 to 700 rooms. It was believed that the management structure created could easily accommodate the assimilation of more properties, although large individual properties may take up more management time.

In the evaluation of all the possible alternatives, the following criteria were used – risk/return, funding requirements, corporate management skills, growth aspirations, corporate business definition and internationalist aspirations.

THE CHOSEN STRATEGY

By mid 1977, a paper was prepared by the hotel group management for presentation to and approval by the management board. The paper set out a plan for the expansion of the hotel group over the period to 1983.

Lex Hotels set itself an objective of twelve additional properties by 1981 to be operated under management contract. These properties were all likely to be in the USA. The hotels would be positioned in the luxury segment of the market and would be in city-centre locations. The market would be mainly the 'mobile senior executive travelling on company business'. The initial search for new properties would focus on Boston, New York and Washington.

Lex would concentrate on smaller luxury hotels with less than 400 rooms. This was seen as a segment largely neglected by the major chain operators. Lex recognised that competition for hotel management contracts would be fierce but through this segment concentration, they would be able to compete.

Lex would also compete more effectively for management contracts by introducing modifications to the traditional form of hotel management contract placing emphasis on equity contributions and incentive (profit-based) fee structures. Lex would also seek to employ all hotel staff itself rather than acting only on the owners behalf in this respect. Lex predicted an increase in 'owner-developers' with whom Lex could cooperate in the establishment of luxury hotels. Lex would use their proposed equity contributions to 'buy into' the developments and would demonstrate their commitment by their willingness to be rewarded through profit-based fees. As Lex predicted a strengthening of the US economy in the 1978–82 period, the availability of contracts as a result of existing operators' bankrupticies would be restricted. Lex would therefore derive its additional properties from two main sources:

    (i) Cooperation with property developers at the instigation of Lex who would have researched the need for a luxury hotel in an area.

   (ii) The 'repositioning' of existing hotel properties in the market place.

Lex Hotels would actively resist the implementation of a chain image which was seen as inappropriate to the chosen luxury segment. Lex Hotels would differentiate its properties from the competition through high levels of personalised service in its city centre locations and friendliness and efficiency at the airport locations. The Lex name would not be actively promoted to the final consumer but every attempt would be made to establish the name with travel agents, a major source of business in the hotel market.

The hotel group management also made long term plans for the existing hotel portfolio including the opening of the Gatwick International Hotel at London's Gatwick Airport. This opening had been deliberately delayed awaiting a market resurgency. Because of the predominantly holiday oriented traffic mix at Gatwick, a different market position from The Heathrow was planned with a concentration on the training/seminar market in the winter months.

The Lex Hotel management was confident that its plan for the future would enable Lex to satisfy some of its international expansion aspirations and that they matched the expressed corporate interest in high quality service industries utilising the accumulated management skills base. In particular, they were confident that Lex's skills in the operation and financial control of luxury grade hotels would be sought after by property developers.

9

The International Shipping Industry

The shipping industry is made up of a series of different markets which can be distinguished by product, type of service, regularity of sailing and a host of other criteria. It is a truly international industry and still relatively free of direct government restrictions. As such the market in many ways most closely mirrors the economist's definition of classical competition. At the end of the 1970's however there were signs that this position might be changing as the industry reached the trough of perhaps the worst depression it had ever known: massive amounts of the world fleet were laid up, potential bankruptcy faced many companies, and there was growing concentration of ownership in the hands of large corporations and governments. Some indication of the relative importance and diversity of the various segments of the industry are shown in Table 1 which gives a breakdown of world tonnage by type of vessel for 1977. The most important distinction is between the dry cargo and oil trades and the vessel types indicate the range of different ships within these broad categories.

REGISTRATION & OWNERSHIP

A small number of countries are predominant in terms of the size of their registered fleets. The 5 largest account for nearly 60 per cent of the world's registered tonnage and are Liberia (24 per cent), Japan (10 per cent), U.K., Greece and Norway (each with around 8 per cent). The tonnage registered on a country does not, however, give an exact picture of ownership because for various reasons owners do not always trade under their national flag. In practice there are 5 main categories of country:

- Traditional shipping nations which for reasons of Empire, trade etc., have large merchant fleets.
- Countries in which financial and other incentives have encouraged a merchant marine.
    - Countries like Liberia and Panama which enable non-nationals to operate vessels without meeting a variety of obligations related to crew wages, taxation, safety regulations etc., of other countries.

113

E

Table 1
World Tonnage by Type of Vessel 1977

Type	Number	mn. dwt	% of total dwt.
General Cargo	21,783	108.3	16.9
Cellular Container	507	7.3	1.1
Ore/Bulk Carrier	3,961	127.1	19.9
Combination Carrier	445	47.8	7.5
Passenger Liner	152	0.9	0.1
Ferry	966	1.4	0.2
Other Dry Cargo	391	1.6	0.3
Total Dry Cargo	28,205	294.3	46.2
Oil Tanker	6,912	335.3	52.6
Chemical Carrier	492	2.9	0.5
Liquefied Gas	493	4.5	0.7
Other Tanker	106	0.2	0.03
Total Tanker	8,003	343.0	53.8
TOTAL ALL SHIPS	36,208	637.2	100

Source: General Council of British Shipping

- Countries like Greece, where post-second world war tax and other incentives have encouraged a rapid growth in tonnage operated by indigenous owners.
· Countries like Japan and an Arab countries' consortium where rapid industrialisation and/or oil production or consumption have encouraged the build-up of their fleets.
· Many developing countries which have developed small national and usually state-owned fleets to participate in liner trades.
· Special cases such as the recent rapid increase in the Eastern Bloc and Chinese fleets.

TRADING PRACTICES

There are a number of important trading practices which help define the character of the industry and are major determinants in the strategies of individual companies:

The Concept of Liner Shipping and the Conference System

The term 'conference' is generally applied to standing arrangements agreed between operators of liner services for a particular route or routes. As a result operators in a particular trade collaborate to provide regular sailings and tariff structures often sharing expenses and profit on a proportional basis. The system is basically protective and designed to ensure economic load levels and steadier earnings in return for regularity of service. The effects of cost inflation overtaking those of productivity and the inability to increase rates or load factors to realistic levels, have encouraged ship owners to rationalise their sailings in this way and today there are around 350 liner conferences worldwide.

Conference members face competition from three different outside sources. Airlines compete for high value low weight cargo while deep sea, tramps[1] and the operators of bulk carrier scheduled services compete for low value high, volume traffic. Competition also comes from the operators of liner services (now usually containerised) who are not conference members and who usually charge less than conference rates. These are known as outsiders, and many dry cargo vessels operate outside the conference system.

Charter and Spot Bulk Carrier Operations

The oil, gas, bulk and combination carrier segments operate differently from the liner trade. Although there may be consortia agreements, vessels usually operate on their own account, accepting full cargoes from one shipper either on a time charter or individual voyage basis. Bulk and combination carriers operating in this way are referred to as tramps.

Vessels are usually operated by negotiating a price for one voyage (spot) or longer-term arrangements (charters) are agreed. Charters typically produce a lower return but are financially more secure. The rates for these two methods provide a general picture of the level of demand for ships. They also help to characterise the attitudes of different companies. At one extreme, total reliance on the spot market indicates a fairly cavalier approach; at the other, trading solely on long-term charters suggests conservatism.

The long-term market operates in a way very like the commodity futures market with such refinements as hedging, shorts and the like. There are also several major variants of long-term charters:

(1) Time Charter – where the charterer provides capacity in a ship at a fixed rate per deadweight ton per month for a fixed period (usually between 3 and 15 years).

(2) Bareboat Charter – like a time charter except that the charterer undertakes to operate the ship at his own expense (crew, maintenance etc.)

(3) Contract of Affreightment – whereby the owner undertakes to transport using any ship within specified limits, a given quantity of a

---

[1]Vessels engaged in casual trade or on a contract between a ship operator and a charterer for the carriage of goods on a stated voyage or for a period of time but not a regular service.

116

commodity per annum between two or more specific points at a fixed rate. (Contracts vary from 1 to 10 years).

(4) Consecutive Voyages – whereby the owner undertakes to provide a specific ship for consecutive voyages at a given rate per ton of cargo transported. Contract duration might state a number of voyages or years.

INDUSTRY PERFORMANCE AND PROSPECTS

At the beginning of 1979 the world shipping industry was entering its sixth year of depression, with in general massive overcapacity in most sectors of trade as shown in Figure 1.

The immediate cause of the slump was the 1973 oil crisis. The ensuing worldwide recession drastically reduced international trade. The slump was worsened by major ship ordering programmes that had been placed by owners at the beginning of the decade, when prospects looked bright and grants and cheap credit were freely available. The dry bulk cargo initially escaped the cutback in the tanker trade but when it became obvious that many tankers on order would never find a charter, owners converted their ships on order to dry cargo vessels. This, in turn produced a glut in the dry cargo market from the end of 1977.

The growth in world seaborne trade is shown in Table 2 indicating that overall trade had grown at around 6 per cent per annum in the decade from

Figure 1

World Fleet – Trade Balance

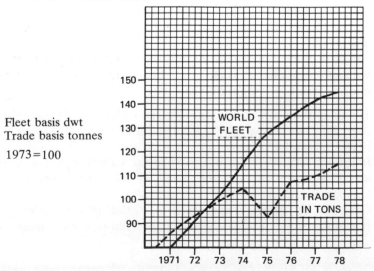

Fleet basis dwt
Trade basis tonnes

1973=100

Source: Fearnley & Egers.

Table 2
Growth in World Seaborne Trade by Weight

Year	Million Tonnes	Dry Cargo Inc. on Previous Year %	million Tonnes	Oil Inc. on Previous year %	million Tonnes	Total Inc. on Previous Year %
1968	930	8	1,130	12	2,060	10
1969	990	6	1,260	11	2,250	9
1970	1,110	12	1,420	13	2,530	12
1971	1,120	1	1,520	7	2,640	4
1972	1,180	5	1,650	9	2,830	7
1973	1,350	14	1,865	13	3,215	14
1974	1,450	7	1,800	-3	3,250	1
1975	1,400	-3	1,690	-6	3,090	-5
1976*	1,535	10	1,895	12	3,430	11
1977	1,600	4	2,000	6	3,600	6

*Estimated
Source: United Nations Monthly Bulletin of Statistics, and Hoare Govett Estimates.

1967. At the end of 1978 the world fleet was, however, still expected to grow as ships on order were delivered as shown in Table 3.

Other industry figures published by the General Council of British Shipping estimated that 75 million dwt or 17% of the world oil tanker fleet was currently surplus to requirements. This was equivalent to 150 VLCC's.[1] At the end of 1978, 361 tankers totalling 43.2 million dwt (12 per cent of the world tanker fleet) were laid up while many more were 'Slow Steaming'

Table 3
1978 World Fleet: Delivery Programme (million dwt)

	Existing Fleet	To be delivered	% addition to fleet
Tankers	325	20.2	6.2
Bulk carriers	132.6	13.4	10.1
Combined carriers	48.4	2.7	5.5
Liquid petroleum gas carriers	4.6	1.9	41
Liquid natural gas carriers	3.5	3.7	105.7
Containerships (twenty-foot equivalent units)	585,914	237,566	40.5
General Cargo (m grt)*	80	8.8	11

*Financial Times estimate.
Sources: Lloyd's Register and H.P. Drewery.

[1]Very Large Crude Carrier

around the world with unwanted cargoes, while many others had been scrapped since 1973. Figure 2 indicates the tonnage of tankers and dry cargo vessels laid up to mid 1978.

THE TANKER MARKET

The tanker market was made up of company owned vessels and those concerned with third party operations. Some 60 per cent of world tanker capacity was owned by major oil companies most of whom were US or European owned.

Figure 2
Growth in laid up tonnage 1977–78

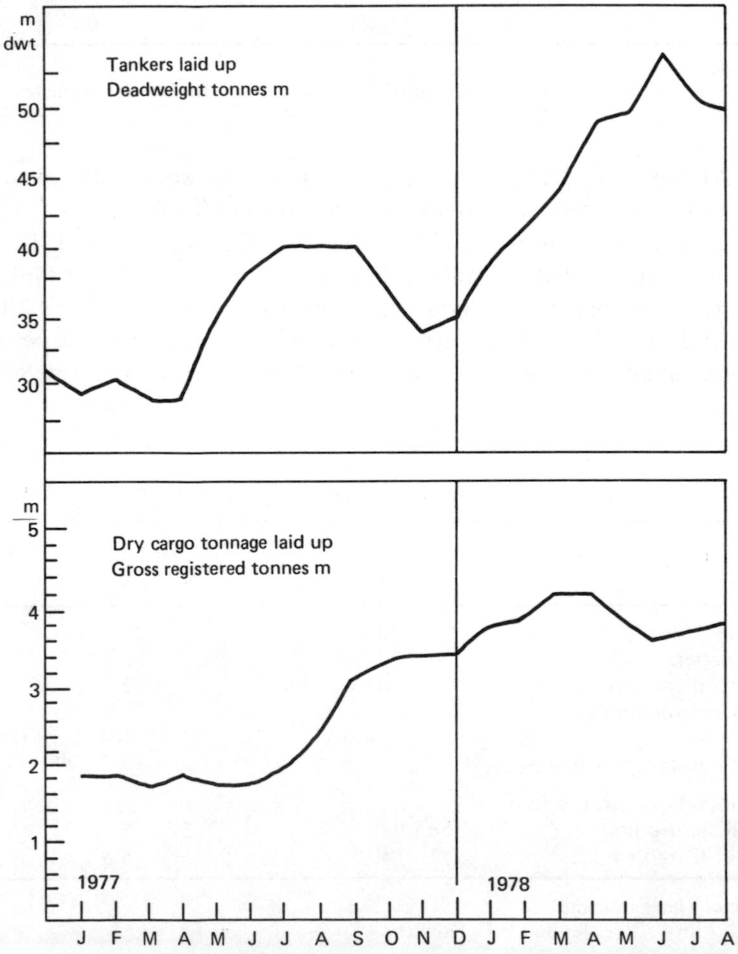

Source: Investors Chronicle.

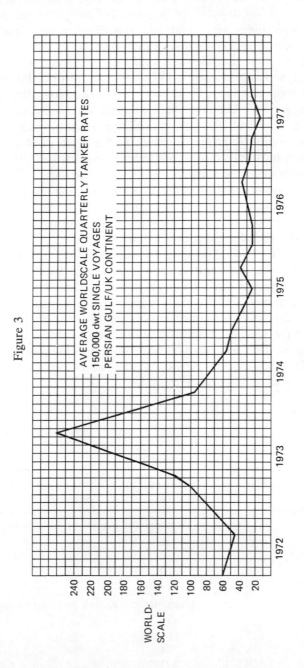

Figure 3

AVERAGE WORLDSCALE QUARTERLY TANKER RATES
150,000 dwt SINGLE VOYAGES
PERSIAN GULF/UK CONTINENT

The tanker market provided the clearest indication of the impact of the 1973 oil crisis on the shipping industry in general and on specific operators in particular. A key indicator of the extent of the problems this has caused is the Worldscale Index which plots the prevailing average level of spot tanker rates achieved by tankers as shown in Figure 3.

The figures show that the rates paid for spot tanker and the related rates for new charters rose steeply in 1972–1973 and dropped dramatically in late 1973 to a level that typically has covered voyage costs but not capital costs or operating costs. Although the spot rates vary considerably for different types of tankers and different routes, there are few deviations from the Worldscale Index. A further measure of the state of the market is by the need owners have felt to renegotiate long time charter rates because of the threat of default by the shipper.

At the beginning of 1979 the medium to long-term prospects for the tanker sector were bleak. On the basis of the supply/demand analysis in Table 4, it is evident that overcapacity in terms of tonne miles was equivalent to 88 million dwt at the end of 1977.

Moreover, if world oil movements were to increase, some laid up tankers would re-enter the market to depress rates again. Another critical factor was the likely scrappage rate. Although it was estimated to cost £500,000 per year to lay up a VLCC the likely scrap value was insufficient to encourage owners to dispose of unwanted vessels in this way. Moreover, most of the world tonnage was less than five years old. Offsetting these pressures for prolonging the glut, was the likelihood that maritime law would be changed in the aftermath of the Amoco Cadiz wreck so as to encourage the accelerated scrapping of older ships.

Table 4

Year	Fleet size	Required Fleet	Surplus	Surplus as %
		(Assumes 3% growth pa in oil tonne miles)		
1977	337	249	88	26
1978	342	256	86	25
1979	338	264	74	22
1980	330	272	58	18
		(Assumes 6% growth pa in oil tonne miles)		
1977	337	252	85	25
1978	342	267	75	22
1979	338	284	54	16
1980	330	301	29	9

Source: Hoare Govett

Actual and potential bankruptcies in both the shipping and banking sectors could be seen as a direct result of the collapse of the tanker market. The Norwegian Government's rescue fund for its over-extended tanker owners amounted to hundreds of millions of pounds. The banking sectors of many countries had also suffered heavy losses from generous loans extended to tanker owners when the market was booming. In the UK Edward Bates had to be bailed out by the Bank of England. Merchant Banks like Hambros and Kleinwort Benson and clearing banks like the National Westminster also have considerable outstanding tanker loans with little immediate prospect of full interest or capital repayments. UK shipowners' exposure to these problems had been less acute than for others. Even so, tanker assets had proved a drain on the resources of those companies with diverse shipping interests. For instance the heavy losses of London and Overseas Freighters was largely attributable to their extensive tanker commitments.

THE BULK CARRIER MARKET

Markets rates in this sector were particularly affected by the general conditions. The supply/demand analysis in Table 5 (which assumes two different levels of world growth in millions of tonne miles and projected fleet levels based on current figures and new buildings) shows that the very optimistic estimate of 8% growth leaves a substantial supply surplus until 1980.

Voyage rates which were equivalent to oil tanker spot rates, were in 1978 at levels generally so low that shipowners could not break even although

Table 5
Bulk Carrier Supply/Demand

Date	Fleet size	Required Fleet	Surplus	Surplus as %
(Assumes 5% growth in tonne miles)				
31.12.77	154.0	128	26	17
31.12.78	160.5	135	25.5	16
31.12.79	163.5	141	22.5	14
31.12.80	162.5	148	14.5	9
(Assumes 8% growth in tonne miles)				
31.12.77	154.0	130	24	16
31.12.78	160.5	140	20.5	13
31.12.79	163.5	152	11.5	7
31.12.80	162.5	164	NIL	NIL

Source: Hoare Govett.

Table 6
World Seaborne Trade 1966–77 in Million Metric Tonnes

	Iron Ore	Coal	Grain
1966	153	61	92
1967	164 + 7.2%	67 + 10%	83 – 10%
1968	188 + 15%	73 + 9%	78 – 6%
1969	214 + 14%	83 + 14%	71 – 7%
1970	247 + 15%	101 + 22%	89 + 25%
1971	250 + 1%	94 – 7%	91 + 2%
1972	247 – 1%	96 + 2%	108 + 19%
1973	298 + 20%	104 + 8%	139 + 29%
1974	329 + 10%	119 + 14%	130 – 6%
1975	292 – 11%	127 + 7%	137 + 5%
1976	294 + 1%	127 N/C	146 + 7%
1977	283 – 4%	125 – 2%	143 – 2%

Source: Compiled from Fearnley & Egers statistics.

they usually covered operating costs. However, these rates operated within wide bands for different commodities and routes. For instance, grain from the U.S. to Japan commanded US$11.50 per tonne in January 1978 whereas equivalent coal rates were US $3.50.

Bulk cargoes could be roughly divided into industrial raw materials (iron ore, coal, phosphate rock and bauxite) and agricultural products (such as grain and sugar). World sea-borne trade in these commodities which accounted for roughly 40% of bulk cargoes are shown in Table 6.

The iron ore and coal movements relied heavily on levels of industrial production – notably on the steel industry which was operating at very low levels. The grain market relied upon harvests for much of its trade and crop failures created erratic demand patterns. In addition, two large grain importers, Russia and China, had built up and were extending their bulk fleets at the end of the 1970's.

To measure the extent of overcapacity, in April 1978 there were 13.2 million dwt of dry cargo (which includes bulkers) laid up, and industry estimates suggested that bulkers accounted for between 2.4 million dwt of this figure. The world order book which had been increased by substitution orders was, according to Lloyds List, as follows:

	Building	Ordered	Total
Bulk Carriers	5.8	4.8	10.7
(million deadweight tons)			

Thus in 1978 the bulk carrier market was depressed and overtonnaged. The OBO carrier fleet of 44 million dwt, (of which 50% trades oil) were expected to be further encouraged to switch to dry bulk if rates improved.

Voyage freight rates reflected these conditions and in the charter market several companies had defaulted on charter payments.

THE LINER TRADE MARKET

Two principal types of ships operated in this sector: cargo liners and container ships, the latter increasingly replacing the former on specific conference routes. An important factor that distinguished liner trades from bulk and tanker operations was the use of cargo space by a variety of cargoes carried for different shippers: it was unusual for vessels to operate exclusively for one customer.

The conference system made it difficult to estimate supply/demand factors accurately. However, one rationale for conferences was to reduce aggregate sailings on a specific route to ensure greater load factors for owners operating in concert than would be the case if they traded independently. Ship owners could be sure that within the Conference their proportion of the trade would remain relatively stable and that there would be no price competition among members.

Rate levels varied considerably on different routes. Rates were constrained by a variety of factors, including relations with importing/exporting nations (which operated international committees to negotiate rates); the level of capacity utilisation on the trade; and the rates quoted by non-liner competitors. Any port or import surcharges were passed directly on to the shipper and were not regarded as an operators' cost. Revenue earnings were often biased in the sense that traders frequently had a controlling leg, i.e. an outward voyage carried a full cargo, whereas the return trip was relatively empty. The Europe/West Africa and Europe/Middle East services provided examples of this.

The traditional general break-bulk cargo liner still accounted for a high proportion of the market. However, an increasing number of combination carriers had come into service in the last ten years. These vessels were able to carry break-bulk cargoes and containers, and were used on liner trades which did not have purpose built handling facilities but had some container throughput. Container ships were a fairly recent phenomenon, and several important liner routes had switched predominantly to them. The types of container ships are shown in Table 7. An indication of the growing importance of this sector was the fact that ships on order represented 38.5% of current TEU capacity (Twenty foot Equivalent Unit)[1].

Container based traffic had grown substantially from 15.0 million TEU's in 1973 to 23.1 million in TEU's in 1977. This trend was expected to continue as more capacity was delivered, and represented a threat not only to established conference container ships but also to conventional cargo

---

[1]Containers are measured in lengths of 20 feet. Maximum load limits are 20 tons for a 20 foot length container to 30 tons for a 40 foot container.

Table 7
Twenty Foot Equivalent Unit (TEU) Capacity

Type of container carrying vessel	In service Oct 1, 1977		On order Oct 1, 1977		Total in service & on order		Percentage of Total TEU
	No. of Ships	TEU Capacity	No. of Ships	TEU Capacity	No. of Ships	TEU Capacity	
Fully cellular vessels	301	354,656	109	117,158	410	471,814	56.24
Converted to fully cellular	105	77,158	8	9,872	113	87,030	10.37
Semi-container (cellular and/or lo-lo)	232	101,538	89	46,632	321	148,170	17.66
Cellular with ro-ro capability	31	24,740	18	12,318	49	37,058	4.42
Barge carrier with cellular space	9	5,445	0	0	9	5,445	0.65
Pure ro-ro multi-deck	62	42,092	55	47,296	117	89,388	10.66
TOTAL	740	605,629	279	233,276	1,019	838,905	100.00

Source: Containerisation International.

liner business. Hoare Govett estimated that by 1980 the general cargo fleet would grow by 25–30 per cent over 1977 without a corresponding growth in world trade.

Container shipping represented a considerable capital investment both for new tonnage and the necessary port infra-structure. The tendency had been for container ships' demand to move in quantum jumps as new routes switched to container operations. When ports switched to container handling facilities, the resulting economies to shippers severely cut the demand for cargo liners, as each large container ship displaced 6 to 8 cargo liners.

In 1978 no major new routes were scheduled to be containerised. Thus, it appeared that some of the container ships' order book represented speculative building. Some of these ships were destined for non-liner trades and would cause problems for the Conferences. They were also likely to have knock-on effects in the general cargo sector because the 109 cellular vessels on order were equivalent to about 600 cargo liners. To add to this problem, the current cargo ship order book represented 11.4% of the current world cargo fleet.

NEW FACTORS

To compound the problems that shipowners faced from the imbalance between supply and demand a number of new factors were becoming important:

- The Eastern Bloc countries were rapidly increasing the size of their cargo and bulk fleets and this had had a severe effect on certain liner routes. In cross trades,[1] these ships, undercut Conference rates by between 10% and 40%. The Russians, for instance, generated 1.6% of all non-oil seaborne trade, yet their cargo capacity in 1978 represented 9.6% of world capacity. Between 1974 and 1978, the number of Russian ships operating in cross trades rose by 600%.
- The TransSiberian Railway carried an increasing amount of potential Far East marine freight. For instance, it was estimated to carry over 25% of the Europe/Japan trade. The railways planned to double capacity by 1982. As a measure of its competitiveness, it took one month to ship ex Tilbury via Leningrad and the railway to Japan. At the same time, a containership ex Southampton could only just beat that time, assuming there was an appropriate sailing.
- The UNCTAD 40–40–20 resolution. This was a much debated United Nations proposal to replace the Conference system. It proposed that 80% of trade between two countries should be shared equally by their respective ships and that 20% should be available to cross traders.

[1]Trades between two or more countries other than that in which the shipowner resides.

This had particular implications for many U.K. shipowners, operating in Conferences, where such a rule would mean a major re-allocation of the trade in someone else's favour. Although the code was unlikely to be ratified, some form of compromise would have important effects on U.K. interests.

· National fleets: many developing countries were building up their own national fleets and demanding representation (usually within the Conferences) on relevant routes. This happened mainly on a small scale (e.g. W. African countries such as Nigeria). However there were some important examples (e.g. United Arab Shipping Co., which by 1980 was expected to operate a fleet of at least 61 vessels in the dry cargo trades).

· Second hand re-tonnaging: two countries, Greece and China, had acquired considerable tonnage in the general cargo and bulk fields during the slump. Other low-cost shipping nations such as Hong Kong were also taking advantage of the weak demand to buy up cheap good quality second hand ships.

Chinese Fleet

1973	1.2 million grt	end 1977	3.6 million grt

(Source: 'Shipstats')

Spent US $ 75 million on 33 vessels of 527,600 million dwt between May and August 1977.

Greek Fleet

New tonnage in 1976.	99 Cargo/Bulkers	8.2 million dwt
On order (Feb 1977)	211 Cargo/Bulkers	4.7 million dwt
Second hand 1977	336 Cargo/Bulkers	5.6 million grt

· Changing strategy of non-shipowning nations: the U.S.A. and Germany had small merchant fleets relative to the amount of trade that they generated. However, the introduction of protective legislation in the U.S. and a desire by Germany to profit from its own economic success, was expected to affect the countries currently operating in these trades.

· Most UK shipowners' costs were in sterling, and most of their earnings in U.S. dollars, or a basket of European currencies. This had recently worked to their disadvantage – OCL, with a pre-tax profit of £49 million claimed to have lost £7 million pre-tax profit because of the upward movement of sterling in 1978.

· Worldwide shipyard overcapacity had encouraged many countries to provide direct subsidies and other incentives to save this labour and capital intensive industry from collapse. With considerable shipping overcapacity this was likely to prolong the slump for shipowners and provide cheap ships, able to undercut established rates and to operate on cross trades outside the Conference system.

BRITISH SHIPPING COMPANIES

There were in 1978 over 200 British shipping or ship management companies. The fleet which had always been strong in traditional cargo liners, bulk carriers, tankers and coastal vessels was also among the world leaders in container ships, chemical carriers, refrigerated ships, gas carriers, offshore supply ships, ferries and passenger liners. The make-up of the fleet which was the fourth largest in the world is shown in Table 8. The shipping industry made a direct contribution of over £1 billion to the U.K. balance of payments and accounted for over 70 per cent of the order book of British shipyards.

Container ships and gas carriers, which accounted for 19% and 18% of the world fleet respectively, indicated the willingness of U.K. owners to adopt and in many cases pioneer new concepts of transportation. On the other hand, the current U.K. oil tanker fleet of 28 million dwt. represented a modest 8.4% of the world fleets. Overall U.K. tonnage figures do not give an accurate picture of individual company fleets. Table 9 lists twelve of the largest U.K. public and private shipping companies. The fact that they accounted for only 30% of the U.K. merchant fleet indicates that many much smaller companies made up the balance.

Table 8

Merchant Ships Owned and Registered in UK 1977
(100 grt or over)

	No.	Million dwt
Passenger/Cargo Liner	141	0.2
Cargo Liner	403	3.8
Cellular Container	90	1.4
Total Liner	634	5.3
Ore/Bulk Carrier	215	8.7
Combination Carrier	37	5.3
Other Tramp	451	1.7
Total Tramp	703	15.7
Oil Tanker	359	27.0
Chemical Tanker	39	0.3
Liquefied Gas Carrier	35	0.8
Total Tanker	433	28.1
TOTAL FLEET	1,779	49.0

Source: General Council of British Shipping.

Table 9

Leading U.K. Shipping Companies

	No. of Ships	Size (Million dwt)	Legal Status of Company
P and O	130	3.3	Public
Silver Line	24	1.3	Private
Alva Shipping	6	0.9	Private
Bibby Line	21	1.4	Private
Ocean Transport	55	1.3	Public
Furness Withy	65	1.1	Public
Globtik	4	1.1	Private
Ben Line	29	0.9	Public
British and Commonwealth	30	0.9	Public
London and Overseas Freighters	18	0.8	Public
Bank Line (Andrew Weir)	49	0.7	Private
Ellerman Lines	56	0.7	Private

The principal public shipping companies and their representation in various marine sectors are shown in Table 10.

Although the actual tonnages are not shown, the table does give an indication of the breadth of interests of companies like P & O and Ocean and the heavy reliance upon dry and liquid bulk shipping for a company like London and Overseas Freighters.

The shipping industry until the late 1960's tended to be extremely

Table 10

	P & O	Ocean Transport & Trading	Furness Withy	British & Commonwealth	London & Overseas Freighters
General Cargo Ships	*	*	*	*	*
Ore Bulk Carriers	*	*	*	*	*
Oil Tankers	*	*	*		*
Product Tankers	*	*	*	*	*
Gas Carriers	*	*	*		
Cruise Ships	*				
Ferries	*				
Offshore Supply Vessels	*	*	*		
Tugs	*	*			
Container Ships	*	*	*	*	

Source: Annual Reports

conservative and traditional. Many managers had extended family connections with their companies and many senior executives were descendants of the original founders of particular shipping lines. Then in 1968 the shipping world was shaken out of its traditional attitudes by the dramatic take-over by Trafalgar House Investments, a rapidly growing conglomerate, of the Cunard Steamship Company, the doyen of the British merchant fleet. The purchase gave Trafalgar House access to Cunard's valuable unused tax losses and to its accumulated depreciation allowances. This take-over made other shipping companies aware of both their vulnerability to such aggressors and also the hidden strength of their own extensive assets which were not being adequately utilised. Thus in the 1970's, there had been a major trend toward increased diversification by many of the major shipping concerns. Many had diversified into other areas of distribution and freight management although a number had moved into property and hotels, while others had developed certain aspects of their traditional business such as marine engineering and insurance broking. Table 11 shows the development of the non-shipping activities of the major shipping companies.

The 1977 financial performance of the leading shipping companies reflected the severe market conditions. The decline of the container trade hit P & O, Furness Withy, Ocean Transport & Trading and British and Commonwealth as their jointly owned subsidiary Overseas Containers

Table 11

	P & O	Ocean Transport & Trading	Furness Withy	British & Commonwealth	London & Overseas Freighters
Non-national Shipbuilding		*	*		
Ship repair	*	*	*		*
Engineering	*	*	*		
Oil Exploration	*				
Oil Support	*	*		*	
Air Freight	*	*			
Banking	*				
Insurance Broking	*	*	*	*	
Property & Construction	*	*			
Hotels			*	*	
Warehousing & Distribution	*	*	*		
Road Transport	*	*	*		
Others	*	*	*	*	

Source: Annual Reports

Limited suffered a rapid slowdown in its growth rate in the second half of 1977. This trend continued in 1978 when OCL's interim profit fell sharply. P & O and Furness Withy were also affected in their own container operations while Ocean T & T, with substantial liner services to West Africa were hit by disruptions in Nigeria in 1977 and early 1978. Further Ocean T & T and P & O reported greatly reduced profits in the first half of 1978 as the bulk and liner trades reeled under competitive pressure. Furness Withy, strong in liner trades and container operations stood up to the decline relatively well as a result of its spread of operations. The only bright spot amongst the British shipping concerns was European Ferries which continued to increase its share of the lucrative 40 million people market for cross channel ferry services. Brief details of the recent financial performance of the major British shipping concerns are shown in Table 12.

OTHER RESULTS OF THE CRISIS

The world shipowning fraternity and the various governments of maritime nations had offered a number of quasi solutions to the various problems facing the industry.

In 1977 the "Internal Tanker Services" scheme was suggested designed to improve tanker rates by laying up a minimum of 40 million dwt of tonnage. Although there were some important supporters, the scheme lapsed in June 1978 well short of its minimum target, due to Greek owners' disinterest.

In the dry cargo market, the Greeks had formed the Union of Greek Shipowners to try and marshall dry cargo shipowners into an international association.

Governments had also taken a hand. Japan started a scheme to store several years oil supply in some of its surplus tankers, rather than provide onshore facilities. The U.S. government was contemplating changes to favour U.S. flag vessels on trade routes to the USA. The EEC, divided over whether or not to support the UNCTAD 40 : 40 : 20 resolution, was concerned at the growth of the Soviet maritime fleet and was considering discriminatory action against this threat. Finally, in Britain the Government had allowed applications for a moratorium on shipbuilding loans on government guaranteed schemes.

A further result of the crisis was a sharp change in the relative strengths of national fleets. The British fleet was being seriously depleted by the recession as owners moved to sell of surplus vessels. No fewer than 87 bulk and combination carriers were sold in 1978 totalling 3.5 million dwt, representing more than a quarter of the British bulk and combined fleet. In total during the year 165 ships of 4.8 million dwt were sold by 78 different owners from the British flag to foreign companies with a further 38 vessels totalling 1.0 million being scrapped.

The Norwegian fleet had also been depleted by 3 million dwt in 1978

Table 12

| | Performance | | | | | | Financial Status | | | | | |
	Year End	Turnover £m's	Turnover % change	Return on assets %	Profit margin %*	Stock turnover	Debtor turnover	Cash flow £000	Gross debt/Group Sh. funds %	Net debt/Group Sh. funds %	Interest Cover	Current ratio	Acid test
Brit & Comm' Shipping	12–77	238	+ 9.2	12.9	7.0(8.0)	13.2	4.5	22,554	48.4	29.4	4.3	1.5	1.2
European Ferries	12–77	127.9	+36.8	19.0	19.8(14.5)	8.6	5.9	22,315	80.8	51.5	5.4	2.0	1.5
Furness Withy	12–77	184.6	+ 9.6	11.3	6.1(8.4)	36.1	3.8	18,495	80.4	60.6	2.2	1.2	1.2
London & Over's Freighter's	3–78	13.0	–20.7	nil	nil (nil)	n/a	n/a	–2,583	75.5	41.8	nil	4.3	4.3
Manchester Liners	12–77	62.4	+23.8	4.9	4.5(6.3)	23.3	4.0	2,690	222.5	203.7	2.8	1.0	0.9
Ocean Transport & Trading	12–77	459.0	+19.9	11.0	3.7(5.7)	21.0	5.5	42,552	74.3	60.0	1.8	1.1	0.9
P & O Steam Navigation	12–77	980.4	+32.4	7.7	4.2(4.8)	7.6	6.0	50,944	88.76	76.76	1.8	0.9(a)	0.9(a)

*Previous year in brackets. (a) Excluding banking subsidiaries.
Source: Investors Chronicle.

whilst the Swedish fleet had declined from 12.6 million dwt in July 1977 to 8 million dwt by the end of 1978. Ship demolition was also running at unprecedented levels with more than 18 million dwt being scrapped in 1978.

Despite the crisis there was no shortage of buyers for good quality ships sold at bargain basement prices. These had featured maritime countries with either very low operating costs such as Hong Kong, Taiwan, Korea, Singapore and the Phillipines which enjoyed very low crew costs and relatively few trade union problems. Another group of purchasers had been countries developing their own fleets as a matter of policy to gain a greater share of their own and the cross trades. These included the USSR and China and a number of third world countries.

Also seriously affected by the prolonged crisis was the world's shipbuilding industry. By 1980–81 the Association of West European Shipbuilders forecast the level of output could be less than half that for the last boom years of 1975–6. The forecast for 1981 was a mere 8 million gross registered tons compared with 1976 output of 34 million GRT. These figures issued in 1978 represented a 3 per cent reduction on the similar forecast issued in 1977, and suggested that employment would need to be halved by 1980.

Some governments had already anticipated this suggestion. The Swedish parliament had a plan to almost halve its shipbuilding industry workforce of 20,000; Spain expected a 40 per cent reduction by 1982; the Dutch were battling with trade unions to rationalise its RSV group; the Norwegian Government had decided to cut most of its subsidies to shipbuilders; the state owned British Shipbuilders were preparing plans for substantial redundancies; and finally the Japanese were planning to reduce capacity by 35 per cent.

10

Furness, Withy & Company

Sir James Steel, Chairman of Furness, Withy, had little comfort to offer shareholders when he reported to them in 1978. 'Shipping is in a sad state the world over', he noted. 'The depression is the worst experienced in 40 years and the end of it is not yet in sight. It started with the collapse of the market for supertankers in 1973 and spread through all kinds of tankers and bulk carriers to general cargo ships engaged in open market trading. Freight rates scarcely cover operating costs. Close to 9% of world shipping is laid up and each month more ships have been joining the mausoleums in dock and fjord whilst shipyards continue to launch more unwanted ships, built at a loss and subsidised with taxpayers funds, to force rates yet further below economic levels. The market for secondhand ships has literally collapsed under this intolerable pressure. Few fleets will escape this trauma. Only a dramatic revival of world trade will end it quickly or a sensible control of new building end it eventually.'

Against this gloomy background the board of Furness, Withy continued the difficult task of formulating a successful and profitable strategy and despite the problems of the industry achieved a pretax profit of £20.7 million in 1977—less than £2 million down on the previous year.

COMPANY BACKGROUND

Furness, Withy (FW) was one of the leading British shipping companies with sales of £184.6 million in 1977 and assets employed of over £200 million. Details of recent financial performance are given in Exhibits 1 and 2.

The company was incorporated in 1891 as an amalgamation of the ships, investments and offices of Christopher Furness with the Middleton shipyard and dry docks owned by Edward Withy & Co. In 1898, four years after the opening of the Manchester Ship Canal, Sir Christopher Furness took the lead in forming Manchester Liners Ltd. (ML), a shipping company in which FW held slightly less than half the share capital established to trade mainly with North America. Ever since FW had continued to expand by acquiring other shipping companies and their

EXHIBIT 1

Furness Withy Profit & Loss Accounts 1973–1977 (£'000)

	1973	1974	1975	1976	1977
Turnover	115800	142600	154100	168400	184600
Profits from Trading	8485	16451	9291	15375	11247
After Depreciation	6483	7420	8403	8098	9735
Ship and plant hire	2798	2792	3605	2650	3850
Sale of Ships	1709	1626	1457	1116	3350
Investment income	3807	5042	4607	4386	3747
	14001	23119	15355	20877	18344
Interest payable	3537	4100	5514	6470	6780
	10464	19019	9841	14407	11556
Share of profits less losses of principal associated companies	3403	5702	4294	8235	9162
Profit before tax	13867	24721	14135	22642	20718
Tax	5273	10456	7026	7087	7223
Profit after tax	8594	14265	7109	15555	13495
Attributable to minority interests	1128	1180	450	581	909
Profits before extraordinary items	7466	12385	6659	14974	12586
Extraordinary items	708	3582	2720	(3958)	1059
Profit attributable to FW	6758	8803	3939	11016	13645
Dividends	1560	1693	1835	2013	2260
E.P.S.	27.66p	46.01p	24.65p	55.67p	46.76p

fleets. By 1951, FW was established as a leading shipping group with a fleet of 81 ships and a total tonnage of 680,000 gross registered tons.

In the post war period FW continued its acquisitive growth. In the 1960's the group bought out the minority interests in Prince Line, Cairn Line, Shaw Savill, British Maritime Trust and in 1965 those in Royal Mail Lines. In 1968, FW acquired control of the Houlder group, in which it already held a substantial stake, and complete ownership in 1974. Then in 1970, FW attempted to buy all the outstanding ML ordinary shares, but was successfully resisted by the then ML board and others. FW ended up with a controlling interest of 53.6 per cent.

In 1978 the principal business of FW remained that of shipping and ancillary services such as ship management, ship agencies, ship broking and stevedoring. In addition the group had diversified into a number of other activities of which the principal interests were insurance underwriting,

EXHIBIT 2

Furness Withy Balance Sheets (1973–1977)

	1973	1974	1975	1976	1977
			(£'000)		
LONG TERM ASSETS					
Fixed Assets	99373	108088	116836	132954	155833
Ships	85719	92532	99150	113621	136749
Land & Buildings	9426	11047	12331	12717	12535
Plant & Furniture	4228	4509	5355	6616	6549
Investment in associates	8521	10675	11456	12450	16917
Other Investments	12751	13846	13292	13062	11681
Economic Insurance (Net Assets)	1406	2145	2160	—	—
TOTAL Long Term Assets	122051	134754	143744	158466	184431
CURRENT ASSETS					
Govt. Securities	1365	1118	1216	1187	3479
Short term deposits	18016	17377	14176	17219	13762
Stocks & Stores	1989	3429	5194	5818	5109
Net balance on open voyage accounts	793	1915	3453	3899	2439
Debtors	41053	42615	41038	45487	49146
Bank & Cash	5134	4398	3940	3381	4583
TOTAL Current Assets	68350	70852	69017	76991	78518
CURRENT LIABILITIES					
Creditors	38181	40295	39463	49344	50349
Bank Overdraft	4608	3784	3110	2946	6874
Tax Payable	361	103	—	1086	1165
Provisions	3708	5451	4769	2699	2337
Dividends Payable	1517	1650	1792	1970	2217
TOTAL Current Liabilities	48375	51283	49134	58045	62942
NET CURRENT ASSETS	19975	19569	19883	18946	15576
NET ASSETS EMPLOYED	142026	154323	163627	177412	200007
Ord. Shares	26803	26803	26803	26803	26803
Reserves	36837	43129	45264	59746	71263
Pref. Shares	1500	1500	1500	1500	1500
Minority Interests	11214	2679	2686	2683	3393
Investment Grants	11507	9803	8230	7122	5567
Deferred Tax	5643	11018	12695	8042	8211
Loan Stocks	48522	59391	66449	71516	83270
	142026	154323	163627	177412	200007

EXHIBIT 3

Furness Withy Group: Principal Activities Dec. 31st 1977

General Shipping Division   Trading Profits £5,334,000
  Houlder Lines & Royal Mail Lines
  Pacific Steam Navigation Co.
  Royal Mail Lines joint service
  (Central America Service)
  Prince Line
  Shaw Savill Line.
  Cairn Line
  General Trading

Houlder Bulk Shipping Division   Trading Profits £310,000
  Ship & Tanker broking   Share of associate co. losses
                                         (£46,000)

  4 Bulk Carriers
    Bulk/ore carrier
    Tanker
    Associate company: Ocean Gas Transport—LPG transport.

Houlder Offshore Division   Trading Loss £109,000
  Drilling rig (30% interest)   Share of associated co. profit
  North Sea support vessels   £984,000
  Associate company: Kingsnorth Marine Drilling (44%)

Manchester Lines   Trading Profit £2,802,000
  Manchester/Montreal container ships
  Manchester/Mediterranean Cellular service
  Great Lakes feeder service
  General ship trading

Overseas Containers Ltd. (16.01% Interest)   Trading Profit £7,514,000
Furness Withy (Chartering)   Trading Profit £239,000
Brantford International   Trading Profit £54,000
  Freight forwarding & port agency activities
  Furness travel

Furness Houlder (Insurance)   Trading Profit £719,000
Furness Withy (Engineering)   Trading Profit £247,000
  Compugraphics International—photomark technology
  Fescol Ltd.
  Valve & Tool merchanting

Saxon Inns (Regional motels)   Trading Profit £325,000
Furness Trinidad   Trading Profit £926,000
  Partly owned ship repairing activities, ship agents   Share of associated company
  and general trading.   profits £117,000

Source: Annual Reports.

insurance broking, road haulage and warehousing, engineering, hotel ownership, travel and portfolio investment. A number of subsidiaries were overseas. The principal subsidiaries, their activities and recent financial performance are shown in Exhibit 3.

EXHIBIT 4

Furness, Withy Group Abstract of Fleet (17 June 1976)

Vessels Operated by the Group (Including Associates and 3 Vessels Owned by FW and Operated by OCL)

	Number of ships and rigs	Number under construction and on order	Tonnage DWT	Trade	Asset spread on market value (incl. proportion in association) 1976 per cent	1978 per cent
1. Owned and chartered by demise*						
Refrigerated ships	15	—	174,000	Liner		
General cargo ships	6	1	72,700	Liner/ chartered out	32	24
Multi-purpose ships	8	2	116,300	Liner	29	29
Container ships	13	2	194,000 (9,200 TEU)	Liner/ chartered out		
Bulk carriers	11	7	625,000	Chartered out	21	18
Oil tankers	2	2	222,000	Chartered out	1	14
Product tankers	—	1	104,000	Chartered out	2	3
Gas carriers	5			Chartered out		
Offshore rigs and support vessels	4	1	—	Chartered out	15	12
2. Time chartered in†						
Bulk carriers	11		178,000			
General cargo ships	5		41,000			
Container ships	5		14,000 (750 TEU)			
Total DWT			1,741,000			
Proportion of bulk carriers			46%			

*The terms of the contract amount to a virtual change of ownership during the period of hire; the charterer provides the crew.

†The hire of the ship for a stated period of time; the shipowner provides the crew.

Source: Monopolies Commission Report p. 117.

SHIPPING POLICY

Unlike many shipping groups, FW's policy was to invest in many market segments each with different degrees of risk, profit potential and flexibility. Sir James Steel believed, 'We are able to protect our profits better than many shipowners for three reasons. First, many of our ships are engaged in liner trades in which we have a long history of good service to shippers; these ships are not exposed to the same cutthroat competition. Secondly, our tramp ships were not generally fixed on long charters and so we are already experiencing the worst of running the market in 1977 and do not have to face a further fall in revenue on the termination of charters. Thirdly, our fleet is designed to cover a broad spread of the market—high and low risk activities, liners and tramps, conventional and container cargo ships, dry bulk carriers and tankers, offshore oil and other marine business'.[1] (See Exhibit 4 for details of the fleet in mid-1976.)

SHIPPING OPERATIONS

Before 1960 FW had had a loose federal organisation in which were held both directly and indirectly by the parent company. By the mid 1970's the group had been restructured and the main shipping operations integrated into a General Shipping Division. In addition two other divisions, Houlder Bulk Shipping and Manchester Liners were mainly engaged in shipping activities. The volumes of cargo carried on various regular routes operated by the FW group were as follows in 1975:[2]

	Volume of cargo
	1975 (in '000 tons)
(i) U.K. and continent/New Zealand and also West Indies, Mediterranean, west coast South America, South and West Africa	401
(ii) U.K./Brazil & River Plate and thence Continent/U.K.	152
(iii) West coast U.K./Bermuda, Bahamas, West Coast South America, Caribbean	385
(iv) Continent and U.K./Panama and Pacific Coast Central America	57
(v) East coast U.K./Malta, Cyprus, Israel, continent and east coast U.K./Libya, Egypt, Lebanon, Syria, South Turkey	230
(vi) Manchester, Liverpool, Greenock and Dublin/Montreal (ML)	583
(vii) Manchester/Mediterranean (ML)	102

[1]Annual Report, 1977, p.4.

[2]Monopolies Commission Report on the proposed merger of the Canadian Shipholdings Ltd. with Furness Withy & Company and Manchester Liners Ltd., HMSO 1976.

FW GENERAL SHIPPING DIVISION OPERATIONS

The General Shipping division was responsible for most of the group's liner trade activities. These were subdivided to reflect both geographic and the historic interests of the group's individual lines:

(1) *United Kingdom, Continent and New Zealand*

Until mid-1977, the Shaw Savill subsidiary provided a fully rationalised schedule of sailings in both directions between Europe and New Zealand. Most of this trade was subject to freight and cargo pooling arrangements, covering both conventional and container carryings. In mid-1977 the Shaw Savill service was replaced by a fully cellular container service operated by Overseas Containers Ltd. (OCL)[1], and from that time, Shaw Savill assumed responsibility as managing agents for the OCL residual service which operated conventional vessels to supplement the container service. In addition a number of conventional refrigerated ships were chartered to OCL while two others were time chartered to outside interests.

Shaw Savill also operated a separate service between New Zealand and the Caribbean Area calling upon U.S. Gulf ports for southbound cargo. In 1977 this service was merged with a similar one owned by Bank Line to create the Bank & Savill Line, which began operations in January 1978.

(2) *United Kingdom/East Coast South America*

The Royal Mail and Houlder Lines operated a service between the U.K. and the east coast of South America. They cooperated with other British lines and the national flag lines of South American countries. In recent years a rationalisation of tonnage had provided some improvements in performance.

(3) *United Kingdom/West Coast South America*

The FW subsidiary Pacific Steam Navigation Company (PSNC) was the only British flag operator on this route. In the southbound trade PSNC was in a full freight pool[2] with European shipping lines and national lines. No pooling arrangement existed on north bound traffic. This service enjoyed a good performance with increased trade. There was a growing trend to increased containerisation on the route which was being handled by multi-purpose vessels introduced by FW.

---

[1]OCL is a consortium of British Shipping concerns operating containerised services.

[2]A freight pool is an arrangement whereby each member is allocated a share of the cargo on offer.

(4) *United Kingdom and Continent/Central America*

Royal Mail operated on this route in partnership with a number of European shipping companies. During 1977 this service performed poorly as a result of a decline in a market share of profitable westbound trade from Europe to Central America.

(5) *United Kingdom and Continent/Mediterranean*

Prince Line, either on its own or in conjunction with British and other shipping lines, offered a variety of services to the Mediterranean. This activity was expanding satisfactorily and had been enhanced by the introduction of specialist container vessels and, in July 1977, a new container service to Arab areas in the Eastern Mediterranean.

(6) *Middlesea Trading*

Through the Cairn Line the FW group operated a fleet of 6 small bulk carriers and one general cargo vessel engaged in short and middle sea trading. These ships traded marginally profitably in 1977 despite a severely depressed market.

Houlder Bulk Shipping Division

FW also operated in a number of specialised markets. Bulk shipping activity was managed by the Houlder Bulk Shipping Division. Until 1976, FW had participated in a consortium formed to pool the bulk carrier tonnage of a number of companies. However FW disagreed with the operating policies of the consortium and withdrew.

The severe slump conditions in the bulk carrier market had meant that Houlder had made little contribution to group profits in recent years. At the beginning of 1977 39 million tons deadweight were laid up in the bulk trade and by mid-1978 this had risen to 53 million tons. An associate company of FW had similarly been forced to lay up a 137,000 ton bulk ore carrier while in 1977 FW had sold its 168,000 ton OBO carrier 'Furness Bridge'. All other vessels remained trading.

Houlder Bulk was also responsible for the management of a fleet of liquid petroleum gas (LPG) tankers owned by Ocean Gas Transport Ltd., a company jointly owned by FW and Gazolean SA of Paris. This company was one of the world's leading companies engaged in the trading and transportation of LPG. Although the shipping depression had affected the LPG market, the profits of Ocean Gas Transport were maintained since its ships were all on long term charter.

Houlder Bulk Division also ran small units in shipbroking and in tanker broking. Both units traded profitably.

Manchester Liners

Manchester Liners (ML) provided services mainly to Canada and a number of other destinations in North America. When the St. Lawrence Seaway opened in 1959 ML expanded and by 1966 operated a fleet of 20 owned or chartered ships on the South Atlantic and Great Lakes. The company anticipated the trend to containerisation on the North Atlantic and was the first British company to offer a regular deep sea container service in 1968.

The company decided that the greatest efficiency could be obtained if it had control of its container terminals on both sides of the Atlantic at Manchester and Montreal. In 1968, ML therefore entered an agreement with the Manchester Ship Canal Company to lease part of the port of Manchester for a container terminal. A similar area was leased in Montreal.

The container service was immediately successful. ML expanded its base by purchasing a number of haulage and warehousing companies in the North of England and Scotland, plus many of FW's operations in Canada connected with the distribution business.

In order to reduce its dependence upon the North Atlantic trade ML embarked upon charter operations with container ships. ML had also diversified into ship repairing, engineering and other activities and had extended its shipping services into the Mediterranean and Middle East.

By 1978, ML operated a fleet of four container ships sailing between Manchester and Montreal. During the eight months 'open water season' ML operated a feeder service using chartered vessels between Montreal and the Great Lakes ports. The company also operated a small conventional North Atlantic service through an associated company, and four cellular container ships on two liner services to Mediterranean ports also through a subsidiary company.

The position of Manchester Liners was unusual in the FW group in that although it was majority owned, the company maintained an independent position and was not subject to the same degree of group control as wholly owned subsidiaries. This position had been confirmed in 1975 when ML had been the target of a take over bid by Eurocanadian Shipholdings. The conditions of the relationship between FW and ML are set out in Exhibit 5.

Overseas Containers Ltd. (OCL)

In 1966 four of the largest British shipping companies, British and Commonwealth Shipping Company, Ocean Transport and Trading, the Peninsular and Oriental Steam Navigation Company and FW established a

EXHIBIT 5

A letter from Sir James Steel to RB Stoker Esq of 9 September 1975

R B Stoker Esq,
Manchester Liners Limited,
POB 189,
Port of Manchester,
Manchester M5 2XA.   9th September 1975

Dear Rob,

I believe that the moment is opportune to clarify the relationship between the Boards of Furness Withy and Manchester Liners, and I hope you will find the following both acceptable and helpful.

1. So long as ML have a substantial minority, the Board of ML will continue to have a greater degree of autonomy than applies in wholly owned subsidiaries of FW.

2. It follows that all matters of consequence, to which I refer later in this letter, should be reported to and submitted for decision by the Board of ML as a whole.

I am sure, and I would appreciate your confirmation on this point, that you and your executive colleagues accept that in cases where there are divergent opinions on matters affecting FW the views expressed by the FW nominees should be allowed to prevail. The Board as a whole should, however, have proper regard to minority interests.

3. The present policy of diversification, based on the following four points, should continue:

(a) Shipping operations on the North Atlantic and to Mediterranean destinations.
(b) Chartering or leasing out of owned container ships or containers.
(c) Road haulage and warehousing particularly concerned with shipping and container traffic.
(d) Engineering concerned with ships and containers.

However, should you have plans for extending your diversification into other areas of operation, these should be submitted to the Furness Withy Board for ratification after full discussion and on the recommendation of the ML Board.

4. You should know that in the existing circumstances FW will not give guarantees in support of future ML borrowings and will not be prepared to consider any capital reconstruction which results in a dilution of their equity.

5. The FW nominees on the ML Board will wish to discuss and agree with you and your colleagues the matters and subjects to be put before the ML Board from time to time for consideration and/or approval. To give you some idea of our thinking, the attached list*, which you might care to think of as a discussion document, may be helpful.

Yours sincerely,

James.

*Matters of consequence to be put before the ML Board to include:
(a) Operating budgets.
(b) Capital budgets.
(c) Requisitions for capital expenditure not included in budget.
(d) Proposals for raising finance for approved capital expenditure.
(e) Proposals for entering into any new shipping operations or material change in the operation of any existing liner trade.
(f) All intended charters out of owned tonnage (having regard to the OCL Agreement).
(g) Any intended extension of existing non-shipping operation.
(h) Periodic statements of:
   (i) trading accounts of all operations for comparison with budgeted profits—monthly.
  (ii) cash flow for comparison with budgeted cash flow—quarterly.
 (iii) expenditure of a capital nature for comparison with budgeted capital expenditure—quarterly.
(i) Terms and conditions of staff employment.

Source: Monopolies Commission Report p. 123–4.

consortium. Its purpose was to operate container shipping services on those trade routes served by the partners, thereby preserving a major British interest. In 1969 the UK/Australia trade was containerised, soon followed by the Far East trade. In 1977 the New Zealand trade was added. It was proposed that the UK/Europe/South Africa trade and three trades in the Pacific basin should follow suit in the future.

OCL, when incorporated, issued to each of the four member companies an equal number of shares. Once a firm's programme for containerising a particular trade had been agreed by the procedures laid down in the agreement covering the formation of the company, each of the members became liable to provide its share of the additional capital or its share of guarantees given for money borrowed to finance the new trade, any UK capital expenditure being shared equally. In trades in which more than one constituent company participated, each company share of the new containerised trade was related to the gross freights earned on its old conventional service. Each company's interest in OCL thus varied. If any of the partners defaulted, the others had to make good the deficiency in their respective basic proportions within 60 days. FW's total share of the firm programmes financed stood at 13.4 per cent for a number of years but in August 1977 rose to 16.01 per cent as a result of the containerisation of the New Zealand trade.[1]

[1]Monopolies Commission Report *op cit* p.26

OCL had been an extremely successful development with profits rising steadily throughout the 1970's despite growing competition and often difficult industrial relations problems at the UK container ports of Southampton and Tilbury. By 1978, OCL had grown to be one of the world's largest shipping enterprises.

Furness Withy (Chartering)

FW also operated a ship chartering subsidiary which chartered out FW's own ships. This company was also responsible for a tramp trading venture using chartered tonnage which was set up in 1971 in South East Asia. The subsidiary operated contracts of affreightment[1] as well as acting as brokers.

Houlder Offshore Division

Diversification had led FW into supply services for offshore drilling and, via an associated company, to offshore drilling. These activities were managed by the Houlder Offshore Division whose main concern was with under water maintenance and offshore construction work. Houlder Offshore owned the support vessel 'Oregis', and used a separate subsidiary Houlder Comex Ltd. as a vehicle for supplying the diving and sub-sea services provided by the British subsidiary of a leading French diving contractor Comex S.A. In June 1977 Houlder Comex also took delivery of 'Uncle John', the world's first dynamically positioned semi-submersible diving support and sub-sea construction vessel.

Houlder Offshore also owned a 30 per cent interest in 'Ross Rig', a drilling rig on long term charter to the Norwegian State Oil Company. In addition FW participated in drilling through its 44 per cent participation in Kingsnorth Marine Drilling of which Houlder Offshore was the manager. This company operated two semi-submersible rigs chartered out for offshore drilling.

FW saw this division as an area for growth and was actively seeking new ventures across the whole spectrum of offshore oilfield contracting from high-risk wildcat exploration to run-of-the-mill maintenance.

NON-SHIPPING ACTIVITIES

By 1978 FW operated a number of non-shipping ventures, as shown in Exhibit 3.

The Engineering interests managed by a holding company included Compugraphics International (a leading company in the high technology

---

[1]A contract between a shipper and a ship operator under which the latter undertakes to carry specified quantities of a bulk commodity over a specified route or routes over a given period of time using ships of his own choice.

photomark industry), Fescol Ltd. (a firm engaged in the chemical deposition of metals), Brooks & Walker and Trent Valve (engaged in the merchanting of valves, pipe fittings and tools). The hotel interests in Saxon Inns comprised three motor hotels in Blackburn, Northampton and Harlow. Further expansion was envisaged with similar types of hotel in secondary centres.

FW operated a number of overseas non-shipping ventures. These included: Empire Stevedoring, a ship stevedoring and terminal operating company based in Vancouver, Canada; Furness Trinidad—trading operations in Trinidad the majority of which were joint ventures with others outside a FW group. Most important of these was Swan Hunter (Trinidad) Ltd., a joint venture with Swan Hunter, and engaged in ship repair. FW also operated the Mahé Beach Hotel in the Seychelles, and held a substantial investment portfolio of equities and other investments around the world. These made a useful contribution to group profitability.

THE 1970's REORGANISATION

After buying out most of the minority interests in subsidiary companies FW began to overhaul its organisation in the early 1970's. In 1973 the company appointed its first outside chairman in Lord Beeching, former Chairman of British Rail. *The Sunday Telegraph* described the organisational change that subsequently took place.[1]

' "There was a change in the West Coast South America trade", says John Gawne who headed Furness General Shipping Division, "which made our ships unsuitable for the trade. Certain of our trades turned sour and we were having to build a new generation of ships".

The new ships were in a different financial league. "We were replacing ships costing £750,000 with £3½ million ships" says Herbert Suffield one of Gawne's Lieutenants.

Beeching was quickly aware that the archaic structure was no match for the modern shipping world and certainly not right for the emerging forces at FW. Under him the major work of restructuring the individual companies along functional lines went ahead fast'.

Beeching decided that the group needed a professional chief executive and he went outside for him. Ironically he found his man at Bovis, a company whose experience in the shipping world had hardly been a happy one.[2] The appointment proved controversial. Paddy Naylor did not find complete support from Beeching's fellow directors.

[1]*Sunday Telegraph* 15.10.78.
[2]In 1973 Bovis a small construction company bid for P & O. This led to a boardroom split in the shipping company and ultimate rejection of the Bovis bid. Following a reorganisation of P & O the shipping company subsequently bid for and won Bovis in a takeover.

F

'He split the board right down the middle' says one man. The opponents won, Naylor never took over, and soon after that Beeching, under doctors orders to ease off, left, too. (Sir James) Steel replaced him.

'Beeching had set up a management committee which in his absence was chaired by Brian Shaw, a young Liverpudlian who had come into the group with the Royal Mail acquisition and had later become chairman of Shaw Savill. After the Naylor battle, Shaw emerged as the strong man and after Beeching left no one seemed to feel any need or desire to look outside again. Shaw soon became managing director and the man who in the past three years has been largely responsible for completing the company's transformation.

'Around him Shaw had already built a team of younger men; Tom Pulley, the group finance appointment, John Keville, the executive director, planning manager Walter Cairns and ex-British Leyland personnel advisor Tony Miller.

'The group still has its close ties with the old family companies. Geoffrey Murrant, deputy chairman and the man responsible for key non-shipping business, is the son of a former chairman. So is John Keville although he is one of the younger generation.

'At Manchester Liners Bob Stoker is grandson of the founder, although he is expected soon to pass over the reins to the highly professional and tough Tony Roberts. John Houlder . . . is of course a Houlder of the Houlder Line and the last chairman of the company before it was absorbed'. (The structure of FW is shown in Exhibit 6.)

'Shaw is happy that he has arrived at the right balance of activities and of management style. "We've spent £100 million on new ships in the past three years", he says. That keeps the group on the right end of the business still maintaining its strong position in the liner trades and able to support its bulk division until the time when the market turns up.

At the same time FW is arriving at a 60 : 40 mix between shipping and non-shipping. Counting John Houlder's burgeoning North Sea business as non-shipping to be sold off—each one of the lines had its own often hair-brained ideas for diversification, all of which eventually ended up with FW—but in the end the non-shipping end will probably resolve itself into an insurance broking business, Saxon Inns . . . an engineering business . . . and two good businesses in Trinidad and in Canada. Then there is Houlder Offshore, which is possibly the most exciting bit of the new FW'.

THE THREAT OF TAKEOVER

FW until the early 1970's was seen by many as a sleepy, asset-rich shipping company and a potential target for acquisition. In 1971 the merchant

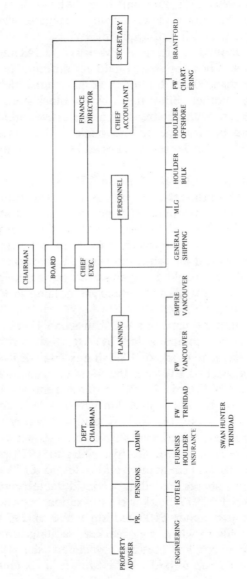

EXHIBIT 6
Furness Withy Organisation 1978

bankers Rea Brothers came forward to advise the FW board that it represented between 30 and 40 per cent of the equity capital, a figure that astonished the company. Rea Brothers had in fact accumulated a large block of shares for its clients and in this case was also acting in concert with Hambros, the major merchant bank, who in turn were acting for Hilmar Reksten, the Norwegian shipping magnate who was at the time interested in the possibility of acquiring FW.

Speculation about the future of FW was rife. At the end of 1978 there were three large blocks of shares held by different parties which together made up more than 50 per cent of the equity but which were used to counterbalance one another. First, there was a block held by Rea Brothers of around 25 per cent with apparently no aggressive intentions although many approaches had been made to the bank to purchase these shares. The Chairman of FW, Sir James Steel was also a deputy Chairman of Rea Brothers.

Second, there was a block of around 20 per cent of FW shares held by the Canadian Mr. Frank Narby via his company Eurocanadian Shipholdings. This company also held 37.6 per cent of the shares of Manchester Liners and in 1975 had bid for ML. FW held 61.6 per cent of the shares of ML. The Eurocanadian approach had been subjected to a Monopolies Commission investigation which concluded that the transfer of ML to Canadian ownership would be against the public interest and had further ordered that Mr. Narby should reduce his holding in FW to 10 per cent or less by the end of 1979.

The third rumoured aggressor was European Ferries, the very profitable cross channel ferry company led by Mr. Keith Wickenden which had acquired a 5 per cent block of FW shares from Eurocanadian. European Ferries had approached FW with the view to a takeover but this had been rejected by the FW Board.[1] However it was rumoured that there might be a deal between Narby and Wickenden whereby Wickenden would purchase all Eurocanadian's stake, bid for FW and sell Narby the controlling stake in Manchester Liners. European Ferries had shown a consistent record of growth in the 1970's, and in the five years to 1978 profits had expanded from £4.7 million to £22 million and sales to £122 million. As a result European Ferries shares traded at a considerable premium over the assets per share value. In 1977 market capitalisation became slightly more than that of FW at just under £100 million while in 1978 this value grew to nearly £150 million while the market capitalisation of most shipping companies including FW actually declined sharply. The share price performance of FW up to mid 1977 is shown in Exhibit 7.

[1]*Sunday Telegraph* 15.10.78.

149

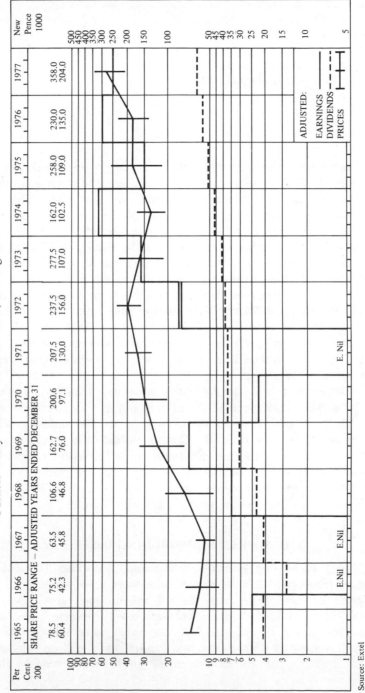

EXHIBIT 7

Furness Withy—Record of Share Price, Earnings and Dividends

Source: Extel

11

British Shipbuilders

After a bitterly fought parliamentary battle lasting over three years, Callaghan's Labour Government finally succeeded in placing on the statute books the Aircraft and Shipbuilding Industries Act 1977. This Act took into public ownership the great majority of the private shipbuilding and aircraft industry sectors and created British Shipbuilders. On vesting day, July 1st 1977, the Corporation took over the shares of 27 companies and their subsidiaries engaged in shipbuilding, slow speed diesel marine engineering and allied industries throughout Great Britain. Excluded from the Act were a number of ship repairing concerns and the major Belfast yard of Harland and Wolff. Many of the ship repair firms subsequently voluntarily joined British Shipbuilders and by the end of 1978 the Corporation was engaged in five industrial sectors, namely, merchant shipbuilding, warshipbuilding, diesel engine building, ship repair and general engineering.

The Corporation was the largest shipbuilding company in the world. Sales in its first year were £548 million and the Corporation employed over 85,000 people. Due to the dire state of the industry worldwide, however, Sir Anthony Griffin, the Chairman, had little comfort to offer Mr Eric Varley, Secretary of State for Industry, in his report on the first nine months of operation by British Shipbuilders. In this period Sir Anthony reported the Corporation made a pre-tax loss of £108 million. Details of the Corporation's finances are given in Exhibits 1 and 2.

THE WORLD SHIPBUILDING INDUSTRY

In 1950, world ship launchings amounted to some 3.2 million gross registered tons (grt). Of this, British yards were responsible for 1.4 million tons gross and Japanese yards for 0.2 million tons gross. By 1977 the positions of the UK and Japan were effectively reversed, and of the 25 millions tons gross completed, Japanese yards were responsible for 11.7 million tons gross or 43 per cent, and the UK for 1 million tons gross, or 4 per cent. In large part the decline in the market share held by the British

EXHIBIT 1

British Shipbuilders' Consolidated Profit & Loss Statement (£000)

9 months ending March 31, 1978

Turnover		
Shipbuilding		455258
Ship repairing		47389
Engine building		38665
Engineering		49331
Other activities		10397
		601040
Less intra group		53160
Net Sales	547880	
Trading loss for period		
Shipbuilding		(83770)
Ship repairing		(9894)
Engine building		(9250)
Engineering		3175
Other activities		(2267)
		(102276)
Less intra group		(2214)
Net Loss before tax	(104490)	
Investment income	98	
Interest payable net	(3934)	
Share of associate company profits	17	
Loss before tax	(108309)	
Tax credit	14660	
Loss after tax	(93649)	
Outside shareholders' interests	266	
Loss for period	(93383)	

Source: Annual Report.

industry was caused by its failure to expand capacity while other industries had substantially developed theirs.

Other major shipbuilding nations included the Scandinavian countries, West Germany, France and the Netherlands. Some had substantially developed their shipbuilding industries in the post-war period and had been joined by a number of Eastern Block countries, notably Poland and East Germany. In addition, South Korea was showing signs of developing as a major threat in the Far East and Brazil was emerging as an important centre in Latin America. The tonnages completed by selected countries are shown in Exhibit 3.

At the end of 1978 the world shipbuilding industry was in a state of crisis as capacity dramatically outstripped demand; there was massive excess tonnage in virtually every shipping sector. The roots of the problem

EXHIBIT 2

British Shipbuilders' Consolidated Balance Sheet (£000)

At 31st March 1978

Fixed Assets		
Land & buildings	79938	
Plant & machinery	56824	
Capital projects in progress	24341	
		161103
Investment in associated companies		36364
Other investments & loans		618
Current Assets		
Stocks	25408	
Work in progress (less provision		
for losses)	1084354	
Less instalments received	(1018878)	
	65476	
Debtors	113495	
Short term deposits	74650	
Cash & bank balances	23904	
		302933
Current Liabilities		
Provisions for net losses	71595	
Instalments in excess of cost of WIP	175120	
Creditors	136710	
Loan instalments due	14031	
Current tax	4898	
Bank overdraft	9764	
		412118
Net current liabilities		(109185)
Net assets		88900
Financed by		
Capital account[1]		119542
Less adverse balance on revenues		(93183)
		26359
Loans	36360	
Deferred tax	25283	
Outside shareholders' interest	898	62541
		88900

Source: Annual Report
1. Pending agreement of the commencing capital for the Corporation with the Secretary
   of State the capital account was taken to be equal to:
   (i) the book value of the total net assets of the subsidiaries acquired on
   vesting day
   (ii) loans taken over from the Secretary of State.
   The capital account was to be adjusted in future and apportioned between Public
   Dividend Capital and the commencing debt to the National Loans Fund in proportions specified by the Secretary of State.

EXHIBIT 3
New Vessels Completed by Country of Build 1967–77 ('000 grt)

	1967	1971	1975	1977
Denmark				
Tankers	220	557	674	437
Total	488	806	961	709
France				
Tankers	260	717	763	402
Total	553	1112	1301	1107
West Germany				
Tankers	205	380	1623	375
Total	1002	1649	2549	1595
Italy				
Tankers	151	370	610	378
Total	507	813	847	778
Japan				
Tankers	2707	5007	12999	2745
Total	7497	11992	17978	11708
Netherlands				
Tankers	97	584	736	38
Total	339	821	951	241
Norway				
Tankers	219	346	670	106
Total	522	831	1029	567
Spain				
Tankers	212	356	1026	1422
Total	406	916	1638	1814
Sweden				
Tankers	519	1251	2139	1949
Total	1161	1837	2460	2311
United Kingdom				
Tankers	260	369	564	435
Total	1298	1239	1304	1020
United States of America				
Tankers	—	213	695	688
Total	242	482	1004	1012
Brazil				
Tankers	—	2	99	37
Total	59	147	389	295

EXHIBIT 3 (*continued*)
New Vessels Completed by Country of Build 1967–77 ('000 grt)

	1967	1971	1975	1977
Poland				
Tankers	40	1	1	2
Total	400	489	608	479
South Korea				
Tankers	1	—	390	164
Total	14	7	441	562
World				
Tankers	4990	10424	24051	10222
Total	15780	24860	35898	27532

Source: Lloyd's Register

went back to the latter half of the 1960s when forward projections indicated a steady increase in world oil demand and consequently of tanker tonnage. Further, the closure of the Suez Canal, coupled with the development of new supertankers of over 200,000 deadweight tons (dwt), stimulated shipbuilding demand.

The industry in Japan boomed and output expanded from 1.7 million grt in 1960 to 10.09 million grt in 1970, reaching a peak of 16.9 million grt in 1975. The shipbuilding industry in Europe by comparison consistently underestimated the growth of demand for new ships and the industry only grew from 4 million grt in 1960 to 7.8 million grt in 1975. In Britain, no expansion at all took place and, indeed, a small fall in output occurred from 1.3 million grt in 1960 to 1.2 million grt in 1975.

In 1973, following the massive rise in the price of oil, the Western economies went into recession, thus reducing the demand for oil. By the end of 1975 there was a huge surplus of tankers, especially for very large crude carriers, and the situation was likely to worsen as the result of new ships on order. Where possible, shipowners converted orders building to bulk cargo ships, and by the end of 1978 this had led to excess supply in this sector, too. A special Forum established by a number of independent tanker owners, bankers, shipbuilders and some major European oil companies was established to investigate the size of the problem in 1976. The Forum reported in late 1977 that there would be an expected surplus of about 75–100 million dwt in 1979 and this would still be between 45–85 million dwt by 1985. Further, there would also be a smaller but still serious excess demand in the bulk market in the 1980s.

The Forum report also noted that governments contemplating financial assistance for the building of ships for which there was not true commercial demand, could exacerbate the period of depressed shipbuilding rates brought on by overcapacity and so force many owners into bankruptcy. The estimated tanker operating losses of $455 million in 1977 were expected to rise to nearly $2,000 million in 1980.

The inability of owners to obtain an adequate rate structure was causing problems in raising additional long-term finance for new tonnage from internal funds. At the same time, the international banking community was growing increasingly concerned about providing further funds for ship finance. As a result, the shipping industry was increasingly reliant on government finance. This seemed to be directed largely at stimulating new shipbuilding tonnage which could only increase the pressure on rates and also help build-up new competitors, such as the Eastern Bloc and some third world countries. The Forum suggested that as a result many shipping companies, some with long experience and an excellent reputation, would be forced to withdraw from the industry or else go into liquidation.

It was estimated that in 1975 the world shipbuilding capacity was 39 million grt, while by 1980 demand for new tonnage was expected to be only 12–13 million grt. In order to fill the excess capacity, governments were pursuing four specific policies which seemed might add to the problems of the international shipping industry. First, many governments were selling ships at heavily subsidised prices to the Soviet Union and other Eastern Bloc countries. These ships were then expected to be used in competition with Western shipping companies, helping to reduce shipping rates. Second, some governments were selling ships to developing countries keen to build their national fleets at below cost prices. These ships, too, would increase competition and replace developed country ships in trades on specific routes in conjunction with proposals such as the UNCTAD 40 : 40 : 20 rule.[1] Third, there was a threat by some countries intent upon providing subsidised ships produced in their national yards for domestic shipowners. Fourth, some countries were contemplating the introduction of flag preference schemes to stimulate the building of national flag ships to carry reserve freights which would normally be carried by open competition.

Despite these measures, the outlook remained gloomy. In 1978 there was a fall of 34 per cent in the volume of shipbuilding orders placed compared with 1977 and the established shipbuilding nations continued to lose market share to the growing yards of the developing countries. Orders placed in 1978 slumped to 915 ships totalling 13.7 million dwt compared with 20.8 million dwt in 1977.

The fierce competition for orders had led to a proliferation in government subsidies for shipbuilders to enable them to quote lower prices

---

[1]The United Nations proposed that the trade between two countries should be subdivided on a 40 : 40 basis between the ships of the countries with the remaining 20 per cent being available to open competition. The acceptance of such a system was expected to severely affect the fleets of some countries such as the UK whose shipping lines were heavily engaged in the cross trades.

and extend credit terms. The height of the bidding was reached according to *Fairplay International* when Japan won an order for six, 16,500 dwt cargo ships for Pakistan with a bid based upon 100 per cent credit spread over 30 years with no payments in the first 10 years and a 3 per cent rate of interest thereafter.

Despite such terms Japan lost market share in 1978, taking orders for 308 ships of 5.5 million dwt—a share of 40.5 per cent of the total market compared with 47 per cent in 1977, reflecting the problem for Japanese shipyards of the rising value of the yen. Other leading nations to lose ground in 1978 included Holland, Norway, Spain and the UK with shares of 1.8 per cent, 0.7 per cent, 2.9 per cent and 2.3 per cent respectively.

Countries gaining market share included Brazil (1.8 per cent), South Korea (5.8), Poland (5.9), Sweden (7.8) and Taiwan (3.1). This trend toward the new shipbuilding countries was a growing cause for concern for the Shipbuilding Committee of the Organisation for Economic Co-operation and Development (OECD).

Moreover, the industry in 1978 was producing new ships at almost twice the rate new orders were being received. At the end of December 1978 *Lloyd's Register* reported a total world ordering book of 25.8 million grt compared with 36.7 million grt a year earlier. Almost 69 per cent of this order book was due for delivery in 1979, while in the last quarter of 1978, new order intake slumped to a 13 year low. Japan retained just over 25 per cent of the orders on hand but second place was taken by Brazil with 2.8 million grt on order largely due to government backed orders. Behind these countries came the following with the figures for orders on hand at the end of 1978 and that for the end of 1977 shown in brackets (in millions of grt): USA 2.6 (3.6); France 1.5 (2); Poland 1.4 (1.8); Spain 1.3 (1.8); UK 1.2 (2.2); Sweden 1 (2.1) and South Korea 0.7 (1.1).

In December 1977 there were 10.3 million grt of oil tankers on order compared with 6.6 million grt at the end of 1978 and 10.7 million grt of bulk carriers compared with 5.9 million grt. There was a slower rate of order decline in general cargo vessels with an order book of 8.3 million grt at the end of 1978 indicating continued overcapacity in this sector.

THE RESOURCES OF THE CORPORATION

In 1978, British Shipbuilders consisted of 30 shipyards, 19 repair establishments and six firms building medium and slow-speed diesel engines. The publicly owned sector accounted for about 97 per cent of merchant shipbuilding in the UK, 99 per cent of warshipbuilding, all slow-speed marine diesel production and about half the ship repairing activities. Shipbuilding capacity was something over 1 million gross tons of merchant shipping annually and most classes of naval tonnage were also built, together with the fabrication and repair of offshore structures and modules.

At the time of nationalisation, much of the industry was in serious financial difficulty, with some companies appearing close to bankruptcy. Further, the industry had on hand an order book which in many cases was destined to lose money and in its first 9 months' operation, some £47 million of British Shipbuilder's reported losses were due to contracts taken on prior to nationalisation. The principal activities of the Corporation were as follows:

Merchant Shipbuilding

Merchant shipbuilding represented the major area of the Corporation's activities. The new organisation combined many world famous shipbuilding names which, although co-ordinated with the introduction of a centralised marketing organisation, still operated in a largely autonomous manner. The principal yards concerned with merchant shipbuilding were:

Ailsa Shipbuilding Company

Located at Troon in Scotland, this yard specialised in the production of small vessels below about 6000 dwt, such as passenger ferries, small dry cargo and bulk carriers, dredgers and offshore fast patrol craft. The yard had been significantly re-equipped in the decade prior to nationalisation and with its covered building berth rated as one of the most modern small building units in Europe. Ailsa was not originally nationalised but requested to join British Shipbuilders in 1978 when the yard ran out of work.

Appledore Shipbuilders

Developed as a private enterprise organisation, Appledore had created a successful niche for itself in Devon, building series produced bulk carriers and container ships of 3–5000 dwt. The yard also built dredgers and offshore supply ships. Its facilities were considered to be very advanced using fully covered integrated assembly techniques where ships were built in dock and floated out. As a result Appledore had an efficiency and output record that rivalled similar Japanese yards.

Austin and Pickersgill

One of the larger shipbuilding units located in Sunderland, Austin and Pickersgill had been the subject of a £30 million major development programme to double its building area, making it one of the most advanced yards of its kind. The redevelopment had also led to modernisation of stockyards, improved manufacturing facilities, including the installation of panel lines and the erection of a covered and enclosed block assembly area.

Austin and Pickersgill had developed a range of standardised dry cargo ships and more than 140 of its SD14 type ships were at sea by 1978. Standardisation had allowed the yard to be competitive by obtaining longer production runs and further additions to its range of standardised models were being developed. Austin and Pickersgill had been one of the most profitable merchant shipbuilding companies.

Brooke Marine

A small yard based on the East coast at Lowestoft, Brooke Marine was still in the process of redevelopment. The yard specialised in the production of small naval vessels.

Cammell Laird Shipbuilders

Based at Birkenhead, Cammell Laird had undertaken a £22 million modernisation scheme replacing four open berths with two covered berths plus a large construction hall. The company produced a range of product carriers and fast freighters and was also a builder of naval vessels. The company was already 50 per cent State owned and had been losing money before full nationalisation.

Clelands Shipbuilding Company and Goole Shipbuilding and Repair

These two small yards both located on the East coast built to a maximum size of around 6500 dwt and produced trawlers, coasters, dredgers, small dry cargo carriers, container ships and product carriers.

Govan Shipbuilders

An amalgamation of several famous Clydeside yards, Govan had developed out of Upper Clyde Shipbuilders, which had already been the subject of a controversial rescue operation by the Heath Conservative administration. Substantial public funds had been provided to Govan, although losses had continued. Despite these, a £28 million investment programme had been undertaken to improve facilities and yard productivity. The revised facilities allowed Govan to build ships up to 80,000 dwt although marketing efforts immediately prior to amalgamation into British Shipbuilders had been largely devoted to smaller vessels, especially series-produced dry cargo ships.

Hall Russell and Company

Another small yard based in Aberdeen, Hall Russell conducted traditional building on three conventional berths with a maximum capacity of around 6000 dwt. Over the past few years the yard had concentrated on building specialist ships such as chemical tankers, Ro-Ro vessels and trawlers. The yard had also diversified into the production of naval offshore patrol and fishery protection vessels.

Robb Caledon Shipbuilders

A small Dundee based builder producing small and medium sized ships up to 15,000 dwt, Robb Caledon offered a range of specialised products such as Ro-Ro vessels, ferries and salvage ships.

Scott Lithgow

One of the largest groups to be taken into British Shipbuilders, Scott Lithgow operated a series of yards in Glasgow and Greenock. These yards had received substantial capital investment before nationalisation, including the installation of NC turning machines, introduction of a panel line and the construction of a large building pad. The larger yards in the group built a range of vessel types from oil tankers to dynamically positioned drill ships and complex warships. The smaller yards constructed specialist vessels such as trawlers, offshore supply vessels and dredgers.

Smiths Dock Company

This company operated two yards in the North East specialised in the production of series-built refrigerated ships, containers, reefer containers and Ro-Ro vessels. One of the yards could accommodate large vessels up to 170,000 dwt and had in recent years been producing large bulk/oil carriers.

Sunderland Shipbuilders

Also based in the North East, Sunderland Shipbuilders was another of the larger concerns in British Shipbuilders. The yards had just been extensively redeveloped at a cost of £20 million and had the capacity for side-by-side construction of two vessels of up to 25,000 dwt. Designed as one of the most advanced totally enclosed ship construction facilities in the world it had comprehensive steel fabrication and outfitting facilities. The yards offered series construction of 16,300 dwt cargo liners and were also capable of constructing vessels up to 150,000 dwt.

Swan Hunter Shipbuilders

Swan Hunter was one of Europe's largest shipbuilding groups and had recently invested heavily to restructure its facilities. Its yards in the North

East could produce medium and large tankers, product carriers and other bulk vessels. In addition, Swan Hunter was skilled in producing specialist vessels such as gas and chemical tankers, ferries and containerships. The group was also an important builder of naval ships.

Naval Shipbuilding

Three companies in British Shipbuilders—Vickers Shipbuilding Group, Vosper Thornycroft (UK) and Yarrow (Shipbuilders) were specialists or 'lead' warship builders supplying ships to the Royal Navy and foreign navies. These yards designed and built an extensive range of warships and fleet auxiliaries, to fast patrol craft and offshore protection vessels. In addition, a number of other yards, known as 'follow on' yards, combined both merchant and naval work. These yards were those of Cammell Laird, Brooke Marine, Scott Lithgow and Swan Hunter.

General Engineering

Six companies within the Corporation specialised in general engineering offering a wide range of marine related products, together with an extensive array of products and services outside of shipping. Included in the range of products and services offered were: deck machinery; switchboards; electrical installation and distribution systems; steering gear; stem frames; missile launchers; armaments; ships support equipment; combustion equipment; stabilising installations; specialist machinery; ferrous and non-ferrous casting and hydraulic equipment.

Engine Building

British Shipbuilders could supply almost all types of main machinery for ships and at its engine building establishments produced slow and medium speed diesels to the Corporation's own designs and under licence. A number of these engines were also employed for industrial purposes on land where they were used to drive compressors, blowers and pumps.

Ship Repairing

This was initially excluded from nationalisation, largely as the result of a successful fight by the small, entrepreneur-led Bristol Channel Ship Repairers. However, British Shipbuilders had subsequently acquired over half of the ship repair capacity in the UK as a result of voluntary agreements with the private owners of these facilities. Most came as integral parts of the purchase of shipbuilding assets. The companies within the ship repair division offered comprehensive and competitive facilities for all types of repairs, conversions and overhauls in 46 fully equipped dry docks and floating repair facilities.

ORGANISATION

The Corporation established its head office in Newcastle-on-Tyne, a traditional centre for the shipbuilding industry. A second office in London provided a centre for a separate marketing division created to co-ordinate the marketing activities of the Corporation's subsidiaries.

The blueprint drawn before vesting day had been designed to give the maximum possible decentralisation for the individual companies. All the traditional trading names had been retained to help keep customer confidence. Individual yards or groups of companies were retained as profit centres. A small headquarter's staff acted as a holding company, concerned with the central functions of corporate planning, marketing, industrial relations, financial control and budgeting. These departments were to provide the policy framework for the profit centres and then monitor their performance.

A strong central marketing division had, however, been created to co-ordinate the selling activities of the individual companies, and to launch an intensive marketing programme. Commenting upon the value of this arrangement, Mr Michael Casey, Chief Executive of British Shipbuilders, said:

> 'As a unified organisation we are able to structure and support the financial packages designed to assist member companies in the sale of ships. The raising of large scale, long term foreign currency loans when negotiating and financing the building of ships would have been beyond the strength of the individual companies before nationalisation. The fact that we are dealing as a publicly owned corporation also strengthens our position when dealing with foreign governments for both merchant and warship contracts.[1]'

Mr John Parker, former managing director of Austin and Pickersgill, who had joined the Board of British Shipbuilders as group marketing director, was in charge of this central effort.

A second central division had been created responsible for research and development. This division was specifically concerned with improving ship design and yard productivity, and in the longer term the exploitation of opportunities for improving or introducing new processes and products.

Controls on finance and accounting had been introduced to the subsidiaries, together with cost and production control systems in the shipyards. A headquarters monitoring system to vet performance against forecasts was also created. Headquarter's staff were also engaged in the assessment of the strengths and weaknesses of various yards with a major initial task being to establish improved techniques for measuring relative levels of efficiency and productivity in yards producing different types of ship.

[1]British Shipbuilders' Report and Accounts, 1977/78, p. 13.

The Board was appointed by the Secretary of State for Industry, and consisted of a maximum of 20 members. Early in 1979 the actual composition of the Board consisted of 13 members, 7 of whom served in a part-time capacity. Several of these members also held executive positions in subsidiaries and three were executive officers of trade unions. Finding suitably qualified candidates for some full-time appointments proved difficult. The Chairman of the Board, Admiral Sir Anthony Griffin, acted in a part-time capacity and the Chief Executive Officer and Deputy Chairman was Mr Michael Casey. Mr Casey had been appointed to his position when, following delays in implementing the Nationalisation Act, the first choice had resigned. Mr Casey was a former civil servant who had been Under Secretary at the Department of Industry in charge of its shipbuilding division.

STATUTORY DUTIES OF THE CORPORATION

Laid down in the Aircraft and Shipbuilding Industries Act were a number of duties the Corporation was expected to fulfil. These were as follows:

- to promote the efficient and economical design, development, production, sale, repair and maintenance of ships and slow speed diesel marine engines and research into matters relating thereto
- to have full regard in carrying out its activities to the requirements of national defence
- to promote industrial democracy in a strong and organic form in its undertakings
- from time to time, when it considers it appropriate or the Secretary of State so requires, to undertake a review of its affairs for the purposes of determining how the management of the activities of the Corporation and its subsidiaries can most efficiently be organised, what steps are necessary to promote industrial democracy and of seeking the largest degree, consistent with the discharge of its function, of decentralisation of management and decision-making to separate profit centres and to make a report to the Secretary of State thereon
- after consulting any relevant trade union to formulate in each year a corporate plan relating to the conduct of the operations of the Corporation and its wholly owned subsidiaries.

INTERIM STRATEGY

Until it had formulated a long term strategic plan, British Shipbuilders adopted a holding action strategy based upon five main objectives. These were also expected to remain important elements in future policy. Mr

Casey outlined these objectives as follows:

- maximising the volume of new business while reducing the heavy financial losses
- concentrating business in the most efficient yards
- raising levels of productivity
- improving industrial relations
- preserving as much capacity as possible by diversification mainly into offshore business and a wider range of warship building.

The Pursuit of Shipbuilding Orders

In maximising the volume of new business generated, British Shipbuilders had pursued an aggressive marketing policy since its formation. As a result in its first nine months the Corporation won orders for 60 ships of 348, 321 cgrt.[1] The largest single contract won during the period was for the building of 24 ships for Poland. This order was won with the help of aid of around £28 million given to the Poles and drawn from a £65 million fund established in February 1977 by the British Government as an 'intervention' fund to be used to encourage ship orders.

The Polish order was negotiated for over a year and consisted of 22 ships and two floating cranes worth £115 million. Apart from the £28 million provided from the government intervention fund, British Shipbuilders raised a further $65 million on the Eurobond market to cover one-third of the financing. Commenting on the deal, the *Economist* noted:

'Poland will chuckle all the way to the bank now that the deal . . . is clinched. On the face of it, the order, proudly flourished before the Labour Party Conference by the Prime Minister . . . , will help stave off redundancies in Britain's ailing shipyards. But scratch the surface of Mr Callaghan's glossy words and it becomes apparent that Poland will benefit more than Britain.

'The British taxpayer is donating a £30 m subsidy to cut the price of the ships . . . and the State owned British Shipbuilders is giving the Poles invaluable help to raise the finance to pay for them. To bolster Britain's lame duck shipbuilders the government is subsidising the expansion of the Comecon fleet whose cheap freight rates are already threatening the prosperity of the British merchant navy (which unlike the shipyards, is a profitable foreign-exchange earning industry).

'With the Polish state shipping company building in Britain, Polish yards are free to build for export; 90% of Polish output is exported, including over 60% to the Soviet Union.[2]

[1] Compensated gross registered tonnage—a measure adopted by British Shipbuilders to reflect the relative difference in complexity between, say, warship and merchant shipbuilding.

[2] Economist, 8.10.77.

EXHIBIT 4

Main British Shipbuilders' Companies: Their Record and Prospects

Company	Last full year pre-nationalisation			Yr ended March 1978 Pre-tax Profit/(Loss)	Unemployment in area %	Orders for delivery beginning January 1979
	Turnover	Pre-Tax profit/losses	Employees			
	(millions)	(millions)		(millions)		
Brook Marine (end March 31)	£9.9	£0.9	875	£0.9	6.6	2 small naval craft for Nigeria and Oman (1978) 4 fast patrol craft
Vickers	£59.1	£3.8	14,000	£4.9	6.7	1 cruiser 4 nuclear submarines 1 Type 42 destroyer
Smith's Dock	£22.3	£1.7	3,500	£(6.5)**	9.7	3 bulkcarriers (1979)
Appledore	£15.7	£0.5	1,100	N/A	7.7	4 container ships (1979) 1 diving support ship (1979)
Swan Hunter (1976)	£72.4	£1.4*	11,000	£(11.4)	8.5	1 container ship (Jan. 1979) 1 cruiser + 2 Type 42 frigates
Sunderland	£56.9	(£2.4)	7,000	N/A	13.5	2 cargo vessels 1 cargo vessel 6 cargo vessels (16,000 dwt)

Company						Orders
Cammell Laird	£34.0	(£9.2)*	5,200	£(25.0)	12.5	2 type 55 tankers 1 Type 42 destroyer
Vosper Thornycroft	£62.0	£5.6	4,600	£4.5	4.8	1 minesweeper 2 Mk 9 frigates 3 October class patrol ships
Austin & Pickersgill	£36.9	£2.5	2,800	£0.4	13.5	13 SD 14 cargo ships 2 SD 16 cargo ships
Govan Shipbuilders· (June 1977)	£47.9	(£6.9)*	5,700	£(10.0)	9.7	13 multi-purpose
Robb Caledon (June 1977)	£16.7	£0.2	2,300	£(7.6)	9.3	3 multi-purpose cargo ships for Poland
Yarrow (June 1977)	£35.6	£3.1	5,400	£1.8	9.7	4 tugs
Scott Lithgow (major companies)	£63.4	(£0.7)	7,600	(£23.8)	11.0	3 21,000 dwt cargo liners for Ocean 2 small multi-purpose cargo ships for Poland 1 supply ship—Navy off- shore emergencies craft—BP

Source: Financial Times 19/10/78 and Company accounts.
*Accounts qualified by Auditors.
**Haverton Hill Yard only.

Other deals of a similar but less contentious nature were done with other countries, while as an alternative, overseas development aid funds were also used to encourage orders from the Indian subcontinent. Despite the policy of heavy subsidies for orders placed, British Shipbuilders were relatively unsuccessful in generating further orders. During 1978, orders for only 17 merchant ships were taken of 86,000 grt against completions of 714,000 grt. These orders were valued at £80 million compared with the 1977 order intake of 67 ships totalling 517,000 grt and worth £343 million. As a result, the plight of many individual yards was grave, as shown in Exhibit 4.

The subsidisation attempts by British Shipbuilders had been attacked in some countries as unfair competition. However, most had responded with the introduction of similar or even more generous schemes. Many shipowners especially in Britain were, however, bitter, believing that such schemes served only to help build up competition, especially from Eastern Bloc countries and developing nations, which would help continue the economic slump in shipping rates and permanently damage the financial viability of established British shipping lines.

Commenting upon the controversy surrounding the high level of aid given to Poland for its large order in 1977, Mr Casey said:

'I do not know of any action more misunderstood, nor one so deliberately distorted by those who should, *and do,* know better.

'Loose talk of giving away ships to competitors really does not stand up to examination. It is a lie and it was time it was nailed.[1]'

However, the deal was subsequently sharply criticised by the Comptroller and Auditor General, Sir Douglas Henley, in his report to Parliament reviewing payments authorised for the financial year 1977–78, Sir Douglas noted that the Corporation was unable effectively to assess the scale of large contracts. He stated that while the accounts of British Shipbuilders for the first nine months resulted in a £104 million loss after assistance from the Government Intervention Fund totalling £45 million, the scale of this loss was not known until June 1978.

At this time the Corporation had assured the Department of Industry that orders secured with help from the intervention fund had not been taken at below break-even prices. Later, however, it was stated that losses would be shown. Sir Douglas had asked the department whether they had found the cause of the losses and was told that the Corporation was still building up its organisation when the nationalised company became effective and that top management had concentrated on winning orders.

[1]*The Times*, 27.7.78.

Sir Douglas, referring specifically to the use of the intervention fund, said:

'My staff found little evidence that the department had adopted a selective approach or had made offers of assistance conditional on any restructuring of the industry.

'They also noted that the Treasury had expressed concern that the department had not used the large Polish order to apply the selective subsidy strategy, though accepting that the department had been hampered by the lack of an interim plan from British Shipbuilders.

'The department told me that in 1977–78 they had not found it possible to link offers to a formal selective strategy for achieving a viable industry in the long term. Such a strategy had to await the formulation by British Shipbuilders of its corporate plan, the preparation of which has been affected by the delay in bringing the industry into public ownership.'

Although in November 1977, British Shipbuilders had initially felt that £28 million would be an insufficient subsidy this had quickly been revised. By March 1978, however, British Shipbuilders again forecast a significant loss on the contract. Sir Douglas went on:

'At that time British Shipbuilders remained unable to provide detailed cost estimates as they had not been prepared by its subsidiaries.'[1]

Concentration in Efficient Yards and Productivity

The Corporation first set out to try and produce productivity figures for its own and rival yards. Finance Director, Maurice Elderfield, declared later that the attempt had been abandoned because there was no way of comparing like with like. The Corporation noted, however, that the productivity of the British yards devoted to merchant shipbuilding were among the least productive of major shipbuilding countries, with an output of 16 cgrt per employee per year. This was 50 per cent worse than typical Western European ratios and even farther behind Scandinavian and Far Eastern performance.[2]

There were also reports that since nationalisation, productivity in a number of yards had actually fallen, due in part to the introduction of

[1]*Daily Telegraph*, 2.2.79.
[2]*Financial Times*, 7.12.78.

another layer of bureaucracy on already inefficient yards. The *Sunday Telegraph* reported:

> 'In the summer Derek Kimber . . . created a furore when he announced that productivity at his Austin and Pickersgill yard . . . had fallen more than 20 per cent since nationalisation. The fall, he said, was "deplorable", adding that before nationalisation a standard SD14 ship . . . was produced off the line in 16 weeks. Now it was down to 20 weeks or more.
>
> 'He also added another key point which is repeated by managers elsewhere: the workforce, said Kimber, had quickly sensed that the management at the yard was no longer able to manage as it had done before but had to keep referring decisions to headquarters.
>
> 'Senior executives argue that productivity in the yards has fallen as the workers have tried to spin out the last orders. This was not the case in Germany and Japan despite a similar lack of orders.'[1]

Mr John Parker, the board member for shipbuilding revealed in an article published in the British Shipbuilders' House Journal that each yard on average lost another 3 hours production time per day through late starts, early finishes, waiting time and other factors. As a result the average production performance of each man was only half that of Japanese yards and some in Europe.[2] The financial consequences of such performance were severe, as Exhibit 4 shows.

Improving Industrial Relations

For many years before nationalisation, the British shipbuilding industry had had poor labour relations. Demarcation disputes between particular trades were notorious. After nationalisation the Corporation placed the highest priority on establishing a close working relationship with trade unions at all levels. Most of the Corporation's employees were members of the Confederation of Shipbuilding and Engineering Unions (CSEU) and regular monthly meetings were held between the Corporation and CSEU's Shipyard Negotiating Committee. A number of important national agreements had been reached. Joint monitoring committees were set up to maintain production targets, and to negotiate flexible manning in some of the worst yards. However, this had only happened with the help of equal pay awards which had added over £15 million to the Corporation's wage bill. The Corporation's proposals that its fragmented wage bargaining system involving 168 sets of separate negotiations with a common date for all negotiations of January 1st had however received a mixed reception.

[1]*Sunday Telegraph*, 17.12.78.
[2]*Shipbuilding News*, March 1979.

Although accepted in principle by the government, British Shipbuilders and leaders of the CSEU, some rank and file members were opposed to the system and the General and Municipal Workers Union rejected the proposals.

Despite some progress labour difficulties persisted. Shortly after winning the order for Polish ships, a dispute at Swan Hunter between outfitters and boilermarkers had resulted in British Shipbuilders shifting all the order to other yards, mainly in Scotland and had led to over 1000 redundancies at Swan Hunter. Other orders had been lost through failure to meet delivery dates. Another problem emerged when the Corporation recognised the Engineers' and Manager's Association (EMA) which represented a significant number of managers within the industry.

FUTURE STRATEGY

By the end of 1978 British Shipbuilders had announced about 3400 redundancies at Swan Hunter, Haverton Hill and Cammell Laird. Despite union resistance, further redundancies were felt to be inevitable in the long term. In November 1978, the Corporation produced its first corporate plan. This was outlined in a series of detailed papers submitted to the Secretary of State.

The aim was to achieve an average merchant shipping annual output of 560,000 compensated gross registered tons per annum over the period 1980–85. This represented a cut back on existing capacity of only around 14 per cent, and implied continuing and substantial subsidies on future orders. Compared with other nations, this cutback seemed modest. Japan was planning a reduction of 35 per cent, while Norway expected a 48 per cent fall. West Germany planned to reduce its labour force by 30 per cent by 1980, and France planned a 20 per cent cutback by the end of 1979. Similar reductions were planned or had been announced in Italy, Belgium, Holland and Sweden.

Union leaders were provided with details of output targets for the seven years to 1985. In 1978 and 1979, expected output was 600,000 cgrt falling to 430,000 cgrt in 1980 and rising slowly to stabilise at 560,000 cgrt between 1983–1985. The projections were based upon a mixture of the British industry's ability to maintain its traditional share of the world market for different types of ship. Since 1973, the UK had built about 5 per cent of the world's dry cargo vessels and 2 per cent of the world's tankers and non-cargo fleet.

The British Shipbuilders' paper stated:

'in the short term, it may be impossible to maintain historical product market shares due to the high level of world shipbuilding capacity relative to demand, and the consequent competition from countries with tanker capacity seeking to maintain employment by switching to dry cargo construction. Under these conditions a constant aggregate market share of 3.2 per cent can be regarded as a realistic objective.'[1]

The new plan called for a reduction in capacity of 32 per cent by 1980–81 and the loss of 12,300 jobs. In addition to the favoured option, three other alternatives had been considered. One was to retain merchant shipbuilding at its existing size by using an intervention fund of £300 million per year to support the workforce of 33,000. The other two possibilities involve 20,000 and 25,000 redundancies which were a total shutdown of merchant shipbuilding. The favoured option required an annual intervention fund of £110 million in 1979–81, £85 million in 1981–82 and £50 million in 1982–3. It was also hoped that around 6,000 of the jobs lost in merchant shipbuilding could be redeployed into warship building and offshore oil work

The new plan envisaged further growth taking place in the three main naval yards. Vickers, Vosper Thornycroft and Yarrow. In addition, some contracts were expected for the other naval yards. Export orders might also form the basis for possible increased employment.

The warship yards were, however, expected to be inhibited by the imposition of overdraft limits on the Corporation by the Secretary of State and only vital or necessary capital expenditure for health and safety reasons would be allowed in the short term. Although employment was expected to remain constant at around 20,000, productivity improvements were needed.

There were three options for engine building. First, the Corporation could continue without change, giving a financial break-even position. Second, Kincaid and Scotts Engineering could be amalgamated; Hawthorn Leslie allowed to diversify into medium-speed engines; Clarke and NEM concentrate on slow-speed Sulzer engines; and Doxford continue to make its own engines. Third, Doxford could be closed down and its production concentrated at Hawthorn Leslie.

The four major ship repairing groups were expected to lose £14.4 million in 1978–79—a substantial proportion of the £45 million maximum target loss expected by the Secretary of State. The chosen strategy was therefore to continue operations at the six Tyne yards plus Brigham and Cowan at Hull. River Thames Shiprepairers was expected to face a halving of its 1100 workforce, sale of its facilities at Felixstowe and closure of facilities at Gravesend and Sheerness. Vosper was to be expanded and Falmouth, which had suffered losses from poor productivity and poor labour relations, was to be closed down. This last move was announced in January 1979, together with the closure of the Haverton Hill merchant shipping yard, resulting in a loss of 2,000 jobs.

---

[1]*The Times*, 13.11.78.

REACTIONS TO THE PLAN

These plans were not endorsed by the trade unions. Union leaders were given an assurance that no government decision would be taken on the future of the industry without further consultation. Mr Eric Varley, Secretary for the Industry, also promised the unions to take into account their alternative proposals on diversification and on a "scrap and build" policy aimed at preserving jobs.

In deciding which course of action to adopt, Mr Varley had several reasons for supporting the case for maintaining the British industry at something like its existing size. First, the industry, unlike others abroad, had not expanded in the post-war period. Second, the demands of the British merchant fleet, still the fourth largest in the world, provided a home demand absent in many other shipbuilding countries. In 1977, UK shipyards produced around 1 million grt of ships, while at the same time the British fleet took delivery of 1.8 million grt from yards at home and abroad. Third, labour costs in Britain had become low by European standards. Fourth, there could be a case for stating that there was a minimum viable size for the industry in terms of retaining labour skills, research and development potential, back-up supply industries and economies of scale. Finally, most of the shipyards were located in areas of high unemployment. These areas were also important political centres for the Labour Party, virtually all returning Labour members of parliament.

Managing the External Environment

12

Norcem (D)

'Norcem will never be highly profitable, but neither will it ever be bankrupt. The Government will not allow either to happen'.

Gerhard Heiberg, Managing Director of Norcem, Norway's monopoly cement manufacturer, was commenting on the relationship between the Government and his company. 'Because of our monopoly position in the supply of a basic commodity for the construction industry and our use of raw materials which are a national resource, the Government wants to know of our plans. Also we are one of the largest industrial concerns in Norway, so naturally the Government expects us to help them fulfil their general industrial policy. However, I do not believe they have any desire to nationalize us so long as we continue to manage the company efficiently'.

'The essence of the dilemma for a company like Norcem can be highlighted by its plant in Kjøpsvik, the northernmost cement plant in the world. If Norcem were a privately owned company acting to maximize profitability, we would close down the Kjøpsvik plant because the costs are very high. On the other hand, if Norcem were government-owned the social benefits of keeping the plant open would outweight the additonal costs for inefficiently produced cement. Kjøpsvik is an isolated community, completely dependent on Norcem's cement plant. In reality Norcem is neither independent of government forces or free market forces given its major participation in export markets.'

In addition to the dilemma above Mr. Heiberg identified numerous factors which impinged on present and future decision-making.

- 'Should the Government take an ownership stake in our company and if so, on what conditions? While there is to-day much debate in Norway on the question: "Who should own what?" and "What should be nationalized?", many business leaders feel that the question of ownership is becoming less important.'
- 'Who should be elected to the Board of Directors?'
- 'What will be the sources of Norcem's future capital funding? It could come from the Government in exchange for equity. As time goes by,

the Government will have larger resources than private sources, particularly given the anticipated levels of oil revenues and taxation.'
- 'Would Government ownership affect cement prices in Norway? At the moment Norcem obtains permission from the Price Agency of the Department of Consumer and Administrative Affairs to raise prices. One topical problem is to explain to this Agency that the impact of inflation on Norcem's financial performance would be reduced if the Price Agency would consider replacement cost depreciation instead of historical cost depreciation.'
- 'How can Norcem generate a growth rate sufficient to continue to challenge its management?'

Mr Heiberg continued 'These factors are all part of the Norwegian political, social and economic environment. Also you must recognise that, Norway is a country with one of the most developed welfare states in the world. Politics have been dominated by the socialist party for most of the past 35 years. Norway is a large country with a small population and hence a small home market compared with most European countries. Norwegian labour rates are amongst the highest in the world. High personal income taxation results in small differentials in after tax income between the shop floor worker and the middle manager. A growing state involvement in industry may occur as the Norwegian economy becomes more and more dominated by North Sea oil, an activity controlled by Government agencies. Increased worker involvement in the company management seems probable although the recently established Corporate Assemblies have perhaps caused relatively few changes.'

More detail about Norway and Norwegian Industry is given in Appendix A.

ACTIVITIES OF NORCEM

Norcem was founded on November 4th, 1968 by the three major cement companies in Norway merging to form a single company. By 1976, the company operated three groups. These were:

(1) *Cement*
This group ran both the Norwegian and International cement divisions. There were three plants in Norway, two in the south and one in the north. Total sales in 1975 were 2.89 million tons with 2.72 million tons being produced by Norcem. The remainder was purchased from other manufacturers in Sweden, the United Kingdom and Germany, and resold. The two southern plants accounted for 48.3 and 39.0 percent and the northern plant for 12.7 percent of Norcem's output respectively. The home market took 1.74 million tons and 1.15 million tons were exported in 1975. Cement accounted for 52 percent of sales, and 42 percent of company employment.
Two of the three plants operated by what is known as the wet process

and the third plant by the dry process. The wet process required a greater amount of heat to dry out the final product and made Norcem the second largest consumer of fuel oil in Norway. With the post 1973 increase in oil prices, the economics of the wet process declined considerably compared with the dry process.

In the late 1960's and in the early 1970's Norcem was the largest European exporter of cement. By the middle 1970's Norcem was surpassed by one or two other European companies as a result of over capacity in the cement industry.

The main reasons for the high level of export were twofold. With a small home market of about 1.7 million tons, a 3 percent per annum growth rate in home demand, and incremental increases in plant capacity of 500,000 tons, exporting was essential to ensure that new capacity was taken up when created. Secondly, Norwegian ship owners required bulk products to ship to the U.S.A. and West Africa on return journeys after bringing commodities to Europe. Thus very cheap shipping was available to transport cement. All the three plants were located by the coast with access for vessels of 35 to 40,000 tons. Thus Norcem was ideally placed to exploit export opportunities.

Bulk export prices were tyically somewhat below home market prices. However transportation and handling costs resulted in prices to the final user higher than those prevailing in Norway.

The International cement division was concerned with the export of cement from the cement division, the sale of cement acquired from third parties in export markets, and joint ventures in cement manufacturing. The two major export markets were Ghana and the U.S.A. (New York and Florida) which took 61 and 31 percent of 1975 exports respectively. The remainder was sold to Liberia. This represented a major change from 1974 when the U.S.A. took 52 percent of the 1.22 million tons exported, Ghana 40 percent, Liberia 5 percent and the Ivory Coast 3 percent.

The division also supplied the top management for a joint venture in Ghana in which Norcem had a 25 percent ownership. The Ghana plant processed clinker imported from Norway. Annual capacity was 300,000 tons in 1975. A further management contract was agreed in 1974 with the United Arab Emirates for Norcem to manage a new 250,000 ton per year cement plant. This became operational in 1975. Joint feasibility studies for new cement plants were also being undertaken with local interests in Saudi-Arabia and other Middle Eastern and developing countries.

(2) *Building Products*
This group contained the following building product divisions:

(a) *Concrete*
This division sold sand, gravel, concrete and concrete products.

In 1975 it accounted for 10 percent of sales, 8 percent of employment.

(b) *Eternit and Siporex – Ytong*

This division produced building materials made from fibre reinforced sheets (Eternit) and low density cellular concrete slabs (Siporex – Ytong). Both sheets and slabs were used for roofs and walls. Slabs were also used for floors and were capable of taking a considerable load. The products could be decorative and construction was relatively quick from the standard sized modules. A major export contract (for Siporex-Ytong products) was completed in 1973/75 to the Ivory Coast. The division accounted for 13 percent of turnover and 18 percent of employment in 1975.

(c) *Leca*

This division also made building products, mainly lightweight blocks. The light expanded clay aggregate (LECA) could also be used to make precast panels and slabs and in loose condition for insulation and filling. The division accounted for 15 percent of sales and 18 percent of employment in 1975.

(3) *Miscellaneous activities*

This group contained the remainder of Norcem's manufacturing activities accounting for approximately 11 percent of the total sales in 1975. The principle activities were Fjordplast, a boat building subsidiary (see below), Norcem Plast, a fibre glass products company and Norcem Paper Mill. Norcem also had various activities related to North Sea oil exploration.

NORCEM AND THE PLEASURE BOAT MARKET

In 1970 the Norwegian authorities expressed the view that Norway's competitiveness in the pleasure boat market would be greatly enhanced if four of the major competing companies merged to form one large producer. Norcem accepted the role of trying to integrate the four companies in a joint venture involving State ownership. In 1972 a refinancing of the project took place and Norcem became the owners establishing the Fjordplast Division. There were three factories with sales of approximately 100 million kroner per year.

The results of the new division turned out to be far from satisfactory. Polyester and fibre glass, the major raw materials involved proved to be too expensive. Demand for pleasure craft was seriously affected by the oil crisis in late 1973. By 1974 it was clear that there would have to be a major reduction in the boat building activities. Two plants were closed and employment reduced from 500 to 300 during 1974. Further severe rationalisation followed in 1975 with employment falling to only 95 people. Sales fell from 58.5 million kroner in 1974 to 39.7 million kroner in 1975 with exports accounting for 83 percent of sales. By the end of 1975, total operating losses had totalled 33.5 million kroner. Of this amount Norcem contributed 20.2 million kroner and the Norwegian government 13.3 million kroner.

Commenting on the closures, the Commercial Director Mr. Tisthammer said:

> 'There was close cooperation with employee representatives on this matter. The good relationships between these representatives and the management developed in the board, the corporate assembly and during the day-to-day operations, proved to be of great importance in solving very difficult problems in a way acceptable to those involved.
> When the market situation and the company's financial situation was explained in detail, the employees accepted that some radical changes had to be made. They contributed very positively to the solution of the problem, even though they knew that the inevitable result would be that the majority of their colleagues would lose their jobs'.

In spite of the problems experienced in Norway, Fjordplast established a 51 percent owned joint venture in the Phillipines in 1975. Production of boats mainly for export to Japan and Australia was due to start in early 1976.

FINANCIAL ISSUES

(1) Performance

Reported sales almost doubled between 1971 and 1975 from 617 million to 1188 million kroner. These figures did not however take into account the impact of inflation. The profit and loss accounts and balance sheets for 1974 and 1975 are shown in exhibits 1 and 2. Selected figures for the five year period 1971 to 1975 are shown in exhibit 3. Although sales increased by over fifty percent between 1972 and 1974, profits after tax declined. Profitability improved in 1975 largely as a result of a cement price increase allowed by the Government in February 1975. Commenting on the results Mr. Heiberg said: 'Profitability should improve again in 1976. However our depreciation is not at an adequate level to allow for future plant replacement'.

(2) Share Ownership in Norcem

Fifty percent of the share capital in Norcem was held by five companies; one, an insurance company, holding approximately 20 percent. The other 50 percent was held by approximately 6000 shareholders. Norcem was one of the ten most traded shares in Norway, but the Norwegian stock market was not a major source of capital for Norwegian companies.

EXHIBIT 1

The Norcem Group Consolidated Profit and Loss Account
(000 kr)

	1975	1974
Sales and operating revenues	1 188 257	1 133 067
Operating expenses:		
Materials and services	795 043	797 068
Wages and social costs	256 682	229 611
Ordinary depreciation	58 103	54 787
Operating result	78 429	51 601
Financial income:		
Interest from subsidiaries	—	—
Other interest income	6 473	5 553
Dividends from subsidiaries	—	—
Other dividends	260	267
Financial expenses:		
Interest charges	39 171	31 674
Profit after financial charges	45 991	25 747
Provision for bad debts	—	416
Profit before taxes	45 991	25 331
Provision for taxes	11 069	9 154
Profit after taxes	34 922	16 177
Extraordinary income:		
Profit on sale of fixed assets	684	637
Other extraordinary income	10 784	—
Extraordinary expenses	15 106	7 604
Profit after taxes and extraordinary items	31 284	9 210
Correction for minorities	—	2 613
Transferred from free reserves	—	9 648
Available for distribution	31 284	21 471
Which the Board proposes should be applied as follows:		
Extraordinary depreciation	7 390	5 753
Free reserves	2 235	—
Regional Development Fund	7 070	1 000
Legal reserve	2 725	2 851
Dividend	11 864	11 867
Total	31 284	21 471

EXHIBIT 2
Norcem Group Consolidated Balance Sheet, December 31
(000 kr)

	1975	1974
Assets		
Cash and bank deposits	20 585	9 304
Short term loans	65 000	22 200
Accounts receivable etc.	162 856	160 972
Inventories	120 097	147 618
Total current assets	368 538	340 094
Long term investment and loans etc.	54 686	40 680
Properties and plant	566 919	545 489
Total assets	990 143	926 263
Liabilities and equity		
Acceptance credits	5 795	16 246
Tax credits and assessed taxes	11 172	10 465
Accounts payable etc.	208 968	191 372
Total short term liabilities	225 935	218 083
Overdraft facilities	19 476	28 764
Mortgage loans	353 526	296 927
Other long term liabilities	69 176	71 518
Total long term liabilities	422 702	368 445
Sundry provisions	26 431	19 713
Minority interests	—	619
Share capital	128 000	128 000
Legal reserve	111 565	108 840
Free reserves	56 034	53 799
Total equity	295 599	290 639
Total liabilities and equity	990 143	926 263

(3) Debt Capacity

As Exhibit 3 indicates, equity represented less than 30 percent of total capital in 1975. Raising long term debt within Norway was partially controlled by the Government. Legislation required insurance companies to make a proportion of their funds available to industry in the form of favourable mortgage loans. Government permission was necessary before a company could issue more mortgage loans. Companies were free to find other sources of private capital within Norway if possible. Government permission was also necessary to borrow money outside Norway. In 1975, it was difficult to raise long term debt within Norway, and many companies were obliged to go abroad for money. During the first half of 1976, Norcem

EXHIBIT 3
Norcem Group in Figures
(million kr)

From the profit and loss account	1975	1974	1973	1972	1971
Turnover	1188,3	1133,1	838,6	742,1	617,3
Operating costs:					
Materials and services	795,1	797,1	540,9	467,4	399,3
Wages and social costs	256,7	229,6	183,8	155,2	122,0
Ordinary depreciation	58,1	54,8	62,4	59,2	54,0
Operational result	78,4	51,6	51,5	60,3	42,0
Financial expenses less financial					
income	32,4	25,9	21,6	23,4	23,0
Provision for bad debts	—	0,4	0,6	4,1	6,1
Profit before taxes	46,0	25,3	29,3	32,8	12,9
Taxes	11,1	9,1	11,7	8,9	5,1
Profit after taxes	34,9	16,2	17,6	23,9	7,8
Extraordinary income less expenses	÷3,6	÷7,0	÷0,6	÷10,5	0,7
Profit after taxes and extraordinary					
items	31,3	9,2	17,0	13,4	8,5
From the balance sheet					
Current assets	368,5	340,1	343,8	274,4	242,0
Short term liabilities	225,9	218,1	202,4	157,1	135,6
Current assets as % of short-term					
liabilities	163	156	170	175	178
Fixed production assets	566,9	545,5	544,8	507,5	456,5
Long-term investments	54,7	40,7	33,2	29,2	30,2
Total long-term assets	621,6	586,2	578,0	536,7	486,7
Long-term liabilities	442,2	397,8	403,7	363,4	334,2
Long-term assets as % of long-term					
liabilities	140	147	143	148	146
Provisions	26,4	19,7	18,3	28,5	13,0
Share capital	128,0	128,0	128,0	95,0	85,0
Share capital at market value 31/12	144,0	162,3	192,0	134,9	110,5
Equity at book-value	295,6	290,7	297,4	262,1	245,9
Equity as % of total capital	29,9	31,4	32,3	32,3	33,7
Total capital at book value	990,1	926,3	921,8	811,1	726,7

borrowed 100 million kroner from the United Arab Emirates Currency Board. It was anticipated that by the early 1980's oil revenues would result in capital being readily available within Norway.

ORGANISATION

Norcem's structure in 1976 is shown diagramatically in exhibit 4. The Board of Directors reported to a Corporate Assembly elected by the shareholders and employees. The executive management group was headed by Mr. Heiberg who reported to the Board of Directors. The Board of Directors contained two employee representatives, four non executive directors and the Chairman.

The small headquarters staff was responsible for planning and development, finance and personnel. These staff groups reported to Mr. Tisthammer, the Commercial Director. He, together with the General Manager of each of the three product groups, reported to Mr. Heiberg.

Organisational Development 1969 to 1976

This period was essentially one of consolidation during which the three original companies merged together. After the merger the chief executive of one of the three companies retired, while the other two chief executives became President and Chairman of Norcem respectively. A divisional structure emerged in 1971. There were no major management changes at the top of the organisation during this period.

Mr. Heiberg was appointed as Managing Director in August 1973 having joined the company in April 1972 as assistant to the Managing Director. Between 1973 and 1976, Mr. Heiberg developed the organisation by appointing several new, young general managers, and moving from cost centre responsibility to profit centre responsibility.

EXHIBIT 4
Organisation Structure of Norcem 1976

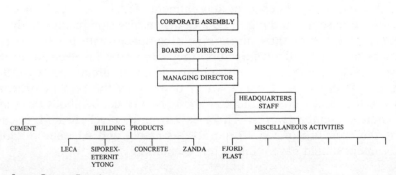

Source: Company Records

EMPLOYEE PARTICIPATION IN MANAGEMENT

The employees participated in the management process in two ways. First through elected representatives to the Corporate Assembly established by law in 1973 and secondly through elected representatives on the Board of Directors.

Corporate Assembly

The Corporate Assembly was made up of 24 members. Two thirds were elected by the shareholders and one third by the employees. The election of the employee representatives took place every two years.

The purpose of the Corporate Assembly was

(1) To agree any substantial new investments proposed by the Board of Directors. The definition of substantial was a function of the size of the existing assets and was determined by each Corporate Assembly.

(2) To approve any decisions of the Board of Directors which significantly changed the number of employees in the company.

(3) To elect the Board of Directors every two years.

The Corporate Assembly met at least twice per year. One meeting was held just before the presentation of the annual report since the Corporate Assembly must recommend acceptance of the results to the Annual General Meeting.

Election to the Corporate Assembly involved lists of nominees being presented by at least 25 employees. In the first election at Norcem two lists had been presented, each with 18 nominees for the 8 available places. One list was put forward by the official trade union, which represented 75 per cent of the workforce, the other by the non-union employees. In the event six of the trade union nominees were elected and two of the non-union nominees.

Commenting on the working of the Corporate Assembly Mr. Heiberg said: 'Frankly it has been a disappointment. It has not really been very effective because it is too big to be an efficient decision making body. With meetings only two or three times a year compared with the ten to twelve meetings of the Board of Directors, they cannot be involved in all major decisions. Basically they can only approve decisions already made, or if they wish impede decisions of the Board. I don't think the present structure is very practical and I do not think anybody is very happy about the way the Corporate Assembly works. There is currently much heated discussion about the structure of the Corporate Assembly and whether or not the Government should have a direct representation'.

Elected Representatives on the Board of Directors

Since 1973 all companies employing more than 50 people in Norway must have at least two members of the Board of Directors elected by the workers. In Norcem both these elected Directors were senior trade union officials. However, if the non-union employees were to obtain three of the eight elected representatives of the Corporate Assembly, one of the worker directors would be nominated by the non-union employees.

MANAGEMENT MOTIVATION

Commenting on the issue of management motivation, Mr. Tisthammer said:

'As yet we have not had any trouble filling management positions at Norcem. There are always plenty of well qualified applicants for the jobs. However, I do not think the main motivation is now financial. The difference in pay between people at the different levels in the organization is not that big, especially if taxation is taken into account as Norway has very steep progressive personal tax rates (see Exhibit 5). A plant worker would earn about 60,000 kroner per year and a member of middle management about 90,000 kroner before tax.

'The incentive for taking on additional responsibility has to come from the challenge which the job offers. It is vital that Norcem continues to be able to offer a range of interesting jobs with future potential.

'If we were simply cement manufacturers with Norway as our market I do not think this would be possible. We need the opportunities created by new products here in Norway, and selling cement and other products in foreign markets.'

EXHIBIT 5
Personal Income Taxation Rates

Monthly taxable income (after allowances)	Total tax	Marginal tax on last 1000 kr (percent)
1000	208	20.8
2000	555	34.7
3000	1055	50.0
4000	1505	50.0
5000	2075	57.0
6000	2727	65.2
7000	3453	72.6
8000	4202	74.9

All income above 8300 Kr per month is taxed at 80 percent.
June 30 1975 £1 = Kr 10.95 = \$2.22.

NORCEM'S RELATIONSHIP WITH THE GOVERNMENT

Commenting further on Norcem's relationship with the Government Mr. Heiberg said: 'As I have already said our prices are closely controlled by the Government. Although the politicians do not fully understand all our problems I do not think there is a big communication gap. One of the advantages of a small country is that leading industrialists and politicians can get to know each other. I see it as an important part of my job to know the politicians and to meet them often and discuss my problems.

'Norcem is an effective management resource available for the Government to use, as it did when we became involved in the management of the boat building companies. The risks of entering ventures at the request of the government are slightly different from normal business risks. On the one hand the Government may for social reasons restrict our freedom to close down operations that we consider to be uneconomic. But on the other hand, the Government may absorb part of the operating loss.

'Also I believe companies like Norcem will be needed to help the Government invest the oil revenues. Much of these revenues will have to be invested outside Norway. It is probably not politically acceptable for the Government to invest directly in other countries. Therefore, they are likely to make loans to leading companies who have experience in operating outside Norway so that they can invest and manage the funds in foreign countries.'

THE FUTURE

The future environmental conditions for Norwegian industry were perhaps not difficult to predict. Labour costs would remain high. Labour would also remain in short supply within Norway since it was the stated intention of Government not to permit large numbers of immigrant workers. The Government would eventually have large quantities of capital to invest as a result of the oil revenues and would tend to become more and more the major source of capital within Norway.

The problem for Norcem was therefore not so much identifying the nature of the future environment but deciding how to operate within that environment. Speaking of the future Mr. Heiberg said: 'Eventually cement production facilities will have to be renewed. The issues of location and raising of perhaps 2 to 3 billion kroner will then have to be faced. Also I think we must broaden our base in the building materials and other markets. Although we are already in a significant market position I do not believe there would be any opposition from the Government if we were to increase our market share. We must also actively pursue opportunities outside Norway. Many of the developing countries see Norway as a non-aligned nation and therefore presenting no political threat. This perhaps makes it easier for us to embark on joint-ventures compared with the larger European countries and the U.S.A. I believe we must employ more and more international specialists to seek out these opportunities'.

Appendix A

Norwegian Industrial Background

MAJOR NORWEGIAN INDUSTRIES

Norway's population passed 4 million in 1975. This small population was spread over a land mass larger than the U.K., West Germany or Italy. Four cities, Oslo, Bergen, Trondheim and Stavanger contained 23 percent of the population and most people lived within 20 kilometers of the sea. The sea, the availability of cheap hydroelectric power and large areas of forest land have shaped the structure of Norwegian industrial activity. In the mid 1970's, Norway's merchant fleet of 44 million tons was the fourth largest in the world. One of the largest industrial employers in Norway, Aker, was primarily involved in ship and deep sea oil rig construction. Fishing and fish processing have over the centuries been a significant activity particularly in Northern Norway.

The availability of cheap hydro-electricity has made Norway into Europe's major producer of Aluminium and Magnesium. With 21.3 percent of the total country productive forest land, paper and wood products play a significant part in the overall economy. Finally the sea is once again to play a further major role in Norway's development with the discovery of oil and gas in the North Sea.

Norway's per capita GNP of approximately $5900 in 1974 placed it with France, Belgium and Denmark but still significantly behind Sweden, West Germany and Switzerland. Some predicted that by 1980 when North Sea oil and gas would be flowing in quantity, Norway would have one of the highest per capita GNP's in the world. However the recession of the mid-1970's did not leave Norway unaffected. With 92 percent of the merchant fleet engaged in trade between third countries, 52 percent of the fleet oil tankers and a further 14 percent combined oil and dry cargo carriers, Norway's fleet was particularly vulnerable. By the second half of 1976, 47 percent of Norway's tanker fleet and 27 percent of its combined carrier fleet were laid up. Surplus oil tanker capacity throughout the world was forecast to beyond 1980.

THE BALANCE OF PAYMENTS

Norway expected a deficit on its balance of trade of about 20 billion kroner for 1976. This would exceed the 1975 deficit by about 50 percent. The 1975 deficit on a per capita basis was about six times greater than the U.K. deficit. However, in spite of the deficit on the balance of trade the kroner had tended to strengthen against most currencies. This in turn had the effect of making the export of manufactured goods more difficult. The future of Norway's balance of trade was coming to rely more and more on the export of oil products, an industry entirely controlled by the State.

POLITICS AND STATE OWNERSHIP OF INDUSTRY

The Labour Party has dominated Norwegian politics over the past 40 years. This party was in power continuously (with a brief one month break in 1963) from 1935 to 1965. Since 1965 there have been two non-Labour coalition governments and two Labour governments. Labour have been the ruling party since 1973. An extensive welfare state has been established together with high personal income taxation.

The State has acquired ownership in industry either to preserve Norwegian control of natural resources which might otherwise become foreign owned or to promote regional policies particularly with regard to employment. As a result the State has a controlling shareholding in approximately ten percent of Norwegian industry. The three major companies in which the State has a majority holding are Norsk Hydro, Norway's major chemical and fertiliser producer, Ardel and Sunndal Verk, aluminium smelters, in which Alcan has a 25 percent stake and Statoil which controls North Sea oil operations.

During 1975 there was further growth of State ownership. First, Statoil endeavoured to acquire the Norwegian British Petroleum (B.P.) network of 1300 filling stations together with its 40 percent stake in a new oil refinery built jointly with Norsk Hydro. Eventually they were restrained by the politicians who decided to establish a new State owned company to acquire Norwegian B.P. Statoil had a 15 percent interest in the new company. Second the ship owner Hilmer Reksten ran into serious financial difficulties and was eventually obliged to sell large holdings of shipping and industrial shares to the State.

Third as a consequence of the collapse of the world tanker market, the Government made a direct loan of 25 million kroner and guaranteed a further loan of 100 million kroner to the Aker Group. Also a Guarantee Institute for shipping was established in late 1975. This was in the form of a joint stock company with a majority State participation. The purpose of the Institute was to prevent the sale of Norwegian ships to other countries at very low prices. Each shipowner was obliged to make a minimum contribution of 1 million kroner. The Government guaranteed up to 2,000 million kroner.

All this growing involvement of the State in industry caused considerable disagreement in political circles together with much comment in the press.

GOVERNMENT INDUSTRIAL POLICY

In April 1975 the Norwegian Government presented a White Paper outlining the outlook for industry and the policies and measures needed to ensure that future developments were in the desired direction. The basic view stated that industry was an important factor in social development and must therefore be subordinated to social objectives determined by the Government for the development of the Norewegian society as a whole.

Within this overall objective various sub-objectives were formulated. These included:

(1) that an adequate range of employment opportunities should be available throughout Norway,
(2) the working environment should be improved and industrial democracy and participation in decision making further developed,
(3) industrial pollution should be eradicated or reduced over the next ten years. This it was considered, would require 3 percent of total industrial investment,
(4) control over industry and commerce should be mainly in Norwegian hands. If control over the development of new physical facilities and the use of natural resources was considered necessary, the State would consider purchasing foreign owned enterprises,
(5) further State ownership was envisaged. Although this would be primarily in the oil industry, where social considerations made it necessary, purchases might be made in other important industrial sectors.

The White Paper recognised that Norwegian labour rates would continue to rise thus causing some manfacturing industries to lose international competitiveness. It was anticipated that these sectors, mainly textiles, clothing, furniture and selected parts of the engineering industry, would lose 35,000 employees by 1980. This represented between 20 and 45 per cent of total employment in these sectors. Total industrial employment was expected to fall by 20,000 by 1980.

Responding to the White Paper the Federation of Norwegian Industries questioned whether it was desirable to permit a reduction in the contribution of industry to Norwegian society thus increasing Norway's dependence on imported products. The Federation suggested that the industries which would be most affected by a reduction in employment would be those in the regional areas. These were areas where the White Paper had expressed the need for maintaining or even increasing employment. The Federation argued that it was important to prevent petroleum revenues from distorting the future structure of Norwegian industry. This might best be achieved by exporting a great proportion of the available capital, particularly to developing countries. They also stressed the importance of maintaining the confidence of foreign investors in Norway since they had made considerable contributions to Norway's technological and industrial development. Finally although accepting that industry must be profitable in total socio-economic terms, it was stressed that this should not mean operating at a loss in business economic terms.

13

F. Hoffman-La-Roche & Co. A.G.

Although it had never published turnover figures, F. Hoffman-La-Roche & Co. A. G. of Basle, Switzerland, was considered to be the largest producer of ethical drugs in the world by 1970. Sales were estimated at $1.2 billion and earnings $200 million, eight times the reported figure for 1970. The company had not raised money in the form of debt or equity externally since 1920. The 16,000 voting shares were closely held largely by descendants of Fritz Hoffman, the company's founder. In over the counter trading, single shares were sold for $40–50,000.

Worldwide Roche was one of the top 3 or 4 ethical drug companies in almost all major markets. The company operated more than 60 subsidiaries in over 30 countries, employing some 30,000 people. These subsidiaries operated 42 pharmaceutical and blending plants for aromatics, and during the late 1960's and early 1970's sales had grown on average at 15 per cent per annum.

The operating subsidiaries were grouped under two holding companies. One, F. Hoffman-La-Roche & Co., was based in Basle and included all operations in continental Europe, North Africa and the Middle East. The other, SAPAC, was a Canadian corporation with headquarters in Motevideo, Uruguay.[1] SAPAC included all Roche's operations in North and South America, Asia and the British Commonwealth.

Some two thirds of Roche sales came from ethical drugs, 20–25 per cent from the supply of bulk vitamins, and the balance largely from aromatics and flavours. The company's sales were dominated by the range of benzodiazepine tranquilizer drugs including Librium and Valium. It was estimated that Hoffman-La-Roche held some 50 per cent of the world market for this type of drug.

[1]*Note:* Until legislation was introduced in 1973, Canada was a good location for international holding companies for tax purposes since under certain conditions non resident companies registered in Canada were not subject to local taxes, but at the same time had the advantages of Canada's wide range of double taxation treaties. As a management centre, Montevideo similarly offered favourable tax advantages for a headquarters operation and the executives who staffed it.

Librium was first sold in the USA in 1960 and thereafter was rapidly introduced in other countries. Valium which had similar tranquilising properties but was much more effective as a muscle relaxant and as an anti-convulsant was first sold in 1963. The greatest ethical drug disaster, thalidomide (also a tranquiliser) took place in 1962. The two drugs gained widescale acceptance and were considered by industry observers to be 'the most profitable products ever produced by the pharmaceutical industry'. By the early 1970's they probably accounted for a very large proportion of the company's total ethical drug sales.

The company operated extremely conservative accounting practices, particularly in relation to capital investment and research. Effectively all capital expenditure was fully depreciated in the financial year it was incurred. All research expenditure was charged as a current expense. In 1970 capital expenditure and research costs were estimated by industry observers to the S.F.1 billion and S.F. 600 million respectively ($1 = S.F. 4.32).

The company was firmly controlled by Dr. Adolf Jann, the Chairman and Chief Executive, and Dr. Alfred Hartmann, Vice Chairman and Vice President, both of whom had previously worked for the Union Bank of Switzerland. They managed the company through weekly meetings of an executive committee comprised of Dr. Jann, Dr. Hartman and the heads of five functional departments. Top management made frequent visits to overseas subsidiaries which were usually managed by local nationals. Top management had no significant stock holding in the company and were rewarded by high salaries and bonuses based on performance. The nine member board of directors contained three family representatives and three members of management but met only about twice per year.

THE BRITISH MARKET FOR PHARMACEUTICALS

The total world market for pharmaceuticals in 1970 was estimated at £7,100 million.[1] At manufacturers' prices, total consumption in the United Kingdom amounted to about £280 million. Industry structure in the U.K. was similar to that in many other developed countries, consisting mainly of a few large manufacturers, usually multinational in operation, together with many smaller firms. Foreign owned companies, mainly American or Swiss, supplied some 64 per cent by value of prescription drugs in 1970. No company held a dominant position in the market for ethical drugs as a whole and the leading manufacturer in any year accounted for less than 10 per cent of the total market. However, within specific therapeutic groups it was common for a particular company to achieve a relatively high market share. Nevertheless market shares fluctuated among companies as a result of

[1]National Economic Development Office, *Focus on Pharmaceuticals*, HMSO, 1972.

competition in product innovation from high levels of R & D which averaged 7–12 per cent of turnover for the leading companies.

The cost of new product development had been constantly increasing world wide partly due to more stringent requirements on safety and efficacy on the part of national governments. These requirements also substantially increased the time before a new product could be introduced to the market. Smaller producers thus tended to find it difficult to remain research oriented and in the main copied the innovations of the major companies either via license agreements or after the expiry of patents.

The demand for prescription drugs world wide depended heavily upon prescribing doctors who did not themselves pay for the medicine. In the United Kingdom the patient also did not pay for medicines except for a small flat rate prescription charge. The real cost was borne by the State in the form of the National Health Service, which in turn was funded by taxation. The success of prescription drugs depend on acceptance by doctors. The producers endeavoured, therefore, to promote their products through brand names rather than generic names.

In the U.K. the market for branded ethical products was product-competitive rather than price competitive. This therefore produced little incentive to reduce prices, but it did encourage new product introduction. Price restraint in the U.K. thus came not from the consumer but from the Department of Health and Social Security (DHSS), the ministry responsible for the National Health Service. The DHSS attempted to advise doctors about the comparative costs of similar drugs, and the advantages of generic prescriptions. However, the DHSS counter promotion effort was very limited compared with the extensive advertising promotion, and personal selling efforts of the drug companies. The main method used by the DHSS to control costs was through price negotiations with individual manufacturers within the operation of the Voluntary Price Regulation Scheme (VPRS). The Department also had power to control maximum prices for medical supplies to the NHS.

In 1972 a revised VPRS came into effect between the Association of the British Pharmaceutical Industry (of which Roche Products was a member) representing manaufacturers and the DHSS. This agreement provided for the submission of annual financial returns, price restraint and for negotiations about the reasonableness of profits. Where raw materials, intermediates or finished goods were supplied from an affiliated company, the receiving company had to satisfy the DHSS that transfer prices were arms length. If the DHSS considered transfer prices were too high, the company should inform the Department of any profit margins or contributions to overheads within the transfer prices.

The British Patents Acts normally provided a monopoly for a period of 16 years. However for medicines, food and surgical or curative devices, it was possible for a compulsory licence to be issued against the patent holder to an appropriate applicant unless the Comptroller of Patents refused such an application. In return the patent holder was entitled to royalties.

ROCHE PRODUCTS LTD.

Roche Products Ltd., the group's U.K. subsidiary was one of the five largest operating companies (along with the U.S., Switzerland, West Germany and Japan). Between 1960 and 1970 sales doubled from £9.25 million to £18.6 million. The 1970 sales figure represented over 7 per cent of the total U.K. ethical drug market. Reported profits rose from £634,000 to £886,000.

The company's total investments in the U.K. were about £20 million. By 1972, 500 people were employed in the firm's vitamin plant in Dalry, Scotland, 780 at the Welwyn Garden City factory, and about 150 scientists and technicians at the Welwyn research facilities. British operations contributed about £5 million (S.Fr. 45 million) to the whole of Roche's research in 1972.

In 1970 the £8.15 million sales of Librium and Valium accounted for nearly 70 per cent of all ethical drug sales by Roche products. The active ingredients for the two drugs were imported from other group companies at a cost in 1970 of £4.49 million. This cost was subsequently reduced by a rebate from the parent company to Roche products of £603,000 related to all ethical products. There was a further rebate to the U.K. company of £376,000 related to other products. Thus the profit of £886,000 in 1970 was only arrived at after receiving rebates from Basle of £979,000. Rebates were a regular feature of Hoffman la Roche's business practice. The DHSS had received rebates of £200,000, £500,000 and £900,000 in 1967, 1968 and 1970 respectively. The first two rebates covered a 12 month period, the third an 18 month period. All but £100,000 of this money had come from the parent company in Basle. These rebates were given in response to a request in 1966 by the DHSS for Roche Products Ltd. to reduce their prices (the request was refused) and because Roche Products decided not to participate in the existing Voluntary Price Regulation Scheme.[1] The U.K. company also supplied, free of charge, Librium and Valium to NHS hospitals and the armed services valued at £400,000 in 1970.

Roche spent heavily on sales and marketing. The 1970 expenditure was almost £1.5m. Drug advertising accounted for 43 per cent and 44 per cent represented the cost of a 66 person field sales force. This sales force aimed to visit 90 per cent of general practitioners and about 50 per cent of hospital doctors at least once a year. This effort was heavily supported by direct mail and promotion campaigns and extensive journal advertising.

Some 90 per cent of Roche Products ethical drugs were distributed through pharmaceutical wholesalers, and the balance direct to hospitals. The wholesalers in turn supplied retail pharmacists.

Wholesale chemists were allowed a $12\frac{1}{2}$ per cent discount off trade list prices established by Roche. Retail chemists purchased at listed trade prices

[1]*Source:* Hoffman la Roche company document 'A Report on the Supply of Chloridiazepoxide and Diazepam – The Roche Position'.

without discount. Retail prices charged by chemists for private prescriptions were 50 per cent above trade list prices. Doctors, dentists and veterinary surgeons were allowed 10 per cent off the retail price except NHS dispensing doctors who were allowed 20 per cent. All products were sold subject to strict observance of the fixed prices.[1]

From July 1969, in the case of Librium, and July 1971, in the case of Valium, until June 1972 supply to NHS hospitals and the armed forces was free of charge under control contracts between Roche and DHSS. Then from July 1972 Roche was awarded a central contract to supply these two users at discounts between 60 and 86 per cent off trade list prices.

U.K. COMPETITION

In its evidence to the Monopolies Commission Roche claimed that although its original price levels for Librium and Valium in the U.K. were based on prevailing world prices, subsequently prices had declined due to local conditions. In particular this was due to negotiations with the DHSS and the granting of compulsory licenses to competitors.

In reality prices were maintained at the same price from product introduction (in the case of Valium 1963) until May 1972. During this period the average cost of consumer goods increased 58.6% in the U.K.

Librium and Valium were covered by patents in the U.K. Between 1964 and 1971 nine requests for voluntary licences to produce the drugs were made to Roche Products. None were granted. The company claimed that granting licenses diminished the intensity of competitive research and Roche did not therefore grant such licenses as a matter of policy. By 1971 however two small British pharmaceutical companies, Berk Pharmaceuticals and DDSA, had applied for, and been granted, compulsory licenses by the British Patent Comptroller.

Despite the granting of compulsory licenses to DDSA and Berk and lower prices from these companies, Roche's market position remained virtually unaltered. Further, other tranquillizers had made little impact.

There were several reasons why Roche had maintained its virtual monopoly position. As a large manufacturer Roche could exert significant pressure on wholesalers who derived a substantial part of their income from the products of the major manufacturers. The wholesalers in turn could discourage retailers from ordering low price drugs. Thus doctors prescribing such medicines would be advised that they were not readily available. They then stopped prescribing them. These processes were reinforced by the much greater scale of Roche's sales and promotional efforts.

By supplying hospitals free of charge until 1972, Roche denied its licensees access to this market. On release from hospital, patients naturally continued to use the same brand name drug. Even after free supplies ceased,

---

[1]Ethical drugs and proprietary medicines were exempt from the U.K. legislation against Resale Price Maintenance introduced in 1964.

the high royalty terms in the compulsory licenses made it impossible for Roche's competitors to compete for low price special contracts for the NHS.

Finally Roche Products Ltd. did reduce prices. For example following the launch of Atensine by Berk Pharmaceuticals in May 1972, Roche twice reduced the price of Valium, the final price representing a 36% reduction overall. Berk responded by also dropping prices twice finishing with prices approximately 19% lower than their original price and 14% below Roche prices.

INVESTIGATION OF ROCHE PRODUCTS LTD. BY THE U.K. MONOPOLIES COMMISSION

In September 1971, the Department of Trade and Industry asked the Monopolies Commission to investigate whether the prices of chloridiazepoxide and diazepam (the generic names of Librium and Valium) operated against the public interest. An 18 month inquiry took place before findings were published in April 1973.

During the inquiry the Commission endeavoured to establish the costs associated with the sale of Librium and Valium in the U.K. From information supplied by the company, it was established that the manufacturing costs of Librium and Valium were £437/kilogram and £979/kilogram respectively. By far the greatest part of these costs were the transfer prices for the active ingredients imported from the parent company. These were £370/kilogram and £922/kilogram respectively. (See Columns 3 and 9 of Exhibit 1.) The Commission also established that the raw materials could be purchased in Italy for £9 and £20 per kilogram respectively.

To enable the Commission to consider the reasonableness of the transfer prices Roche was asked to obtain a breakdown of the prices charged by Basle. The Swiss parent at first replied it did not understand what was meant by such a breakdown but eventually stated:

  (i) that the 'manufacturing cost of Roche would probably not be very different' (from the prices charged by an Italian producer)
 (ii) that the difference between the Italian prices and the Group's prices (£361 and £902 per kilogram in 1970) were 'merely differences', and were not obtained by reference to any particular items, and
(iii) that the Basle company's prices 'have not in fact been made up or arrived at on a cost calculation'.[1]

Roche stated that the price charged had to cover certain research costs but that fixing prices was largely a commercial operation based on what the market would bear. Its reasonableness was tested by considerations of what was reasonable for taxation purposes.

[1] A Report on the Supply of Chloridiazepoxide and Diazepam, The Monopolies Commission, HMSO, 1973, p. 39.

The cost of contributions to research also received considerable attention from the Commission. Roche expected to recover its research costs out of current sales. The U.K. for historical reasons made a direct contribution to central research. This had been calculated in conjunction with the U.K. tax authorities.

It involved calculating the current cost of Group research as a percentage of net world sales to independent customers. This percentage plus a profit margin on the capital employed in the central services (22.1% in 1970) was applied to the company's total world sales of ethical products. Finally a deduction was made to allow for the research actually conducted in the U.K.

Roche advised the Commission that they considered research recoveries should be based on the world average prices. Since the U.K. prices of Librium and Valium were approximately half the world average, a further substantial contribution had to be recovered via the transfer price mechanism. The Commission requested that Roche quantify this sum with particular reference to the difference between its own transfer prices and the Italian raw material prices. Roche were not prepared to provide this calculation unless the Commission accepted the principle of the world average price method. The Commission refused to accept the principle.

The company argued that each kilogram of drugs sold in the U.K. should contribute the same amount in money terms as a kilogram sold in any other country irrespective of the sales price. The Commission demanded support for this claim, and requested from Roche details of the value of world wide ethical drug sales, world wide research costs, and world wide sales figures for Librium and Valium by value and weight. Roche refused to supply this information.

As a result the Commission produced its own calculations for the profit of Librium and Valium using the Italian raw material prices instead of the Roche transfer prices. The results are shown in Exhibit 1.

As Exhibit 1 shows, the Commission calculated that Roche had made the

	Librium		Valium	
	£ per kilo	£'000	£ per kilo	£'000
Average Selling Price (net)	734	3,082	1,962	3,720
Costs as in Columns 4, 2, 10 and 8 in Exhibit 1	329	1,377	752	1,427
Profit	405	1,705	1,210	2,293
Profit as in Columns 3, 1, 9 and 7 in Exhibit 1	1	5	191	363
Additional Profit	404	1,700	1,019	1,930

EXHIBIT 1

F. Hoffmann-La Roche & Co., A.G. Statement of Sales, Estimated Costs and Profits for Librium and Valium, 1970

	Librium						Valium					
	£000		£ per kilo		% of net sales		£000		£ per kilo		% of net sales	
	1	2	3	4	5	6	7	8	9	10	11	12
	A*	B*	A*	B*	A*	B*	A*	B*	A*	B*	A*	B*
Net Sales	3,082	3,082	734	734	100	100	3,720	3,720	1,962	1,962	100	100
Cost of Manufacture												
Net Cost of Imported Active Ingredients	1,555	38	370	9	50.3	1.2	1,748	38	922	20	46.9	1.0
Raw Material from the U.K.	7	7	2	2	0.3	0.3	13	13	7	7	0.4	0.4
Production Costs	245	245	58	58	7.9	7.9	61	61	32	32	1.6	1.6
Production Overheads	28	28	7	7	1.0	1.0	35	35	18	18	1.0	1.0
Total Cost of Manufacture	1,835	318	437	76	59.5	10.4	1,857	147	979	77	49.9	4.0
Other Overhead Expenses												
Distribution	39	39	9	9	1.3	1.3	46	46	24	24	1.3	1.3
Sales Promotion	346	346	83	83	11.2	11.2	418	418	221	221	11.2	11.2
General and Administrative	153	153	37	37	5.0	5.0	186	186	98	98	5.0	5.0
Contribution to Research	517	445	123	106	16.8	14.5	625	538	330	248	16.8	14.5
Contribution to Central Overheads	60	38	14	9	1.9	1.2	72	46	38	24	1.9	1.2
R & D–U.K.	127	38	30	9	4.1	1.2	153	46	81	24	4.1	1.2
Total Cost of Sales	3,077	1,377	733	329	99.8	44.8	3,357	1,427	1,771	752	90.2	38.4
Profit	5	1,705	1	405	0.2	55.2	363	2,293	191	1,210	9.8	61.6

*A. Figures based on estimates of Roche data. Other overhead expenses apportioned in proportion to sales revenue.

*B. Figures based on Monopolies Commission assumptions of appropriate transfer price for imported active ingredients and overhead allocations.

Source: "A Report on the Supply of Chlordiazepoxide and Diazepam", The Monopolies Commission, April 11, 1973; pages 75–76, Appendix C.

following levels of additional profit from that shown in their accounts for 1970.

Although the Commission recognised the reservations that could be placed on their calculation without better information from Roche they conservately calculated using the same assumptions that the true profits for the Roche group over the period 1966 to 1972 were approximately £24 million compared with the reported figure of £3 million. Return on capital for Librium and Valium was thus calculated at over 70 per cent.

Conclusions and Recommendations

In spite of the existence of the compulsory licences, the counter promotion activity of the DHSS and the fact that the DHSS was a monopsony buyer the Commission still concluded that Roche Products Ltd. enjoyed a monopoly position and its pricing policies were strongly directed to preserving this.

The Commission noted that while it did not have power to demand evidence from the overseas members of the Roche Group and had therefore been unable to get relevant information in some areas, its calculations with the exception of the charge for research costs were not disputed by Roche. Even if the world average price argument was accepted, thus increasing the charge for research costs in the transfer price, the profits obtained would still amount to nearly 40 per cent of sales for Librium and about 50 per cent for Valium implying a return on captial of some 60 per cent.

The world average price was not, however, accepted and the Commission added:

'If, because the United Kingdom prices for the drugs are below the world average . . . the Group recovers through the research "contribution" a smaller amount per kilo sold than it recovers from sales in countries where prices are higher, this does not imply any deficit in the recovery; the higher priced sales make an above average contribution to research. An additional research charge applied to United Kingdom sales, if it were made, must mean that the Group would "recover" . . . more than its total research expenditure.'[1]

The Commission considered that the profit figures calculated in Exhibit 1 were a reasonable assessment of the true position and that they were quite unjustified in the latter part of a patent's life. It was also seen as undesirable that Roche should supply free drugs to NHS hospitals thus keeping competitors out of this market. The level of prices charged by Roche was found to be against the public interest.

The Commission made the following recommendations

(i) the price of Librium should be reduced to not more than 40 per cent of the 1970 selling price

[1]Monopolies Commission, *op cit*, p. 65.

(ii) the price of Valium should be reduced to not more than 25 per cent of the 1970 selling price

(iii) the selling price between customers should not be differentiated except to the extent justified by normal commercial considerations.

The Commission also recommended that the company should enter into negotiations with the DHSS over the repayment of past excessive profits.

CHARGE AND COUNTERCHARGE

The Monopolies Commission report was published on April 11, 1973. It was rumoured that because of the poor relationships which had developed between the Commission and Company, Roche had not had a preview of the report, as was customary. The Commission's recommendations became legally enforceable on April 23 when the House of Commons approved a Special Order presented by the Department of Trade and Industry.

Roche responded to the findings in two ways, through the media and by use of the law. On April 25 a full page advertisement headed 'Librium and Valium: The Comments of Roche on the Monopolies Commission Report and the Government Action' appeared in four leading newspapers. In it Roche addressed issues of price, profits, compulsory licenses, research and the government's allegations. The following extracts are typical of the comment in the advertisement:

'The whole nature of the drug industry is such that if a costing exercise, such as that attempted by the Commission, were applied to any of the major break-throughs so rarely resulting from research, and these costs compared with the selling price, profits similar to those earned on Librium and Valium would be shown, so long as patent protection exists.'

'Roche, in fact, has used a very large part of their after tax profit from these two drugs to expand its research at a rate greater than any other major research-based drug firm. During the last three or four years this rate of expansion has been, as the Report stated, between 25% and 30% per annum. The result is that Roche is now spending considerably more on research than any other drug firm in the world.'

'Apparently like every similar enquiry before it, and like the DHSS itself, the Commission has found it impossible to state how fair and reasonable prices can be determined on a costing basis. Nor has it explained how they could be made generally and equally applicable to all those supplying drugs to the NHS.'

On April 27, Dr. Jann, accompanied by a number of company directors, gave the firm's first press conference in Basle to a group of European journalists. As reported in the press, he considered the profits made in the past to be '100 per cent justified and we therefore see no reason why we should repay them'. Dr. Jann went on to criticize the British Government for singling out Roche:

'It has issued special rules with regard to just one company, thereby establishing a kind of special decree to one entity among the many forming the pharmaceutical industry,' he said.

'We consider this a lack of fair play against which we shall fight. We will argue for an equal treatment which is the least one should be able to ask for in a system of law and equity.'[1]

Dr. Jann averred that Roche did not intend to 'retire' from the British market nor did it intend to stop supplying Britain with Librium and Valium. He noted that in the company's view, the British measures would have "grave financial repercussions' on Roche Ltd. and that its future profits situation would hamper its development in every respect. He added that the parent company could not countenance a major subsidiary making a continuing loss.

On the legal front the company submitted a petition to the House of Lords Special Orders Committee contesting the findings of the Monopolies Commission. This led to a series of legal battles which continued throughout 1973 and 1974. From time to time both sides in the dispute appeared to make progress but Roche's advances were usually followed by a later setback. In the meantime the recommended prices remained legally enforceable although at one stage Roche threatened to raise them in defiance of the Government order. At the last minute, however, the company backed down.

REACTION TO THE DISPUTE

By and large press and public reaction to the Commission report was considerably unfavourable to Roche. Commented the Economist[2]

'The managers deserve no sympathy, this is a misfortune they have brought on their own heads ... Roche had the kind of watertight patents on some drugs which give it an effective monopoly. Without competition to worry about Roche saw no reason to cut its prices ... What must be obvious to everyone in the industry is that Roche would probably have got a much better deal if it had been prepared to strike a reasonable bargain with the DHSS ...The efficiency of research and development in Britain's drugs industry is the highest in the world ... The industry is still claiming that because prices in the British market are probably the lowest in the developed world they must be raised otherwise the flow of new drugs will dry up.

[1]*The Financial Times*, April 28 1973
[2]*Economist*, April 14, 1973

However, in those countries where prices are less strictly controlled, only two introduced more new drugs than Britain in the period covered by a recent study (by the Pharmaceutical Industry).'

By the end of May 1973 the results of the Monopolies Commission findings and the subsequent imposition of price reductions was rapidly echoing around the world. Investigations of the Hoffman La Roche tranquillizer had been begun or were under discussion in Germany, Holland, Belgium, Sweden, Australia, New Zealand, South Africa and Greece and at the EEC Commission in Brussels.

The threat to raise prices in defiance of the Government order brought sharp criticism. The most outspoken critic was Mr. Wedgwood Benn, 'shadow' Minister for Trade and Industry, who denounced Roche as

... 'a militant, multi-national monopoly' and argued that international companies of this type have now grown so powerful that they are threatening the sovereignty of national States.'[1]

In the same article, Mr. Christopher Tugendhat, author of the book *The Multinationals,* was quoted as saying:

... 'The behaviour of Roche has caused grave disquiet among many industrial companies, especially in the pharmaceutical industry where it is regarded that the company has behaved in an extraordinary and unreasonable fashion.'[2]

In late October 1974 the first of the domino chain reaction moves feared by Basle occurred in West Germany where the Federal Cartel Office ordered cuts in the factory prices of Librium and Valium by 35 and 40 per cent. Roche responded by taking the issue to the German courts.

[1]*The Financial Times*, June 28, 1973
[2]*Ibid*

14

Lonrho*

The London and Rhodesian Mining Company (Lonrho) was founded in 1909 to acquire mining rights and shares in mining companies in Rhodesia. Over the next fifty years Lonrho developed these assets and also acquired interests in property, ranching and agriculture, which by 1961 were earning pre-tax profits of £158,000 on assets of £3.41 million.

A decade later, Lonrho had been transformed into a multinational conglomerate of some 400 companies, employing 100,000 people throughout fifteen countries in Africa and five in Europe. Interests ranged from automobile sales franchises and mining to electricity generation and ground nuts, giving an annual turnover of £216 million by 1972. A summary of Lonrho's principal activities is shown in Exhibit 1. Over this period pre-tax earnings rose to £18.3 million on total assets of £231.6 million giving an (unadjusted) earnings per share of 11.32p, and a share price increase more than eight times. Exhibit 2 and 3 give financial data for 1967–72. The company's share price is given in Exhibit 4 for 1962–1972.

Lonrho owed much of its transformation to its managing director and chief executive, Mr Roland Rowland, who joined the board in 1961 at the request of Harley Drayton's 117 group, a major shareholder. After successfully building up Lonrho's operations in Rhodesia in the pre-UDI phase (Unilateral Declaration of Independence, Autumn 1965), Mr Rowland embarked on an ambitious acquisition programme, taking over well-established colonial companies which were sensitive to the new political climate of the emergent African states. Earnings before tax for 1969 were boosted to £13.8 million and the share price reached a peak of 316p in March of that year.

Then, a turn of fortune saw a number of promising mining ventures fall through when talks collapsed with African governments concerned. Technical difficulties in the development of a major venture in South Africa,

*Note: This case is an abridged version of the case published in British Business Policy (Macmillan, 1975). All the information in this case has been collected from publicly available sources.

EXHIBIT 1

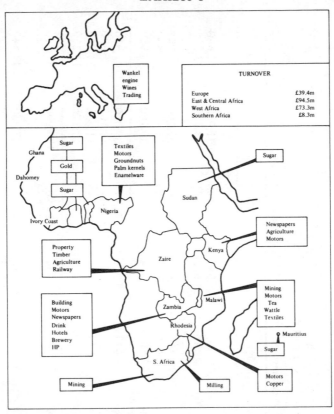

EXHIBIT 2

Lonrho Group Consolidated Six-year Operating Summary (£ millions)

	1967	1968	1969	1970	1971	1972
Turnover	N/A	101.0	154.00	184.00	191.88	215.90
Net profit before tax	3.60	6.83	13.75	14.23	15.06	18.28
after Depreciation	1.47	2.37	4.39	5.29	5.75	6.49
Long-term interest	0.08	0.20	1.16	1.23	1.45	1.38
Short-term interest	—	0.98	1.64	2.22	2.36	2.86
Tax	1.38	3.04	6.79	6.67	8.05	10.38
Minority interests	0.79	1.50	2.78	2.83	2.63	3.01
Profit attributed to parent Co.	1.42	2.04	3.19	4.73	4.19	4.89
Dividend	0.81	1.42	2.48	3.13	1.38	2.43
Retained profit	0.61	0.61	0.71	1.60	2.81	2.46
Earnings per share (adjusted) (pence)	5.60	5.60	6.75	9.00	7.95	7.85

Source: Extel Statistical Services Ltd.

EXHIBIT 3

Lonrho Consolidated Group Balance Sheets (£ 000) (Year ended 30 Sept.)

	1967	1968	1969	1970	1971	1972
FIXED ASSETS						
Freehold and leasehold properties		36,780	45,053	48,128	51,980	52,680
Mining properties		4,807	23,662	26,904	33,400	33,230
Plant, equipment, vehicle, aircraft and others	N/A	13,376	48,940	54,398	62,200	66,240
Pipeline		3,590	3,590	3,590	3,590	3,590
Less Depreciation	8,244	14,574	33,964	35,973	45,160	45,920
	19,106	43,979	87,281	97,047	106,010	109,820
Nationalised assets suspense accounts	—	1,081	1,252	2,143	1,160	530
Investments	1,413	4,835	11,201	12,715	11,650	14,920
Wankel patents rights[1]	—	—	—	—	12,170	12,250
TOTAL FIXED ASSETS	20,519	50,793	99,734	111,905	130,990	137,520
CURRENT ASSETS						
Stock and W.I.P.	—	—	34,410	38,682	47,780	47,540
Project expenditure[2]	8,597	15,797	1,344	1,260	760	—
Debtors	8,213	14,514	27,447	37,743	36,300	34,060
Cash and deposits	1,631	2,774	8,899	8,191	7,120	12,440
TOTAL CURRENT ASSETS	18,441	33,086	72,100	85,876	91,960	94,040

CURRENT LIABILITIES						
Bank Overdraft						
Secured	} 6,569	} 8,638	19,551	6,260	6,830	6,020
Unsecured				15,840	17,160	11,790
Creditors and accruals	8,879	17,035	33,878	44,153	52,210	47,350
Taxation	3,045	5,850	10,714	10,621	13,670	13,410
Dividends	490	1,424	2,483	3,128	1,380	2,430
Others	46	61	—	—	—	—
TOTAL CURRENT LIABILITIES	19,029	33,008	66,626	80,000	91,250	81,000
Share capital	3,860	7,061	12,286	12,521	12,521	16,210
Surplus on consolidation of net assets	325	3,956	6,467	6,004	5,440	4,240
Capital reserves	313	7,332	33,532	35,132	30,020	40,720
Revenue reserves	1,989	2,376	3,429	7,482	9,810	14,480
Future tax	—	926	1,899	2,413	2,500	3,970
Minority interests	6,570	22,075	23,489	29,060	31,470	33,920
Convertible loan stock	1,916	546	12,400	11,810	12,980	12,520
Long-term loans	1,142	2,520	5,508	6,199	15,940	10,220
Short-term loans[3]	3,816	3,181	6,198	7,160	5,760	12,340
Deferred Purchase Consideration	—	—	—	—	3,260	1,940
TOTAL CAPITAL EMPLOYED	19,931	49,973	105,208	117,781	131,700	150,560

Source: Annual Reports.
Notes:
1. Increase in 1972 due to currency realignment.
2. The amount represents expenditure on mining and other projects in course of investigation or development.
3. Repayable in less than five years.

206

EXHIBIT 4
Lonrho Share Price Movements 1962–72

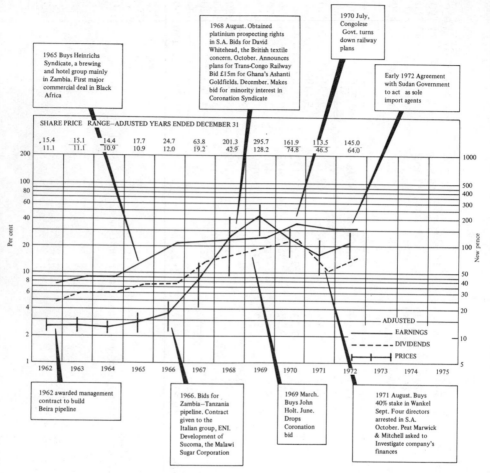

Source: Extel Statistical Services Ltd.

the Western Platinum Mines, caused a serious drain on capital and in September 1971, the acquisition of the Wankel Group, owners of patents of the revolutionary Wankel rotary engine forced a liquidity crisis over which two directors and Lonrho's financial advisers, S. G. Warburg, resigned. Simultaneously news arrived of the arrest of four directors in South Africa on fraud charges.

Peat, Marwick and Mitchell, the accountants, were called in to review the company's financial and managerial state of health. Their subsequent report, issued in March 1972, made certain recommendations which led to a strengthening of the board.

However, by March 1973 the board had split over a resolution to remove

Mr Rowland from office, on the grounds that he was unsuitable to administer the diversified conglomerate Lonrho had become. Mr Rowland immediately sought a court injunction to prevent his dismissal. The issue was finally resolved at an Extraordinary General Meeting requisitioned by Mr Rowland in May 1973.

This case describes the development of Lonrho's strategy under Mr Rowland's leadership and its implementation, leading up to the liquidity crisis in 1971, the subsequent boardroom controversy, together with the reactions of governments and other interested groups in the 'Lonrho affair'.

MR ROLAND ROWLAND

Mr Rowland's invitation to join the board arose after the 117 Group, an investment group owned by Mr Harley Drayton, acquired an equity interest in Lonrho in 1960. The following year, Lonrho's profits fell sharply and the slump in share price prompted Mr Drayton to send Mr Angus Ogilvy, a junior member of the 117 Group and husband of Princess Alexandra, a member of the British Royal Family, to find someone capable of putting the company back on its feet. Mr Ogilvy's enquiries brought him into contact with Mr Rowland, 'Tiny' Rowland, a successful six-foot entrepreneur from Salisbury, who had built up a substantial fortune in Rhodesia.

Mr Rowland was born in Rawalpindi, West Pakistan, in 1917, son of a well-to-do German merchant who, he claimed, was financial adviser to the Dalai Lama. The family settled in England before the Second World War, and when war was declared Mr Rowland and his father were interned as a security precaution. He was released before the end of the war and started his entrepreneurial career.

When peace came he moved to Holland, where he used his salesman's skills to persuade a number of Dutch local authorities to allow him to act unofficially as their buying agent in England. Large purchases of goods were made at substantial discounts, on which Mr Rowland was able to make a handsome profit by way of commission. But then, after a spell as a director of a London-based refrigerator company, he moved to Rhodesia.

On his arrival in 1955, he set up as a farmer, growing maize at Gatooma, a small town some ninety miles from Salisbury. He quickly made a number of important Rhodesian friends, among them a government minister of foreign affairs. At the same time he expanded his interests, buying among other things the Mercedes motor dealerships in Salisbury and interests in two gold mines. Just as significant, he started to act as contact and go-between for a number of mining companies, the most prominent being Rio Tinto (Rhodesia), a subsidiary of the international Rio Tinto Mining Company of London. During the next seven years he brought Rio Tinto a number of important deals. One of the first was the Isandhlawana Emerald Mine, discovered by Mr Rowland on his own initiative, who then organised its sale to Rio Tinto in return for a substantial commission.

Mr Rowland's first encounter with Lonrho came in 1960, when he succeeded in persuading Lonrho to sell its most profitable asset, the Cam and Motor gold mine, to Rio Tinto. Mr Rowland arranged that three of Lonrho's directors, the late Sir Arthur Ball, his son Alan Ball and Brigadier Thorburn, representing the 117 Group, be paid 'compensation for loss of office' of £11,000 each.

It was this operation that convinced Angus Ogilvy, a year later, that Mr Rowland was the man for Lonrho. Mr Rowland joined the board on 29 August 1961. Mr Rowland's strategy for the transformation of the company from a somnolent ranching and mining company to a multinational conglomerate in the space of ten years can be conveniently divided into three main phases.

PHASE 1: DEVELOPMENT IN RHODESIA (1961–5)

The first phase brought growth primarily in Rhodesia until UDI was declared by Rhodesia in 1965. Upon joining the board Mr Rowland agreed to the transfer of assets held in his Rhodesian holding company, Shepton Estates, to Lonrho. These included two gold mines, the Mashaba and the Kanyemga; two companies dealing in cars, one of which dealt in spare parts, while the other, Morton Developments, owned a chain of distribution outlets and held the sole franchise in the Rhodesias for Mercedes Benz vehicles; and a company negotiating to build an oil pipeline from Beira in Portuguese Mozambique to Umtali, Rhodesia. In exchange he received the managing directorship of Lonrho, and together with the chairman, Mr Alan Ball and executive director, Mr Angus Ogilvy, these three formed the main executive body. In addition, Shepton Estates received 1.5 million Lonrho shares, which represented 19 per cent of Lonrho's equity, and an option to buy 2 million more at 35p in five years' time.

After the negotiations Mr Rowland also offered to Lonrho his interest in the Shamrock Copper Mine in Rhodesia, the sole assets of a Rhodesian company, Nyaschere Copper (PVT) Ltd. This interest comprised a 50 per cent holding in Nyaschere and the management rights. Lonrho made an engineering appraisal which showed development to be uneconomic and the offer was declined. Lonrho also immediately appraised the prospects of the Kanyemba gold mine. Although it was believed to have a commercial life of twenty years, the appraisal showed that the mine had commercial prospects for less than one year.

These were the only initial disappointments, for there remained the interest in building the Beira pipeline, one of Mr. Rowland's most profitable deals, and described by a colleague as 'his masterpiece'. Mr Rowland formed a company called Associated Overland Pipelines in which he had a 51 per cent interest after spotting the profit potential in supplying land-locked Rhodesia with oil, via pipeline, from the port of Beira. It was reputed that Mr Rowland made no less than sixty-five journeys to Lisbon in an attempt to gain Portuguese approval and he was finally awarded the management contract in 1962. Backed with South African money, the pipeline came into operation seven months before UDI was declared, showing a profit potential of £2 million annually before it was shut down.

In 1962/3 Mr Rowland also managed to extend Lonrho's interests to neighbouring Malawi, (formerly the British colony of Nyasaland) when he bought the management contract of the almost profitless Nyasaland Railways. After selling off the monopoly fuel rights to Total, Mr Rowland approached Mozambique with the offer to sell them the company's railway bridge over the Zambesi. Malawi was approaching independence, and this proposal was fiercely contested by her (British) civil servants. However, Mr Rowland succeeded in gaining the support of the President of Malawi, Dr Hastings Banda, in return for the promise of additional investment in the future. The cash raised from this deal then enabled Mr Rowland to undertake further expansion.

Lonrho expanded further into ranching with the acquisition of Willoughby's Consolidated and into more motor dealerships in both Rhodesia and Malawi. At the end of 1963 Lonrho strengthened its position in Malawi with the formation of Lonrho (Nyasaland) to administer Lonrho's estates and to conduct a feasibility study for a £4 million sugar scheme.

In South Africa Lonrho acquired a controlling interest in a gold mining company, Coronation Syndicate, which owned several mines in Rhodesia. The deal enabled Lonrho and Coronation to rationalise their holding into one Rhodesian subsidiary, Corsyn. This was followed by the acquisition of Klanderson's Transvaal Estates, owners of substantial coal assets in Rhodesa, held by its subsidiaries, Tweefontein United Collieries and Witbank Consolidated.

At Lonrho's general meeting in March 1964, Mr Ball advised shareholders that he estimated 65 per cent of the group's investment was represented by mining, 4 per cent by railways, 11 per cent by tea and 20 per cent by commercial and industrial activities which were spread mainly in Central Southern Africa, but with a 16 per cent interest in the UK.

However, recognising the political uncertainties facing Rhodesia, Lonrho strengthened its ties with neighbouring African countries. By 1965 the company had made significant acquisitions in Zambia (formerly the British colony of Northern Rhodesia), including interests in brewing, hotels, a newspaper company and the formation of the Lonrho Construction Company to meet Zambia's growing economic needs.

PHASE 2: EXPANSION NORTH OF THE ZAMBESI (1965–9)

In the mid-1960s Africa was undergoing a dramatic change, emerging from the grasp of past empires into a collection of new and independent countries. Europeans, who had established businesses in the colonial days had become nervous about their future, fearing that hotheads in the new administration would push through threats to expropriate or nationalise foreign-owned assets. Mr Rowland sensed however, that the new Black African leaders wanted to reassure world opinion as to their stability and responsibility. He therefore embarked on an acquisition programme to purchase such assets with a singular display of initiative, drive and business acumen which earned him an image which the *Observer* described as belonging to 'a man of action who hops from country to country in his Mystère executive jet, clinching deals and building up goodwill, so that if there is business to be done, it will come Lonrho's way. He is not a man who works through committees and close consultation with colleagues.'

European businessmen were moving out of Africa as fast as they could sell. Mr Rowland offered them low cash multiples, and mopped up valuable earnings and debt-free assets at knock-down prices. Moreover the businesses acquired had a well-trained and sound local management so that Mr Rowland foresaw little need for reorganisation. He used Lonrho's new acquisitions to secure loans which were then ploughed back into the newly independent economies, and high returns on low outlays created impressive earnings and growth records. Mr Rowland gained the new leaders' favour, the new states prospered, and Lonrho boomed.

In the four years between 1963 and 1966 the group's equity base expanded by just five per cent from 15.7 million to 16.5 million shares. But earnings over the same period multiplied fivefold, from £0.22 million to £1.22 million, and earnings per share rose from 1.4 p to 7.41 p. Net assets per share doubled from 17p to 34p, against a fivefold expansion in capital employed from £3.21 million to £15.84 million. The group spread rapidly in Zambia, Zaïre (the former Belgian Congo), Uganda, Lesotho, Botswana, Swaziland, Kenya and Malawi, acquiring companies dealing in newspapers, cars, sugar, tea, ranching, bricks, electricity, textiles, beer and others.

Rhodesian operations were also built up with the acquisition of more mining interests in 1966. These included a 50 per cent holding in Nyaschere Copper, which formerly belonged to Mr Rowland's partner and acceptance of the mine's management duties together with the acquisition of the Luyati Copper Mine which lay just inside the Rhodesia/Mozambique border.

In 1967 and 1968 Lonrho's growth rate slowed a little. The group doubled its equity from 16.5 million to 33.9 million shares with a successful bid for Anglo-Ceylon and General Estates that took it into Sri Lanka (formerly Ceylon), a one-for-five scrip issue, and Mr Rowland's subscription for his option at 35p per share against a market price of 71p.

Nevertheless, just after the end of the group's financial year in October 1968, Mr Rowland pulled off his biggest coup with the acquisition of Ashanti Goldfields Corporation Ltd in Ghana. The Ashanti mine was reputed to be the richest in the world. Its acquisition was typical of Mr Rowland's style and was the culmination of this period of rapid expansion. First, Mr Rowland had made an important political contact in the inspector of mines for the Ghanaian government, which was threatening to revoke Ashanti's mining leases. Lonrho, with government backing, then made an offer of £15 million to the Ashanti board, which at that time included Mr Duncan Sandys, the former Commonwealth Secretary, and chairman Major-General Sir Edward Spears. This offer was accepted and Sir Edward Spears joined the Lonrho board as a director with a salary of £10,000 p.a., while Mr Duncan Sandys remained as a director of Ashanti, although he was subsequently engaged by Lonrho South Africa in the summer of 1971 as a consultant for £10,000 p.a. The acquisition was completed in December 1968. The political difficulties facing Ashanti were solved by giving the Ghanaian government 20 per cent of the equity together with an option for a further 20 per cent.

Simultaneously news broke of a highly significant platinum discovery in South Africa, know as the Western Platinum Mine. Mr Alan Ball, Lonrho's chairman, announced that it was destined to be 'one of the major producers of the world' with reserves worth up to £600 million.

By the end of 1968 Lonrho had grown into a multinational conglomerate operating well over 300 companies involved in a variety of mining interests such as diamonds in Lesotho, rare earths in Malawi, copper in Rhodesia, asbestos in Swaziland and platinum in South Africa. Mining interests had become less important, however, being estimated to account for 40 per cent of profits; agricultural activities consisting of tea, sugar and cattle ranching were estimated to account for 10 per cent of profits. Industrial and commercial interests, such as motor trading throughout Africa, hotels in Zambia, building and construction in Zambia and Malawi, and printing and packaging in Kenya, Uganda and Tanzania, had expanded in importance at 45 per cent of profits; finally, finance and other activities, including building societies in Malawi, made up the remaining 5 per cent.

PHASE 3: CHANGES OF FORTUNE (1970–71)

The pace of acquisition continued. In February 1969 and in the aftermath of the Nigerian civil war, Lonrho launched an £8 million bid for the John Holt motor trading group in Africa and then followed up its West African success by buying Slater Walker's wattle and cattle ranching interests in Central and East Africa for £6 million. By March Lonrho's shares had reached a peak of 316p.

In September Lonrho made its first venture into shipping with the acquisition of The Watergate Steamship Company Ltd, which was expected to yield profits of £200,000 p.a. This was quickly followed by the acquisition of a 51 per cent interest in Rogers and Company Ltd, a merchant shipping company in Mauritius which also had extensive interests in aviation and tourism.

Towards the end of 1969 however, the first problems began to appear. With a head office staff of only eighty and no formal corporate planning, rationalisation proved difficult and, as one director observed, ' 'Tiny' (Mr Rowland) is the only one who knows the whole picture'.

In some African countries various motor franchises were competing with each other, and in Zambia nationalisation of the commercial vehicle fleet operators, Smith and Youngson, had provided little compensation. The many makes, depreciation and spare parts difficulties made valuation difficult and finally Lonrho paid the Zambian government £210,000 to wipe out losses and provided a loan of £1.08 million for working capital, in return for a nominal amount which bought 100 percent of the equity.

Whereas, Lonrho's successful past growth was emphasised by Mr Rowland in his message to shareholders in the 1969 annual report, it was the group's mining ventures that were gaining the attention of management. At the AGM in July 1969, Lonrho's chairman, Mr Alan Ball, stated, 'I want to emphasise that we regard ourselves primarily as a mining finance house and there is certainly no intention of changing this policy . . . we will look at mining propositions of all sorts anywhere in the world.'

In Ghana, Ashanti Goldfield's expansion continued at a cost of £1 million annually, and through its South African subsidiary, Coronation Syndicate, Lonrho was busily extending its Rhodesian copper interests. Coronation Syndicate, which held all Lonrho's Rhodesian mining interests, was itself fully engaged in developing the Inyati copper mine which lay close to the Mozambique border. In August 1969 Lonrho's 50 per cent holding in the Shamrock copper mine was transferred to a wholly-owned Rhodesian subsidiary, after which locally-raised development expenditure of £3.05 million was made. In Mozambique, Coronation Syndicate acquired an option on the Edmundian copper mine in September 1969, and then transferred the mine to a wholly-owned Lonrho subsidiary in early 1970 for development. The Western Platinum Mine in South Africa produced highly favourable drill test results and Lonrho stated, 'the first mine should start production early in 1971 and it is planned that the second mine should begin operations during 1973'. Development costs amounting to £26 million were estimated to be recoverable in three years, eventually yielding profits of £3.5 million per annum.

Other mining ventures, however, were not so successful. In mid-1969 Mr Rowland attempted to secure a marketing contract for Sierra Leone diamonds in a deal involving the Sierra Leone government. At the time, diamonds worth £11.5 million were being mined by Consolidation African Selection Trust (CAST) along with William Baird. It was reported that if Lonrho managed to secure the marketing contract, they planned further deals with Tanzania, Russia and Israel to establish a world-wide marketing organisation. A 'shell' company, Diminco, was formed in which Lonrho orginally aimed for 51 per cent control, but as talks continued a new company, Cominco, was formed with the Sierra Leone government taking a 55 per cent stake. However, Mr Rowland was distrusted by Sierra Leone top civil servants and strongly opposed by De Beers, the diamond marketing concern responsible for over 80 per cent of world diamond sales. Unfortunately, Mr Rowland's main contact, the Governor-General, had no executive power and resigned at a critical time in the negotiations. Finally, a *coup d'etat* occurred during which the president was deposed and the mines nationalised although the management contract was eventually awarded to CAST.

At the same time Lonrho sought to gain a major share in the management contract of the Congo's Copper Mines and untapped mineral wealth, which was held by the Belgian group, Union Minière. Mr Rowland's plan was to link the management contract with an offer to build a £300 million railway in Zaïre to be independent of the Benguela railway which ran through Portuguese West Africa, and managed by a major shareholder of Union Minière. Finance was to be arranged with the World Bank by the Zaïre government. Originally the deal appealed to the Zaïre government on the basis of a partnership with Lonrho and removal of Union Minière, who were perceived as supporters of the former colonial regime. However, in July 1970, the Zaïre government accused Lonrho of publicising as a certainty a deal yet to be concluded and refused to have any future dealings with them.

The collapse of a partnership with the Nigerian government to build and run an oil tanker fleet and a change of government in Ghana emphasised the political uncertainty of operating in Black Africa. In March 1971 Lonrho found Ashanti under the axe of annexation, with the Ghana government taking 55 per cent of the equity instead of the negotiated 40 per cent. Zambia too was posing problems for Lonrho's substantial motor vehicle distribution franchise. In an effort to reduce the balance of payments deficit in late 1971 Zambia restricted imports of all cars under 1200 cc, and imposed a double import tax on those of over 2000 cc to assist the penetration of locally produced Fiat cars. Tanzania too followed up its 1967 nationalisation of sisal estates with the purchase of Lonrho's two local newspapers.

PROBLEMS OF EXPANSION

The explosive growth of Lonrho into a multinational conglomerate had also brought special problems. After UDI all Rhodesian profits had been blocked, although Lonrho contined to foot the annual maintenance bill of £300,000 for the Beira pipeline. Capital expenditure had been mounting and the 1970 accounts showed commitments of £13.3 million of which three ships accounted for £11 million, Ashanti Goldfields for £1 million, without accounting for the Western Platinum Mine. Furthermore not all African countries allowed profits to be remitted to the UK. The 1972 accounts showed that £2.40 million of 1971 profits were remittable and £3.56 million remittable in 1972.

To improve the return of income earned abroad, Lonrho appointed Mr A. S. Sardanis in early 1971. Formerly a prominent secretary in the Zambian Ministry of State Participation and managing director of Zambian Industrial and Mining Companies Ltd, he had particular expertise in rationalising diversified organisations in Africa. Mr Sardanis was given the post of joint managing director (together with Mr Rowland) of a new subsidiary, African Industrial and Finance Corporation (AIFC), as well as a directorship of Dominco for the purposes of the Sierra Leone negotiations. AIFC held all the group's interests in Africa north of the Zambesi and these were to be regrouped and rationalised with a view to further expansion from a firmer base.

In May 1971, however, Mr Sardanis resigned, 'because I found myself in basic disagreement with Lonrho's objectives and its style of management.' He added that foreign investment must have capital to supply and earn its profits through efficient management, in order to be consistent with the interests of the developing countries. He also found that Lonrho's policy was geared towards acquisition and in his view not enough attention was paid to long-term management.

Meanwhile technical difficulties had arisen at Western Platinum and the downward spiralling commodities price caused doubts about the forecast profitability of the operation. Lonrho had entered into partnership with Falconbridge Nickel and Superior Oil in July 1970 to offset development costs. Falconbridge paid £2.9 million for a 49 per cent stake and a further £2.1 million for subscription rights and the intent to raise long-term capital for future development. Fifteen months later Mr Rowland estimated that Western Platinum had spent around £13.3 million in development and a further £8.3 million was planned to bring the first stage into production by the end of 1972. Full production was postponed until 1975. To finance their 51 per cent commitment, Lonrho applied to the First National City Bank to form a syndicate to raise a further $8 million, in addition to their original $8 million loan. This was rejected on the grounds that it was not advisable, although Lonrho's main bankers, The Standard Bank agreed to increase its stake to $20 million.

At the same time the company had made a commitment to purchase the Wankel rotary engine patents. These were held by Wankel GmbH and Rotary Engines GmbH (the Wankel Group), and in the summer of 1971 a partnership of Lonrho, Rio Tinto Zinc and British Leyland had made a bid when the opportunity had arisen. This bid was rejected, but Mr Rowland decided to bid again, this time alone, and successfully acquired the Wankel Group on 30 September. Lonrho claimed that the deal would eventually be self-financing in terms of income from subscription rights, and details in the press indicated the deal involved a sum of £10 million, of which some £6.8 million was required immediately as a down payment to give Lonrho a 40 per cent share in future licence income. Finance was arranged by a $7\frac{1}{2}$ per cent Swiss loan repayable over five years. As a result of this commitment, however, Lonrho's merchant bankers, Warburg's, and two of the group's main board directors, Andrew Caldecott, a director of Kleinwort Benson and Philip Hunter, former chairman of Cammell Laird, resigned. Further, rumours of a liquidity crisis spread in the press and the London Stock Exchange urged Lonrho to give more details to shareholders on the Wankel deal.

Then came the news that the South African government had issued warrants of arrest for four directors on fraud charges and that one director, Mr Fred Butcher, had been arrested on 25 September. The government alleged that Lonrho had been engaged in intercompany dealings to the detriment of outside shareholders and charged four directors in all. Three of the directors charged were directors of local South African subsidiaries. Mr Butcher, the main board finance director, was charged on behalf of Lonrho.

According to the *Observer* the events precipitating the charges could be traced back to 1967. An 'administrative error' then occurred when the local Rhodesian subsidiary of Lonrho sold its 50 per cent share of Nyaschere to the Rhodesian subsidiary of Coronation Syndicate, Corsyn. In August 1969 this holding was retransferred by Fred Butcher to a wholly-owned Rhodesian subsidiary. Over time, a variety of mining claims were transferred out of Coronation in this manner including the Edmundian mine which lay near the Mozambique-Rhodesian border. Then, in January of 1969 Lonrho made a bid for the minority holdings of Coronation Syndicate and Tweefontein Collieries which controlled Coronation Syndicate via a 60 per cent holding. The bid fell through, but it gave rise to later allegations that the offer document did not disclose an important copper find in Rhodesia, thereby undervaluing shareholders claims. Although this referred to the Inyati mine, allegations were also made that Lonrho bought the Edmundian mine from Coronation at a bargain basement price. Eventually the charges were withdrawn in the Regional Court, Johannesburg on 12 January 1973, but the papers were passed to the South African attorney general for a final decision.

As a result of these events Lonrho's share price sank to 48p and shortly afterwards, in mid-October 1971, Mr Angus Ogilvy insisted on calling in Peat, Marwick and Mitchell, the accountants, with the mandate to conduct an independent audit of the group's affairs and a complete reappraisal of its management methods.

PEAT, MARWICK AND MITCHELL REPORT

At the beginning of March 1972, Peat, Marwick and Mitchell (PMM) submitted a report to shareholders, providing information on the group's operations and recommendations to the Lonrho management. The report included details of unaudited results for the year ended 30 September 1971 and a profit forecast for 1972. The report also provided information such as analysis of turnover which had not been available to shareholders before (see exhibit 5).

The main findings of the report were as follows:-

Accounting Procedure

When a subsidiary was acquired it was Lonrho's practice to include in their accounts that subsidiary's profits from its previous accounting date. It

EXHIBIT 5

Analyses of Turnover, Profit Before Tax and Net Assets (Year Ended 30 September 1971) (£ millions)

	East and Central Africa	West Africa	Southern Africa	Europe and other	Total
Turnover	104.0	57.0	7.0	24.0	192.0
Profit before tax					
Agriculture	1.2	—	0.9	0.6	2.7
Finance	0.1	0.4	(0.2)	(2.4)	(2.1)
General trading	2.5	1.2	—	0.5	4.2
Mining	0.3	2.8	0.2	—	3.3
Motor distribution	2.7	0.5	—	—	3.2
Printing and publishing	0.8	—	—	—	0.8
Shipping	—	—	—	0.1	0.1
Textiles	1.6	—	—	0.2	1.8
Wines, spirits and beers	0.8	(0.2)	—	0.4	1.0
TOTAL	10.0	4.7	0.9	(0.6)	15.0
NET ASSETS (before deducting minority interests)	37.9	28.2	26.1	(0.5)	91.7

Territories included are as follows

East and Central Africa: Kenya, Malawi, Rhodesia, Tanzania, Uganda, Zaire and Zambia
West Africa: Ghana, Ivory Coast and Nigeria
Southern Africa: Botswana, Lesotho, South Africa and Swaziland
Europe and other: Belgium, Ceylon, France, Mauritius and U.K.

PROFIT AND FUNDING RECORD (£ million)

Year ending 30 Sept.	1962	1963	1964	1965	1966	1967	1968	1969	1970	1971
Profit before tax	0.4	0.5	1.0	1.8	3.0	3.4	6.1	12.5	15.0	15.0
Profit after tax	0.2	0.3	·0.6	1.1	1.8	2.1	3.5	6.8	8.8	7.0
Profit attributable to										
Lonrho[1]	0.2	0.2	0.3	0.6	1.2	1.4	2.6	4.0	7.7	5.0
Shareholders' funds	2.6	3.0	3.7	4.8	5.7	6.5	21.6	55.7	61.1	60.22[2]
Bank overdrafts						6.6	8.6	19.6	22.1	24.8
Loan stocks						1.9	0.6	12.4	11.8	13.0
Debentures and other loans						5.0	5.6	11.7	13.4	21.7
Total borrowings						13.5	14.8	43.7	58.7	28.7

Source: Peat, Marwick & Mitchell Report (March 1972).
Notes:
1. Profit attributable is stated after crediting extraordinary income.
2. Decrease in shareholders' funds due to provision of £5.3 million for diminution in value of nationalised and mining assets and the write-off of £0.5 million project expenditure incurred in prior years.

was recommended that only that part of the accounting year's profit from the date of acquisition should be included.

Expenditure incurred on projects under examination or in the negotiation stage was carried forward in stock and work in progress. This project expenditure was either capitalised or written off when it was known the project was to succeed or be abandoned. PMM recommended that such expenditure should be capitalised as an asset only when there were reasonable prospects of the development producing revenue in the near future.

It was also Lonrho's practice to include extraordinary items in the profit-and-loss account, for example, the £2.1 million subscription rights fee from Falconbridge. Since this was not recurrent income, PMM advised that such items should not figure in profit before tax but should be shown separately in the accounts.

Nationalised assets were kept on Lonrho's books at the old book value without provision for depreciation, the argument being that the company would be in a better position to negotiate greater compensation. It was recommended that a consistent depreciation policy on mining assets should be adopted throughout the group, which PMM showed would reduce profit before tax by £0.3 million and constitute an assets write-off of £5.3 million.

Capital Commitments

At 30 September 1971, capital commitments totalled £12.7 million of which £1.4 million was authorised but not contracted for.

Finance external to the group had been arranged for £6.3 million of this capital expenditure, and liabilities amounted to £3.8 million.

PMM noted that the Western Platinum Mine had demanded an increasing investment on the part of Lonrho. Although Falconbridge were responsible for 49 per cent of the capital development, they were unable to raise long-term finance! This had so far involved Lonrho in development costs amounting to £4.8 million which were in addition to its original investment of £3 million. Further costs of £2 million seemed likely before the first sales of platinum, which were scheduled to commence in late 1972. Lonrho had also agreed to build a precious metal refinery for £1 million near the mine, with finance arrangements under negotiation in South Africa.

In Peat, Marwick's view, Western Platinum was the major cause of Lonrho's liquidity problems. However, another project was also discussed which, together with Western Platinum, had involved Lonrho in a heavier cash commitment than any it had undertaken in the past – the Wankel deal of 30 September 1971.

It was revealed that Lonrho had paid £12.2 million for Wankel GmbH and Rotary Engines GmbH which had a 40 per cent interest in the exploitation of patents in Europe and Japan. Of the principal, £7.8 million was payable immediately on acquisition with annual instalments of £1.28

million for three years and the remainder in the fourth. This was financed by a Swiss loan of £7.9 million bearing $7\frac{1}{2}$ per cent interest, of which 8 per cent was repayable in December 1972, and the remainder in eight equal half-yearly instalments. Third party interests arose over the outstanding claim of another party to buy a 100 per cent interest in the Wankel companies. They agreed to accept a 20 per cent equity interest at no consideration although the management rights had yet to be settled.

PMM further noted that provided income was received in accordance with the terms of existing licences (although dependent on successful renegotiation with one important licence holder) and no dividends paid, the cash forecast of the Wankel group indicated that the total cost of this deal would be recovered by the end of 1976. Lonrho had agreed to issue a circular giving full details of the Wankel takeover.

Liquidity Crisis

Since late 1970 remittances had been inadequate to finance the group on projects such as Western Platinum and Wankel, and pay dividends. In particular bank overdrafts had risen to £24 million and, due to the diverse nature of the group losses arising in a number of subsidiaries, these were not available to relieve profits earned elsewhere so that the company's tax rate had been high.

Cash flow projections indicated that Lonrho's overdraft with its main bankers, the Standard Bank would increase from £6.1 million to £11 million by 30 September 1971. Standard Bank's expectations were that the overdraft should be reduced to £2 million by that date. PMM estimated that if this was to be met, funds of the order of £10 million were needed. Apart from not making the approaching dividend payment they therefore recommended that, if an actual loan was not forthcoming, the sale of a major asset should be considered.

Management

PMM observed: 'The group is currently managed in effectively the same manner as it was in the early 1960s. Due to the rapid expansion of the group in recent years, the existing management organisation is now unsuitable for administering the complex and diversified group that Lonrho has become.'

They further disclosed that the group's chairman since 1947, Alan Ball, had announced his intention to leave this post to become executive deputy chairman and Mr Rowland would become chief executive as well as managing director. Mr Fred Butcher, who had been with Lonrho since 1944, had also expressed a wish to resign his post as group finance director, as soon as a successor could be found. He would remain on the board as an executive director.

At the same time recommendations were made to appoint an independent chairman from outside the group, along with two independent non-executive directors, and to increase the number of permitted main board directors from twelve to twenty. Subsequently, three of Lonrho's senior executives, Mr T.R. Prentice, Mr W. H. M. Wilkinson and Mr R. F. Dunlop, were then invited to join the board.

The Future

Peat, Marwick argued that ventures such as Western Platinum were entirely dependent on the vagaries of a currently depressed platinum price, although they saw a good potential in Wankel on the basis of licences already granted. For the immediate future, they saw current operations yielding profits for the year ended 30 September 1972 at least equal to those of 1971. This represented a return of 8 per cent on shareholders' funds, which they regarded as adequate.

However, they stressed that the liquidity problem should not be recurrent and made recommendations to maximise the remittance of funds to the UK, dispose of assets which showed an inadequate return on capital employed, and obtain finance for overseas developments and projects from sources outside the UK, in order to reverse the flow of funds from the UK. In conclusion, Peat, Marwick and Mitchell remarked of Lonrho that 'in common with other groups of this nature profits must be viewed in the light of the territories in which they arise and the ease with which profits and capital can be remitted to the UK'.

THE AFTERMATH OF THE REPORT

Following the report's recommendations, the group's management structure was strengthened by the appointment of Mr Roger Moss to the post of group chief accountant on 28 February 1972. Initially he found Lonrho to be a 'group rich in assets and people with demonstrable entrepreneurial genius which had not been subjected to central financial controls'. He added, 'The [group's] legal structure was like a cat's cradle ... the only management control information that was centrally available was the sum of 165 profit-and-loss accounts and balance sheets submitted each quarter and added up.'

Mr Moss immediately organised back-up teams in financial accounting, management accounting, development accounting and tax to strengthen the group accounting function; he also restructured group reporting. 'Basing the changes principally upon the former regional offices we now have seventeen standard regional operating statements coming into London monthly ... instead of the 260 standard quarterly submissions and the great variety of other forms ... ,' he reported.

In addition two non-executive directors, Sir Basil Smallpeice and Mr Edward Du Cann MP, and a new chairman, Mr Duncan Sandys MP, were appointed to the board in April 1972. Sir Basil Smallpeice, aged sixty-six and an experienced professional manager, was formerly managing director of BOAC and chairman of Cunard until 1971. He joined the board as non-executive deputy chairman after Lord O'Brien, Governor of the Bank of England, and Sir Ronald Leach, senior partner of Peat, Marwick and Mitchell had expressed the hope that he would be appointed. Mr Edward Du Cann was also chairman of Keyser Ullman, the merchant bank that had agreed to succeed S. G. Warburg as the group's financial advisers. Keyser had subscribed for 500,000 new shares involving an initial outlay of £350,000 with an option on another 500,000. The new chairman, Mr Sandys, had been associated with Lonrho for some time, and had extensive knowledge of those parts of Africa in which the group traded. Known as a strong personality and respected but not too well known in the City, he was appointed chairman of a board of sixteen directors at a salary of £40,000 p.a. Of the appointments and boardroom moves in general, Mr Ball commented that the board were 'unanimous that we have come up with the right sort of package for Lonrho'.

In line with the recommendations to divest loss-making and incompatible activities, the annual report for 1971 gave details of five holdings sold in its 'rationalisation programme'. Among these the shipping and general services company, Rogers and Company, of Mauritius, was sold in October 1971, and a 50 per cent interest in Chibukeu Holdings, the group's only brewing interests south of the Zambesi was sold in December, both at a profit. Other interests sold in December included diamond mining in Lesotho and an insurance company in Mauritius. Sales of these assets realised £2.5 million.

More cash was raised on 25 May 1972 by a rights issue of over 14 million ordinary shares of 25p nominal. These were readily subscribed for at 73p per share and raised approximately £10 million, thus reducing the group's short-term borrowings to £1.5 million. Mr Rowland took up his rights at a personal cost of £1.8 million, although this was partially offset by the repayment of a £1 million loan he had made to Lonrho during the previous year's liquidity crisis. As a result of the successful issue, the Standard Bank agreed to increase substantially its £2 million overdraft facility.

Shareholders were provided with more information on the Wankel deal in a circular issued in March 1972. The circular gave details of complex arrangements between Wankel, Audi-NSU and Curtis Wright in the United States that reduced Lonrho's nominal 40 per cent share of royalties to 36 per cent of most non-American sales, 22 per cent of payments from General Motors, and 10 per cent of other American receipts. It also provided some guide to the overall value of Wankel royalties by pointing out that Audi-NSU had issued non-voting participatory warrants which shared in the royalties on a decreasing income basis, and that the market price of those warrants effectively capitalised the royalties as a whole at £61 million.

The group was also able to report the completion of the first stage of development of the Western Platinum Mine, and that shipment of milled ore to the refineries had begun. At the AGM in April, Mr Sandys informed shareholders that production had reached 60 per cent of the designed capacity and that capital expenditure was falling away, although he noted, 'the viability of such a venture depends very much on the price of platinum'. However, in July, Ford announced that it had agreed to buy 0.5 million ounces of platinum from Lonrho on a three-year contract, and commodity prices for platinum began to rise. This was followed by General Motors' announcement to begin commercial production of Wankel engines in 1975 and to install them in some of their Chevrolet models.

New ventures were in accord with the group's policy of taking initial steps 'toward an expansion of our activities into North Africa and the Middle East'. In particular Lonrho Exports, a wholly-owned subsidiary, signed an exclusive purchase agreement with the Sudanese government to act as their sole agents for imports. The deal, which involved no financial commitment on Lonrho's part, provided income in the form of a fixed percentage of the value of goods involved.

Lonrho then announced in October their intention to undertake a feasibility study for a £45 million sugar project in the Sudan, in which Lonrho would participate on a 49/51 per cent basis with the Sudanese government. At the same time an agreement was signed between Lonrho and the government of Dahomey to survey, finance and manage a £24 million sugar project – Dahomey's largest investment project since independence.

THE BOARDROOM DISPUTE

By April 1973, however, public speculation was rife over the delay in the publication of Lonrho's mid-March accounts. Although unanimously approved by the board, the group's auditors, Peat, Marwick and Mitchell felt that publication without revealing a deep boardroom rift would be unfair to shareholders.

Following the recomposition of the board after the 1972 Peat, Marwick Report there had been mounting boardroom fears over a new impending liquidity crisis as well as growing criticism of Mr Rowland's style of management. In order to avert a major rift within the board Mr Rowland, backed by Keyser Ullman, produced a plan to inject a further £8 million into the company. This involved Mr Rowland, highly placed Zambian interests, and Dr Khalil Osman, a Sudanese and managing director of the Gulf International Group of Kuwait, subscribing for new capital at 115p per share, a premium of 23p per share. It was hoped that this would boost confidence in Lonrho as well as strengthen its finances and bring Middle East oil and African interests together.

However, the plan was rejected, and on 18 April a resolution calling for the dismissal of Mr Rowland as chief executive and managing director in the interests of shareholders was signed by eight of the Lonrho board. Those involved were Sir Basil Smallpeice; Mr Gerald Percey, one-time protégé of Mr Rowland and his proposed replacement; Mr Wilkinson, an ex-merchant banker; Major Colin Mackenzie, a director since 1963 and ex-rancher; Mr Stanley Dalgleish, non-executive director since 1970 and second largest single shareholder with 763,721 shares, which were acquired when his family shipping business, Watergate, was taken over in 1969; Mr Nicholas Elliot, Sir Edward Spears and Dr Adolf Gerber, who became joint managing director with Mr Rowland of Wankel GmbH and an executive board member in 1972.

In opposition to the resolution were seven directors: Mr Rowland; Mr Duncan Sandys; Mr Alan Ball; Mr Edward Du Cann; Mr Prentice; Mr Dunlop; and Mr Butcher. Mr Angus Ogilvy, who represented the Drayton Corporation which had recently halved its 10 per cent holding, did not vote and resigned the following day. Mr Sandys was holder of 267,072 shares, 200,000 of which had been bought from Keyser by means of a loan from them – Keyser's holding being thus reduced to 300,000 shares.

Mr Rowland, Lonrho's largest shareholder with a 20 per cent holding, acted immediately by applying for a temporary injunction to prevent the passing of such a resolution on the grounds that his dismissal would be disastrous for Lonrho's African interests. This was granted pending a full court hearing in May. Kleinwort Benson came to the support of the directors headed by Sir Basil Smallpeice, while Keyser Ullman resigned as Lonrho's merchant bankers but remained as advisers to Mr Rowland. An extraordinary general meeting to allow shareholders to settle the issue was also called for 31 May by Mr Rowland.

THE COURT HEARING (MAY 1973)

The court hearing called by Mr Rowland to prevent his dismissal before the general meeting commenced on 8 May. Mr Rowland had received many affidavits from chairmen of Lonrho's overseas companies which Alan Ball described as 'all supporting Mr Rowland to a man'. Notable among these were statements from the Zambian President, the son-in-law of President Kenyatta of Kenya, Udi Gecaga (managing director of Lonrho East Africa), Colonel Gil Olympio, son of the former president of Togo (in charge of development in Central, East, and West Africa), and the governments of Ghana and Zambia. Mr Rowland also had the support of Mr Chapman, Lonrho's most senior executive in French-speaking West Africa, and Mr Hossy, the Lonrho Group's consultant mining engineer.

The essence of Mr Rowland's case was that Lonrho had substantially benefited from his personal commitment. He stated, 'Accounts show that the net profits before taxation of the company have grown from £158,000 in 1961 to £19.3 million in 1972 . . .. A large part of this expansion is, I believe, due to my knowledge and understanding of Africa which I have obtained from living there for over twenty five years . . .. I have helped to build turnover from about £800,000 to about £230 million in the current year. I do not believe that this could have been achieved in the aftermath of the British Empire in the areas concerned without close personal knowledge and understanding . . .. Since I joined the company I have been solely responsible, with one or two minor exceptions, for the negotiations which brought about 400 subsidiary companies into the Lonrho group. In the course of my negotiations I have met the principals concerned. Many of them have become my friends . . .. When I am in London because of my personal connections I spend my time by day, in the evening, and at weekends, as all who know me will confirm, to the total exclusion of all social life, on the company's affairs.'

In putting the defendant's view, Sir Basil Smallpeice rejected this argument. He stated, 'I came to the conclusion that Mr Rowland was unfit by reason of his temperament and lack of commercial probity to be chief executive of a public company . . .. None of the defendants denies the vigour, energy, and speculative ability of Mr Rowland . . .. In the considered opinion of the majority of the board the time has now arrived when the damage which has been done . . . by the irresponsibility of Mr Rowland greatly outweights any benefit to be derived from his abilities and contacts . . .. In order to get his own way, he is prepared not only to override and disregard decisions of the board and to refuse to consult with the board but also . . . actively to deceive and conceal from the board material information . . .. In specific circumstances Mr Rowland appears to have acted without any regard whatsoever to the true interests of the company or indeed, to what are in my view, elementary standards of propriety. The total UK bank overdrafts are now forecast to grow from £1½ million immediately after the rights issue to approximately £9 million by the end of 1973.'

Mr Rowland, however, thought that he and Sir Basil were in opposition because they held 'ideologies so opposed as to make a meeting of the minds impossible'. he added, 'In the thirteen months he [Sir Basil Smallpeice] has been director of Lonrho he has never visited any of the group's mining operations, nor, I understand, any of its activities outside head office.' Mr Rowland also admitted that apart from board meetings he had rarely if ever spoken to Sir Basil since the latter's appointment.

The court hearing produced conflicting opinion about Mr Rowland's management style. Those supporting him described him as an entrepreneurial leader who delegated day-to-day affairs to the local management. Those against him described him as deceitful and a man who would not share information and abide by majority decisions. One of the major critics of Mr Rowland's style was Mr Percy. His criticism was such that Mr Rowland was reported as describing him as a 'dirty double crossing rat'. There was also considerable discussion about Mr Rowland's personal holdings, albeit indirect, in the Nyaschere copper mine, a company to which Lonrho had advanced substantial loan funds. The terms and conditions of

Mr Sandys appointment as Chairman of Lonrho received detailed examination. It transpired that Mr Rowland, together with Mr Ball and Mr Ogilvie, had agreed terms of employment without advising the remaining members of the board. There terms had included a £130,000 compensation payment for terminating a previous consultancy contract, and major payments via the tax free Cayman Islands.

The judge, in his summing up, described the case as one that 'involves issues which transcend the legal problems involved', and ruled against Mr. Rowland. However, an agreement was reached between the two parties which allowed him to keep his position until the EGM on 31st May. At a press conference following the hearing, Mr Rowland stated that he thought the boardroom dispute had arisen because of a 'complete clash of personalities between Sir Basil Smallpeice and myself.' Mr Rowland explained that his vision of Lonrho's future would be to combine 'the potential of independent Africa, the cash resources of Middle East Oil and Western technology in an unbeatable force'.

REACTIONS TO THE COURT HEARING

The case itself provoked a number of reactions from African governments and their spokesmen, some in affidavit form, and from government bodies and institutions in the United Kingdom.

The Zambian government, commenting upon the possible dismissal of Mr Rowland stated in an affidavit:

'The Government was strongly of the view that in these circumstances it should take immediate control of the assets of Lonrho in Zambia . . .. It was only as a result of urgent representation from Mr Rowland that the Government of Zambia has refrained from taking such a step'.

The Ghanaian government voiced a similar opinion:

'The Government of Ghana supports the stand taken by our brother countries of Zambia, Kenya and the Sudan . . . and warns that it will not be party to any decision taken unilaterally which may be detrimental to the smooth and efficient operation of Ashanti Goldfields . . . of which Lonrho is a minority shareholder. The Government would like to warn all concerned that it will not hesitate to take measures to protect its interests in any appropriate circumstances.

Kenya and the Sudan also supported Mr Rowland.

Nevertheless British public opinion was shocked by the disclosures of the hearing and in an unusually strong statement in the House of Commons, the British Prime Minister, Mr Edward Heath, called the Lonrho affair 'the unpleasant and unacceptable face of capitalism', but added that one should not suggest that the whole of British industry consists of practices of this kind. He went on, 'As far as the boardroom procedures are concerned they can obviously be examined by the department concerned from the point of view of tax affairs or from the point of view of company law.'

Although the Confederation of British Industry declined to comment specifically on Lonrho, a statement stressed its deep concern at the 'personal conduct and integrity' of directors, and in its annual report on the responsibilities of the public company issued in May 1973 declared, 'companies must recognise that they have functions, duties and moral obligations that go beyond the immediate pursuit of profit and the requirements of the law.'

Mr Anthony Wedgewood Benn (former Labour Minister for Trade and Industry) gave one view from the major opposition party. In a speech he stated, 'The abuse of business and financial power is now a direct threat to our democratic institutions and must be checked . . .. That is one reason why the Labour Party must allow the public to control or own key industries or financial centres on a far greater scale than in the past.'

The press continued to speculate about the affair with suggestions that Mr Sandys might have used his influence to persuade the South African government to drop the charges against the Lonrho directors. It was also suggested that Lonrho might have helped Rhodesia to export copper thus breaking the trade sanctions imposed by the United Nations.

Two weeks before the Extraordinary General Meeting, the Department of Trade and Industry announced that they would conduct a full scale investigation into the affairs of Lonrho. Mr Rowland than released a statement disclosing a series of complicated share dealings linking him with Mr Ball and Mr Ogilvie. It transpired that both Lonrho's and Mr Rowland's interests in Nyaschere were held half by a South African company (of which Lonrho held 50 percent) and half by a Swiss company. The Swiss company was in turn owned by a Bahamas company, Yeoman Investments. Yeoman had been originally set up to allow Mr Rowland access to otherwise blocked dividends from his Rhodesian company, Shepton Estates. In 1967 when Yeoman had been nominated to take options on two million shares of Lonrho (at a cost of £725,000), Mr Rowland gave Mr Ball and Mr Ogilvie options on substantial stakes in Yeoman. These two men had not, however, paid for their options so that in 1973 Yeoman was still shown in its accounts to be wholly owned by Mr Rowland.

Meanwhile, the eight directors produced a seven point plan on which, in their view, Lonrho's future should be based. In summary, these were:

To save £1 million in supporting Mr Rowland's personal initiatives, including £300,000 operating expenses for the Mystére jet and expenditure on 'uncontrolled development schemes' undertaken by him. To implement the Peat, Marwick report in full and recruit top managers.

Develop a long-term strategy of backing activities where Lonrho is strong and dispose of weaker ventures.

Put greater concentration on remittable profits and acquire immediately £2 million of annual profit generated in Britain in order to close the current balance of payments gap in the Lonrho group amounting to £2.5 million per year.

Develop local management in independent Africa and build on broadly-based local support.

THE FINAL DECISION

Against this background the shareholders of Lonrho were scheduled to meet on 31 May 1973, for an extraordinary meeting, where they were to determine Mr Rowland's future role in Lonrho by vote on two resolutions:

(a) Whether to retain Mr Rowland as chief executive.
(b) Whether to remove the eight dissident directors from office.

15

INMOS

In March 1978, Mr James Callaghan, the British Prime Minister, announced the formation of three working parties to advise the government on the expected future impact of the microcomputer. The first of these was to look specifically at the industrial applications of micro electronics; the second was to consider 'how we can improve the present process by which scientific, discoveries are converted into profitable industrial activities', and the third was to look ahead at the 'wider social consequences and social acceptability of technological change, including the important effects on employment'. Britain was beginning to realise the potential implications of the new industrial revolution promised by the microprocessor. A few months later, Britain's state owned industrial holding company, the National Enterprise Board (NEB), announced the provision of an initial £50 million of taxpayers' money for investment in a new company, INMOS, which would attempt to launch Britain into the mass market for standard semiconductors. Commented Sir Leslie Murphy, Chairman of the NEB. 'We felt that the whole use of the micro chip in this country would suffer unless we developed something'.

CHIPS WITH EVERYTHING

Semiconductors were first developed commercially in the 1950s. Since then progress has been rapid and discrete semiconductors have given way to the production first of integrated functions and, more recently, integrated systems. Integrated functions consisted of moderate complexity products which were expected to continue to be developed into higher performance components. However, the main growth in the world semiconductor market in the 1980s was expected to come from the rapid development of Very Large Integrated Systems (VLISs) which contained the capability of reproducing the functions of a mini computers on a single chip of silicon.

VLIS products consisted of more complex memory and logic products such as magnetic bubbles, large metal oxide semiconductor (MOS) memories, microprocessors and microcomputers. Since 1960, the number of

Active Element Groups (AEGs) that could be contained on a single chip had increased by the power of four. By the early 1980s it was expected that technology advances would permit the building of a 32 bit microcomputer with one million bits of memory on a single chip less than one half inch on a side. As a result the cost and size of computing capability had been dramatically reduced.

The impact of the development of the microprocessor on a chip was expected to be profound. In the 1980s the equivalent of the largest computer systems of the 1970s might be shrunk to the size of a hand calculator and retailed for under $300. Voice activated machines would be produced to increase productivity in the factory, office and home. Machines operating in the language of one's choice would simplify the interface for the user. Automatic self diagnosis and self repair of electronic equipment would become commonplace, machine intelligence was expected to improve productivity through the development of industrial robots, computer controlled cars and other scarcely imagined military and computer developments. Microprocessors were also expected to have a major impact on jobs in manufacturing industry, and result in large scale redeployment of labour.

THE CHIP INDUSTRY

The market for semiconductor products was extremely competitive. Its value in 1978 was some $7.4 billion and expected to rise by around 13% per annum to some $24 billion by the late 1980s, as shown in Exhibit 1. Because

EXHIBIT 1
World Semiconductor Market
(BILLIONS OF $)

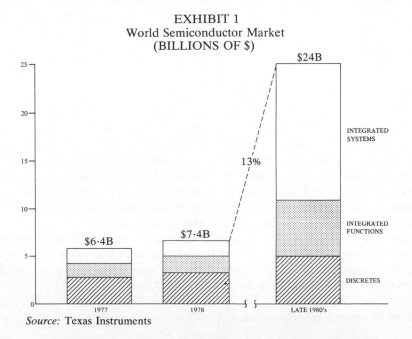

Source: Texas Instruments

EXHIBIT 2
Leading Integrated Circuit Manufacturers 1978

	1978 Integrated Circuit Sales $m	Market Share %
Texas Instruments	660	15
Motorola	580	13
National Semiconductor	330	7.5
Intel	300	6.8
Fairchild	275	6.3
Signetics	200	4.5
Mostek	120	2.7
ITT	70	1.6
Others	1865	42.7
Total	4400	100

the production of advanced chips was becoming increasingly capital intensive, the minimum level of sales viability was estimated to be around $100 million in 1978. Half the world's sales were in the USA, although this was expected to change as Japanese and European demand grew in the 1980s. By then it was anticipated that the world electronics industry would be the fourth largest after automobiles, steel and chemicals.

Most of the world's advanced semiconductor products in 1978 were produced by a number of US companies which held an estimated 70% share of world integrated circuit sales (see Exhibit 2). The leading company was Texas Instruments (TI), with semiconductor sales of around $700 million a year. TI, which had expanded aggressively in electronic products since the early 1950s, had corporate sales of over $2 billion in 1977 and had target sales of $10 billion by the late 1980s.[1]

Motorola was the second largest producer of semiconductors with a 1978 turnover of over $500 million. The company was not however a market leader in either microprocessors or memory units. In 1977 the company moved its microprocessor production from Phoenix, Arizona to Texas, resulting in reduced production availability, but by 1978 the new plant was operating smoothly and shipments doubled. Motorola operated a plant in Scotland which was doubled in size to become Europe's largest MOS based technology unit. Motorola announced a 64K RAM unit in January 1979 and anticipated volume production by the end of the year.

Ranking third in world semiconductor sales in 1978 was National Semiconductor. After a fire in 1977 it had rebuilt its UK plant at Greenock with the most advanced plant. National was also expecting to establish a major new plant in a joint venture with Saint-Gobain.

[1]See the case *Texas Instruments* for details.

Intel had been formed by a breakaway group from Fairchild and was a pioneer in integrated circuit (IC) memory units in which it was a market leader, together with Mostek. Intel was also the leader in the 8 bit microprocessor market, and in 1978 sales of semiconductor products reached $300 million. Intel had not announced its 64K RAM product as of mid-1979.

Mostek, although smaller than Intel, was currently a joint leader in the 4 and 16K RAM market. Dr Richard Petritz (a co-founder of INMOS) was one of its founders after leaving TI. It was a pioneer of MOS products and announced its 64K RAM design in January 1979. Mostek had also announced plans to start operations in Europe with a plant based in Eire, Initially testing microprocessors shipped from the parent company in Dallas, but later assembling and fabricating ICs.

Fairchild was one of the longer established contenders in semiconductors and in August 1978 announced a joint venture with GEC to manufacture advanced IC products in the UK, with a factory employing some 1000 people to mirror Fairchild's plant in California. The new venture was scheduled to begin volume production in 1981.

Although American-owned ITT had concentrated its IC production in Europe, with its plant at Footsray in Kent being the company's centre for MOS memory products, in September 1978 ITT announced a $10 million expansion programme for its UK plant in anticipation of the introduction of a 64K RAM unit into production in 1980.

The industry has been characterised by 'quantum' jumps in the level of complexity of chips with the discovery of a new technique allowing a sudden increase in the number of components which could be located on an individual chip. Mostek and Intel both succeeded with such quantum changes. Another characteristic of the micro electronic industry was the struggle to produce the 'industry standard' device. This was the chip accepted by the majority of users as being the best, in terms of ease of use, reliability, supply availability and designer reputation.

The economic success of semiconductor production depended crucially on achieving large volume production for each design. Those competitors failing to reduce costs down the experience curve risked being overwhelmed or even elminated by production and development costs. This tendency had already been demonstrated in a number of micro electronic products such as calculators, transistor radios and digital watches. Efficiency was vital as chip production was wasteful, with scrap rates as high as 60% per batch, especially for new and more complex circuits.

The proportion of good chips obtained from each four inch circular slice of silicon was the yield. Minute variations of temperature or chemicals used in processing the silicon wafers could offset the yield. To obtain good yields was often considered to be more alchemy than science. Circuit design was a further crucial element in commercial success.

The companies were therefore constantly striving to improve productivity and drive down prices. Increased complexity was, however, leading to steep rises in capital expenditure for each new production line. This was estimated at $5 million per line in 1978, excluding assembly of chips into plastic packages and testing. The increased complexity of the new advanced chips of the 1980s was expected to lead to further capital increases. For example, new methods of producing superfine circuit lines by techniques such as electron beam lithography for 64K RAM units was estimated to be 8 times as expensive as conventional projection equipment used for existing chips.

The fastest growing and newest sector of the market centred on MOS memory devices used for high density computer memories and microprocessors. In 1978, sales of MOS memory chips began to show phenomenal growth of around 40%. In the USA, total MOS memory sales were expected to reach $700 million in 1978. By the early 1980s the market was expected to reach $1.3 billion rising to over $7 billion by the late 1980s. In 1978 the main MOS product in use was the 16K RAM unit with market leadership being held by Mostek and Intel, each selling between 4 and 5 million units, giving a combined market share of more than 50%.

By 1983 it was expected that the 64K RAM unit would be the leading random access memory product, and competition for dominance was expected to be extremely tough. To the surprise of the industry, TI announced a 64K RAM unit at the end of 1978 and it was known that the MOS pioneers, Mostek and Intel, were close behind. Others, including Motorola, Fairchild and National Semiconductor were known to have products under development.

One further major threat to the established contenders was the expected Japanese competition. Mr John Nesheim, treasurer of National Semiconductor, noted 'It is clear that the Japanese have decided to put a major effort into semiconductors and we think it will be a life-or-death struggle'. At the end of 1978, five Japanese companies, led by Fujitsu and the Nippon Electric Company (NEC) were working on a $300 million programme to develop the next generation of very high density chips. Already, too, the Japanese had achieved a high reputation for the product reliability of their memory components which were strenuously tested for up to six months before shipment to the USA. In late 1978, Fujitsu also announced the availability of a 64K RAM unit.

The Japanese threat seemed likely to lead to even greater competition in the industry. Prices tended to be dictated by TI which aggressively employed experience curve pricing practices, by driving down unit prices in anticipation of productivity gains from cumulative production gains and by stressing on design within rigorous cost targets. TI aimed to dominate each of its chosen market segments. They predicted a dramatic decline in the cost of AEGs, as shown in Exhibit 3, as output volume grew.

TI's president, Mr J Fred Bucy, believed that the company's understanding of the learning curve effect was crucial to competing successfully with the Japanese.

EXHIBIT 3
Increasing Complexity &
The Decreasing Cost of Active Element Groups
(Dollars per AEG)

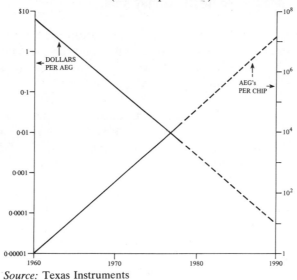

Source: Texas Instruments

'Manufacturing costs can be brought down a fixed percentage each time cumulative volume is doubled' he noted. 'Therefore selling price can be brought down by the same percentage. Exhibit 3 shows a 60% learning curve for worldwide shipments of AEGs. The key to using the learning curve is "design-to-cost" where you determine the cost required for the product to realise high volume production and then design the product and the system to manufacture it to hit that cost goal.'[1]

Based upon the learning curve effect, TI predicted that the cost of their 64K RAM, assuming volume production began in mid-1979, would have an initial price of $55 which would fall to about $38 by the end of 1979, $18 in 1980, $8 in 1983 and $4 by 1985.[2]

EUROPEAN RESPONSES

Although there were major electronic manufacturers in Western Europe, in the high growth MOS sector the Europeans were weak. As a result, various governments were investing some half a billion dollars in the five years to 1983 in an attempt to catch up with microprocessor technology.

[1]Texas Instruments Report to Stockholders, First Quarter, 1978.
[2]*Sunday Times*, 10.9.78.

Although the chances of success were not seen as good in view of the highly competitive nature of the market, the penalties of failure appeared to be even worse. Commenting upon this effort by the Europeans, Mr Bob Heikes, vice president of Motorola commented:

> 'Micro electronics will be the basis of civilisation for the next 25 years. Of course, the Europeans feel a desperate need for the technology, but it's like if you jump off a building 50 storeys high and say "I must learn to fly". Maybe you should try something different.'[1]

Governments and companies were using different routes to establish the technology. In France, government subsidies were used as a bait to tempt Motorola into a joint venture with Thomson CSF. In the UK, General Electric Company was setting up a similar venture with Fairchild. In Germany, Siemens was endeavouring to develop an independent international position by a combination of its own resources, government subsidy and acquisitions in the USA. In 1977, the company paid $30 million for a 17% share of Advanced Micro Devices, and as a contribution to a microcomputer joint venture. Phillips in Holland had adopted a similar policy when, in 1975, it purchased Signetics, the sixth ranking US semiconductor producer at a cost of $45 million.

A different approach was being adopted in the UK by the state owned NEB. This was to provide subsidies and financial support to smaller companies to help them carve out specialist niches in the advanced electronics market.

THE NATIONAL ENTERPRISE BOARD

The NEB was created by the Labour Government in late 1975 as an instrument of industrial intervention. By the end of 1978, it had acquired a portfolio of some 52 companies. Given a budget of £1 billion, the growth of the NEB had been gradual. By the end of 1976 it had 13 companies with assets of £959 million, the largest of which were the 'lame ducks' of Rolls Royce and British Leyland (BL) which, at the end of 1978 still accounted for the bulk of the NEB's assets. At the end of 1977 the NEB held 33 companies with combined assets of £1,132 million. By this time the NEB was amongst the 10 largest industrial groups in the UK, a conglomerate with a turnover of £4 billion.

The NEB was first led by Lord Ryder, formerly of Reed International. On his retirement in August 1977, he had been succeeded by Sir Leslie Murphy. The strategy of the NEB was to invest in industries and companies which contributed significantly to exports, import substitution, employment growth or advanced technology. It also gave preference to companies whose

[1]*Financial Times*, 19.9.78.

activities were relevant to the NEB's evolving strategy of encouraging the expansion, modernising, or restructuring of certain key industries. In the area of industry restructuring, the NEB was active in sectors such as telecommunications, diesel engines, offshore technology, nuclear engineering and hydraulics. No major results had been announced however by the end of 1978.

Most NEB investments over £100,000 were in the form of equity. The NEB preferred not to have less than a 20% stake in any company. Where a significant equity base existed, the NEB's normal policy was to provide share capital in a form which enabled the existing shareholders to retain control with the NEB providing money alongside existing shareholders. It was also possible for shareholders to buy out the NEB at the end of some specified period.

While it preferred to take equity stakes, the NEB did make loans to its companies, and at the end of September 1978, had outstanding loans of about £236 million, of which £160 million was loaned to BL and £62 million to Rolls Royce.

The NEB operated within general financial criteria laid down by government which stated that it should make a 15 to 20% return on capital employed on all its investments taken together (apart from BL and Rolls Royce which were treated separately) by 1980–81.

The organisation of the NEB was outlined by the *Financial Times:*[1]

'The NEB is run by a Board led by Sir Leslie as full-time chairman and Mr Richard Morris who joined as full-time deputy chairman from Courtaulds.

Sir Leslie takes direct responsibility for the main "lame ducks" such as BL and Rolls Royce while Mr Morris has special responsibility for the regions (where he heads the two regional boards) and other strategic work and new acquisitions.

Then there are nine part-time board members – four industrialists, four union leaders and one management consultant.

There are 83 staff, about half of whom have clerical and other support jobs while the rest are executives recruited mainly from industry who have experience in line management, accountancy, banking, and other fields. The day-to-day work is run by four divisional directors whose average age falls in the early 40s beneath whom are other staff in their late 20s and 30s.

Each of the divisional directors has about six executive staff: but the work of the NEB has not yet developed sufficiently for all the companies to be categorised neatly into divisions.

There are eight other posts at the same level in the NEB hierarchy as

[1]*Financial Times,* 19.9.78.

the divisional directors. Two of these are the regional directors in Newcastle and Liverpool who have a staff of four or five each.

In London there is also a finance director, a planning director, a director of information, and the Board's secretary who, as a career servant on secondment from Whitehall, is in charge of the regular contacts between the Board and Government Departments.

The final two posts are the heads of the support staff for BL and Rolls Royce, each of whom has a staff of one executive and one secretary.

The job of all these staff is to monitor their companies' progress and to give advice where necessary, especially when top management changes are considered necessary. They also look for new acquisitions and investment opportunities.'

The NEB Electronics Industry Strategy

The electronics industry had been chosen by the NEB as an area for special attention. As a result the Board had embarked upon a series of moves forming an overall strategy for the industry. This was outlined in the *Financial Times* as follows:

'The strategy, now being drawn up by the National Enterprise Board, envisages four simultaneous thrusts into areas of business at present dominated by foreign multinationals. The plan, costing a total of perhaps £150m will therefore be the first major test of the NEB's ability to exercise leadership in the borderlands of new technology. (See Exhibit 4.)

It has grown out of a combination of accident and design, to create a new capacity in sections of high growth which private capital has largely failed to exploit.

It is therefore very different from the rescue operations which have taken up most of the NEB's time and money since it was founded three and a half years ago.

The electronics sector is the first for which the NEB has formulated a coherent long-term strategy, mainly because it is the sector in which it happens to have the largest number of investments.

Of its 16 subsidiaries, half can be classified as being in the electronic or data processing field. Out of the total portfolio of 42 companies in which the NEB has substantial shareholdings, just under 20 come into this category.

The largest of the electronics subsidiaries is Ferranti. The NEB inherited a controlling share in the company from the Government in 1976, after a rescue operation in 1975. With the help of new management, Ferranti has pulled sharply out of its nose dive. A 1975 loss of £500,000 has been turned into a pre-tax profit of £11m last year

EXHIBIT 4
National Enterprise Board Electronics Strategy

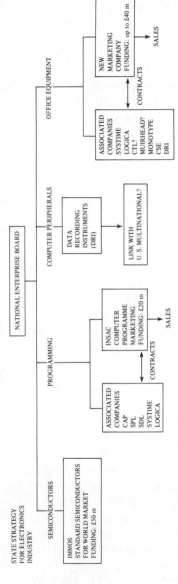

STATE STRATEGY
FOR ELECTRONICS
INDUSTRY

NATIONAL ENTERPRISE BOARD

SEMICONDUCTORS

PROGRAMMING

COMPUTER PERIPHERALS

OFFICE EQUIPMENT

IMMOS
STANDARD SEMICONDUCTORS
FOR WORLD MARKET
FUNDING: £50 m

ASSOCIATED
COMPANIES
CAP
SPL
SDL
SYSTIME
LOGICA

INSAC
COMPUTER
PROGRAMME
MARKETING
FUNDING: £20 m

CONTRACTS

SALES

DATA
RECORDING
INSTRUMENTS
(DRI)

LINK WITH
U. S. MULTINATIONAL?

ASSOCIATED
COMPANIES
SYSTIME
LOGICA
CTL?
MUIRHEAD?
MONOTYPE
CSE
DRI

NEW
MARKETING
COMPANY
FUNDING: up to £40 m

CONTRACTS

SALES

CAP   COMPUTER ANALYSTS AND PROGRAMMERS (SOFTWARE)
SPL   SYSTEMS PROGRAMMING LIMITED (SOFTWARE)
SDL   SYSTEMS DESIGNERS LIMITED (SOFTWARE)
SYSTIME SOFTWARE AND MINI COMPUTERS
LOGICA   SOFTWARE
CSE   COMPUTER AND SYSTEMS ENGINEERING – MODEMS MULTIPLEXING & OFFICE SYSTEMS
DRI   DATA RECORDING INSTRUMENTS – DISC DRIVES FOR COMPUTER MEMORIES

Source: Financial Times

on a greatly increased turnover of £86m. In the long term Ferranti could have a central position in the NEB's strategy for electronics, but there is no evidence as yet of any major plan to integrate it with the other companies in the NEB fold. The other large company is International Computers Limited (ICL) in which the NEB holds a 24.4 per cent stake. ICL has also been a successful example of the marriage of public money and private enterprise, but, like Ferranti it will probably be left to its own devices for the next few years.

ICL has emerged from its early difficulties to become the strongest European computer company with sales approaching £500m a year of which about half come from overseas. The cost to public funds has been £12m for the equity stake plus a £40m loan for development costs.

The NEB has taken a very passive role in the running of ICL. However it is an example of the general way in which the NEB hopes to use public money as "pump priming" to co-ordinate and stimulate the efforts of private companies in newly emerging markets. On the other hand, ICL's formation out of English Electric and ICT in 1968 cannot be expected to provide an exact pattern for the future. One reason is the dearth of high technology companies in the UK which could form the basis of new groupings in the four areas selected for the NEB's thrust into electronics.

These are:

· Semiconductor integrated circuits
· Computer programming (software)
· Computer peripheral equipment (printers, magnetic storage devices, etc)
· Office equipment

The NEB strategy for the first two groups has already been disclosed. It intends to enter the risky market for standard mass-produced semi-conductors with a completely new subsidiary called Inmos, which it plans to fund with £50m.

The setting up of Inmos was more of a commercial accident than the result of a carefully laid policy. The NEB had been wondering for some time what, if anything, it ought to do about the integrated circuit industry, and it had come to the conclusion that one of the keys to the emerging technology lay in mass produced standard circuits like computer memories. Unfortunately none of the three UK owned manufacturers had an entrée to this market, since they all concentrate on tailor-made custom circuits.

However it just happened that Dr Dick Petritz, a Dallas venture capitalist, and two associates wanted cash to set up a new semi-conductor company. The NEB did a deal with them in surprisingly quick time. And it certainly showed flexibility in being prepared to make one or two Americans into millionaires as the entry price into a US dominated technology.

The NEB's entry into computer software has been by an entirely different route. Rather than buying US expertise as in the case of Inmos, it aims to co-ordinate the talents of a number of relatively small UK companies and market their skills in America. The venture is based on the premise that programming expertise in the UK is good, and in US terms, relatively cheap. However, most of the companies which sell software are used to producing tailor-made systems for individual customers. They do not have enough capital to devise standard programmes off the cuff, which could then be sold to large numbers of different customers abroad.

To fill this gap, the NEB set up a marketing company called INSAC, whose main job will be to sell abroad computer programmes devised by UK companies. INSAC will not actually write programs, but it will aim to discover what programs it thinks need to be written. It will then place development contracts with one of a group of software companies which have agreed to co-operate. The NEB meanwhile is taking minority shares of generally about 27 per cent in these companies. Four companies have been signed up so far, and negotiations with a fifth, Logica, are at an advanced stage.

If INSAC is successful it will bring new business to member companies, while at the same time building up a generally co-ordinating role over the British software industry. But its influence over the software companies in the scheme will depend entirely on its success in bringing in new business. If INSAC fails to do this, the companies will continue on their independent ways much as they did before.

Like Inmos, INSAC is a fairly risky business, and sceptics are easy to find. The main question facing both is whether the big computer groups in the US will be prepared to place significant business with government-owned companies across the Atlantic. Investment in INSAC and associated companies could reach £20m, and there is always the risk that it will be money down the drain. On the other hand if it is successful the return on the investment will be very high, and the spin-off could be important.

The NEB's strategies for the other two sectors in electronics have not yet been published, although some fairly detailed plans have been made internally. The development of computer peripherals centres on the Data Recording Instrument Company (DRI) in which the NEB bought a controlling share for £5m in July, 1976. DRI makes disk drives for magnetic storage. With sales of £20m a year it is the largest independent European company in its field but is dwarfed by the major US competitors like Control Data Corporation (CDC).

The fourth part of the NEB's strategy – for the office equipment industry – is in many ways the most interesting. British companies have badly failed to take advantage of the new micro electronics technology to develop a range of new products from accounting machines and small business computers to automatic typewriters and word processors. Although the UK is still relatively strong in the production of copying machines and duplicators, most computer-like products have to be imported from abroad. Moreover, the market is dominated by large multinationals like IBM, Phillips and Olivetti.

A possibility would be to set up a marketing organisation on the lines of INSAC, as a way of co-ordinating the efforts of a number of smaller independent companies. This is in fact the direction which the NEB is expected to take. To be effective, the new company would have to be given complete control over the marketing of a range of products from companies within the scheme. The NEB company would probably also take over a general responsibility for the funding of research and development. In this way it would control strategic planning for future products.

Although the NEB is now thought to have agreed in principle to the scheme, the question remains whether companies will be prepared to cede their all-important marketing rights to a state-owned company. Unless they agree to this, the scheme would not have much chance of success. Even then it remains an open question whether a state marketing company can become a credible competitor with the multinationals without integration between marketing, manufacturing design and development.

The four sections of the electronics industry to which the NEB is giving its first priority will clearly start to overlap in a few years' time.

So the NEB may soon need a much more complex management structure to co-ordinate all the various strands of activity. If it is to compete with big multinationals, it will probably be forced to behave like one. This would probably mean much more specific plans for integrating Ferranti and ICL into the overall strategy.

However, so far the NEB does not appear to have paid much attention to this longer term question. Its major effort is being spent trying to make the four new enterprises successful, on the principle that you must walk before you can run.'

THE DEVELOPMENT OF INMOS

In early 1976, Dr Richard Petritz, a co-founder of Mostek in 1969 conceived the idea of breaking away and establishing a new enterprise to produce advanced MOS memory units just as a group of engineers had done to form Mostek. By mid-1977 he had interested Dr Paul Schroeder, one of Mostek's main architects of its successful random access memory units. In August the two met Mr Ian Barron, an Englishman who had been conducting a consultancy study on the implications of microprocessors, and who suggested the NEB might be a possible source of finance for the new venture. In December 1977, a plan outlining the establishment of a new venture to produce advanced MOS RAM units was submitted to, and accepted by, the NEB. At this time INMOS had no contracts, no products, had done no design work and had not finally decided what to design.

The NEB decided to back the new venture with £50 million because, as Sir Leslie Murphy explained, private investors would not put their money into 'leading edge' technologies because of the high risk. The new venture was announced at a press conference at the NEB on July 21st 1978 after which the three founders sped back to their small temporary headquarters in a nondescript building in Dallas, Texas. Although exact details of the financial arrangements were not released, the NEB investment was in the form of a mixture of convertible preference and ordinary shares. The founders and key employees were to be allowed to purchase up to 27.5% of the equity.

Almost immediately, Mostek slapped a law suit on them to stop them from revealing to INMOS confidential information gained at Mostek. Mr L. J. Sevin, Mostek's president, although not relishing the action since Dr Petritz had been one of the founders of Mostek, declared: 'It's war. The semiconductor companies are out to destroy each other.'[1]

The action failed, but three of the defendants, other engineers hired from Mostek, left INMOS after less than two months to form their own fledgling company. INMOS was left with Dr Schroeder, Dr Petritz and David Wooten, a former Mostek engineer who had been concerned with the design of a microcomputer on a single chip. The depleted team returned to the task of developing its research and design team and prospecting for sites for its technical centres, one to be located in the USA and another in the UK.

Critics of the INMOS venture within the industry considered it would be difficult for a newcomer to break in. Second, it was felt that any venture financed by government would not be able to shake off politicians who would want to intervene in the company, and finally, some US companies had a low opinion of European state enterprise. It was also considered that many US chip users might be reluctant to purchase from a British chip producer, and for success it was felt that INMOS had to be international in its outlook.

Commenting upon these criticisms, the *Financial Times* reported[2]:

'Dr Petritz had a major defence against these views. The semiconductor business, he believed, took periodic technological "leaps". One such was the leap from medium-scale integration (MSI) to large-scale integration (LSI). The next leap would be to very large-scale

---

[1]*Financial Times*, 8.11.78.
[2]*Financial Times*, 17.11.78.

integration (VLSI), and the 64K RAM would be one of the first products of this new technology. To effect such a leap, and fully to take advantage of it, Dr Petritz argued, a new corporate structure was required unencumbered by old ideas (that is, last year's) and, more practically, with no outdated capital equipment making obsolete LSI products. For each "leap" requires new machine tools, and even new machine tools for the new machine tools, and these had often to be designed and specified by the semiconductor companies themselves.

All the new advances in technology, said Dr Petritz, have been made by new companies – notably Intel and Mostek. The entrepreneurial spirit required independence and a sense of new challenges to make breakthroughs – and if its capital came from a government which was socialistic or worse, it hardly mattered, as long as the principle was recognised.

The NEB – and the British Cabinet – accepted Dr Petritz's logic, and backed his faith. Soberly, he says he is conscious of the responsibility this places upon him.'

By the end of January 1979, INMOS had established its corporate headquarters in Colorado Springs, near Denver, Colorado, where it had set up a research and development centre and pilot plant production. In addition, the company had begun to recruit for its UK research centre which was to be located near Bristol. Professor Ian Barron, the managing director of INMOS (UK), noted that he had received several hundred high quality applications for the 50 scientific jobs to be created at the new Bristol centre.

Meanwhile in the USA, the US division of INMOS had begun to recruit key executives at Colorado Springs and Dr Petritz, the INMOS president, said they were some of the top men in the industry. Although INMOS was saying little about the precise product range it intended to produce, it was understood in the industry that the initial focus would be on 64K RAM MOS memory units. Dr Petritz was also able to announce that pilot production of the first devices would be available by the end of 1979 and samples could be ready by August 1979. Full production would be initially developed at Colorado Springs which would employ between 750–1000 people over the succeeding 5 years. If the products were successful, three further manufacturing sites would be developed, the first of which would be located in the UK and many local councils in development areas were offering suitable sites to INMOS.

The research centre at Bristol was expected to concentrate on microcomputer development, working in close conjunction with the research team at Colorado Springs.

Organisation

INMOS had put together a design team that Dr Lester Hogan,

vice-chairman of Fairchild had described as 'the best in the world'[1]. Dr Petritz was for many years Technical Director of TI and was responsible for the development of the series 74TTL logic which was one of TI's most successful IC developments. He left TI in 1968 to help form Mostek, before which he had started New Business Research Inc, a venture capital company that financed bright scientific ideas. INMOS co-founder Dr Paul Schroeder had worked at Bell Laboratories before joining Mostek. While at Mostek he was the chief designer of the industry standard 4K RAM and the current industry standard 16K RAM. As a result he was recognised as the leading designer of RAM devices. Some measure of Schroeder's esteem could be seen in the comment by Peter Bagnall, marketing manager of Motorola, who said that his initial impression on hearing about INMOS was that a new company would be too late 'but when I heard Dick Petritz and Paul Schroeder were involved, the company's chances in my view significantly improved'.[2]

Ian Barron was the only one of the three INMOS founders who was not a micro electronics expert. His field was computers where he had previously worked with Elliott Automation before operating as a consultant and visiting professor at Westfield College.

INMOS had yet to decide upon a definite top management structure, but a possible form is shown in Exhibit 5. Dr Petritz headed the company while Dr Schroeder led the US operations and Professor Barron the UK technical centre. John Keightley, formerly of Bell Laboratories, would develop advanced memory products and Dr Thomas Hartman would be in charge of worldwide production. Hartman was formerly head of wafer fabrication at Intel, and was regarded by Petritz as the industry's best production man. Assisting Hartman would be Dr Alfred Griadinger, former head of R & D at Fraselec of Switzerland, who would be in charge of process development and Ralph Bohanan, from TI, who would supervise prototype production at Colorado. Other personnel included David Wooten from Mostek who was to be responsible for product marketing and Michael Burton director of financial planning and control and formerly of TI.

The senior executives of INMOS were expected to end up with a substantial interest in the company if it were successful, and it was expected that the founders could accumulate over $1 million each. This aspect had been the source of some criticism amongst Left wing Labour MPs.

Future Developments

Commenting on the development of INMOS, Professor Barron added that initially £10/15 million of capital would be employed to make 5000 direct step on wafers per week or around 20 million devices per year using

[1] *The Guardian*, 3.4.79.
[2] *Electronics Weekly*, 26.7.78.

244

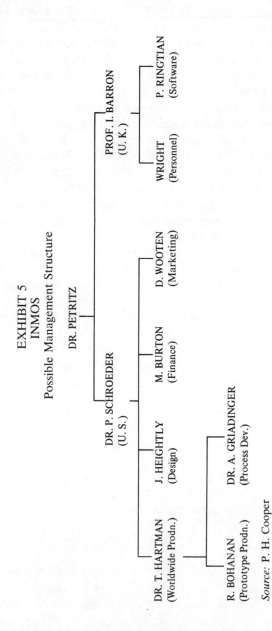

EXHIBIT 5
INMOS
Possible Management Structure

DR. PETRITZ

DR. P. SCHROEDER
(U. S.)

PROF. I. BARRON
(U. K.)

J. HEIGHTLY
(Design)

M. BURTON
(Finance)

D. WOOTEN
(Marketing)

WRIGHT
(Personnel)

P. RINGTIAN
(Software)

DR. T. HARTMAN
(Worldwide Prodn.)

DR. A. GRIADINGER
(Process Dev.)

R. BOHANAN
(Prototype Prodn.)

Source: P. H. Cooper

200 people. The expected selling price of a 64K RAM chip was to be about $200. The anticipated cost structure of INMOS was expected to be as follows:

Raw Materials	5%
(purified silicon imported from USA)	
Energy	5%
Depreciation	12%
Chip Fabrication Labour	28%
Assembly Process Labour	10%
R & D and Management Salaries	40%

Ultimately it was planned to set up four UK factories.

The Impact of Political Change

Early in 1979, the announcement of a general election brought on the prospect of the election of a Conservative Government and with it the question of what would happen to the NEB, and in particular its investment in INMOS. Sir Leslie Murphy the Chairman of the NEB noted 'Government involvement in industry is a fact of life and is here to stay'. As a result he argued that there was a strong case for maintaining the NEB.

However, it was anticipated that any incoming Conservative administration would severely curtail the activities of the NEB which was seen as an instrument of Socialist intervention in industry. Mr Michael Grylls, Conservative spokesman on industry indicated his party's attitude. He insisted 'The NEB cannot act as a merchant bank punting with taxpayers' money'. He added that new money going into the NEB should be frozen and priority given to returning investments to the market in healthy companies such as Ferranti and ICL.

By contrast the Labour Party had proposed to increase the NEB's borrowing powers from £1 billion to £3 billion (rising to £4.5 billion after a further Parliamentary vote) although this had not been implemented due to the government's defeat. Further, the Labour Party were hoping to use the NEB as an increasing instrument for industrial intervention.

Sir Leslie stressed that his attitude to returning investments to the private sector was 'flexible'. He saw no objection to some investments becoming public again. However, he appeared less flexible regarding the disinvestment of ICL which was regarded as a component element in the NEB's computer and electronics strategy. This was unlikely to be a strong argument for the Conservatives who felt that INMOS also would probably not get off the ground.[1]

On May 3rd 1979, the Conservative Party, led by Mrs Thatcher, won the general election with a comfortable working majority.

[1] *Sunday Telegraph.*

Competitive Developments

Although TI, Motorola, ITT and Fujitsu had all announced 64K RAM prototypes and predictions had been made that the market for such a product would only last until 1984, by mid-1979 the target date for volume production appeared to be slipping. At the US Analyst Conference in May 1979 attended by, amongst others, L. J. Sevien, president of Mostek, Robert Noyce of Intel and Alfred Stein of Motorola, the general opinion was that volume production of the 64K RAM would not begin until the early 1980s. It also became apparent that TI had unofficially withdrawn its prototype product having experienced extremely poor production yields.

Planning Systems

16

Ameri Chem Corporation

Ameri Chem Corporation (ACC) was one of the ten largest chemical manufacturers in the world in 1974, producing a wide range of mainly organic chemicals including polyolefines, nylon polymers, polystyrene, a range of ethylene oxide and propylene oxide derivatives and a number of surfactants in Europe. The company was organised into a series of product and overseas geographic divisions reporting to corporate headquarters in Baltimore, Maryland.

ACC's first European investment was in the UK during the 1950's. The first plant produced a range of speciality polymers primarily to serve the British market, but with added capacity to supply markets in continental Europe. With the formation of the European Economic Community the company had switched its pattern of investment away from Britain, and in 1962 opened a major complex in Rotterdam using naphtha feedstocks from a neighbouring refinery. Later the company built another complex alongside a refinery near Naples and expanded both its UK and Rotterdam operations.

The company's initial European organisation was a series of local marketing and production subsidiaries each reporting to an International Division in Baltimore. In 1967, however, the International Division had been replaced by area-based divisions covering Europe, Latin America, the Middle East and Africa, and Asia and the Pacific. The headquarters of ACC in Western Europe were in Geneva, and all local national companies reported monthly to the corporate board of ACC on all material matters. In Geneva, the European board included vice presidents for marketing, production and project development.

STRATEGIC PLANNING

Formal planning in ACC was introduced during the 1950's, and the company considered itself to be highly planning oriented. Each year an annual corporate plan was produced throughout the corporation with projections forward for the coming five years, the first year of the plan forming the basis for the annual operating budget.

The company's planning cycle began with the establishment by the President and Board of ACC of a series of overall corporate objectives for the coming planning period. These objectives, together with a number of philosophical guidelines indicating the company's posture toward social responsibility and aims to be a good corporate citizen, were passed to the divisions. The objectives were subdivided between the divisions and specific targets allocated to each. The same expectations were not made of each division.

PLANNING FOR EUROPEAN OPERATIONS

Once he had received the corporate targets and guidelines, the President of ACC (Europe) arranged a meeting for his board and all the national chief executives in the region to be held in Geneva. The meeting included a brainstorming session to discuss anticipated movements in local markets, national economic conditions and rates of inflation together with possible plans to cope with environmental change. In addition, the meeting was provided with independent economic and functional assessments prepared by the headquarters staff in Geneva and by a number of outside economic consultants. The end result of the meeting was the production of a series of broad operating objectives for ACC (Europe) and the national subsidiaries, all consistent with the expectations of the US parent.

The Role of the Product Group Managers

Planning was then handed over to the 32 Product Group Managers who were each responsible for a specific group of chemicals throughout Europe. These executives were directly accountable for both the turnover and profit contributions of their products; they supervised all functions, both line and staff involved with their products. They undertook market acceptability, and the like. Selling was the responsibility of the national product sales managers who reported both to the Product Group Managers and to the national chief executives. The Product Group Managers, however, established the availability of products, the production source, and the local pricing policies.

The Product Group Managers were in close contact with the field sales managers. In this way they kept abreast of developments and could deal with current operational problems and devise future action programmes. They also drew up five-year volume targets consistent with overall area targets and environmental inputs provided by the sales managers and the European President's meeting.

Their sales forecasts at first assumed an unlimited supply of products and a finite market requirement derived from estimates by the sales managers and central functional staff departments. It was also assumed that ACC would be competitive on price, and that technical support services would be adequate. In conjunction with the local sales managers, the forecasts were turned into national sales targets, and a first attempt at consolidation made.

Next, reconciliation was conducted in Geneva between the various product groups, as the demand for one product could influence the capacity to produce others; plants and feedstocks were to a degree interrelated. Once these interrelationships had been resolved, and cost and price projections prepared, plans were consolidated and presented to the ACC (Europe) Board with profit projections and cash flow expectations for the next five years.

The plans produced by the Product Group Managers were critically examined and evaluated by the area board, and tested for consistency with the divisional targets. If these objectives were met the plans were then ready for presentation to corporate headquarters. If not, they were passed back down the line for revision.

Once it was accepted by the ACC (Europe) Board, the President presented the area division plan in Baltimore for critical review by the Planning Executive Committee of the parent board. Again the plans were carefully scrutinised. Once accepted they became a firm and binding target for the division.

The detailed implementation of the plan then became the responsibility of the Product Group Managers. Together with the Vice President Production and his staff, each allocated production of finished products to the local sales managers, and monitored their performance against the plan. The sales managers in turn were responsible for allocated sales targets to individual salesmen who were also monitored against their performance.

Capital Investment Decisions

Although the Product Group Managers were responsible for their products throughout Europe they had no authority for recommending new capital expenditure, and were not accountable for return on investment. These were the responsibility of a group of project managers who reported to the European Vice President for project development. These individuals were required to develop capital expenditure proposals for existing products and for all new product introduction plans. They also monitored return on investment for existing operations to ensure that this was consistent with divisional targets.

Capital expenditure plans were also produced with five year projections. For existing products projections from the Product Group Managers were used, whereas for new products future demand estimates were derived from discussions with potential customers and the local sales managers. New plants tended to be erected to service all or a large part of Western Europe, as there were usually substantial economies of scale to be gained.

The capital budgets prepared by the project managers were first received by the Vice President of project development, and if approved passed to the ACC (Europe) Board. If the plans were approved by the area board, projects of less than $250,000 could be authorised by the division up to a limit of $1 million in one year. This sum was, however, small in relation to the cost of capital plant in the industry, so all significant projects tended to be referred to Baltimore for ultimate approval. At corporate headquarters the capital spending plans were examined carefully both for their expected return on investment and payback and for their impact on the total corporate strategic goals and distribution of resources. The President of ACC (Europe) considered that if he and his board strongly recommended any capital project it was very likely to be approved at the corporate level.

PROBLEMS

ACC (Europe) was experiencing serious problems in forecasting because of the great uncertainty in the demand and supply of many chemicals at the end of 1974. In recent years, the five year forward financial projections had become increasingly inaccurate as a result of rapidly changing economic conditions, rising rates of inflation and discontinuities in the supply of vital feedstocks due to the oil and energy crisis. At the same time the increasing size of new chemical plants suggested to management the need to try and plan even further ahead as a plant building time stretched from around two years to more than three. These uncertainties seemed more significant in Western Europe than in the USA. There, although the reliability of future forecasts had also deteriorated, there were no wide differences in national conditions to handle.

17

Lex Service Group (D)

In mid-May 1977, a strategic planner at Central Staff Headquarters stated in an internal memo:

> 'The thrust of Lex development from now on is intended to be related to proved "product" superiority in the market places in which we choose to operate. In order to achieve proved superiority we will have to limit the number of markets in which we operate and increase, particularly, the product-based skills that we apply in these markets. Since we are operating entirely within service business which, by definition, require a high level of personal motivation, and are not particularly capital intensive, we require to manage the operating environment to support, in the best means possible, the service activity. Our aim in the current strategic development process is to identify the right organizational structure and skills necessary to produce the superior product quality we seek. We have moved into industrial markets where the buyers are more sophisticated and the standard competitive offering is high. By the same token, our consumer markets have increased in sophistication and through the pressure of inflation have become more selective in their buying patterns. Having defined our individual business strategies in all cases, the major task must be to inject the highest possible level of specific skills necessary to achieve real product differentiation.'

Yet, by July, one of the 'fast trackers' recently moved to corporate headquarters observed:

> 'The Centre is certainly different from working out in the businesses, and I guess I can describe my present position as having less job satisfaction than any I have had in Lex to date. My present position involves more thinking than task orientation—it is "responsibility without authority". I have no routine. My main area seems to be development of new concepts and I am constantly

frustrated both by organizational overlap and the fact that my boss doesn't have the authority to progress most of my ideas, even if he agrees with them. The bulk of the decisions are still taken by the Chairman. When I came into the department to establish this new function, essentially from a much more responsible job in which my views were mostly implementable by the business head—I was surprised that I received absolutely no training at all on my new role. I find here that I am very dependent on my boss's relationship with the Chairman; and I am not sure how good that fact is, especially with regard to changing things. I believe the Chairman and Managing Director function should be split and that the Managing Director should play a strong coordinating role to get the corporate heads really working together. At the moment, they are all going in to see the Chairman on the same issue. It's of course part of the evolution of a family business which accounts for the Chairman's taking so much authority.'

HISTORY

Lex Service Group Limited (known until 1969 as Lex Garages Limited) was incorporated as a public company, quoted on the London Stock Exchange in 1928, to operate parking garages and petrol stations; taking its name from a street near the company's office in Soho. In 1945, Norman and Rosser Chinn (brothers) became Directors of the Company. Lex became a privately-owned family company in 1955, when the Chinn brothers, through Chinn Family Holdings Limited, acquired the total issued share capital and withdrew the Stock Exchange quotation. From 1945 the Company expanded and acquired distribution franchises for a variety of British, European and American passenger car manufacturers. Lex began importing Volvos in 1958. In 1960 the Chinn brothers wanted to raise capital to expand Lex's businesses and they returned to the stock market with an offering of Lex's shares. Lex went into BMC (later British Leyland) and Rolls-Royce distribution and service, buying up R. S. Mead, Gelston of Dartford, Bristol Motor Co., and Richards of Bexleyheath by 1965.

The motor business grew rapidly in the early 1960's and was split into Sales, reporting to Trevor Chinn and Service, under Harold Meacock. Charles Singer headed Volvo. While non-family managers began to rise in influence, there was essentially no staff at the head office. Decision-making belonged to the Directors. Charles Singer made up the car orders and set the margins himself. Once the stocks were high, he sent out a decision to cut margins at the retail level, hoping to stimulate demand, which it did. However, Mr. Singer didn't send out an order to increase margins again—and they stayed low. When he chastised a line manager for losing profit by not raising margins once stocks came down, he was told, 'You are getting the margins you asked for.' By 1965 the strains created by the sales/service split were too great and a move towards a general management structure began.

Transition

By the mid-1960s, a strategic reassessment of the company's corporate direction resulted in the objective that Lex should become a major force in vehicle distribution, concentrating on the Volvo, BL Cars and Rolls-Royce franchises and the heavy truck business. (This was achieved by 1970.) The parking garages and petrol stations were to be gradually sold off. By 1968, Lex was the No. 2 Rolls Royce distributor in the U.K. and was among the leading distributors for British Leyland. Volvo, under Charles Singer, was England's fourth largest car importer. Property was still in the news. The garage business had brought Lex into the property market and it was too profitable to leave. London property values grew at a rate of 15%–20% per year through the sixties.

A New Managing Director

In 1968 Rosser stepped back from the day-to-day operations of the company to become joint Chairman of the Board of Directors with Norman Chinn. Trevor Chinn, Rosser's son, took over as Managing Director. An energetic man, he had an entrepreneurial spirit and a strong sense of personal responsibility to Lex employees, shareholders, customers, and suppliers. He wanted to head a large company. The general goal was that: 'Lex should grow steadily in profits and size.'

EXHIBIT 1

Criteria for Potential New Industries

1. The total industry must be large enough to allow Lex to establish a business entity complete in line and staff management of the highest calibre.

2. It must have a good growth potential in the following decade that will allow the activity in that industry to at least match the rate of profit growth of the existing businesses.

3. The structure of the industry must be such that it will be possible for Lex to establish itself among the market leaders, qualitatively, if not quantitatively.

4. The opportunities for growth in sales and profits must be such that Lex can expect within a maximum of five years to draw a significant contribution to total Company earnings from that service industry.

5. It must be possible to base successful performance in the industry on a high level of service to the customer, achieved within the Lex system of management through a decentralised organisation structure, coupled with the application of highly developed management skills in the areas of planning, financial control, marketing and personnel management.

Shortly before this, Mr. Chinn had attended a marketing program at the Harvard Business School which helped to crystallise his thoughts regarding his company's future. He realised his company needed to consider growth strategically. Trevor Chinn personally wrote the first draft of Lex's strategy, which defined the nature, management style, and structure of the new Lex. Exhibit 1 shows the final criteria adopted as a result of this initial effort.

An analysis of Lex's opportunities found the vehicle distribution industry always subject to external force which could arbitrarily limit Lex's growth. The Government's hire-purchase policy could cause unanticipated shifts in demand. Reliance of manufacturers' franchise meant Lex could be bound by another company's strategy. Trevor Chinn decided to develop the existing franchises but to seek growth through diversification. If the motor business was essentially a service business, Lex was a service business. A strategy was developed which said that any service delivery system required some general skills which Lex had already learned in the business. The strategy of diversification through acquisition was described in *Financial World* (20, Feb. 1971, pp. 118–119):

> 'The change of attitude has been symbolised by a change of name—Lex was formerly known to the market as Lex Garages. Yet while the move into motor assesories and petrol, into leasing and even into freight and transport may seem natural enough, the group's more recent sorties into property, hotels and travel agencing appear at first sight to be taking it out on a new limb.
>
> But the key lies in the group's new title—Lex *Service* Group. Group managing director Mr. Trevor Chinn defines its expansion in terms of the application of the skills of Lex built up on the original car side to other major service areas—areas where quality of service, management efficiency and expanding demand can marry to create a business of rapidly expanding dimensions.
>
> Such rapid growth can of course bring problems, even in the very field which the group knows best. The tripling of turnover in the B.L. Division in 1969 produced badly overstretched management . . . and similar problems arose in the Albany division, then embracing both travel and freight . . . but although the travel division clearly harmonises well with both the group's new interests in hotels and its established interest in freight handling and even car leasing, Lex still had some doubts as to whether this sort of activity can in fact respond particularly well to large scale operation.'

Management Responsibility

Trevor Chinn infused his personal values into the Lex organisation. Lex publicly commited itself to the highest standards of honesty and morality

EXHIBIT 2
Salary Comparisons

Employee Pay and Conditions

If a service is to offer high standards, its employees have to be adequately remunerated and motivated. Lex claims that its working conditions, pay levels and pension arrangements are among the best in the respective industries in which it operates. Whilst it is difficult to make completely accurate comparisons, a survey of wages per employee amongst the quoted motor distributors in 1976 does suggest that Lex pays sufficiently well to attract and maintain its staff:

Average Pay Per Employee-1976

Lex Service Group	£3,234
Caffyns	£2,297
Dutton Forshaw	£2,559
Godfrey Davis	£2,522
Heron Motor	£2,383
Henlys	£2,391
Kenning Motor	£2,195

Source: Phillips and Drew Research.
22, September, 1977.

towards all its stakeholders. The Managing Director understood that high quality service delivery required loyal, happy, long-term employees. Lex personnel policy assured employees good working conditions, excellent benefits, and job security, (see exhibit 2). One Lex manager commented:

'For example, the Lex pension system is non-contributory and takes generous account of the wife in the event of a pensioner's death. The system is liberal due to Trevor Chinn's initiative.'

Liberal benefits were more than a motivating device; they reflected Trevor Chinn's strong sense of fairness, decency, and generosity. A company's responsibility to employees was not limited to the formal, traditional channels. A manager in the automotive area remembered:

'The parents of one of our apprentices were killed in a plane crash, leaving our 18 year old employee to fend for himself. When I brought the matter to Trevor's attention, he immediately agreed to make a generous donation to an endowment to ensure the boy could pursue any opportunities that arose in his future.'

A Reorganisation in 1968

Since 1960 turnover had doubled from £16 million to £33 million. In the same period, profit before tax rose from £300,000 to £1 million. Most of

EXHIBIT 3

Financial Record (1960–68) £'000

	1960	1961	1962	1963	1964	1965	1966	1967	1968
TURNOVER (Note 1)	£15,168	16,786	17,610	20,139	24,205	24,308	22,756	25,539	32,614
Profit before charging interest on long and medium term debt	£ 337	339	242	473	551	329	402	844	1,169
Profit before taxation	£ 311	302	208	411	450	209	292	728	1,038
Net Assets	£ 2,639	2,460	2,684	3,184	4,018	4,191	4,396	4,512	6,111
Shareholders' Funds (Note 2)	£ 1,917	1,926	1,915	2,028	2,096	2,346	1,484	2,613	3,431
Earnings per Ordinary Share (Note 3)	1s. 3d.	1s.	6d.	1s. 8d.	1s. 7d.	10d.	9d.	1s. 11d.	3s. 2d.
Profit before Taxation as a percentage of Shareholders' Funds	16.2%	15.7%	10.9%	20.3%	21.5%	8.9%	11.8%	27.9%	30.2%

Notes:
1. Up to 1962 turnover includes purchase tax on new cars. From 1963 onwards it has been excluded.
2. The ordinary share capital was increased in 1964 by a bonus issue of 1 'A' Non-Voting ordinary share for every 10 ordinary shares held.
3. Up to 1964 profits were subject to income tax and profits tax and tax deducted from dividends paid was retained by the Company. From 1965 profits have been charged to corporation tax and (subject to transitional relief in respect of 1965) tax deducted from dividends paid has had to be accounted for to the Inland Revenue. Earnings per ordinary share have been computed on a similar basis.
Source: Company Records.

the other key measures doubled also. (See exhibit 3 for Lex financial record 1960–1968.) In 1968 Lex was split into five separately managed and profit-accountable groups: Volvo, British Leyland, Rolls-Royce, Albany Travel and Freight, and Accessories Petrol and Parking.

Trevor Chinn's conception of the Lex management structure was reported as:

> 'The key note throughout is the operation of a decentralised line management structure and the delegation of a high degree of responsibility and authority to profit-responsible line managers, with the centre providing the framework of a highly developed business philosophy and control of policy. While acquisitions must perform a role of achieving this end, Mr. Chinn emphasizes that the main objective is to increase sales and profit organically, and expresses his confidence that the quality of the management team will enable the group to meet that objective.'

(*Financial World*, London. 5 May 1971)

The Staff Arrive

Around 1970 a central office staff, reporting directly to Trevor Chinn, began to grow: Charles Murray in Public Affairs, Oswald Dockery in Financial Control, Lionel Harvey in Planning, and Haydn Jones in Personnel. Trevor Chinn wanted these men to develop, implement, and monitor the mechanisms to provide the control from the Centre that must balance decentralisation. Lex was to be an integrated business not a conglomerate. Close relationships developed at the head office. Any or all of the staff frequently attended held informal meetings in Charles Singer's office at 8:45 a.m. These men began to exert increasing influence on the Chairman. (Exhibit 4 shows the organisation chart for 1971.)

NEW SYSTEMS

Planning

Planning was the channel chosen for communicating the goals of the centre to the business groups. One of the central office staff stated:

> 'The implementation of planning was set up in the finance function. By late '69 or early '70 we had several steps of planning. Trevor wrote half of it himself.'

The planning system was based on corporate Targets of Performance, drafted by the Planning Manager to Trevor Chinn's brief. In 1972, the

260

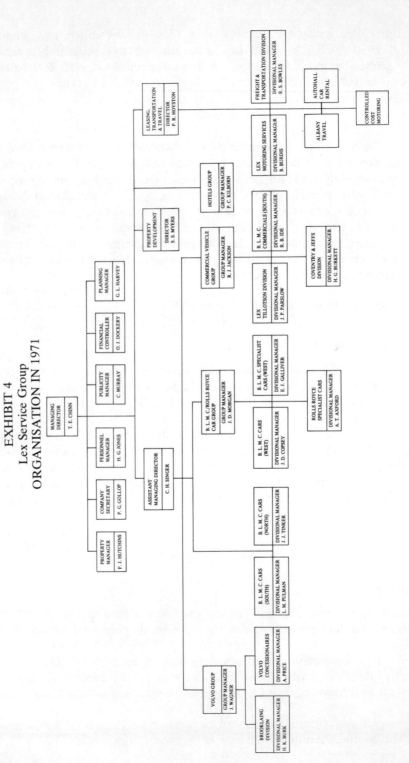

EXHIBIT 4
Lex Service Group
ORGANISATION IN 1971

Source: Company Records

managers were told:

'1. Profits before tax of each division were to be at least one third up on 1971.
2. Control of resources to be achieved were to show a return of 10% on properties and 33% on current assets.
3. Particular emphasis should be paid to Net Profit before tax expressed as Return on Sales as a key financial ratio through control of trading margins and detailed control of all expenses. Specific target ratios have been allocated to each Business Group.'

There were five more targets to meet. Group managers submitted a one year plan showing how they would meet their responsibility to make Lex grow. A participant in the early meetings commented on the Lex brand of decentralisation:

'Although Lex called it a plan, it was a target. Plans were turned back for insufficient profit. The line managers weren't making the strategic decisions about where their businesses could or should go. They were pursuing the short-term targets on their plans. And, until 1973, they were tactically achieving remarkable increases in profit every year.'

Financial Control

The management information needs created by the planning process were met in the financial control system. Every month the Board Report, a consolidated and individual comparison of actual results against plan, was reviewed by the Directors. In contrast to the wide-ranging concerns of Lex strategy and the variety of its businesses, the Board focused on two measures: turnover (sales) and trading profit.

In the early 70's, a planning and a financial control system were the head office's management systems. They comprised the formal channel of communication between the centre and the operating groups. The staff saw line managers as short-sighted

'Some line managers never lifted their eyes above daily operating details. They were short-term thinkers. Some managers would sacrifice a good customer—and next month's profits—to squeeze more profits into today's account.'

The line managers' perspective was quite different:

'We were given targets; then measured on and rewarded for our ability to generate profits. Certainly some poor business decisions were made in getting those profits. But, at the same time, the head office did not pay much attention to where the profits came from.'

Personnel

The recruitment and development guidelines echoed the logic of 'common skills' that Lex felt were necessitated by the similarities of service businesses. Managers hired in the early '70's were of the 'new breed', schooled in the techniques and analytical frameworks of business theory, and getting their industry training on the job. Exhibit 5 shows the numbers recruited during this period. At the same time older managers came up through the ranks. The head office Personnel function (responsible for developing managers) began a series of general management programmes to bring professional management skills to Lex and to establish training as a necessary corollary of service business management. These programmes ranged from short courses on communication and personal skills for general managers to courses on techniques of management for experienced departmental level managers to specialist courses on industrial relations.

EXHIBIT 5

Managers Recruited 1970–1976

	1970	1971	1972	1973	1974	1975	1976
Volvo Group	20	20	41	40	11	14	24
Lex Motor Company	66	46	52	42	9	13	12
Commercial Vehicles Group	—	20	10	22	11	3	10
Hire and Leasing	—	—	—	14	13	8	7
Transportation	17	9	27	11	5	8	16
Hotels	9	9	36	30	31	48	26
Corporate	23	23	29	27	10	11	15
TOTAL	135	127	195	186	90	105	110

Source: Company Records.

The Service Concept

Rapid growth was the prime objective during the acquisitions stage. In October 1971 the chairman began to address the quality of Lex service. One of the 'Corporate Targets of Performance for 1972' called for:

' . . . a dynamic commitment to the improvement of the level of customer satisfaction in each location through the implementation of the "Customer Service Programme." The level of Customer Service is to be improved by 25% in each location as measured by:

a) the number of complaints

b) repeat business

c) sample questionnaires on customer satisfaction developed and administered by the Publicity Department.'

and the Corporate Policy Statement from the Customer Service Manual (see Exhibit 6) specified:

'Improvement in customer relations in the future will depend chiefly on a policy directed towards giving a service which is more personal and which looks after each customer's individual needs.'

EXHIBIT 6

Customer Service Manual

Part I

The following three essentials from the Corporate Policy Statement form the bases for Customer Service:–

1. We aim to offer high quality goods and service at prices necessary to meet our profit objectives. WE WILL MAINTAIN AN OUTWARD IMAGE WHICH WILL REFLECT THIS ATTITUDE.

2. We believe we must OPERATE UNDER THE HIGHEST STANDARD of honesty and morality towards our customers, our shareholders, our employees and our suppliers.

3. We are strongly orientated towards our customers knowing that the VALUE-SATISFACTION OF OUR SERVICE IS THE ONE THING THAT CAN DIFFERENTIATE US FROM OUR COMPETITORS.

Remember, at all times, that a satisfied customer is. THE BEST POSSIBLE SALESMAN.

The Manual advocated improvements on a twelve-point program covering improved customer contact in person, on the phone, and in correspondence; good working conditions and training to ensure a long-tenured, motivated staff; and the establishment of a communications system to handle complaints efficiently.

An interview with a line manager at that time recorded this comment:

'We are always trying to provide customer satisfaction, of course, but making it an objective gives just that much more weight to it. It is not contrary to operational things. So it should enable us to grow. There are basic conflicts too. There is the obvious one between short-term and long-term profits. We are not measured on profits three years from now, but in the car business that is when you reap the benefits of a satisfied customer who returns to buy a car. Maximising our profit on today's dealing with him may lose him next time.'

Diversification through acquisition
(as seen by the Business Press)

'Shares in Conduit Holdings jumped $52\frac{1}{2}$ p to $147\frac{1}{2}$ p yesterday on the news that the employment agency and advertising groups had agreed to merge with motor distributors. Lex Service Group.

The deal takes Lex into an entirely new field and there is no opportunity currently seen for integration of activities, according to Mr. Trevor Chinn, Lex managing director, yesterday. On the other hand, it was felt Conduit "will benefit from our management philosophy".'

(*Financial Times*, London, 2 April 1971)

'Where Lex has been able to outpace all its competitors in the business is simply on its aggressive and shrewd management ability. Its earnings growth has not been the result of clever paper financial takeovers at knockdown prices, but the efforts of management on trading situations that were previously poor.'

(*Guardian*, London, 1 Feb. 1971)

'Work started today on the £2,000,000 plus hotel being built by the Lex Service Group at Stratford-on-Avon, just in time to qualify for the Government grant scheme which comes to an end on March 31.

The new Lex hotel and one at London Airport, already started and believed to be costing from £6,000,000 will be managed by American hotel groups Hyatt and Hilton. Lex has, however, now appointed Mr. Paul Kilborn, 41 year-old American hotel and catering management expert, as managing director of its hotels subsidiary.

The company, says Mr. Kilborn today, is interested in building up an international hotel chain, and a search for sites is now going on, not only in Britain, but also in Europe and America.

"We are planning to build three or possibly four hotels a year" he says, "As we build up perhaps we can accelerate that".'

(*Evening Standard*, London, 8 March 1971)

Exhibit 7 lists these and other acquisitions during the period 1960–73.

EXHIBIT 7

Lex Service Group—Major Acquisitions, Disposals and other changes 1960–73

Date	Company	Activity
1960	London Trading Estates Ltd.	Garages, auto distribution and servicing
	B. S. Gelston & Co. Ltd.	BMC auto distributors
1961	R. S. Mead Ltd.	Rootes and Rolls Royce distributors
1962	Albany Travel Services Ltd.	Travel and package holiday operators and freight forwarding agents
1963	Bristol Motor Co. Ltd.	BMC and Rolls Royce distributors
	Lex appointed Renault distributor for London	
1964	US Concessionaires	Pontiac (GM) auto importers and distributors
1965	W. T. Richard (Bexleyheath) Ltd.	BMC auto distributors
	Sold 35 petrol stations	
1968	Joseph·Cockshoot & Co. Ltd.	BLMC auto distributors
1969	Leased their principal parking garages to NCP	
	Controlled Cost Motoring	Fleet vehicle hire
	Westover Garage (some assets sold for £1,247,299 cash)	BLMC auto distributors
	Disposed Renault business, US Concessionaires and Lendrum & Hartman (for Cadillac, Buick, Oldsmith and Chevrolet)	
1970	Steels Garages Ltd.	BLMC auto distributors
	Stour Valley Trucks Ltd.	BLMC truck distributors
	Stour Valley Motor Co.	BLMC truck distributors
	Phoenix Travel Ltd.	Travel agents
	Roy Bowles Transport Ltd.	Specialist transport company
	Pondust Ltd.	Owned site and planning permission for hotel at Stratford-on-Avon
	Motor interest of Hanson Trust Ltd.—comprising of	Truck distributors
	Tillotson Commercial Motors, Sellers & Batty (Sales) Ltd., Swain Group Ltd: (Swain group later sold for £1,025,000 cash)	Auto distributors
1971	Conduit Holdings Ltd.	Personnel Employment Agency
	Friendship Hotel Corp.	Hotel operator
	The Carlton Tower Ltd.	Hotel operator
	Heathrow Airport, Gatwick Airport and Stratford Hotel Projects	Hotels

EXHIBIT 7 (*cont.*)
Lex Service Group—Major Acquisitions, Disposals and other changes 1960–73

Date	Company	Activity
1971	*Disposals*:	
	Streets Consumer Advertising	Advertising subsidiary of Conduit
	Other small Conduit subs.	Translation and School of English
	Some Property interests	
	Cathedral Garage (subsidiary of Steels)	Chrysler auto distributors
1972	Sparshatts (Standard/ Triumph) Ltd.	BLMC auto distributors
	Wilkinson Transport Group Ltd.	Road haulage operators
	15.5% Cavendish Land Co. Ltd.	Property developers
	Distribution rights for JCB	Contractors Plant sale and hire
	Disposals:	
	28 branches of Conduit Bureau	
1973	Townsends Carriers Ltd.	Transport haulage operators
	Harvey Plant Holdings Ltd.	Plant hire operators
	Royal Orleans Hotel and Hotel Sonesta, Houston	Hotel operations
	Disposals:	
	15.5% Cavendish Land	
	Distribution rights for JCB	

Exceptions and Reservations

Although Trevor Chinn said that Lex did not view itself as a conglomerate, financial observers did not always concur:

'*A New Conglomerate*

Lex Service Group increased its market share of vehicle sales in the first half of 1971—and the outlook for car sales in Britain as a whole is better than at any time since 1964. So why is Lex diversifying hard out of motoring? Because it thinks of itself as a general provider of services, whose management abilities can be developed widely. Another conglomerate is in the making, and one with international ambitions.'

(*Economist*, London, 18 Sep. 1971)

Nor were all analysts convinced that Lex was capable of managing for long on it's 'general service industry' skills:

'*A Grand Design*

A week in politics is a long time. So are a couple of months in business. In April, with merchant banker Rothschilds acting as marriage broker, Lex Service Group bought Mr. B. Z. Immanuel's Conduit Holdings for a little over £5 millions.

Conduit came to the market in December, 1969, when employment agencies were in vogue. Subsequently, a series of acquisitions aimed at diversification brought Conduit into the public relations, technical writing and publishing businesses.

Just before the Lex bid in April the shares were valued at $99\frac{1}{2}$ p compared with a high of 230 p and an issue price of 150 p. The 154 p per share bid by Lex rescued Rothschilds from some embarrassment.

Lex, following the threadbare traditions of the takeover game, issued a statement commending the bid and its logic to shareholders. The ingenious phrase "service to commerce group" was used to explain how the hotch potch of Conduit interests fitted into the Lex Service Group.'

(*Guardian*, London, 13 July 1971)

THE EFFECTS OF GROWTH

The years of acquisition brought the growth the Chairman wanted. Between 1968 and 1972, turnover increased from £32.6 million to £129.4 million, resulting in profit growth (before tax) from £1 million to £7.4 million. Employment rose from 2500 to 6700 during these years. (See exhibits 8 and 9 for financial and personnel statistics.)

Middle managers became critical actors in 1972, and a 3-level line and staff management structure was in place, Divisional Managers, General Managers and Departmental Managers.

In 1972, 62 out of 637 managers were employed by the Lex Service Group head office. One-third of the managers at the divisional manager level were based at the central office.

The Boom Tops Out

Despite continuing profitability, Lex began to lose favour with the financial community:

'The £5.4 million rights issue by *Lex Service Group* of $8\frac{1}{2}$% unsecured loan stock of 1992–97 with warrants attached has flopped. There were subscriptions for £280,159 of the stock and excess applications for a further £101,284. The balance of £5,018,557, representing 92.9% of the offer, has been taken up by the underwriters.'

(*Daily Telegraph*, London, 29 Sept. 1972)

EXHIBIT 8

Financial Record 1968–76

		1968	1969	1970	1971	1972	1973	1974	1975	1976
Turnover	£000	32,614	45,179	85,016	111,325	129,432	154,194	165,400	190,866	251,467
Operating profit	£000	1,274	1,809	3,376	5,298	8,181	9,443	10,336	10,185	14,252
Profit before interest on long and medium term debt	£000	1,169	1,479	2,922	5,120	8,059	8,261	8,244	8,325	12,752
Capital employed	£000	8,587	10,620	21,575	36,795	54,938	76,161	80,724	83,330	95,380
Return on capital employed	%	19.7	13.9	15.2	17.3	14.8	10.9	10.2	10.0	13.4
Profit before taxation	£000	1,038	1,250	2,455	4,382	7,352	6,011	3,702	4,086	7,835
Shareholders funds	£000	3,431	5,950	10,811	25,392	29,570	34,031	34,612	33,032	33,900
Return on shareholders' funds	%	30.2	21.0	26.5	26.3	25.2	17.7	10.7	12.4	23.1
Profit before taxation as a percentage of turnover	%	3.2	2.8	2.9	3.9	5.7	3.7	2.2	2.1	3.1
Earnings per ordinary share (note 2) Basic	p	3.79	4.16	6.69	9.15	10.96	6.70	3.43	3.09	8.79
Fully diluted	p	3.34	3.64	5.68	7.48	10.56	6.64	3.41	3.09	8.71

Notes:
1. Turnover figures for years up to and including 1971 include sales of used cars to the trade.
2. Earnings per ordinary share are computed on the basis of the United Kingdom taxation system applying at the time which from 1973 onwards has been the imputation system. Under the previous system, earnings per share benefited from a substantially lower rate of corporation tax, but the payments of dividends gave rise to a liability to Income Tax Schedule F, which no longer arises.

EXHIBIT 9

LEX SERVICE GROUP

Managers and Total Employment 1969–76

	Dec 1969	July 1970	Dec 1971	Dec 1972		Dec 1973	
				Total	LSG*	Total	LSG*
Regional/Divisional Managers	19	21	29	32	10	38	12
General Managers	33	37	117	162	19	226	19
Dept. Managers	182	221	426	443	33	572	33
Mgmt. Accs.	47	61	n/a	n/a	—	n/a	—
Supervisors: Office			73	162	—	216	—
Ops.	36	44	123	171	—	341	—
Tech.			144	140	—	170	—
Total Employment	2817	3023	5214	6744	126	9704	156

	Dec 1974		Dec 1975		Dec 1976	
	Total	LSG*	Total	LSG*	Total	LSG*
Divisional/Group Managers	38	11	50	15	51	15
General Managers	125	20	230	35	243	37
Dept. Managers	550	31	557	25	599	29
Supervisors	669	—	793	1	761	1
Total Employment	8978	134	8313	123	8637	147

*Lex Corporate Headquarters Managers and Staff.
Source: Company Records.

The ever-increasing profits Lex had enjoyed were not forthcoming in the economic conditions of 1973. The energy crisis and the threat of petrol rationing seriously affected demand in the passenger car business and drove up operating costs in the transportation industry. Initial operating losses at the Heathrow Hotel rounded out the bleak picture which resulted in a drop in profit of £1.3 million (down from 7.4 million in 1972) despite a £35 million increase in turnover.

The Financial Crunch

During 1973, interest rates rose to record levels when Lex's borrowing was at its peak:

'Lex's aggressive acquisitions have traditionally been funded from long and medium term loans. Last year's balance sheet showed that it was already heavily dependent upon loans and overdrafts to pay for its expansion. But the offer documents for Harvey Plant Holdings reveal that the level of borrowing has been increasing at an alarming rate since the beginning of the year. And the cost of servicing this debt is bound to make severe inroads into the group's profits for the year.'

(*Investor's Guardian*, 4 Sept. 1973)

Lex's interest expense rose from £3.5 million to £6.6 million between 1973 and 1974. Depressed conditions in the automobile and hotel industries continued. The profits needed to cover interest expense did not come easily.

The cash crunch caused by interest expense and debt repayment can be seen in Lex's overdrafts and trade credit:

	1972	1973	1974	1975
		(in millions of £)		
Overdrafts	4.5	13.8	9.4	4.5
Debt to creditors	15.3	19.1	22.1	24.1

Financial Control

Drastic steps were taken in 1974. Gil Black, then Financial Controller, recalled:

'We had planned to spend £15.5 million in 1976, then decided to cut out £6.7 million. The actual figure was £8.9 million. Things were very critical. I came to the centre in August 1973 just as we bought Harvey Plant for £10.5 million in *cash*. The system whereby the centre provided the cash to all groups without any knowledge of what the total cash position would be—day to day or long term—collapsed in 1974. There was no mechanism to monitor cash. In December 1973, I insisted we get cash flow forecasts (based on best and worst projections) that actually tied into the balance sheet.

There seemed to be a belief that Lex could borrow money and earn such enormous margins because it had cracked the profit formula. We had no choice about clamping down on everyone. We had to have cash flow forecasts because they were a selling weapon with the banks. We had to demonstrate we had regained control to keep our credibility. Oswald Dockery worked hard to keep current lenders "sweet" with cash flows and profit forecasts. He also managed to persuade several lenders to refinance overdrafts into medium-term money.

We got into working capital control as well. People were naive about how costs mounted up. In June 1974 working capital (stock plus debtors minus creditors) was £16.4 million; by June 1975 it was £9.8 million. There were times I wasn't sure we'd make it through the day.

The crisis was good for financial control within Lex. People have a wider skillbase; there's a greater element of discipline. Things are better now, but a slight sloppiness has raised its head.

I've heard people say "now that we're flush with cash." Working capital will never be taken for granted in Lex again.'

Three financial principles were adopted to avoid a similar situation in the future:

1. Lex must set a limit on its level of gearing.
2. Lex will avoid short term debt vulnerability and bunching of maturities on longer term debt.
3. A policy of interest cover must be defined.

During 1975, a re-appraisal of the current and future viability of each of the Company's operating units identified certain businesses which were not capable of earning a satisfactory return on investment or were seen as strategically irrelevant to the future of Lex. The 1975 organisation chart (see Exhibit 10) reflected the new directions taken. The staff still reported directly to Trevor Chinn. Charles Singer had reached retirement age at Lex (65 years) and had been replaced by John Hirsch as Assistant Managing Director.

THE SERVICE CONCEPT REVISED

By 1974 it became clear that the new acquisitions were less profitable than Lex management had anticipated they would be.

Looking back on that period, one head office manager said:

'We had the five criteria, but they were not always the guidelines for the acquisitions. If a deal looked good, there was a willingness to rationalise the company's fit within Lex. We wanted companies which would require our brand of management. We called it decentralised and needed a profit-responsible line manager to head up each unit.

We ran into problems because we didn't always take the criteria seriously. We bought Conduit and St. Paul's and there was no way we could have each little bureau a separate profit centre. I think if we had pushed the analysis, we would have seen some drawbacks.

Wilkinson Transport is another case of blind imposition of our management system. We wanted separate depots, but it was a network business. It took time for us to understand that each depot was dependent on every other depot to get the package to its destination. We saw a profitable business run into the ground. That woke us up. We began thinking about a business's operating and cost structures; its "profit formula".'

The service concept came under scrutiny again in 1974. The strategy considered this concept as a key to Lex's success. Although Lex might

272

EXHIBIT 10
Organisation in 1975

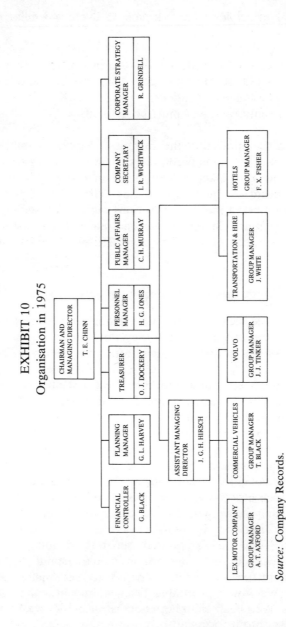

Source: Company Records.

have had no experience in an industry, their service skills from the motor business would be the basis for success in these new ventures. The 1972 efforts to focus on and monitor improvements in Lex service had been diverted by the financial crisis. Charles Murray, as Public Affairs Manager, was conscious of the effect that poor service would have on Lex's strategic objectives. Supported by the head office, he attempted to set service standards at Lex. Looking back on what he considers an unsuccessful programme, Mr. Murray said:

'This was a project that made good marketing sense and was based on logical business reasoning. However, it was organised from the centre and failed because it was done to keep the head office happy.'

One business did adopt service standards in 1974. It was Wilkinson Transport. They were running into major delivery problems. In order to stop the declining profits, Wilkinson management developed standards for service and a measurement system to determine if standards were being met. Jim White, the Transportation and Hire Group Manager, said:

'We had to get into service standards in 1974. We had no fundamental understanding of the business and how to make money in it. We had to find the profit formula for Wilkinson. Service standards were the answer.'

THE MANAGING DIRECTOR

The most influential man in Lex from the mid-1960's was Trevor Chinn. First as the head of Sales during Lex's drive to become a leading force in U.K. auto distribution, then as Managing Director (appointed Chairman in 1972) during the years of growth and crisis, he had largely determined Lex's direction. A young man (42 years old in 1977), Mr. Chinn's entrepreneurial spirit and intense energy set a rigorous pace. His quick and searching intelligence ranged over the strategic, managerial, and operating aspects of Lex. One Lex manager who had been in contact with the Managing Director for many years said:

'Trevor Chinn is brilliant, and he's right very often. He masters incredible detail of what goes on within Lex and in its markets. His ability to integrate this detail into coherent arguments make him a formidable presence in planning meetings. His style has changed since 1976. He used to be more directive, somewhat autocratic perhaps. He could get quite angry if he was presented with a plan he didn't consider "comprehensive", and he let his feelings be known. People didn't stand up to him very often.

Since the financial crisis, it's been clear that line managers could

K

take responsibility for their businesses. Trevor consciously tried to delegate more. He began to listen to the line managers. Influence was shifting to line management. This signalled an important change in Lex.

Other characteristics of Trevor Chinn's style are that it is personal, benevolent, challenging, and inconsistent. That last one leads to problems for both staff and line managers. He can be very enthusiastic about a manager or project and then change his mind suddenly.'

This was changing as well. Most managers saw consistency start to grow in 1976.

PROFITS AGAIN

Lex's profits for 1976 hit a record high of £7.8 million, with non auto-distribution activities contributing 37% to operating profit.

'These were very hard days. No one who lived through them wanted to go through that experience again. Lex came out of that crisis thinking about management as well as profits. When the survival of Lex became a certainty, the focus easily switched to skilled, experienced management to ensure we wouldn't fall back.'

(A Line Manager)

The management ranks were also growing. By 1976, Lex had a 20-point grading system with management levels beginning at grade 7. The grades assigned to job title are listed below:

17–19 Group and Head Office Managers
14–16 Division managers
10–13 General managers
 7 – 9 Departmental managers

The improved financial climate in 1976 allowed Lex to broaden its horizons from cash flow management to the long-term strategic issues it faced. The period of rapid growth followed by a financial crisis led Trevor Chinn seriously to look for any structural or management resource weaknesses which could limit the organisation's capacity to respond to Lex's strategic aims. In early 1976 he hired two organisational consultants (one professional and one academic) to work with the Personnel Manager and himself on these problems.

18

Big Buy Supermarkets (A)

Big Buy Supermarkets[1] was one of the early pioneers of the supermarket revolution in food retailing in the United Kingdom. Originally founded in the early 1950s by Mr Phillip Green, the company initially consisted of 6 small food stores based in East London. Mr Green, however, had noted the trend toward self-service retailing and supermarkets emerging in the United States and proceeded to experiment with the concept for his own small operation. Mr Green had a simple formula for retailing success. His policy was to offer good quality merchandise at the lowest possible prices and to supply all the housewife's basic grocery needs. The business flourished and by 1959 Mr Green had to open a small warehouse in Deptford to service a growing number of retail stores which were all converted to self-service outlets, and as new stores became larger, to supermarkets. The East London warehouse soon proved inadequate to service the additional stores and in 1963 Mr Green moved the company's head office and central warehouse to Sevenoaks in Kent. Big Buy expanded rapidly during the early 1960s as a supermarket food retailing company and in 1964 made a public share issue of part of the company's equity capital which was oversubscribed a staggering 112 times. After the public flotation new store openings proceeded even faster and by 1966 Big Buy was operating over 40 supermarkets and superettes while pre-tax profits had reached £0.7 million on sales of £16.9 million.

Then in 1966 Mr Phillip Green died suddenly and he was succeeded as Chairman by his son who had been involved with the company since his father had founded it in 1953. Despite going public in 1964 the Green family was still left with a majority of the ordinary capital and following his father's death Mr David Green had effective control of some 54 per cent of the stock including his own holdings of some 30 per cent, and those of his mother and various family trusts holding an additional 24 per cent. This

---

[1]This case was made possible by the cooperation of a company that wishes to remain anonymous. All names, places and operating results have therefore been changed.

case describes the subsequent strategy of the company under Mr David Green against the background of trends in the industry up to the middle of 1972.

THE FOOD RETAILING INDUSTRY

Although food sales in Great Britain were the largest single shopping item representing a market of some £7,000 million per annum or 20 per cent of total consumer expenditure this share was steadily declining. It had dropped from 22.3 per cent in 1966 to 20.7 per cent in 1971 while forecasts by the National Economic Development office suggested a continuing decline to 1980.

The number of grocery stores was also declining from some 261,000 stores in 1961 to 202,000 by 1971. This decline was largely attributable to the rapid growth of self-service and supermarket stores and was more marked among grocers than specialist food retailers. At the same time, self-service and supermarket outlets had grown substantially in number from 7,100 in 1960 to almost 30,000 by 1971. The development of supermarkets, with at least 2,000 sq. ft. of selling space, accelerated in the mid 1960s, reaching an estimated 4,800 stores in 1971. At this point the opening of new stores was being increasingly offset by the closure of smaller units. An estimate of outlets by size for 1971 indicated that 78 per cent of self-service stores were under 2,000 sq. ft in size and a further 13 per cent were between 2,000 and 4,000 sq. ft. Only 0.4 per cent were over 10,000 sq. ft, but since 1969 the trend to larger store sizes had increased markedly with the advent of superstores and hypermarkets, and in 1971 27 per cent of new supermarkets were over 10,000 sq. ft.

Food retailing was also beset by relatively low price mark-ups in comparison to other goods. Packaged groceries, for example, typically offered a gross margin of less than 10 per cent to traders, against a 25 per cent mark up on household textiles or 30 per cent on domestic utensils. Competition was intense and margins on many basic goods were often reduced to break-even point.

Food retailers had two advantages however. First, the overall market was the largest single retail area in the United Kingdom. Secondly, food retailers dealt in necessities. Thus stock turns were high and shopping patterns meant that housewives visited grocery stores between 2 and 4 times per week, although only one of these trips resulted in major purchases. The large multiple supermarket groups were attempting to capitalise on these advantages.

In 1972 the retail industry was going through a period of dramatic change and renewal. It was estimated that 25 per cent of stores standing in 1975 would not have been in existence at the start of 1969. These major changes were occurring where new towns were being built, where existing towns and suburbs were being extended and where deteriorating older areas of towns were being renewed. New developments were therefore of three main types. First, there was the development of neighbourhood precincts replacing small rows of shops or providing new centres for suburban neighbourhoods. Second, new town centres or suburban precincts were being developed frequently as extensions of existing store groupings. Finally there were major new 'greenfield' developments in new towns or on the edges of suburbia. Such developments included 'out-of-town' hypermarkets and superstores, although reluctance to grant planning permission was slowing the growth of these large stores.

During the 1960s there had been a significant gain in the share of the food market held by the leading multiple retailers. These groups had exhibited rapid growth, increasing their share of trade from 25.3 per cent in 1961 to nearly 40 per cent in 1972. This growth had been given a special impetus by the abolition of retail price maintenance in 1964 and the introduction of selective employment tax in 1965 which had allowed the multiples to emphasise a price differential over traditional retailers. The multiples were also able to demand improved discounts from suppliers over small independent stores, could build their own private label sales, and engaged in considerable promotion principally by the use of local press advertising.

The major multiples were all attempting to develop large store sites which would enable them to broaden the range of goods offered and better cater for car-borne shoppers. As a result competition for good sites was intense and the largest groups with the best financial resources tended to be offered the best opportunities. Shoppers were, however, fickle and store loyalty was low for most of the food retailing groups.

In 1972 five major groups dominated the grocery trade: Tesco, Fine Fare, Allied Suppliers, J. Sainsbury and International Stores. In addition Marks & Spencer had developed its food activities to such an extent that it was a leading competitor. These six groups accounted for approximately 30 per cent of grocery expenditure nationally but their relative shares differed considerably from region to region. Sainsbury was the market leader in the South East but held a minor share of other southern regions, was growing rapidly in the Midlands, but was unrepresented in the north. Tesco was very strong throughout the South Midlands and North West. Fine Fare had a good base in Scotland and was important in the North and East Midlands. Allied Suppliers operated nationally but traded under a variety of names. The group was the major multiple in Scotland and was important in the North, East Anglia and the South West. International was represented in most areas under various names but was strongest in East Anglia and the South West. Marks & Spencer held a small but significant share in all areas. The five main grocery multiple groups had a turnover of some £1,216 million from over 4,600 stores of which some 50 per cent were supermarkets.

Tesco (turnover £395 million from 679 stores of which 421 were supermarkets) pioneered self-service stores in the 1950s. The company grew rapidly in the 1960s assisted by the introduction of stamp trading and low prices. The company had also moved away from traditional grocery lines by introducing household goods and clothing which by 1972 were stocked by 75 per cent of stores in addition to 60 exclusive Home 'n' Wear outlets. This product range was still being extended to furniture, footwear and consumer durables and it was estimated that non-foods made up some 40 per cent of turnover. Small stores were also being converted to Fresh Food units, off licences were included in all new stores and own label wines were sold. The company had developed over 500 private label lines. By 1972 Tesco had adopted a policy of only developing superstore sites with more than 20,000 sq. ft of selling space. Some 250,000 sq. ft of new selling area was being introduced in 1972, 600,000 was planned for 1973 and over 1 million more was in the pipeline. Many of the new developments were to be stores of over 50,000 sq. ft located at the edge of towns.

J. Sainsbury was a family firm, expanding rapidly, based on a reputation for high quality fresh perishable foods which had been successfully transferred to a wide range of own label dry goods and a growing non-food range. By 1972 the company had some 196 stores, 138 of which were supermarkets, and turnover had reached nearly £300 million.

Allied Suppliers with a turnover of some £330 million formed part of the Cavenham Foods retail division which also included the Wrights/Moore chain. Most of the 2,650 stores operated by the group were small grocery outlets trading under a variety of names. The group was being rapidly rationalised to strip away unproductive property assets and it was intended to concentrate developments on supermarkets in the future.

Fine Fare, with a turnover of £205 million from 1,000 stores, was a subsidiary of Associated British Foods. 471 of the groups' stores were supermarkets. Increasing emphasis was being placed on the development of large stores and increasing non-food sales which by 1972 were approaching 10 per cent turnover.

International Stores operated some 930 stores mainly of small size. It was acquired in 1972 by British American Tobacco, the world's largest tobacco company, as part of a major diversification programme. Only some 50 of International's stores were over 4,000 sq. ft and it was considered that substantial investment would be needed to make the group into a leading competitor.

In addition to the leading multiple groups there were a number of smaller chains operating, which were composed essentially of two types—subsidiaries of major companies or independent groups strong in a limited geographic area. MacFisheries (owned by Unilever) and Keymarkets (a subsidiary of Fitch Lovell) each operated some 200–400 stores emphasising fresh food. Safeway Stores, a subsidiary of a major US chain, operated some 50 supermarkets using American merchandising methods. The regional groups included Big Buy, F. J. Wallis, and Pricerite in the South East, Lennons in the North and Wrensons, David Greig and Redmans in the Midlands and North West.

A recent development in food retailing had been the rapid growth of discount stores whose positioning was based on the establishment of low prices mainly on national brands. These stores varied in size and the number of lines offered: at one extreme Kwik Save Stores carried only some 700 lines compared with some 4,000 in the average supermarket; at the other was Carrefour a hypermarket operator selling a complete range of goods in one location. By 1972 discount operators accounted for some 5 per cent of total grocery turnover although their importance in dry goods was greater. Discounters such as Kwik Save and Asda had established the highest recent growth of retail food operators, and due to better availability of sites this form of trading had developed most rapidly in the Midlands and North.

The largest retail organisation in the UK were the cooperatives, with 15,000 shops owned or controlled by retail Cooperative Societies responsible to their own membership. The Coops had been losing ground despite efforts in 1968 to create a national identity and a drive for greater marketing coordination.

To combat the competitive thrust of the multiples two developments had occurred to assist the independent retailers. First, many small retailers had joined voluntary groups, the most successful of which were linked to one or more wholesalers with centralised buying control. The largest ten of these groups had approximately 25,000 members and in all some 33 per cent of independent grocers were participants in voluntary groups. The top

EXHIBIT 1

Big Buy Supermarkets—Profit and Loss Statements 1966–71 Year ended 25 December (£000)

	1966	1967	1968	1969	1970	1971
Sales	16,905.1	23,019.4	29,039.9	32,119.3	33,368.2	38,072.9
Profits before tax	699.7	906.6	1,014.8	1,077.8	772.4	579.9
Taxation	293.4	384.3	464.9	505.5	328.9	261.8
Profits after tax	406.3	522.3	549.9	572.3	443.5	318.1
Dividends						
Declared (net after tax)	96.9	100.3	103.4	129.3	131.7	134.8
Less waived	55.8	55.1	41.4	57.3	60.0	67.4
	41.1	45.2	62.0	72.0	71.7	67.4
Retained earnings	336.3	445.3	444.3	450.0	323.9	208.1
Depreciation	136.5	195.6	357.2	323.5	378.1	404.5
Directors' emoluments	22.9	21.5	40.8	46.5	43.9	69.3

Source: Company Records.

EXHIBIT 2

Big Buy Supermarkets Ltd. Balance Sheet as at 25 December 1966–71
(£000)

	1966	1967	1968	1969	1970	1971
Current assets						
Stocks at lower of cost or market	1192.4	1348.6	2587.8	2409.6	2665.0	3275.4
Debtors and prepayments	174.9	258.5	278.0	439.1	354.5	375.2
Cash at bank	71.5	29.7	81.0	140.0	4.1	0.0
	1438.8	1636.8	2946.8	2988.7	3023.6	3650.6
Fixed assets						
Freehold properties	677.6	1252.9	1133.8	1238.4	1535.3	1731.5
Leasehold properties	—	—	570.8	738.1	850.8	866.6
Fixtures, fittings and motors	790.9	1082.3	1521.8	1733.3	1908.1	2029.6
	1478.5	2335.2	3226.4	3709.8	4294.2	4627.7
TOTAL ASSETS	2917.3	3972.0	6173.2	6698.5	7317.8	8278.3
Current liabilities						
Creditors	1202.3	1622.5	2722.3	3041.2	3202.5	4068.6
Bank overdraft (secured)	—	—	436.6	—	193.7	231.2
Current tax	98.0	132.6	330.0	404.5	459.1	345.3
Proposed dividend	18.6	24.3	31.4	48.2	57.8	68.8
Tax payable 1 January	94.7	124.6	388.9	470.3	310.2	198.0
	1413.6	1904.0	3909.2	3964.2	4223.3	4911.9
Share capital in 25p shares	275.0	1100.0	1100.0	1100.0	1100.0	1100.0
Reserves	1228.7	968.0	964.2	1395.6	1737.1	1945.2
Future tax	—	—	199.8	238.7	257.4	321.2
	1503.7	2068.0	2264.0	2734.3	3094.5	3366.4
TOTAL LIABILITIES	2917.3	3972.0	6173.0	6698.5	7317.8	8278.3

Source: Company Records.

four (Mace, Spar, Vivo and VG) had a combined turnover of over £400 million, provided merchandising know-how, private label products, promotion and advertising, and assisted with finance for conversion and modernisation. Second, cash and carry wholesaling had developed rapidly to provide lower prices for independent grocers.

BIG BUY IN 1966

When Mr Phillip Green died in 1966, Big Buy operated some 40 stores principally in London and the home counties. During the early 1960s the number and size of stores had expanded resulting in a rapid growth of sales and profits. Details of recent financial performance are shown in Exhibits 1 and 2.

Mr Green had operated the business in a highly personalised style. He personally had taken all the major decisions and had not been over-concerned with sophisticated accounting and control systems. In 1963, in response to the growing number of branches, a computer system had been introduced under Mr Simon Henderson to help control purchasing, stock levels and goods movements between the central warehouse and the stores. Wage payments were later also dealt with on the computer. Nevertheless, little information was available to guide top management decision making. No budgetary systems were in force and the only full-scale corporate accounting undertaken was the result of annual visits from the company's auditors, Peter J. Cobb and Company, a small accounting firm who also acted as personal accountants for the Green family. Mr Green, however, was able to maintain adequate control by knowledge of store sales, goods bought in and estimates of gross margins. This was supplemented by frequent visits to the branches by Mr Green from his office at the company's headquarters and central warehouse at Sevenoaks. As a result, profits had grown by over 500 per cent between 1960 and 1966 and Big Buy's performance was considered to be amongst the best of retail food companies.

The company organisation was also kept along simple functional lines. Apart from Mr Green, the Big Buy Board consisted of his wife, Mrs Sara Green, his son David and the family solicitor and friend, Mr Abraham Goldstein. Mr Green called board meetings at irregular intervals, with the meetings being used to approve formally the annual results or to sanction specific decisions Mr Green wished to undertake. Apart from Mr David Green, the board members were not involved in Big Buy's operations.

A small number of senior executives reported to Mr Green (see Exhibit 3). Apart from Mr Henderson who had joined the company when the

EXHIBIT 3
Big Buy Supermarkets Ltd.—Organisation structure 1966

| Chairman and Managing Director Phillip Green | Non-Executive Directors Mrs Sara Green Mr Abraham Goldstein |

| David Green Retail stores and site development (Director) | Sales Managers N. Symonds J. Fielding | Buying D. Phelps | Chief accountant A. Flynn | Computer services A. Henderson | Company secretary A. North |

Source: Company Records.

computer system was introduced, these executives had joined Phillip Green shortly after he had entered the food retailing business and their responsibilities had grown with the expansion of the company. Mr David Green, who started in the company first as a store manager, then as a supervisor and store controller, was responsible for sites and property developments, but also maintained a strong interest in retail operations.

DEVELOPMENTS TO 1970

Following the death of his father, Mr David Green assumed the chairmanship of Big buy late in 1966. He decided that the policy of rapid expansion should continue at all speed mainly by means of a substantial new store opening programme and within the next four years the number of Big Buy stores more than doubled to over 100. In addition, Big Buy extended a number of its existing stores wherever this was possible. As a result of new openings, Big Buy began to expand its geographic coverage with new stores being opened in South Wales and the West Country. The company also moved northwards and into the eastern counties from its base in the south of England. To help service the new stores two new warehouse operations were opened, a major depot in Bristol to service South Wales, the West and the Midlands and at Micheldever in Hampshire to service the western home counties.

The company also began to expand its range of private label merchandise wherever possible and made a number of applications for off-licences for its stores to enable it to include wines and spirits in the product range. Big Buy began to develop non-food sales in its larger outlets as well as improving its range of fresh foods and meats for which specialist packaging operations were set up at the Bristol and Sevenoaks warehouse. In addition, the company extended its stamp trading operations offering alternatively Green Shield or Sperry and Hutchinson pink stamps in its stores.

The new stores opened by Big Buy tended to be of increasing size in line with a national trend toward larger food stores. However, being one of the smaller supermarket chains, Big Buy tended not to be offered the prime sites in new shopping developments and in consequence many of the new stores were located either in smaller towns, or outside city centres or other major shopping areas. It was also Mr Green's conscious policy to seek outlets in locations where there would be no direct competition with the largest supermarket operators especially Tesco and to a lesser extent Sainsbury's who Mr Green considered were the most aggressive competitors Big Buy faced. In addition, relatively few stores had their own parking facilities. The location and size breakdown of the principal Big Buy stores in 1972 is shown in Exhibit 4.

At the same time, Big Buy was faced with increased pressure on trading margins caused by increased operating costs including higher bills for

EXHIBIT 4

Big Buy Supermarkets Ltd.—Store Size and Location 1972

	Sales area in sq. ft					
Location	less than 2000	2–4000	4–8000	8–25,000	over 25,000	Total
Area 1						
London	3	8	6	1	—	18
Kent	3	6	5	2	—	16
Sussex	2	5	5	1	1	14
Surrey	—	3	4	—	—	7
Essex	—	1	2	1	—	4
Area 2						
Hampshire	2	4	3	1	—	10
Berkshire	1	3	1	—	—	5
Wiltshire	1	2	2	—	—	5
Dorset	2	2	3	1	—	8
Somerset	—	3	2	—	—	5
Devon	—	2	—	—	1	3
Cornwall	—	2	1	—	—	3
Area 3						
South Wales	2	2	2	—	—	6
Gloucestershire	1	2	1	1	—	5
Oxfordshire	—	1	1	—	—	2
Buckinghamshire	1	2	1	—	—	4
Northamptonshire	—	1	2	1	—	4
Cambridgeshire	—	1	1	—	—	2
Norfolk	—	1	2	—	—	3
Suffolk	—	1	1	—	—	4
Leicestershire	—	1	3	—	—	4
Lincolnshire	—	3	1	—	—	4
Nottinghamshire	1	2	2	1	—	6
Derbyshire	—	1	2	—	—	3
TOTAL	19	59	53	10	2	143

Source: Company Records.

wages, higher rents and rates and the introduction of selective employment tax. More important, the company was faced with greatly increased competition from other supermarket operations, which were also expanding rapidly. Some were substantially larger than Big Buy and thus able to obtain better supply terms or improved promotional deals, which provided increased margins that could be passed on to their customers in lower prices. Moreover, despite Big Buy's store location policy, the increased geographic coverage by other supermarket operators meant that Big Buy began to face new competition in many areas where its early stores had been established. The major groups in expanding into these areas with new stores, which were generally larger than the earlier Big Buy stores, represented a considerable threat and led to significant pressure on Big Buy's trade margins in an attempt to maintain the turnover of its smaller outlets. Commenting on the increased competition, Mr Green stated 'At a time when we had to absorb sharply increased operating costs we were also faced with intensive competition in many areas in areas in which we operated, mainly from new supermarkets with a far greater sales area than our own. Aggressive competition, is of course a fact of life for us, but in 1970 for example we were particularly hard hit by the opening of major competitors of new stores in no less than 30 areas in which we operate, nearly one in every three of our stores was faced with competition from new and larger store.'

The result of this increased competition was some reduction in sales turnover per square foot in 1970 although overall turnover continued to advance as a result of new store openings. More important, trade margins declined markedly and profits reached a peak of £1.1 million in 1969 before falling back to £0.7 million in 1970.

Big Buy's managers were poorly placed to make a careful response to the pressure on margins largely due to continued deficiencies in the company's control system which had little changed since the death of Mr Green's father. The personalised system developed by Phillip Green became increasingly inadequate, however, as the number of stores increased and strong localised competition emerged at branch level. Mr David Green recognised many of the inadequacies in organisation and control left by his father and took a number of steps to correct these. First, shortly after his father's death which in turn had made Mrs Sara Green seriously ill, Mr Green invited his uncle, Mr Michael Jacobsen, who had been a close friend and confidant of his father, to join Big Buy as managing director. Next, early in 1968, he took steps to strengthen the main board by appointing Mr Phelps, Mr Symonds, Mr North and Mr Fielding as directors. Then, early in 1969 he took advantage of an offer from one of Big Buy's main suppliers and called in Mr Gerald Battersby the managing director of the British subsidiary of international consultants, Muller Day Associates Inc., to undertake a brief examination of the company's organisation and control systems.

THE MULLER DAY REPORT

Mr Battersby, who had previously held a senior executive position with a leading food retailer before turning to consultancy, had also acquired a reputation as a successful company doctor reviving the flagging fortunes of several companies in various industries.

In February 1969 Mr Battersby, after a brief examination of Big Buy, reported to Mr Jacobsen and made recommendations for organisational and control system changes.

He considered that changes in the administrative systems were required as a matter of urgency in view of the prospective growth in shops and turnover. A proper budgetary system was also required as soon as possible including capital expenditure and cash flow, purchases and sales, stocks, expenditure, profit and loss account and balance sheet.

Mr Battersby considered that the company's computer system was adequately staffed and Mr Henderson appeared confident that the systems he had designed were adequate. Nevertheless, he felt that independent advice upon computer performance might be useful and if the company's auditors were not up to this task Muller Day would be a suitable alternative. Mr Battersby also believed that, despite Mr Henderson's reluctance, some new systems should be contemplated, namely four-weekly profit and loss accounts for each shop, the bought ledgers and purchase invoices, the issue of cheques, statistics to buying and selling departments, and expense accounts.

Big Buy's accountancy systems were considered to be under pressure largely due to physical space restrictions. Mr Flynn was considered competent but again Mr Battersby thought that independent advice might be useful on the efficiency of the accountancy department and its paperwork systems and, failing the use of the auditors, Muller Day were recommended as suitable. Mr Battersby also believed that the production of monthly or four-weekly profit and loss accounts within two weeks of the end of a period for the company and for individual departments and shops was an urgent necessity, if senior management was to maintain their existing sensitive control over operations.

Mr Phelps was seen as a competent buyer, who had poor support from his team. Further, the buying department was thought to have too little knowledge of the detailed pattern or real profitability of purchases of 'directs'. Comparisons of 'direct' suppliers' invoiced prices, with buying department's negotiated prices, and with consequent adjustments of selling prices, was by test sample only. As a result, until goods inward or delivery notes could be endorsed with the buying department's cost and selling prices, profit and loss accounts for the shops, individual departments and the company itself could not be produced.

Mr Battersby reported that at present the computer gave a detailed analysis of warehouse stocks and of their movement, from which the 'average number of weeks' stock holding could be seen. Stocks requiring reorder were starred. On the other hand he felt less attention seemed to be given to overordered, slow-moving or 'special' stocks and of the consequent finance locked up in these stocks. The stock position had been excellent, but in view of the present cash position and of high interest rates, the size of the stock holdings was of increasing importance.

It was not clear to Mr Battersby exactly how the buying department worked out their gross margin policy on individual commodities so as to reach a desired overall gross margin for individual shops or indeed for the company as a whole.

Mr Battersby visited a number of Big Puy stores and was impressed with the quality of their personnel, the good control of staff costs, low wastage figures and small stockholdings. He considered lines of communication and management structure to be well planned and well under Mr Fielding's control. Mr Battersby also received the impression, however, that profit and loss information and budgetary controls were not deemed to have a high priority.

He discovered that most managers were not given information on gross margins as a matter of policy, and their results and rewards were judged solely on total sales. He believed that although this observation had little present importance it could be a weakness as the company grew to be a major national group.

The warehouse operation seemed extremely well managed and efficient compared with other supermarket groups. Space occupancy at Sevenoaks was 95 per cent and 75 per cent at Bristol. Mr Battersby was somewhat concerned however about large stocks of 'special' purchases which could be in the warehouse for several months, so tying up capital, despite the fact that they represented additional discounts from manufacturers when purchased. In addition, large consignments of 'own label' products were also taken from manufacturers.

Mr Battersby personally believed in education for top management and recommended that both top and middle managers should spend on average between seven and ten days per annum attending conferences, lectures, seminars, exhibitions and the like to keep themselves abreast of affairs.

Finally, Mr Battersby considered the size of Big Buy and its plans for expansion meant that the managing director would find it necessary increasingly to divorce himself from detailed operations. He therefore recommended the appointment of a new director of administration to coordinate and control all the administrative systems throughout the company. This individual should be about forty with a professional qualification and a successful background as a financial controller. Mr Battersby believed that this appointment should be made with urgency before the present strains on the administrative system led to a breakdown in financial controls.

MANAGEMENT RESPONSE

Although Mr Battersby's report made a number of recommendations these were not all acted upon immediately since Big Buy were in the process of moving to a new administrative building being completed at Sevenoaks. During 1969 a number of new computer systems were introduced but little progress was made on the introduction of new accountancy procedures, budgetary controls or long-term plans. In April 1970, following further discussions with Mr Battersby, it was decided that a director of administration should be appointed and subsequently Big Buy's auditors,

Peter J. Cobb, who had merged with the large city accountants, Fitch, Henry, Sullivan and Company, were requested to undertake a comprehensive review of the company's basic systems and control procedures relevant to the accounting function.

Muller Day Associates, for a fee of 20 per cent of initial remuneration, were requested to draw up a specification for the new board post and to submit a short-list of suitable candidates. This was done and a specification submitted in May 1970 and, as the consultants did not recommend advertising the position, an initial candidate was put forward. This individual eventually proved unavailable and Muller Day suggested a second candidate, Mr Cyril Mellor, for consideration. Mr Mellor had had two years' experience in computer systems with the same major food retailer that Mr Battersby had worked for, but had left following a disagreement with a member of the main board to join a major electrical products manufacturer.

Mr Mellor was accepted by Mr Green and Mr Jacobsen and joined the company in October 1970. As administration director Mr Mellor was initially responsible for the introduction and maintenance of accounts and statistics, for the introduction, operation and control of budgets, and for finance and financial policy as laid down by the chairman and managing director. He was also to assist in the formulation of short- and long-term policy planning and was responsible for all accountancy, computer and administrative personnel, including Mr North, Mr Flynn and Mr Henderson.

Following his appointment Mr Mellor moved swiftly to fulfil his new function. He initiated a review of the company's computer-based systems by International Computers, introduced a new system of warehouse stock control, requested Muller Day to help recruit additional accountancy help, and in December, before the report on control procedures by Fitch, Henry, Sullivan, commissioned Muller Day to provide consultancy services to produce an expense control system capable of later computerisation. This contract, worth £2,500 plus expenses, was later increased to £4,500 as the Muller Day assignment was widened to include help in the preparation of a budget for 1971.

Following the completion of this project, Muller Day reported to Mr Green that in the course of its investigation a number of other defects had emerged which they wished to bring to his attention. Muller Day considered first that there was no agreed organisation structure or reporting structure in Big Buy and they had therefore defined the responsibilities of each manager within the existing day-to-day working arrangements. It was still felt that a detailed organisation structure should be spelt out; that the relationships between buying and marketing should be clearly established; that buying and selling operations for meat and fresh produce under the nominal control of the sales director was too flexible; and that the sales operation was weak, with some question as to whether the existing personnel were sufficiently forward-looking to manage a modern budgetary system. Second, it was considered intolerable that the company only knew its gross profit once a year as the existing accounting system could only give an indication of trends in gross profits. Third, their investigation of sales per square foot on the most recent sales figures revealed that the least successful stores were those opened in most recent years and it was recommended that formalised systems of site appraisal be introduced.

Then, early in 1971, following a series of disagreements between Mr Green and his uncle, Mr Jacobsen left the company. Mr Green turned to Mr Mellor as his new deputy, appointing him in effect the company's chief executive. This position was confirmed by the board in August 1971 on the appointment to the board of Mr Stephen Cleary. He had been recruited by Muller Day from Mr Mellor's former company to fill the slot left vacant by Mr Mellor's promotion.

CHANGES IN STRATEGY AND STRUCTURE

With the approval of Mr Green, Mr Mellor moved quickly: first, to place the existing business on a new footing by improving Big Buy's eroding competitive position; and second, to prepare the company for a new leap forward so as to become one of the major food retailers by 1980. Mr Mellor proceeded to accomplish the first of these objectives by reorganising the company and introducing new professional management; introducing new control procedures; broadening the company's retailing formula and expanding non-food sales in particular. To implement the second, in 1972 he brought in consultants to assist in the development of a corporate long-term plan which would provide the blueprint for Big Buy's proposed expansion.

The 1971 Reorganisation

Following the comments from Muller Day, Mr Mellor wrote to all branch managers outlining a revised structure for Big Buy with the objectives of creating lines of communication where these did not exist, giving each manager the authority that went with responsibility, which was to be carefully determined jointly between the individual and top management and, having established agreed performance targets, adequately rewarding managers who met their targets. In this way, Mr Mellor intended forging a closely knit organisation which would act as a team with the common aim of improving the profitability of the company.

The Big Buy organisation was subdivided into a series of major functions as shown in Exhibit 5. The first of these functions covered finance and administration and was headed by the newly appointed Mr Stephen Cleary. Reporting to Mr Cleary were a series of departments covering

EXHIBIT 5

Big Buy Supermarkets Ltd.—Organisation, October 1971

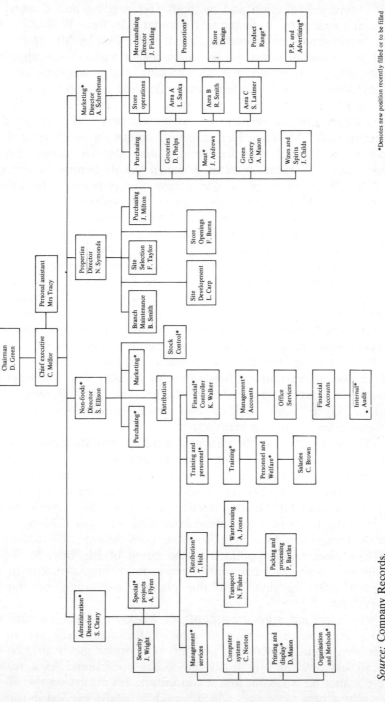

Source: Company Records.

*Denotes new position recently filled or to be filled

management services headed by Mr Jack Strong, responsible for computer operations, organisation and methods and printing and display; financial control headed by a financial controller Mr Ken Walker, a new cost accountant from manufacturing industry recruited by Muller Day; training and personnel for which no overall manager was initially appointed; and distribution, responsible for warehousing and transportation. No head of distribution was appointed initially pending a comprehensive review of all distribution systems and procedures by International Management Consultants Ltd. Subsequently, distribution was hived off as a separate function under Mr Tony Holt, a new appointment and former distribution manager with another leading food retailer. Mr Henderson, formerly responsible for computer systems, resigned shortly before the reorganisation and Mr Flynn was appointed to a new post responsible for development projects. Mr Mellor considered that in this position Mr Flynn's long experience in Big Buy could be utilised on financial aspects of new ventures and later on corporate planning, when an executive had been appointed to take charge of this activity.

All aspects of purchasing and retail operations were centralised under a new marketing department led by Mr Al Schreibman, a newly appointed marketing director. Mr Schreibman was a Canadian recruited from the British subsidiary of a North American food retailing company. Reporting to Mr Schreibman were purchasing, which was in turn subdivided into grocery purchasing, headed by Mr Phelps, a main board director, and separate buying functions responsible for meat, fresh produce and beverages; merchandising, headed by Mr Fielding who was responsible for advertising and promotion, store design, and product range; and retail stores, which were divided into three geographic areas, each the responsibility of an area manager.

The third area was the property development function headed by Mr Symonds whose department was responsible for site selection, store development and equipment, new openings and store maintenance.

The final area was non-foods which was expanded in responsibility since Mr Green and Mr Mellor intended to develop this area substantially as part of Big Buy's plan for future expansion. Mr Stan Ellison was recruited to head non-foods from his position as sales director of a leading non-food variety retailer and appointed to the board of Big Buy. Mr Ellison then built up a team to incorporate buying, marketing, distribution and stock control staff, in line with the planned expansion of the non-food operations.

With the final appointment of Mr Mellor as chief executive and the introduction of a number of new professional managers to lead the functional areas, Mr Green's position as chairman meant that he needed to spend less time on Big Buy's day-to-day operations. As a result, it was agreed that he would in future concentrate his efforts on the all-important search for new store sites which would be vitally needed if Big Buy were successfully to accomplish its ambitious expansion objectives.

New Control Procedures

During the remainder of 1971 and the first half of 1972, new controls and systems were gradually introduced by members of the new management team aided by the supplementary assistance provided as a result of previous or new consultancy contracts. In particular, new computer systems were introduced to replace those developed originally by Mr Henderson, new accounting controls were developed by Mr Walker, a system of management by objectives was introduced, a new incentive plan for store managers was adopted, annual budgeting became fully established, and in May 1972 the company began to draw up its first long-term strategic plan.

Nevertheless, in 1971 although turnover continued to grow to £38 million, pressure on margins caused profits to fall yet again to £580,000, and Mr Green and the executors of his father's estate waived their entitlement to dividends on 5 million of their shares. Big Buy were therefore continuously searching for new ways of reducing costs and improving efficiency, and in April 1972 Mr Mellor and Mr Cleary reported to the board on an encounter they had had at a seminar on 'Store Profitability'. There they had met an executive of Starshine Inc., an American retail food company. Mr Mellor and Mr Cleary had been extremely impressed with the results claimed for the Starshine control system that they had visited Starshine in the United Stats to see the system in use. As a result the board agreed that Starshine executives should come to the UK to install their methods experimentally in two Big Buy stores at a cost of $15,000 on condition thay they achieved their specified targets. If the system was as successful as it was claimed, resulting in substantial improvements in efficiency, reduced labour requirements and more rapid stock turnover, consideration was then to be given to converting all Big Buy stores.

Changes in Retail Policy

In an effort to halt declining profit margins in the retail branches Big Buy introduced a number of policy changes in its trading formula. In August 1971 Big Buy operated 111 stores with a total sales area of 480,000 square feet, 107 of which offered trading stamps and of these 61 gave Green Shield with the rest offering S and H pink stamps. Although the average size of the stores was around 4,500 square feet, 10 were over 7,500 square feet and 53 were considered to be supermarkets. The remainder were self-service superettes, 19 of which had a sales area of less than 2,000 square feet. By mid-1972 the number of stores had grown to 143 and the company's total sales area to 620,000 square feet. These stores were serviced either from the company's three warehouses or direct from Big Buy's suppliers. Approximately half of deliveries were made through the company's own warehouses.

In its average supermarket Big Buy reckoned to have a product range of some 4,000 drygoods grocery lines which made up some 80 per cent of group turnover. Private label merchandise sold under the Big Buy brand name represented some 15 per cent of turnover and covered a product range, including beverages, biscuits, bakery products, canned fruit and vegetables, soups, cereals, confectionery, desserts, fats, frozen foods, jams and preserves, dairy products, pet foods, prepared meats, cooking aids, household and paper products, and soaps and toiletries, in all, some 350 items in various pack sizes. Meat, fresh provisions and greengrocery represented a further 14 per cent of total turnover with the larger supermarkets offering a wider range of merchandise. In addition, the larger stores provided a choice between prepacked or counter-assisted service in meat and counter-assisted service in greengrocery.

Non-foods represented only 5 per cent of total turnover and because of the limited availability of selling space in the majority of stores the product range offered was usually limited to household products, such as kitchen accessories. Larger stores where more space was available for home and wear products carried an extended range of household goods and cheap men's, women's and children's clothing and footwear.

In order to improve Big Buy's competitive appeal and to reduce the rate of obsolescnce of its small first generation superettes, a number of changes were made to this pattern.

Conversion to discount operations

In September 1970 Mr Green introduced discount trading in one store as an experiment aimed at combating intense local competition. A small superette store in Wandsworth was converted from normal trading stamp operations to discounting. Under this method of trading the number of lines sold was substantially reduced from around 3,000 in the average superette to about 1,000, the merchandising displays were largely converted from the traditional supermarket gondolas to more emphasis on cheap, cut-case display, trading stamps were terminated and gross margins were reduced from the average of between 19 per cent and 20 per cent obtained in normal trading stamp supermarkets to an average of between 12½–14 per cent. Furthermore, prices were cut across all lines of merchandise to at least some extent whereas in conventional supermarkets only certain lines were reduced, and although some lines were treated as loss leaders or special offers, most were sold at recommended prices or even in some cases 'bunced' to above recommended price. For discounting to be successful a turnover increase of between 30–40 per cent was necessary to break even in comparison with conventional operations.

The Wandsworth experiment proved highly successful and during 1971 and the first half of 1972 a further 26 of Big Buy's stores converted from superette operation to discounting and 7 new discount stores were opened all operating on a 'baby shark' limited product range. Not all of these new stores were equally successful, however, and although Mr Green and Mr Mellor anticipated further increases in the number of discount stores, a number of outlets were still considered to be too small to remain viable.

Changes were also made in the stores which remained unconverted. The budget for advertising and promotion was stepped up to over £80,000 in 1972. This was primarily spent on special promotions and local newspaper advertising. Increased attention was paid to store layout, changes were made to the product range offered placing increased emphasis on sales of fresh food, garden produce and meat, and in some stores changes were made in trading stamp policy, switching from pink stamps to green wherever this was found to be possible under contracts and franchise arrangements with the trading stamp suppliers.

The Opening of Superstores

Most important, however, was the opening during 1972 of Big Buy's first two out-of-town stores at Eastbourne in Sussex, and Plymouth in Devon. These new stores had a sales area of at least 25,000 square feet, together with ample parking places for between 150 and 250 cars. The Eastbourne store was typical of the new superstores. It formed the major part of a new shopping centre established some 3 miles from the town centre as part of a large new housing development on reclaimed shingle beach, and first became available as a site early in 1970. Big Buy submitted plans to the local council which gave planning approval in October 1970. Construction began immediately and was completed on schedule in March 1972, when shop-fitting began, leading to the new store opening in May. Details of the store are shown in Exhibit 6.

These new stores were expected to provide Big Buy with valuable experience in the management of large out-of-town centres which Mr Mellor believed would provide a major source of the company's future growth. In particular, these stores provided the opportunity for a substantial increase in the sales area available for non-foods which were the largest single department in the new superstores with nearly 50 per cent of the available selling space. As a result, the range of non-food goods was broadened to include a wide range of soft goods, clothing and footwear. Many of these goods represented new additions to the non-foods catalogue and to cope with this increase in activity, Mr Ellison rapidly built up a team of 30 non-food staff responsible for buying, marketing and merchandising, promotion and display, and stock control. As many of the new lines were imported and made for Big Buy under contract, the buying function tended to differ somewhat from grocery buying, requiring a number of visits to suppliers, frequently including trips overseas to Western Europe, Hong Kong and the Far East in order to secure the best deals.

EXHIBIT 6

Eastbourne Superstore Details

		Departments:	
Gross area	36,480 sq. ft		
Sales area	27,640 sq. ft	Bacon	—open service
Warehouse area	4,170 sq. ft	Provisions	—open service
Preparation area	1,930 sq. ft	Delicatessen	—open service
Car parking	176 places	Fruit & vegetables	—pre-packed
Check-outs	15	Meat	—open/pre-packed
		Fish	—open service
		Frozen food	
		Bakery	—open service
		Cigarettes & tobacco	—open service
		Wines & spirits	—open service
		Home and wear	
		Car accessories & tyre services	—(Associated Tyre Services)

Size of departments:
1. Refrigerated

Cooked meat (incl. Deli & Bacon)		8 m single side
Provisions (incl. Dairy)		14 m island
Produce		5 m 2 deck
Meat (fresh)		8 m single side
Meat (frozen incl. Home Freezer Pack)		16 m
Poultry		8 m
Ice cream		$2 \times 6' \times 3'6''$
Patisserie		1×14 m island; 1×9 m s/s
Frozen food		9 m single side

2.	Produce	36' gondola	12' wall fitting	4
3.	Home & wear	508' gondola	198' wall fitting	48
4.	Grocery	340' gondola	36' pallet	25

Source: Company Records.

THE FOODFAIR ACQUISITION

Mr Ellison considered that non-food retailing was sufficiently different in that not only did it require a specialist staff but it would also be best if it were able to undertake its own warehousing and distribution function. This problem was solved in January 1972, when Big Buy acquired Foodfair Ltd, a company formed by Mr Michael Levene and operating a chain of 23 supermarkets and superettes mainly in South and West London, Surrey and Middlesex. These stores were serviced from a small 25,000 square foot warehouse with office accommodation in Putney near the South Circular Road which was made available to Mr Ellison as a headquarters and storage area for the non-food operation.

Foodfair, with an annual turnover of some £5.5 million, had moved into a loss position during 1971 and in the half year to December 1971 losses had increased to nearly £80,000. At this point, Mr Green had approached

Mr Levene who was a personal friend and suggested that Big Buy purchase his company. This was agreed and terms of £300,000 cash were offered and accepted, Mr Levene joining Big Buy to help Mr Green in the search for new store sites.

Big Buy moved quickly to rationalise the new acquisition in an endeavour to turn Foodfair around as well as utilising the additional purchasing power the increased turnover provided. Within 6 months, 5 of Foodfair's stores had been shut down realising nearly £45,000 and the remaining operations restored to profitability. In addition, Foodfair's purchasing, administration and distribution functions had been integrated into Big Buy resulting in the saving of over 50 staff. It was estimated that Foodfair's remaining stores had a profit potential of over £100,000 p.a. pretax which Big Buy hoped to achieve by 1974, and these earnings would be protected by the accumulated tax losses of some £300,000 incurred earlier by Foodfair.

HYPERMARKET DEVELOPMENTS

Mr Mellor believed that for the future large out-of-town stores with a minimum sales area of 40,000 square feet and ample parking facilities would become an increasingly important aspect of Big Buy's retail strategy. Mr Green and Mr Mellor had therefore undertaken a special study of hypermarket developments in France, where this type of store had shown spectacular growth in the late 1960s and early 1970s, and stores of up to 250,000 square feet had been developed.

Mr Mellor reported to the board in November 1971 that despite this spectacular growth there had, however, been 30 hypermarket failures in France. He therefore considered that despite the opening of Big Buy's own superstores which were in effect small hypermarkets, Big Buy had neither the personnel nor the expertise to risk the development of hypermarkets on its own. Mr Mellor was in favour of being able to call on the expertise of successful French hypermarket operators for at least the company's first hypermarket. Although some members of the board disputed the necessity to obtain this help, it was eventually agreed that Mr Mellor should explore the possibilities of working with a successful French operator.

As a result of further investigations, Mr Mellor was able to present to the Board in April 1972 a draft agreement for consideration between Société Générale des Grands Magasins Provinciales S.A. (SGGMP) and Big Buy. SGGMP was a company registered in France by a group of French retail operators for the purpose of developing hypermarkets in the southern and central part of France and especially around such cities as Lyons, Toulouse and Marseilles. The company operated a total of seven hypermarkets with net selling areas ranging between 44,000 and 110,000 square feet under the trade name Hypermarché de Lyons.

Under the suggested agreement with SGGMP it was proposed that a new company would be created, 51 per cent owned by Big Buy, 49 per cent by SGGMP, which would own and operate hypermarkets in the United Kingdom. SGGMP were to provide the initial expertise for the new company in exchange for 33 per cent of the shares in the new company worth £75,000 which would be paid for by Big Buy. Apart from this, however, all further capital in the new company would be provided jointly in proportion to their shareholdings. SGGMP were also to train Big Buy's own personnel in France in hypermarket operations. Although Big Buy had no specific sites available for hypermarket operations, it was hoped that an initial site would be found to permit opening of the joint venture's first store by the end of 1973 or early in 1974.

PLANS FOR THE FUTURE

Mr Mellor believed that Big Buy should become one of Britain's leading retailers by 1980. He hoped that by 1976 the number of Big Buy stores would be reduced from 143 to about 110 but that the average store size would be increased from around 4,500 square feet to nearer 17,550 square feet of selling space due to a strategy of concentrating on new superstores while phasing out superettes.

Having introduced a budgetary system in 1971, Mr Mellor moved on in 1972 to the preparation of Big Buy's first 5-year plan which would serve as the basis for identifying what needed to be done to fulfil the company's objectives for 1976. To help in the preparation of the company's plan, Mr Mellor turned to Total Strategic Systems Inc., an American consultancy company whose president, Mr Harvey Wainwright, had developed a unique system of strategic planning. This system included both top-down and bottom-up features in order to ensure the active participation in the planning process of all the company's senior and middle management.

As a result of the planning exercise, Mr Mellor predicted that Big Buy would reach sales of £180 million in 1976 or, allowing for an annual rate of inflation of 7 per cent, £236 million. Retail store selling space was expected to expand to nearly 2 million square feet with a major expansion coming in non-foods which were expected to account for 880,000 square feet in 1976 as compared with only 80,000 in 1972 and as a result non-food sales were expected to reach £41 million by 1976 (in constant £). Although pressure on trade margins was recognised and margins were expected to continue to decline, Mr Mellor nevertheless predicted pretax profits would expand to £5 million by 1976. Mr Mellor, commenting on Big Buy's expansion plans, added

> 'Food and non-food retailing to the mass consumer market is steadily growing and providing an increasing market for those companies interested in retailing. This pattern of expansion has been demonstrated in America and hypermarkets have opened on the Continent.

British consumers are as price conscious as consumers elsewhere, and this presents a massive opportunity to service their requirements for both foods and non-foods.

Tesco, for example, during 1971 and up to February this year, expanded their retail space by 500,000 square feet. Their business increased by about 16 per cent to almost £300 million. Forty new stores were opened in 1971 alone with an average floor space of about 12,000 square feet or more and they are planning 5 to 10 years ahead.

Sainsbury too pushed up their sales in 1971 by 18 per cent. During the past 3 years they opened 26 stores with a total of 353,000 square feet and in the next 3 years they plan to open 50 new stores adding to a total of 800,000 square feet more than they are managing now.

Our strategy, therefore, can be seen in these terms. First. administratively we must get the company into a streamlined, efficient and well-run operation. Second, we have to design and maintain an organisation and a management style which will maximise individual participation, provide good communications, gain above average motivation and keep out employee skills high. Third, we have to improve our corporate marketing image so that our sales per square foot go up to £2 per week on foods. Fourth, we want to establish distribution as a viable business so that we can distribute ourselves up to 96 per cent of the products sold through our retail space both internally and by joint ventures and acquisitions so that by 1976 we are operating over 1.5 million square feet of retail space.

This is an ambitious plan but with the new management team we have built I am confident it can be readily achieved.'

Critical to the success of Mr Mellor's plan was the search for new large store sites. Mr Green, who was especially involved in this activity, sounded a note of caution on this. 'Our main problem, as I have often told the board, is that we never get the "first bite of the cherry" as far as property is concerned and we only get offered the "leftovers" from the larger supermarket operators.' The South of England was proving extremely difficult for good sites especially for superstores or hypermarkets and as a result he and the property development department had begun investigating sites in the North of England. Indeed, in view of the company's proposed expansion the property development department's brief had been broadened to allow them to consider sites anywhere in the British Isles although 'adequate consideration of every circumstance was given to all aspects in each new instance'.

Nevertheless, Mr Mellor was confident, that, despite Mr Green's claim that Big Buy got the last bite of the cherry on new sites, good sites would become available. 'Furthermore.' he added, 'the company has now embarked on an ambitious expansion programme, and if we cannot find enough space in the South, it is therefore inevitable that we move North.'

EXHIBIT 7

Big Buy Supermarkets Ltd. Trading and Profit and Loss Account to 13 May 1972
(£000)

	Actual	%	Actual	%	Budget	%	Variance	%
SALES			15805.6	100	15498.3	100	(392.7)	
Cost of sales			12360.0		12668.7		308.7	0.5
BRANCH GROSS PROFIT			2845.6	18.7	2829.6	18.2	16.0	0.5
Add depot operating margins								
Meat			66.0					
Greengrocery			44.4	0.7	—	110.4		
GROSS MARGIN			2956.0	19.4	2829.6	18.2	126.4	1.2
Add Promotion allowance			68.7		—		150.2	1.0
Cash discount			81.5	1.0	(61.9)	0.4	34.7	0.2
Less Stock losses			(27.2)	0.2		2.0	(70.8)	0.5
Cost of trading stamps			380.8	2.5	310.0			
Stamps issued	405.2							
Deduct allowance and discount	24.4							
NET MARGIN			2698.2	17.7	2457.7	15.8	240.5	1.9

	Detail							
Deduct Branch expenses								
Net rents	270.8	1.8						
Rates	101.4	0.7						
Light and heating	140.0	0.9						
Insurance	25.2	0.1						
Wages and salaries	933.0	6.1						
Cleaning	40.8	0.3						
Repairs and maintenance	49.7	0.3						
Depreciation	117.3	0.8						
Other	17.9	0.1	1697.5	11.2	1648.4	10.6	(49.1)	0.6
BRANCH NET PROFIT			1001.7	6.5	809.3	5.2	191.4	1.3
Deduct Distribution expenses	200.6							
Retaining expenses	174.7							
Administration expenses	374.1		749.4	4.9	597.7	3.8	(151.7)	1.1
COMPANY NET PROFIT			252.3	1.6	211.6	1.4	40.7	0.2

*Excluding Foodfair Ltd. which showed a net profit of £11,000 over the period.
Source: Company Records.

BOARD CHANGE

In March 1972 Mr Abraham Goldstein died, and in April Mr Green and Mr Mellor recommended to the board that this loss meant Big Buy urgently needed someone with financial and management expertise to assist the company. It was therefore agreed that Mr Gerald Battersby of Muller Day be invited to replace Mr Goldstein. Mr Battersby therefore joined the Big Buy board in May 1972.

THE SITUATION IN MID-1972

Following 1970's profit decline, the first half of 1971 saw a further fall in pretax profits to only £163,000 on sales of £18 million. But in the second half of the year the first benefits started to show through from the various changes made, and profits began to recover. Although traditionally the second half of the year was better than the first half, sales expanded to £20 million and profits to £416,000.

The early results for 1972 now available monthly to management showed a continuation of the improved trend. By June the latest available figures for Big Buy's fourth-week period (see Exhibit 7) revealed sales and profits running ahead of budget. It appeared that for the year overall pre-tax profits would comfortably exceed the £825,000 budgeted as a result of the opening of the company's new superstores and further developments of new discount operations.

Styles of Management

19

Securicor Limited

Securicor Limited was the largest commercial security organisation in the United Kingdom with a group turnover in 1978 of £121 million and pre-tax profits of £5.4 million (detailed financial statistics are given in Exhibits 1 and 2). In addition, the Securicor Group, of which Securicor Limited was a member, operated a range of security services throughout Europe and in Hong Kong and several African countries. The Group also owned interests, engaged in office cleaning, specialist parcel deliveries and property. In the UK, Securicor was estimated to hold a market share of

EXHIBIT 1

Securicor Profit and Loss Account 1971–1978

(£000)

	1973	1974	1975	1976	1977	1978
Group Turnover	40,659	46,730	61,554	81,806	100,828	121,080
Group Profit Before Tax						
Hotel Division	473	—	—	—	—	—
Security Division	1,719	1,996	2,095	2,688	3,541	4,085
Finance Division	—	632	660	738	979	1,066
Associated Company Profits	—	—	—	—	—	265
	2,192	2,628	2,755	3,426	4,520	5,416
Taxation	1,026	1,553	1,550	1,209	1,275	1,618
Profit After Taxation	1,166	1,075	1,205	2,217	3,245	3,798
Outside Shareholders Interest	495	437	488	956	1,424	1,634
Extraordinary Items		140	10	—	20	187
Net Profit Available for Distribution	671	498	707	1,261	1,801	2,351
Dividends	144	146	155	165	182	356
Profit Retained	527	352	552	1,096	1,629	1,995

Source: Annual Reports.

EXHIBIT 2

Securicor Group Consolidated Balance Sheet for Year Ended September 30th

Year	1973	1974	1975	1976	1977	1978
Fixed Assets	6,513	7,895	10,777	13,100	20,661	27,029
Development Expenditure	565	989	1,265	585	515	415
Subsidiary Companies	1,419	1,327	1,227	1,254	1,252	1,232
Investments	162	31	574	1,174	2,008	—
Associated Company						
	8,659	10,242	13,854	16,113	24,436	28,988
Current Assets						
Investments	—	—	—	—	—	4,402
Stocks	635	1,218	1,969	2,402	3,290	3,669
Debtors	6,831	8,538	9,412	8,533	11,521	11,631
Bank & Deposit Balances	6,317	5,313	4,395	6,358	4,580	7,193
TOTAL ASSETS	13,783	15,069	15,776	17,293	19,391	26,895
Current Liabilities						
Trade and Other Creditors	5,844	6,689	7,522	9,672	13,425	15,407
Hire Purchase Creditors	—	354	1,183	2,005	4,443	6,708
Taxation	1,826	2,276	2,280	2,197	1,815	1,713
Bank Overdraft & Advances	2,179	2,447	3,138	1,118	2,535	1,311
Proposed Dividends	107	89	95	103	115	223
	9,956	11,855	14,218	15,095	22,333	25,362
Net Current Assets	3,837	3,214	1,558	2,198	(2,942)	1,533
Total Net Assets	12,486	13,456	15,412	18,311	21,494	30,521
Financed by Share Capital	2,275	2,275	3,074	3,074	3,074	3,257
Reserves	5,573	5,898	5,623	7,150	8,750	11,408
Shareholders Funds	7,848	8,173	8,697	10,224	11,824	14,665
Outside Shareholders Interest	559	3,769	4,178	5,576	6,627	10,343
Loans	3,631	595	612	2,302	2,341	4,546
Deferred Taxation	448	919	1,925	409	702	967
	12,486	13,456	15,412	18,311	21,494	30,521

Source: Annual Reports.

around 65% in 1978. The strategy which had led to this dominant position is the subject of this case.

THE SECURITY INDUSTRY

The security industry in Britain grew rapidly and profitably after the end of the 1950s, once the police had almost completely withdrawn from escort services for cash in transit. The termination of this service coincided with a sharp increase in attacks on money on the move and with greater insurance pressures upon management for higher levels of security. A rapid expansion in private cash-in-transit services filled the void left by the withdrawal of the police. Comparable internal losses in industrial and commercial establishments to which the police had no automatic rights of entry led to a similar demand for guard services. This trend had continued as awareness of the need for better fire protection and security had increased.

Industrial and commercial organisations could set up their own security systems, but many recognised the advantages of using professional services, particularly as security technology became more sophisticated. Public sector enterprises, too, had found they needed supplementary custom-designed security services. By 1978 the British Security industry Association (BSIA) had over 800 members, although the Metropolitan Police estimated that there were some 2000 firms operating in the security industry.

Most security firms were very small and operated solely on a highly localised basis. Only about a dozen firms operated nationwide. The services most commonly provided were alarm system installation (47% of companies), guard dogs (39%), mobile guards (38%) and static guards (32%). Other services were offered much less frequently and a majority of firms (60%) offered only one service.

A few large firms dominated the market with Securicor being by far the largest. Group 4 was Securicor's nearest competitor and was the British subsidiary of Securitas International, a Swedish company and the largest non-American security organisation in the world. Group 4, with a turnover of around £22 million, held about 12% of the UK market. Security Express, a subsidiary of Thomas de la Rue was active in the cash transit and guarding segments but was much smaller than Securicor. Brinks MAT, a subsidiary of the US Brinks Corporation, was an important competitor in the transport of bullion and other precious metals.

There were no legal barriers to entering the security industry, although the main participants were actively pressing the Home Office for the introduction of some form of licensing system. This was expected to help weed out the many small operators who, it was felt, did not possess the resources, ability and perhaps integrity required for security work. Moreover, with a licensing scheme in being the security companies hoped

L

EXHIBIT 3

Insurance Losses Through Crime

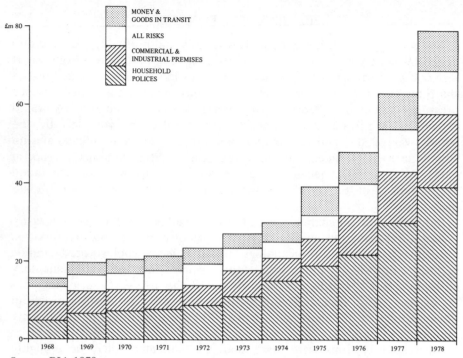

Source: BIA 1979.

to gain access to police records to assist in vetting potential employees. The other major difficulty faced by would-be competitors was the cost involved in establishing a nationwide system of communications and logistics to rival that of Securicor in particular.

At the end of the 1970s, crime rates were still increasing annually as was the value of property lost by crime, fire or vandalism, as shown in Exhibit 3, and leading to a growing demand for security services. Some changes were also occurring in the technology of the industry, with a growing use of electronic surveillance systems and the introduction of new systems such as electronic fund transfer to reduce the amounts of cash transported. In the 1980s therefore it was expected that there would be some reduction in the use of labour, an increase in skill levels and greater dependence on electronic systems.

EARLY HISTORY OF SECURICOR

In 1935 a group of London householders, disturbed by the amount of theft and petty crime in their neighbourhood, clubbed together to form a small company called Night Watch Services Limited to protect their interests. The company provided uniformed guards to patrol (often on bicycle) private property such as flats and penthouses in Mayfair. In 1939 the Hampstead branch broke away and formed another company, Night Guards Limited, which provided similar services.

During the war, the companies all but disappeared and by 1945, Night Guards Limited consisted of just two guards. Then, in late 1945, Henry Tiarks and Lord Willingdon (later Chairman of Securicor to 1966) revived Night Guards Limited, mainly as a means of providing work for ex-servicemen. Very soon after this the services offered were extended to cover commercial premises. The company thus formed became Securicor.

The security industry at that time consisted of Securicor and a few others (such as Factory Guards Limited, later Group 4), but no great growth occurred with services essentially those of guarding premises. Then in 1955, a young man called Roy Winklemann, who had spent some time studying the more developed security industry in the USA, returned to the UK and started the Armoured Car Company, based in West Drayton. This organisation carried cash between banks and to and from bank customers in armoured vans. Winklemann imported many ideas from the USA, such as American-style uniforms and helmets and the guards in the vans carried shotguns. The 'paramilitary' image did not endear the company to either the public or the press. However, as organised crime was on the increase in the UK, the idea quickly won support and soon Securicor had three of its own vans. Other firms such as Security Express (founded by Thomas de la Rue and Wells Fargo) also entered this new market and competition increased. In spite of the increase in business. Securior's financial performance was not very good, and by 1956 the company looked as if it would fail.

One of Securicor's clients was the Allied Hotels–Kensington Palace Hotel Group, which was in the control of the Erskine family and run by Denys Erskine. Keith Erskine (Denys' younger brother) persuaded him to buy Securicor for the hotel group. At the same time, Securicor was earning some £50,000 on a £450,000 turnover and the purchase price was £125,000. The Erskine family took little interest in the company and Securicor's fortunes continued to decline and it was not long before the company was losing money. As a result, Keith Erskine began to take a more definite interest in Securicor's activities. In 1960 a Securicor guard was seriously beaten up and largely as a consequence of this Keith Erskine took charge.

THE KEITH ERSKINE ERA

Keith Erskine's main work at the time was as senior partner of Hextall, Erskine and Company, the firm of solicitors he had founded and who acted as legal advisers to the hotel group and the Erskine family. In 1960 he pushed this work aside and set up his bed in the Securicor headquarters. He remained there for the next five years, going home only at weekends, in an attempt to put the firm back on its feet again. He followed a hard regimen for a man in his early fifties, rising at 5.00 am every day and taking a swim in the Serpentine before starting his 18 hour working day! Members of his staff were often invited to join him on these early morning outings.

UK Developments

Such determined action paid off and by 1963 Securicor was well established on an upward growth path. It as also in 1963 that Securicor purchased the Armoured Car Company where the effect of a series of criminal raids and a critical public inquiry had left the company in a perilous financial state. Keith Erskine seeing a big future for the cash-carrying business in other areas, apart from banks, bought it.

Erskine examined the trends of organised crime in the UK and saw that the generally improved road communications made it much easier for criminals based in London to do a job in a provincial town and make a quick getaway. In this manner major crime was extending into areas that had been relatively free hitherto. Also, because of the national operations of Securicor customers, Erskine saw the advantage of nationwide coverage from a competitive point of view. These thoughts, coupled with the introduction of the cash-carrying service, started (1960) the construction of a widespread branch network which had reached 280 by the mid-1970s.

Effective control and communications was seen as fundamental if the increase in the number of bank raids and other crime was to be contained. Therefore, the programme of expansion included the building of customised communications centres, of which there were nearly sixty by the mid-1970s, and the linking of all centres with sophisticated facilities including telex, radio and links into an on-line computer system. In the early days the situation had been somewhat different. Rather than wait for the business to come to Securicor, Erskine sent out almost raw recruits into the provinces to set up new branches. This was quite a risky business since Securicor had no real services to offer in the new areas and the 'branch' would often be set up in a vacant shop with just one chair, one table and a telephone. Security Express, the main competitor in the cash-carrying business, followed a different strategy and only built up branches in areas where business had first been found. The more positive approach of Securicor combined with some shrewd property speculation by Keith Erskine resulted in a complete national coverage for Securicor unrivalled by any competitor.

The result was that in the 14 years Erskine was in control, profits multiplied 45 times on a turnover that increased nearly 85 times. Virtually all of the growth was achieved without recourse to acquisition, except for the purchase in 1973 of a small firm of combined security guards and cleaning contractors at a cost of £375,000.

EXHIBIT 4
Securicor Group Shareholding Structure

Securicor Group Ltd.
| (52.05%)

Security Services Ltd.

Securicor Subsidiary Holdings Ltd.
Securicor Ltd.
Securicor Mobile Ltd.
Night Security Ltd.
Janitorial Services Ltd.
Securicor (Malaya) SDN. BHD.
Securicor (Malawi) Ltd.
Securicor (Kenya) Ltd.
Securicor (Zambia) Ltd.
Securicor (Copperbelt) Ltd.
Securicor (Hong Kong) Ltd.
Securicor (Singapore) Ltd.

---

*There are also minor operating subsidiaries in Norway, France, Germany, Holland, Belgium, Luxembourg and Cyprus.

The growth in the security side of the hotel group's business was such that by 1966 it had become the major profit earner. In 1973 most of the hotel interests of the group were sold and the security services were reorganised into a new company. Keith Erskine, who had been Chairman and Managing Director of the hotel group since his brother had died some years earlier, was now in control of Securicor Group Limited (formerly Associated Hotels Limited) which had a majority shareholding in Security Services Limited (formerly Kensington Palace Hotels Limited), of which Securicor was one of a number of UK and overseas subsidiaries. The shareholding structure of the group is shown in Exhibit 4.

Overseas Expansion

From the early 1960s, Securicor followed a policy of expansion overseas. The first moves were into Australia and New Zealand, but because of a multitude of well-established local operators, these ventures did not do well. As Erskine's strategy was to avoid confrontation with entrenched competition, the Australian branches were closed down in 1972. Securicor next entered Singapore and Malaysia where the company was more successful and branches were operating satisfactorily by 1968.

Sir Derek Erskine, Keith's elder brother, had settled in Kenya and was chief whip in Jomo Kenyatta's African National Party. Securicor was therefore attracted to East Africa and three subsidiaries were set up in Kenya, Uganda and Malawi. These were still operating in the late 1970s, except for the Ugandan subsidiary which had been nationalised in 1973. By 1970, another subsidiary had been established in Zambia.

Securicor had attempted to get a firm footing in Europe, but here again there were many well-established firms and the business was of a different nature to that in Britain. The branches that had been established were small and were basically European depots for the Special Delivery Service. In the company report of 1973, Erskine outlined his strategy for growth in Europe which was to be through opening up new branches rather than by acquisition, as this was seen as a safer method and would save money in the long run. He had hoped to build up the European turnover to about £4 million over the next three years, at a cost of £2 million.

Securicor had experienced some cultural problems in trying to introduce its 'mutual company' concept to countries where the local staff could not seem to grasp its significance, where money was more important and corruption a common occurrence. Nevertheless, by 1973 turnover from overseas branches had reached £3.9 million and profits were £400,000.

KEITH ERSKINE—CHIEF HELPER SECURICOR

The success of Securicor owed a great deal to the personality and philosophy of Mr Erskine. He came from a family with a tradition of public service, his father having been an MP. He was born in Scotland in 1908 and was a Kings Scholar at Westminster School. After qualifying as a Solicitor in 1933 he saw war service in the Middle East and Italy with the Eighth Army. He reached the rank of Captain in the Royal Artillery having joined as a ranker. His army experience taught him the importance of communications as later became apparent with Securicor's use of radio control and telex linkages between the branches.

Keith Erskine was a founder of Hextall Erskine and Company, a firm of London Solicitors. Due to his involvement with Securicor and other companies he ceased practicing as a Solicitor but remained a senior partner in the firm until his death. While practicing law he first got his taste of management by being invited onto the boards of various companies for whom his firm worked.

Amongst his industrial appointments, Erskine was a Director and past Chairman of the London Advisory Board of the Norwich Union Assurance Company. This connection proved fruitful for a number of reasons. First, for arranging mortgage finance and leaseback agreements for the acquisition of property in which to house the growth of Securicor. Second, it helped in the provision of insurance, an important point considering the high risk of either injury to a member of Securicor's workforce or of a substantial loss of clients' property. Third, it introduced Erskine to the idea of a mutual company which he later adopted as part of Securicor's defence against nationalisation.

Erskine was an active and energetic man who ate sparingly and did not smoke or drink. Fitness was almost an obsession and he brought this attitude to the operations of Securicor where he said 'In our job we have to keep fit. Frugality is our watchword, luxury is wasteful and weakening'. He was very self-disciplined and believed this was a characteristic that should be developed in all Securicor's employees.

With his family background and the reinforcement of his professional training, Erskine developed a very idealistic philosophy. This idealism became absolute in the case of Securicor when, in the late 1960s and early 1970s, it was used as part of a strategy both to defend and develop the company.

Erskine believed that 'People do not want to be managed, they want to be helped'. His own position in Securicor, which would conventionally have been referred to as Managing Director, was known within the company as Chief Helper. He encouraged all managers within Securicor to be referred to as helpers. The formal company hierarchy was removed ('There are no gradations, just people') as were all the perks that traditionally went with advancement. Erskine said 'I don't believe that one man can be worth £20 week and another £30,000 a year. There are differences in what a man can do for a company but not such enormous differences'.

It was partly because of this belief that Erskine pursued a policy of decentralistation. He aimed to drive the level of decision-making right down to the individual man, at the same time recognising that this would lead to involvement and job enrichment. This was considered particularly crucial in a job such as that of a night watchman which was generally extremely boring and tedious. With such jobs, or where there was the high risk associated with handling large quantities of cash, the morale of the company's workforce was vitally important. To maintain morale Erskine felt it important that the top management team should 'get out into the field'. In line with this, he himself occasionally did a nightwatch or took part in a cash-in-transit run. In referring to this involvement, Erskine used military analogies saying that all the best generals in history were never aloof from the battle and they were always in touch with the ordinary trooper.

Erskine did not believe in long-term planning but was more concerned with actually getting things done. One of his mottos within Securicor was 'Get down to the NITTY GRITTY, never mind the AIRY FAIRY, the TALKIE TALKIE must lead to the DOEY DOEY'.

ERSKINE'S POLICIES

Erskine displayed essentially an entrepreneurial style in his approach to Securicor. He considered that market research was a substitute for action. He said 'We must go in and do it and if it does not work we get out'. Erskine never moved into an area or service where there existed an established competitor. When he sent out people from London to establish branches throughout Britain there was no guarantee that there would be any business for the branch. Conversely, if there was any business, the branch could rely on being the market leader. In 1960 there were 3 branches, while in April 1974 there were some 280 branches throughout the UK.

The growth of Securicor brought with it the problem of property financing. This was solved by arranging leaseback agreements with the Norwich Union Assurance Society. However, Erskine also anticipated Securicor's growth and he set up a department to search for property bargains which could be bought out of the company's retained earnings and held until expansion required it to be used as a functional company building.

The property department within Securicor was originally responsible for devising conversions of suitable premises, but it came to supervise the construction of purpose-built security centres, of which there were over 60 in Britain. Erskine claimed that Securicor was the only security organisation in Europe to have developed a specialised building programme on any scale.

Erskine also broadened the range of services that Securicor offered, usually by developing extensions to already existing services. Thus the Special Delivery Service started in 1965 to carry computer tapes was extended to carry good less risk-prone than cash and could deliver to anywhere in the UK within 24 hours.

Erskine produced a high morale within Securicor's workforce in a number of ways. His policy of egalitarianism throughout the company removed any perceived unfairness in the distribution of rewards for the job done. At the same time this policy had the sound business logic of cutting down overheads for such items as personal secretaries, large offices and plush furniture. He also encouraged the senior management to become involved in some of the company's actual operations.

The egalitarian ethic also promoted the desired decentralisation. In the mid-1960s, Securicor was growing rapidly and had been based in a central office situated in London. Decentralisation cut the London office staff and Erskine subsequently profitably sub-let one half of the 100,000 sq ft of office space that Securicor had on lease in London. The company operations became largely local in character but were based on an extensive branch network.

In order to reinforce the spirit of commitment to the corporate culture, Erskine devised 'good housekeeping' meetings. These occurred weekly at each branch and involved all the workforce of that branch, except the night watchmen who might nominate a representative. This meeting was charged with the management of the branch. Although Erskine believed in democracy, he only believed in what he termed 90% industrial democracy.

The missing 10% was to made up by 'wise guidance' which could provide leadership rather than driving force and could veto any stupid decisions. Who decided if a decision was stupid was left begging, but presumably the ultimate appeal would have been to Erskine himself as the Chief Helper on 'the continuous sitting National Goodhousekeeping Department'. These measures had the effect of producing a commitment to the corporate culture. This aim was highlighted by another of Erskine's company mottos, 'Not "I" but "WE"'.

Erskine wrote of himself that 'being a Scotsman by origin, I sought to reconcile ethics with practical business'. As a result Erskine formed Securicor into a mutual company in 1966. Overseas subsidiary companies did not become mutual companies because of the higher risks. Shareholders' profits were thus limited to no more than 5% of turnover, everything else going to the benefit of the company's workers, the customers and the State.

The workers benefitted through higher wages and annual merit awards. The pay of guards rose by nearly double the national wages index over the period 1961 to 1971. Morale improved as the workers no longer perceived that they were being exploited. Erskine said 'when profits are moderated, the workers know they are getting a fair deal'. The customers benefitted because the prices were not determined by demand but rather by a moderate fixed percentage of the turnover. The State benefitted because the wealth which Securicor would have accrued had it charged more for its services could instead be invested elsewhere. Thus Securicor could be seen to be asssisting in reducing inflation.

Such were the ethics of the mutual company. There were also practical advantages. First, the growth in Securicor by the mid-1960s had given rise to suggestions by politicians that Securicor should be nationalised. By pointing to the fact that Securicor was not exploiting its virtual monopolist position by making undue profits, Erskine erected a defence against this threat. Second, by limiting its profits to 5% of turnover, Securicor's pricing was extremely competitive. Erskine was quoted as saying: Like Henry Ford, I believe in big turnover and low margins'. In 1968 the profit limitation was reduced to $4\frac{1}{2}$% and in the 1970s the profit had averaged out at 4%.

Throughout their growth, Securicor and other security organisations had come under attack for being private armies. Keith Erskine was very sensitive to this charge and invited distinguished men to be members of the board of the operating company. In 1970 he began a scheme to change the corporate image of Securicor so that it appeared to be less of a public threat. The slogan 'Securicor Cares' was developed and appeared on all Securicor vans and trucks. Company advertisements in the press appeared with the headline that 'Securicor Cares for Customers, Co-Workers and the Common Good'.

These advertisements were also used by Erskine to set out his corporate philosophy:

'They say it is love that makes the world go round. Certainly, we could not take hate or fear as recipes for Securicor.

'Leaning on men more than machines, we have obeyed Pope's edict: "The proper study of Mankind is Man". Our answers have met with some success. Indeed we have figured in the *Management Today* list of the ten most successful companies.

'Until I was pitchforked into Securicor 13 years ago, as its head, I was a lawyer and much concerned with justice. I could not accept the present company law as adequate—so we formed the mutual company, both as a unilateral amendment and a reply to Karl Marx's prospect of dreary and eternal conflict.

'Justice, our first pillar, has a cold ring. Care was the second and missing motive. Four years ago we proclaimed that "Securicor Cares". But how to demonstrate it?

1. 'We eliminated the conflict of interest by the mutual company. All profits over the safe minimum go to the workers and customers.
2. 'We respect the Dignity of Man.
3. 'We rebuke prejuduce, whether of race, class, religion, rank or sex.
4. 'We judge merit by character, rather than slickness.
5. 'We regard self-discipline as ennobling, enforced discipline as degrading.
6. 'We treat our men as educated and adult, capable, with a little help and guidance, of running their own show.
7. 'We lift motivation, whether for employers or employees, above the lowest common denominator of greed or necessity—men we have found will join together in a "common effort to a noble end". So we have introduced the theme of Caring for the Common Good . . . .
8. 'We have invented a new machinery of management and a new nomenclature. Each of our branches is run by a weekly meeting of the Good Housekeeping Team. The loose ends between branches are tied up by a sub area aid team, and anything else by a regional aid team. The aim is management in depth. Specialists exist but their job is mainly to teach our men to become all-rounders, batsmen and bowlers. In Caesar's 10th Legion each man carried the tools for fighting and for building roads. Our critics have said these are our old friends the Works Councils. Maybe, but they have teeth. They don't just debate the canteen food. Increasingly they run the show. Decisions for the faint hearted are refused: but not help or advice.
9. 'Men do not want to be managed—they want to be helped. But the need for leadership and for inspiration is as vital as before, only of

a more quiet patient and unselfish kind, giving credit to the men. Human relations pose a challenge as exciting and rewarding as music, art or writing. They demand the same dedication.

'As for names: Manager equals Helper. Management equals Guidance. Supervisor equals Career-Trainer. Supervision (that stunting work which promotes "them" and "us") equals caring/training. Training after initial schooling is continuous by telephone, radio themes and visits (the sharing of skills is part of caring) . . . If service is the central element in our lives, we must care for those we serve.

'Does it work! The proof of the pudding! Not all the time in all places, not without some inevitable reactions, but better than any of us dreamed. The success of democracy depends on people being responsible. Our workers, like our voters, are basically responsible. "The third bulwark of all human endeavour is Truth". In Securicor fighting dishonesty, honesty is our stock in trade. We have made it one of our aims to observe the highest code of this. But it is human to err, and we only claim to be steering towards the peak of integrity.

'But if success is the result of these aims, it can be toppled by pride. So in humility one finds the last and surest bulwark. All of us at the top in Securicor inform and work alongside the men. There are no separate lavatories, close covered carpets or luxury cars. We eschew ostentation. We avoid over-indulgence because in our job we have to keep fit. But democracy means equity not equality. We reward merit by higher salary, but not star salary, for none of us are stars. We are all in shirt sleeves. We are all co-workers.

'In Securicor we have ceased to follow the false gods of doubt and division. We try in all modesty to follow the true gods of brotherhood and service. As Emerson said: "When the half gods go, the gods arrive".'

On 23rd of April 1974 the company was devastated by the news that Keith Erskine had been killed in a car crash.

THE SMITH YEARS

After the death of Keith Erskine, he was succeeded by Peter Smith. Also a solicitor, Smith had joined Hextall Erskine in 1951 and by 1966 was concentrating solely on Securicor. In 1968 he joined the board and was joint Vice Chairman before becoming Chairman in 1974. Smith, although an admirer of many aspects of Erskine's approach, believed that Securicor with a turnover of £50 million and interests extending across Europe, was ready for change. He stated, 'It was my job to inject some conventional management'.

Under Smith's leadership, Securicor diversified further. Making use of the £6.5 million cash received from the sale of its hotel interests, the company expanded in office cleaning and by 1975, 2000 people were employed in this activity. Smith also noted the falling growth rate in the cash-in-transit market. Although one of Securicor's major activities, this service operated on low margins yet was labour intensive and required expensive armoured vehicles.

Making use of the widespread branch and communications network, Securior started a special parcel delivery service aimed at the gap between a normal parcels service and freight traffic. Offering guaranteed next-day delivery at a rate about double that charged by the Post Office the service proved popular and was extended to Europe with daily trucking based in Brussels. Since 1975 the average growth rate for the parcels service had been around 35% per annum. In 1978 via rights issue, Securicor raised £3 million to finance an entry into a specialist freight service which permitted the carriage of items up to 100 kilos vs a 40 kilo maximum for the parcels service. The new freight service was carefully segregated from existing operations and 16 special depots were established. Securicor invested a further £2 million in 1979 to build up its overnight parcels division by providing new vehicles and establishing 7 new depots.

Smith reversed Securicor's earlier policy of avoiding the security equipment market. Securisound was established as a joint venture with an electronics manufacturer, Sound Diffusion, to develop electronic systems to combat the growing number of attacks on security vehicles.

The traditional policy of financing investment from earnings had also been modified by Smith toward a more conventional approach, making use of new debt and equity funds. Thus, by 1978, leverage had reached 44% and was more in line with the industry average. The company continued to invest heavily in custom developed property for the needs of the security division.

Group Financial Structure

The financial structure of the Securicor Group was somewhat unusual. The ultimate holding company, Securicor Group Limited, owned 52.05% of Security Services Limited, an intermediate holding company which in turn held all the shares of 24 operating companies including Securicor Limited. The majority of both the voting and non-voting shares in Securicor Group were owned or controlled by the directors. In total they had control of 2.36 million enfranchised stock units out of a total of 2.83 million issued shares. Mrs Denise Delaney, a member of the Erskine family, was the largest equity holder with 1.4 million shares of 48.99%. Other directors collectively owned 0.46% of the voting stock while other shares were held in trusts to which Securicor Group directors were trustees. Mrs Delaney and other directors held only small holdings in Security Services Limited, but had control of this company and its subsidiaries via their control of Securicor Group. The Group had come in for criticism for its capital structure but there had been resistance to any change by Mrs. Delaney and other members of the Securicor Group Board.

THE SECURICOR RANGE OF SERVICES

Securicor offered a comprehensive range of nearly 40 specialised services covering most aspects of security. Further, the company claimed that if a client had a need for a service not in the current range, then within reason the company would initiate it. Indeed, many of Securicor's services had originated in this way. The main services offered by Securicor were Guarding, Money Movement and Paypak, the Parcel Service, Office Cleaning and Radio Telephone Services.

Guarding

The original foundation of Securicor, the Guarding service, could be subdivided into two: internal guards and mobile, radio-controlled operations.

The internal guards service was primarily concerned with providing adequate protection of invariably high value premises against break-ins, fire and flood, arson, terrorism and other acts of vandalism. Guards could work alone or as part of a team in some cases using dogs. The team was supported by a network of control centres and monitoring by a team of night supervisors including telephone contacts at regular intervals. Each Securicor guard was carefully screened before acceptance and was also trained in fire prevention and as a doghandler.

Where the value of property or its contents did not justify the use of an internal guard, Securicor offered a mobile patrol service. This was regarded as a deterrent against vandals, thieves and fire and flood. Coverage could be tailored to the requirements of the user and included internal and external visits, round the clock coverage and immediate contact with the operations centre to ensure rapid alerts to the police and/or other public services.

Money Movement and Paypak

The foundation of Securicor's growth in the 1960s, the cash in transit services covered every kind of cash movement. In addition, Securicor offered its Paypak service which involved breaking down bulk cash into wage packets for bulk delivery or individual distribution at a work site. Securicor took full responsibility for the cash and valuables it carried until the moment they were handed over to the user. All cargo was fully insured, and should the guards be attacked and the money stolen, Securicor undertook to replace the amount with the minimum of delay.

Special Parcel Service

A development of the cash in transit operations, Securicor offered a range of special parcel delivery services. Based on a network of around 300 branches in the UK, Securicor delivered between more than 18,000 collection and delivery points each day. With an emphasis on security and reliability, Securicor employed a National Planning Department to co-ordinate its fleet of some 2000 vans. A number of specialist supplementary services had evolved around the parcel service, including a contract parcel service for volume users, the Inter City Flier service emphasising speed and maximum security, Securicor Data Services which specialised in carrying computer data, Air Cargo service, Radiac, a service specialising in the carriage of radio-active materials and the European Parcel Service.

Office Cleaning

Securicor offered a general cleaning service using up-to-date equipment, some of which was specially designed to provide dust-free cleaning in computer centres, laboratories and other special case areas. The normal service included the cleaning and maintenance of both internal and external office and factory premises.

Radio Telephone Services

Centred upon its extensive communications network, Securicor had developed a wide range of radio telephone services for both business and private individuals. These services included Highway Link, aimed at the commercial haulage operator designed to help combat the theft of high value loads; Linkline, a service co-ordinated with the Automobile Association for use by salesmen, business executives and the like to provide information on travel and weather conditions; and Maritime, a similar service for coastal waters and inland waterway users.

Securicor also offered a wide range of other security related services including store detectives; security hardware and alarm installation; security consultancy, ID card preparation and dog kennels and training.

ORGANISATION STRUCTURE

Under Peter Smith the organisation structure of Securicor had changed little from the personalised system created by Keith Erskine. With its emphasis upon industrial democracy there was no formal structure, although within each branch there were a number of permanent positions such as Branch or Business Manager, Cash in Transit Manager and Security Delivery Services Manager. Other positions within a branch might be allocated on a rota basis amongst the guards and patrolmen. This was facilitated by a union agreement to ensure no demarcation disputes.

Upon joining the company, each new recruit spent time at one of the training schools spread throughout the country to learn how the organisation operated. Industrial democracy was developed through the weekly branch Good Housekeeping Meeting. When first conceived these meetings had been permitted to make up their own agendas but this had later been replaced by the creation of the National Good Housekeeping Department to provide 'wise guidance' for the democracy by drawing up a very precise and comprehensive agenda. Decision-making rested with the branches with the helper there to provide guidance and advice, although he could impose a veto if he judged the meeting to have acted irresponsibly.

This system meant that each branch could be almost autonomous, a fact which gave rise to problems when there were customers whose service was covered by several branches. To overcome this Erskine had formed Aid Teams. These consisted of some 15 people drawn from a geographic sub-area which in turn was defined by a group of between 4 and 6 branches. The Aid Teams included men who had experience in all branches of Securicor plus 2 or 3 ladies on the administrative side. Erskine defined their role as being such that 'if there is a problem at one of their branches, the Aid Team can converge on it and give whatever help is required from first aid to a more lasting therapy'. Sub-area Aid Teams met fortnightly and were co-ordinated through regional Aid Teams, which in turn were run through a national Aid Team originally led by Erskine himself. The country was divided into 10 regions which were further divided into 50 sub-areas incorporating all the branches.

The branch and sub-area helpers were largely responsible for appointments and recommendations for the merit reward scheme. Promotion was based on merit only and this was judged in terms of integrity, industry and unselfishness. As Erskine had noted, 'We promote on character'. This was further enhanced by Erskine's dislike of using experts. Under Erskine Securicor had never employed a chartered accountant, although for a while it farmed out the preparation of the monthly accounts to a professional firm. Erskine was eventually advised to recruit a £15,000 a year finance man. In reply to this he dismissed the external accountants and persevered with a system of management that he developed and which was maintained by a 'collection of girls'.

The regional Aid Teams were known as CATs (Co-Workers Action Teams) and they provided much of the leadership and encouragement that was given by Erskine in the days before decentralisation. A similar function was provided at the weekly branch meetings through the appointment within the company of some 500 'Professors'. These were older men within the organisation who could provide wisdom and guidance through a half-hour lecture and a half-hour question period given before each Good Housekeeping Meeting.

In line with the corporate image that Securicor 'Cares', the company had also appointed some 400 night and day 'Carers'. Erskine had defined their jobs as to 'care for the men, to act as an elder brother, or perhaps in the case of the young'uns as a father—to explain and to teach—to solve all their problems. Also to care for the customers, who prefer to get it from the horse's mouth than from a salesman however silver tongued'.

With operating control extablished at branch and regional level, there had been no need for a large head office staff and no specialists. The Chief Helper had a small knot of 'assistants' and staff officers, some of whom performed reasonably well defined co-ordinating functions, while others were there to carry out any task that might be set them, such as developing a new line of business or checking up on the competition. Certain non-executive directors were occasionally called in to help with specific operations. Members of the board of the operating company had been chosen for the specific help they might be able to give in certain situations, as well as for their distinguished reputations and influential connections.

AIMS OF SECURICOR

Despite the death of Keith Erskine, his philosophy largely lived on and was reflected in the Aims of the organisation which had remained unchanged from those stated by Erskine in his 1972 Chairman's Review:

'Aims of Securicor (a mutual company):
1. To observe the highest code of business conduct.
2. To devolve and involve; to enrich both jobs and lives; to combine private enterprise with social justice; to care for the individual.
3. To put principle before expediency and make sure our word is our bond.
4. Whilst not deviating from what is practical to enrol the idealism of youth.
5. To ignore class or race; to judge only by merit; to work in comradeship.
6. To divide more fairly the fruits of investment and work by means of the mutual company.
7. To combine what is best in public services, e.g. devotion to duty, with what is best in private endeavour, e.g. adaptability.
8. To express in the terms of guarding and watching Man's regard for his neighbour and wish to serve him.
9. In sum, to seek Love, Truth and Justice.

It is human to err. We in Securicor regret our errors; but slowly, painfully and persistently we are climbing to a peak of unimpeachable integrity where Service is an end, not just a means.

To the cynic we reply that these aims result in higher morale, goodwill and reward to our mutual company partners, i.e. the customers, co-workers, shareholders and the Nation. Business cannot be divorced from living; both should be nobly done.'

20

Scott Bader Company Ltd.

Early 1977 was a period of change for Scott Bader. Firstly the organisation was being restructured to afford its members a greater degree of involvement in company affairs. Although the employees already 'owned' the company, a number of people felt that changes were necessary to fulfil the objectives underlying common ownership.

Secondly, the company was about to recruit a new managing director, the former managing director having left to take up another appointment. The method of selection and appointment would, of course, have to be consistent with the company's philosophies, and the person appointed would have to work within these while ensuring that the company's past performance was at least maintained.

COMPANY BACKGROUND

Ernest Bader was the youngest child of a Swiss farmer. Following a clerical apprenticeship he came to London in 1912, aged 22. He set up his own company, Scott Bader & Co. in 1920, Scott being his wife's maiden name, and registered it as a private limited company in 1923.

The company started as the sole UK agent for a Swiss manufacturer of Celluloid. Other products were added during the 1920's—an improved type of paint for vehicles, and oil-soluble synthetic resins for the paint industry, both imported from Germany, and a phenolic resin from America, for example. The depression of the 1930's squeezed these merchanting activities, but Mr Bader responded by moving into manufacturing.

In 1940 the company moved from its central London offices and dockland factory to Wollaston Hall in Northamptonshire. The old hall provided adequate accommodation, a stable block became laboratories, and the 44 acre site offered ample room for a new factory and future expansion of production facilities.

The company grew with the development of plastics. By 1951 Scott Bader was a leading manufacturer of polyester resins and also manufactured intermediate chemical products such as alkyds, polymers and plasticisers. The company employed 151 people, had a sales turnover of £625,000 per year, and net profits of £72,000.

Ernest Bader had long been concerned about the concept of such things as a 'labour market' and 'wages systems'. He believed that men should employ capital rather than capital employ men. In an article in the American magazine 'Journal' he stated:

'Let me try in a few words to indicate the motives which inspired me to introduce revolutionary changes in my firm, based on a philosophy which attempts to fit industry to human needs. The problem was two-fold: firstly, how to organise or combine a maximum sense of freedom, happiness and human dignity in our firm without loss of profitability, and secondly, to do this by ways and means that could be generally acceptable to the private sector of industry.

I realised that—as years ago when I took the plunge and ceased to be an employee—I was up against the capitalist philosophy of dividing people into the managed on the one hand, and those that manage on the other. The real obstacle, however, was Company Law, with its provisions for dictatorial powers of shareholders and the hierarchy of management they control.'

Mr. Bader did not consider profit sharing was an adequate way of fulfilling these aims. In 1951, therefore, he established the Scott Bader Commonwealth as a charitable trust. Mr. Bader and his family gave 90% of the shares in Scott Bader and Company Ltd. to the Commonwealth. The remaining 10% (carrying over 50% of the voting rights) were held back until 1963 when they too were transferred to the Commonwealth. All eligible employees could apply for membership of the Commonwealth and thus share in the ownership of the company.

The structure evolved over the following 25 years. A further major change occurred in 1971 when a new constitution was adopted. This was the outcome of the contributions of many people and was agreed in general meeting.

ORGANISATION STRUCTURE

The structure in 1976 is shown diagrammatically in Exhibit 1.

Operating Company

The five executive directors of the operating company represented the finance, manufacturing, resources (R & D), marketing and information functions. The directors had been employees of the company for between 14

EXHIBIT 1

Scott Bader Commonwealth & Company—Organisation Structure

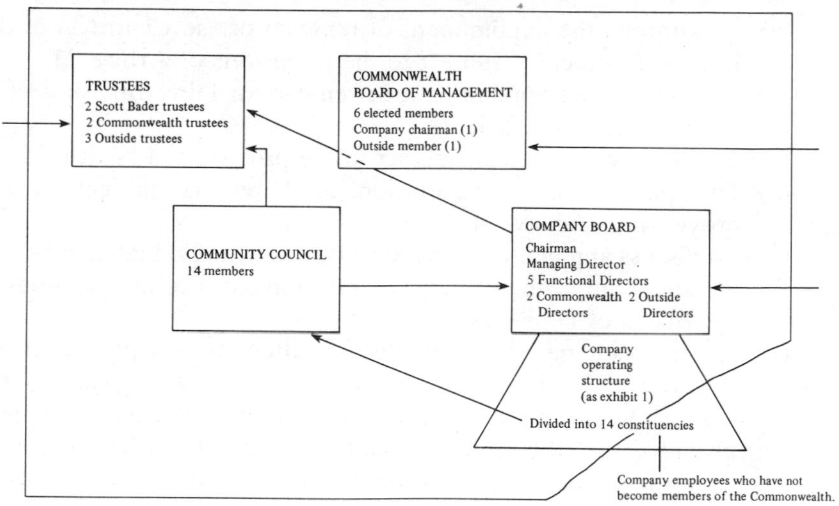

and 32 years and directors for between 1 and 16 years. The manager responsible for personnel was not a director although he reported to the managing director. Every employee was also a member of a 'constituency'. At the end of 1976 there were 14 constituencies, each of about 30 people, covering the 420 staff. Nine constituencies were allocated on a geographical basis, i.e. covering a particular section of the plant, laboratories or offices. Four were 'shift' constituencies, one covering each of the shifts engaged in the continuous production processes; and one constituency was 'hierarchical', representing the plant production management.

Community Council

Each of the constituencies elected a member to the Community Council. Every employee who had completed satisfactorily six months probationary service with the company was entitled to vote, but only Commonwealth members were eligible to stand for election. The chairman and directors of the Company were not eligible to stand for election to the Community Council, excepting the two 'Commonwealth Directors' referred to below.

The elected members of the Council were appointed for a period of two years, half retiring each year. The retiring members were not eligible for re-election until after one year's absence from the Council. At the first meeting of the Council the members elected a chairman from amongst themselves to act for that year.

'The Community Council is the standing Committee representing the interests of the members and staff of the Company. Its functions shall be:

(a) To approve the appointment of removal of the Chairman of the Board of Directors, subject to the provisions of Article 21.

(b) To approve the appointment or removal of Directors, subject to the provision of Article 22.

(c) To elect two Directors, subject to the provision of Article 22.

(d) To approve the remuneration of Directors subject to the provision of Article 24.

(e) To discuss any matter referred to it by any individual member, or by any organ of the Company, and to make recommendations to the Board of Directors.

(f) To consider any matter or dispute affecting disciplinary action referred to it by individual members or any organ of the Company and to give a decision on a grievance or appeal provided that the ordinary channels have been exhausted. Such decisions shall not be set aside by any individual member or any other organ of the Company.'

(Scott Bader Co. Ltd., Articles of Association, para. 16)

There have, in fact, been occasions on which the Community Council has reversed managerial decisions and the Community Council's view has prevailed.

Company Board

The provisions concerning appointment of Directors are defined in the Company's Articles of Association as follows:

21 'Ernest Bader and Godric Ernest Scott Bader shall be Directors of the Company and notwithstanding anything contained in any other Article they shall be entitled to hold office for life. The said Ernest Bader shall be entitled to be Chairman of the Board of Directors during his life or until he shall retire as a Director, and from and after his death or retirement the said Godric Ernest Scott Bader shall succeed him as Chairman to hold office for life or until he shall cease to be a Director. Any succeeding Chairman shall take office or be removed from office by resolution of the Board, subject to the approval of the Community Council.'

22 'There shall not be more than ten other Directors of the Company all of whom shall be members of the Scott Bader Commonwealth Limited and not more than eight of these shall be appointed or removed by the Chairman of the Board of Directors, subject to the approval of the Community Council. Not more than two Directors (herein called

"Commonwealth Directors") shall be elected by the Community Council from among its members. Any two members of the Community Council will be eligible for election provided neither holds the office of Chairman of the Community Council.'

At the end of 1976, the board consisted of eleven people, as shown in Exhibit 2. The two directors elected by and from the Community Council were referred to, confusingly, as Commonwealth Directors. Their duties as Community Councillors and as Commonwealth Directors occupied a significant part of their working time in addition to the work involved outside normal working hours.

All other directors were appointed (and could be removed) by the Chairman of the Company subject to the approval of the Community Council. Although the Community Council could request changes in the appointment of directors, it was generally thought that such a request would be considered rather harsh, and was unlikely. Therefore, on the last occasion when Mr. Godric Bader had asked the Council to approve a director's appointment, the Community Council had approved the appointment for an initial period of three years only.

During the moves towards a new organisation structure in 1976, the Community Council had also requested that all the Company Directors should resign and offer themselves for re-appointment on three-year terms of office. This proposal had been left in abeyance while the organisational changes were being discussed. A senior manager saw this request as a welcome sign of maturity with the Community Council:

'They are starting to grow into the role that is implicit in common ownership.'

The Commonwealth

The Commonwealth was established in 1951 to hold the share capital of Scott Bader Company Limited. (The term 'Commonwealth' is used in the Cromwellian sense of wealth in common.) This structure was adopted to allow members to share in company ownership on a common basis, as opposed to individual share holding. The Commonwealth was established as a charitable trust. It was registered as a company limited by guarantee and not having share capital. In accordance with its charitable status its objectives, as defined in the Memorandum of Association, were to carry out charitable work. The prime investment in 1976 was the entire share capital of Scott Bader Company Ltd. Registration as a charitable trust imposed considerable constraints on disposal or transfer of the assets.

The Commonwealth was administered by a Board of Management consisting of six people elected by and from the Commonwealth members plus the Chairman of Scott Bader Company Ltd. and one outside member co-opted by the other seven to represent the interests of the local community. The elected members served for a period of three years, and were not eligible for re-election until one year after retirement from office. One third of the elected members stood down each year.

Powers of the Commonwealth Board

The Board, apart from managing the running of the Commonwealth as an organisation, was charged with the following responsibility:

'The Board shall at all times exercise a philosophical oversight of the community as expressed in the forewords to this constitution and in the Memorandum and Articles of Association of the Commonwealth and of Scott Bader Company Limited.'

The ideals referred to are summarised in the foreword to the constitution shown in Exhibit 2a.

Commonwealth Membership

All employees of the Company could apply for membership of the Commonwealth 12 months after satisfactory completion of an initial 6 months probationary service. Applicants would then be interviewed by a member of the Commonwealth Board of Management, and an applicant's work colleagues would be questioned, to ensure that members understood and accepted the Commonwealth ideals. Everyone joining the Company would have received a copy of the Code of Practice for Members (Exhibit 2b) when they first applied for employment.

About 70% of employees were Commonwealth members, i.e. 295 out of 420 employees in December 1976. Forty people were not eligible, having been employed for less than 18 months. The remainder had chosen not to join for various reasons. Reasons given included apathy; to avoid any pressure on them to serve on the community council, and some younger people did not see Commonwealth membership as appropriate for themselves: 'its just security for the old men'.

David Ralley, the full-time Commonwealth Secretary commented:

'Many of those who are eligible but who haven't applied to join have been here less than three years. I think it takes that long before they understand what common ownership means. Then they start to get more interested, attending meetings and asking questions, and then often apply to join. I don't think we should try to pressure people to join: they should join voluntarily when they understand our philosophy.'

Very few applicants had been refused membership permanently, although

EXHIBIT 2(a)

Foreword to the revision of this Constitution

On this twenty-third day of March 1963 as we adopt these revised Articles of Association we, the members of The Scott Bader Commonwealth Limited, happily renew our dedication to the ideals which inspired the founding of the Commonwealth in 1951. Twelve years of working together on a common-ownership basis endeavouring to live out these ideals has developed in us a deeper consciousness of their fundamental truth and purpose. The following is intended to give expression to this development. The Commonwealth was born out of a growing realization of the incompatibility of the existing industrial and social order with a Christian concept and we continue to be moved and inspired by the spiritual force behind such a concept. The Commonwealth is an expression of the age-old ideal taught by all great religions of a brotherhood of all men knowing no restriction of race, sex or social class and owing allegiance to a living creative spirit. It is seeking through, and beyond, all material ends to foster conditions for the growth of personality truly related to God and man.

This means we endeavour to provide opportunity for the full development of us all, both materially and spiritually, unhampered by unjust conditions or crushed by economic pressures, and to take steps towards developing a way of life free from bondage or material things and mere conventions.

Power should come from within the person and the community, and be made responsible to those it affects. The ultimate criteria in the organization of work should be human dignity and service to others instead of solely economic performance. We feel mutual responsibility must permeate the whole community of work and be upheld by democratic participation and the principle of trusteeship.

Common-ownership of our means of production, and a voice in the distribution of earned surplus and the allocation of new capital, has helped us in our struggle towards achieving these aims.

The Commonwealth has responsibilities to the wider national and international community and is endeavouring to fulfil them by fostering a movement towards a new peaceful industrial and social order. To be a genuine alternative to welfare capitalism and state-controlled communism such an order must be non-violent in the sense of promoting love and justice, for where love stops power begins and intimidation and violence follow. One of the main requirements of a peaceful social order is, we are convinced, an organization of work based on the principles outlined here, a sharing of the fruits of our labours with those less fortunate instead of working only for our own private security, and a refusal to support destructive social conflict or to take part in preparations for war. We must strive to release the best in man within a free community to live up to the highest that he knows and recognize the interdependence of means and ends as we continue working towards a new and better society.

23rd MARCH, 1963.

there had been cases where applicants had been told that their attitudes and behaviour were not suitable, and were advised to re-apply at a later date.

Company directors were required to be Commonwealth members, and there used to be an understanding that senior managers would also join. The pressure on managers had since weakened and at least one senior manager who was eligible had chosen not to apply for membership.

EXHIBIT 2(b)

Code of Practice for Members

A We recognize that we are first a working community and that it is our basic attitude to our work and to our fellow workers that gives life and meaning to the Commonwealth.

B We have agreed that as a community our work involves four tasks, economic, technical, social and political, neglect of any one of which will in the long term diminish the Commonwealth. We feel that the practical working out of a balance between the four tasks is a continuing study for the membership as a whole.

C We are conscious of a common responsibility to share our work among ourselves in such a way that it becomes a meaningful and creative part of our lives rather than merely as a means to an end.

D We recognize that there are some members in a position of authority. Such members have a greater opportunity and hence a special responsibility to facilitate the building of jobs which are capable of fulfilling us as people; to act as 'catalysts of common effort' and not as authoritarian 'bosses'.

E We recognize that since management by consent rather than coercion is an appropriate style for the Company, a corresponding effort to accept responsibility is required from us all. This will show in a desire to attend meetings and to participate in the affairs of our community; it will show in increased communication between person and person and between groups and departments; it will show in an effort to understand the problems encountered and the contribution made by those in other areas of our organization; above all it will be seen as a genuine willingness to learn, to develop and grow.

F We try to be open and frank in our relationships with our fellow workers, to face difficulties rather than avoid them and to solve problems by discussion and agreement rather than through reference to a third party.

G We are agreed that in the event of a downturn in trade we will share all remaining work rather than expect any of our fellow members to be deprived of employment, even if this requires a reduction in earnings by all.

H We have agreed not to hold second jobs if our doing so is likely to deprive others (in the community at large) of employment or to affect our interest at work adversely.

I We are agreed that, as the foundation of our Commonwealth abolished here the power of share ownership, we shall strive to discourage our money from being used to profit from other people's work or to control other people's lives.

J We recognize that we have a responsibility to the society in which we live and believe that where we have some special talent or interest we should offer this to the wider community. Thus most of us are engaged in some form of social, political or public service, however small.

K We are agreed that (in addition to such disinterested services that we offer as individuals) our social responsibility extends to:

1 Limiting the products of our labour to those beneficial to the community, in particular excluding any products for the specific purpose of manufacturing weapons of war.

2 Reducing any harmful effect of our work on the natural environment by rigorously avoiding the negligent discharge of pollutants.

3 Questioning constantly whether any of our activities are unnecessarily wasteful of the earth's natural resources.

L As members of the Commonwealth we support the basic ideas expressed in the Preamble to the Constitution and reaffirm that the Commonwealth stands for a new approach to the problems of work and society. Therefore we accept that commitment to the principles of the Commonwealth implies an active concern for the expression of these principles both in our working lives and in the other areas of our lives.

Adopted at a General Meeting
held on the 19th day of July 1972

Trustees

Finally, there were the trustees of the Commonwealth who had the power to act as holders of the Trustee shares, although the shares were in fact held by the Commonwealth. In addition to Ernest Bader, who was entitled to hold office for life, there could be between 4 and 8 other trustees; at the end of 1976 there were 7 others. There could be up to two 'Commonwealth Trustees' elected from the Community Council, one of these being the Council Chairman. There could be up to two 'Scott Bader Trustees', these being the Company Chairman and one other Company director.

The Commonwealth and Scott Bader trustees jointly nominated three other trustees. Nominated trustees were appointed for 5 years but were eligible for re-appointment.

The share capital of Scott Bader Company Ltd. was divided into 100,000 shares of fifty pence each. There were two classes of shares. The ordinary shares, of which there were 90,000, each carried a single vote; the remaining 10,000 shares were termed 'Trustee shares' and carried 10 votes each.

14 'The holders of the Trustee Shares or all but one of the Trustee Shares may do any of the following acts:

(a) Require the Board of Directors or the Community Council to seek the approval of the Trustees for any change in the Memorandum and Articles of Association of the Company and to veto any measure taken or proposed to be taken by the Board of Directors or the Community Council if in the opinion of the majority of the Trustees a breach of the principles upon which the Company is intended to be managed as laid down herein (1) is or would be committed if such measure were taken.

(b) Require the Board of Directors to take such steps as the Trustees shall think fit to restore the profit-making capacity of the Company, if at any time the Auditors of the Company shall certify that the business of the company is in their opinion being run at a loss, so that the power under this paragraph shall continue until such time as the Auditors of the Company shall certify that in their opinion the business of the Company is no longer being run at a loss.

(c) Determine any matter in the event of a disagreement between the Board of Directors and the Community Council on an issue of fundamental policy.'

COMPANY MANAGEMENT

By 1977 Ernest Bader was in his eighties. He took no active part in the management of either the Company of the Commonwealth, except as one of the eight trustees, but still made his views known by writing strongly worded letters to managers and members on a wide range of issues. He had relinquished the post of Managing Director of the operating company in 1957 and the chairmanship in 1966. His son, Godric, has taken over both appointments.

In 1970, Mr. Godric Bader, then 47, relinquished the Managing Directorship. Nicholas Broome was appointed from outside the company; he had formerly spent some time at Rothschilds on new ventures, following management training in the textile industry and work in both the chemical and engineering industries. Mr. Broome was a strong believer in the ability and efficacy of small and medium sized concerns, and he developed a greater emphasis on commercial criteria. The Managing Director's committee became the focus for operating decisions: the Community Council and the Commonwealth Directors adopted a more remote, supervisory and guidance role on general policy. This change in emphasis became pronounced during the 1973 oil crisis and the period of power restrictions in early 1974 during a national miners' strike. One manager commented that the company's performance in those critical times was largely due to Mr. Broome's commercial astuteness. However, there were also criticisms from members that 'it is under just such conditions that the value of common-ownership and cooperation should be most valuable; but members had not been allowed to participate fully in reaching the important operating decisions.'

These criticisms were perhaps reflected in the motion discussed by all the workforce in January 1977. The motion was:

> 'To accept in principle a democratically appointed Community Board, accountable to the Community and to whom management will be accountable.'

During the meeting the motion was amended, and subsequently passed, to read:

> 'To accept the principle of a democratically appointed Community Board, demonstrated by its majority being elected by members.'

PERSONNEL

The Commonwealth was based on the belief that the ultimate criteria in the organisation of work should be human dignity and service to others, instead of solely economic performance. Personnel policies were, therefore, of importance within the company. The staff were well distributed throughout the 16–65 age range. Over a quarter had worked for the company for more than 15 years and about a quarter for 4 years or less. Staff turnover was low,

EXHIBIT 3
Extracts from the 1976 opinion survey

The figures quoted in the following summary are in precentage terms and where these do not add up to 100%, answers were not provided by the remainder. As the form of the questions are different from last year direct comparison is not exact, however, the trend can be seen.

Communications

(a) Do you get enough information on what is going on in your department?
Almost Always: 47. Often: 11. Occasionally: 35. Rarely: 5.
(b) Do you get enough information on what is going on in the Company as a whole?
Almost Always: 18. Often: 23. Occasionally: 44. Rarely: 16.
(c) Have communications improved in the last year?
Very much: 5. To some extent: 37. No change: 47. Have got worse: 7.

Decisions

(a) Do you feel you have enough say in those decisions which affect your department?
Almost Always: 21. Often: 33. Occasionally: 18. Rarely: 26.
(b) Do you feel you have enough say in the broad aspects of the Company as a whole?
Almost Always: 5. Often: 18. Occasionally: 30. Rarely: 42.
(c) If there are changes in your own work are you given the reasons why?
Almost Always: 47. Often: 12. Occasionally: 30. Rarely: 9.

Community Council

(a) Are you satisfied with the performance of the Community Council?
Satisfied: 23. Fairly Satisfied: 40. Some dissatisfaction: 23. Not satisfied: 12.
(b) Do you think that the Community Council are given a real chance by management?
Yes: 14. To a reasonable extent: 56. To a little extent: 14. No: 5.
(c) How interested are you personally in the Community Council?
Strong interest: 32. Some interest: 46. Little interest: 16. No interest: 7.
(d) Do you think that your individual interests are represented in the Community Council?
Well: 14. Fairly well: 53. Not so well: 28. Badly: 5.

Commonwealth Membership

(a) How much does membership and the Code of Practice mean to you?
A great deal: 46. To some extent: 30. Only a little: 14. Nothing: 9.
Members only %: 59.
(b) How should membership be decided?
Automatically on joining: 12.
Automatically after a certain time with Scott Bader: 28.
By interview after a certain time with Scott Bader: 56.
(c) Should members have meetings with the elected representatives of the Board of Management?
Annually: 74. Less frequently: 9. Initial interview only: 11.

(d) Do you understand the functions of the Board of Management?
    Yes: 42. More than last year: 49. No: 9.
(e) Are you satisfied with the performance of the Board of Management?
    Satisfied: 46. Fairly satisfied: 26. Some dissatisfaction: 19. Not satisfied: 5.
(f) Should there be a financial benefit in becoming a Commonwealth Member?
    Yes: 18. No: 75.

Company Board

(a) Recognising that the four tasks of the Company are interwoven, are you satisfied with the performance of the Board in the:

    (i) Economic task
    Satisfied: 53. Fairly satisified: 40. Some dissatisfaction: 5.
    Not satisfied: 2.
  (ii) Technical task
    Satisfied: 26. Fairly satisfied: 47. Some dissatisfaction: 14.
    Not satisfied: 7.
 (iii) Social task
    Satisfied: 26. Fairly satisfied: 32. Some dissatisfaction: 14.
    Not satisfied: 26.
 (iv) Political task
    Satisfied: 28. Fairly satisfied: 39. Some dissatisfaction: 12.
    Not satisfied: 9.

(b) Since last year how successful has the Board been in:

    (i) Involving people
    Successful: 11. Fairly successful: 39. Not very successful: 32.
    Not successful: 18.
  (ii) Improving working conditions in your area
    Successful: 12. Fairly successful: 28. Not very successful: 32.
    Not successful: 25.
 (iii) Stimulating job satisfaction
    Successful: 5. Fairly successful: 37. Not very successful: 30.
    Not successful: 23.

(c) Do you think enough money has been spent in improving conditions as a whole?
    Yes: 26. No: 72.
(d) Are you prepared to forego salary increases or bonus to provide social facilities?
    Yes: 32. No: 63.

typically 5–6% per year, compared with 15–20% per year for the synthetic resin industry.

Each year the company carried out an opinion survey among the employees, and reported the results in the company's fortnightly staff magazine, The Reactor. The survey consisted of a questionnaire and interview (by an outsider) and involved 10–15% of the employees selected at random. Responses to some of the questions in 1976 are shown in Exhibit 3.

Number of Personnel

The constitution was first drawn up on the basis that the company would not employ more than 250 people. If necessary, separate operations would be established as had been done with RP Structures. But by 1976, Scott Bader employed 420 people, and the scale of operation was, therefore, larger than that which the founders visualised as being the maximum for effective involvement and participation.

Pay

The pay structure had been based on a Hay/MSL job evaluation scheme, but had become somewhat distorted over time. 'Average pay' was £3,500 per employee at June 1976, including fairly generous shift premiums where appropriate. In addition, anyone employed for the full year would have recieved a bonus of nearly £300, and company-financed benefits of £830. Pension fund contributions (55%) and national insurance (33%) were the most important of the latter.

Pay was above the average for the area, which was predominantly rural. The pay structure was, however, rather 'flatter' than normal within similar industries. Lower-paid employees were considerably better off than in comparable companies, and enjoyed good 'staff' conditions irrespective of job. The pay for middle management was about the same as within other companies, but senior managers probably received less than they could have earned in other organisations.

Trade Unions

A number of employees were members of trade unions and the company operated a 'check-off' system for about 60 members of TGWU and ASTMS.

The company did not negotiate wages and conditions with trade unions, and did not differentiate in any way between members and non-members. In the event of a grievance an individual could ask to be represented by a shop steward, or by his constituency Community Councillor, at any stage of the grievance procedure up to an interview with the Chief Executive. Anyone who wished to take an issue further could also appeal to the Community Council but in this case should be represented by a 'colleague' and not by a 'trade union representative'.

It seemed that the main reason for joining a trade union was for 'security' particularly in the event of an industrial injury leading to a claim for compensation.

COMPANY PERFORMANCE

Products and Product Development

Scott Bader's key products were unsaturated polyester resins used for glass reinforced plastics. The company was the UK market leader, and sold at least three times as much tonnage of these resins as any one of its UK competitors, which included ICI and BP. Other suppliers were British Industrial Plastics (a

EXHIBIT 4

Scott Bader Company Ltd. Certain Financial Statistics Since Formation of Commonwealth

Year to 30 June	Fixed Assets	Current Assets	Liabilities (including Tax)	Worth of Company	Sales	Pay (including overtime)	Number of staff	Average pay	Sales per staff	Fixed assets per staff
	£'000	£'000	£'000	£'000	£'000	£'000		£	£	£
1951	91	241	202	130	624	67	161	417	3876	565
1952	86	196	149	133	635	56	150	375	4233	573
1953	79	154	78	155	407	61	138	441	2949	573
1954	86	187	93	180	423	71	138	514	3065	623
1955	95	196	104	187	442	82	162	508	2728	586
1956	108	193	95	206	556	85	155	547	3587	697
1957	116	344	218	242	874	102	177	575	4938	655
1958	137	428	272	293	1106	128	199	643	5558	688
1959	173	495	322	346	1179	138	209	658	5641	828
1960	189	524	332	381	1531	161	228	704	6715	829
1961	230	481	297	414	1467	186	250	745	5868	920
1962	269	510	323	456	1496	200	260	768	5754	1035
1963	282	577	364	495	1627	232	262	886	6210	1076
1964	388	694	492	590	2088	276	289	954	7225	1343
1965	434	834	568	700	2533	331	312	1062	8119	1391
1966	484	902	574	812	2694	351	323	1087	8341	1501
1967	507	1114	723	898	2887	363	320	1144	9022	1587
1968	590	1428	997	1021	3912	416	337	1254	11608	1760
1969	732	1748	1404	1076	4712	464	357	1300	13200	2050
1970	721	1837	1375	1183	5010	525	376	1396	13324	1917
1971	799	1854	1286	1367	4990	587	379	1548	13166	2160
1972	.849	1943	1238	1554	5250	663	385	1722	13636	2205
1973	1968	2646	2226	2388	6991	826	423	1952	16527	3765
1974	2173	3745	3307	2611	9429	977	429	2332	22654	5186
1975	2318	4376	3334	3360	12204	1177	419	2809	29216	5532
1976	2497	5373	3694	4176	14898	1493	419	3563	35556	5959

subsidiary of Turner and Newall), Synthetic Resins Ltd. (Unilever) and Pinchin Johnson (Courtaulds).

Scott Bader occupied a much smaller niche in the supply of emulsion polymers, which are used in textiles, paint and carpet backings. The competition included another Unilever subsidiary, Vinyl Products Ltd. Other products included plasticisers used in making PVC, and polyurethanes from which foamed products were made for textile coatings, shoe soles, etc.

The most important products were originally produced under licences from United States chemical companies in the 1940's. Scott Bader had subsequently extended the range. One significant development was an

Operations Profit £'000	% Assets (gross)	% Sales	% Pay	Tax £'000	% Profit	Dividend for charitable purposes (inc. CDF)[1] £'000	% Profit	Bonus to Staff £'000	% Profit	Plough back and to meet exceptional items written off £'000	% Profit
72.7	21.9	11.7	108.5	36.5	50	1.5	2	5.8	8	28.9	40
18.5	6.6	2.9	33.0	9.5	51[2]	0.4	2	1.7	9	6.9	37
39.7	17.1	9.7	65.1	15.7	40	4.0	10	4.0	10	16.0	40
56.3	20.7	13.3	79.3	22.7	40	3.9	7	3.9	7	3.9	46
13.3	4.6	3.0	16.2	6.3	47					7.0	53
45.0	14.9	8.1	32.9	17.2	38	4.5	10	4.5	10	18.8	42
87.3	19.0	10.0	85.6	35.3	40	8.7	10	8.7	10	34.6	40
120.5	21.4	10.9	94.1	44.6	37	9.6	8	9.6	8	56.7	47
101.9	15.3	8.6	73.8	39.9	39	8.2	8	8.2	8	45.6	45
84.2	11.8	5.5	52.3	33.4	40	5.9	7	5.9	7	39.0	46
68.4	9.6	4.7	36.8	28.8	42	3.4	5	3.4	5	32.8	48
96.1	12.4	6.4	48.1	43.9	45	9.6	10	9.6	10	33.0	35
117.6	13.7	7.2	50.7	47.1	40	9.4	8	9.4	8	51.7	44
179.0	17.0	8.6	64.9	61.9	35	16.0	9	16.0	9	85.1	47
160.1	12.7	6.3	48.4	46.6	29	9.0	5½	9.0	5½	95.5	60
176.3	12.7	6.5	50.2	65.6	37	3.0	2	3.0	2	104.7	59
172.8	10.7	6.0	47.6	72.2	42	10.0	6	10.0	6	80.6	46
262.8	13.1	6.7	63.2	113.4	43	15.0	6	15.0	6	119.4	45
285.7	11.5	6.1	61.6	136.0	48	20.0	7	20.0	7	109.7	38
215.6	8.4	4.3	41.1	86.9	41	7.5	3	7.5	3	113.7	53
299.1	11.2	6.0	52.8	94.0	32	25.0	8	25.0	8	155.1	52
377.0	13.5	7.2	56.8	159.0	42	50.0	13	50.0	13	118.0	32
452.0	9.8	6.5	54.7	142.0	31	61.0[2]	14	72.0	16	177.0	39
635.0	10.7	6.7	65.0	346.0	54	18.0) 27.0)	3 4	54.0	9	190.0	30
1072.0	15.3	8.4	87.3	561.0	55	18.0) 27.0)	2 3	54.0	5	367.0	35
1181.0	15.0	7.9	79.1	554.0	47	39.0) 60.0)	3 5	120.0	10	408.0	35

1. Payment to CDF equal to dividend started 1971.
2. Dividend imputation tax started.

emulsion polymer for gloss emulsion paints, a technical breakthrough for which the company won a Queen's Award for Industry in 1975. Others included the use of polyvinylidene chloride emulsions to produce low permeability packaging film coatings and improved fire resistant materials. A number of developments had been patented, and Scott Bader licensed production by a number of other companies throughout the world.

EXHIBIT 5

TEN YEAR REVIEW for Scott Bader Company Limited including SOURCE and USE of Funds. Year to 30th June in £'000

	1967	1968	1969	1970	1971	1972	1973	1974	1975	1976
NET ASSETS EMPLOYED:										
Land, Buildings, Plant etc.	495	578	695	688	765	798	1,593	1,746	1,833	1,894
Investment in Subsidiary and Associated Companies	12	12	37	33	34	51	376	427	485	603
Net Current Assets	391	431	344	462	568	705	420	438	1,042	1,679
	898	1,021	1,076	1,183	1,367	1,554	2,389	2,611	3,360	4,176
FINANCED BY:										
Share Capital	50	50	50	50	50	50	50	50	50	50
Retained Profits	819	939	986	1,092	1,240	1,369	1,887	2,049	2,336	2,843
Deferred Taxation	29	32	40	41	77	135	452	512	974	1,283
	898	1,021	1,076	1,183	1,367	1,554	2,389	2,611	3,360	4,176
SALES	2,887	3,912	4,712	5,010	4,990	5,250	6,991	9,492	12,204	14,898
PROFIT BEFORE TAX	173	263	223	208	279	363	321	617	937	1,230
Operating Profit	180	271	286	216	299	377	451	635	1,027	1,181
Subsidiary Companies Profit (Loss)	(7)	(8)			(8)	3	(47)	(17)	(6)	(43)
Associated Companies Profit (Loss)			(63)	(8)	(12)	(17)	(83)	(1)	(8)	8
Non-operating income (costs)					—	—			(76)	84
TAXATION	96	113	136	87	94	159	142	342	561	554

NET PROFIT AFTER TAX	77	150	87	121	185	204	179	275	378	676
Staff Profit Sharing	10	15	20	7.5	25	50	72	54	54	120
Dividend for charitable purposes	10	15	20	7.5	12.5	25	25	18	18	39
Allocated for Commonwealth Development Fund	—	—	—	—	12.5	25	36	27	27	60
RETAINED PROFIT	57	120	47	106	135	104	46	176	277	457
Depreciation	57	75	121	100	104	106	157	186	207	218
CASH FLOW	114	195	168	206	239	210	203	362	484	675
Investment Grants	17	41	37	14	12	—	—	(3)	—	—
Increase (Reduction) in Bank borrowing	24	(49)	112	(137)	91	(115)	646	(32)	(39)	(375)
Increase in Commonwealth Development Fund balance	—	—	—	—	13	25	10	6	8	49
Increase in deferred tax provision	29	3	8	1	36	58	56	75	462	309
TOTAL SOURCE OF FUNDS	184	190	325	84	391	178	915	408	915	658
Additions to Fixed Assets	87	199	275	107	193	139	232	339	294	280
Additions to Associated Company Shares and Advances	10	—	25	(4)	1	17	324	51	58	118
Increase (Reduction) in working capital	87	(9)	25	(19)	197	22	359	18	563	260
TOTAL USE OF FUNDS	184	190	325	84	391	178	915	408	915	658

Notes: Non-operating items:
1967 to 1970 are goodwill costs written off.
1973 Exchange losses (£73,000), Profit on Engineering Contracts £25,000, Extra depreciation (£35,000).
1974 Exchange losses (£6,000), Profit on Engineering Contracts £5,000.
1975 Exchange losses (£30,000), Goodwill written off (£79,000), Profit on sale of investments £33,000.
1976 Exchange losses (£24,000), Goodwill written off (£36,000), Change in basis of stock valuation £66,000, Doubtful Debt provision in previous years no longer required £75,000, Asset revaluation adjustment £3,000.

M

Markets

Customers were primarily industrial users. In the U.K. many were small companies with little or no technical expertise. Scott Bader therefore provided a technical service for customers, and undertook a fair amount of product and application development on behalf of customers.

Overseas sales were achieved mainly by licensing other manufacturers, although in 1976 exports from the U.K. exceeded £2 million. Apart from the normal commercial advantages of using local manufacturers and suppliers, this policy was necessary in many cases because of the limited shelf life of the resins; also because in some countries import barriers favoured local production. Licencees covered most of the world except Japan and North America and included such well known companies as Monsanto in Australia and Borden in Brazil. In 1976 Scott Bader established an International Division within the marketing function to incorporate and integrate exports as well as to provide a technical service to licensees, and manage the licensing operations.

Subsidiaries and Associate Companies

In the U.K. Scott Bader had established a subsidiary company R.P. Structures Ltd. on the Wollaston site in 1972. R.P. used Scott Bader's resins in the manufacture of glass reinforced plastics products. It was expected that eventually it would grow into a viable common ownership company and it was hoped that the employees were beginning to appreciate the real meaning of the term.

Scott Bader also held a 50% interest in a small German company, Crystic Kunststoffe GmbH, and a 25% stake in a Swedish company, A. B. Syntes. The other shareholder in the latter was a chemical company, Berol Kemi, belonging to the Swedish state ownership body, the Statsföretag. A. B. Syntes employed over a hundred people and under Swedish law was therefore required to appoint two worker directors. Berol Kemi was sympathetic to the Scott Bader philosophy, and the company was managed on 'democratic' lines.

Financial Performance and the Distribution of Profit

A summary of Scott Bader's results since formation of the Commonwealth is shown in Exhibit 4, and in further detail for the last 10 years in Exhibit 5.

A number of companies offered products in direct competition to Scott Bader but in most cases these were subsidiaries or divisions of major chemical companies with a wide range of other interests. Direct financial comparison is not therefore possible. However some comparative financial data for a range of chemical companies is given in Exhibit 6.

The company's Articles required profits to be distributed as follows. At least 60 percent of the before tax profits must be used for taxation and

EXHIBIT 6
Comparison of Scott Bader Co. Ltd. With Some Major Chemical Companies

	1971	1972	1973	1974	1975	1976
NUMBER OF EMPLOYEES						
Scott Bader Co. Ltd.	379	385	423	429	419	419
Laporte Industries (Holdings Ltd.)	5,600	5,500	5,100	5,100	4,700	4,500
Ciba Geigy (UK) Ltd.	7,200	7,300	7,500	7,800	11,900	10,900
Albright & Wilson – total	12,700	12,400	11,900	10,800	10,400	10,100
– UK	9,100	8,800	8,300	7,600	7,300	6,700
ICI Ltd. – total	190,000	199,000	199,000	201,000	195,000	192,000
– UK	137,000	135,000	132,000	132,000	129,000	125,000
SALES/EMPLOYEE £						
Scott Bader	13,200	13,600	16,500	22,700	29,200	35,600
Laporte	8,000	7,100	9,800	12,000	13,100	19,200
Ciba Geigy (UK)	10,100	11,800	13,100	16,200	16,600	23,300
Albright & Wilson	9,800	10,800	13,100	18,900	21,900	28,200
ICI	8,000	8,500	10,900	14,700	15,900	21,500
PROFIT BEFORE TAX/EMPLOYEE £						
Scott Bader	740	940	760	1,440	2,240	2,940
Laporte	170	380	1,170	1,510	610	2,680
Ciba Geigy	360	320	450	520	(360)	465
Albright & Wilson	220	210	620	2,090	1,770	3,100
ICI	680	460	1,570	1,290	990	1,420
LABOUR COST/EMPLOYEE £ (UK only) (Including profit sharing bonus)						
Scott Bader	1,650	1,850	2,120	2,420	2,940	3,850
Laporte	1,650	1,750	1,950	2,200	3,310	3,790
Ciba Geigy	1,785	2,000	2,180	2,670	3,240	3,720
Albright & Wilson	1,660	1,850	2,040	2,390	3,200	3,770
ICI	1,950	2,120	2,460	2,950	3,650	4,360
NET ASSETS/EMPLOYEE £						
Scott Bader	3,600	4,000	5,600	6,100	8,000	10,000
Laporte	11,500	12,300	13,800	14,700	17,100	20,400
Ciba Geigy	8,400	8,300	8,500	10,900	11,700	13,500
Albright & Wilson	9,100	9,500	9,800	12,700	15,400	18,000
ICI	9,300	9,400	10,800	12,000	14,100	18,300
RETURN ON NET ASSETS, % (Before Tax including investment income, and after interest charges)						
Scott Bader	20.4	23.4	16.5	24.2	28.5	26.8
Laporte	1.9	3.1	8.5	10.3	3.6	13.1
Ciba Geigy	4.2	3.8	5.2	4.8	(2.8)	10.9
Albright & Wilson	2.4	2.2	6.3	16.5	11.5	17.3
ICI	7.3	7.6	14.6	19.1	12.3	14.1

retained earnings. Not more than 20 percent was to be paid as staff bonus, the actual amount being determined by the Community Council and approved by members in general meeting. A dividend equal to at least half the staff bonus must be paid to the Commonwealth to be used for charitable purposes. A further sum at least equal to the dividend must be transferred to the Commonwealth Development Fund. This fund is used to give grants or loans to enterprises operating on common ownership principles.

EXTENDING COMMON OWNERSHIP

A major social objective of Scott Bader was the extension of the Common ownership principle. This was fostered in several ways, e.g. by financial and other assistance to common ownership ventures, and by publicising the work and results of the Company and Commonwealth. Latterly, the company had tended to take more direct action with its subsidiaries and licencees. In one case Scott Bader laid down in a draft agreement with a potential licencee that it would 'expect the Scott Bader style of management to be adopted within five years'. In another case where a joint subsidiary was proposed with a Californian distributor, the agreement noted:

'The (U.S. company) understands the common ownership basis or which Scott Bader is constituted and accepts that Scott Bader may wish that any future joint company established by Scott Bader and (the U.S company) reflect the philosophies on which Scott Bader is founded.'

The Distribution of Commonwealth Funds

The charities which were supported were nominated and approved by Commonwealth members and were often those in which members took an active role. Over the years about £80,000 had been loaned at preferential interest rates by the Commonwealth Development Fund (CDF) to organisations operating on common ownership principles.

'We're rather inexperienced at assessing the risks in such ventures. People tend to react emotionally rather than rationally when assessing whether to give financial assistance. Some of the groups we have helped are still going, but others have not been successful.'

The Commonwealth was a founder member of Demintry (Democratic Integration in Industry) in 1958. Demintry became the Industrial Common Ownership Movement (ICOM) in 1971. Industrial Common Ownership Finance (ICOF) grew out of this movement and in 1976 most loans and aid were made via ICOF, which acted as an agent for the CDF. Further assistance to ICOF was made available following the passing of the 1976 Industrial

Common Ownership Act which provided up to £250,000 over a five year period from government funds. Scott Bader saw this Act as indicative of government recognition of the concept of common ownership, as well as the provision of financial help.

THE FUTURE

Whatever changes were made in the company, the effectiveness of the structure and the executives would be assessed not only by commercial criteria but also by the extent to which they contributed to the following requirements stated in the company's articles.

'The basic purpose of the Company is to render the best possible service as a corporate body to our fellow men. Towards this end we strive particularly:

(a) to develop the strength of the Company, its efficiency and means of production.

(b) to provide economic security to members and to relieve them of material anxiety or striving for personal advancement at the cost of others.

(c) to produce goods not only beneficial to customers of the Company at a fair price and as high a quality as possible but also for the peaceful purposes and general good of mankind.

(d) to conduct research and provide technical education mainly in synthetic resins and their application in the paints, plastics and allied industries.

(e) to contribute towards the general welfare of society, internationally, nationally and in the Company's immediate neighbourhood.

For the purposes aforesaid the Directors of the Company and either of the other said organs of the Company shall take such measures as they think fit, and in particular:

(a) limit the product of the Company to those beneficial to our fellow men, in particular by excluding any products for the specific purposes of manufacturing weapons of war.

(b) direct everyday affairs so that the members and staff may fully participate in the firm's activities in relation to their ability, knowledge and experience and co-ordinate all tasks and purposes in terms of service.

(c) encourage the desirable principle that members in all meetings should reach decisions without need for a formal vote. To achieve a decision in this way may not be easy, but it is an intent that it will carry the goodwill of all.

(h) ensure that the highest salary paid in the Company shall not be excessive when compared with the lowest basic pay for a Commonwealth member. This ratio having been established any variation will require the approval of members in General Meeting. At 1st January 1971 this ratio is less than 7:1.'

21

Yoshida Kogyo KK (A)

Yoshida Kogyo KK, better known as Y.K.K., was the largest manufacturer of zip fasteners in the world and was also Japan's leading producer of aluminium sashes. Y.K.K. opened its first overseas manufacturing plant in 1960 and by mid-1976 the company's overseas interests had expanded to 29 subsidiary plants producing zippers in 24 countries, employing over 4500 foreign employees led by some 180 Japanese managers on overseas assignments. In 1976 Y.K.K. was estimated to hold around 22 per cent of the world market for zippers and 95 per cent of the market in Japan. Manufacturing subsidiaries were established in the U.S.A. and Canada while in Europe plants were operating in the Netherlands, the U.K., Germany, France and Belgium.

Normally Y.K.K. established local plants to assemble, package and sell completed zips, using sliders produced at the parent company's plants in Japan. Slider production was the most expensive and capital intensive component in zip manufacture. Over 50 per cent of Japanese production was exported to over 125 countries. The company also manufactured zipper making machinery, most of which was exported to the company's overseas subsidiaries.

COMPANY PHILOSOPHY—THE CYCLE OF GOODNESS

Y.K.K. was founded in 1934 by Tadao Yoshida. After leaving elementary school Mr. Yoshida was apprenticed to the Aima Importing Company in Tokyo before forming his own company, San S, to sell zip fasteners. Two years later the company began exporting to South America and Australia. Sales to these areas and throughout South East Asia soon became a feature of the business. After the war Mr. Yoshida was forced to rebuild his business and the name was changed to Yoshida Kogyo Kabushiki Kaisha.

Mr. Yoshida believed deeply in a business philosphy which had become widely known within Y.K.K. and elsewhere as the 'cycle of goodness'. Mr.

Yoshida outlined this personal philosophy which had guided his company to such swift success:

'Since my boyhood, I was very fond of reading biographies of great men and when I read a biography of Andrew Carnegie, I was deeply inspired by his "Unless you render profit or goodness to others you cannot prosper". At the same time I wondered if and how I could do as he had said. Gradually I came to believe that it is not good to make money without working so hard as to sweat, and that to buy things other people made when their prices fall and sell them back to others when their prices rise is nothing but a rip-off. What is important is to make things by yourself. What is most precious in man, I believe, is the ability to create something tangible out of nothing. By means of creativeness, man can make his life richer and can also gain much profit.

'Now suppose that we succeed in reducing the cost of a certain product to ¥50 while other companies make the same product for ¥100. Then, we will pass on two-thirds of the balance of the cost saved to consumers and related industries, and we will retain the remaining one-third ourselves, which we will use as much as possible for future investments. This is my idea of profit. Savings make the difference between human beings and animals. Inventiveness and savings are the two indispensable wheels for human progress.

'I would say that those people who make money without working but just by raising prices in a concerted way, as you have seen recently, are committing a sin against society. Some people are said to have earned as much as ¥100 million by merely buying and selling stocks of the companies for which they are not working. In my view point, this is one of the shortcomings of capitalism. As I cannot favour speculation to make money from shareholdings in companies which are not your own, Y.K.K. does not put its stocks on the market; we are trying to give Y.K.K. stocks to Y.K.K. employees as much as possible. As we cannot afford to pay our workers as much as we would like, we make them our shareholders so that they can get dividends and enjoy a better life. Because our employees have a sense of responsibility to the company performance as shareholders of Y.K.K., and try to work hard and exercise their creativeness, Y.K.K. can make products with better quality at lower costs. The 40 years of history of our company is a history of realising the idea of the "cycle of goodness" in this way.

'From last year to this year, costs of our raw materials went up more than 50 per cent, and some of them as much as 200 per cent. Even if we had boosted prices of our products by 50 per cent, our competitors could not have competed against us and we could have earned profits amounting to hundreds of million yen. But we did not. We did increase our prices last year, but we made our utmost efforts to make our price-hike as small as possible. As a result, we decided to squeeze this year's production cost on an assumption that we could have purchased raw materials ¥10 billion less than what we actually paid. Even with this, we will not go into the red.

'We can rely on our own excellent production facilities. Our investments since the "Nixon shock" alone amounts to ¥80 billion. But our wages have not been on the high side in the country and some of our people wanted larger price increases and bigger bonuses. I admonished them and reminded them, making money by buying things at low prices and selling them at high prices is not compatible with the Y.K.K.'s principle because that money is not earned by our own efforts and toils. I told them that now was the time for the Y.K.K. group to exert itself to serve society better by keeping prices as low as possible even if we were to use up the last bit of our stockpile. I also told them, "Situations are very bad, we cannot deny it. We are now, so to speak, in winter. But for Y.K.K. the winter will be crisp and clear. We need not be miserable because we are sure that at this time next year we will be able to get raw materials more cheaply and abundantly. Let's prepare ourselves, therefore, for a new spring when we can offer society newly developed materials and products". I believe this is the way to contribute to society. Y.K.K. achieved the present position of the world's largest zipper manufacturer because we were and are aiming to serve society.

'Y.K.K. investments made in the past years amounted to ¥190 billion—some ¥160 billion in Japan and ¥30 billion in foreign countries—including our plant in Kurobe which is unique in the world. We are confident that our products are of the best quality and the cheapest in the world. It is because we not only produce zippers and zipper parts but also we develop and produce ourselves machinery used in our factories all over the world.'

INNOVATION AND INTEGRATION

Y.K.K. had been a major innovator in the zip market. In 1953 the company had introduced its own automatic slider manufacturing machines. In 1957 it produced the world's smallest zipper, concealed zips were introduced in 1958 and in 1959, nylon zips were unveiled. Production was also increasingly integrated. By 1960 Y.K.K. had established two major zip production units, a copper drawing plant, an aluminium alloy plant, a nylon zip plant and a dyeing plant.

Y.K.K. had constantly sought to increase its production integration. There were seven key departments; the metal zipper department; the metal department making flatwires for zippers, and rolled copper components; the aluminium building product department which made aluminium doors and window frames; the machinery department producing automatic zip making machines and in addition automatic machinery for window frame manufacture and machine tools; a textile department making cotton yarns, cords and zipper tapes; a plastic zipper department; and a zipper components department producing sliders, top and bottom stops and bale chains. The integrated nature of Y.K.K. production allowed the company to control its prices closely and to pursue the aim of highly automated, low labour content processes.

Mr. Yoshida had personally developed many of the technological advances which had given Y.K.K. part of its competitive edge. He was attributed with some 400–500 patents, and was constantly on the lookout for new and improved ways of production or materials and energy savings. As a result Y.K.K. was able to produce zips and sell them at a profit at a price below many competitors' costs.

OVERSEAS EXPANSION

In 1964 Mr. Yoshida went on a world tour and returned to Japan convinced that 'zippers offered a barometer of civilised life'. As a result he launched a 10-year expansion plan to transform Y.K.K. into a multinational corporation. By the late 1950's the company had re-established its export markets in South East Asia, Latin America and the Pacific Basin. Import restrictions and the like led to the subsequent establishment of joint venture manufacturing in Indonesia, Malaysia and Thailand. In the 1960's the number of joint ventures was increased with new activities in Costa Rica (1963), New Zealand (1963), Taiwan (1965), Trinidad and Tobago (1965), Australia (1968), El Salvador (1968), Singapore (1960) and Lebanon (1971). In addition a wholly owned subsidiary was established in Hong Kong (1966) to serve the local market and also the U.K.

In 1960 Y.K.K. began its advance into the developed country markets with the opening in New York of its first plant in the U.S.A. Subsequent expansion had made the Y.K.K. the second largest supplier in the U.S.A. In 1964 Y.K.K. opened a sales office in the Netherlands and this had been expanded to a network of six assembly and production units in the Netherlands (1964), France (1976), U.K. (1967), West Germany (1967), Belgium (1971) and Spain (1971). In each case the new plants had been established in areas offering regional financial incentives providing the subsidiaries with advantages such as lower taxes, financial assistance and lower tariffs. The subsidiaries in the developed countries had also been established as wholly owned ventures. Describing the company's international progress Mr. Yoshida commented:

'Now Y.K.K. has about 30 plants throughout the world. It is just like seeing seeds spread over the soil by wind developing into a forest.

But Y.K.K. in the United States, in the Netherlands, in Britain, etc., are not Japanes companies. They have their roots deep into the soil of the countries where they are operating. When I send out employees on foreign assignments, I always tell them, "As you are going to work, for instance, in Britain, try to get acclimatised to local conditions and to behave as the British do. You are Japanese. You can do nothing about it. But try to be good citizens in your new community. Respect their manners, customs and traditions even when you may find them strange or funny. Do not forget to contribute your share to the progress of the local economy and welfare; remember that if you do not render services to your new community, you will neither be accepted by them nor succeed".

'In advanced countries there are fewer restrictions and we can do our business with more satisfaction than in developing countries, where we are required to tie-up with local partners. From the viewpoint of the Y.K.K. management principles, local shareholders tend to be obstacles rather than partners. Many of them lack the willingness to consider the betterment of employees. More often than not, they are eager to let employees work for as low wages as possible and to put all the profits into their pockets. When establishing joint ventures in Southeast Asian countries, most of the Japanese companies go into business with Chinese residents with whom they have dealings. But in many cases, that choice turns out to be the cause of failure. I always recommend those people who seek joint venture partners to choose nationals of the host country. If you have overseas Chinese as your partners, it can lead to local people boycotting your company. People in many Southeast Asian countries seem to have a feeling that they have been economically oppressed for a long time by Chinese merchants. They tend to think, therefore, that the Japanese come into their country to exploit them hand in hand with the Chinese living in their country. You should not forget that every country has its own nationalism. It is all right to have a Chinese manager in the sales department, but management of factories should be put in the hands of local nationals. Unlike commercial business, a manufacturing company must have its roots deep in the soil of the host country. You cannot pull it out easily even if you come to face unforeseeable and unfavourable situations. A factory is like a bridge; once you have built one at a certain place, you cannot move it to another place for many years to come. In many cases, local businessmen are short of money and are not good at doing business. But we must think in long-run terms and help them in financing and transferring technical and management know-how.'

THE MANAGEMENT OF OVERSEAS SUBSIDIARIES

The top management of Y.K.K.'s overseas subsidiaries was usually Japanese although the company had adapted its domestic approach to allow for cultural differences and encouraged local employees to participate in the management of the business. Mr. Yoshida explained:

'In the management system prevalent in Japan you must wait for ten or fifteen years before you are a department manager, and an additional five or ten years to be a member of top management. If we tell our local employees to wait as their Japanese counterparts do just because it is the Japanese way, they will not be fully persuaded. In our overseas companies, therefore, we promote capable employees of two or three years service to the level of departmental manager or temporal members of the board of directors. Because we do not fully understand their abilities and character, they sit at the table of the board of directors for one term and are replaced by other candidates in the next term. We are hoping that in this way we can develop them into good executives.

'I always tell my local employees, "Make your best efforts in your work since all of you have the ability and opportunities for advancement to directors, whether you work in an office, or a warehouse or a factory". When I visit our plants abroad, the first person I would speak to is a warehouseman or a delivery man. I tell them in this way, "You are doing a very important job for your company. And when you make delivery to plants or offices of our customers, you will find there one or two small things which can be easily improved but to which no one ever paid attention. Then, put forward your suggestions to them. They will appreciate your attentiveness and suggestions. They will realise that you are different from ordinary delivery men. Thus, you will win good reputation among them and they will come to listen to what you tell them. And then, you will be entitled to join our sales staff". Some of them were moved by my words to tears, some would blush with joy. They would tell me that they would work for Y.K.K. as long as they could. It is surprising to find that in the United States and European countries as well as in developing countries there exists too wide a gap between executives and workers to allow effective communication. I cannot help feeling that workers in these countries sell themselves for daily or monthly wages. In this respect the situation in Japan is much better than in other countries.'

The Japanese general managers responsible for individual subsidiaries overseas were not especially prepared for their new positions. The company did not feel it could afford to give a great deal of attention to this. As Mr. Yoshida explained;

'They are sent to their international assignments without any special preparation and training. To speak frankly, they are sent to their new post of general manager of an overseas company without any well advanced notice and go right to work visiting their new customers one after another. Because they are not especially trained for their new assignments abroad it can happen that we have complaints from our foreign customers that our new general manager cannot fully understand what they tell him over the phone. If I could find in our company some people who could act in my place, I would happily send such people abroad. But I cannot, and I will not be able to. Although our international assignees have to develop their capability still further and they have to deepen their understanding of the basic philosophy of Y.K.K., they have a very valuable asset; their youthfulness. They should work diligently fully utilising their vitality. I always tell them, "You are to be pioneers of the country where you are going to work. You are expected to work not only for our company but also for the benefits of your host country. You should have pride that you are doing a task which may make your name written in the history of that country".'

Planning for international operations took place at an annual meeting held at the main Ikuji plant in Japan. Some 125 overseas managers met with the home country management to discuss long term plans and performance objectives. This meeting was also used to invite a large group of guests from overseas countries including bankers, customers, and government officials to observe how Y.K.K. conducted its world-wide operations.

In the main local managers enjoyed considerable autonomy. All decisions at the local level were made on the basis of full discussion among both the expatriate Japanese and local national managers by means of 'officers' meetings (known as teirei yakuin kai in Japan).

EMPLOYEE MOTIVATION AND REWARD

Mr Yoshida believed strongly in gaining the commitment of all employees to the company. In Japan this was achieved partially through the share participation scheme. This system had not, however, been extended overseas and although Mr. Yoshida was anxious that this should be done he was also worried that shares in the company might fall into the wrong hands. He commented:

'I hope to distribute Y.K.K. stocks to overseas employees as we do in Japan as soon as possible. But we must be careful in doing so in foreign countries. They could sell Y.K.K. stocks at a good price. Once we have distributed stocks among local employees, they as shareholders have legitimate rights to keep or sell their stocks. If they want to sell them, we can do nothing about it. Suppose that our employees in the United States sold their stocks to one of our American competitors. If he comes to see our plants, we cannot refuse him. Or, if someone could obtain a certain amount of stocks and wanted to sit on our board of directors, we cannot do anything but accept him. The question is how we can give them a sense of participation in the management of their company as worker-shareholder; and how we can prevent stocks distributed among our local employees from being sold to outsiders. If and when we can find a solution of this problem, we will carry out our stock-sharing plan in our subsidiaries abroad.

'However lofty and noble ideas one may have, it is only pie in the sky unless we translate it into practice. So, we are giving serious consideration to stock-sharing plans in our overseas companies. At the beginning of this type of plan, foreign employees will agree not to let their shares go at any price. But since they are not accustomed to our way of thinking, avarice may make them change their mind. Even in Y.K.K. there were some employees who did not want to have Y.K.K. stocks which we offered them and some others who sold their shares to people other than Y.K.K. people. And some portion of our stocks are held by outsiders. Today our employment increases more rapidly than our issued stocks. Therefore, we must now ask our older worker-shareholders to transfer their stocks to newcomers upon their retirement, or at the time of capital increase we ask them to turn over a part of their right for new stocks to younger employees to that as many employees as possible can participate in the stock-sharing plan.'

Mr. Yoshida did however recognise that not all Y.K.K. workers would necessarily agree with his basic philosophy. He believed, however, by winning the trust of employees it was possible to forge a common bond which would allow the company to maintain its dynamic leadership position in the zip fastener market. He concluded:

'In these days, even in Japan, you cannot expect to find simply honest people any more. Almost all people are slightly tainted with the socialist ideology. In the past 40 years our company was exposed to one crisis after another and every time we overcame difficulties by unifying our strength. The only way to win the trust of our foreign employees, therefore, is to put into practice what we are telling them, however trite or seemingly insignificant that may be. We do not hope to have only good workers. I think that all the workers of our company joined us, led by a certain bondage which is invisible to us.

We must treat them kindly and it is our duty to make good workers of them. They are just like transplanted trees; it takes time before they are accustomed to new environments.

'The basis of the management philosophy of Y.K.K. should not be changed. But when my son and his colleagues assume responsible positions in the company, it will reflect their own value judgements and will be slightly different from what it is now. Similarly, our principal idea must take different forms from country to country. Management philosophy must have flexibility to adapt itself to different times and different countries. Through this process, we can make it closer to the ideal one.'

Mr Yoshida was a major stockholder in the company. Other significant holdings were held by Vice President Kyamatsu Yoshida, the Yoshida family, Yoshida Realty and the Nihon Kogyo and Hokkaido banks.

22

Yoshida Kogyo KK (B)

In 1967 Yoshida Kogyo KK, better known as Y.K.K., the largest manufacturer of zip fasteners in the world established a sales company, Y.K.K. Fasteners (UK) Ltd. as a prelude to trying to penetrate the British market for zippers. To get round the tariff wall established by the British to protect their own industry Y.K.K. proposed to import from its Hong Kong based subsidiary thereby taking advantage of the tariff position of the Crown Colony. However this initial strategy proved relatively unsuccessful due to problems of meeting local delivery schedules and an inability to meet the product range required by the British market.

In 1960 it became clear that Y.K.K. needed to manufacture in the U.K. if it was to penetrate the market. Mr. Susuma Takahashi was appointed as general manager of the British subsidiary and charged with the responsibility of achieving a market share of around 40 per cent within 5 years.

THE BRITISH ZIP FASTENER MARKET

In 1976 there were 12 zip fastener manufacturers operating in the U.K. Industry sales of fasteners to the home market were £15.8 million in 1975 and expected to reach £18.7 million in 1976. Three manufacturers dominated the market each producing a full line of metal and plastic zips. The market leader was Y.K.K. which held around 40 per cent of the total market, next came the Aero Zip Division of the U.S. conglomerate, Textron with about 23 per cent and finally Lightning Fasteners a subsidiary of Imperial Metal Industries, itself a majority owned subsidiary[1] of Imperial Chemical Industries (ICI).

Since their introduction zip fasteners had substantially expanded the range of applications for which they were used, largely replacing buttons. Zips were included as integral components in clothes for men, women and children; they were used in shoes, furniture covers, bed clothes, sports

---

[1]Imperial Metal Industries has since become independent of I.C.I.

EXHIBIT 1
U.K. Zip Fastener Sales 1973–6 (£000)

Item	Year	1973	1974	1975	Until September 1976
Metal	Sales	7,464	6,938	6,756	5,729
	Export	1,494	954	1,646	1,827
	Import	1,813	687	773	838
Plastic	Sales	10,205	9,382	9,120	8,472
Total	Sales	17,669	16,320	15,876	14,201
	Export	1,494	954	1,646	1,827
	Import	1,813	687	773	838

goods, fishing nets, luggage and the like. The market was divided between plastic and metal zips with the plastic overtaking metal since the late 1960's. Details of the U.K. market are shown in Exhibit 1 which indicates that demand had actually fallen over the period from 1973 to 1976.

Y.K.K. IN THE U.K.

Y.K.K. began manufacturing in the U.K. on the Astmoor Estate in Runcorn in 1970. It was housed in a temporary factory equipped with two finishing machines, until a new factory was completed nearby. The permanent plant came on stream in 1972 employing a total of 76 people, including 5 Japanese staff. From the start it made over two million zips a month. In 1973 employment doubled while production tripled and Y.K.K.'s market share grew to 17% in sales, placing it equal second in sales with Aero and behind Lightning Fasteners. By 1976 the Runcorn plant had been expanded to 5 times the size its original size and provided jobs for 300 workers, 6 British managers and 12 Japanese staff under Mr. Fujisake, the factory manager. At Y.K.K's London sales office there were 2 Japanese and 6 British salesmen, a Japanese accountant and 35 British office staff under Mr. Takahashi, Chairman of Y.K.K. (UK). Production had reached 12 million zips per month and Y.K.K.'s share of the U.K. market had risen to over 40 per cent.

Commenting upon Y.K.K.'s success in Britain Mr. Takahashi said 'Everybody can sell—it's very easy but production is very difficult. If we can supply zips at the same quality and prices as our competitors we will get the contract because we can guarantee 24 hour delivery and we can do that because, even though our quality is good, our production is even better. We, for example, are always buying new machines, normally every 5 years, where some UK companies use the same machines for anything up to 20 years[1] Details of Y.K.K. (UK's) financial performance are given in Exhibits 2 and 3.

Y.K.K. concentrated on a number of factors. First, its products were high in quality and were priced competitively. Second, the company aimed to provide an extremely fast service for its customers, an important factor in the fashion garment industry. Finally Y.K.K. concentrated on servicing large accounts such as Littlewoods, Marks & Spencer and G.U.S.

In the fashion garment business, manufacturers planned several seasons per year. As a result the decision on colour, length and kind of zipper came relatively late in the planning cycle and the ability to deliver zippers quickly could be a competitive advantage. Y.K.K. was able to supply over 200 zipper colours in lengths varying from 4 to 26 inches and in a choice of metals or plastics. Upon receipt of an order the desired colour and type of zipper was selected from coils of zippers produced at the main plant in Japan. Banks of Y.K.K.-produced machines then cut the coils to length and attached end stops and sliders. As a result Y.K.K. could provide a delivery service which its competitors found difficult to match.

THE EXERCISE OF JAPANESE MANAGEMENT AT RUNCORN

At the Runcorn factory as in Japan itself, it was impressed upon every employee that he mattered as an individual and that his contribution to company success was vital. Describing the system at Runcorn, *Management Today* contained the following comments from employees:

'The company is now a much more human organisation. The difference is harmony—working together', said one.

'They are sociable, and they are fairer than English bosses. They consider you more. If you have complaints, they listen. Because they are fair with us, we pay them back by pulling our weight'—so says Lillian Gallager, 41, a British housewife, and a packer in Y.K.K.

John Davies, 45, who represented the employees on the Runcorn plant's Japanese-style 'Works Committee', said: 'We asked to finish at 4.30 p.m. instead of 5.0 p.m. on Friday, they gave us that. We asked for a Christmas holiday; they gave us that. We asked for a sickness scheme, and they gave us that too. These Japanese seem to understand us, I wouldn't want to work for an English firm again'.[2]

Neither Mr. Minami, the production director nor Mr. Takahashi spoke very good English, although they were supported by other Japanese managers who were more fluent. Despite this handicap, they had won and maintained the respect of their staff and labour force precisely because

[1]'The Confident Cycle of Y.K.K.', *Management Today*, Jan. 1974, p. 66.
[2]*Ibid.*

YKK Fastener (U.K.) Balance Sheets for Fiscal Years 1970–1975 (£)

	1970	1971	1972	1973	1974 (From April to Dec.)	1975
Fixed Assets						
Machinery	49,700	119,000	390,000	450,000	284,000	1,200,000
Motor Vehicles	4,500	9,000	12,000	17,000	13,500	24,000
Furniture and Equipment	7,000	15,150	23,000	25,000	23,000	29,000
Factory Building		173,618	345,984	521,713	753,357	999,510
Total Fixed Assets	61,200	317,568	770,984	1,013,713	1,673,857	2,252,510
Current Assets						
Stock	222,232	497,917	1,009,850	1,490,265	1,843,317	1,835,628
Debtors	133,837	291,529	489,570	702,383	897,792	1,310,342
Prepayments	13,798					56,410
Import Deposits						
Bank Balances and Cash	260,967	354,423	181,734	969,673	1,029,887	1,835,237
Corporation Tax Receivable			4,800			
Total Current Assets	630,854	1,143,869	1,685,954	3,162,321	3,771,176	5,037,617
Current Liabilities						
Creditors	17,019	140,507	102,681	387,357	378,261	490,625
Bank Loans	300,000	538,218	1,029,381	1,129,381	1,629,381	1,859,381
Associated Companies	198,158	305,216	603,579	836,645	1,074,426	1,419,688
Corporation Tax	4,000	10,000		55,000		
Total Current Liabilities	519,177	993,941	1,735,641	2,428,883	3,082,068	4,019,694
Total Net Assets	173,098	467,516	721,297	1,747,151	2,362,965	3,270,433
Ordinary Share (£1)	160,000	320,000	320,000	1,000,000	1,000,000	1,000,000
Reserves	13,098	147,516	401,297	747,151	1,362,965	2,270,433
Total Capital Employed	173,098	467,516	721,297	1,747,151	2,362,965	3,270,433

Source: Directors Reports.

EXHIBIT 3

YKK Fasteners (U.K.) Six-year Operating Summary (£)

	1970	1971	1972	1973	1974	1975
				(From April to Dec.)		
Sales	605,203	1,455,286	2,964,094	4,320,112	4,194,761	7,961,177
Depreciation	11,196	28,077	74,640	146,990	197,002	457,399
Profit Before Tax	79,619	88,566	228,691	373,729	519,476	1,000,943
Tax	4,000	7,613	10,000	55,000	55,000	266,431
Profit After Tax	75,619	80,953	218,691	318,729	464,476	734,512

YKK Financial Performance Analysis 1970–1975

	1970	1971	1972	1973	1974	1975
Sales Growth %	13	240	203	146	129	142
PBT/Sales %		6	7.7	8.6	12.4	12.6
C.A./C.L.	1.21	1.15	0.97	1.30	1.22	1.25
C.A.—Stock/CL	0.79	0.65	0.39	0.69	0.63	0.80
Debtors/Sales × 365 (days)	80.6	73	60	59	78	60
Creditors/Sales × 365 (days)	10.2	35	12.6	32.7	33	22

Source: Directors Reports.

they made no attempt to differentiate themselves from the rest of the company's employees. All the managers at the London head office or at the factory wore thin nylon wind-cheaters, so that the effect was not to differentiate them in terms of clothing. They were also prepared to turn their hands to anything that needed to be done, showing that they were not above the common or garden tasks. Mr. Takahashi, at the sales end, still did jobs like packing and opening cartons one day a week.

For Mr. Minami, a qualified mechanical engineer, it was a little different. He frequently spent half a day working on a machine in the factory. For him, the principle was the same as for Mr. Takahashi, but he also radiated a love of his machinery. Walking round the factory, he would often dash off to perform some quite small deed, such as refilling a paint tray.

The Japanese had imported two key personnel management concepts to Runcorn. One is 'WA' which can be roughly translated as 'unity and harmony'. The other is 'RINGI' the process of giving everyone concerned a chance to participate in making proposals and arriving at an ultimate decision. The inevitable delays of this system could cause frustrations, but its strength was that once a decision was taken it was one that everyone understood and agreed with.

In Japan all company decisions were based on a consensus of managerial opinion and even the most junior executive expected to put forward his views and be listened to. As a result policy ideas often came from below instead of being sent down as directives from above. Although the process was time consuming, it ensured that everyone felt involved and that all managers understood the issues entailed in a particular decision. It also meant that people accepted unwelcome decisions more easily because they knew their opinions had been fully considered. The management of Y.K.K. (UK) enjoyed a great deal of autonomy. They could make plans for purchasing materials, machines, production, sales, new factory buildings, personnel hiring and the like in response to local market conditions.

Employees were encouraged to discuss and learn from their mistakes. This was only one of the changes that Japanese managers were attempting to introduce in the West. Also, if an employee was inefficient, he was not casually dismissed, Japanese managers would try several times to find him the right job in the factory. Therefore, most of the employees felt more secure in terms of it being unlikely they would lose their jobs, than in any British company.

No Y.K.K. plant employed more than a few hundred workers. Consequently the management could know workers personally, and grievances could usually be sorted out informally. At this size, the works committee could also 'negotiate' about matters which would be too trivial for the management's time in a larger set-up. The workers at Runcorn were, for instance, stopped from smoking in the factory because of fire regulations, and had to negotiate a five-minute time allowance for smoking in the toilets. Then there were other things like a shop in the canteen and a telephone.

In 1972, the workers heavily rejected the idea of joining a union; in such a small factory it was doubtful if a union could do much except clog up the works. In any case there had been no serious grievances to contend with. Workers' job aspirations could be very flexible because there was no distinction between staff and factory workers. Thus a factory hand could, if he was so inclined, become a white collar worker.

Small size allowed each factory to be a more human place of work. Two or three times a year, there were factory parties—not just the usual Christmas events—at a hotel as a way of thanking the employees. Even more spectacular, there was an annual trip to Japan, worth about £500 a person, for ten employees. Selection was based on criteria like length of service and seniority. Usually it worked out at five from London and five from Runcorn. The smaller the labour force, the more valuable this kind of perk was, as everyone had a reasonable chance of going.

THE REACTION OF ZIP FASTENER MANUFACTURING ASSOCIATION

Y.K.K's immediate and rapid expansion made the British Zip Fastener Manufacturing Association members irritated and they sought to bring government pressure to bear against what they saw as unfair competition. Describing Z.M.A's action, the *Financial Times* reported, on 17th May 1974:

'In the past five years one Japanese company, Y.K.K., has captured an estimated 20 per cent of Britain's £15m zip fastener market, according to the Zip Fastener Manufacturers' Association.

Y.K.K., the biggest zip maker in the world, has done so by importing finished and semi-finished zips, thereby destroying all the work the UK makers had done to build a useful balance of payments surplus through their export efforts.

That is what representatives of the Z.M.A. claimed when they met officials at the Department of Industry in London. They went along at the invitation of the Parliamentary Secretary for Industry, Mr. Gregor Mackenzie, yesterday.

In the House of Commons earlier this week, Mr. Jeffrey Rooker, Labour MP for Perry Barr, whose constituency happens to be next door to the factory of Lightning Fasteners—largest of the U.K. manufacturers—went even further and maintained that the British market was in danger of being overrun by imported Japanese products. Several thousand jobs were at stake, he warned.

Mr. Rooker seems to have somewhat overstated the U.K. industry's concern about the Japanese company's ability to "overrun" the market completely but British manufacturers have been annoyed by the way Y.K.K. was encouraged by the Government to set up two years ago in Runcorn new town in a development area.

They maintain that before then British had a self-sufficient and efficient zip industry which was beginning to develop a healthy export business. (The £15m market is equivalent to roughly 300m zips around 60 per cent of them made from plastics and most going to the clothing industry).

They also estimate that without Y.K.K's appearance on the scene the balance-of-payments situation last year would have still shown £3.5m of exports, but only around £1m of imports instead of the £3m actually recorded.

Y.K.K's managing director, Mr. Susuma Takahashi, agrees that his organisation does import from Japan and Hong Kong semi-finished goods for finishing off at Runcorn. But within five years the company hoped that 80 per cent of the components needed would be made at Runcorn, with only speciality items being imported. This would entail increasing the number of employees at Runcorn from 200 to around 600.

Mr. Takahashi maintained that Y.K.K. itself had begun to contribute to Britain's export performance, and would continue to build up its export business. This point is received with some puzzlement by the rest of the industry, an industry at present dominated by Lightning Fasteners, part of Imperial Metal Industries, with the U.S. group Textron's subsidiary Aero Holding about the same kind of market share as Y.K.K.

For Y.K.K. already claims 22 per cent of total world sales of zips. On its home ground in Japan it has 95 per cent of the market. It has manufacturing subsidiaries in the U.S., and Canada, and its European operations include Italy and the Netherlands, apart from the U.K.

"So, where is it going to export to?" asked one of its rivals yesterday.

After the meeting between the ZMA and the Department of Industry last night a joint statement said that the Department "took sympathetic note of the Association's representations" which the Department undertook to "bear in mind" in discussions it proposed to have with Y.K.K.'

The Y.K.K. Response

To cope with the political and social pressure in the U.K. market, Y.K.K. decided to build a new factory in Runcorn for manufacturing fastener sliders. Describing Y.K.K's quick response to the political and social pressure in the U.K. *Asahi*, one of the leading Japanese newspapers, reported on 17th November 1976:

> 'Y.K.K'S 100 per cent subsidiary Y.K.K. Fastener (UK) started to build a new factory in the Runcorn plant for manufacturing fastener sliders by investing ¥500m, . . . Y.K.K. has a policy to export fastener sliders to its overseas subsidiaries with the exception of some South East Asian countries where they set a high tariff barrier. This is partly because the investment in a slider manufacturing plant is quite expensive and partly because it costs too much to manufacture small volumes of sliders. The fastener sliders which will be manufactured in the U.K. will cost 50 per cent higher than those imported from Japan . . . This is mainly because the regulation of EEC countries importing zip fasteners becomes more stringent as with motor cars, steel, etc. . . . When the manufacture of fastener sliders in the U.K. is running smoothly, the company estimates that 80 per cent of the components needed will be made at Runcorn and that they will then cope with the zip fastener dumping problem which has been a cause of trouble for the last three or four years.'

RECENT EVENTS

Despite the assurance given by Y.K.K. Mr Alan Williams, Minister of State for Industry, in reply to a question from Mr. Jeff Rooker, advised Parliament in March 1978 that imports from Japan had not been reduced. Indeed imports of complete slide fasteners rose in value terms by 63 per cent in 1976 and by 45 per cent in 1977. Imported slide fastener parts by value rose by 44 per cent in 1976 and 19 per cent in 1977. The Y.K.K. assurances given in 1974 were made when imports of complete fasteners had risen by 53 per cent and parts by 47 per cent. The following year the rise in complete fasteners fell back to just under 7 per cent, although parts were up nearly 37 per cent.

In 1977, Y.K.K. had taken between 40 and 50 per cent of the British market and was the acknowledged market leader. Since 1972 Lightning Fasteners, the subsidiary of Imperial Metals located in Mr. Rooker's Birmingham constituency with about 30 per cent of the market, had closed two factories and made redundant about a third of its workforce.

Y.K.K. answering Mr. Williams, claimed that his comments had placed the company's reputation at risk. The company told him there had never been an undertaking given to the Government on the level of imports which would be brought in from Japan or the level of exports that would be made. Mr. Takahashi said that what the company had submitted was a plan 'which was merely an estimate and not in any way a duty to be carried out to the letter'.

The company maintained that the 1974 plan was still going ahead but imports from Japan had been necessary to make good the shortfall on fastener components caused by construction delays on the Runcorn plant extension. The Department of Trade and Industry noted 'We shall be watching the level of fastener imports from Japan very, very closely. The company have told us they intend to reduce the import level'.

Decision Making and Leadership

23

General Trading Company

VIEW FROM THE CHAIRMAN

The following comments are taken from the Chairman's statement in the 1975 Annual Report on General Trading Company:

'The last year has been a difficult period for your company, due to the generally low level of economic activity in most of the countries in which we operate, and to the continuation of price increases for many of our oil-based raw materials. In view of these constraints the financial results can be regarded as reasonably satisfactory and already we are starting to see improvements in the operating results of many subsidiaries—particularly those in Europe and North America. The profitability of our Australian region is still rather low, due partly to low sales and reduced margins in the Singaporean market. However, recent reorganisation within this area is expected to contribute to improved profitability within the next six months.

This report would not be complete if I failed to recognise the contributions made by all our staff, who now total over 110,000, based in almost 70 countries. The year has been a trying one for them but the results are a testimonial to their loyalty and effort.

We are continuing our policy of training and developing management throughout the Group and, wherever possible, appointing nationals to the senior positions in the countries in which we operate. Your directors recognise that a multinational enterprise such as ours owes much of its success to its behaviour in foreign countries and to the high opinion in which it is regarded by governments and consumers. Our policies of non-involvement in the domestic affairs of host countries, and the appointment of nationals to senior positions, all help to retain the high esteem in which the Company is held.'

BACKGROUND INFORMATION

General Trading Company (GTC) was a major European based multinational company manufacturing and distributing a wide range of consumer products, mainly in the plastics, domestic housewares, clothing and packaging businesses. The group controlled about 200 manufacturing units and had over twice as many sales and distribution centres throughout the world. Because of the need to react flexibly to conditions in each country each subsidiary was allowed considerable autonomy in such areas as product development, marketing strategy and conditions of employment. Headquarters were involved in major capital investment decisions and in the development and promotion of top executives. Control was exercised via Zone Managers, to whom the General Manager of each subsidiary reported.

VIEW FROM SINGAPORE

The Chief Accountant in Singapore had a perspective on the Company's managerial practice that differs somewhat from the Chairman's. The rest of this case tells the story as seen by this man.

The Australian zone covered Australia, New Zealand, Hong Kong, The Philippines, Malaysia and Singapore; Mr. Adrian Fawley has been the Zone Manager since 1967. I had been appointed Chief Accountant of the Singapore operation a short while later. Although I was responsible to the Singapore General Manager I was, of course, involved in most meetings with Mr. Fawley when he visited us to discuss operating results and future plans. While this involvement allows me to appreciate Mr. Fawley's reasons for selecting new General Managers, it had not made the consequences of his decisions any easier to bear.

THE BUILDER

Mr. Hamish Trubshaw had been transferred to Singapore from England in 1959. His terms of reference included the establishment of an independent subsidiary—Singapore had been under Malaysian control since operations started in the 1940's.

He was certainly a man with a mission. In 1961 a new sandal factory was opened, and in 1964 shoe manufacturing was transferred from its old location into new premises alongside the sandal plant. Product development progressed at a very fast rate and by 1969 the subsidiary was manufacturing 308 different lines. In 1969 a new plastics moulding plant was built on the same 117 acre complex and the company transferred into a modern head office.

Staff at all levels were enthusiastic as they were all sharing in this rapid development in terms of involvement, promotional prospects and generally in the overall success of the company; turnover increased over 500% during this period.

When in August 1970 Mr. Trubshaw was transferred back to Europe as a Zone Manager the company was, to say the least, well established with a competent team of divisional managers and support staff.

THE CARETAKER

Mr. Brian Thomas was a man of 63 who had been General Manager in Japan for many years. He had recently retired and was living in England when he was asked to come to Singapore and hold the reins for about a year pending the appointment of a replacement for Mr. Trubshaw.

For the twelve months or so that Mr. Thomas was with us little effort was given to product development—although countless hours were spent playing with a new design of ski boot.

THE DEVELOPER

Len Erikson came to us from GTC Japan, where for two years he had been in charge of the Leisure Products Division. Naturally the senior staff were disappointed that yet another outsider had been imposed on them and the general feeling was that he would have to be "bloody good" to gain anybody's cooperation. Fortunately he was outstanding and when he left at the end of 1972 to become General Manager of the larger Indian subsidiary everyone was sorry to see him go.

In a very short time this man summed up the market. He salvaged our Sportswear Division by withdrawing from the Manufacturers' Association which set trading terms within the industry, he cut out about a quarter of our customers, who we were calling on unprofitably, and established a major programme of product development which was enthusiastically received.

Senior management were allowed considerable freedom and emphasis was placed on the development of junior and middle managers by in-company training and participation in outside courses.

THE ORGANIZER

The Malaysian General Manager was due to retire at the end of 1973 and Adrian Fawley decided that his successor, who had been in charge of marketing in Malaysia, should have outside experience before taking over. It was, therefore, convenient to appoint him General Manager in Singapore for twelve months.

Kok Doo Chan was a very capable man who had some interesting ideas about organisation structure which he would be able to evaluate in this period. He took distribution away from marketing, separated wholesale and retail sales, and relieved Product Sales Managers of administration and distribution, putting them under a new National Sales Manager; he also created another new position of National Distribution Manager. Needless to say there were a few casualties as a result of the reorganisation, the most significant being the Marketing Manager who, in his sixtieth year, decided he was not going to be pushed around any more. Another colleague, the Personnel Manager, also approaching sixty, told me one day that he was thinking of leaving but shortly afterwards was appointed to the Board and is still with us.

The changes were frustrating to many middle managers who, after receiving sound training in Mr. Erikson's reign, found that the jobs they expected to hold had either disappeared or been taken by other men.

We also started a new product development programme, concentrating on small domestic housewares which had apparently been very successful in Malaysia.

THE EVALUATOR

Joe Munroe, from GTC (U.K.) Ltd., was the next General Manager. He was a very successful management accountant who had gone into marketing and risen through the ranks very quickly. Obviously talented he realised that the company was losing ground in terms of profitability and concentrated on a rigorous programme of cost control. The distinction between marketing, sales and distribution probably helped in the identification and control of costs in these areas.

The emphasis in product development was also changed. Joe insisted on far more detailed evaluation of forecast sales revenue and production costs before authorising a development proposal. Unfortunately the delay this causes often results in us 'missing the boat' in the introduction of new products.

THE BUREAUCRAT

When Joe returned to Europe in mid-1975, Ian Rosser from the United States was appointed General Manager. (The last two appointments seem to be part of a wider policy of transferring managers between zones in the interests of achieving greater consistency in management style throughout the world.) He has already made it perfectly clear that he expects to return to the States within two years.

Although Mr. Rosser's track record in Sales is pretty good, he is not at all popular. He has imposed his own style of management throughout the company, with detailed job descriptions, procedures and tightly controlled budgets—we don't talk to each other now—we put it in writing. Once again the organisation structure is being re-shaped; we now have two National Sales Managers, one for household good and one for other products.

In order to increase turnover and market share—both have fallen over the last year—we have just signed a contract to become sole distribution agent for a small sports-good manufacturer, which will mean calling on many of the customers cut out by Len Erikson. New product development is mainly based on existing American products, in the interest of reducing development costs. Even so, we're going to need a miracle to live up to the Chairman's expectations.'

24

Crown Company

Mr. Edward Woodstock had recently received word of his appointment as general manager of plant X, one of the older established units of the Crown Company. As such, Mr. Woodstock was to be responsible for the management and administration at plant X of all functions and personnel except sales.

The Crown Company conducted marketing activities throughout the United Kingdom and in certain foreign countries. These activities were directed from the head office by a director in charge of sales.

Manufacturing operations and certain other departments were under the supervision and control of a deputy managing director. These are shown in Exhibit 1. For many years the company had operated a highly centralised-functional type of manufacturing organisation. There was no general manager at any plant; each of the departments in a plant reported on a line basis to its functional counterpart at the head office. For instance, the personnel manager of a particular plant reported to the director in charge of personnel at the head office, and the plant accountant to the financial controller, and so on.

Mr. Woodstock stated that in the opinion of the top management, in particular the managing director, deputy managing director and the sales director, the record of plant X had not been satisfactory for several years. The board had recently approved the erection of a new plant in a different part of the city and the use of new methods of production. It was anticipated that the relocation of plant X would take place quite shortly after Mr. Woodstock's appointment as general manager. Lower costs of processing and a reduced manpower requirement at the new plant were expected. Reduction of costs and improved quality of products were needed to maintain competitive leadership and gain some slight product advantage. The proposed combination of methods of manufacturing and mixing materials had not been tried elsewhere in the company. Some features would be entirely new to employees.

According to Mr. Woodstock the top management of the Crown Company was beginning to question the advisability of the central control of

N

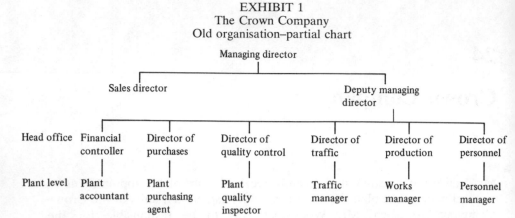

EXHIBIT 1
The Crown Company
Old organisation–partial chart

manufacturing operations. The board had consequently decided to test the value of a decentralised operation in connection with plant X. They apparently believed that a general management representative in plant X was needed if the new experiment in manufacturing methods and the required rebuilding of the organisation were to succeed.

Prior to the new assignment Mr. Woodstock had been an accounting executive in the financial controller's department of the company. From independent sources the case writer learned that Mr. Woodstock had demonstrated analytical ability and general administrative capacity. He was generally liked by people; however, although he was personally acquainted with the head office executives, Mr. Woodstock had met few plant personnel. From top management's point of view he had an essential toughness described as an ability to see anything important through. By some at the head office he was regarded as the comapny's efficiency expert. Others thought he was a perfectionist and agressive in reaching the goals that had been set. Mr. Woodstock was aware of these opinions about his personal behaviour.

Mr. Woodstock summarised his problem in part as follows: 'I am going into a situation involving a large number of changes. I will have a new plant; new methods and processes but most of all I will be dealing with a set of changed relationships. Heretofore all the heads of departments in the plant reported to their functional counterparts in the head office. Now they will report to me. I am a complete stranger and in addition this is my first assignment in a major "line" job. The men will know this.'

'When I was called into the deputy managing director's office to be informed of my new assignment he asked me to talk with each of the functional members of his staff. The directors in charge of production, traffic and personnel said they were going to issue all headquarters instructions to me as plant general manager and they were going to cut off their connections with their counterparts in my plant. The other head office

EXHIBIT 2
The Crown Company
New organisation–partial chart

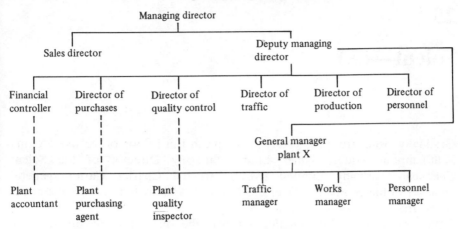

executive admitted their functional counterparts would report to me in line capacity. They should obey my orders and I would be responsible for their pay and promotion. But these executives proposed to follow the common practice of many companies of maintaining a dotted line or advisory relationship with these men. I realise that these two different patterns of head office plant relationships will create real administrative problems for me.'

Exhibit 2 shows the organisation relationships defined in these conferences.

25

Solent—(A)

Gradually rising from his chair, in his plush third-floor office overlooking Southampton Water, James Lind, Managing Director of the Solent Chemical Company Limited (SCC), greeted Charles Carter, general manager of the company's Overseas Division, and invited him to take a seat across from his desk.

'You have many fine qualities—I was the one who recognised them when I promoted you—but I have been reviewing your progress these past few months and the results have not met our expectations'. 'Charles', he added as Carter remained standing, 'I am sure that something has gone wrong'.

Carter fidgeted at the window, watching the October morning across the harbour. His face reddened, his pulse quickened, and he waited for Lind to continue.

'The costs in your division are higher than budgeted, the morale is low, and the branch managers are unhappy with your stewardship', Lind said. 'And your cooperation with Pat Harris has fallen short of satisfactory'.

Carter grew angrier at the mention of Harris, an aggressive young man with a master's degree from a leading British business school. Although Harris was a latecomer to SCC, Carter knew that everyone was pleased with his performance.

'Charles, I was speaking to one of our suppliers at my golf club last week. He intimated that your dealings with him had not been entirely clean. And that is what hurts me the most.'

'I must ask for your resignation, and I will do my best to help you find a more suitable opportunity', Lind concluded awkwardly as Carter stared out of the window.

'James, I can't believe it', Carter finally replied. 'It's just all wrong.' He turned slowly from the window, his face blood-red.

'I have been with this company for nearly ten years. I built my division. I agree, this year's results are not quite what you expected, but my division is still the largest contributor to corporate profits. I'll bet your friend Pat has been telling you about the "supplier deals". Well there is absolutely no truth in it, and I won't stand for it! He won't stop at anything to get power.'

There was a long silence as Lind and Carter stared at opposite corners of the large office. 'I will not resign', Carter suddenly declared, and he left the Managing Director's office coughing, his face flushed and his heart pounding.

Lind stood motionless as he watched the door close. He was uncertain about what to do; it had never occurred to him that Carter might refuse to resign. He decided to proceed as he had originally planned, but with one modification.

'Janice please take a letter', he said to his secretary. First he dictated a letter to Charles Carter informing him that his employment with SCC was terminated as of that afternoon, 10 October, 1977. Then he dictated a memo for release to all departmental heads informing them that Carter had resigned and that Joseph Ward, the planning manager in the Operations Division, would take over as acting general manager, Overseas Division.

Carter, meanwhile, was trying to contact his previous boss and old friend, Roy North. North was past Managing Director of Solent and an influential member of the company's board of directors. Carter was determined not to let this happen to him; he planned to take his case to the board for deliberation.

COMPANY BACKGROUND

The Solent Chemical Company was a manufacturer and marketer of a range of rubber products and in 1976 had £30 million in sales and an e.p.s. of £0.92. The company was listed on the London Stock Exchange with one million shares outstanding, yielding a stable dividend of £0.75 per share over the last five years. During these five years, sales had grown at an average rate of 6%, but market share had dipped slightly. As one competitor put it, 'a certain amount of "creative accounting" must have been used to maintain that dividend'. Board members held under ten percent of outstanding stock; the rest was widely owned.

Solent Chemical Company sold rubber piping and hoses to industrial and commercial customers throughout the UK. A large part of the overseas business was in South America, developed many years earlier by a Sales Director whose family was Brazilian. Its manufacturing plant and London and Southern Sales office were located in Southampton. Its two other UK Sales offices were in Manchester and Glasgow. Within Overseas there were seven selling companies: five in South America and two smaller offices in Dubai and Lagos.

The company usually negotiated hard for its basic raw materials with an affiliate of an international oil company, the only local supplier able to meet the specifications required by their manufacturing process. It was deemed uneconomic to obtain this raw material from other parts of the UK.

The company also sold rubber footwear, mainly beach sandals in the Overseas markets, but not in the UK. These were purchased locally in the

UK from several manufacturers; Solent being in no way involved in their manufacture.

Solent had two close UK rivals in its industry: the larger company had annual sales of £60 million; the smaller, sales of £15 million a year. It was a fiercely competitive industry, and special favours or discounts were sometimes granted to win customers from another company. Customers were precious: just ten clients accounted for one-quarter of Solent's sales.

PEOPLE IN SOLENT

Exhibit 1 shows Solent's organisation structure in skeletal form. The Board consisted of a part-time chairman, managing director, financial director, personnel director, operations and manufacturing director (presently vacant) and three non-executive directors. The sales function was divided between two general managers, UK and Overseas, who though not members of the board, were always invited to attend when major issues of sales policy were discussed; in particular the long range plans and annual budgets.

EXHIBIT 1
Solent Chemical Company Ltd.
Organisation Structure, September 1977

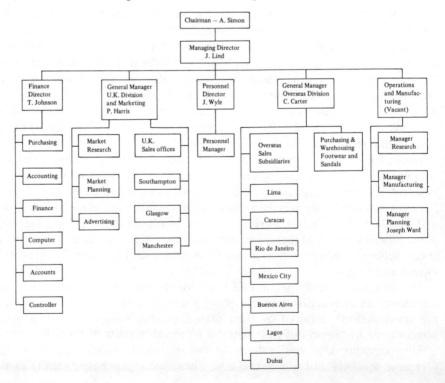

In addition to managing five divisions, and the normal duties of the Managing Director, Lind took a special interest in the negotiations with the unions and the purchase of the principal raw materials and the footwear and sandals for overseas markets. The specific responsibility for labour relations rested with the Personnel Director. (Exhibit 2 provides basic details on all the directors.) Control of the purchase of raw materials lay with the Operations and Manufacturing Director. The General Manager, Overseas Division, was responsible for buying the footwear and sandals. That individual was Charles Carter.

The Personnel Director, John Wyle, 51, had been with the company the longest. However, he had suffered two serious heart attacks since joining the company in 1945. According to Roy North, the former Managing Director, 'John is one of the best industrial relations men I've met and he is a good personal friend; but his health concerns me and several of the other directors'.

Since joining the company as a clerk in 1952, Thomas Johnson had risen in 1973, at the age of 44, to the position of Finance Director. Johnson was often involved in negotiations in which Lind took part. When Roy North retired in December 1974 Johnson had been under serious consideration. But as one member of the selection committee later said, 'Johnson was quite happy in his present situation. He is a little lazy. He never wanted the top job'.

James Lind was selected—over Johnson and a few other unsuccessful candidates from Solent and other companies in the Southampton area—to succeed North. He joined the company in January 1976 from a top executive position in an Employers' Federation based in London.

One month after Lind arrived, the Sales Director, Robert Grant, 46, had been killed in a motor accident late at night on the M3 on his way home from Heathrow after a business visit to South America. Grant had been responsible for company-wide sales and UK advertising. After this tragedy Lind consulted Andrew Simon and the other directors to seek their support for creating two new divisions; the UK division and the Overseas division. He was anxious to avoid a repetition of the tragedy by cutting down the work load and travelling of his top sales executives.

The head of each division was to be a General Manager with the courtesy title of director for use when dealing with customers. The General Manager UK Division was also to be personally in charge of marketing. Lind felt that it would be undesirable to create two new directors in the place of one sales director at this stage, though it was understood privately between Lind and Simon that at a later date, one or both General Managers might be appointed to the board if company growth warranted it. This had never been mentioned to either General Manager and was not known within the company. The UK and Overseas divisions were officially created by Lind in February 1976 with the board's unanimous approval.

In March, he promoted Charles Carter, who had been with Solent for

EXHIBIT 2

Solent Chemical Company

Board of Directors

Name	Age	Position	Background	Outside interests	Years of Association with		Shares held
					Industry	Company	
Simon, Andrew	65	Chairman	Entrepreneur	Construction	20	20	30,000
Lind, James	59	Managing Director	Engineer	—	28	2	4,000
Johnson, Thomas	48	Finance Director	A.C.W.A.	—	24	24	1,000
Wyle, John	53	Personnel Director	—	—	26	26	1,000
Fields, Anthony	54	Non executive	F.C.A.	Chairman of International Company.	—	15	12,500
North, Roy	56	Non executive	Engineer	previous M.D.	16	10	15,000

over eight years, to general manager of the newly-created Overseas division. Carter, 47, had responsibility for the conduct and profit performance of all the Overseas sales offices and the small volume of exports to other parts of the world. He participated in marketing decisions such as advertising and promotion. His division was charged a pro-rata share of expenses on the basis of divisional sales.

Carter spent the first six months after his appointment almost entirely out of the UK, working closely with the subsidiaries and getting to know the staff in each office, returning only for major policy discussions and to negotiate with footwear suppliers. Being a strong delegator, once he had the right people who were loyal to him in each of the seven sales offices, he spent most of his time in the Southampton office.

Three months after consultation with the board, Lind suggested to Frank Adams that he resign as Operations and Manufacturing Director. Financially the company was not prospering, as rising material and labour costs had squeezed margins. Lind felt that Adams, after 27 years at Solent as Manufacturing and Operations Director, was utterly lacking in ability to negotiate raw material contracts and that he had directly contradicted his new boss whilst negotiating with a supplier. Adams was so upset at being asked to leave the company that he resigned without pressing his rights as a director to demand an extraordinary general meeting. Adams, then 53, became an estimator for a local construction firm at one quarter of his former salary. The position of Operations and Manufacturing director was left vacant and the three managers who had been working for Adams—in charge of manufacturing, planning and research—were reporting directly to Lind.

Lind's third major organisational change was to bring an old friend of his who he hoped would develop new marketing strategies for the entire company. Pat Harris, from a chemical company in Manchester, became general manager of the UK division, with additional responsibilities for company-wide marketing. In this capacity, Harris, 33, was responsible for the conduct and performance of the three UK sales offices and for company-wide market research, market planning and advertising campaigns.

CARTER RETALIATES

'Tony, thank you for meeting me here, and for cancelling your other engagement to see me. I'm sorry, but I had to talk to you. Something has happened that I think you should know about.'

Leaning heavily on the table in the restaurant in the Yacht Club, Carter related his story to Anthony Fields, who as well as being a non-executive director of Solent was chairman of one of the biggest companies in the Southampton area. He was also on the board of a company whose South American subsidiaries were major customers of Carter's division.

As Carter told him the details of his forced resignation, Fields fingered the stem of his wine glass and looked puzzled.

'I control the company's three biggest customers, you know' Carter was saying, 'I can easily take them to the competition. And he still has the gall to accuse me of accepting gifts from suppliers, with absolutely no proof. I think Harris has put him up to it. He's been charging a substantial proportion of his division's expenses to my division. I have been arguing with him about these expenses during the past month, and he finally told me he'd have my head if I went to Lind about it'.

'I'm truly sorry to hear about this Charles', Fields said, 'And it comes as such a surprise. I was in the office this morning with James and Andrew. James never mentioned to me that your resignation was being considered. I cannot understand the secrecy; that's not the way the company is run'.

'After almost ten years with this company' mused Carter, 'what do I get? Not a mention of recognition by the board meeting, just a letter and the legally required redundancy money.'

'I'd like to help in any way I can' said Fields. 'What I suggest is that you wait and see what happens at the next board meeting, scheduled in two weeks. Let's hope that we can work out an appropriate way to deal with the matter.'

'Well', said Charles, 'I just hope the board takes this chance to finally straighten up the organisation. The board's relationship to the company, the delegation of responsibility, the criteria for employee evaluation—there are a lot of things that have remained garbled and unclear ever since Frank Adams was asked to resign. The morale of the executive staff is low. Earnings are not improving. Everyone is concerned about his own skin. Who will be axed next?'

'I think this is a case of wrongful dismissal and am going to my solicitor this afternoon to find out what my rights are.'

LIND STICKS TO HIS GUNS

Carter's refusal to resign shook James Lind, who spent the rest of the day trying to analyse the situation. He realised that he had made a mistake in promoting Carter a year and a half ago at a salary of £10,000 p.a.*, even though his sales experience and past performance had pointed strongly to Carter as the man for the job. But then Lind remembered that Carter had been warned about a year ago to take it easy for a couple of months, and he had been watching his diet ever since.

'I must stick to my guns', Lind decided. 'I refuse to be blackmailed by the three powerful customers Charles has in his pocket. I cannot let my

---

*In addition Mr. Carter was provided with a Rover 2000, a non-contributory pension amounting to 15% of salary, life insurance, BUPA at top grade for self and family, telephone rental and membership in several professional bodies.

authority be challenged, especially by a man I believe has taken back handers.'

After a sleepless night Lind telephoned the Chairman, Andrew Simon, to inform him of Carter's resignation.

'Yes, Jim, John Fields called me yesterday about it.' Simon told him. 'He was quite upset. And I saw Roy North at a cocktail party last night. He too knew about the event, and looked disturbed. It is a sad situation, Jim. But you are the boss. We will try to handle the matter appropriately at the next board meeting.'

Simon replaced the receiver thoughtfully. For the first time in his 20 years as Chairman, he felt that there was a conflict between the management of company affairs and the way he thought they ought to be managed.

Approaching sixty five, Simon was still active and healthy, and never missed a board meeting. He had been the caretaker Managing Director for one year in 1956. His deep concern for the company was reflected in the way he usually helped in its decision-making process: carefully and after long consideration and debate. He had discussed the matter of Adams' resignation privately first with Lind, and then with other members of the board before becoming fully convinced that Adams should go. Similarly he had spent long hours deciding on Lind's appointment and had talked over the matter exhaustively with several members of the board individually. Both Mr. and Mrs. Lind were interviewed thoroughly before the board selected him as managing director.

THE BOARD MEETS

The board of directors of the Solent Chemical Company Limited met at 11.00 a.m. on 24 October, and, as usual, the meeting promptly came to order. The items on the agenda were: the company's performance for the third quarter; the economy for the coming year; the contributions that SCC made annually to three local charities, and a proposal to spend £100,000 replacing an extruding machine.

26

Carter Ltd. (A)

The Directors of Carter Ltd. were nearing the end of their monthly board meeting. Peter Gascoigne, the managing director, asked Bob McCall, the group chief executive of the Elmec product group, to introduce the final item entitled 'Letter from the Department of Industry'.

'Basically, gentlemen', McCall started, 'we have been approached by the Department of Industry (DOI) with respect to possible aid for development of our new generation of electronic products. Although the letter you have with your papers talks only in general terms, I have already had a preliminary discussion with Harry Miller of the DOI and he has indicated that they see this as a major project which fits into the Government's general support of microprocessor applications. We could eventually be talking of thirty or forty million pounds of Government money over the next five to seven years. It is, of course, difficult to be certain about the conditions on which the aid would be granted but Miller appeared to be thinking along the lines of a possible joint venture between Carter and a State controlled organisation, possibly the National Enterprise Board. You can see this poses some major decisions for us, given our uncertainty about the future of the Elmec group.'

CARTER LTD. AND THE ELMEC GROUP

Carter Ltd. had grown into a significant company in the U.K. during the first thirty years of the twentieth century serving Britain's engineering industry with a range of components and sub-assemblies. The second world war had created major growth and this was followed during the post war period, particularly the 1960's and 1970's by major diversification moves. Sales of approaching £800 million at the end of the 1970's were spread across six major product groupings which involved both manufacturing and distribution.

The Elmec group operated in the original business of the company supplying components and sub-assemblies to a major consumer goods industry. The Elmec group accounted for about 10% of Carter's total sales.

The manufacturing division of the Elmec group had sales of approximately £40 million per annum. Roughly three-quarters of these sales were original equipment supplies to the consumer goods industry. The remainder were sold internally to the sales and service division which sold both Elmec's products and products sourced from other manufacturers in the after market. For the past four years the manufacturing division had done little better than break even. However the sales and service division was one of the most profitable activities in the whole of the Carter company.

The other activities of Carter were spread at home and abroad. About 35% of Carter's total sales were sold to a wide variety of State owned or controlled organisations in the U.K. The proportion for each of the six main product groups ranged from 70% to 5%.

EUROPEAN STRUCTURE

The Elmec Group produced components and subassemblies in very high volumes. The consumer goods industry involved, and all its principal component and sub-assembly supplying industries had experienced considerable rationalisation since the second world war. By the 1970's Carter's Elmec Group was the only major supplier of its particular product line in the U.K. In a similar way there was only one major manufacturer in each of France, Germany and Italy. Each of the four national suppliers dominated their home markets. Unfortunately for Carter, its home market had, like much of U.K. manufacturing industry, lost considerable ground compared with its continental competitors. Consequently Elmec had only about 9% of the European market compared with the 33% of its Italian competitor, 22% of its French competitor and 18% of its German competitor. The remaining share of the market was supplied either by vertically integrated subsidiaries of the end product manufacturers or by a number of small specialist suppliers.

In general it was informally accepted that none of the four big suppliers would make major inroads into the others' home markets. During the past two years though, the Elmec group had obtained a number of orders from the Continental end product manufacturers in an effort to offset the general decline of their home market. To obtain these new orders, Elmec had to offer prices below those obtained in the U.K. market. No retaliation had yet been provoked, but many felt that any further inroads would produce some reaction from at least one of the other three companies.

IMPACT OF MICROPROCESSORS

Elmec together with most of the rest of the industry had been aware for the past four to five years that their current electro-mechanical product had only a limited future life. Microprocessors offered the opportunity of a more effective product at a lower price. The exact form the new product would take was however uncertain. Research was currently being conducted on at least four major variants with no company in the world able to invest in research in all possible areas. The timing of the new product introduction was also uncertain. By 1979 a few very expensive end products had electronic equipment incorporated in them. Introduction in the mass market was probably unlikely to occur earlier than 1984 or later than 1990.

Elmec and its competitors had entered into a number of cross licensing agreements with each other to try and cover the possibility that someone else's research would create a successful widely accepted product. Elmec's customers were inherently conservative and not noted for major innovations. Product mistakes in the market place were very expensive, and thus represented a barrier to the introduction of the new generation of electronic products. However once one major manufacturer introduced the electronic equipment into their product, it would be difficult for the rest of the industry not to follow suit.

U.K. GOVERNMENT INVOLVEMENT

The U.K. Government was involved in many ways in industrial activity. In this it was no different from its counterparts in other developed countries, although the extent and mechanisms varied from country to country. Most basic industries in the U.K. were state owned including coal, gas, electricity, railways, steel, and the post office. In the engineering sector, British Leyland (cars) and Rolls Royce (aero engines) were state owned. The 1974–79 Labour government had also taken the aerospace and shipbuilding industries into state ownership. Other segments of the transport industry were state owned and through the British National Oil Corporation the State had a considerable involvement in North Sea Oil. All told, the state employed 28% of the total U.K. workforce. In the industrial sector the state employed 2.0 million out of a sector total of 9.3 million employees.

The Government also sought to influence industrial activity through the National Economic Development Office (NEDO), through the National Enterprise Board (NEB) and through the use of a wide range of grants.

NEDO consisted of 18 sub committees each covering a major industrial sector. These sub committees in turn were broken down into a total of 39 sector working parties, each of which covered a narrower sector of industry. The purpose of NEDO was to bring representatives of management, the trade unions and government together to identify and discuss problems affecting a particular industry sector and to plan future strategies aimed at making the sector more successful in world markets. As a result of several years work NEDO had identified about six industrial sectors in which it was felt the U.K. could be particularly successful in the future, either in reducing import penetration or in gaining additional exports. Elmec's products fell within a small part of one such sector.

The NEB was essentially a state holding company. Its main holdings were British Leyland and Rolls Royce. However, during the past four years, it had acquired significant holdings in a range of small companies often providing funds for product development in return for an ownership stake.

Microprocessors and their applications had been identified by the Department of Industry as a major and crucial area requiring government support. £50 million had been committed to the creation of INMOS, a company established to make microprocessors. Grants were available to encourage companies to invest in product development which involved the application of microprocessors. Typically these grants covered about 25% of development costs. Elmec was already making use of such grants. Approximately £1 million would be received over the next two to three years.

THE ELMEC DECISION

After several minutes discussion during which various facts, mostly related to the above sections, were established, Peter Gascoigne took up the conversation. 'This potential offer comes at a time when the future of the Elmec's manufacturing activities are under serious review. As you are all aware, we have experienced considerable difficulty during the past few years. The industry we supply has steadily lost ground against its European competitors, causing us in turn to lose ground to our competitors and to suffer continual cost disadvantages. We are already faced with a 10% redundancy of 300 people because of falling volumes. Elmec obviously does not have a long-range future if it is not eventually able to manufacture a successful range of microprocessor based products. To pursue the research and development programme vigorously for the next five to seven years will probably require Carter to invest at least £30 million in Elmec products and manufacturing facilities. Carter would have no problem providing the funds but it is extremely difficult to forecast a satisfactory return on the investment with any degree of certainty and more importantly Carter has many other investment opportunities in its other divisions which promise a better and more certain return. We are unlikely to be able to fund all these investment opportunities.

'There appears therefore to be three basic strategies we can pursue with Elmec. First we can treat it as a run down situation with a view to leaving manufacturing in 5 to 7 years. This would, from our point of view, be highly profitable since we could drop our low profitability contracts rapidly, consolidate the activity in one site and stop investing. It would, however, be a one-way route because the new generation of electronic products would eventually take our remaining business. This might cause some problems for the sales and service activity but these could probably be resolved by buying in from our competitors. Our customers would of course be obliged to source from outside the U.K. and all the current

3,000 jobs in manufacturing would go. I don't suppose the politicians or the DOI will be very pleased about either of these issues.

'Our second basic choice would involve selling Elmec's manufacturing, and possibly the sales and service activity, to one of our major European competitors. We have reason to believe that at least one might be interested. If we choose to pursue this strategy, we could act as soon as possible because our negotiating position can only get weaker as time goes by. Such a sale could of course run into problems with either or both the EEC and the U.K. government. If the purchaser were French or German, the U.K. government might well remember the Lucas-Ducellier and GKN-Sachs situations. A possible alternative selling opportunity might exist with one of the major electronic companies who could see Elmec's market as a new product area to integrate forward into.

'The third major route would be to go along with the DOI and accept the opportunity to form a joint venture with a Government controlled agency. It can certainly be argued that from a national standpoint this is the strategy we should adopt. If we succeed with the product development ahead of our three main European competitors, there would be a major opportunity to take customers on the continent and radically alter the current market share situation. With a £30 to £40 million investment the DOI are certainly not going to be interested in honouring gentlemen's agreements about who controls which part of the market. Success would ensure the maximum number of jobs in the U.K. even though there would probably be a substantial drop, perhaps to between a third and a half, of today's level. It would also make a significant contribution to the U.K. balance of trade. Of course there is no guarantee that we would succeed. We might simply dissipate the tax payers money in an investment into which frankly we are not prepared to put Carter's money. Also it is very unclear what form this joint venture with Government would take and how it would be related to the rest of the Carter organisation. As you all know, I believe there is too much Government interference in industry and I have expressed this view publicly on more than one occasion. Some of my colleagues in other companies will certainly give me some strange looks if they hear that we at Carter have set up a joint venture with the Government.

'Gentlemen, we have a very complex decision ahead of us. If we offend the DOI and the politicians, many other areas of Carter business might be affected. Obviously we do not have to make a final decision today. However, Bob will have to have further discussions with Harry Miller at the DOI within the next two weeks and we really ought to try to be consistent in our approach throughout our handling of this issue.'

Managing Complexity

27

The Volvo Group

In 1977 the Volvo Group celebrated its 50th anniversary as a manufacturer of cars. During this time it had become the largest industrial organisation, in terms of sales, in the Nordic region accounting for 8% of total Swedish exports. The group's product range included cars, trucks and buses, tractors, construction equipment, forest machinery, marine, industrial and aircraft engines and a range of leisure products. Between 1973 and 1978, cars had averaged 54% of total sales, trucks and buses 26%, tractors, construction and forest equipment 11%, engines 7% and other products 2%. Although small variations in the breakdown of sales took place from year to year depending on the economic conditions of various markets, the group clearly belonged to the world's automotive industry. By the standards of the automotive industry, Volvo was very much a small company. Disregarding the U.K. and Japanese automakers, Volvo came only in 9th place in the European table of automotive manufacturers for 1977 (see Exhibit 1).

By the the late 1970's the car product range consisted of essentially two models. The 200 series was produced with 4 and 6 cylinder engines in saloon and estate versions and accounted for about 75% of unit output. The acquisition of DAF cars in Holland had added a small car (the 66) and then a medium car (the 343) to the range. The 66 and the 343 together accounted for the remaining 25% of unit output.

The main emphasis in trucks and buses has been on large vehicles. Typically 80% of trucks produced were in or over the 16 ton gross vehicle weight ranges. The Volvo Penta inboard marine engines have been significant in volume terms on a world scale for small craft. Aircraft engines however have been sold only to the Swedish airforce.

All told, the company manufactured over 100 products which were sold via 2600 dealers in 160 countries. The company operated 29 plants in Sweden and had major factories in Belgium, Holland and Canada. Details from the profit and loss account and balance sheets for the period 1971 to 1978 are given in Exhibits 2 and 3. Profitability and profit margins by pro-

EXHIBIT 1
Tables of Sales & Output for European Vehicle Manufacturers, 1971 & 1977

	1971			1977		
	Sales ($m)	Car Output (000's)	C.V. Output (000's)	Sales ($m)	Car Output (000's)	C.V. Output (000's)
Volkswagen	4720.0	2078.0	267.8	10410.5	1977.2	241.6
Ford of Europe	3178.0	1104.4	198.9	8324.0	1448.0	199.0
*Fiat	2677.6	2001.9	69.3	8240.1	2167.1	122.6
Daimler-Benz	3650.0	284.2	188.1	11148.3	401.3	248.1
British Leyland	2860.1	852.0	174.2	4554.0	629.0	143.0
General Motors (Europe)	2414.7	1039.5	118.9	5050.0	1016.0	92.0
Renault/Saviem	2138.7	1318.3	148.8	10006.1	1584.5	209.0
Volvo	1258.6	214.4	15.4	3477.0	225.7	25.2
Peugeot	1677.7	559.5	61.4 }	8513.2 }	1451.0 }	208.0
Citroen	1035.7	615.0	100.0 }			
Saab-Scania	854.4	73.7	12.8	2321.7	76.5	21.7

Source: Company Annual Reports.
*These figures represent Fiat's turnover in cars and commercial vehicles only. The total turnover of the Fiat Group in the two years was respectively $2,936m and $12,975m.

duct group for the same period are shown in Exhibit 4 and sales by product group and geographic region are given in Exhibit 5.

Mr. Pehr Gyllenhammar became managing director of Volvo in 1971. During the 1970's he embarked upon a number of major strategic moves designed to strengthen Volvo's position both in terms of its international capability and in relation to the other European automotive companies. This case describes the major strategic moves during the 1972–1979 period. Other major international moves by Volvo not described in the case include:

(1) The opening of an assembly plant in Ghent, Belgium in the 1960's. This plant was opened as insurance against Sweden's continued exclusion from the EEC.
(2) Investment in a joint engine plant to produce a 6 cylinder, 2.7 litre engine with Renault and Peugeot. This plant came into production in 1973 providing engines for the Volvo 260 models, the Peugeot 604 and Renault 30. Each of these models represented the top end of the respective manufacturers' product range.
(3) Negotiations with Berliet the French truck manufacturer aimed at amalgamating both companys' truck operations. These negotiations were dropped in October 1973.
(4) A shortlived attempt in 1973 to form a working relationship with Toyota.

EXHIBIT 2
Volvo Profit & Loss Accounts, to December 31 (millions SKr)

	1978	1977	1976	1975	1974	1973	1972	1971
Sales	19,133	16,168	15,743	13,692	10,537	8,996	7,346	6,104
Less: Cost of Operations	17,625	14,935	14,430	12,563	9,477	7,834	6,389	5,496
Operating Income before Depreciation	1,508	1,233	1,313	1,219	1,060	1,152	957	608
Less: Planned Depreciation	658	599	558	488	358	285	237	166
Operating Income after Planned Depreciation	850	634	755	641	702	867	720	442
Interest Received Less Paid	(204)	(170)	(173)	(142)	(7)	40	36	19
Other Income/(Expenses)	—	(113)[3]	—	2	42[4]	2	2	2
Income before Allocations & Taxes	646	351	582	501	737	909	758	463
Less Allocations to:[1]								
General Inventory Reserves	122	49	343	375	384	179	102	85
Extra Depreciation	(74)	(21)	3	32	(11)	41	21	39
Investment Reserve	103	—	91	42	30	191	212	89
Others[2]	20	6	(14)	(8)	141	10	20	10
Income before Taxes	475	317	159	60	193	488	403	240
Less: Taxes	152	130	112	74	86	240	228	113
Minority Interests	12	(11)	(16)	(22)	2	2	1	—
Net Income	311	198	63	8	105	246	174	127
Swedish Purchasing Power of SKr (1971 = 100)	51	59	65	72	80	87	93	100

Notes:
1. All allocations except write-down of shares represents untaxed reserves provided by Swedish legislation.
2. Special investment reserve, work environment reserve, extra appropriation to insurance reserve and write-down of shares.
3. In this amount extraordinary capital gains on sales of fixed assets of SKr 40 million and extraordinary exchange losses on loans of SKr 154 million have been included.
4. In this amount an extraordinary capital gain of SKr 40 million made by Volvo BM on sale of fixed assets has been included.
Source: Company Annual Reports.

EXHIBIT 3

Volvo Balance Sheets (SKr millions)

	1978	1977	1976	1975	1974	1973	1972	1971
Assets								
Current Assets:								
Cash, bank and short-term notes	2,385	1,868	1,837	1,589	1,414	1,578	1,298	981
Accounts Receivable	3,888	3,929	3,336	2,918	2,102	1,743	1,481	1,222
Inventories	6,903	6,643	6,015	5,137	3,922	2,588	2,014	1,857
Total Current Assets	13,176	12,440	11,188	9,644	7,438	5,909	4,793	4,060
Block investment accounts with Bank of Sweden	54	115	93	115	127	128	32	20
Fixed Assets	4,482	4,435	4,424	4,273	3,271	2,777	2,326	1,851
Total Assets	17,712	16,990	15,705	14,032	10,836	8,814	7,151	5,931
Liabilities & Shareholders Equity								
Current Liabilities	7,295	7,174	6,898	6,081	4,749	3,717	2,894	2,534
Long-term Liabilities	3,867	3,661	2,923	2,583	1,447	1,049	883	648
Untaxed Reserves	4,194	4,019	3,984	3,565	3,115	2,581	2,109	1,776
Minority Interests	199	185	65	80	10	8	11	5
Shareholders' Equity	2,157	1,951	1,835	1,725	1,515	1,459	1,254	968
Total Liabilities & Shareholders' Equity	17,712	16,990	15,705	14,032	10,836	8,814	7,151	5,931

Source: Company Annual Reports.

EXHIBIT 4

Volvo Profitability and Profit Margin by Product Group (%)

Profitability[1]	1978	1977	1976	1975	1974	1973	1972	1971
Cars	4	0	2	2[3]	6	14		
Trucks & Buses	11	11	11	11	13	15		
Marine & Industrial Engines	−3	4	5	3	14	9		
Construction Equipment, etc.	−1	3	7	11	14	9	N.A.	
Aircraft Engines, etc.	10	13	10	11	11	11		
Recreational Products	N/A	−1	−1	−18	1	—		
Group Total	5	5	6	6	9	12		

Profit Margin[2]	1978	1977	1976	1975	1974	1973	1972	1971
Cars	2	−1	1	1[4]	3	9	11	8
Trucks & Buses	10	11	9	7	11	12	11	10
Marine & Industrial Engines	15	1	1	−1	9	15	16	11
Construction Equipment, etc.	−5	−1	3	9	12[5]	9	5	3
Aircraft Engines, etc.	18	21	19	15	15	15	11	10
Recreational Products	N/A	−5	−5	−18	13	—	—	—
Group Total	3.4	2.9	3.7	3.7	6.6	10.1	10.3	7.6

Notes:
1. The profitability of the various product groups has been calculated on the basis of a model applied within the Group, whereby product group earnings are related to capital employed. Capital employed includes all assets, except liquid funds, with no deduction for liabilities. Assets have been determined at the net current replacement cost of property, plant and equipment.
   The stated profitability for the Group shows the return on total capital employed, including cash and short-term notes.
2. Profit margin reflects the relationship between the respective product groups' shares of Group income after financial income and expenses, and the product groups' invoiced sales.
3. Excluding products from Volvo Car B.V. the profitability is 4%.
4. Excluding products from Volvo Car B.V. the profit margin is 3%.
5. Excluding capital gain made by Volvo B.M. of SKr 40 million.
Source: Company Annual Reports.

ACQUISITION OF DAF CARS

In November, 1972, Volvo acquired 33% of the Dutch car manufacturer, DAF. The consideration was 110,000 new Volvo shares. This gave Volvo, at this time manufacturing only large cars, an interest in a manufacturer of small cars. Prior to November 1972 DAF had manufactured both cars and trucks but the company had been split into two separate operations. International Harvester, of the USA, acquired 33% of the new DAF truck company. Volvo increased its ownership in DAF cars to 46% in 1974 and 75% in January 1976 at a cost of SKr. 70 million. Of the remaining 25% the original DAF company still held 15% and DSM, the Dutch state owned mining and chemical company, held 10%.

Although DAF cars made a small profit in 1973 of SKr 20 million, losses of SKr 147 million had been incurred in 1974. Immediately after the

EXHIBIT 5

Volvo Sales by Market Areas and Product Groups (SKr millions)

I. By Market Area	1978	1977	1976	1975	1974	1973	1972	1971
Sweden	4,874	4,716	5,009	3,993	3,385	2,703	2,209	1,923
Nordic Area, excluding Sweden	2,453	2,266	2,069	1,625	1,388	1,258	1,043	947
Europe, excluding Nordic Area	7,272	5,382	4,741	3,848	2,594	2,543	2,054	1,489
North America	2,357	1,855	1,708	2,165	1,851	1,592	1,406	1,271
Other Markets	2,177	1,949	2,216	2,061	1,319	890	634	476
Total	19,133	16,168	15,743	13,692	10,537	8,986	7,346	6,104
II. By Product Group								
Cars	10,257	8,310	8,441	7,525	5,569	5,132	4,332	3,640
Trucks	4,830	4,059	3,634	2,990	2,307	1,854	1,396	1,127
Buses	455	447	428	321	211	134	112	61
Marine & Industrial Engines	911	802	747	601	507	424	335	256
Construction Equipment, Farm & Forest Machinery	1,773	1,729	1,778	1,588	1,349	986	819	745
Aircraft Engines, etc.	504	433	379	372	330	290	255	189
Recreational Products	403	153	155	112	84	—	—	—
Others		235	181	183	180	166	97	86
Total	19,133	16,168	15,743	13,692	10,537	8,986	7,346	6,104

Source: Company Annual Reports.

1976 move which gave Volvo managerial control, Mr. Gyllenhammar commented that there were two tough years ahead and that efforts would be made to step up sales immediately through the large Volvo sales organisation in order to use up DAF's spare production capacity. DAF car losses for 1975 amounted to SKr 82 million.

In February 1976 Volvo launched its new middle-range car, the Volvo 343. It was a 1.4 litre engine, three-door hatchback which was designed to fill the gap between the small Volvo 66 (originally the DAF 66) and the large 240 series. It was hoped that the three models would give Volvo a more comprehensive coverage across the whole of the car range and in particular provide a significant presence in the faster selling medium/small car sector of the market.

In February 1977, after further losses in 1976, Volvo initiated talks with the Dutch Government to negotiate additional finance. At that time, breakeven was not forecast until 1978. A major contributor to the company's unprofitability had been difficulties with the new 343. These difficulties were two-fold. The car had suffered from an 'expensive image' despite no price rises since the original launch. There had also been difficulties with component suppliers, caused by the demands of larger car makers taking precedence over Volvo orders. Consequently, parts often had to be installed after the cars had come off the assembly line or even after shipment. In July 1977 the Dutch Government turned down an offer of a larger stake in Volvo's Dutch subsidiary. By this time the government controlled the other 25% of the company.

On January 5th, 1978, a rescue plan was announced for Volvo's Dutch operations. The Dutch Government would increase its stake in Volvo Car B.V. from 25% to 45%. This would provide a cash injection of SKr 165 million. The government also promised further financial support equivalent to SKr 288 million until the end of 1980. Losses of the Dutch subsidiary from the time of its takeover to 1977 amounted to approximately SKr 500 million, and losses for 1978–80 were predicted to total a further SKr 475 million. Breakeven, estimated at an output of 100,000 units, was not expected until 1981. At that time Volvo and the Dutch Government would have the option to return to the previous 25%–75% shareholding ratio. One condition of the agreement was that Volvo would not develop or produce another car in the 343 class outside Holland. During the rescue negotiations, the largest Dutch union, the Metal Workers, accused Volvo of blackmail. They claimed the company would close down its Dutch operation, employing 5,500, unless the Dutch government provided finance. The union also criticised Volvo's marketing policy for Dutch made models, particularly for the 343, and claimed that this was the reason for the disappointing sales of the models.

After ironing out many of its faults, the Volvo 343 was relaunched early in 1978.

In March 1979, it was announced that Volvo and the Dutch

Government were discussing long-term plans for Volvo Car which would take the Dutch company up to the end of the 1980's. A Volvo Car spokesman denied suggestions that Volvo would pull out of its Dutch subsidiary unless the government increased its aid. Volvo Car B.V. accounted, at that time, for more than a quarter of the company's total car production.

THE U.S. CAR PLANT

In September 1973 it was announced that Volvo were to establish a car assembly plant in Chesapeake, Virginia. The plant, which was to become operational in 1976, would employ 3,000 workers and produce 100,000 cars per year. This would be a major contribution in raising Volvo's worldwide capacity from 250,000 to 400,000. The plant would be the first foreign-owned car plant on U.S. soil.

The reasons behind the move were several. The U.S. was Volvo's largest overseas market. Over fifty thousand cars had been sold in 1972, one-quarter of Volvo's total production, and sales had grown consistently since 1956 when Volvo entered the U.S. market, selling 5,000 cars. Volvo was the second largest European importer of quality cars behind Daimler-Benz.

Volvo could expect to save little from assembling in the U.S. Despite the fact that Swedish wage rates were the highest in Europe, they were still lower than those of American car workers. Also the U.S. levied a relatively modest tariff on car imports. Pehr Gyllenhammar, Volvo's managing director, explained the move, 'We are past the export stage. We must now move into assembly and manufacturing in our important markets, in order to get closer to those markets'.

The opening of the plant was postponed several times and then indefinitely. The reasons for this were the fall in U.S. demand for Volvo cars, sales falling from 58,400 in 1975 to 43,700 in 1976, and the underutilisation of capacity in its European plants. In 1979 the plant was being used to prepare imported cars for the Eastern U.S. market.

THE KALMAR PLANT

In June 1974 Volvo opened its newest car assembly plant at Kalmar in south-east Sweden. The new factory was hailed as 'the greatest event in production technology since Henry Ford introduced the assembly line', and its inauguration was attended by the heads of some of Europe's leading motor manufacturers.

The new plant was based on group assembly methods. Instead of a production line, Kalmar was equipped with some 200 electrically driven trolleys. These ran automatically along guide lines laid into the concrete floor and were controlled by a sophisticated computer system. In effect the trolleys, carrying their part completed bodies, from station to station replaced the assembly line. The computer system allowed groups of workers to work at their own pace, so that work could pile up temporarily at different parts of the plant.

The workers were split into groups of about 15. Each group was responsible for one part of the car, e.g. doors, chassis, electrical system, etc. Within the group, each worker could become a specialist in a particular type of job, or could change job every few days. Alternatively the group could be split into teams of two or three people who carried out all the jobs on one particular body.

Working conditions were exceptional compared to other car plants. Workers had plenty of space and light. Conversation was possible since all power tools were specially silenced and walls and ceilings included sound absorbing materials. Trolleys had special lift and tilt devices to avoid inconvenient working positions. Workers could stop at any time to have a coffee in separate carpeted rooms, each equipped with coffee machines, refrigerators and ovens. They had their own washing and changing facilities complete with saunas. The only provision laid down by management was that each group should complete its agreed production programme each day.

Kalmar was designed to eliminate the grinding rhythm and repetitive tedium of the assembly line which was becoming unacceptable in developed countries where affluent, well-educated, labour forces had a wide choice of employment opportunities. Volvo were experiencing very high labour turnover and absenteeism rates in their conventional plants despite wages among the highest in Europe.

At a cost of SKr 96 million for an eventual output of 30,000 cars a year, Kalmar was considered to be 10–15% more expensive than a conventional plant. With a workforce of 600, labour productivity was expected to be similar to an assembly line plant but the labour force required much more job training.

Volvo was convinced that group assembly was the way of the future. Part of the engine plant at Skovde was already operating on the same principle and the new U.S. plant at Chesapeake was to be constructed on the same lines.

Towards the end of 1976, an independent report published by Sweden's main national employers' and trade union organisations, showed that the Kalmar plant had been a reasonable success although the results had not matched up to all of Volvo's initial hopes.

The report's main critical finding was that the company's reported 10–15% extra investment cost had not been offset by savings. Also quality was not up to expected standards and expensive rectification work had been necessary. Output and labour efficiency were about the same as in Volvo's more traditional assembly line factories.

Volvo's major aim of reducing chronic absenteeism and turnover among its workforce was only partially successful, although reduced supervisory and back-up staff produced some savings.

In the first half of 1976, absenteeism at Kalmar was 14%, a significant improvement on the 19.6% at Torslanda the main traditional assembly plant, but not as low as Volvo had hoped. Comparative absenteeism figures for the same period were 16.3% and 20.8%.

THE PROPOSED MERGER WITH SAAB-SCANIA

On the 6th May 1977, proposals were announced for a merger between Volvo and Saab-Scania, the other major Swedish vehicle manufacturer. If the merger went ahead it would be the largest in Swedish industrial history. Volvo sales in 1976 totalled SKr 15.74 billion and those of Saab-Scania SKr 9.6 billion. The new company, to be named Volvo-Saab-Scania AB would be overwhelmingly Sweden's largest industrial concern with a turnover of SKr 25 billion and 100,000 employees. The merger plan still had to be approved by the shareholders, workers' representatives and the Swedish Government. The government had just been informed and Mr. Pehr Gyllenhammar, the proposed new managing director of the merged group, stated that the Minister's reaction had been favourable.

The motivations behind the planned merger were both economic and national. A joint communique issued by the two companies stated, 'Our choice was to enlarge the cooperation with foreign car makers or to create a coordination within Sweden, but the latter alternative has emerged as the most favourable one for the country and the industry'. The two manufacturers both needed to rationalise their joint production and reduce costs to meet international competition. At the time of the proposed merger, both companies were making a loss on their car operations. However by merging the truck and bus divisions, both of which were profitable, the new company would have one of the three largest truck operations in the world.

On the 29th August 1977 it was announced that the planned merger had been abandoned. The Volvo board decided to discontinue negotiations after waiting for 2 months beyond the agreed July 1st deadline for a decision from the Saab-Scania board. Mr. Gyllenhammar said that it was not worthwhile to continue talks 'as Saab-Scania is so negative'. He added that further delay would harm Volvo's planning for the future.

Opposition to the merger had developed first within the Scania truck division, whose managers could find little advantage in a fusion with Volvo. The Saab-Scania board then split over the merger when the car division management, with support from the white-collar union, also raised objections. It pointed to the problems of fitting Saab's front-wheel drive cars into the Volvo range.

Since the breakdown of the merger talks, Saab has improved its financial performance. For fiscal 1978, the company announced profits before allocations and taxes of SKr 465 million, up 54% on the previous year, a 9% dividend boost, a share split and a new share issue.

THE PROPOSED SALE TO NORWAY

On the 22nd May 1978, it was announced simultaneously in Oslo and Stockholm that Volvo was to be reorganised as a joint Swedish-Norwegian concern with a 40% Norwegian holding. The Norwegian Government would guarantee a SKr 750 million investment in the share capital of the new company.

Volvo was to become Volvo (Swedish-Norwegian). Its present shares were to be transferred to a holding company, Svenska (Swedish) Volvo AB, which would in turn own 60% of the share capital in the new joint company. A holding company, Norwegian Volvo AS, would be set up in Norway and would own 40% of the stock in return for its investment of SKr 750 million.

The highlights of the agreement were:

1. The new concern would develop and produce aluminium and plastic components for automobiles and manufacture a new car model in Norway.
2. The head office of Volvo Penta was to be moved to Norway where a new series of marine diesel engines would be developed and produced.
3. 3–5,000 jobs would be created in Norway.
4. Volvo Flygmotor, the subsidiary which manufactured Swedish military aircraft engines, was to be excluded from the agreement for security reasons.
5. Swedish Volvo would establish an oil company which was to be granted North Sea exploration rights.

Mr. Pehr Gyllenhammar said the agreement would strongly reinforce the company's capital base, give it a development potential it would not otherwise have had and allow investment in new techniques. The bulk of the capital injection would be used to fund Volvo's new car development plans.

Mr. Odvar Nordli, the Norwegian Prime Minister said the agreement 'broke new ground for Norwegian and Swedish cooperation in the fields of energy and industry'. The main aim was to help Norwegian industry through a difficult transitional phase by using oil wealth to create a more lasting industrial base.

Mr. Thorbjaern Faelldin, Swedish Premier, thought Volvo's agreement would help to secure Sweden's future energy supplies. Sweden had been trying to gain access to Norwegian North Sea oil and gas for a long time.

Details of the agreement were to be completed by October 15th 1978.

The agreement was to be signed on December 8th and come into effect by 1st July 1979.

Reaction to the deal in Norway could best be described as unenthusiastic. The opposition political parties were against it. A poll of 100 business leaders showed that only 4 would buy shares in the new company. Eighty of those polled felt it would be more sensible to use the money to provide direct support to viable Norwegian industry, e.g. by offering incentives for the establishment of new activities.

On December 8th 1978, the agreement was finally signed in Oslo by Mr. Nordli and Mr. Gyllenhammar. Norway would now pay SKr 850 million instead of the previously agreed SKr 750 million for a 40% share of Volvo. The extra SKr 200 million was to be paid to the new company, free of tax, as compensation for the reorganisation of the company and Volvo's planned investment in Norway.

At the same time Mr. Nordli and Mr. Olla Ullsten, Sweden's new Prime Minister, signed a 30 year agreement on industrial and energy cooperation. The main elements of this were a Norwegian commitment to supply Sweden with up to 4–5 million tons of oil per year for 20 years and the Swedish government's recognition that Norway should import between 1.5 and 2 million cubic metres of Swedish timber over the same period. This agreement was conditional on the Volvo deal going through.

On 26th January 1979, the Volvo Board acknowledged that it had lost its fight to obtain the necessary two-thirds support from shareholders for the Norway deal, and that it had cancelled the shareholders meeting scheduled for the 30th January. This effectively killed the proposed acquisition by Norway of 40% of Volvo.

The reasons behind the shareholders' revolt were:

1. Norway was acquiring 40% of Volvo too cheaply.
2. Volvo's commitment to creating jobs in Norway and paying dividends to the Norwegian holding company would have a harmful effect on the company's cash flow.
3. Volvo's capital requirements could be met more cheaply through the Swedish financial market without commitments to spend money and finance new jobs in Norway.
4. Volvo's entry into the oil industry entailed too much risk, since there was no guarantee exploration would be successful.

The rejection by the shareholders also rendered invalid the Swedish-Norwegian Government deal over oil and timber supplies.

After this setback Volvo announced plans to press ahead with its new model developments. It was implied that they would shortly be calling upon the shareholders for substantial new funds with a possible rights issue worth about SKr 400 million. It was not clear whether the shareholders, having rejected the board's chosen strategy, would now be prepared to cooperate with the present management.

Victory by the shareholders was seen as having possible political ramifications which might affect the future manoeuvrability of Swedish companies. Trade unions, who had strongly favoured the deal, and left-wing parties saw the shareholders' action as a classic example of capitalism subverting national interests. The chairman of the Volvo branch of the Metalworkers' Union stated that the shareholders' action should 'open the eyes of the whole people to the necessity for some form of wage-earner share-holding funds'.

The Swedish media had speculated that rejection of the agreement, which Mr. Gyllenhammar had negotiated, would result in his resignation. He had repeatedly said that the agreement did not involve his personal future but that of the company.

28

FIAT s.p.a.

In the latter part of 1975 Gianni Agnelli the President of FIAT was nearing the announcement of a decision on the future structure of the company. For some years he, together with his brother, Umberto Agnelli, the Managing Director, had been piecing together a coherent strategy to take the company as successfully into the 21st Century as it had come through 76 years of the 20th. The old monolithic form of the FIAT group was being changed into individual operating entities, but of the two groups of activities still undevolved from the original company, the steel group and the car group, the former posed particularly difficult problems. The steel group was a captive supplier to all of FIAT's companies. It had been built up only to serve FIAT's requirements and it was now a question of whether this group should or could stand on its own as an independent operating company, with or without a special relationship to the FIAT group companies.

EARLY HISTORY

The company was founded in 1899 by a group of Turin notables to make 'any type of engine, cars and automobile or road cars, trams and other rolling stock, electrical equipment, along with accessories and components, vessels of any size or system (even aeronautical) their spare parts, accessories, repairs and fuel treatment'.

Until the end of the sixties the company's guiding strategy had been to expand the automobile sector and to a lesser extent the commercial and industrial vehicle sector, to develop related product lines that were subject to production economies of scale (eg engines) and to develop other lines of semi-finished, intermediate or capital goods that were difficult to find on the Italian market.

The result was that for cars, the group made nearly every component part. Besides the steel making capacity, which had been installed in the 1920's, the steel group made forgings, (valves, axles etc), fasteners (nuts and bolts), springs, tubes, machine tools for its vehicles, plus a wide range of other items for which these components and others were used for end products. Activities of FIAT ranged through vehicle assembly (cars, commercial vehicles, (CVs) buses, tractors and earth moving plant) to annex activities (steel, components, machine tools) to the directly related fields (civil engineering, energy, rail transport) and to very different interests (tourism, newspapers, telecommunications).

The whole FIAT organisation was heavily centralised both for tax reasons (Italy operated a non-shiftable general revenue tax) and to obtain the benefits of a functional corporate organisation. The company structure was the classic pyramid style with a great deal of the management decisions taken at the top. All accounting was done on a cost centre basis: FIAT SpA was the only profit centre. Individual production units kept records of their direct costs but little else and did not run rigorous financial controls such as might be found in say, North American companies. All financial management and reconciliation of profits and losses was undertaken centrally in the name of the FIAT SpA Group.

Giovanni Agnelli, who was one of the founders, did not become chairman of the company until 1920 by which time FIAT was already building aircraft, had its own steel plant, had developed successful diesel engine designs and was a reputable producer of cars and commercial vehicles. Agnelli was strongly influenced by and a friend of Henry Ford. The latter had realised his own dream of constructing on one site a car starting with original basic materials and thus his operation was very similar to that of FIAT. Ford's ability to divine what was the right product to sell to the emerging car owning class was mirrored by Agnelli's similar ability and the early success of FIAT owed as much to Agnelli as that of Ford did to its founder.

When Agnelli died in 1945, his son having been killed in an accident, the place of President was taken by Professor Vitorio Valletta who had already been with the company some 20 years. Valletta's style was autocratic; reputedly every decision was taken by him. Even so, he saw the company through an enormous expansion, quintupling its turnover (to 1,065 billion lire) and quadrupling the labour force (to 135,374) by the time he stepped down in 1966. Notable developments during his period in control included moves into construction and power generating (diesel and gas turbine) equipment, jet aircraft production, licensed assembly in Spain (SEAT), the Kariba dam construction (by the Impresit off-shoot of FIAT), new advanced foundry investment, the passing of the 1 million cars production per year mark (1965) and the signing of an agreement with the USSR for a car production plant. FIAT's first experience in USSR had been in the 30's with various component factories and assembly in Poland had started in 1934. Other countries which had benefited from FIAT know-how or investment included China (aircraft), France (Simca cars), Argentina (tractors, diesel cars, commercial vehicles and rolling stock), Yugoslavia (cars and CVs) and Turkey (tractors).

o

The internal atmosphere that Gianni and Umerton Agnelli inherited was unusual even for an Italian company due to the almost feudal way in which Valletta had run the company. It was not unknown for him even to arrange marriages within the firm between couples he considered to be likely partners. Buttressing his own approach, two other factors were relevant. First, the Piedmont people, having provided the Royal House of Italy, were more disposed to accept a central authority than other Italians. Second, many of the technical staff, and hence much of the management were trained in the Turin Polytechnic. This excellent engineering school produced engineers who were very analytical, very precise, and very focussed on the immediate (preferably technical) problem in hand. The combination of these two factors helped Valletta to achieve the extraordinary dominance he had over the company, and to impose the high degree of management centralisation.

Neither Gianni nor Umberto Agnelli resembled Valletta. Gianni Agnelli had at one stage of his life been better known for his frequent appearance in the social pages of the newspapers than in the business sections. But after a serious car accident in the sixties he seemed to have changed his approach and to have developed a desire to make a more substantial contribution to the world than in the past. He was by nature a visionary, a man concerned with the long term, with the overall strategy, with concepts. Umberto Agnelli in contrast had what the Italians call a 'steel backside'; happiest when behind his desk dealing with administrative problems. A tenacious man, very interested in implementation of policies, he was an excellent complement to his brother.

The return of the Agnelli family to the control of FIAT in 1966 came in the final years of the 1960's boom. Even before the energy crisis the external environment was changing to make outmoded FIAT's policy of emphasising cars above all other activities. Continued integration within the EEC was not only increasing the competition in the car sector but also in the ancilliary sectors in which FIAT had invested. Thus for example, components which FIAT had previously made for itself, in part because it had no alternative on the Italian market, now became available from elsewhere at lower prices that those used for internal supply and external sales. The quantity sold outside FIAT varied with each division, but most intermediate product companies (eg. springs) sold about 15% of production outside.

When proposals were made in the middle seventies for the introduction of value added tax to Italy to conform with EEC legislation it became clear that some alterations in the legal structure of the company was desirable. This spur to change coincided with others. The car market showed every sign of becoming a mature market in Europe with correspondingly different growth prospects from those that had prevailed through the sixties. The size of the company was such that centralised corporate management needed a staff of 8,000 to keep in touch with its 30-odd sectors of activity. The very centralised structure which Valletta had left, where everything was subordinated to the car, did not seem appropriate for the future. A new policy was therefore set in motion to adapt the company to the changed conditions of the seventies.

THE MOVE TO DECENTRALISATION

The loosening up of the central administration was a gradual process. The accounting systems had to be changed so that inter-group transfers were not longer conducted on a cost basis with all profit grouped under FIAT SpA. Indeed any losses by a supply company like the steel group were passed on to end products rather than borne by the division. As far as was possible individual business units were set up with clearly defined responsibilities. The start of the process was in 1972 and in 1973 the first change in company structure was announced. The monolithic FIAT SpA was broken into 3 operating groups: Automobiles, Commercial and Industrial Vehicles and Diversified Activities (which included the steel group and indeed all the other activities other than cars and CVs). Within these areas the individual companies within each area were encouraged to adapt to a more open stance so that they could stand on their own in the international market, both for marketing their products and, eventually, for raising their own capital.

Independence was to be as total as possible. Where the activity was felt to be too weak to survive on its own or where it needed strategic strengthening, joint ventures were encouraged with other manufacturers. Thus in 1973 FIAT ALLIS was set up (with FIAT share 65%) making it the 4th largest construction equipment company in the world. In 1974 IVECO was established as a commercial vehicle venture with Klöckner-Hunboldt-Deutz of Germany and Unic of France (FIAT held 80%). The newly combined firm had 20% of the Western European truck and bus market.

In 1974 cars and light commercial vehicles accounted for no more than 56% of the group total turnover of 2,951 billion lire. The next most important activity was commercial vehicles (23%) and then the iron and steel group (including foundries and forges) (6%). Agricultural tractors accounted for the same percentage, and the next largest activity was FIAT ALLIS (3%). The remaining activities, representing each between 1 and 2% of turnover were fork lift trucks, rolling stock, mechanical and electromechanical products, plastics, rubber and chemical goods, aviation engines and frames, turbines and marine products. None of these activities was separately accounted for in 1974, though plans were in hand to publish an activity breakdown in the 1975 report and so recognise publicly the thrust of central policy. Group employment, including IVECO, was over 180,000, most of whom were in Italy.

The greater part of Fiat's international business was exports. 44% of the cars produced in Italy were exported. For tractors, exports accounted for over 70% of output. For IVECO the figure was 47% and so on. Licensees in the USSR, Yugoslavia, Poland, Spain and Turkey together produced as many cars as did FIAT for its own account in Italy. Foreign manufacturing was limited to Argentina, though plans were in hand to start production in Nigeria and Brazil. In addition, there were a few small assembly plants in such countries as Chile.

In explaining his new strategy, Agnelli insisted that FIAT would continue to be managed so as to make its full contribution to the Italian economy. In 1972 Agnelli restated the company's commitment to invest in the Mezzogiorno, hoping it would make it one of the poles of the European car industry. A second consistent theme of Agnelli's strategy was FIAT's international outlook. The various mergers sought out and completed by FIAT were seen as evidence of Agnelli's belief that the way forward for a company such as FIAT was through closer European integration. His belief was unshaken by the failure of a merger with Citroen, which fell through in 1973. The need for a central European strategy was a theme of the 1973 Annual Report.

Within the group the thrust behind the changes was justified by Agnelli as necessary to change the management from autocratic to participative. In his view the future required 'a larger body of competent, qualified managers', a new structure with a multiplicity of entrepreneurial forces, with suitable responses to the demands of the various markets'. However, the group would ensure that each unit 'had a common frame of reference that there was a unified administration of strategic resources and that there was coherence between the long term lines of development'. One initiative that Agnelli took that was to be of great value during the changeover and subsequently was to establish a company management school ISVOR. Courses and regular meetings between managers at all levels including the board, took place regularly at the school from the early seventies onwards.

The practical implications of Angelli's new approach were spelt out by a member of the senior management:

'Our philosophy is centralised control and strategy, and decentralised operations. Its impossible for us to have all the capabilities in the central staff for managing with different activities, so we control 4 or 5 ratios, but the manager is completely responsible'.

Such remarks, however, could disguise the fact that management decision making would remain distinctively Italian in character. Thus personal relations would perhaps weigh more heavily than in an anglo-saxon environment, and politics, in the widest sense, would be more in evidence. A notable national characteristic was ability to improvise, to be ingenious and another was the greater emphasis put on the importance of appearance or form. Empire building, a derogative term elsewhere, in Italy would be considered a normal function of Italian leaders of all sorts. Industrial enterprises were often considered the fief of X or Y, and while Agnelli was wholly sincere in his wish to decentralise, one could be sure that central control would remain strong, and yet each independent divisional leader would vigorously defend his territory.

Fiat was, after IRI, the second largest employer in Italy. Consequently, relations with the unions were of crucial importance. The image of the group as paternalistic was not without justification, but in general relations with the unions were good. Notable investments had been made in equipment to eliminate boring or unpleasant jobs with the encouragement of the unions. But in the aftermath of the energy crisis, 1974 was a year in which relationships deteriorated considerably and this culminated in an agreement which considerably altered the existing relationships. To manage the crisis the management agreed to maintain employment (a policy which had immediately resulted in a big rise in car stocks and a consequential worsening of the short term debt), and gave the unions access to production statistics and more freedom in shop floor organisation. In return the unions conceded greater job mobility. One newspaper saw the agreement as impossible to finance without some subsidy from the State. Agnelli, a sensitive negotiator, emphasised the need to cooperate with the unions in the 1974 Annual Report, and called for common European Industrial policies as the only way to a future involving cooperation, planning and investment on at least a European scale for all industries. As president of Confindustria (the Italian employers federation) he was also an eloquent defender of the market system, but remained open to development of state initiative.

For FIAT Agnelli saw the prospects for 1975 and beyond again internationally, with diversification into growth areas. 1974 investment was its highest ever figure (2483 billion lire) devoted to CVs, tractors and earth-moving equipment plus strengthening FIAT's position in the car market. (Exhibits 1 and 2 show the overall financial state of the Group at the end of 1974.)

All these issues had been brought together in the carrying out of the decentralisation of management, but in 1975 there remained the problem of deciding on the new policy and structure of the captive steel group. This group and the automobile group were the only two still not established as separate operating entities from FIAT SpA and for both of them 1975 had every sign of being one of their worst years ever. (Exhibit 3 shows the overall management structure in simplified form.)

THE STEEL GROUP IN FIAT

In 1975 the diversified activities were still one accounting entity and were managed by a single group director. Among the activities was the Steel Group, which was itself in effect a number of businesses involving the

EXHIBIT 1

Fiat Balance Sheet at December 31st, 1974 and at December 31st, 1973 (Comparison)
(in billions of lire)

ASSETS		31.12.1974	31.12.1973
1 Industrial accounts			
Fixed assets			
Property	L.	491	433
Plant-machinery-tooling	»	1,821	1,568
Furniture and fittings	»	160	136
	L.	2,472	2,137
Work in progress	»	3	2
	L.	2,475	2,139
2 Repair of war damages			
(expenditure on buildings, plant and machinery qualifying for government war damage compensation)	»	8	9
	L.	2,483	2,148
3 Patents	»	0.2	0.1
	L.	2,483	2,148
4 Current assets			
Raw materials, goods and stock in hand (incl. amounts spent on replacements qualifying for G'ment war damage compensation totalling about 6 billion lire)	»	567	326
	L.	3,051	2,474
II Commercial accounts			
1 Customers			
payable from customers	L.	{732	349
Notes and acceptances	»		54
2 Receivables from associated co's	»	154	143
3 Advances to suppliers	»	4	7
4 Sundries debtors	»	57	20
5 Accruals and prepayed charges	»	27	11
	L.	975	583
III Financial accounts			
1 Cash and securities on hand	L.	5	5
2 Bank credits	»	70	57
3 Fixed income securities	»	16	17
4 Shareholdings	»	403	362
	L.	494	440
TOTAL ASSETS	L.	4,520	3,497
Contra Accounts	L.	422	396
TOTAL	L.	4,942	3,893

EXHIBIT 1 (*contd.*)

LIABILITIES		31/12/1974	31/12/1973
I. Capital accounts			
1. Capital stock			
– no. 200 million ordinary shares	L.	100	100
– no. 100 million preferred shares	»	50	50
	L.	150	150
2. Legal reserve	»	30	30
3. Special reserve	»	21	21
4. Stock premium reserve	»	43	43
	L.	244	243
II. Reserve against revaluation of fixed assets	L.	0.5	0.5
III. Monetary revaluation			
1a. Fixed assets revaluation up to 1945 acc. to Decrees No. 436 dated 27-5-1946 and No. 49 dated 14-2-1948	L.	4	4
1b. Alignment revaluation of fixed assets according to Law No. 74 dated 11-2-1952	»	32	32
2. Alignment of shareholdings acc. to Decree No. 436 dated 27-5-1946 and Decree No. 49 dated 14-2-1948 and alignment rev. acc. to Law No. 74 dated 11-2-1952	»	13	13
3. Revaluation of stocks of raw materials and goods according to Law No. 25 dated 11-1-1951 and No. 74 dated 11-2-1952	»	18	18
	L.	68	68
IV. Special fund according to Law No. 170 dated 18-3-1965 and subsequent regulations	L.	34	24
V. Soc. welfare fund—Decree No. 1523, dated 30-6-67 art. 102	L.	2	1
VI. Law Reserves No. 823 dated 19-12-1973	L.	88	39
VII. Tax reserves	L.	8	28
VIII. Dividend fluctuation and retained profits fund	L.	10	19
IX. Fixed assets depreciation fund	L.	1,744	1,568
X. Provision for Bad Debts	L.	5	—
XI. Debenture loans	L.	16	27
XII. Long term loans	L.	232	129

(*contd.*)

EXHIBIT 1—Liabilities (*contd.*)

XIII. Commercial accounts

1. Due to suppliers	L.	859	670
2. Due to associated companies	»	7	1
3. Advances by customers	»	74	5
4. Sundry creditors	»	90	140
5. Accruals and deferred liabilities	»	167	111
	L.	1,208	987

XIV. Financial accounts			
1. Due to banks	L.	396	4
XV. Personnel severance bonus fund	L.	463	363
XVI. Operating surplus	L.	0.03	0.3
Total liabilities	L.	4,520	3,497
Contra accounts	L.	422	396
Total	L.	4,942	3,893

EXHIBIT 2

Profit and Loss Account for 1974 and comparison with 1973
(in billions of lire)

Income		1974 Operating year	1973 Operating year
Outside sales	L.	2,837	2,370
Internal production of fixed assets	»	30	19
Other income and recoveries	»	13	59
Rents and real estate income	»	2	2
Dividends on industrial shares—Interest on fixed-income securities, and profits arising from investments outside the industrial sector	»	5	4
Total income	L.	3,005	2,453

Expenditures		1974 Operating year	1973 Operating year
Brought forward from previous year	L.	326	291
Outside purchases	L.	1,603	1,192
Labour and related charges	L.	1,065	909

(*cont.*)

EXHIBIT 2—Expenditures (*contd.*)

Production and operating expenses	L.	222	110
Losses on shareholdings	L.	65	30

Financial charges:
  Interest payable, bank commissions and charges,
  capital increase charges
	L.	25	8

Interest and expenses on debenture issues	»	1	1
	L.	26	10
Direct taxation	L.	39	25
Fixed assets depreciation ordinary	L.	150	98
accelerated	»	77	54
	L.	227	152
	L.	3,573	2,779
Less: Carried forward	L.	−567	−326
Total Expenditures	L.	3,005	2,453
Net profit	»	0.03	0.3

Note: Totals do not always add up due to rounding.

production and conversion of steel and steel products. With a total conversion capacity of well over 2 million tons per year and sales outside the FIAT group of 235 billion lire, the Steel Group was a sizeable business. It employed 37,000 people of whom 7,000 were engaged in producing steel. The other employees were employed making springs (FIAT was Europe's second largest producer with an approximately 7 billion lire turnover); tubes in stainless and ordinary steels for hydraulic cylinders and shock absorbers; tools (a 3.5 billion lire business); cold forging of screws and bolts and hot forging operations (second only to GKN in size and turning over 20 billion lire); castings of all types in the biggest foundries in the world, and a business producing refractories for making steel and also glass. With the exception of the last activity nearly 85% of all the production of these companies was absorbed by FIAT.

The steel producing operation supplied these businesses and others in the FIAT group. These supplies were in general classified in one of three ways: stainless, flat and long products. The first was essentially stainless

410

EXHIBIT 3
Fiat Management Structure

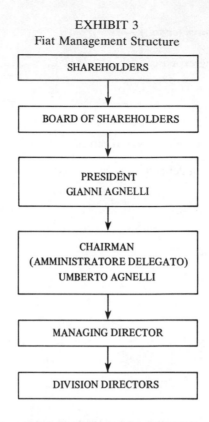

sheet, the second ordinary steel sheet and the third bars and billéts of áll steel types, ordinary and special. The classification of products' followéd usual steel industry practice. A more complete list of products was as follows: semi-finished products, bars, wire, rods in alloyed and non-alloyed special steels; hot rolled and cold rolled strips; hot rolled and cold rolled sheets made in quality steels for hulls, boilers, pressure vessels, for general use and for pressing; sheets and strips in stainless and heat resistant steels; drawn and ground bars; standard and special sections.

The production facilities of the steel making division were generally modern, though somewhat hybrid. There were a number of small (100 ton) electric furnaces with associated rolling equipment which could produce all the stainless and special steel long products required. For flat products, however, as the consequence of a long term contract which had been pivotal in securing the necessary investment for the steel mill at Genoa, FIAT bought hot coils from the state comapny ITALSIDER, which it then rerolled for its own purposes, principally vehicle body pressings. The capacity for rerolling was 800,000 tons, that for long products, 800,000 tons and for stainless about 60,000 tons. (Exhibit 4 gives a flow diagram of the plant.) Thus on flat products FIAT did not have a fully integrated works while for long and stainless products it was fully integrated. This

EXHIBIT 4
Fiat Steel Division
Production Flow

Not Controlled by FIAT

SHEET STEEL COILS → COLD ROLLING TO SIZE → SHEET STEEL USERS

from State Steel Plant

STAINLESS STEEL SHEET → HOT ROLLING REDUCTION → COLD ROLLING TO SIZE → STAINLESS STEEL USERS

from State Steel Plant

Typical End Products

Car bodies

Household Appliances

Furnaces

SCRAP → INGOTS → BLOOMING → BILLET MILL

from inside and outside FIAT

reduction to size

BAR MILL

HEAT TREATMENT

INGOTS → STRIP MILL → COLD ROLLING

from outside FIAT

TUBES

FOUNDRIES

Forgings
Fasteners
Tools
Springs

Pressure
Vessel
Plate

Pneumatic
Cylinders

Castings

made sense economically as the returns to scale were different; plant for normal steel (generally flat steel) was only economical at much greater throughputs while special steels (high carbons or alloys) could be produced in smaller quantities, indeed needed to be for quality control.

The production facilities of the other parts of the steel group were also up-to-date. The foundry division had new facilities which were reputedly the best in the world. The division took billet (a long product) and ingot from the steel making division which it then converted into castings like engine blocks. Facilities existed for very sophisticated castings in special alloys and aluminium which were sold outside FIAT to industries like the aircraft industry and the petrochemical industry. The forging division also took billet from the steel makers, as well as wire and rod (also long products) and produced items like crankshafts springs and steering rods. These were hot forgings. Cold forging, for which higher quality steel was usually required, was another activity, producing items such as fasteners (nuts and bolts). Items such as tubes were produced by hot and cold extrusion processes, for which again steel quality was quite important, and which was supplied by the steel making division.

All, or nearly all, of these many products found their way back into other parts of the FIAT group where they were assembled into end products. Even the approximately 15% of all the steel division activities sales that were made outside FIAT were necessarily affected by the rhythm of captive sales as the remark by a car division manager indicates:

'It is also important that so many of the smaller mechanical companies are linked to our car production. Of the outside suppliers I would say 70% are really captive. So when there is some kind of variation in our production, this creates a big change to the whole system and really affects more of the steel business than what they supply directly to us. Other producers have a wider spread in their portfolios'.

The management structure of the Steel Group was oriented towards production. The FIAT end product companies tended to order large quantities which they kept on stock in their own plants. The steel users ordered their steel likewise, and themselves kept the necessary stock. Research and development was generally undertaken under the responsibility of the customer companies and as mentioned above most transfers took place on what was essentially a cost basis. Marketing in the steel division companies was practically non-existent.

The component businesses of the steel group when compared with companies outside FIAT were clearly dominant in Italy. Outside Italy they were as good as the best component companies in other countries, most of which did not operate outside their national boundaries. Despite their dependence on FIAT they had little to fear should they be required to operate on a less direct basis with the group than the present.

With steel making the picture was more confused. The breakdown into steel types produced approximately 40% ordinary steel (mainly sheet) and 60% special steels. The company could therefore compare itself with both the bulk and special steel sectors in Italy.

FIAT STEEL MAKING IN ITALY AND EUROPE

The bulk steel market was dominated by the Italian State company FINSIDER and its principal off-shoot ITALSIDER which itself produced some special steel but it was generally a small percentage of production.

Bulk Steel Producers
1974

	Tons '000	% Special Steel
ITALSIDER	13,561	1
Acciarerie di Piombino	1,500	16
AFL Falck	N/A	23
Terni	300	32

The special steel companies, so called because of their greater emphasis on special grades as a percent of their steel production produced smaller quantities.

Special Steel Producers
1974

	Tons '000	% Special Steel
FIAT	860*	60
Nacionale Cogne	358	99
Breda	310	73
Acciaierie de Bolzano	199	100
Redaella	227	85
Idssa – Viola	95	60
Aveg	55	100

*Note that the steel re-rolled by FIAT is not included in this figure.

The first four companies in the list above in 1974 produced 41% of Italian special steel, and in the special steels sector there were about thirty companies, although about seven accounted for most of the volume. In general the Italian steel market had four important characteristics. It was largely based on scrap, as sources of iron ore were limited. Facilities were in general quite modern, certainly when compared with some parts of European industry. The role of the State was important, although usually it had not interfered with local producers who had created profitable markets for themselves (in general the special steel producers). However, exceptions to this statement were the companies Cogne, Breda and Piambino, which were in financial difficulty and had received various degrees of state support. Italy was an early producer of higher grade steels, but its European rivals had now caught up and overtaken it in this respect.

It was in the special steels sector that one found a particular feature of the Italian steel market, the Bresciani, small producers of steel for special purposes and markets. By careful selection of markets and tightly integrated mini-mills these producers were able to manufacture certain products (like reinforcing bars) at particularly low prices. Because of abundant hydroelectric power in the Alps there was extensive use of electricity for steel making in Italy. Low cost electricity permitted smaller scale activity than was possible in Germany where coal was the predominant power source. These small Italian mills had little tradition of high technology and individually were not commercially strong.

Outside Italy a comparison with other major producers of special steels on the basis of the tonnage and special steel percentage showed that Krupp produced 1.6 million tons, 35% in special steels, Thysen—8,000,000 tons, 5% in specials, Kluckner—350,000 tons, 10% in specials, Rockling—500,000 tons, 15% in specials, Ugine—530,000 tons all special steels, Crusola—1.4 million tons, all special steels.

At the European level, by 1975 it was obvious that a radical shakeout in the steel industry was in prospect. The boom years of the 60's had both encouraged investment in increased capacity and put off difficult restructuring decisions. In Europe as a whole capacity seemed to be 7 million tons per year too much and the labour force 80,000 employees too large. Italy was no exception to this pattern, the state company FINSIDER having previously followed a policy of investing to anticipate demand now looked as though it might have gone too far with its proposed new works at Taranto. But the picture was by no means uniform, and there were a number of companies with particular structures or markets which were remaining profitable.

Nonetheless, some factors appeared determinant for the shape of the future in European steel. Output from the large Japanese integrated mills was penetrating Western Europe, particularly in flat products, and if the Americans were ever to curb imports, then Japanese pressure on Europe was likely to be even tougher. The mini-mills had grown to be competitors with the large mills in certain long products, and the Bresciani had become a force on a European scale. It was estimated thay they produced some seven million tons of medium quality steel at highly competitive costs with European producers. The emergence of Third World producers and growth in the supply of steel from Eastern European states, was another factor to be considered. Generally designers were tending to use less steel, which was having a further impact on the world excess capacity of bulk steel. Moreover, the growing power of organised labour, particularly when it was fighting for the maintenance of employment, had become a critical force influencing the future of the industry.

It appeared that for 1975 as a whole, FIAT's steel making sector was to be hit harder than many by the downturn in demand. Total tonnage (produced and re-rolled) was likely to be 24% lower. Capacity utilisation rates would be only 65% in the steel making sector, 59% in the foundries, and 68% in the conversion operations. Prices had plummeted from October 1974 but by October 1975 they had then stabilised and sales of basic steel products to third parties had dropped by 10%. Thus the Fiat stéel group found itself in a turbulent and uncertain national and international environment where the avenues to a successful future for any steel company were far from obvious.

OTHER CAPTIVE COMPANIES

In pondering what to do with the steel division Agnelli had in mind two contradictory examples. The Ford company still had its own steel plant in the USA. Indeed it was the only other car company to have a steel plant. The result of Henry Ford's original investment, it had been continuously up-dated and it was still profitable. No sales were made to third parties and all pricing was done on a rigorous arms-length or market basis, as the plant was not Ford's sole supplier, 50% of its requirements being bought outside. Although Ford executives were of the opinion that the investment would never have been undertaken in the present time, they were well satisfied with its performance on technical, profit and cash generating grounds.

Against this experience could be laid that of Baltimore Steel, the former captive steel company of Philadelphia Tractors. More than half the sales were on the open market, though preferential treatment had always been given to Philadelphia Tractors, to which sales were made on a cost basis. When Philadelphia Tractors decided to buy only on a market-price basis, they had wanted to sell off the steel division. Baltimore Steel had had the greatest difficulty in re-adjusting and went through many years of extensive losses as it tried to re-orientate its thinking from being production orientated to being market and quality orientated.

By looking elsewhere Agnelli could see that companies with their own captive steel production tended to follow a certain pattern. Own steel production was started to support the parent business either to give guaranteed control over supply or over quality or both; parent company demands would determine the investment in plant, and the product range. The steel industry had then matured faster than the end product industries, and the captive production plant had become no longer competitive in many products. Lack of efficiency was camouflaged by end-product value. Finally the end product industry had matured revealing the inadequacy of the captive steel plant.

At this stage successful companies had done one of four things. They had moved from just being producers to being total suppliers (involving production and purchase of materials) to the parent company (SKF was an example). They had refocussed their own steel products range (like GKN). They had exploited both a focussed production and a purchase and distribution capability on the external market, while maintaining the advantages of being a major supplier to the traditional business. Or they had retreated.

THE CONTEMPORARY ENVIRONMENT

Italy was hit harder than many countries by the oil crisis, being very heavily dependent on oil for energy. As in other countries there had been a rise in the rate of inflation, increasing industrial disruption and rising losses in private companies, some of it due to price control attempts by the State. The political tendency seemed to be towards the left; the Christian Democrats seemed increasingly unable to hold the confidence of the country and the Communists were becoming ever more credible as a party with a really mass following. To an industrialist like Agnelli, who showed no distinct political predilictions, the future lay in European integration, a theme that occurred increasingly in his public utterances. His view of the means to greater prosperity was to invest, advance into new markets, constantly improve productivity. In one address he remarked that export studies had shown that the highest shares of export markets were held by those countries most technologically advanced which continued to invest substantially nonetheless in mature sectors. Was this the way forward for the steel division? Would it ever be able to stand on its own feet, or would only be able to remain of use to FIAT as a captive supplier? The pros and cons of these two possibilities were obviously central to the decision on the future of the division's management.

29

Bancil Corporation

Struggling to clear his mind, Remy Gentile, marketing manager in France for the toiletry division of Bancil, stumbled to answer the ringing telephone.

'Allo?'

'Remy, Tom Wilson here. Sorry to bother you at this hour. Can you hear me?'

'Sacre Bleu! Do you know what time it is?'

'About 5:20 in Sunnyvale. I've been looking over the past quarter's results for our Peau Doux . . . '

'Tom, it's after 2 A.M. in Paris; hold the phone for a moment.'

Remy was vexed with Tom Wilson, marketing vice president for the toiletry division and acting division marketing director for Europe, since they had discussed the Peau Doux situation via telex no more than a month ago. When he returned to the phone, Remy spoke in a more controlled manner.

'You mentioned the Peau Doux line, Tom'

'Yes, Remy, the last quarter's results were very disappointing. Though we've increased advertising by 30%, sales were less than 1% higher. What is even more distressing, Remy, is that our competitors' sales have been growing at nearly 20% per year. Furthermore, our present cost of goods sold has not decreased. Has Pierre Chevalier bought new equipment to streamline the factory's operation?'

'No, Pierre has not yet authorized the purchase of the machines, and there is little that can be done to rationalize operations in the antiquated Peau Doux plant. Also, we have not yet succeeded in securing another distributor for the line.'

'What! But that was part of the strategy with our increased advertising. I thought we agreed to . . . '

Tom Wilson hesitated for a moment. His mind was racing as he attempted to recall the specifics of the proposed toiletry division strategy for France. That strategy had guided his earlier recommendation to Gentile and Pierre Chevalier, the Bancil general manager in France, to increase advertising and to obtain a new distributor. Tom wanted to be forceful but tactful to insure Gentile's commitment to the strategy.

'Remy, let's think about what we discussed on my last trip to Paris. Do you recall we agreed to propose to Chevalier a plant to revitalize Peau Doux's growth? If my memory serves me well, it was to increase advertising by 25%, groom a new national distributor, reduce manufacturing costs with new equipment, increase prices, and purchase the "L'aube" product line to spread our marketing overhead.'

'Oui, oui. We explored some ideas and I thought they needed more study.'

'Remy, as you recall Peau Doux has a low margin. Cutting costs is imperative. We expected to decrease costs by 5% by investing $45,000 in new equipment. Our test for the new strategy next year was to increase advertising this quarter and next quarter while contracting for a new distributor. The advertising was for naught. What happened?'

'I really don't know. I guess Pierre has some second thoughts.'

Tom spoke faster as he grew more impatient. Gentile's asking Tom to repeat what he had said made him angrier. Tom realized that he must visit Paris to salvage what he could from the current test program on Peau Doux. He knew that the recent results would not support the proposed toiletry division strategy.

'Remy, I need to see what's going on and then decide how I can best assist you and Chevalier. I should visit Paris soon. How about early next week, say Monday and Tuesday?'

'Oui, that is fine.'

'I'll fly in on Sunday morning. Do you think you can join me for dinner that evening at the Vietnamese restaurant we dined at last time?'

'Oui.'

'Please make reservations only for two. I'm coming alone. Good night, Remy.'

'Oui. Bon soir.'

COMPANY BACKGROUND

Bancil Corporation of Sunnyvale, California, was founded in 1908 by pharmacist Dominic Bancil. During its first half century, its products consisted primarily of analgesics (branded pain relievers like aspirin), an antiseptic mouthwash, and a first-aid cream. By 1974, some of the top management positions were still held by members of the Bancil family, who typically had backgrounds as pharmacists or physicians. This tradition notwithstanding, John Stoopes, the present chief executive officer, was committed to developing a broad-based professional management team.

Bancil sales, amounting to $61 million in 1955, had grown to $380 million in 1970 and to $600 million in 1974. This sales growth had been aided by diversification and acquisition of allied businesses as well as by international expansion. Bancil's product line by 1970 included four major groups:

	Sales (in millions of dollars)	
	1970	1974
Agricultural and animal health products (weedkillers, fertilizers, feed additives)	$ 52	$141
Consumer products (Bancil original line plus hand creams, shampoos, and baby accessories)	205	276
Pharmaceutical products (tranquilizers, oral contraceptives, hormonal drugs)	62	107
Professional products (diagnostic teagents, automated chemical analyzers, and surgical gloves and instruments)	60	76

In 1974, Bancil's corporate organization was structured around these four product groups which, in turn, were divided into two or three divisions. Thus, in 1973 the consumer products group had been divided into the Dominic division, which handled Bancil's original product line, and the toiletry division, which was in charge of the newer product acquisitions. The objective of this separation was to direct greater attention to the toiletry products.

INTERNATIONAL OPERATIONS

International expansion had begun in the mid-1950s when Bancil exported through agents and distributors. Subsequently, marketing subsidiaries, called National Units (NUs), were created in Europe, Africa, Latin America, and Japan. All manufacturing took place in the United States. Virtually the entire export activity consisted of Bancil's analgesic Domicil. An innovative packaging concept, large amounts of creative advertising, and considerable sales push made Domicil a common word in most of the free world, reaching even the most remote areas of Africa, Asia, and South America. A vice president of international operations exercised control at this time through letters and occasional overseas trips.

By the mid-1960s, overseas marketing of pharmaceutical and professional products began, frequently through a joint venture with a local company. Increasing sales led to the construction of production facilities for many of Bancil's products in England, Kenya, Mexico, Brazil, and Japan.

Bancil's international expansion received a strong commitment from top management. Jon Stoopes was not only a successful business executive but also a widely read intellectual with an avid interest in South American and African cultures. This interest generated an extraordinary sense of responsibility to the developing nations and a conviction that the mature industrial societies had an obligation to help in their development. He did not want Bancil to be viewed as a firm that drained resources and money from the developing world; rather, he desired to apply Bancil's resources to worldwide health and malnutrition problems. His personal commitment as an ardent humanist was a guideline for Bancil's international operations.

While Bancil had been successful during the 1960s in terms of both domestic diversification and international expansion, its efforts to achieve worldwide diversification had given rise to frustration. Even though the international division's specific purpose was to promote all Bancil products most advantageously throughout the world, the NUs had concentrated mainly on analgesics. As a result, the growth of the remaining products had been generally confined to the United States and thus these products were not realizing their fullest worldwide potential.

According to Bancil executives, these problems had their roots in the fact that the various product lines, though generically related, required different management strategies. For consumer products, advertising consumed 28% to 35% of sales; since production facilities did not require a large capital investment, considerable spare capacity was available to absorb impulses in demand created by advertising campaigns. For agicultural and animal health products, promotion was less than 1% of sales, but the capital-intensive production (a facility of minimum economic scale cost $18 million) required a marketing effort to stimulate demand consistently near full production capacity. Furthermore, the nature of the marketing activity for the professional and pharmaceutical products placed the burden on personal selling rather than on a mass-production effort.

In response to this situation, a reorganization in 1969 gave each product divison worldwide responsibility for marketing products. Regional marketing managers, reporting to the division's vice president of marketing, were given direct authority for most marketing decisions (e.g., advertising, pricing, distribution channels) of their division's products in their area. The manufacturing division, with headquarters in Sunnyvale, had worldwide responsibility for production and quality control. (See Exhibit 1 for the 1969 organization chart.)

Corporate management also identified a need in key countries for a single local executive to represent Bancil Corporation's interests in local banking and political circles. There was no single criterion for selecting,

EXHIBIT 1

Bancil Corporation

1969 Organization Chart

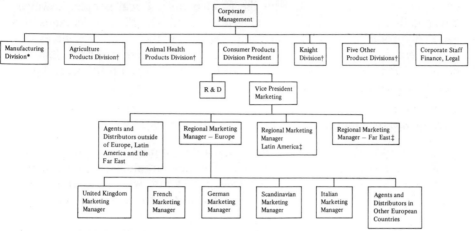

*The manufacturing division manufactured products for all the product divisions. Overseas manufacturing (not shown) reported to the manufacturing division in Sunnyvale.

†Organization similar to that of the consumer products division.

‡Organization similar to that for Europe.

Source: Company records.

from the divisions' representatives in each country, the Bancil delegate, the title given to this position. A corporate officer remarked: 'We chose whom we thought was the best business executive in each country. There was no emphasis on functional specialty or on selecting an individual from the division with the greatest volume. In one country, the major candidates were opinionated and strong-willed, and we therefore chose the individual who was the least controversial. The Bancial delegate generally had a marketing background if marketing was the primary Bancil activity in the country or a production background if Bancil had several manufacturing facilities in the country.'

While international sales had grown from $99 million in 1970 to $147 million in 1972, profit performance from 1971 to 1972 had been disappointing. A consultant's report stated:

'There are excessive communications between the NUs and Sunnyvale. The marketing managers and all the agents are calling for product-line information from the divisional headquarters. Five individuals are calling three times per week on an average, and many more are calling only slightly less often.'

It appeared that a great deal of management time was spent on telex, long-distance communications, and travel. In response to these concerns the divisions' staffs increased in each country. Overheads nearly tripled, affecting the growth rate of profits from international operations.

With the exception of financial decisions which were dictated by corporate headquarters, most decisions on inventories, pricing, new product offerings, and facility development were made by corporate headquarters in conjunction with the local people. Local people, however, felt that the key decisions were being postponed. Conflicting demands also were a problem as every division drew on the local resources for manpower, inventories, receivables, and capital investment. These demands had been manageable, however, because even though profits were below target no cash shortages had developed.

Current organization of international operations

To improve the performance of its international operations, Bancil instituted a reorganization in mid-1973. The new organization was a matrix of NU general managers and area vice presidents, who were responsible for their product lines worldwide. (See Exhibit 2 for a description of the matrix in 1975.)

The general manager was the chief executive in his country in charge of all Bancil products. He also was Bancil's representative on the board and executive committee of local joint ventures. The Bancil delegate usually had been chosen as the general manager. He was responsible for making the best use of financial, material, and personnel resources; pursuing approved strategies; searching for and identifying new business opportunities for Bancil in his NU; and developing Bancil's reputation as a responsible corporate citizen. The general manager was assisted by a financial manager, one or more plant managers, product-line marketing managers, and other financial managers as required.

The divisions were responsible for operations in the United States and Canada and for worldwide expertise on their product lines. Divisions discharged the latter responsibility through local product-line marketing managers who reported on a line basis to the NU general manager and on a functional basis to a division area marketing director. The latter in turn, reported to the divisional marketing vice president. Where divisions were involved in other functional activities, the organizational structure was similar to that for marketing. The flow of product-line expertise from the divisions to the NUs consisted of (1) operational inputs such as hiring/termination policies and the structure of merit programs and (2) technical/professional inputs to the NU marketing, production, and other staff functions on the conduct of the division's business within the NU.

Only the Dominic division was represented in every NU. Some divisions lacked representation in several NUs, and in some cases a division did not have a marketing director in an area. For example, the Rodgers division had area marketing directors in Europe, the Far East, and Latin America, all reporting to the divisional vice president of marketing to whom the division's U.S. marketing personnel also reported. However, the Knight

EXHIBIT 2
Bancil Corporation Shared Responsibility Matrix

Vice President, International Operations
Clark B. Tucker

Product Group Vice Presidents	Division Presidents	Area Vice President, Europe Andre Dufour			Area Vice President, Latin America Juan Vitas			Area Vice President, Far East
		General Manager, France P. Chevalier	General Manager, Germany D. Rogge	General Manager, Four Other National Units	General Manager, Argentina and Uruguay S. Portillo	General Manager, Brazil E. Covelli	General Manager, Two Other National Units	General Manager, Four National Units
Agricultural and Animal Health (3 divisions)	Rodgers Division / Division B / Division C							
Consumer Products (2 divisions)	Dominic Division / Toiletry Division (Robert Vincent)							
Pharmaceuticals (2 divisions)	Division A / Division B							
Professional (3 divisions)	Knight Division / Division B / Division C							

division, which had a structure similar to that of the Rodgers division, could justify area marketing directors only in Europe and Latin America.

The new matrix organization established for each country a National Unit Review Committee (NURC) with its membership consisting of the general manager (chairman), a financial manager, and a representative from each division with activities in the NU. Corporate executives viewed the NURC as the major mechanism for exercising shared profit responsibility. NURC met quarterly, or more frequently at the general manager's direction, to (1) review and approve divisional profit commitments generated by the general manager's staff; (2) insure that these profit commitments, viewed as a whole, were compatible with and representative of the best use of the NU's resources; (3) monitor the NU's progress against the agreed plans; and (4) review and approve salary ranges for key NU personnel. When the division's representatives acted as members of the NURC, they were expected to view themselves as responsible executives of the NU.

Strategic planning and control

NURC was also the framework within which general managers and division representatives established the NU's annual strategic plan and profit commitment. Strategy meetings commenced in May, at which time the general manager presented a forecast of Bancil's business in his NU for the next five years and the strategies he would pursue to exploit environmental opportunities. The general manager and the divisional representatives worked together between May and September to develop a mutually acceptable strategy and profit commitment. If genuine disagreement on principle arose during these deliberations, the issue could be resolved at the next level of responsibility. The profit commitment was reviewed at higher levels both within the area and within the product divisions, with approval coming from the corporate executive committee (CEC) which required compatible figures from the vice president of international operations and the product group executives. CEC, the major policy-making forum at Bancil, consisting of the chief executive officer, the group vice presidents, the vice president of international operations, and the corporate secretary, met monthly to resolve policy issues and to review operating performance.

For each country, results were reported separately for the various divisions represented, which, in turn, were consolidated into a combined NU statement. The NU as well as the divisions were held accountable, though at different levels, according to their responsibilities. The division profit flow (DPF) and NU net income are shown in the following example for the Argentine National Unit in 1974:

	Rodgers division	Dominic division	Toiletry division	National unit
Division sales	$250,000	$800,000	$1,250,000	$2,300,000
Division expenses	160,000	650,000	970,000	1,780,000
Division profit flow (DPF)	$ 90,000	$150,000	$ 280,000	$ 520,000
NU other expenses				
(general administrative, interest on loans, etc.)				350,000
NU income before taxes				$ 170,000
Less: Taxes				80,000
NU net income				$ 90,000
Working capital	$100,000	$300,000	$ 700,000	

The product divisions were responsible for worldwide division profit flow (DPF) defined as net sales less all direct expenses related to divisional activity, including marketing managers' salaries, sales force, and sales office expenses. The NU was responsible for net income after charging all local divisional expenses and all NU operating expenses such as general administration, taxes, and interest on borrowed funds. Because both the general managers and the divisions shared responsibility for profit in the international operations, the new structure was called a shared responsibility matrix (SRM). The vice president of international operations and the division presidents continually monitored various performance ratios and figures (see Exhibit 3). In 1975 international operations emphasized return on resources, cash generation, and cash remittance, while the division presidents emphasized product-line return on resources, competitive market share, share of advertising, and dates of new product introductions.

The impact of the 1973 organizational shift to the SRM had been greatest for the general managers. Previously, as Bancil delegates, they had not been measured on the basis of the NU's total performance for which they were now held responsible. Also, they now determined salary adjustments, hiring, dismissals, and appointments after consultations with the divisions. In addition, general managers continued to keep abreast of important political developments in their areas, such as the appointment of a new finance minister, a general work strike, imposition of punitive taxes, and the outbreak of political strife, a not-infrequent occurrence in some countries.

Under the new organizational structure, the area marketing directors felt that their influence was waning. While they were responsible for DPF, they

EXHIBIT 3

Bancil Corporation Control Figures and Ratios

Vice President of international operations for national unit		Division president for product line
X	Sales	X
X	Operating income: % sales	X
X	General manager expense: % sales	
X	Selling expense: % sales	X
X	Nonproduction expense: % operating income	
X	Operating income per staff employee	
X	% staff turnover	
X	Accounts receivable (days)	X
X	Inventories (days)	X
X	Fixed assets	X
X	Resources employed	X
X	Return on resources	X
X	Cash generation	
X	Cash remittances	
X	Share of market and share of advertising	X
X	Rate of new product introduction	X

X indicates figure or ratio on organization's (national unit or division) performance of interest to the vice president of international operations and the division presidents.
Source: Company Records.

were not sure that they had 'enough muscle' to effect appropriate allocation of resources for their products in each of the countries they served. This view was shared by Nicholas Rosati, Knight division marketing manager in Italy, who commented on his job:

'The European marketing director for the Knight division keeps telling me to make more calls on hospitals and laboratories. But is is useless to make calls to solicit more orders. The general manager for Italy came from the consumer products division. He will neither allocate additional manpower to service new accounts for the Knight division nor will he purchase sufficient inventory of our products so I can promise reasonable delivery times for new accounts.'

Divisions, nevertheless, were anxious to increase their market penetration outside the United States and Canada, seeing such a strategy as their best avenue of growth. The recent increase in international sales and profits which had by far exceeded that of domestic operations (see Exhibit 4), seemed to confirm the soundness of this view. Not all NU general managers shares this approach, as exemplified by a statement from Edmundo Covelli, the general manager of Brazil:

EXHIBIT 4

Bancil Corporation Sales and Profits for Bancil Corporation Domestic and International
(in millions of dollars)

Year	Domestic		International		Total	
	Sales	Profit	Sales	Profit	Sales	Profit
1955	$ 61	$ 5.5	—	—	$ 61	$ 5.5
1960	83	8.3	$ 6	$ 0.2	89	8.5
1965	121	13.5	23	1.3	144	14.8
1969	269	26.7	76	9.2	345	35.9
1970	280	27.1	99	12.3	379	39.4
1971	288	28.7	110	14.2	398	42.9
1972	313	32.5	147	15.8	460	48.3
1973	333	35.3	188	21.4	521	56.7
1974	358	36.7	242	30.9	600	67.6

Source: Company Records.

'The divisions are continually seeking to boost their sales and increase their DPF. They are not concerned with the working capital requirements to support the sales. With the inflation rate in Brazil, my interest rate of 40% on short-term loans has a significant effect on my profits.'

The Peau Doux issue

The telephone conversation described at the beginning of ·the case involved a disagreement between Tom Wilson, who was both marketing vice president for the toiletry division and acting division marketing director for Europe, and Pierre Chevalier, Bancil's general manager for France. It also involved Remy Gentile, who reported on a line basis to Chevalier and on a functional basis to Wilson.

Pierre Chevalier had been a general manager of France for 18 months after having been hired from a competitor in the consumer products business. Upon assuming the position, he identified several organizational and operational problems in France:

'When I took this job, I had five marketing managers, a financial manager, a production manager, and a medical specialist reporting to me. After the consumer products division split, the new toiletry division wanted its own marketing manager. Nine people reporting to me was too many. I hired Remy for his administrative talents and had him assume responsibility for the toiletry division in addition to having the other marketing managers report to him. That gave me more time to work with our production people to get the cost of goods down.'

In less than two years as general manager, Chevalier had reduced the cost of goods sold by more than 3% by investing in new equipment and had improved the net income for the French NU by discontinuing products which had little profit potential.

Remy Gentile had been the marketing manager for the toiletry division in France for the past year. In addition, five other marketing managers (one for each Bancil Corporation division operating in France) reported to him. During the previous six years Gentile had progressed from salesman to sales supervisor to marketing manager with the Knight division in France. Although he had received mixed reviews from the toiletry division, particularly on his lack of mass-marketing experience, Chevalier had hired him because of his track record, his ability to learn fast, and his outstanding judgment.

The disagreement involved Peau Doux line of hand creams which Bancil Corporation had purchased five years earlier to spread the general manager's overhead, especially in terms of marketing, over a broader product offering. Wilson's frustration resulted from Chevalier's ambivalence toward the division's strategy of increasing the marketing effort and cutting manufacturing costs on the Peau Doux line.

The total market in France for the Peau Doux product line was growing at an annual rate of 15%–20%, according to both Wilson and Gentile. However, Peau Doux, an old, highly regarded hand cream, had been traditionally distributed through pharmacies, whereas recently introduced hand creams had been successfully sold through supermarkets. The original Peau Doux sales force was not equipped to distribute the product through other outlets. To support a second sales force for supermarket distribution, the toiletry division sought to acquire the L'aube shampoo and face cream line. When Gentile had informed Chevalier of this strategy, the latter had questioned the widsom of the move. The current volume of the Peau Doux line was $800,000. Though less than 10% of Chevalier's total volume, it comprised the entire toiletry division volume in France.

Tom Wilson viewed the Peau Doux problems primarily in terms of an inadequate marketing effort. On three occasions within the past year, he or his media experts from Sunnyvale had gone to Paris to troubleshoot the Peau Doux problems. On the last trip, Robert Vincent, the toiletry division president, had joined them. On the return flight to Sunnyvale, Wilson remarked to Vincent:

'I have the suspicion that Chevalier, in disregarding our expertise, is challenging our authority. It is apparent from his indifference to our concerns and his neglect in allocating capital for new machinery that he doesn't care about the Peau Doux line. Maybe he should be told what to do directly.'

Vincent responded:

'Those are very strong words, Tom. I suggest we hold tight and do a very thorough job of preparing for the budget session on our strategy in France. If Chevalier does not accept or fundamentally revises our budget, we may take appropriate measures to make corporate management aware of the existing sensitivity to the toiletry division in France. This seems to be a critical issue. If we lose now, we may never get back in the French market in the future.'

After Wilson and Vincent had departed for Sunnyvale, Chevalier commented to Dufour, his area vice president:

'I have the feeling that nothing we say will alter the thinking of Wilson and Vincent. They seem to be impervious to our arguments that mass advertising and merchandising in France do not fit the Peau Doux product concept.'

Andre Dufour had been a practicing pharmacist for six years prior to joining Bancil Corporation as a sales supervisor in Paris in 1962. He had progressed to sales manager and marketing manager of the consumer products division in France. After the untimely death of the existing Bancil delegate for France in 1970, he had been selected to fill that position. With the advent of SRM he had become the general manager and had been promoted to vice president for Europe a year later. Dufour had a talent for identifying market needs and for thoroughly planning and deliberately executing strategies. He was also admired for his perseverance and dedication to established objectives. Clark B. Tucker, vice president of international operations and Dufour's immediate supervisor, commented:

'When he was pharmacist he developed an avocational interest in chess and desired to become proficient at the game. Within five years he successfully competed in several international tournaments and achieved the rank of International Grand Master.'

In the fall of 1974, Dufour had become the acting vice president of international operations while his superior, Clark Tucker, was attending the 13-week Advanced Management Program at the Harvard Business School. Though Dufour had considerable difficulty with the English language, he favorably impressed the corporate management at Sunnyvale with his ability of getting to the heart of business problems.

The toiletry division had only limited international activities. In addition to the Peau Doux line in France, it marketed Cascada shampoos and Tempestad fragrances in Argentina. The Cascada and Tempestad lines had been acquired in 1971.

Tom Wilson and Manual Ramirez, toiletry division marketing director for Latin America, were ecstatic over the consumer acceptance and division performance of Cascada and Tempestad in Argentina. Revenue and DPF had quintupled since the acquisition. In his dealings with Gentile, Wilson frequently referred to the toiletry division's success in Argentina. Given this sales performance and the division's clearly stated responsibility for worldwide marketing of toiletry products, Wilson felt that his position in proposing the new strategy for France was strong.

On the other hand, Sergio Portillo, general manager of Argentina and Uruguay, and Juan Vilas, vice president for Latin American operations, had become alarmed by the cash drain from marketing the toiletry division products in Argentina. The high interest charges on funds for inventories and receivables seemed to negate the margins touted by the division executives. In describing the Cascada and Tempestad operation to Vilas, Portillo commented:

'I have roughly calculated our inventory turnover for the toiletry division products marketed in Argentina. Though my calculations are crude, the ratio based on gross sales is about four, which is less than one-half the inventory turnover of the remainder of our products.'

Neither Portillo nor Vilas shared the toiletry division's enthusiasm and they suspected that Cascada and Tempestad were only slighly above break-even profitability. Chevalier and Dufour were aware of this concern with the toiletry products in Argentina.

As Chevalier contemplated the toiletry division strategy, he became convinced that more substantive arguments rather than just economic ones would support his position. In discussing his concerns with Dufour, Chevalier asked:

'Are the toiletry division product lines really part of what John Stoopes and we want to be Bancil's business? Hand creams, shampoos, and fragrances belong to firms like Colgate-Palmolive, Procter & Gamble, and Revlon. What is Bancil contributing to the local people's welfare by producing and marketing toiletries? We have several potentially lucrative alternatives for our resources. The Rodgers division's revenues have been increasing at 18%. We recently completed construction of a processing plant for Rodgers and we must get sales up to our new capacity. The Knight division is introducing an electronic blood analyzer that represents a technological breakthrough. We must expand and educate our sales force to take advantage of this opportunity.'

Chevalier sensed that Gentile was becoming increasingly uneasy on this issue, and the feeling was contagious. They had never faced such a situation before. Under the previous organization, NUs had been required to comply, although sometimes reluctantly, with the decisions from

Sunnyvale. However, SRM was not supposed to work this way. Chevalier and Gentile stood firmly behind their position, though they recognized the pressure on Tom Wilson and to a lesser degree on Vincent. They wondered what should be the next step and who should take it. Due to the strained relationship with Wilson, they did not rule out the possibility of Wilson and Vincent's taking the Peau Doux issue to the consumer products group vice president and having it resolved within the corporate executive committee.

30

Albion International Petroleum Company

In November 1977 Tom Faulkner was extremely concerned about future strategy for the benzacrylate product area. As General Manager of the Industrial Chemicals Division's (I.C.D.) benzacrylate product group of Albion International's chemical operation, he was wondering what actions he should propose at the Benzacrylate Policy Group meeting to be held at Head Office in December, to hear revised plans for 1978 and the following years to 1980. Mr. Faulkner believed that no clearly defined strategy for this range of products had been established, and that his own ideas on the future direction differed sharply from those of his colleague, Charles Pearson, Commercial Director of Albion Chemicals Europe S.A. (ACE). These two men shared responsibility for benzacrylate operations world-wide. Especially worrying was the fact that in 1977 for the fifth consecutive year the benzacrylates had failed to match up to budget projections for growth and profitability.

Mr. Faulkner was also aware that I.C.D. as a whole was under severe pressure from top management to improve its poor return on capital and slow growth rate. Until this had been achieved further expansion capital was likely to be difficult to obtain. Already talk of possible redundancies was rife, and people in the division pointed to the high capital requirements and unsatisfactory performance of the benzacrylate product area as a major reason for overall poor divisional results.

ALBION'S CHEMICAL OPERATIONS

Albion International Petroleum was a British based international company engaged in all areas of the oil industry. Operations were divided into a series of five functional areas—exploration and production, transportation, refining, marketing and chemicals. Forseeing the potential of downstream operations, Albion had expanded rapidly in the chemical industry initially by the internal development of petrochemicals. As these interests had grown they had been supplemented by a series of acquisitions both at home and overseas. By 1977 Albion was one of the world's leading chemical manufacturers with sales of some £1.8 billion worldwide.

Chemical operations had first developed in the U.K. Product divisions were created as the company diversified its product line. In the U.K., which still accounted for some 65 per cent of total chemicals sales including exports, there were six product divisions: Petrochemicals, Industrial Chemicals, Plastics, Synthetic Fibres, Agricultural Chemicals and the smallest and most recently formed division, Pharmaceuticals.

Overseas chemical operations were organised in four geographic divisions: Europe, Asia and Pacific, Africa and the Middle East, and North America. After starting in Commonwealth countries, Albion had since the late 1960's been increasing its operations in Europe and North America. The European division was established in 1968 and the North American one in 1971 after the Orion Chemical Corporation in the U.S.A. had been acquired.

Each chemical division was a separate profit centre. In the U.K., they were virtually self supporting with their own marketing, production and research facilities. The overseas divisions, however, with the exception of North America relied on the U.K. for their research, maintaining in the overseas territories only limited technical service support. The U.K. divisions were also responsible for all exports of production both from the U.K. and among the overseas divisions, but they had no control over local operations which were the responsibility of local divisional management.

Each division had its own board of directors responsible to the board of Albion International Chemical Company, which in turn reported to the parent board. Divisional boards were responsible for operating the assets in their charge successfully.

Albion International had a matrix form of organisation for both oil and chemical products. Thus each director had both a functional and/or area and product responsibility. The performance of product divisions was monitored and interdivisional operations co-ordinated by a system of Policy Groups made up of three members of the main board, each of whom looked after two divisions. Overseas divisions were treated in a similar manner, although the membership of the Overseas Policy Groups was designed to overlap with that of the product division Policy Groups. Following the move to a portfolio planning system the central office had introduced Product Policy Co-ordination Groups to monitor specific business unit areas. The benzacrylates formed one such business area, and was composed of two Albion International Chemicals directors, one of whom was also a member of the I.C.D. Policy Group, while the other was chairman of the European Area Policy Group.

A similar matrix system responsibilities also existed within divisions. Thus, Mr. Faulkner, who was responsible for the benzacrylate business area for I.C.D., was also the divisional marketing director. An abbreviated version of the Albion International Organisation structure is shown in Exhibit 1.

P

EXHIBIT 1

Albion International Chemicals Company Organisation 1974

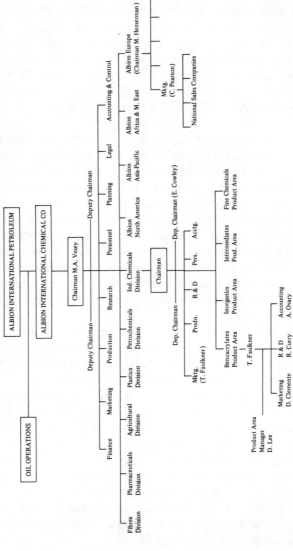

*In process of handing over to M. McAllister.

Source: Case Writers Notes.

THE STRATEGIC POSITIONING MATRIX

In 1974 Albion had adopted a system of portfolio planning to highlight the attractiveness of specific businesses and/or divisions. Different policies were then pursued according to where businesses were positioned on a Strategic Positioning Matrix which reflected industry attractiveness and company strength. The Strategic Positioning Matrix is illustrated in Exhibit 2.

In conjunction with the corporate planning department of Albion International Chemical Company the managers responsible for product groups were involved in establishing the position of each business on the positioning matrix. A number of critical factors were assessed for each product group and the business assigned a value of 3, 2 or 1 the higher the

EXHIBIT 2
Albion Strategic Positioning Matrix

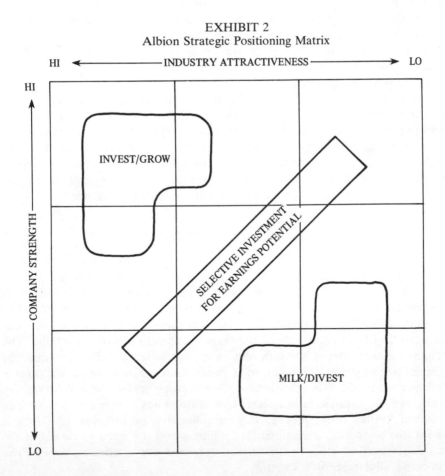

number the better the company or industry position. The main factors included were:

Company Strength	Industry Attractiveness
• Relative Market Share	• Market growth rate
• Company research and development position	• Rate of technical change
• Raw materials availability	• Production capacity/demand
• Relative product quality	• No. of competitors
• Relative market price	• Analysis of self industry cost factors
• Relative productivity	• Trends in investment

When all the factors had been scored, they were added together and divided by the total sum possible. For example, if management believed the market share of a product group was significantly greater than that of any of its competitors it would assign a value of 3 for that factor. Summing the scores for all company strength factors would lead to a score out of 18. Those businesses scoring six or less would score low on company strength, those between 6 and 12 average and those with 12 or more would score high. In this way each business could be assigned to one of the boxes of the strategic positioning matrix.

The location of a business within the matrix suggested the appropriate strategy. For those businesses which scored highly in both dimensions a growth strategy was advocated; those falling in the selective investment area were to adopt a strategy of segmentation into high return segments under stable management aimed to maximise contribution; finally those falling in the milk/divest area were candidates for divestment or savage pruning in order to maximise cash flow which could be redeployed elsewhere.

BENZACRYLATE PLASTICS

Benzacrylate plastics were important speciality products with many applications. They were formed by mixing together two liquids, a resin (the benzacrylate component) together with a curing agent (an isodiamine). A chemical reaction occurred between these two creating a solid plastic. The properties of the plastic could be varied substantially by choosing different varieties of resin and/or one of the three main varieties of isodiamine. The range of resin varieties had different molecular weights and were formed by converting acrylene monomer in a batch process reaction kettle into a polymer or resin. The difference in molecular weight was achieved by using various catalysts and different reaction times and temperatures. The reaction kettles could theoretically produce the entire range of different resins but to reduce contamination problems and the need to clean out the vessels, specific kettles were usually retained for particular resins. The process is illustrated in Exhibit 3.

EXHIBIT 3
The Production and Usage of Benzacrylate Resin Systems

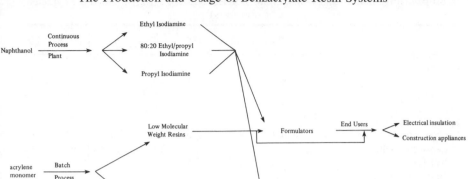

The isodiamine curing agents were produced by a continuous production process from a feedstock raw material, naphthanol. Usually an isodiamine production plant was designed to produce one of the two main variants of isodiamine, ethyl or propyl, but some plants were capable of producing both. The third isodiamine variant was an 80:20 mixture of the ethyl and propyl variants and was only produced on variable production plants.

The European market growth rate of benzacrylate plastics had been high historically averaging 18–20 per cent per annum since 1968 due to a number of factors including rapid technological development and the identification of new users. In some sectors, notably low molecular weight resins, formulating houses had had an important intermediate role between the raw material makers and end users. Low molecular weight plastics were largely used in the electrical and construction industries as insulators and specialist components, whereas high molecular weight plastics found outlets as chemical intermediates, adhesives, shoe components and speciality paints and surface coatings.

The Market

Overall European consumption and production of benzacrylate polymers is shown in Exhibit 4 together with Albion International's position and the projected supply and demand position to 1982. Present and expected national demand and capacity is shown in Exhibit 5.

The market for benzacrylate resins in Western Europe was dominated by the German chemical company Deutsche Glanzstoffe GmbH, which in 1977 held some 30 per cent of the market for benzacrylate, 50 per cent of the isodiamine market, and was the world's overall leading producer. As one of

EXHIBIT 4

European Production and Consumption of Benzacrylates; Historic and Projected[1]

('000 tons)

	1972	1973	1974	1975	1976	1977	1978	1982
Benzacrylate Resins								
Production	20.2	28.0	33.5	37.5	49.7	56.3	82.3	95.1
Consumption	19.3	23.3	27.5	33.2	40.9	45.6	54.0	68.5
Net Export	0.9	4.7	6.0	4.3	8.8	10.7		
Isodiamines								
Production	14.2	16.7	18.9	22.8	26.3	33.4	62.8	78.2
Consumption	11.8	14.3	17.2	20.9	24.4	27.8	34.2	44.3
Net Export	2.4	2.4	1.7	1.9	1.9	5.6		
Albion's Position								
Resins								
U.K.					2.5	2.5	3.0	3.5
Benelux					2.0	3.0	4.0	4.0
Spain*					—	1.0	3.0	3.0
Isodiamines								
U.K.					3.2	3.5	3.7	3.9
Benelux					—	1.0	3.0	3.0

*Part owned.
[1]Projected estimates for 1978 on are based on plant capacities rather than actual production.
Source: Company Records.

the world's largest chemical companies, it had a near monopoly of benzacrylate manufacture in Germany, and was the leading producer of isodiamine. The company also operated plants in Belgium and France for benzacrylate, an isodiamine plant in Spain and joint venture isodiamine plants in France and Belgium. Other leading producers included DKZ, a major Anglo-Dutch manufacturer, American Pacific Oil Corporation, and Eastern Chemicals, two major U.S. corporations, and Chimie Suisse, a Swiss-based chemical and pharmaceutical company. In addition there were large producers in France, Italy and the United Kingdom who predominantly served their home markets and had not established manufacturing facilities abroad. Details of market shares by company are shown in Exhibit 6.

Albion sales of benzacrylate systems in 1977 were some £34 million, about £12 million of which was generated in the U.K. and a further £14 million in Europe. Resin sales represented some 58 percent of the total, about half of which was generated in Western Europe. The main production of isodiamines was located in the U.K., although some 53 per cent of the 3300 tons produced were exported largely to ACE at works cost. Total capital invested in Europe and the U.K. was £23 million approximately, two-thirds of which was in resin plants. Pretax profits amounted to £2.2 million in 1977 against a budgeted figure of £3 million. The decline in profits was largely due to pressure on margins from

EXHIBIT 5

Plant Capacities and Consumption by Country 1977–82 ('000 tons)

| | BENZACRYLATE | | | | ISODIAMINES | | | |
| | 1977 | | 1982 | | 1977 | | 1982 | |
	Capacity	Consumption	Capacity	Consumption	Capacity	Consumption	Capacity	Consumption
W. Germany	18.8	12.9	20.2	19.9	21.7	8.2	33.0	12.9
Italy	3.0	7.1	10.6	9.8	1.2	4.9	10.8	6.9
France	10.3	6.5	13.6	10.3	6.6	3.8	11.6	6.8
U.K.	7.6	5.5	10.1	7.8	4.9	3.5	5.2	5.2
Benelux	28.6	6.7	33.8	8.2	4.5	3.2	14.8	4.8
Spain	2.7	3.4	5.3	5.6	1.2	2.0	2.8	3.8
Switzerland	1.0	3.5	1.5	6.9	—	2.2	—	3.9
Total	72.0	45.6	95.1	68.5	40.1	27.8	78.2	44.3

Source: Company Records.

EXHIBIT 6

Market Share % Analysis by Country and Producer 1976

	W. Germany		Italy		France		U.K.		Benelux		Spain		Switzerland		All Europe	
	B.A.	I.D.	B.A.	I.D.	B.A.	I.D.	B.A.	I.D.	B.A.	I.D.	B.A.	I.D.	B.A.	I.D.	B.A.	I.D.
Deutsche Glanzstoffe	59	72	24	57	44	40	5	6	20	52	21	90	20	16	33	50
Chimie Suisse	17	18	10	20	25	32	—	—	10	—	9	—	40	32	12	11
Eastern Chemicals	9	—	18	—	4	—	7	—	12	32	19	—	—	—	11	—
DKZ	7	10	13	—	4	8	17	7	19	21	6	10	8	10	10	9
American Pacific	6	—	7	—	2	—	14	—	9	6	—	—	—	—	7	—
Albion International	2	—	—	10	11	10	24	44	8	—	22	—	32	33	12	15
Others	—	—	29	13	17	17	33	43	12	—	2	—	—	9	18	15

Abbreviations used: B.A. = Benzacrylate resin; I.D. = Isodiamine.

Source: Company Records.

overcapacity, fierce price competition, and Albion's lack of success in penetrating some markets dominated by its competitors. Plant utilisation, especially for benzacrylates, had been lower than expected, and profits from resin sales had been particularly hard hit at £0.7 million.

Despite its low market share overall in the European market Albion was, after Glanzstoffe, the second largest producer of low molecular weight resins (LMW) and propyl-isodiamine. In these markets formulators were particularly strong. Although representing only some 20 per cent of total raw material sales in these segments, sales to formulators accounted for 43 per cent of raw materials sold. Albion mainly sold direct to large consumers, though in 1974 the company had acquired a formulator in Italy as a way of improving LMW market penetration. In addition the company had formed its own manufacturer of benzacrylate products for the construction industry in the U.K. A similar development was planned for the company's Benelux plant.

Although formulators were particularly strong in the LMW segments, few were highly profitable. They tended to be relatively small suppliers to local markets. Average return on capital for the main formulating houses was less than 12 per cent pre-tax. Such figures were thought to be somewhat misleading in that no great reliability could be placed on the accountancy returns of some of the private family companies. Albion executives believed that several formulators they supplied actually earned much higher returns based on price differentials between Albion's raw material prices and the ultimate prices charged by formulators. In Germany and France, Glanzstoffe had invested heavily in downstream formulating activity, and Albion management believed this accounted for some 15 per cent of its total benzacrylate profits. Nevertheless during 1977 at least six of the larger European formulators were trading at a loss and two were declared bankrupt.

Albion was relatively weak in high molecular weight (HMW) benzacrylates which were more likely to be sold on a price basis. This was higher volume business where end users were mostly sophisticated in formulation. Albion produced most of its HMW resins at Antwerp and sold them largely as a service to its customers or as a back-up facility to sales of its isodiamines where its position was stronger, competitors fewer, and prices more stable. In 1977 HMW resins made up some 37 per cent of Albion's resin volume by weight and 28 per cent in monetary terms, producing a small loss of £0.2 million based on variable cost and a contribution to overheads. Some 25 per cent of HMW production was in the U.K., about half of which was exported outside Europe.

Operations

Albion entered the benzacrylate market in 1965 when I.C.D.'s laboratories hit on a way to manufacture propyl isodiamine when researching into fine chemicals. A plant had been built to supply this product to the fledgling benzacrylate industry. The I.C.D. Intermediates product area produced naphthanol, the raw material for both ethyl and propyl isodiamine, at its plant in Sheffield where the isodiamines were also manufactured. In 1967 Albion added benzacrylate resins to its range when its new petrochemical complex at Ardrossan in Scotland had come on stream. The petrochemicals division, the main operators of the site, supplied acrylene monomer to an adjacent resin plant run by I.D.C.

Since the opening of these first plants capacity for isodiamines had been trebled in the U.K. Resin capacity had been doubled in 1972. Albion had begun to expand its operations in Western Europe in 1967, and in the following year a new division was created in Brussels charged with pursuing this policy. A major petrochemical complex was opened at Antwerp in 1973, and a 2,000 ton benzacrylate plant formed part of the new works. After some serious disagreement between conflicting claims by I.C.D. and A.C.E. in 1974 it was decided that an increase in propyl isodiamine capacity should also be sited at Antwerp. This plant came on stream in mid-1976 with a planned capacity of 3,000 tons which would be reached by 1978, using naphthanol supplied by Intermediates from Sheffield. A.C.E. had also formed a 50:50 joint venture in Spain with Halvados S.A., a local chemical manufacturer, to build a benzacrylate resin plant, and this had been brought on stream in 1976. Further, in 1976 A.C.E. had acquired Acrylosan, an Italian formulating house, based in Milan.

With its acquisition in the United States Albion gained a foothold in the American benzacrylate market where Orion was a minor supplier of resins and merchanter of prepackaged formulations. In 1977 Albion had formed a joint venture in Japan with Toyo Kanataka, a large diversified corporation, which gave Albion a 15 per cent interest in the Kanataka benzacrylate operations.

The primary world-wide responsibility for benzacrylate operations rested with I.C.D. which was profit accountable for the product area outside of Europe, the U.S.A. and Japan. I.C.D. had a watching brief on Orion and the Japanese joint venture, but these concerns were still not fully integrated into Albion's world-wide operations. All sales in Western Europe were however the responsibility of A.C.E., although any excess production for non-continental European markets from the Antwerp plants was sold through I.C.D.

Despite the high growth rate of benzacrylates, and despite its early entry into the market, Albion had failed to make the headway predicted. Return on capital had consistently been below Albion's general target for all product areas of a minimum pre-tax return of 18 per cent. In particular the results of both I.C.D. and A.C.E. in Europe as a whole were the major problem.

After the disagreement between the two divisions over new plant location in 1974 it had been decided to co-ordinate benzacrylate operations on a world-wide basis. The business was identified in the portfolio planning system as a long term investment prospect in view of the growth rate and Albion's market share.

THE FORMATION OF BIPAG

A co-ordinating committee, the Benzacrylate International Product Area Group (BIPAG) was established to prepare strategy, and establish policies for the business. The new group was chaired by Edwin Cowley, Deputy Chairman of I.C.D. Tom Faulkner, Charles Pearson and Dave Lee of I.C.D. were the other members, the latter also being secretary to BIPAG. The organisation of BIPAG in 1977 is shown in Exhibit 7.

BIPAG met on a monthly basis either in Sheffield or in Brussels with meetings usually lasting for about half a day. Dave Lee, the Benzacrylate Product Area Manager, described the function of the committee in 1977 as being

'responsible for making policy decisions on benzacrylates world-wide, although this mainly means drawing together the ideas of I.C.D. and A.C.E. These policy decisions are then converted into action plans by function to be implemented in the two divisions. This used to be a real problem until this year because BIPAG had no control over what each of the divisions actually did. It has now been agreed that Paul Javic, Henry Jones and Reg Curry be appointed to co-ordinate marketing, production and R & D. Paul has come from A.C.E., and will spend his

EXHIBIT 7
BIPAG Organisation Chart 1977

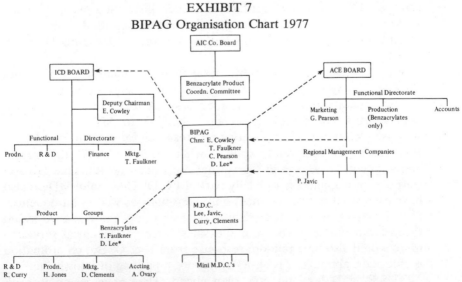

*To be replaced by M. McAllister
Source: Case Writers Notes.

time both here at Sheffield and in Brussels. Henry and Reg are both IC.D. men, but they will also be spending more time in Brussels.'

'BIPAG prepares a one year profit plan for the benzacrylate product area as a whole, and this is then submitted to both the boards of I.C.D. and A.C.E. for acceptance, and before discussion with the Product Policy Group at head office which meets with BIPAG twice a year. Conversion of plans into financial terms is done by Alan Ovary, the Benzacrylate Area Accountant for I.C.D., but he is not a member of BIPAG.'

'Soon after it was established BIPAG also set up the Marketing Development Committee (MDC) which was to provide a mechanism for putting BIPAG policies into action. This used to be made up of Reg Curry and I.C.D. and A.C.E. marketing men, and reporting to Faulkner and Pearson and myself. The MDC was supposed to co-ordinate the marketing plans of I.C.D. and A.C.E. with the laboratories here at Sheffield. Before this A.C.E., in particular, used to claim that R & D did not pay sufficient attention to the needs of their customers, and this was a reason for failing to improve penetration in Europe.'

'I don't believe the MDC has worked, however, for a variety of reasons. Firstly, it had no executive authority. The laboratories are not responsible to BIPAG, but to the research director of I.C.D. and partly to Tom Faulkner as head of the benzacrylate area in I.C.D. Secondly, marketing operations in Europe and in I.C.D. are divided up in quite different ways. Charles Pearson had only two fellows in Brussels on benzacrylates dealing with resins and isodiamines for all industries. The sales effort was out in the individual national sales subsidiaries around Europe. They had few benzacrylate specialists, and were partially responsible to their Area Manager who in turn reported direct to the A.C.E. board, and partially to Charles Pearson as Marketing Director, Europe.'

'Finally MDC led to a proliferation of new committees – the mini MDC's. The MDC had neither the people nor the expertise to actually develop operating plans on a detailed basis. A series of industry based mini MDC's was therefore set up reporting to MDC which were supposed to co-ordinate marketing and research for each main industry. But really they haven't known what to do. Until the recent appointments of Javic and Curry there has been no full time BIPAG staff except me, and I'm officially part of I.C.D. These mini MDC's also have no official status, and meet only informally as well as infrequently. Still, I suppose it's an improvement on 18 months ago when we would receive random requests from the sales force for technical service – there would also be a random response from R & D. But co-ordination is still poor, although it is easier to ensure a pooling of knowledge.'

'The R & D boys do now plan ahead. They have begun to rank customers by business worth, convert research plans into man days, and establish a priority order for customer visits. However, we still don't attempt to establish expected profitability from research programmes, and we have no real system of monitoring or sanctioning behaviour in the laboratories.'

'The system still has many problems, and I shan't be sorry to leave—as you know Malcolm MacAllister is taking over from me. My actual job is very difficult not least because Faulkner and Pearson have totally different conceptions of it. Faulkner sees it as an executive position making sure that the policies adopted by BIPAG are put into practice. On the other hand Pearson sees my role as a staff position, acting as secretary to BIPAG, preparing documents, and so on. As a result, while I can get things done if it's in I.C.D. I can do nothing in A.C.E. Nobody thinks the present organisation is right because there's just too much conflict in the matrix.'

BIPAG Operating Problems

Malcolm MacAllister, who was about to take over as Product Group Manager, confirmed Mr. Lee's view on the different interpretations of his new job, and added

'Edwin Cowley, the Chairman of BIPAG, tends to agree more with Tom Faulkner about the role, but there are many who say that they've chosen a personnel man like me to stop Faulkner and Pearson from always having a go at each other. Of course the job has few formal executive powers, and I see my main contribution being made by diplomacy and generating informal influence.'

'So far my thoughts are only impressionistic, but I can see a number of the problems in BIPAG. Faulkner and Pearson have many fundamental differences. Firstly, their divisional backgrounds have divergent ethics. I.C.D. is said to be too production and tonnage chemical oriented and seeking after technical excellence. A.C.E., on the other hand, thinks of itself as being market oriented and wants to move closer to the end users by buying into systems houses.'

'Secondly, Faulkner would probably be in favour of recommending that the benzacrylates were hived off into a separate new product division because in many ways they have little in common with the rest of I.C.D., either technically, commercially or, in the case of resins, in production. This might become an increasingly serious option because benzacrylates aren't popular in I.C.D., and the division itself is under pressure, new capital is hard to get and we need a lot of it because we are growing at 20–25 per cent a year while I.C.D. as a whole is virtually static. Pearson, on the other hand, would be under pressure from A.C.E. to resist such a move. Benzacrylates represent a significant portion of A.C.E. business which they certainly wouldn't want to lose control of.'

'BIPAG has other problems. It has little commitment at lower levels because for most people their career pattern is tied up with the division they work for, not BIPAG which has no authority to hire or fire at all. Production sourcing is another problem. BIPAG is trying to organise production from the most suitable source, but the plant managers are directly responsible to the site manager of each complex, and these in turn report to the division production directors. Each plant manager is, therefore, measured according to the efficiency of his own unit, and if BIPAG decide to use an alternative source it can make one plant look bad. This is less of a problem in Europe than here at Sheffield. Then there's the unions who are very touchy about shifting production from the U.K. to Europe and can shut down a whole complex if they strike.

'Group capital expenditure procedures can also distort things. BIPAG itself does not have any spending power, but makes recommendations to the respective divisions. The divisions tend to be allocated new capital on the basis of their overall performance and at the moment I.C.D. is being fairly seriously rationed. On the other hand, top management is very keen to build up investment in Europe, so A.C.E. is very anxious to generate capital projects and sees benzacrylates as a good prospect.'

FUNCTIONAL MANAGEMENT VIEWPOINT

In mid-1977, in an attempt to improve some of the perceived defects in organisation, BIPAG had received divisional approval to make a series of functional appointments nominally in A.C.E. or I.C.D., but with informal responsibility for the corresponding function in the other division.

Marketing

Paul Javic, formerly A.C.E. marketing manager for Benelux, was appointed to fill the marketing role for BIPAG. Although nominally still a member of A.C.E. Mr Javic also had an office at Sheffield, and Dick Clements, marketing manager benzacrylates for I.C.D., reported to him. Discussing the BIPAG marketing operation he commented,

'The benzacrylates marketing is essentially divided between I.C.D. and A.C.E. The former handles sales world wide, including the U.K., Scandinavia and Eastern Europe except Yugoslavia and Greece. A.C.E. covers all other European countries. At present 27 men are involved in sales and marketing in I.C.D. and 15 in A.C.E. I.C.D. effort is presently organised on an application basis while in A.C.E. it is on a product basis. I see us, therefore, moving probably to a product rather than an application method of selling.

'As the marketing manager for BIPAG I am now responsible for all marketing in both divisions. It is my job to create and collate the divisional plans and forecasts, innovate in sales methods, to look at sales outlets and make product range decisions. I am profit accountable, although not accountable for overall profitability, and I report to BIPAG itself. We must make the cross divisional teams work together better than at present. The main mechanism for achieving this is by merging the technical service and marketing efforts via the MDC and mini MDC's.

'To understand the difficulties you must see the historic perspective in Albion. A few years ago it was decided to concentrate new chemicals investment in Europe, the Near East and North America. This was a difficult concept to sell to the chemicals management here which were U.K. oriented largely because many of them came in as the result of acquisition. But we are an international company in oil and A.C.E. was, therefore, created to break the insularity of the U.K. product divisions. I.C.D. perhaps in particular had a real stick in the mud mentality, and is still terribly production and technology oriented. A.C.E., on the other had, was marketing and profit oriented, and concentrated on products which were difficult to move around, had high margins and were not the traditional bulk tonnage stuff that is largely the case in the U.K.

'We have a number of problems still to sort out and a fair way to go. By the mid 1980's we would like to hold a 20 per cent market share world wide, but that will be tough to achieve. The HMW benzacrylates are dominated by Glanzstoffe and Eastern Chemicals. We must therefore concentrate on LMW's for electricals and building where we are strong, and new HMW areas like sealants and adhesives. Glanzstoffe has 4 times the technical development we have, and Eastern dwarfs us in the U.S.A. We can't meet these competitors head on without spending £100–200 million, and the returns just aren't worth that.

'What we have to do is to get right the interface between timing and the development of our organisational effort. We are presently actually overstaffed in a way. Our marketing effort is incorrectly deployed, we're short on technical effort of the right quality and in the right areas, and the laboratories are wrongly located here at Sheffield. In A.C.E. they want to support formulating more for specialist activities and move downstream. This is the trend for the majors in the U.S.A. and Eastern and Glanzstoffe are moving more to specialist activities or integrated commercial/technical teams because that's where I think most of the future profits lie.'

These views were not altogether shared by I.C.D. marketing management. Mr. Dick Clements added,

'We've found it essential to organise on an industry basis for everything except bulk sales of isodiamines because our customers expect us to have specialist industry knowledge. A.C.E., who are still principally divided on a product basis, are now finding it the same.

'In Albion the division that controls assets controls marketing. For example the Sheffield plant is the only producer of ethyl isodiamine, and we are therefore responsible for sales of this product even in A.C.E. territories. A.C.E. on the other hand is the main producer of HMW resins. We also establish prices from I.C.D. for all territories including Europe since we deal with the other producers. We tell A.C.E. what prices we want for all products and the profits generated are consolidated in BIPAG.

'There are certainly differences in the two divisions, but I can't see how you can take away the centralised marketing effort from I.C.D. In some ways, however, A.C.E. has better quality people in the field than we do here, but these are regional managers not necessarily anything to do with benzacrylates.'

Production

Henry Jones was co-ordinator of the I.C.D. benzacrylate production plants until the autumn of 1977, when his responsibilities were widened to include the A.C.E. plants also. Commenting on his new position he said,

'BIPAG have now decided we should have a production co-ordinator for the entire operation. I will not be directly responsbile for production, however, since that is under the control of the production directors in each division, and indeed my boss is the production director of I.C.D. I will, however, be able to provide an interface between the plants and the product area. In the past this wasn't as necessary because Dave Lee was an operations man, but Malcolm MacAllister has no plant experience and I expect to play a greater role.

'Personally, although I know that many of the others think BIPAG is a mess, I don't believe there will be much trouble. We all work for the same company after all. Anyway, if there are any difficulties between the plant managers this can usually be solved by talking, and if that doesn't work I'll ram their b . . . . . heads together.'

Research and Development

Mr Reg Curry, head of the benzacrylate technical team, was responsible for all research and development in the area. The I.C.D. Laboratories were located in Sheffield with a small technical service team located in Antwerp. Mr Curry said of the R & D effort,

'We have organised on an industry basis here in the laboratories in order to allow ourselves to concentrate on specific user problems world wide. I.C.D. was a real innovator in the benzacrylate field, and I believe we have one of the best technical teams available. It isn't as big as Glanzstoffe or one or two others, but it is first class in quality.

'In the past it hasn't been possible to provide the service we would like because we have been unable to get out enough to meet the customers and frankly the sales force is very deficient in solving real technical problems especially in A.C.E. I think the creation of the MDC and the industry subcommittees is therefore a very good thing, and is enabling us better to come to grips with what is required.

'At present it is being suggested that the laboratories should perhaps be divided and part of the team placed in Antwerp. I think this is wrong. We have a team here which would be much less efficient if divided up and the expense to move or duplicate the laboratory facilities would be ridiculously high. Further, it takes a long time for a man to become really familiar with this technology, and I am sure we would lose a number of skilled people if we asked them to move away from where they feel their roots to be.'

Control

The accounts for BIPAG were prepared by Mr Alan Ovary, a member of the I.C.D. Finance and Accounting staff, who was assigned to the benzacrylate product area. Although not a member of BIPAG, Mr Ovary prepared the financial analyses for all special exercises, capital investment appraisals, acquisition evaluations and all financial support documents for the I.C.D. division board and the Policy Group Review meetings. Mr Ovary also reported to the finance director of I.C.D. He was somewhat concerned about his position as he did not believe that BIPAG had adequate financial skills for their meetings, and that their actions did not always recognise the implications for the performance of the individual divisions.

He commented,

'Edwin Cowley attempts to optimise the performance of BIPAG as a whole, but to a degree this actually distorts things. Naphthanol is an example. This is supplied by Intermediates to benzacrylates inside I.C.D. at works cost. We then supply it to A.C.E. at the same price. However, company policy is that all interdivisional product transfers should be made at market prices. Thus, I.C.D. is artificially subsidising A.C.E., and while it may help BIPAG it distorts I.C.D.'s profits. When this was raised with A.C.E. they said that if we charged at market prices they would want to build a naphthanol plant at Antwerp, and they are now putting this forward as a real proposal.

'There are also problems with the transfers of finished products. I.C.D. sells a lot of A.C.E. material in non-European markets, but A.C.E. charges us at full market prices less our selling expenses, hence

I.C.D. makes no profit at all. BIPAG says there is no need to bargain on this since the money all shows up in the combined BIPAG figures, but it all helps to reduce I.C.D.'s apparent performance which means that as a division we get more pressure from head office. A.C.E. on the other hand has plenty of capital and is constantly looking for new projects to fund so as to build up its size in Europe. Yet these projects may not be the most profitable for the group. The profits that are made are mainly coming from the bulk sales of isodiamines by I.C.D. whereas some of the specialities that A.C.E. wish to invest more in, are actually losing money.'

THE VIEW FROM BIPAG

The I.C.D. viewpoint of BIPAG's operations was stated by Tom Faulkner.

'Really', he said, 'the objectives of the two divisions are not aligned. I believe BIPAG has not really established a strategy, and when we report to the Product Policy Group it is a sort of uneasy compromise with a pseudo united front. Pearson and I disagree fundamentally on our policy as to what should be our major product lines. On HMW's for instance we want to get out while A.C.E. want to invest more. On our marketing policies, investment and so on we also disagree. These problems have gone on for a long time, too. For example, the isodiamine plant location issue in 1974 finally had to be resolved at deputy chairman of AIP Co. level.

'Nowadays BIPAG won't come out with a really positive statement, and Pearson just says everything is fine. I'm not under pressure from my divisional board like Pearson, however. He is constantly being asked to put up capital projects because A.C.E. wants to build up fast.

'I believe that we will not really solve the problems probably until benzacrylates are hived off into a separate world wide product division. As it is this interdivisional squabbling will go on, and being a high growth product in a low growth division like I.C.D. means we are starved of the necessary resources to become a real force in the market.'

Mr Charles Pearson stated the A.C.E. position.

'The real problem in the past has been that I.C.D. has failed to really commercialise its technology. It was an innovator in benzacrylates, but has now been left far behind by Glanzstoffe. I.C.D. has been far too U.K. oriented, while we have said let's exploit the market. When the isodiamine plant was eventually located in Europe it literally killed the then I.C.D. chairman.

'Today I believe that with the formation of BIPAG we have largely resolved our problems. We now have a unified marketing, research and production organisation, and what problems are left are minor. There is still a need to improve communications, and for BIPAG to convey its policies down the line more clearly, and we must stop the proliferation of committees. We also believe A.C.E. should erect its own naphthanol plant which will cause a bit of a row in I.C.D. because they are so compartmentised.

'Tom Faulkner is really a bit risk averse. He believes marketing and downstream technology are rather an annoying consequence of manufacturing isodiamines, whereas I see isodiamines as a means to an end.

'I think all we really need is to get on with the job and clean up the organisation to smooth communication. We in BIPAG should just set the strategy and then, with the existing team, form one operating committee to manage the day-to-day operations, put our ideas into action, and report back on the results.'

Finally, the part-time chairman of BIPAG, Edwin Cowley, explained his position.

'I was responsible in the first place for helping to set up BIPAG with Mike Hamerman, the chairman of A.C.E. We wanted to cut out all the nonesense between the divisions such as transfer prices, and so on, and run it as one international business. BIPAG is there to set major policy and monitor the activities of the chaps in the field. It's a part time job, and I don't want it to become more than that since I haven't time to do it.

'Compared with about three years ago things are really running a lot smoother. It's true there's probably a few problems like some misunderstandings down the line, some personal problems between Faulkner and Pearson and the location of technical service. Things like the constraint of money in I.C.D. versus the availability of funds in A.C.E. I don't see as a difficulty. It's group policy to invest more in Europe, and provided we use normal common sense we will do the right thing.

'I believe the appointment of the new people in BIPAG who are all carefully chosen, and are strong no-nonsense characters will cut out a lot of the poor collaboration.

'I know that Tom Faulkner is worried, but we have got to resolve our problems in BIPAG, not refer them up to higher authority. I really don't think the main board would entertain the idea of hiving off the benzacrylates, or want to know about what are really minor difficulties that a little common sense and goodwill should be able to resolve.'

31

Norcros Limited

In 1954 John V. Sheffield was concerned with preserving the assets of the Sheffield family from erosion by taxation. These assets, which had already been depleted by death duties following the death of Sir Berkeley Sheffield, mainly consisted of ironstone deposits near Normanby in Lincolnshire. The deposits were leased out for mining and were expected to be depleted by the mid-nineteen-seventies. Income from the mining operations was subject to surtax direction and hence by the time of depletion taxation would erode the majority of the asset value.

Mr Sheffield therefore decided to form a public holding company which would not be subject to surtax direction. Thus, in June 1956, 100,000 ordinary shares in a new company Norcros were offered to the public at a placing price of 5.25 shillings per share. In addition to preserving the asset position of his own family, Mr Sheffield considered, in launching Norcros, that it would meet similar needs of other successful family enterprises not large enough to be floated on their own yet not willing to risk a loss of identity by joining a large industrial group. At the same time an opportunity was offered to the investing public to participate in successful companies which would otherwise have remained private.

The initial assets of Norcros consisted of the Sheffield family ironstone deposits and a small label and specialist printing concern, Dapgag (1943)—later renamed Tickopress—a company acquired by Mr Sheffield.

By 1971 the basic concept of Norcros had undergone significant change. The principal aim made in a statement to shareholders was 'to provide shareholders with the best possible capital and income return over the long term', which was to be achieved by a strategy 'of an industrially-based group which uses its resources efficiently to exploit its opportunities, in order to grow at a better than average rate as measured by its earnings per share'. In 1970 sales of the Norcros Group reached a record £33 million, producing pre-tax profits of over £3 million per annum on net assets of nearly £17 million. Recent financial statements are shown in Exhibit 1.

This case describes the evolution, strategy and stated policies of the Norcros Group from its inception in 1956 until 1971.

COMPANY HISTORY

The development of Norcros since inception in 1956 could be divided into three main phases. Between 1956 and 1961 the company expanded rapidly by a process of acquisition. From 1962 to 1966 problems created by the initial expansion became recognised and a gradual process of rationalisation took place. Following the rationalisation a new strategy and a new structure were forged to lead to the position found in 1971.

1956–61: The Acquisitive Growth Phase

Following the public placement of shares in 1956, Norcros expanded rapidly. The company became a kind of club, successfully attracting owner entrepreneurs concerned about reducing the threat of estate duty. The qualifications for membership of this club included a satisfactory past profit record and the availability of surplus cash. This cash was in effect used to finance the next purchase. This initial philosophy was clearly stated in a foreword to the early annual reports.

> Our subsidiary companies are wholly owned, and have been selected from a wide cross-section of British industry, and, prior to their incorporation within Norcros Ltd, they were controlled and managed by their founders or their families.
>
> Norcros enables the public to invest in some of the soundest and most progressive industrial companies of a limited size, which up to the present have been entirely in private hands.
>
> Norcros provides a means by which the private owners of these companies can avoid the destruction of their life's work by penal taxation and death duties, and yet retain an active interest by continuing to manage their companies, and by investment in their parent company of which they become an active, participating member.
>
> Care is taken when considering new acquisitions that management is progressive and assured for the future, that personalities and business outlooks are similar to existing members of the Group, and that relations with staff and work people have always been happy.
>
> Lastly, great importance is attached to past profit achievements, encouraging growth possibilities and financial self-sufficiency.

Many family companies sought to join Norcros and some twenty-three acquisitions were made in the first five years, extending the interests of the group into a wide variety of product markets. Exhibit 2 contains a summary listing of the acquisition and divestments of the group and indicates the product markets in which the acquired companies were engaged. Profits expanded rapidly, increasing more than five fold in the three years up to financial year 1960 when profits reached £1.9 million

EXHIBIT 1
Norcros Group Financial Statements Year Ended 30 November
(£'000)

	1960	1961	1962	1963	1964	1965	1966	1967	1968	1969	1970
Assets employed											
Stocks	1,821	2,939	2,931	3,165	3,367	3,658	4,411	4,379	4,210	3,873	4,468
Debtors	2,886	3,643	4,367	4,984	5,251	4,471	5,806	5,733	7,230	8,079	8,804
Liquid assets	503	10	19	27	168	1,757	132	124	318	1,480	807
Total current assets	5,210	6,592	7,317	8,176	8,786	9,886	10,349	10,236	11,758	13,432	14,080
Property, plant, equipment and motor vehicles	4,746	6,083	6,670	7,326	7,107	5,530	6,198	6,528	6,985	7,430	8,051
Goodwill	2,076	2,446	3,182	3,179	3,092	2,964	3,391	3,414	2,805	4,211	3,957
Investments	105	307	276	341	317	276	362	404	356	384	490
Total fixed assets	6,927	8,836	10,128	10,846	10,516	8,770	9,951	10,346	10,146	12,025	12,498
Total assets	12,137	15,428	17,445	19,022	19,302	18,656	20,300	20,582	21,904	25,457	26,578
Current liabilities	3,353	6,083	4,828	6,012	5,253	4,000	5,957	6,199	6,867	8,873	9,361
Net assets before longer-term liabilities	8,784	9,365	12,617	13,010	14,049	14,656	14,343	14,383	15,037	16,584	17,217
Loan capital	380	350	2,820	2,787	2,752	2,717	2,687	2,659	2,622	3,950	3,463
Other longer-term liabilities	1,239	1,129	1,162	1,202	1,338	1,077	1,080	1,080	1,316	1,554	1,532
Net group assets	7,165	7,886	8,635	9,021	9,959	10,862	10,576	10,644	11,099	11,080	11,882
Minority shareholders	62	211	182	205	239	510	232	238	244	109	195
Net assets of Norcros shareholders	7,103	7,675	8,453	8,816	9,720	10,352	10,344	10,406	10,855	10,971	11,687

of which:											
preference shareholders	1,943	2,038	2,198	2,198	2,198	2,198	2,198	2,198	2,198	2,198	2,198
ordinary shareholders	5,160	5,637	6,255	6,618	7,522	8,154	8,146	8,208	8,657	8,773	9,489
	7,103	7,675	8,453	8,816	9,720	10,352	10,344	10,406	10,855	10,971	11,687
Trading results											
Earnings per ordinary share	7½p	4½p	4½p	4½p	5p	6p	5½p	6p	8p	8½p	10½p
External group sales:											
UK	n/a	n/a	n/a	n/a	n/a	n/a	21,862	22,944	21,981	24,293	27,069
Exports from UK	n/a	n/a	n/a	n/a	n/a	n/a	2,706	2,648	3,196	2,085	2,717
Overseas	n/a	n/a	n/a	n/a	n/a	n/a	2,222	2,613	2,788	3,392	3,760
	16,670	19,750	24,340	25,860	23,000	22,301	26,790	28,205	27,965	29,770	33,547
Group trading profit	1,870	1,959	2,120	2,166	2,262	2,119	2,073	2,134	2,651	2,947	3,439
Profits available for appropriation	938	890	891	932	999	1,098	965	1,049	1,379	1,443	1,724
Preference dividend—gross	69	129	143	143	143	143	143	143	143	143	143
Earnings for ordinary shareholders	869	770	748	789	856	955	822	906	1,236	1,300	1,581
Ordinary dividend—gross	707	754	764	764	764	764	764	764	791	823	863
Tax retained from dividends	(301)	(342)	(352)	(352)	(362)	(372)	(38)	—	—	—	—
Retentions	463	358	336	377	454	563	96	142	445	477	718

Source: Annual Reports.

EXHIBIT 2

Norcros Limited History of Principal Acquisitions and Disposals

Acquisition date	Name of company	Description of activities	Disposal date
1956 June	Norinco Ltd.	Owners of land and properties in Normanby, Lincs, together with ironstone deposits therein	Dec 1969
1956 June	Tickopress Ltd.	Specialist roll printers, etc.	
1956 Sep.	Bramigk Ltd.	Engineers and suppliers of machines to confectionery trade	Oct 1968
1956 Sep.	Neil & Spencer Ltd.	Manufacturers of dry-cleaning machines	Feb 1969
1957 Apr.	CEC Ltd.	Electrical engineers and contractors	Feb 1969
1957 Apr.	Union Fibres Ltd.	International merchants in textiles, etc.	Dec 1963
1957 May	John Tinsley Ltd.	Designers and builders of haulage and winding machinery	Shut down
1957 May	Wescros Ltd.	Iron, steel and metal merchants	
1957 Aug.	Relay Vision Ltd.	Rental, HP and sales of TV and radio sets	July 1964
1958 Mar.	Autotype Co. Ltd.	Manufacturers of photographic coated papers and films	
1959 Jan.	Hygena Ltd.	Manufacturers of timber and plywood kitchen units	
1959 Feb.	Temperature Ltd.	Manufacturers of air-conditioned equipment	
1959 Feb.	Temperature (Vectis) Ltd. (formerly Island Craft Ltd.)	Manufacturers of air-conditioning equipment	
1959 June	Jensen Motors	Motor car manufacturers	July 1968
1959 Sep.	S. Maw, Son and Sons (75 per cent interest)	Manufacturers of chemists sundries, etc.	
1960 Mar.	Blythswood Ship-building Co. Ltd.	Shipbuilders and heavy metal workers	Mar 1965
1960 June	Rotiss-O-Mat	Manufacturers of rotisserie equipment	Feb. 1965
1960 July	Lantigen (England) Ltd.	Manufacturers of oral vaccines	
1960 Oct.	Fisher Clark & Co. Ltd.	Tag and label manufacturers, printers	
1960 Nov.	Harold Wood & Sons Ltd.	Bulk liquid haulage contractors	Sep. 1965
1961 Feb.	Bulk Carriers Ltd.	Bulk liquid haulage contractors	
1961 Nov.	Aluminium Ingot Makers Ltd.	Secondary metal refiners	
1961 Nov.	Lowton Metals Ltd.	Secondary metal merchants	
1962 Feb.	Dow-Mac Concrete Ltd. (formerly Dow-Mac) Products Ltd.)	Prestressed concrete manufacturers	
1965 Dec.	Profile Publications (Publishers)	Publishers of profiles on aeroplanes, etc.	Dec. 1968
1966 Mar.	Ward Brooke & Co. Ltd.	Plastics and instrument manufacturers, etc.	Mar 1969

EXHIBIT 2 (*cont.*)

Acquisition date	Name of company	Description of activities	Disposal date
1968 Dec.	M. & S. Shifrin Ltd.	Manufacturers of bedroom and dining-room furniture	
1969 May	Raymond Holdings Pty Ltd.	Manufacturers of labels	
1969 Sep.	P. P. Payne & Sons Ltd.	Manufacturers of labels, ribbons and packaging materials	

Source: Annual Reports.

before tax. This rapid growth was reflected in the share price which on an adjusted basis rose over seven times to 34 shillings in September, 1960 compared with the placing price of 5.25 shilliings.

The typical formula adopted for acquisition was to offer one-third preference stock, one-third ordinary and one-third cash. The companies acquired continued to operate as autonomous units, with the original family managements being encouraged to retain all control over decision making. There was a minimum of central direction. Initially, central management was composed only of Mr Sheffield and a secretary. Rapid growth, however, led to an enlarged board, and in 1959 to the appointment of a managing director. This was the Honourable Geoffrey Cunliffe, former deputy chairman and managing director of British Aluminium who was chosen for his familiarity with financial management in a large enterprise. In 1960 an additional managing director, Mr John Boex, was appointed, a former colleague of Mr Cunliffe at British Aluminium. The function of Norcros central management was basically to provide finance and advice when and where called upon. Capital requests were never normally refused and the individual subsidiaries were free to spend and raise capital as they chose. Cooperation between subsidiaries, if it occurred at all, was accidental.

By the end of 1960 the financing of acquisitions and internal capital expenditure began to strain the available liquid resources. In 1961 it gradually became apparent that an overdraft position was developing but the lack of central financial data made precise estimating difficult. Although the rate of acquisition slowed, some new purchases were made. These were mainly for cash, thus further draining the short-term liquidity. For the first time profits failed to advance, causing a decline in stock price and increased difficulties of continued acquisition.

1962–6: The Rationalisation Phase

The short-term liquidity problems of 1961 led to refinancing in early 1962. An issue of £2½ million 6¾% convertible loan stock was timed to coincide with the purchase of Dow-Mac Products Ltd. Profitability remained static throughout 1962 and acquisition was virtually halted. A chief accountant was appointed in an effort to improve financial controls, and late in 1962 a request for a short-term cash budget was sent out to the subsidiaries for the first time. Standardised accounting procedures were slowly introduced throughout the group but there were still no central control on cash or capital expenditure.

In May 1963 Mr John Boex was appointed as sole managing director, on the resignation of Mr Cunliffe. Mr Boex began to rationalise the company in two main ways. First, a number of unprofitable subsidiaries were isolated and gradually disposed of or closed down to improve liquidity and financial stability. Between December 1963 and September 1965 five companies were disposed of and no new acquisitions were made until December 1965. Second, improved budgetary controls were gradually introduced by the central office over the activities of each subsidiary. This proved difficult at first and only slow progress was made. There was considerable resistance from the previously autonomous units to the concept of central controls. Further, central management was not available to attend in depth to the problems of the subsidiaries, and to develop the necessary information and control systems. Central management time was mostly taken up with day-to-day operations. However, in 1963 simple profit budgets were introduced, and the 1964 Annual Report noted a 'marked improvement in financial control and group management'.

In 1965 Mr Boex succeeded in reorganising the printing activities in the way he wished later to apply to the group as a whole. Fourteen separate companies were welded together into a single company, Norprint, which integrated the activities of the individual concerns under a divisional executive group.

The reorganisation was carried out firmly yet considerately. Subsidiary directors were allowed to retain their directorship titles though their new functions were unquestionably those of managers. Minority interests were bought out and as a number of family managements retired initial annual savings of £75,000 were realised on executive salaries.

Nevertheless, profits still remained virtually static and the share price continued to decline as Norcros lost its growth image. By the end of 1965 it had become apparent that the rate of expansion which had characterised Norcros's early years could not be regained with the existing structure. It was therefore decided early in 1966 to conduct a study covering all aspects of the business. In June 1966 the group symbolised its desire for 'rationalisation and modernisation' by moving its head office from central London to a new centre at Reading some thirty miles from London.

1966–71: The New Strategy and New Structure

On 7 July 1966 the following statement of corporate purpose was approved by the Norcros board:

The policy of the Norcros group is to reorganise its corporate and component structure by retaining in operation division form those companies which offer the highest potential in the fields of construction, consumer products, engineering and printing, and to achieve the specified rate of growth by concentrating all resources specifically to the expansion of those divisions, and to provide the necessary management to direct, coordinate and control the overall effort.

This statement marked the beginning of a new phase in Norcros's corporate life. Top management defined the task of the next five years as making the transition from a financially orientated holding company of widely diversified subsidiaries, each operating with a minimum of central direction, into an integrated group with a 'consistent purpose and common planned direction'. The group was to be made up of four operating divisions, namely printing, construction, consumer products and engineering, each having above-average growth potential, a coherent industrial structure and based on a solid industrial logic. Exhibit 3 shows the structure of the group in 1971, the divisions by then having been reduced to three.

In September 1966, with the board now behind him and the study complete, Mr Boex summoned the managing director of each subsidiary to a meeting at the Reading headquarters to advise them of the new strategy and structure.

Shareholders were notified of the change in a booklet circulated in March 1967 with the chairman's statement for the year. This included the following points:

It was therefore decided we should aim to redefine Norcros Limited as an Industrial Group of Companies with the result that in future our energies should be concentrated on those of our businesses which have the strongest growth potential. Accordingly, the fourteen companies which best fit this requirement have been reorganised into four main operating divisions each with a division chief executive who reports direct to top management. No further diversification will be made for the time being, allowing all resources of management, men and money to be concentrated on these four sectors.

The new divisions are construction, consumer products, engineering and printing. These are sectors which all have above-average potential for growth in a modern economy and at the same time are not industries in which massive investment in terms of research and development inhibit profitability.

Just as important is our intention to weld together these four divisions which will comprise Norcros Limited into a corporate body with a common identity having a common purpose and operating with a unified plan. It has always been our constant endeavour continually

EXHIBIT 3
Organisation of the Norcros Group

Board of Directors

Chairman
J. V. Sheffield

Executive
F. J. Briggs (Managing)
P. I. Marshall, FCA (Financial)
W. G. S. Tozer (Personnel and administration)

Non-Executive
D. Kirkness
A. Lyell
The Hon. P. M. Samuel, MC, TD
E. C. R. Sheffield

Norcros Limited
Managing Director
F. J. Briggs

Printing and Packaging Division	Consumer Division	Construction Engineering Division
Chief Executive D. M. Norman	Chief Executive D. H. Standen	Chief Executive W. K. Roberts
Factories 7 in UK Auckland, New Zealand Bergen, Norway Singapore Sydney, Australia Wellington, New Zealand	Factories 5 in UK	Factories 7 in UK
Products: Photographic coated papers and films, paper labels, garment labels, tickets, tags, ribbons, overprinting machines and packaging materials.	Products: Kitchen and bedroom storage units and dining room furniture; nursery goods and pharmaceutical products	Products: Precast prestressed and reinforced concrete; air conditioning and refrigeration equipment fabrication and general engineers; metal merchants

to improve the standard of management and financial control within the company. Management, although the least tangible, is the most important ingredient in any organisation, and a significant improvement in management standards and a much greater centralised control over all the operating divisions is a primary aim of the reorganisation.

Norcros has set itself high targets: a turnover of £50 million by the early 1970s and a coordinated plan designed to raise the rate of return on capital employed by over 18 per cent and before-tax profit margins by nearly 13 per cent. No operating part of the group, even those already bettering the target performance figures, is exempt from the obligation to aim for this standard of improvement. Again, a target attains nothing of itself. The means chosen to achieve the objective are critical and, in the case of Norcros, these means amount to an internal revolution.

Central financial control built on forward budgets imposes on every manager the necessity to think clearly about what he intends to do and how he expects to do it in the short, intermediate and long term, through his forward budget of profits and revenue: and how he plans to built the long-term growth of that part of Norcros under his control, through the capital budget. Capital spending, which means the allocation of the resources of the entire group, and thus the shaping of its future, is now rigidly controlled by top management.

These senior executives of Norcros, from the managing director downwards, now all have detailed 'position guides', or job descriptions, which lay down their precise roles in achieving the group's objectives. The managerial principle throughout is that unless a man knows what he is expected to achieve, and is forced to work out for himself how he will achieve it, the chances of success are seriously reduced, perhaps eliminated.

Managers will, however, receive greatly expanded central assistance in deciding on and arriving at their objectives. A new Management Services Division, providing consultant help in finance, industrial engineering, marketing and personnel, comes under a director of its own who also controls the financial system and who reports direct to the managing director. The separate marketing function of this division is unusual in a British company with only part of its interest in consumer products. The explanation is that Norcros is applying modern marketing techniques right across the group to ensure that the right products get to the right customers at the right price; and this will be a top management function in the subsidiaries.

Together with cost-cutting programmes, group-wide technical training, plant modernisation and other policies stemming directly from the board's July 1966 decision, these innovations will disturb many settled ways in the group. But growth is change; the alternative to dynamic expansion, which is stagnation, is in the long run far more unsettling for all those who belong to a commerical organisation.

Making its people realise thay they do in fact belong to the group is one of the paramount objectives of Norcros and simultaneously one of the main methods by which it plans to achieve those aims. The intention is to build a group identity, to make out of a previously over-diversified holding company an operating unity with a clear and hard sense of purpose, whose members will identify themselves with the success and name of Norcros.

This statement of corporate purpose and organisation was backed up with a fifty-page formal statement of policies and procedures which was circulated to all managers throughout the group.

ACQUISITION AND DIVESTMENT POLICY

The new strategy anticipated that approximately two-thirds of the expected growth in turnover and profit before tax would come from external acquisition, with the remaining third being generated by internal growth. This ratio resulted from the identification of a so-called 'development gap'. The profit potential of the businesses Norcros wished to retain was identified and estimated to amount to approximately £3 million before tax by 1971. The difference between this sum and the 1971 profit objective of £4.5 million represented the gap to be satisfied by acquisition.

The financing of this programme was to be achieved partially by additional long-term borrowing but was expected to mainly come from divestments of interests which did not conform to the new strategy. In July 1968 Jensen Motors, a manufacturer of speciality cars, was sold for £60,000 after producing losses of £58,000 in 1967. This was followed by the sale of Bramigk Ltd, manufacturers of confectionery machinery. In February 1969 Neil and Spencer, manufacturers of dry cleaning machinery, was sold providing the main contribution in a total of £4.3 million raised by divestment. By the end of 1969 most of the former subsidiaries composing the engineering division of 1967 had been sold, and this division was combined with the construction division in 1968.

It was the strategy of the group to identify, in precise terms, appropriate growth sectors towards which the resources of the group could be directed and upon which they could be concentrated. Initially the areas chosen for concentration were to build up the consumer products division around the Hygena furniture interest and to expand the domestic and international interests of the printing division. Therefore, in December 1968 the group acquired M. & S. Shifrin, manufacturers of bedroom and dining-room furniture, followed in 1969 with the purchases of Raymond Holdings and P. P. Payne, manufacturers of specialist printings and labels. In May 1971 the overseas printing interests were further expanded by the purchase of a small specialist concern in South Africa.

PRODUCT MARKET STRATEGY

Each of the three main product divisions operated largely independently of the others. There was little or no interdivisional product flow and each maintained its own contact with its respective markets. As a group Norcros did not engage in much basic long-range research. Concentration of research effort was made on product development and process improvement which was deliberately decentralised within the divisions. Extensive market research was conducted, however, aimed at establishing current and future consumer needs.

The largest product division, printing and packaging, accounted for 34 per cent of total sales in 1970 having grown steadily from 19 per cent in 1966. A breakdown of sales and profits by product group for the period 1966–70 is shown in Exhibit 4.

Printing and Packaging Division

In 1967 the printing and packaging interests of the group consisted of Norprint Ltd, the largest European specialist printer of tickets, tags and labels. Norprint produced over 14 million such labels per annum by all printing processes on almost every type of paper, board, film and foil. In addition, the company specialised in label systems and supplied a comprehensive range of machines, applicators and dispensers for printing

EXHIBIT 4

Sales and Profitability by Divisions 1966–70 (£'000)

		1966	1967	1968	1969	1970
Construction	Sales	9,831	10,274	9,795	6,424	9,371
and engineering	% of total	37	36	35	22	28
	PBT	541	574	621	445	516
	% of total	28	31	26	17	17
Consumer products	Sales	5,403	6,099	7,372	8,702	10,148
	% of total	20	22	26	29	30
	PBT	296	401	466	431	508
	% of total	16	21	20	16	17
Printing and	Sales	4,978	5,307	5,822	9,730	11,319
packaging	% of total	19	19	21	33	34
	PBT	513	638	832	1,394	1,523
	% of total	27	34	35	53	50
Overseas and	Sales	6,578	6,525	4,976	4,914	2,709
other interests	% of total	24	23	18	17	8
	PBT	399	136	443	358	473
	% of total	21	7	19	14	16
TOTAL	Sales	26,790	28,205	27,965	29,770	33,547
	PBT	1,903	1,879	2,362	2,628	3,020

Source: Annual Reports.

and applying every type of label. These systems were sold for a variety of industrial purposes and were also widely used in supermarkets. Norprint was also an important producer of specialised coated papers and films for use in the production of photogravure cylinders and silk screens for the silk-screen printing industry.

Norprint extended the application of self-adhesive labels to the toy market in 1968 with the launching of its Simplay range of print-based charts and games for children. This consisted of a range of products such

EXHIBIT 5

Printing and Packaging Division Financial Statements 1967–70

	Norprint				P. P. Payne		
	1967	1968	1969	1970	1968	1969	1970
				(£'000)			
Sales							
Home	4,182	4,642	5,314	6,092	2,226	1,920	2,249
Export	770	895	1,051	1,312	441	418	499
Overseas	183	206	—	—	—	—	—
Total	5,136	5,556	6,365	7,404	2,667	2,338	2,747
Profit before tax	898	982	1,183	1,406	220	268	247
Profit after tax	523	607	752	1,066	133	149	169
Fixed assets	1,158	588	589	591	1,145	1,187	373
Goodwill, etc.	792	2,336	24	19	—	—	—
Unquoted investments	88	21	21	—	—	—	—
Current assets due from other subsidiaries	4	—	9	98	—	1	857
Stocks and WIP	825	777	938	1,119	402	348	353
Debtors and prepayments	1,122	1,448	1,886	2,294	429	661	720
Quoted investments	21	—	—	—	—	—	—
Cash	973	3	5	2	70	111	1
Total	2,945	2,228	2,838	3,513	921	1,121	1,931
Current liabilities							
Due to other subsidiaries	357	7	14	—	—	—	9
Creditors	488	657	960	1,114	349	295	252
Tax	653	808	871	399	11	90	126
Overdrafts	21	—	—	—	—	—	—
Dividends	506	522	732	1,078	45	50	157
Total	2,025	1,994	2,577	2,591	405	435	535
Net current assets	920	234	261	922	516	686	1,396

Source: Annual Reports.

as Spotters Charts on such subjects as automobiles, wild flowers and Build-a-Map. Backed by advertising including spot TV and a specialist consumer products division, the operation achieved sales of over £100,000 in its first year of operation.

The addition of P. P. Payne in 1969 added further complementary strength to the printing division. This Nottingham-based firm was the UK market leader in printed fabric labels for garments and textiles. In addition Paynes produced decorative ribbons and had interests in packaging products especially heavy-duty industrial strapping and Rippatape, a built-in opening device for corrugated containers. Recent financial performance of the British subsidiaries of the Printing and Packaging Division are shown in Exhibit 5.

The acquisition of Raymond Holdings extended the divisions activities to Australia and New Zealand. Trading under the name of Label House Pty, Raymond had the major share of the Australian and New Zealand markets for labels, tickets and tags. Overseas interests were further extended in 1971 with the acquisition of a similar specialist printing concern in South Africa.

Construction Engineering Division

In 1967 this division was operating as two separate operations—a construction division consisting mainly of Dow-Mac Concrete, and an engineering division composed of a number of specialist engineering concerns. By 1968 these two divisions had been combined following the divestment of a number of the larger engineering interests, leaving two main subsidiaries Dow-Mac and Temperature Ltd, together with a number of small concerns engaged in secondary metal refining and trading. The remaining activities had been carefully chosen as growth areas where Norcros believed that success could be achieved through efficiency, service and technological innovation. The financial performance of the remaining subsidiaries is shown for recent years in Exhibit 6.

Dow-Mac Concrete, the largest of the remaining subsidiaries, was the largest manufacturer of structural prestressed concrete units in the UK, and the world's largest producer of heavy structural units for motorway bridges and industrialised buildings. In addition, it had originated prestressed concrete sleepers for British Rail and currently supplied approximately half of the sleepers for an annual track-relaying requirement of 250 miles. Norcros estimated that in a notoriously unprofitable industry Dow-Mac's return on capital was the highest in its field.

The second main subsidiary, Temperature Ltd, was the largest British-owned air conditioning and environmental control manufacturing company. The British air conditioning market was expanding rapidly and was dominated by American concerns either producing locally or importing finished products. Norcros considered that some American equipment was

Q

EXHIBIT 6

Construction Engineering Division Financial Statements, 1967–70

	Dow-Mac Concrete Ltd.				Temperature Ltd.			
	1967	1968	1969	1970	1967	1968	1969	1970
	(£'000)							
Sales								
Home	3,970	4,495	4,650	4,554	874	1,000	977	1,149
Export	—	—	11	38	365	634	328	602
Total	3,970	4,495	4,661	4,592	1,239	1,634	1,305	1,751
Profit before tax	356	339	370	426	44	125	129	101
Profit after tax	223	269	188	238	34	96	66	60
Net fixed assets	1,110	475	450	426	50	43	55	133
Current assets								
Stock and WIP	440	428	373	459	151	137	126	559
Debtors and prepayments	679	1,134	931	912	300	462	584	638
Cash	1	14	48	4	115	1	4	18
Due from other subsidiaries	—	5	24	17	3	116	—	—
Total	1,120	1,581	1,376	1,392	569	716	714	1,215
Current liabilities								
Due to other subsidiaries	—	—	—	—	20	—	29	—
Creditors	554	805	735	813	60	114	169	308
Tax	194	217	358	376	126	25	63	103
Dividends	433	161	349	239	65	124	80	63
Overdrafts	11	—	—	—	—	18	—	—
Total	1,192	1,183	1,442	1,428	271	281	341	474
Net current assets	(72)	398	(66)	(36)	298	437	373	741

Source: Annual Returns.

not always suitable for application in the UK and forecast an expanding future for Temperature Ltd. The company enjoyed a number of government contracts for air conditioning and environmental control in defence equipment. In 1969 the company moved to a new 78,000 sq. ft. plant on the Isle of Wight which had a further 15 acres available for future expansion.

Consumer Products Division

Norcros placed much effort into researching areas of consumer expenditure, attitudes and needs, and predicting future trends. As a result

EXHIBIT 7

Consumer Products Division Financial Statements 1967–70

(£'000)

	Hygena Ltd.				S. Maws Son & Sons Ltd.				M. & S. Shifrin		
	1967	1968	1969	1970	1967	1968	1969	1970	1968	1969	1970
Sales											
Home	2,970	3,589	4,014	5,559	2,727	3,152	2,745	2,972	1,428	1,858	N/A
Export	34	36	48	76	90	97	164	171	—	—	N/A
Total	3,004	3,625	4,062	5,635	2,816	3,249	2,910	3,143	1,428	1,858	N/A
Profit before tax	244	338	286	684	147	187	57	(17)	274	185	N/A
Profit After Tax	222	335	212	399	85	106	33	(17)	156	113	N/A
Fixed assets	512	845	907	835	172	234	241	281	347	304	N/A
Current assets											
Stock and WIP	345	509	757	623	234	310	395	611	169	260	N/A
Due from other subsidiaries	—	—	—	1	152	—	—	—	—	—	N/A
Debtors and prepayments	734	1,158	1,473	1,758	682	896	713	865	210	218	N/A
Bank and cash	110	3	12	16	78	54	5	5	30	9	N/A
Total	1,189	1,670	2,242	2,398	1,146	1,260	1,113	1,481	409	487	N/A
Current liabilities											
Creditors	403	665	787	1,015	560	523	701	786	190	250	N/A
UK and overseas tax	92	20	13	117	97	143	109	30	64	166	N/A
Due to other subsidiaries	—	—	—	—	1	157	144	129	—	—	N/A
Dividends	410	334	283	399	85	99	22	14	—	50	N/A
Total	905	1,019	1,083	1,531	743	922	976	959	254	466	N/A
Net current assets	284	651	1,159	867	403	338	137	522	155	21	N/A

Source: Annual Returns.

of this activity the efforts of the consumer products division had been concentrated in the fields of furniture, baby-care products and pharmaceuticals. Exhibit 7 provides financial details of these individual activities.

While the industry was characterised by relatively slow growth, Norcros considered the industry was undergoing rapid change, with rationalisation into a smaller number of large efficient units. Two sectors of the industry had been identified as exhibiting above-average growth, namely kitchen and bedroom storage furniture. In 1967 the Norcros interest in this market was centred on Hygena Ltd, the largest manufacturer of kitchen storage furniture in the UK. Its main product line consisted of the System 70 range of kitchen units which sold towards the top end of the price range for kitchen furniture and was the brand leader in the UK. This was sold to both home owners and direct to developers, with each market representing about half of the £34 million industry sales reached in 1970/71. After investigating other sectors of the market Hygena launched its QA (Quick Assembly) range of units aimed at the do-it-yourself market in 1968. Backed by spot TV advertising this range had rapidly grown to be second only to System 70 in terms of the market share. In 1971 a further range, System 2000, was launched to appeal to the luxury market, incorporating a full range of built-in electrical appliances supplied by the German Bauknecht Company.

Norcros acquired M. & S. Shifrin at the end of 1968 in order to enter the market for bedroom storage furniture. Shifrin was primarily a low-price producer specialising increasingly in free-standing bedroom furniture. Wardrobes made up 50 per cent of sales with dressing tables and chests accounting for a further 30 per cent. The remaining 20 per cent of sales was split between dining-room sideboards, tables and chairs, wall units and room dividers.

The remaining subsidiary in the consumer products division, S. Maws Son & Sons was engaged in the manufacture, merchandising and sales of nursery and pharmaceutical products. Maws were brand leaders in teats and feeding bottles in the UK and also had substantial market shares in disposable nappies, baby pants and infant toiletries. A range of Junior Pharmaceuticals was sold through chemists including cough medicine, gripe mixture and teething balm. The company also produced a small range of proprietary and ethical pharmaceuticals including vaccines and eye care products. It was company policy to reduce Maws merchandising activities and increase the level of products manufactured within the group. At the same time substantial investment was being made in TV advertising and point of sale promotion to develop Maws's brand name in the baby products market.

Overseas and Other Interests

Apart from the overseas subsidiaries of the printing and packaging division, Norcros owned a subsidiary company in Canada. This company,

Bulk Carriers Ltd, operated a fleet of about 200 'freight trains'—large bulk tractor-trailer tankers—carrying loads such as cement, fuel oils, chemicals and alcohol. This fleet operated mainly in Eastern Canada and the United States, from three bases in Toronto, Montreal and Windsor, Ontario. In 1970 Bulk Carriers made a profit of £91,000, a reduction of £59,000 on the 1969 results.

Other interests included a group property company which owned the freehold of the operating company buildings and a number of small investments.

THE ROLE OF THE CORPORATE HEADQUARTERS

The adoption of the new strategy and structure resulted in an increased role for the Norcros central office. In addition to Mr Boex and the company secretary, a finance director Peter Marshall was appointed from EMI in 1967. Mr Marshall was responsible for the introduction of improved procedures and played a major role in the acquisition and divestment programme. The staff of the finance director was increased and a management services division was set up. Other appointments included an industrial engineer and a marketing adviser, together with a small staff for each. These appointments more than doubled the head office expenses from £147,000 in 1966 to over £320,000 in 1967.

In 1969 Gordon Tozer was appointed to the position of director of personnel and administration as the group came to recognise the need for developing managerial talent. In the same year John Briggs, formerly managing director of Norprint, was appointed director of operations.

The development of the central office led to the introduction of formalised procedures covering marketing, where annual marketing plans were prepared by the divisions; finance, incorporating both short- and long-term plans; and capital budgeting. Nevertheless the size of the central staff remained small and in 1971 totalled approximately thirty. The appointment of central office executives was restricted first to providing specialist advisory services such as taxation, pensions and legal functions, not normally available in the operating division, and second, for analysing incoming information from the divisions in order to control and monitor performance and allocated resources.

Financial Procedures

The new financial procedures developed to assist inplementation of the new strategy were based on the concept of influencing future events through forecasting likely performance. The control exercised by head office centred mainly on two areas:

(a) a system for four-year plans and annual budgets
(b) central control of cash balances

A system of four-year, long-term plans was introduced for each division to be updated in May of each year, with the projections covering the full financial requirements for the growth of the business in terms of sales increase, capital requirements, cash flow and pre-tax profits over the following four years. These plans enabled Norcros to assess its future financial requirements in relation to its planned growth, and formed the basis for its policy on acquisitions and disposals.

Covering the short term a system of annual budgets was introduced. Each division agreed with Norcros (which was consulted throughout the planning stage) its annual budget in October each year for the following financial year (1 December–30 November). The annual plan was prepared initially at the level of the individual subsidiaries in consultation with the divisional chief executive. A plan for each division was then reviewed and renegotiated by the central office in the context of the group's target growth rates for each division. When finalised, the plan became a divisional profit budget for the year and 'a solemn undertaking which local management was required to accept'.

Each division's performance was measured through its monthly management reports. These reports contained comparisons of actual achievement against budget and forecast performance. The monthly budget performance was phased at the time budgets were agreed. Forecast performance was revised monthly and indicated each month in advance how actual performance was likely to vary from budget.

Three days after the end of each month Norcros obtained a 'flash' report from each division containing estimated sales and pre-tax figures for that month. The period report containing actual figures was available to divisions and to Norcros fourteen days after the end of each month. The forms on which this information was supplied were specifically designed to provide data which divisional executives had to have for responsible, efficient management. The information required by head office was easily extracted for its control and accounting purposes.

Capital expenditure was approved 'in principle' at the time the budgets were approved. Each capital expenditure requirement had subsequently to be applied for with a full project justification. Once final approval was given, Norcros control then took the form of phasing the cash outflow.

Freehold properties of the subsidiaries were owned by a group property company and a fair market rental was charged to the occupier. The accounting result of the division was thus related solely to trading performance. For budget and management accounts purposes, a charge was also made by Norcros on each division in respect of interest on the assets managed. This was currently $6\frac{1}{4}$ per cent. The funds created by this charge were remitted to Norcros each month.

The major day-to-day control of the group was through control of cash balances. No United Kingdom division was permitted a bank overdraft. Cash generated in a division's trade, less an agreed retention immediately required for its business, was transferred each month to Norcros Limited. Further cash required by divisions to finance trade expansion or the 'new' money required for capital assets was supplied by Norcros. All transfers were measured against the phased cash budgets and three-monthly rolling cash forecasts.

Recovery of Central Expenditure System

In November 1967, as mentioned above, the new finance director introduced a charge on capital employed by the subsidiaries. Throughout the group, operating companies bore a charge against their profits each month which was calculated at a standard rate on the opening balances of that month of fixed assets, stocks, debtors and creditors. These balance sheet categories were referred to as 'assets managed' and in the definition there was no deduction for depreciation, and all terms were valued at replacement cost so far as practicable.

The rate of interest charged on the 'assets managed' was determined centrally, designed for a longer term to avoid annual fluctuations and levied on all trading operations in an equitable manner.

The underlying principle of the system was to state the operating company profits at a level which was equal to the pre-tax equivalent of earnings for ordinary shareholders. The system yielded a number of advantages which included the following:

(a) Clarity of purpose—both operating and central managements were considering only one criterion of profitability—earning for ordinaries.

(b) Cost of time—interest charges were made on specific events, viz. the credit periods of debtors and creditors, the length of ownership of fixed assets, and the length of time goods remained in stock, or work-in-progress. The effect was valued and charged to the profit statement.

(c) Gross marginal costing was eliminated.

(d) Loss-making activities were identified in stark relief. Such activities usually contained excessive assets (under-utilised plant, slow-moving stocks, slow debtors, etc.) and these were fairly penalised by specific costs.

(e) Departmental profits were easy to measure. Since the interest was calculated on assets managed the charge to a given factory based on its fixed assets, work-in-progress, stocks, etc., could be further subdivided as required. In the marketing departments the interest charge on debtors could be divided readily between outlets of trade, individual customers, exports and so on, so that the particular manager involved could be aware of the situation.

(f) Overhead departments also bore interest charges so that the interest costs of their assets managed were specifically taken into account. This was particularly important in the case of works engineering departments, computer departments, etc.

(g) Piece parts passing from one department to another were priced including the interest content on the assets involved. Sub-assemblies passing between factories also contained the interest element attracted by the assets employed to that stage.

(h) Finished goods went into stock at standard prices which included the appropriate interest on the assets involved in their manufacture.

(i) Calculations for selling price guidance included interest according to the terms of trade. For example in the case of exports, interest would be provided on the length of time in finished goods stock, goods in transit, export debtors and cash in transit. This was frequently a surprising revelation to commercial managements.

(j) Plant and machinery attracted interest without a deduction for depreciation, so that factory managements were stimulated to dispose of under-utilised or inefficient items. This encouraged modern plants of optimum size.

(k) Profit-sharing schemes for management could be fairly devised, automatically containing the vital element—cost of time.

(l) The interest charge was dynamic, based on monthly opening balances. If stock went up in a month there was an immediate increase in the charge—if debtors went down in a month there was an immediate benefit in the profit statement.

Personnel Policy

The adoption of the new strategy led to substantial change in the top management of the subsidiaries. Many of the former family managements left the group in the first two years of change in policy. Norcros recognised that to achieve better than average performance it needed skilled and highly motivated managers. Where possible it remained group policy to promote from within; however, to fill the vacancies created by the new strategy which could not be met from inside the organisation, Norcros began actively to recruit business graduates from leading British and American universities. In 1968, as a result of recruiting, one PhD in operations research from Lancaster, one DBA in business policy from Harvard and two MBAs joined the group. Exhibit 8 indicates the top management team at Norcros in April 1971.

EXHIBIT 8
Top Management Team

Chairman

John V. Sheffield, Chairman. Norcros Ltd. Age 57. Educated Eton, Magdalene College, Cambridge (MA). Chairman: Portals Holdings Ltd, Anderson Finch

Villiers (Insurance) Ltd. Director: British Assets Trust Ltd, Second British Assets Ltd, Atlantic Assets Trust Ld, Clark Chapman—John Thompson Ltd, Green's Economiser Group Ltd, Royal Exchange (City Branch), Normanby Estate Co. Ltd. Was High Sheriff of Lincolnshire 1944–5.

Executive Directors

F. John Briggs, Managing Director. Norcros Ltd. Age 47. Educated William Hulme Grammar School. Served in RAF from 1942 to 1946. Joined Tickopres Ltd, a founder company of Norcros in 1946. Was appointed Sales Director 1953. Became Assistant Managing Director in 1955, joint Managing Director in 1958, Managing Director in 1960. In 1962 became joint Managing Director Tickopres and Fisher Clark Limited. In 1965 was appointed Managing Director and Chairman of subsidiaries. In 1966 was appointed Director of Norcros and Chief Exectuive Printing Division. Appointed Director of Operations in 1969. Is now Chairman of ten Norcros companies. He is President of the World Packaging Organisation. Director of the European Packaging Federation (Past President), and Chairman of the Board, Institute of Packaging. He is also a Freeman of the Worshipful Company of Tylers and Bricklayers, a Fellow of the Institute of Directors, a Fellow of the Institute of Marketing and a member of the BIM.

Peter I. Marshall, Financial Director of Norcros since 1967. Age 44. Educated Buxton College, Derbyshire. Became Chartered Accountant in 1955. Financial Accountant for Mulllard Ltd in 1956. Was Group Accountant of EMI Ltd, from 1960 to 1963 when he became Financial and Commercial Director of their Industrial Electronics Company to June 1967. Is a Fellow of the Institute of Chartered Accountants. Also a Licentiate of the Royal Academy of Music, conductor and pianist.

W. G. S. (Gordon) Tozer, Director of Personnel and Administration. Age 50. Educated at Harrow, Sandhurst and Joint Services Staff College. After serving in Grenadier Guards from 1940 to 1957, he became Sales Manager then Export Manager for Formica Ltd. In 1962 was appointed General Manager of Formica India Limited and in 1966 became involved with Overseas Development for Formica International Ltd. Joined Norcros in 1967 as Chief Executive, Consumer Products Division and the same year was appointed a Director. Present appointment made in 1969.

Secretary

Victor C. Yaldren, Secretary of Norcros since 1963. Age 51. After education at East Grinstead Grammar School, served in the Army from 1939 to 1946. Qualified as Chartered Accountant in 1948. Specialised in taxation and financial investigation. Worked on Norcros's financial affairs from 1956 while with Deloitte, Plender, Griffiths & Co., and joined Group in 1962. Is Fellow of the Institute of Chartered Accountants, Member of Society of Investment Analysis and Member of BIM.

Chief Executives

David M. Norman, Chief Executive, Printing and Packaging Division, and Managing Director of Norprint Limited. Age 30. After attending McGill University, Canada, where he obtained a BA Degree in Economics, he worked on the West Coast for the US Meat Packers, Armour & Company. Then worked for the Corporate Financial Department of Merrill Lynch on Wall Street. Returned to the UK and joined Dunlop's Central Marketing Department in 1964 and became Marketing Manager of Slazengers, UK. In 1965 he attended

Harvard Business School, specialised in Marketing and Corporate Finance and received his Masters (MBA Degree) in 1967. Returned to UK and joined Norcros Marketing Services. In September 1968 became Marketing Director of Norprint and one year later was appointed Managing Director.

W. K. (Ken) Roberts, Managing Director, Dow-Mac Concrete Ltd since 1954. Age 47. Educated: Dominican Friars School, Bangor, and Bath Technical College. Served in the Admiralty from 1942 to 1946. Joined Dow-Mac in 1946. Is a Justice of the Peace.

Donald H. Standen, Managing Director, Hygena Ltd since 1967. Age 46. Educated at Crofton School. Member of the Institute of Cost and Works Accountants and Chartered Institute of Secretaries. War service with Royal Air Force. Was Navigator, Bomber Command, Europe, Middle East, Far East. Industrial experience covers light engineering (general machine shop ferrous and non-ferrous foundries, hydraulics, metal sintering processing), instrumentation (including airborne navigation equipment), textiles (spinning, weaving, dyeing and making up), electrical engineering (including transformer manufacturing), pharmaceuticals (including toiletries), and confectionery. Previous board appointments: Sterling Industries Ltd in 1956, William R. Warner & Co. Ltd in 1961.

The company began a series of in-company group training courses in 1968 covering the functions of general management, accounting, marketing, production and purchasing. This was later expanded in order to facilitate the building of a strong team of executives in top, second and third line positions who could see a permanent career for themselves with Norcros.

A comprehensive and integrated programme was started to enable each individual to develop his career in the group. The career development programme was closely tied to the annual review of the four-year plans. From the plans information was extracted about future manpower, organisational requirements, succession and career development. These requirements were coordinated centrally in close consultation with the divisions and plans based on a minimum two-year training and development cycle. The training which each individual required in order to further his career with Norcros was planned with him and the recommendation detailed in the four-year plan.

In December 1970 Norcros introduced a special share-incentive scheme for executives making the greatest contribution to growth. These shares were only of value if specific targets were met over a period of time. The scheme was designed to increase profitability in terms of earnings per share and to attract and retain executives of the highest calibre.

In addition, an incentive bonus scheme was introduced for all executives who controlled profit centres. This was based on the achievement of an agreed annual pre-tax profit budget and there were substantial increments for results in excess of budget.

Change of Management

Mr. John Boex resigned as managing director of Norcros on 20 March 1970 on the grounds of ill health. He was succeeded by John Briggs formerly managing director of Norprint from 1966 to 1969, when he became director of operations.

RECENT MARKET PERFORMANCE

The result of the new strategy and structure resulted in a rising market price for Norcros shares as shown in Exhibit 9. Nevertheless, market reaction did not result in much change in the company's price/earnings multiple.

Commenting on the 1970 results, the *Guardian* of 23 February 1971 stated:

> The fortunes of Norcros show how hard it is to convince investors that you are the exception that proves the rule. Norcros is a mixed holding company which is not a fashionable form of organisation. Its management is strong in young business graduates, who have yet to convince the stock market that the methods they learn work in real life.
>
> Result: figures which are excellent by any test were greeted yesterday with little more than a shrug. Pre-tax profits are up 13.6 per cent, and the share price rose 2½p—just over 2 per cent—to 118½.
>
> The profit is a record for the third year in succession, yet the p/e on the new earnings of 10.3p per share is only 11.2. Little recognition here for a consistent record, nor for the more remarkable fact that Norcros managed a shade of improvement in trading margins—from 9.9 to 10 per cent—in a year which has been disastrous for so many companies.
>
> The profits picture is complicated by acquisitions and sales of subsidiaries, but apart from the recession in North America which made life difficult for the Canadian group, the preliminary statement gives the impression of an 'all-go' business.
>
> In fact, all three of the operating divisions, construction engineering, 'consumer' (nursery supplies, pharmaceuticals and furniture) and

EXHIBIT 9

Monthly Share Prices (pence)

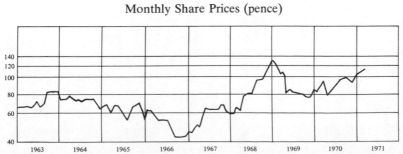

Source: Moodies Investment Handbook.

printing and packaging made 'significant' contributions to the peak earnings performance.

Given reasonable conditions, the improvement in profits could continue, for after the 12.5 per cent profits rise in the first half, growth accelerated to a 14.4 per cent increase in the second half. The synergy, fostered by the Payne and Raymond acquisitions was clearly a stimulus to the printing division.

Norcros now surely deserves a better rating. But it may be some time before investors can believe good news when they see it.

32

Texas Instruments Inc.

In 1978 Texas Instruments was one of the world's leading producers of semiconductors and related products and services. 1977 had been another record year for the company as sales billed reached $2.05 billion, an increase of 23 per cent on the previous year, net income was up by around 20 per cent to $116.6 million and earnings per share reached $5.11. Recent financial performance is shown in Exhibit 1. Despite these sucesses the company still had a long way to go toward the target of $10 billion sales it had set itself to achieve by the late 1980's in some of the world's most competitive and rapidly technically changing markets.

COMPANY HISTORY

Texas Instruments was founded in 1930 as Geophysical Service Inc. (GSI) to exploit the use of the reflection seismograph in oil exploration. The company's first president, Dr. J. C. Karcher, was a physicist generally credited as the principal inventor and developer of this technology. In 1946, Patrick E. Haggerty joined the company when sales had reached $2.25 million, charged with the task of moving the organisation into new areas of engineering and manufacturing. In the next few years the company changed its name to Texas Instruments and gradually began to deliberately set out to innovate, formulating a statement of purpose which expressed that commitment. The statement read: 'Texas Instruments exists to create, make and market useful products and services to satisfy the needs of its customers throughout the world'.

By 1949 the company had more than doubled in size and a deliberate decision was taken to become a good, *big* company instead of a good, *medium sized* company which had been the implicit goal until then. This new ambition was expressed as a company earning at least $10 million a year after taxes and with sales of around $200 million. In pursuit of the new goal the company adopted several strategies, one of which proved to be especially important, namely a major push further into electronics (GSI was already making electronic products such as low altitude bomb sights for the U.S. Navy as well as geophysical instrumentation).

EXHIBIT 1

Texas Instruments Financial Performance

Years Ended December 31	1977	1976	1975	1974	1973	1972	1971	1970	1969	1968
Summary of Operations										
Thousands of Dollars										
Net sales billed	$2,046,456	$1,658,607	$1,367,621	$1,572,487	$1,287,276	$943,694	$764,258	$827,641	$831,822	$671,230
Operating costs and expenses	1,835,619	1,495,981	1,252,833	1,403,105	1,141,824	860,625	705,094	773,113	769,983	621,917
Profit from operations	210,837	162,626	114,788	169,382	145,452	83,069	59,164	54,528	61,839	49,313
Other income (net)	9,261	23,782	11,971	4,159	6,746	7,178	6,840	4,529	3,936	4,258
Interest on loans	(9,179)	(8,310)	(10,822)	(10,741)	(6,654)	(5,676)	(6,526)	(7,014)	(5,474)	(3,209)
Income before provision for income taxes	210,919	178,098	115,937	162,800	145,544	84,571	59,478	52,043	60,301	50,362
Provision for income taxes	94,281	80,678	53,795	73,179	62,309	36,541	25,755	22,182	26,790	24,038
Net income	116,638	97,420	62,142	89,621	83,235	48,030	33,723	29,861	33,511	26,324

Earned per common share (average outstanding during year)†	$1.21	$1.53	$1.35	$1.53	$2.17	$3.67	$3.92	$2.71	$4.25	$5.11
Cash dividends paid per common share†	0.400	0.400	0.400	0.400	0.415	0.555	0.920	1.000	1.000	1.320
Common shares (average shares outstanding during year, in thousands)†	21,819	21,919	22,072	22,085	22,139	22,691	22,854	22,920	22,933	22,842
Financial Condition *Thousands of Dollars*										
Working capital	$157,158	$189,271	$210,957	$261,398	$282,049	$306,968	$314,302	$360,722	$364,754	$348,327
Property, plant and equipment (net)	145,835	182,377	171,436	154,954	154,992	219,941	280,449	253,709	302,873	394,093
Long-term debt, less current portion	52,927	94,595	86,801	94,778	71,373	67,690	72,755	47,530	38,169	29,671
Stockholders' equity	253,462	281,548	303,236	328,702	369,627	469,337	541,372	585,288	660,279	744,618
Employees at year-end	46,747	58,974	44,752	47,259	55,934	74,422	65,524	56,682	66,162	68,521
Stockholders of record at year-end	18,649	17,808	17,738	16,210	15,177	16,135	18,977	21,359	22,425	24,438

†Adjusted for stock split in 1973.
Source: Annual Report.

In 1951, TI began to formalise its strategy by a commitment to develop, manufacture and market semiconductors. A project engineering group was established in 1952 and a research laboratory opened in January 1953. The laboratory developed the silicon transistor and immediately transferred the technology to the newly created Seimconductor Products Division. By 1954 the commercial availability of silicon transistors was announced and for the next three years TI had the market virtually to itself.

Early in 1954 TI concluded that a pocket radio was a technical and commercial possibility. Consequently a tactical R & D programme was set up with the Semiconductor Products Division to develop the necessary devices and circuitry. The germanium transistor was the result, helped by collaboration with the IDEA Corporation. The first pocket radio was on the market in October 1954. TI also integrated back into the manufacturing of its own pure silicon which came into production in 1956. The success of this strategy allowed TI to achieve its goal of $200 million sales by 1960.

From the first semiconductor strategy, a second strategy began to develop following discussions in 1956 which led to research to develop whole circuits processed on wafers of silicon. In 1958, Jack Kilby of TI invented the first practical integrated circuit. TI also did not neglect its original area of technical expertise and in 1953 began development work that led to a new and revolutionary innovation in seismic exploration, using information theory to remove unwanted noise from a desired seismic signal.

By 1960 a new goal of $1 billion a year had been set with net earnings of at least $55 million and a target year of 1973. By 1973 sales billed were nearly $1.3 billion and earnings more than $83 million. In 1966 a new goal of $3 billion was set for the 1970's and in 1974, about halfway to the $3 billion target, a goal of $10 billion sales was set for the late 1980's as shown in Exhibit 2. Each of these goals was subdivided into meaningful segments with corresponding responsibilities assigned to parts of the organisation and individuals by means of a comprehensive system of planning and procedures.

THE HAGGERTY YEARS

From 1946 to 1976 TI was largely guided by Pat Haggerty who finally retired from his position as Chairman of the Board in 1976. Mr. Haggerty's leadership played a major role in formulating the philosophy which had led to the success of TI. Apart from his contribution to the technical achievements of the company and his ability to select and work with a group of outstanding managers, Mr. Haggerty was responsible for the introduction of a number of features which had become symptomatic of the methods employed by TI.

EXHIBIT 2
Texas Instruments – Growth Objectives

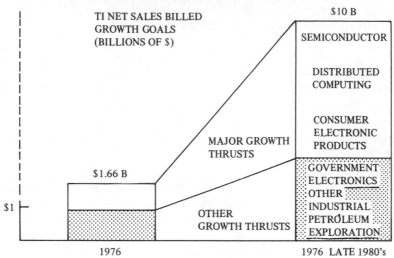

Source: Company Records.

The OST System

TI introduced formal planning at its annual management conference in 1952. However it was around 1959 that the company began to recognise that the successes achieved had come as a result of well conceived strategies and tactics in support of these. Describing the introduction and features of TI's improved system of planning Mr. Haggery stated:

'Around 1961, I finally began to comprehend more clearly the pattern which had existed in these successful strategic programs, and a senior vice president was assigned to spend full time to study and implement a formal system to accomplish these innovative successes.

' A year later we initiated our formal OST (Objectives, Strategies and Tactics) system. This is a system to state in writing succinctly, yet completely, the strategies we intend to follow for further growth and development of TI and the tactics we intend to pursue to implement the strategies'.[1]

The OST system had a number of essential features which TI identified as follows:–

–A system of management
–Hierarchy of quantitative goals

[1]Patrick E. Haggerty—Three Lectures at the Salzburg Seminar on Multinational Enterprise, Texas Instruments Inc., 1977. Subsequent quotes by Mr. Haggerty are all drawn from the same source.

–Performance is measured against goals
–Separates strategic from operational in: thinking; resource allocation; organisation; and reporting
–Strategic funds belong to the entire organisation.

OST began with a hierarchy of quantitative goals. A single statement of quantitative goals was made at the top of the organisation and these were translated into objectives for the individual businesses or 'objectives', strategies that supported each of these objectives, and tactics that supported each of the strategies. Mr. Haggerty considered that it was essential to the system that performance was measured against agreed-upon quantitative goals.

'First of all', said Mr. Haggerty, 'We have a "Corporate Objective", a document that sets forth the overall goals of the corporation. Supporting the Corporate Objective, we presently have eleven "Business Objectives". A business objective is a document that establishes a strategic organisation of people under a business objective manager.

'An actual example of a business objective manager will illustrate how OST managers wear two hats. For many years we had a vice president who had operating responsibility for all semiconductor operations in the U.S.; but not for any overseas locations. However, he was also the manager of our Electronic Functions Objective, and in this role he had strategic responsibility throughout the company, including the related international operations.

'The business objective document defines the scope of the business, including a business charter, appraisal of the market potential within this charter, and projections of the technical and market trends expected.

'The heart of each business objective is its performance measures. These spell out, in quantitative terms, the parameters against which the organisation will be measured. The most important of these measures are sales, profit, return on assets, and market penetration in terms of percentage of served available market. These are specified for five and ten years ahead. Typically, the closest two years are planned by quarter, and remaining years are planned by annual results.'

In addition there was also a fourth loop to the system, a four month forecast which formed the short term profit control system.
TI's four loop planning system is illustrated in Figure 1.

Mr. Haggerty went on 'Each business objective also examines the market and product goals in considerable detail. Technical goals are examined, so that we can identify constraints clearly. Once these

Figure 1

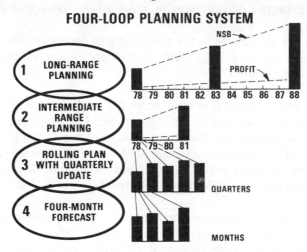

FOUR-LOOP PLANNING SYSTEM

constraints have been identified, it becomes much more obvious what technical innovations will be required. Finally the objective manager includes a critique. It covers evaluations of competition, threats and contingency plans, and possibilities of market shifts. The objective is long range covering the next 10 years.

'Although each business objective is reviewed in detail at least once a year, major revisions are required infrequently in response to (a) success or failure in our pursuit of the specific strategies and tactics, (b) sometimes external economic environmental changes major in scope, or (c) unexpected successes or failures by competitors.

Each of the 11 business objectives was supported by a number of 'strategies'. In 1977 there were a total of 50 such strategies. Each strategy was the responsibility of a 'strategy manager'. Mr. Haggerty outlined how this role worked:

'Under our Consumer Objective, for example, we have a Calculator Strategy Manager responsible for all strategic calculator activity through TI worldwide. He happens also to be the operating manager of the U.S. Calculator Division.

'The strategy document explores the opportunity environment in terms of projected market growth. We try to identify the innovation in technology, manufacturing, and marketing that will be necessary to have a major impact on the business opportunity. We try to understand what competitive reaction might be, and we plan for contingencies. An important part of the strategy is to determine whether major new commitments must be made by the corporation to ensure success of the strategy . . .

'The strategy document also includes major long-range checkpoints, and the expected contribution to the business objective in financial terms.

'Finally we try to weight the probability of success of the strategy as a basis for applying judgement to the projection of the strategy's financial contribution.'

Strategies had lifetimes of several years but were reviewed and revised much more often than were the objectives. Each strategy was then supported by a number of 'tactical action programs' (TAP's) each the responsibility of a 'program manager'. A TAP document included a statement of which it was part. It also set out the quantitative goals for the program. Describing the TAP documents Mr. Haggerty added:

'It is a resource allocation document that both specifies and commits resources in terms of manpower and capital. Moreover it pinpoints responsibilites for accomplishment of each part of the program by listing the individual responsible, his organisation and completion dates to which he has committed.'

The action programmes covered all functions. Many were R & D programmes calling for invention to order and the development of specific new products or services. Some covered deliberate cost reduction programmes, others dealt with feasibility testing while others covered innovative marketing techniques.

Most TAP's had lifetimes between six and eighteen months although others were much longer notably some R & D projects. These normally would be covered by a sequence of TAP's keyed to appropriate stages of the R & D programme.

Mr. Haggery noted 'The TAP is truly an action plan, because it triggers additional steps. As part of our Program Management System, it includes a PERT network, or Schedule Bar Chart, for the project. This schedule, in turn is translated into a Personnel Task Assignment Schedule and an OST Input Form that outlines facilities and support requirements, as well as procurement, manufacturing, and marketing plans'. The system is illustrated in Figure 2.

The OST system had had a profound effect on organisation design creating a form of matrix structure in TI. The organisation of the OST system is shown in Figure 3 and Mr. Haggerty described how it worked as follows:

'The OST organisation on the left side of the matrix, overlays the operating organisation, shown across the top of the matrix. A "PCC"

Figure 2

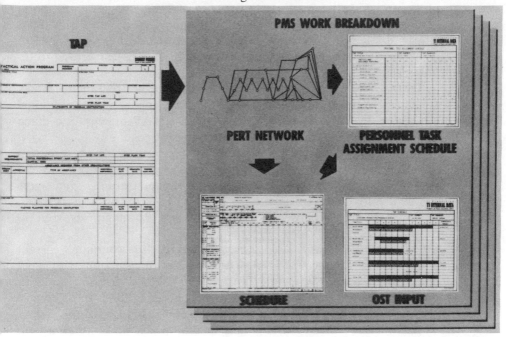

is a "Product-Customer Center", roughly the equivalent of a department, but more nearly self sufficient in that it may have its own engineering, manufacturing and marketing functions. As we define it, each PCC is to have just as much of these three functions—Create, Make and Market—as makes sense. Each rectangle on the chart

Figure 3

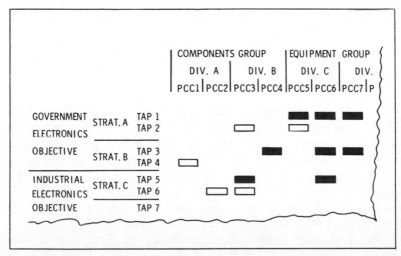

indicates that a TAP, or part of a TAP, is being executed in that part of the operating organisation. In the case of TAP 1, for example, parts of it are being handled by PCC's 5, 6 and 7. Notice that this TAP crosses division lines but not group lines. In the next example TAP 2 involves PCC's 3 and 5. In this case, the TAP does cut across group lines.

'In this way, we can quickly create a strategic program to attack some new business opportunity without creating new organisational structures. Instead we simply pull together a TAP organisation made up of elements from different operating units as required.

'This part of the OST system is similar to other program management systems. Unlike program management, however, most of our TAP managers also manage PCC's, and strategy managers frequently are division heads.

'The Distinction between "operating" and "strategic" is vital to understanding the system.

'"Operating" funds are those necessary to continue current operations at a successful level. They are the funds required to meet operational goals. Operating investments should be sufficient to optimise year-ahead results. In summary, operating funds must be at a level to maintain a strong, healthy, existing business.

'In contrast, "Strategic" funding is that which is discretionary to current operations. It is postponable without hurting the day-to-day business. Strategic funding is project oriented and is devoted to clearly defined project packages. The focus of strategic funding is on optimistic long term results. In summary, strategic funding is aimed at changing the course of the business.

'This clear cut segregation and identification of investment is the key to OST thinking. It does much to resolve the conflict every manager must face between emphasising today's profitability or tomorrow's growth. Also, it helps us keep strategic investments intact and shape our future growth, even during difficult business downturns.

'We also segregate the reporting of operating expenses from strategic expenses to avoid penalising managers who carry out strategic programs.'

The reporting relationships are illustrated in Figure 4. Operating profit was calculated and reported conventionally. Strategic expenses were reported below the line with a high expense level being generally considered desirable as evidence the PCC was devoting resources to innovative programs.

Responsibility, review and reporting of operating expenses and profits followed the conventional operating organisational lines from PCC to division to group. The strategic expense and program progress was the responsibility of OST organisations.

At the TAP level within each strategy, the first step in allocating

Figure 4

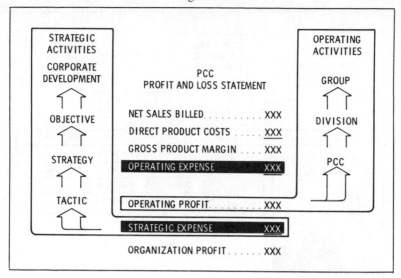

strategic funds was a process of 'decision package ranking' shown in Figure 5. A decision package contained all the resources necessary to implement an innovation.

The appropriate strategy, business objective, or corporate-level committee, depending upon both position within the organisation and judged overall importance to TI, rank ordered all of its decision packages in descending order of strategic advantage. Costs were accumulated from

Figure 5

DECISION PACKAGE RANKING

RANK	PROGRAM	COST	
1	A	$XXX	CUMULATIVE
2	Q	XXX	COST CUT-OFF
3	K	XXX	AT DISCRETIONARY FUNDING LEVEL
⋮	etc.	⋮	
447	X	$XXX	
448	Y	XXX	CREATIVE BACKLOG
449	Z	XXX	
	etc.		

488

Figure 6

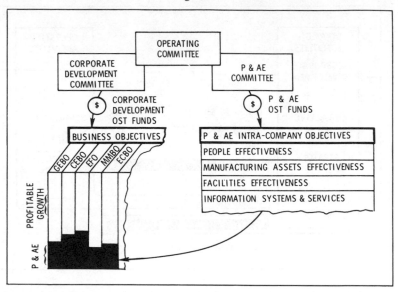

the top down to a cut off point previously set as the discretionary funding level for the year. The programmes above the line received OST funding. Programmes below the line were placed into a 'Creative Backlog' for implementation consideration as funds became available.

OST funds were managed through two corporate committees shown in Figure 6. The Corporate Development Committee allocated the largest portion through the business objectives to create profitable growth.

A smaller portion was allocated by a People and Asset Effectiveness Committee (P & AE) through its intracompany objectives, to implement profit—and performance—maximising innovations. Intracompany objectives were similar to business objectives except they were directed toward critical internal goals such as improving productivity or providing required plant sites and manufacturing facilities.

The TI annual planning cycle is illustrated in Figure 7. The objectives and Policies Committee of the Board of Directors maintained an overview of OST and frequently suggested the investigation of new strategic directions. It met with top management and with the strategy and tactics administration program managers for about 6 full days a year (one to two days at a time).

The Corporate Development Committee monitored objectives and strategies on a regular basis throughout the year. In the third quarter, it determined the level of OST funding for the coming year, then allocated these funds among the business objectives.

Business objective managers, using zero based budgeting techniques,

Figure 7

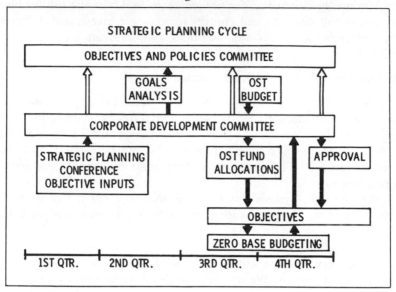

, then determined how their share of OST funds should be allocated among their strategies. Zero based budgeting began with the assumption that no expenditure needed to continue into the next year demanding that each expenditure be justified each year. Plans were then drawn up for the following year. This process involved much negotiation and when the plans had been finally set, everyone throughout the company at all levels had been involved in deciding what should be done for TI's future.

The process culminated in the Strategic Planning Conference, held during the first quarter of the following year. All the members of the Board and 400 to 500 top managers attended this four-day conference. Strategic matters were discussed by managers of objectives, strategies and selected tactical action programmes and resulted in the establishment of quantified 5 and 10 year goals.

Mr. Haggerty believed the OST system had played a major role in the success of the company. 'It's a proven success', he declared, 'But we continue to improve it. It bases our action plans on quantitative goals. It provides mechanisms for the measurement of performance against agreed-upon goals. It permits TI to be more than merely the sum of its operating parts. Many large organisations, both private and public, cannot in practice take on any task which is beyond the resources of their largest division. OST enables TI to tap effectively the resources of several divisions simultaneously or those of the entire corporation if required.

'By segregating operating resources from strategic resources, it keeps us continually mindful of our obligation to build for the future. Finally, by giving full visibility and control to strategic investment, it becomes truly a system for stimulating and managing innovation'.

The Development of the Corporate Culture

Mr. Haggerty's philosophy was that the successful organisation should 'create, make and market'. He believed that effective innovation was an integral of all three functions. Thus, a company could be outstanding at one function but if weak in others could be out-performed by a better balanced enterprise. The planning system was thus really a system for managing innovation.

By 1965 the OST system was in place and by 1969 it had formed the basis for what Mr. Haggerty called the company's 'management culture'. He added:

'Some very definite characteristics are generated by this kind of management system. We are decentralised in that all of TI's business is done through more than 80 product-customer centres. The PCC manager is responsible for the successful operation of that business entity, including satisfying our customers' needs and growing and operating profitably. Yet, we also are strongly centralised. The OST system generates a hierarchy of objectives, strategies and tactics combining the competencies of organisation segments that have no normal supervisory relationship with one another. Thus, a PCC in calculators, is likely to be completely dependent upon the development, manufacture and pricing of an integrated circuit in a product-customer centre in our Semiconductor Group. A strategy manager involved in the successful development, manufacture and marketing of a new and complex calculator is quite likely to be a different man from the general manager of the PCC itself, and he, in turn will have not authority over the actual development, manufacture and pricing of the complex integrated circuit upon which the success of his own technical, manufacturing and marketing program will depend.

'Thus, two extremely significant and important cultural attributes are generated. The OST system itself assigns a variety of decentralised responsibilities and authorities, but it also unites them tightly into a centralised whole. Without this kind of mechanism, one often finds that the overall corporation entity is only as strong as the sum total of the pieces of which it is made . . .

'The OST system ensures that the corporation is not just a collection of patches, but is a well stitched and properly designed patchwork quilt that covers and sustains the overall area intended.

'Further, the responsibility of the individual managers, whether they are the general managers of PCC's or the managers of individual strategies, almost always exceeds their authority ... The OST system recognises this fact and stimulates a culture in which the overall responsibilities are fulfilled and objectives attained while freeing the institution from any organisational approach that attempts to set boundaries for responsibility and authority'.

The Use of Learning Curves at TI

To help establish its corporate culture, TI stressed the significance of market share in a total world market and then exerted constant pressure to design and redesign products to the cost levels required for price leadership as the product price proceeded down a learning curve. Figure 8 illustrates such a curve showing how the average price for integrated circuits had fallen since 1966 as the cumulative production volume had increased. Each time cumulative production experience doubled the average price at which a product was sold fell by a steady percentage. TI had used this tool for over 20 years to anticipate by how much costs needed to fall in order to ensure survival.

'In Figure 9', Mr. Haggerty explained, 'The current industry price is illustrated by the horizonal dashed line. Companies A, B and C have different cost positions depending on their accumulated volume. The volume of market share to Company A with excellent profit margins is clear. Company B is marginal, and Company C operates at a loss. Obviously, a company participating in a world market has an inherent

Figure 8

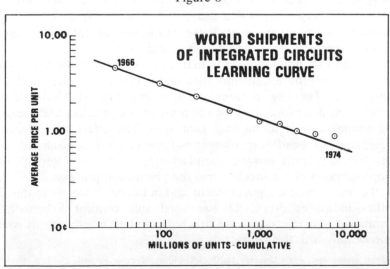

Figure 9

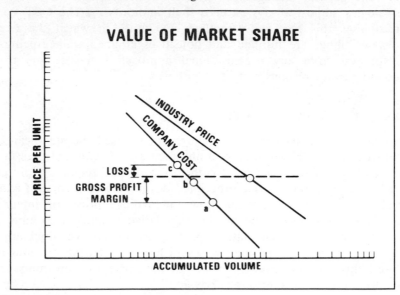

advantage over a company that builds its production base on a national market, but this advantage can exist only if cost reduction is accepted as the responsibility of the entire organisation'.

Mr. J. Fred Bucy, President of TI, emphasised the importance of the learning curve effect for the company:

'TI is competing head on with the Japanese in several major markets, among them semiconductors (where they have a $300 million government sponsored programme for very-large-scale integration (VLSI) development), calculators, and watches. What is to stop the Japanese from taking over these businesses as they have done in radios, stereos, T.V. sets, motorbikes and steel?

'I think the big difference is that TI is the first major non Japanese company they have run into that understands and uses the learning curve. ... The key to using the learning curve is "design-to-cost", where you determine the cost required for the product and the system to manufacture it to hit that cost goal. The effect here is not just spreading overhead over a larger volume of product produced. It also involves constantly forcing manufacturing costs down through design improvements of the product and the production processes.

'In Japan, both the government and industries understand this. Most other industries don't. TI has used this concept informally and formally for many years, and this is absolutely mandatory to compete successfully with the Japanese'.[1]

[1]Texas Instruments Inc., First Quarter and Stockholders Meeting Report, 1978, p. 16–17.

People and Asset Effectiveness Strategy

A second approach used for establishing the corporate culture was the People and Asset Effectiveness Strategy. This was a formal mechanism for involving as many people as possible, not simply professionals and managers, in the effort to achieve overall goals to reward success. The strategy sought to improve the company's ability to solve customers' problems by increasing the productivity of people and using assets more effectively.

Mr. Haggerty explained, 'We believe productivity improvement is basic to achieving all our key company goals. In Figure 10 we show improved productivity as the central block resulting from high people effectiveness and high asset effectiveness. Over the past 10 years, productivity in terms of unit output per man hour has increased at about 15 per cent per year, compared with 2 to 3 per cent per year for the U.S. private sector.

'The line graph at the left of the productivity block illustrates our design-to-cost discipline that bases cost goals on projected price

Figure 10

TI'S INTERLOCKING STRATEGIES
P&AE → PRODUCTIVITY → PROFITS → GROWTH → SUCCESS SHARING

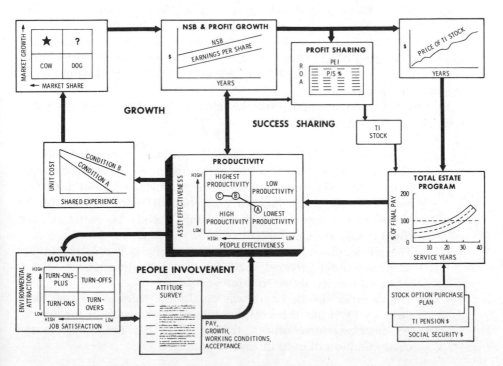

requirements . . . During the past 10 years TI's average prices have decreased each year at about 8 per cent per year.

'These productivity gains and cost reductions have provided the means for NSB (Net Sales Billed) growth which, in turn provides funds for more investments for products and productivity gains, and this represents our growth loop.

'Two key activities for People Effectiveness are People Investment and Success Sharing. For many years, we have involved TI people at all levels in the planning and control of their own work, as well as in the doing. This has been accomplished through widespread work simplification programs and team projects. In addition, we have a "Success Sharing" program, which provides a benefit package that includes a pension plan, a profit sharing plan, and an employee stock option purchase plan. Our goal is to make every eligible employee a TI shareholder. To date, about 80 per cent of TI people are covered by this profit sharing plan. We would like to cover 100 per cent, but the laws of individual companies make it impossible or prohibitively expensive'.

The Evolution of Board Structure

In considering how to create and sustain the appropriate organisation Mr. Haggerty had concluded that the board of directors held the key responsibility. Addressing stockholders at TI's 1967 annual meeting Mr. Haggerty opened the first public discussion of board structure. He commented that it might be desirable to have several directors other than full-time operating officers devoting considerably more time to their duties as directors than would be ordinarily feasible, and that steps would begin to move in this direction.

By 1976 the fundamental principles governing board composition and responsibilities were as follows:

(1) Board members who were employees ordinarily included only the chairman of the board, whose commitment to TI activities might range from full time to part time; the president who was a full time employee; and from time to time, one or more 'officers of the board' whose time commitment would usually be part time, but could in exceptional circumstances be full time.

(2) The president was usually the chief executive officer, although the chairman could serve as such during a transition period seldom expected to exceed two to three years.

(3) The chairman of the board was usually the chief corporate officer but only by virtue of his responsibilities as chairman of the board.

(4) As chief executive officer, the president did not report to the chairman but rather to the entire board.

(5) In addition to the chairman and president, the TI board would be composed of general directors, officers of the board and directors.

Most board members were General Directors. They were not employees of TI (although they could have been in the past) and assumed board duties (including membership on committees, chairmanship of committees, and optional additional activities in TI's direct interests) with a minimum time commitment of approximately 30 days per year.

Officer of the Board was formerly the title for general directors, but was subsequently reserved for a board member who was an employee other than the chairman or president and who also devoted principal amounts of time to his duties as a director. These Directors were expected to spend 15 days per year on TI board business.

The activities of the board included attendance at monthly and special board meetings. attendance at corporate planning meetings, and occasional visits to TI plant and office locations. However, in determining the appropriate amount of time to be spent in such activities, careful organisation was required. To assure the desired relationship between the board and the operating organisation, TI expected most board members to attend at least some of the scheduled operating organisation meetings internally known as Quarterly Financial Reviews (QFR). These were reviews of activities in and performance of product groups and were held quarterly.

EXHIBIT 3

Texas Instruments – Board Structure

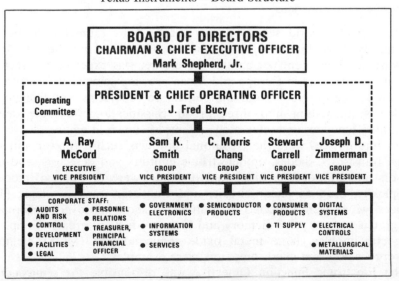

Source: Company Records.

There was also a carefully designed retirement policy for senior officers and directors. TI's chairman, president and executive vice presidents, after serving a specified minimum number of years could choose to retire after 55 and retirement became compulsory at 62 for the chairman, president and executive vice presidents. It was expected that one of the executive vice presidents would become president at the appropriate time while executive VP's who retired at 55 were viewed as first class candidates for election as general directors. The board structure of TI is shown in Exhibit 3.

STRATEGY FOR THE 1980's

Pat Haggerty retired as chairman in 1976. He was succeeded by Mark Shepherd Jnr. who had worked closely with Mr. Haggerty for the previous 24 years and who moved into the chairman's role from his previous position as president. To achieve the company's goal of $10 billion sales by the late 1980's Mr. Shepherd advised shareholders that the strategy of TI would be to concentrate on three major growth areas:

- Semiconductor functions
- Distributed Computing and
- Consumer Electronic products.

Others areas for expansion were government electronics, petroleum exploration and other industrial areas.

Semiconductor Functions

In 1975 the world semiconductor market was estimated to be $4.2 billion. By 1978 this had grown to $7.4 billion and by the late 1980's growing at 13 per cent per annum the market was expected to reach $24 billion with demand in Europe and Japan growing somewhat faster than in the USA. The evolution from components to subsytems was changing the market segmentation into three broad classifications: discrete devices, integrated functions and integrated systems as shown in Figure 11.

Discrete devices were the traditional products such as power and small signal transistors, diodes, optoelectronic emitters and detectors, and other sensors and transducers. Integrated functions were products of moderate complexity, such as linear circuits and transistor–transistor logic (TTL) devices, which were expected to continue to show improved performance. Integrated systems were memory and logic products of greater complexity. Magnetic bubbles, large metal oxide semiconductor (MOS) memories, microprocessors and microcomputers were examples.

The Electronic Function Objective was responsible for semiconductor activities in TI. As shown in Figure 12, all TI's key technologies supported

Figure 11

WORLD SEMICONDUCTOR MARKET
(Billions of $)

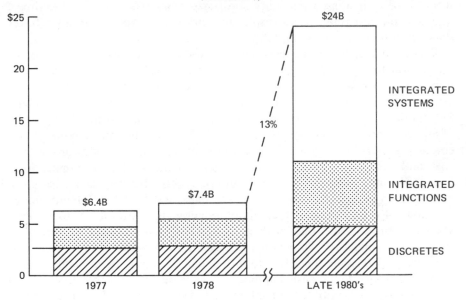

Figure 12

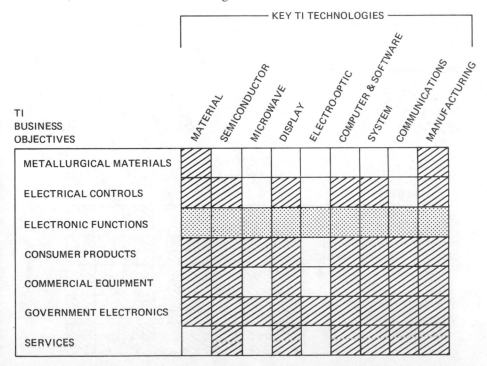

this objective. Besides representing a growing market opportunity in its own right semiconductors were also vital components for most of TI's other businesses. It was felt that advances in semiconductor technology would lead to increased reliability and performance as well as reduced cost in electronic equipment. As a result the market was expected to grow faster than the total electronics market.

The pacing item in the cost and computing was memory, for which semiconductor technology was playing a major role in reducing cost and improving performance. Figure 13 shows how TI's foundation of semiconductor technology supported the solid state memory business. Substantial technical change was expected in memory technology in the 1980's as shown in Figure 14. By 1977 bipolar and metal oxide semiconductor (MOS) components had already overtaken magnetic core in both cost and performance for random access memory (RAM) applications. Charged-coupled devices (CCD's) and magnetic bubble memories were emerging as competitors to fixed head disks and in 1977, TI introduced the first 64K CCD memory component allowing retrieval of stored data about 10 times faster than with a fixed head disk. TI had the broadest spectrum of memory components on the market which was expected to grow from $770 million in 1977 to more than $5 billion by the late 1980's.

Microprocessors, the basic building blocks for electronic products, formed the other major constituent of integrated systems. The TI microprocessor

Figure 13

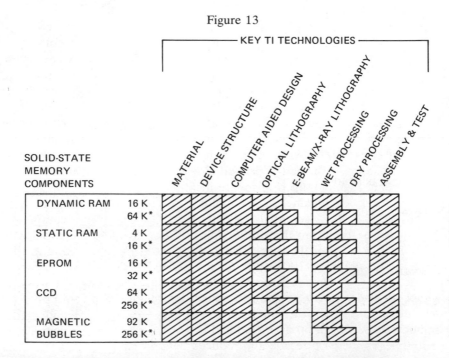

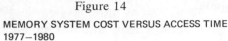

Figure 14

MEMORY SYSTEM COST VERSUS ACCESS TIME
1977–1980

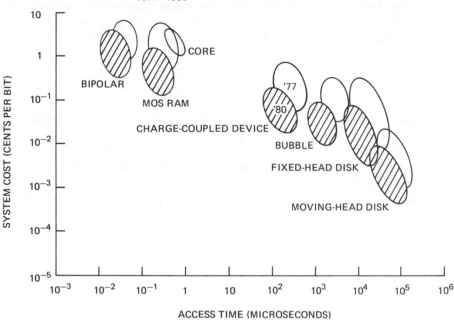

product line was designed for a variety of applications from consumer controls to distributed computing. Considerable growth in microcomputers was forecast for the 1980's. The key to further gains was VLSI (Very Large Scale Integration) a term used to describe semiconductor complexity of 100,000 Active Element Groups (AEGs) on a single chip, no larger than about 1/5 of an inch on a side. By the early 1980's, it was expected that technology advances would permit building a 32-bit microcomputer with one million bits of memory on a single chip less than $\frac{1}{2}$ of an inch on a side. Whereas a single AEG vacuum tube circuit of the mid-1950's had occupied four square inches of printed circuit board, the same unit in 1978 occupied only $2\frac{1}{2}$ millionths of a square inch.

TI intended to remain the technology leader in the VLSI area by capitalising on four essential advantages. First, TI was completely integrated in silicon from the production of pure silicon to preparation of silicon slices. Second, TI was advanced in Electron beam direct slice writing that could write 100,000 AEG's on a single chip and was expected to make this a production process within a few years. Third, TI was the technology leader in dry plasma processing, a technique that could produce finer definitions than the alternative of wet processing. Finally, TI's computer aided design programmes had increased circuit design complexity a 100 times in the past decade and reduced design time to a third.

Distributed Computing

The second major growth area was distributed computing i.e. where computing functions were placed at the point of need whether connected in a network or stand alone. This market was expected to grow from $9.5 billion world wide in 1978 to $37 billion by the late 1980's as shown in Figure 15.

The TI technologies supporting the distributed computing thrust are shown in Figure 16 and were the same as those used to drive down the cost of calculators in the early 1970's. These technologies were being used to develop a broad range of commercial, industrial and consumer products. In 1978, system elements in the TI product line included:

   –the 990/4 and /10 minicomputers as well as the earlier 960B and 980B
   –A broad line of terminals and peripherals, examples being the Silent 700 data terminal family and a new model 700 intelligent terminal
   –Software packages to meet customers' specialised needs.

Consumer Electronic Products

The third major growth area was consumer electronics, also based on semiconductor technology. The market for such products within the scope of TI's interests was projected to grow from $8.1 billion in 1978 to $25

Figure 15

WORLD DISTRIBUTED COMPUTING MARKET
(Billions of $)

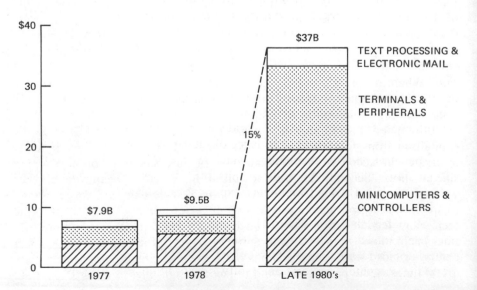

Figure 16

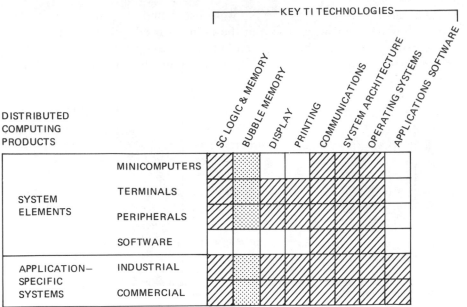

billion by the late 1980's as shown in Figure 17. Calculators were expected to have sales of around $1.7 billion in 1978. Together with personal computing and home information systems this was expected to be the highest grown segment in the 1980's. In 1978 TI products were sold through 75000 retail outlets around the world, an increase of 35 per cent over the previous year.

The pace of technical development of the market was such that an IBM 650 popular general purpose computer of the 1950's was roughly the equivalent of a hand held advanced programmable calculator in 1978. However while the former had cost $200,000 in 1955 the latter cost under $300 in 1978.

Microprocessor learning aids were one major growth sector in calculators and new products were being developed to serve this market and so maintaining TI's position as the world's leading calculator supplier.

TI was also an important producer of digital watches which continued to gain penetration from mechanical watches. In 1977, the industry produced 30 million units and 44 million units in 1978. A major shift to liquid crystal displays (LCD's) was being experienced, with output in 1978 being 75 per cent LCD.

The matrix shown in Figure 18 identifies the key TI technologies used by the Consumer Electronics business. TI's initial consumer products, calculators and time products required semiconductor logic and memory, display, computer, system and software technologies. However it was

Figure 17

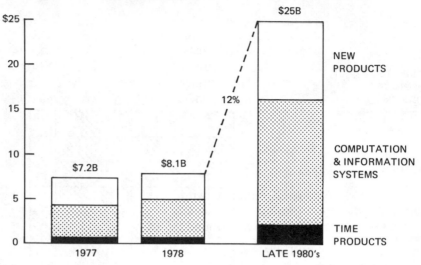

WORLD MARKET
CONSUMER PRODUCTS
(Billions of $)

Figure 18

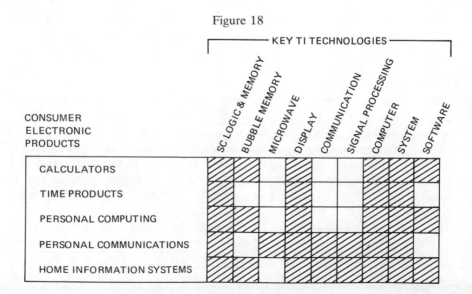

expected that the next generation of consumer products serving the markets for personal computing, communications and home information systems would make use of more of TI's broad technological base.

Other Activities

In addition to its major strategic thrusts TI remained active in a number of other sectors. These objectives were Government Electronic Products, Geophysical Services and Metallurgical Materials. These activities accounted for over $700 million sales in 1977 and produced profits of $75 million before taxes and eliminations and corporate items as shown in Exhibit 4.

International Activities

TI was a multinational company with plants and activities in many countries as shown in Exhibit 5. The company looked upon its markets in world terms and staff were moved around the world on a regular basis.

EXHIBIT 4
Texas Instruments Financial Results by Market Area
($ millions)

| PRODUCT | Net Sales Billed | | Profit | | Assets Employed |
	1976	1977	1976	1977	1977
Components	836	958	112	121	529
Digital Products	396	559	30	54	270
Government Electronics	331	393	33	39	114
Metallurgical Materials	127	148	20	22	60
Services	138	175	2	14	61
Eliminations and Corporate Items	(169)	(187)	(19)	(39)	221
Total	1659	2046	178	211	1255

| GEOGRAPHY | Net Sales Billed | | Profit | | Assets Employed |
	1976	1977	1976	1977	1977
U.S.A.	1271	1569	151	164	734
Europe	344	410	28	39	188
Other Areas	387	463	33	47	144
Elimination and Adjustments	(343)	(396)	(34)	(39)	189
Total	1659	2046	178	211	1255

Source: Annual Reports.

504

EXHIBIT 5

TI Worldwide Plant Locations (and dates of establishment)

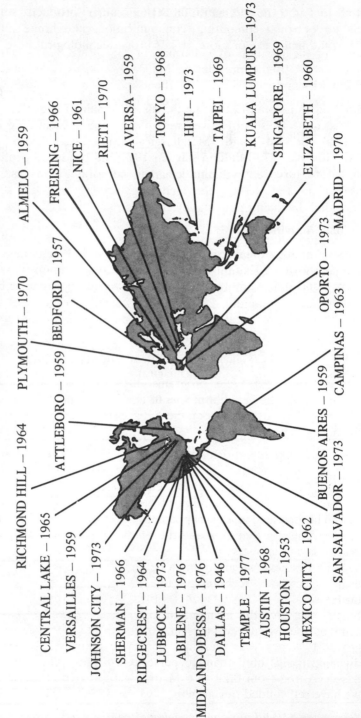

Source: Company Records.

THE PROSPECTS FOR THE FUTURE

Following the retirement of Mr. Haggerty and the appointment of Mr. Shepherd to the position of Chairman of the Board of TI, Mr. J. Fred Bucy succeeded to the presidency. Mr. Bucy, like Mr. Shepherd, was a long term TI employee starting in the Central Research Laboratories in 1953. He became executive vice president in 1972 and had been chief operating officer since 1975 before becoming president a year later.

Mr. Bucy summarised the strategy and outlook of TI to stockholders at the company's annual meeting in Dallas on April 20, 1978 as follows:

'To summarise, we are clearly the leader in semiconductor technology and we are the technology leader in many other areas discussed, including personal electronics, date terminals, electro optics, tactical weapon guidance, and 3D geographical work.

'We have been successful in establishing a large and growing consumer electronics business which none of our semiconductor competitors has been able to accomplish.

'We sometimes stumble in the execution of these complex programs, but we recover rapidly. I believe TI's strategic approaches are sound and that we are accelerating our progress in the important growth segments of our markets.

'The most critical question to all of us is: "Can TI meet its growth and profitability goals?"

'Clearly we have the programs, the managers, the management structure, and the capable people to be a $3 billion company.

Considering attainment of the $10-billion goal, I believe these are the major factors:

First, the market opportunity clearly is there for us. Electronics will take its place as one of the world's largest industries by the late 1980's, driven by the ability of semiconductor technology to increase the problem solving capability of electronics at constantly decreasing cost. The barriers to this happening are minimal. Another advantage of electronics is that is uses little energy and, potentially, can be an energy saving industry.

Second, I believe we are doing a better job than any other company of using electronic technology to leverage a broad spectrum of businesses.

Finally, we have the momentum to do it. Over the last five years, in spite of the worst recession in 40 years, TI's net sales billed have grown 17% per year, earnings per share almost 19% per year and dividends paid more than 26 per cent per year. TI's total debt ratio has decreased from 0.23 to 0.11 over the last five years, which means we have self funded our growth.

I think the $10 billion goal is real and that we'll get there.'

33

Trafalgar House Ltd. (B)

The end of 1979 was expected to see Nigel Broackes reach another milestone in his career at the still early age of 44. The Chairman and Chief Architect of Trafalgar House confidently expected the company he breathed life into a short 22 years earlier to achieve a turnover of over £1000 million in the current financial year. Starting from a small base in property in the last 1950's, Trafalgar had expanded rapidly concentrating in the 1960's largely on property and construction interests while in the 1970's the group had become increasingly diversified. By 1979, largely via a process of acquisition Trafalgar House was engaged in property development and management, contracting, plant hire, civil structural and offshore engineering, mining and other specialist engineering, housebuilding, cargo and passenger shipping, air freight, hotels and newspaper and magazine publishing. Sales for the group in 1978 were £825m up from £587m the previous year while net revenue before tax reached £60.6m compared with the 1977 figure of £46.6m. Total assets were £590m in 1978 compared with £556m in 1977 with long term debt showing a sharp reduction. Full details of recent financial performance are shown in Exhibits 1 and 2.

THE FORMATION OF THE BROACKES-MATTHEWS PARTNERSHIP

The success of Trafalgar House owed much to the close management partnership which had been forged between Nigel Broackes and Mr. Victor Matthews, Trafalgar House's Deputy Chairman and Chief Executive. Over the years these two had also been ably supported by the group's former finance director and present managing director Mr. Eric Parker. Mr. Parker an accountant operated closely with Mr. Matthews and Mr. Broackes and had been largely responsible for the design of the comprehensive financial control systems used throughout the group.

The two leading figures in Trafalgar was in sharp contrast to one another. Nigel Broackes aged 44 in 1979 was born the son of a lawyer, educated at

EXHIBIT 1

Trafalgar House Ltd. Consolidated Revenue Accounts 1972–1978 (£'000)

	1978	1977	1976	1975	1974	1973	1972
TURNOVER	825,003	587,262	448,393	382,707	281,468	268,855	236,492
REVENUE FROM OPERATIONS	64,107	50,248	37,610	31,334	25,015	23,266	17,161
Deduct Provision, Housebuilding for sale	—	—	—	4,700	1,000	—	—
NET REVENUE BEFORE INTEREST ON FUNDED DEBT	64,107	50,248	37,610	26,634	24,015	23,266	17,161
Deduct Interest on funded debt	3,476	3,834	3,995	4,440	4,445	4,453	2,786
NET REVENUE BEFORE TAXATION	60,631	46,414	33,615	22,194	19,570	18,813	14,375
Deduct TAXATION	21,221	16,245	11,765	7,769	5,273	5,643	4,430
	39,410	30,169	21,850	14,425	14,297	13,170	9,945
Deduct REVENUE FROM MINORITIES	765	772	305	261	250	194	136
NET REVENUE AFTER TAXATION	38,645	29,397	21,545	14,164	14,047	12,976	9,809
EXTRAORDINARY ITEMS	1,229	767	70	35	—	—	—
NET REVENUE AFTER TAX AND EXTRAORDINARY ITEMS	37,416	30,164	21,615	14,199	14,047	12,976	9,809
Add TRANSFER FROM RESERVES	—	26	152	215	338	384	247
	37,416	30,190	21,767	14,414	14,385	13,360	10,056
Deduct DIVIDENDS	9,262	8,313	7,117	4,846	3,022	2,736	3,645
ADDITION TO ACCUMULATED REVENUE	28,154	21,877	14,650	9,568	11,363	10,624	6,411
PARENT COMPANY	23,292	17,893	11,487	8,028	9,183	7,900	4,294
SUBSIDIARIES	5,243	1,404	2,048	687	941	1,274	921
ASSOCIATES	(381)	2,580	1,115	853	1,239	1,450	1,196
	28,154	21,877	14,650	9,568	11,363	10,624	6,411
EARNINGS PER ORDINARY SHARE	24.1p	18.6p	14.4p	11.9p	12.2p	11.7p	9p

Source: Annual Reports.

EXHIBIT 2

Trafalgar House Limited Consolidated Balance Sheets 1972–78 (£'000)

	1978	1977	1976	1975	1974	1973	1972
FIXED ASSETS							
Properties	77,484	98,829	80,342	68,685	56,574	125,716	46,625
Associated companies	4,414	4,728	7,657	8,916	3,767	3,775	4,608
Hotels	27,652	24,284	28,132	24,652	23,056	22,432	16,862
Ships and aircraft	162,068	184,023	130,135	117,816	112,122	100,045	79,909
Plant and equipment	47,075	35,951	21,328	18,594	15,778	12,244	13,366
	318,693	347,815	267,594	238,663	211,297	264,212	161,400
OTHER CURRENT ASSETS							
Groundrents	34,693	15,315	13,009	14,128	34,771	35,512	16,247
Developments for sale, and building land	973	894	918	911	960	978	917
Building land	28,965	34,541	37,214	31,983	40,777	10,157	12,603
	16,573	—	—	—	—	26,767	12,116
Work in progress/stocks	84,852	74,619	56,882	52,408	43,337	39,320	33,943
Debtors	91,115	67,986	46,784	38,652	28,841	36,090	37,466
Quoted investments	2,214	2,644	4,682	712	595	—	—
Cash	12,043	12,040	8,524	5,512	2,426	1,630	14,120
	236,735	192,724	155,004	129,818	116,936	114,942	111,164
	590,121	555,854	435,607	382,609	363,004	414,665	288,811
CAPITAL AND RESERVES							
Share capital	33,520	33,510	32,114	25,511	25,011	24,176	19,255
Share premium account	38,846	38,791	34,503	14,592	14,801	13,728	17,899
Reserves	105,536	74,685	24,500	25,858	26,433	41,427	9,376
Accumulated revenue	—	—	—	—	—	22,545	11,921

SHAREHOLDERS FUNDS	177,902	146,986	91,117	65,961	66,245	101,876	58,451
DEFERRED TAX	28,209	14,222	25,546	20,397	15,312	37,012	5,990
MINORITY INTERESTS	4,914	4,566	4,016	2,971	2,917	2,793	2,089
FUNDED DEBT.							
Secured	9,820	10,887	13,352	11,801	14,605	13,217	13,301
Unsecured	35,192	34,761	36,794	35,733	41,316	42,643	39,019
	45,012	45,648	50,146	47,534	55,921	55,860	52,320
Shipbuilding and other loans	94,708	125,801	99,626	106,679	106,813	90,119	59,140
Long term provisions/liabilities	25,145	27,126	11,025	10,446	13,154	18,025	18,133
CURRENT LIABILITIES							
Bank borrowings	9,656	8,088	8,300	14,572	18,151	29,040	31,661
Current taxation	2,240	2,367	4,568	4,052	2,505	3,912	5,105
Portion of shipbuilding & other loans	30,587	31,756	17,796	14,700	12,713	9,705	—
Creditors and provisions	167,074	145,110	119,944	92,157	67,701	64,999	54,156
Ordinary dividend	4,674	4,184	3,523	3,140	1,572	1,324	1,766
	214,231	191,505	153,131	128,621	102,642	108,980	92,688
	590,121	555,854	435,607	382,609	363,004	414,665	288,811

Source: Annual Reports.

Stowe public school and commissioned in a cavalry regiment, the Third Hussars. Victor Matthews, some 16 years Broackes' senior, was born in Islington in 1919 after his father had died in the First World War. He was educated at an elementary school in Highbury and thought himself lucky to get his first job as an office boy in a tobacco company. During the second world war Mr. Matthews served in the Navy, rising from ordinary to able seaman.

The two met for the first time during the formative years of Trafalgar House. Originating in 1956 as a property company known as Eastern International Property Investments, Trafalgar was initially set up as a subsidiary of an investment trust to undertake property investments. Nigel Broackes was the company's managing director and following an introduction by Lord Crowther, Eastern International undertook several developments with the support of the Commercial Union Insurance Group. This relationship with the insurance company was to continue over the years and provided an important source of funds for Trafalgar House.

Broackes met Matthews in 1961 after the latter's building firm, Bridge Walker, had won a contract to convert a block of flats for Eastern International. Describing their meeting, Mr. Broackes commented:

'We went to lunch at Browns Hotel and he explained to me the reason he ran a cream and black Rolls Royce; to make it clear to creditors and suppliers that he was doing very well—which indeed he was. He looked then just as he does today, 18 years later: tough and purposeful, with a pronounced nose, brown eyes and lots of black hair.

'We became friends at our first meeting probably because it was immediately clear to each of us that the other was totally absorbed in his business and our mutual respect was assisted by the fact that in every other way we were quite different: that is to say, in terms of age, education, social background, business experience and recreations.'

In 1963, Broackes having purchased a property company from Commercial Union, introduced the revamped Eastern International to the Stock Exchange under the name Trafalgar House. Within four months of gaining its quotation Trafalgar made its first takeover of a public company, City and West Properties.

This company, which shared offices with two other property groups under the same management, had been a regular takeover target but had consistently beaten off potential bidders by stating that it would not engage in takeover discussions without a firm offer first being made. Further each of the three companies held shares in the other two.

Mr. Broackes therefore hit upon the idea of bidding for all three companies at the same time. He identified the properties owned by the companies by having the staff who paid the porters' wages followed to the properties and evaluated the site size and value from aerial photographs. Despite a market capitalisation of only £1.5 million Trafalgar thus bid around £6 million for the three companies and in September 1964 won the largest of the three with the help of profits made from the sale of share stakes taken in the other two.

In 1964 with the introduction of the new method of Corporation Tax Mr. Broackes realised that property companies which traditionally distributed all their earnings would incur a higher tax liability leading to lower dividends and a lower share price. He therefore decided to buy industrial companies, with the additional money earned from trading being retained. As a result Mr. Broackes added:

> 'In 1964 I compiled, with a colleague, a list of 10 public companies most likely to fail to cope with . . . Corporation Tax, and to become attractive for us to take over.'

Included in this group of 10 companies was Victor Matthews' former employer, the major London based building concern of Trollope and Colls.

By comparison with Mr. Broackes, who launched Trafalgar House in his early twenties, Victor Matthews was much later in starting his own business. After the war he joined the building firm of Trollope and Colls as a trainee, rising to the position of contracts manager over the next 10 years. Initially, Mr. Matthews, brought up in the 1930's, valued the security of a safe salaried job. In 1955 he joined Clark and Fenn, a building products manufacturer and, in 1960, supported by the Chairman, Victor Hosp, Matthews finally decided to buy his own business. He sank his £2,500 savings into a Brixton building contractor called Bridge Walker, which then had a turnover of £250,000. In four years Matthews had increased this tenfold. In 1964 while doing contract work for Trafalgar House it was decided that Broackes should buy a minority stake in Bridge Walker.

In 1967, the partnership between the two men was obviously succeeding and Matthews merged the rest of his company with Trafalgar and joined the Board. The merger with Bridge Walker also brought in Eric Parker who was the finance director of Bridge Walker and who was to prove the important third member of the successful Trafalgar team. The following year Matthews became joint managing director with Nigel Broackes, a position he shared for the next two years. Discussing their approach Mr. Broackes added:

> 'In all issues involving third parties and outside opportunites, we would invariably reach agreement, as we do today—though we often reach identical conclusions for quite different reasons. Neither of us attempts to demolish the reasoning of the other, provided the conclusion is agreeable to us both.'

ACQUISITION AND DEVELOPMENT

Much of the growth of Trafalgar House had occurred by acquisition and the subsequent reorganisation of the companies taken over. Details of the company's major purchases are shown in Exhibit 3. As a result of its

EXHIBIT 3

Trafalgar House Major Mergers & Acquisition 1968–78

Date	Company	Price	Activity
1968	Trollope & Colls	2.7 m 5/- ord., £230K 7% Unsecd. Deb. Stock & £7.5 m 8% Unsecd. Partly conv. loan stock 1994/99	Building and Construction
	South Wales Concrete Pipe Co.	£32,772 8% Unsecd. Part. Conv. Loan Stock 1994/99	Concrete Pipe Manufacturers
1969	J. Nunn & Sons	£134,608 8% Unsec. Part. Conv. Loan Stock 1994/99	Building Contractors
1970	Cementation	8.5 m 4/- Ord., plus £5.1 m 9½% Unsec. L.S. and £1.6 m 7% Unsec. Deb. Stock.	Specialist Engineers and Contractors
1971	Cunard Steamship	16.3 m 20p ord., 1.09 m 'B' Subscription Warrants, £3.6 m 10¼% Unsec. L.S. 2001/06 and £2.0 m 9½% Unsec. L.S. 2000/2005 plus £5.9 m cash	Shipping
1974	Eastern International Investment Trust	2.9 m 20p ord. plus £1.9 m cash	Investment trust
1976	Ritz Hotel (London)	£2.7 m cash	Hotel operations
	Clark & Fenn (Holdings)	315000 20p ord. plus £3.78 m cash	Acoustic materials plaster manufacturers
	Rashleigh Phipps	£1 m cash	Electrical
	British fleet of Maritime Fruit Co.	$85 million cash	10 refrigerated fruit carriers
1977	Direct Spanish Telegraph	5.7 m 20p ord. shares	Investment trust
	Samuel Elliott of Reading	£650,000 cash	High quality joinery and decorative metal work
	Transmeridian Air Cargo	Cash	Long haul air freight
	Beaverbrook Newspapers	£15 m cash	Printing and publishing
	Morgan Grampian	£21 m cash	Magazines and books
1978	Young Austen & Young	Cash	Electrical & mechanical engrg.
	W. J. Simons Sons & Cooke (Northern)	Cash	Contracting & open cast mining
	Robert Stevenson	Cash	Steel fabrication & erection
	Peiner Aliscott	Cash	Crane hire

acquisition programme Trafalgar House had become increasingly diversified. This process of increased diversification occurred in three main phases thus:

THE FIRST LEG—PROPERTY CONSTRUCTION

Trafalgar continued to expand its property interest despite the tax change, buying Woodgate Investment Trust in 1966 and being involved in unsuccessful bids for City of London Real Property in 1968 and MEPC in 1970.

Trafalgar began its diversification by moving into housebuilding. In 1967, the Ideal Building Corporation was acquired at a cost of £4.6m. This company, engaged in domestic housebuilding, was quickly reorganised by Mr. Matthews and introduced to stringent budgetary and financial controls. By 1969 Ideal was the second largest private housing group in the U.K. In the 1970's due to the national economic climate housebuilding had not proved a major source of activity, however.

Trafalgar's first major acquisition in construction was the takeover of Trollope and Colls in 1968. The company was widely respected as a quality building company, had a £10m portfolio of London property but had fallen on hard times and was trading at a loss, although middle management was considered to be good. Trafalgar quietly built up a 9.9 per cent stake in the company, the most that could be held without disclosure, and planned to make its bid for early 1968 after the publication of Trollope and Colls figures which were expected to be poor.

Despite a battle for control Trafalgar won the day and instituted what was to become a familiar post acquisition procedure. Victor Matthews was appointed chairman of Trollope & Colls and embarked upon a study of its operations dividing it into management sections to see whether or not they were profitable. The board of the company was removed and replaced by promising middle managers promoted from within. A system of strict budgets and financial controls designed by Eric Parker was then produced, for the first time in the case of Trollope & Colls. Under Matthews the company was given a clear direction with firm decisive leadership and strict discipline. Within a year Trollope & Colls had returned to profitability.

In 1970 Trafalgar extended its construction and civil engineering activities via the bitterly contested bid for Cementation Construction. Fighting off a bid from Bovis, Trafalgar won control of the specialist mining construction, ground engineering and foundations company. This company also operated a number of overseas subsidiaries mainly in Southern Africa, Canada and the U.S.A.

Closely related to property and construction Trafalgar entered the hotel business in 1969. In its role as a property developer the group had intended to develop hotel sites which would then be managed by Trust

S

Houses, the chairman of Trafalgar at this time being Lord Crowther also chairman of Trust Houses. However Broackes ultimately decided that the joint undertaking should be carried out exclusively by Trafalgar which would undertake the management of the hotels. As a result of this decision Lord Crowther resigned from Trafalgar and Broackes from his board position in Trust Houses. Broackes then became chairman of Trafalgar.

By 1971 after the purchase of Cementation Trafalgar was already a large company with gross assets of £119 million and pretax profits of £6 million. Property was still the largest component of profitability but already, the company had lost its property status despite the fact that its £50m of developments were some of the largest in the City.

Since the early 1970's Trafalgar reliance upon property and construction had been sharply diminished although both activities continued to play an important role in group affairs. Further purchases had been made of specialist companies in the construction and engineering sectors such as Young Austin & Young (electrical/mechanical engineering), W.J. Simms & Sons & Cooke (Northern) (contracting and open cast mining), Robert Stevenson (steel fabrication and erection), Peiner Aliscott (Crane Hire), Clark & Fenn (decorative plaster work and Victor Matthews' old company), Rachleigh Phillips (electrical contractors) and Elliots of Reading (joiners and decorative metalwork producers).

Changes also occurred in Trafalgar's property portfolio with disposals being used to improve cash flow and reduce debt and the balance in the portfolio being adjusted from time to time according to market conditions. By the end of the '1970's Trafalgar covered the entire U.K. property market in terms of shops, offices, factories, warehouses and urban residential property compared with a decade earlier when the group had concentrated mainly on City office accommodation and London residential property.

In hotels, Trafalgar acquired the Ritz in 1976 after a long and abortive siege of the Savoy, another prestige London hotel group. The Ritz was dramatically refurbished and in 1978 won the Egon Ronay Award as Hotel of the Year. With its purchase of the Ritz Trafalgar was one of the leading operators of upmarket facilities in London.

THE SECOND LEG—CUNARD AND THE SHIPPING BUSINESS

July 1971 saw Trafalgar bidding for Cunard, the rationale being that ever since it first moved into hotels, Trafalgar had been looking at cruise ships as 'part of a wider accommodation concept'. Besides the synergy that Broackes and Matthews expected between their hotels and Cunard's cruise ships, they were also looking at Cunard's small but profitable Offshore Marine operation, which specialised in servicing marine oil rigs, and would fit in well with Cementation's work for the same customers on dry land.

The Cunard deal was, in a sense, a continuation of Trafalgar's policy of expansion into related fields. But the move into shipping introduced many more uncertainties than adding another leg to the company's growing marine/industrial and hotel interests.

Cunard's profit record over the previous 10 years had not been a happy one. There had been losses in six out of the previous ten, and three out of the last five years. Cunard was bought as a tax cash box, with £13 million unusable accumulated losses and up to £68 million in depreciation. It effectively allowed Trafalgar to control its profitability after tax for many years. But Cunard was a massive problem which even the efforts of Victor Matthews found formidable. Up to 1970/71, for example, the freight side could not really tell whether any given ship was actually operating profitably. Break-even points and occupancy rates were not available for the passenger ships, though these had been responsible for most of Cunard's problems. When an attempt was made to discover even that simple information, it was found, for example, that the break-even level for the Carmania on its U.K. cruises was a 100% occupancy level at the prices reigning. As the occupancy averaged 35%, the extent of the problem can be imagined.

The QE2 was another problem. A report by McKinsey projected its losses forward to 1975 at a minimum of £1.5 million a year. However, Matthews did not accept that. He felt that with a more flexible pricing and advertising policy, (Cunard having resigned from the North Atlantic conference which operated as a restrictive practices cartel to prevent undue competition), the ship would be in the black the following year.

Apart from these, other problems were to be found. The container investment was only precariously able to break even and with the freight market weak, the other cargo liners, which together with the containers were the largest element in the total package, were in the red. The Sunair-Lunn Poly travel business was also a loser at the time.

In traditional Matthews style, the board was removed and middle managers promoted. The 25 ships of the Port Line which had formerly been managed by Blue Star were brought back into Cunard's management. Financial controls were put in.

Within a year Matthews had managed to turn Cunard round and only felt it necessary to spend about three hours a week on this side of the business. Apart from the management reorganisation and the financial controls instigated, the year saw the sale of 17 smaller and older cargo ships, the improvement in freight rates and the disposal of Cunards travel agency business. Further rationalisation and modernisation of the Cunard fleet followed together with the expansion of the number of oil product and bulk carriers, and offshore supply vessels.

Cunard soon became a major element in the Trafalgar House strategy despite the fact that the world's shipping industry was experiencing a severe slump. Cunard remained relatively unaffected until 1978 with profits tending to increase. In 1976 Trafalgar added substantially to its cargo fleet with the shrewd purchase of ten refrigerated fruit carriers from the creditors of the defunct Maritime Fruit Carriers making Cunard a major force in this specialised sector of the shipping market. By 1977 the profit contribution from shipping and hotels had reached £17.7m including £3.9m generated from the sale of ships. Container interests and refrigerated cargo represented the bright spots in performance but the decline in cargo foreshadowed severe problems which overtook the group in 1978, resulting in the sale of the entire Cunard bulk carrier fleet. Moreover increased operating costs and declining revenue caused problems in passenger shipping with the doyen of the Cunard fleet, the QE2, proving a particular headache by 1979.

A further related extension of Trafalgars marine ambitions was thwarted after making a successful $33m tender offer to acquire a 40 per cent interest in the U.S. based Dearborn-Storm Corporation, a leading offshore drilling and marine supply company. The U.S. Federal Maritime Commission refused permission for Trafalgar to add to its 40 per cent stake and in 1974 this interest was sold.

In 1977, however, Trafalgar entered the air freight business via the purchase of Transmeridian Air Cargo, the operator of a small fleet of longhaul cargo planes which it was hoped to integrate with Cunard's world-wide marketing organisation.

THE THIRD LEG—ENTRY INTO FLEET STREET

In 1974 the U.K. economy was struck by the secondary banking crisis which was triggered by a collapse of the property market. Unlike most of the entrepreneur-led companies created in the 1960's such as Slater Walker Securities, Trafalgar survived the crisis, although from 1974 to 1976 no major acquisitions were undertaken as the group rode out the storm. By 1976 profits and cashflow had recovered and Trafalgar could begin again to assume its course for growth. This was to involve entry into another major area of activity.

Describing how Trafalgar had come to add its third main leg, Mr. Broackes noted:

'It was in May 1977, at lunch at the Ritz, that I persuaded Victor that we could, and should, buy the Beaverbrook Newspaper Group . . . My first contact with one of their directors occurred at a dinner party at Claridges in April 1975 . . . and I mentioned that in my view, Beaverbrook had financial and management problems which would in due course prove to be beyond their ability to solve. If, I said, they ever needed rescue from the unwelcome attention of another company please bear us in mind. Two years later, things came to a head.

'Before I describe the acquisition itself let me revert to Victor and his state of mind at the time. He was morbid and morose, and yearned for the days when we had both run individual operations . . . and I had to face the possibility that we might lose Victor altogether. I do not want to sound flippant, and there were several other good reasons to want to buy a newspaper group which, whatever its problems, sold more than 20 million papers per week, but I must admit that, at the forefront of my mind, was the desire to see Victor once again engrossed with a challenge—something that would gratify and occupy him, leaving free part of his time for all the rest of Trafalgar . . . '

There were many parties interested in Beaverbrook, including Vere Harmsworth, now Lord Rothermere, who controlled the *Daily Mail* and *Evening News*, Rupert Murdoch, proprietor of the *Sun* and *News of the World*, Tiny Rowland and Lonrho and Sir James Goldsmith. These approaches were resisted by Sir Max Aitken and the trusts established by Lord Beaverbrook which controlled the voting shares in Beaverbrook. Following mediation with Evelyn de Rothschild, Chairman of Rothschild Bank, terms were agreed between the Aitken trustees and Trafalgar and on June 30, 1977 Beaverbrook became a subsidiary.

Victor Matthews was appointed as Chairman of Beaverbrook and was almost immediately put to a trial of strength with the Fleet Street trades unions. In early September the engineers at Beaverbrook in London stopped the presses when asked to resume normal work during a union chapel meeting. Mr. Matthews counter-attacked by switching production of the *Daily Express* to Manchester and telling union leaders that he intended to impose new standards of discipline via a code of practice. Commenting, Mr. Broackes added:

' . . . Victor produced a list of 18 conditions without accepting which, those men who had been sacked, would not be re-engaged. The crisis reached its peak on a Saturday, by which time we had lost several hundred thousand pounds. Victor telephoned me four times; the third call was just after lunch and I asked him where he was: "At home, doing the washing up", he told me . . .
"They seem to have agreed to everything", he said, in doleful tones.
"Then why do you sound so depressed", I asked.
"Because its been too easy", he replied.'

Mr. Matthews saw the *Daily Express* as being positioned as a family paper appealing to a pool of people who wanted positive journalism without soft pornography, although the paper was moved downmarket somewhat. To appeal to those who did like nipples, Matthews launched a new morning tabloid, the *Daily Star*, initially based in Manchester. In addition, a new weekly magazine, *Financial Weekly*, was launched in 1979 after efforts to purchase the *Investors Chronicle* from the *Financial Times* had failed. Other new enterprises were also under consideration, including a new London evening and a new Sunday newspaper. Commenting upon these ideas for new products, Mr. Matthews added 'the newspaper industry is not overmanned but under-employed'.

Following the purchase of Beaverbrook Newspapers, Trafalgar increased its penetration into publishing with the acquisition of Morgan Grampian Ltd, the publisher of a wide range of business and specialist consumer magazines in the U.K. and business magazines and books in the U.S.A. At a cost of £21 million cash the company was expected to make a pre-tax return of £3.75m in the year to the end of March 1978 and with Beaverbrook (renamed Express Newspapers) formed the basis of a new Printing, Publishing and Communications Division.

ORGANISATION AND CONTROL

Early in in their partnership Nigel Broackes and Victor Matthews sat down and deliberately mapped out the way they wanted Trafalgar House to develop and grow. The basic idea was to develop expertise and practical experience in fields ancillary to their main original functions of property investment and development for investment. To guide the company in its development an executive committee was established in 1970 composed of Nigel Broackes, Victor Matthews and Eric Parker. For their own purposes they made a distinction between direction, management and labour, with them basically concerned with direction, but on a day-to-day basis. Within the team Matthews regarded Broackes as more of the thinker and himself as the doer. 'I suppose', he commented, 'that the part of Nigel really plays is to be constantly thinking about the next move. Nine out of ten of his ideas (though) don't come to anything for one reason or another . . . '.

'The real difference between Nigel and myself', he continued, 'is that he is basically a property man (and) I have always been a trading man, a commercial man, especially in construction'. Mr. Broackes recognised that when the decision was taken to diversify into more management situations he was 'the thinker, the entrepreneur' and not 'the disciplinarian or the manager of large numbers of people'.

'In my view', Broakes added, 'the Chairman of a large and diverse public company should not handle individual, routine, trading transactions, and should not identify himself too closely with any one particular division. He should be impartially concerned with all of them, and it is they who must deal with the outside world'. Mr. Broackes estimated that the affairs of Trafalgar House took up around 60 per cent of his time. He no longer took a detailed interest in the day to day running of the company, preferring to leave that to Mr. Matthews and Mr. Parker, while he considered the company's long term aims.

Although Matthews, Broackes and Parker dominated the company's

EXHIBIT 4

Trafalgar House Investment Organisation Structure 1979

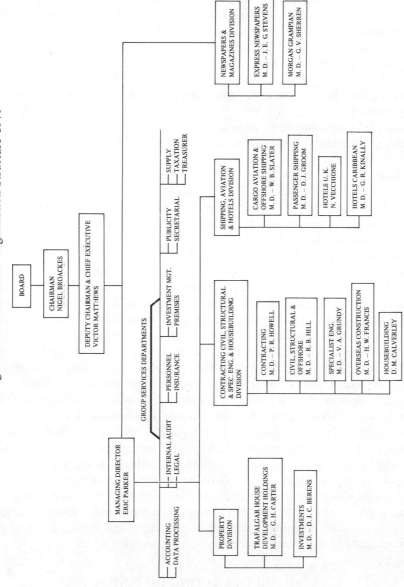

Source: Annual Report

affairs, they had modified their original tight 'cabinet system' of top management to give more authority to the chief executives of the major operating subsidiaries, a number of which had been appointed to the Trafalgar House Board. Details of the group organisation structure are shown in Exhibit 4. Following the acquisition of Beaverbrook the top management responsibilities of Trafalgar had been modifed with Mr. Parker becoming Group Managing Director and Mr. Matthews Deputy Chairman and Group Chief Executive. As a result all the divisions (except Beaverbrook) and head office services reported to Mr. Parker. He in turn reported to Mr. Matthews who was operationally responsible for Beaverbrook.

The initiative for new acquisitions still started mainly at the top, although individual divisions were expected to handle their own infill purchases.

'Once we are in control (of a company) we can use our skills to restore the position', said Matthews. 'But after a takeover you must not rush in and start "cleaning up" immediately—you just might destroy the good and leave the bad. First you must get to know what makes the company tick and the personalities involved.'

This approach had been consistently adopted and having acquainted themselves fully with the company taken over, their most urgent task had been to examine the loss-makers with a view to eliminating them or to making them profitable. At the same time, they had clarified and allocated responsibilities for each operating unit so as to establish a clear and direct chain of command for financial control, targets and reporting.

The basic philosophy had been to secure tight central control of finance and overall policy but to encourage individual operating companies to preserve and enhance their identities in their respective fields. They intended to restrict each operating company to what it did best and back this up with Group service facilities in specialist fields. This was to have three main effects on operating companies: overheads being reduced, technical services being increased in quality and specialist staff who in the past might have been difficult to employ effectively, being employed on a Group basis. Furthermore, a share incentive scheme designed for the senior executives on the Boards of the various subsidiaries had been introduced so as to promote Group loyalties and enable individual participants, each concerned with their particular and individual operation, to participate in the future success of the Group as a whole.

MAJOR OPERATING DIVISIONS

In 1979 Trafalgar House consisted of four major operating divisions, Property, General Construction, Civil, Structural and Specialist Engineering and Housebuilding, Shipping and Hotels and Newspapers and Magazines. Details of recent divisional performance are shown in Exhibit 5.

EXHIBIT 5
Divisional Turnover & Net Revenue Contributions 1972–78 (£'000)

	1978	1977	1976	1975	1974	1973	1972
Property Investments							
Receipts inc. gross rental	65953	29920	14842	20300	11669	13669	12436
Net rental income	2045	3182	3211	1878	1686	1657	1381
Completed development profits	20581	4733	3136	3839	2551	4865	3157
Total property income	22626	7915	5447	5717			
Quoted investment income	1545	528	363	440	385	334	180
Profits on share sales	3877	368	1292	147	(633)	165	768
Interest charged to divisions	9609	7155	6374	5186	4118	1175	382
Total Investment Income	15031	8051	8029	5773			
Contracting, Construction etc.							
Turnover	386109	310486	267616	225253	144369	145491	139502
Net revenue	20296	16857	14758	8582	6678	8668	7156
Shipping, Aviation & Hotels							
Gross Receipts	233158	222596	165935	137154	118757	99752	75122
Net revenue	2954	17664	9376	11262	9632	4967	3236
including ship sales	3213	3886	1725	214	3438	—	—
Newspapers and Magazines							
Turnover	139783	24260	—	—	—	—	—
Net revenue	3200	(239)	—	—	—	—	—
Industrial and General							
Turnover	—	—	—	—	6677	9943	9432
Net revenue	—	—	—	—	598	1435	901
GROUP TOTAL							
Turnover	825003	587262	448393	387707	281468	268855	236492
Net revenue	64107	50248	37610	31334	25015	23266	17161

PROPERTY DIVISION

At the end of 1978 the total book value of group properties was £77.5 million of which investment property represented £47.6 million. This latter value was substantially down on the book value of over £63 million in 1975 as Trafalgar pursued a policy of disposing of a number of its investment properties from 1976 to 1978. Actual values of property were considered to be in excess of their 1970 valuations at which they were included in the accounts plus subsequent additions.

Starting in 1977 Trafalgar began selling its largest completed office developments in the City of London and in 1979 it was intended to sell several smaller ones over the next few years together with Trafalgar's interest in the massive joint venture to develop Whitbread sites for some 400,000 square feet of office accommodation. As a result the property division was becoming less capital intensive. In 1978 property sales produced income of £20.6 million compared with £4.7 million in 1977. By contrast rental income was £2.0 million, down from £3.18 million the previous year.

Trafalgar also operated an investment activity which largely consisted of making group loans to the operating subsidiaries. In 1977 these loans produced nominal interest payments of £7.2m which rose to £9.6m in 1978. The sale of Trafalgar's share stake in the Savoy group also produced a substantial capital profit of around £3 million in 1978.

CONSTRUCTION DIVISION

Construction accounted for some £20.2 million of Trafalgar's profits in 1978, up from £15.9m the previous year. The construction activities of Trafalgar were subdivided into a series of holding companies, as follows:

General Contracting—was managed by Trollope and Colls Holdings and offered a wide range of contracting services each managed by an operating company which maintained its own identity, character and specific skills. Major activities included building and contracting, plant hire, specialist plaster work and ceilings, electrical contracting, joinery and decorative metalwork, open cast coal mining and scaffolding contracting.

Overseas Contracting—Via Cementation International, Trafalgar undertook contracting outside the U.K. The company was active in a number of countries notably in Eastern Europe, but following the collapse of the government in Iran, Trafalgar were taking a cautious attitude to work in some developing countries.

Civil Structural and Offshore Engineering—Under a holding company, Cementation Civil, Structural and Offshore Engineering Holdings,

Trafalgar operated a series of structural engineering subsidiaries including Cleveland Bridge, which was concerned with structural steelwork in the U.K. and via a joint venture in Dubai, oil and gas process engineering via a 50 per cent holding in a Houston based operation and civil engineering constructing via Cementation Construction.

Specialist Engineering—These activities operated under Cementation Specialist Holdings and consisted largely of the specialist engineering activities of Cementation. Specialist engineering was carried out in the U.K. and a number of overseas countries. In recent years Cementation Mining had been particularly active, developing mine shafts and the like.

Housebuilding—This activity operated under the Ideal Building Corporation and consisted of housebuilding largely throughout the South East and North of England. Operations which were started in Western Europe were discontinued in 1978.

SHIPPING AND HOTELS DIVISION

Trafalgar's shipping activities were subdivided into Cargo, Aviation and Offshore and Passenger Shipping. By 1978 both subdivisions were in some difficulty as a result of the world shipping crisis. Trafalgar had reduced the size of the Cunard fleet by disposing of the company's six bulk carriers in 1978, most of its conventional cargo fleet and over half of its product carriers. In November 1976 Cunard's fleet was over 670,000 equivalent gross tons and by the same time in 1978 this tonnage had been reduced to under 500,000 tons, concentrated mainly in container services (127,000 tons), refrigerated cargo ships (87,000 tons), product carriers (88,000 tons) and refrigerated fruit carriers (94,000 tons).

Cunard's passenger shipping interest by the end of 1978 consisted of three ships—the QE2 plus two small specialist cruise ships of 17,500 tons each, delivered in 1976 and 1977 and serving the Caribbean. The size and economics of the QE2 proved a threat to its long term viability.

Hotel operations consisted of a number of London luxury hotels spearheaded by the Ritz which had been extensively refurbished and two hotels in the Caribbean linked to the Cunard cruising programme. The value of Trafalgar's hotel properties amounted to £27.7 million at the end of 1978.

Shipping and hotel operations in 1978 showed a net loss after profits of £3.2m from the sale of ships were taken into account.

NEWSPAPERS AND MAGAZINES

The newest addition to the group, Newspapers and Magazines Division, consisted of Express Newspapers and Morgan Grampian. In 1978 these interests produced £3.2 million profits after charging those operations with notional interest of £3.5m on the cost of their acquisition. Under Mr. Matthews guidance a substantial improvement in the profitability of Express Newspapers had occurred although it was still too early to decide whether this improvement would be maintained.

ACQUISITIONS AND DISPOSALS POLICY

Matthews and Broackes both had a clear idea of what they were looking for in an acquisition prospect. 'We like', said Matthews, 'the best companies with the best names where they have been going through a thin patch but are in a recovery situation'.

Unlike other aggressive acquirers in the late 1960's and early 1970's Trafalgar did not believe in merely buying sleepy companies, ripping out and selling off loss makers to build the profitable core. Mr. Broackes elaborated:

'We only wanted Trafalgar to develop with enterprises which we would cherish and retain. Victor's personality and nature coloured this paternalistic attitude. Eric had installed systems to service enterprises which would be integrated and improved and I was concerned with a ratchet-like concept to built brick by brick, a structure that would endure.'

In December 1976 Mr. Broackes revealed that Trafalgar's relatively high level of debt, then standing at £230 million, would be reduced by 1981 to £50 million as shown in Exhibit 6. This was to be achieved by a programme of ship sales and improved group cash flow. At the same time gross assets were expected to rise to over £500 million. In addition property sales of some £60m were expected with the recovery of the property market. Other disposals were also possible in line with the routine reallocation of assets.

Following the purchase of Beaverbrook and Morgan Grampian, Trafalgar had no major acquisitions in mind in 1979 although the company was interested in opportunities where, after acquisition, substantial and worthwhile further investment in plant, machinery and the like could follow. Mr. Broackes recognised, however, 'Such occasions are hard to find for not only in this country is it the case that most direct capital investment offers only inadequate returns. For this reason we may incline somewhat more than in the past towards service and non-capital intensive industries . . . '.

He also advised shareholders at the end of 1978 that Trafalgar would continue to buy small companies as the opportunity arose and where the activity in question fitted directly into one of the existing operating divisions.

EXHIBIT 6

Trafalgar House – Projected Corporate Borrowings to 1981

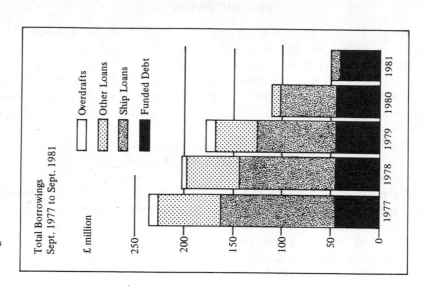

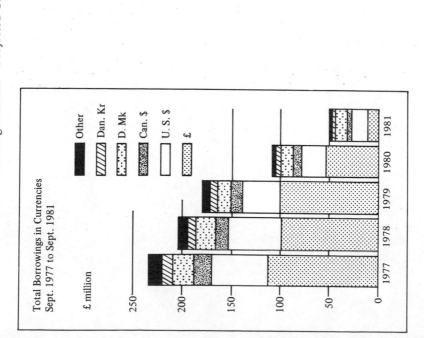

Source: Annual Report 1976.

FUTURE PROSPECTS

Results in 1979 showed a sharp decline on 1978 for the half year. Severe losses occurred in shipping which lost £8.1m and as property sales diminished profits from property were sharply down. In all, net revenue before tax was £16.3m compared with £29.5m for the first half of 1978.

While the figures for 1979 were not as bad as some City analysts predicted, there were still questions over the future strategy of the group. As the *Daily Telegraph* noted:

> 'Trafalgar is still working hard at changing its image from a financial/property group to an industrial company but so far the only trading leg which makes a solid contribution to profits is construction and here the progress is likely to be steady rather than exciting.
>
> Moreover, while the shipping side is operating at a probable loss rate of around £14m per year and until the group's new shape becomes better defined, the longer term prospects will remain shrouded in uncertainty.'

Appendix

Writing Case Reports

Reports are one of the main methods of business communication. The objectives of this guide are to help you, the reader of this book, write good case study reports and to provide a model which will help you in writing good business reports in the future. A case report is intended to provide an opportunity to apply the analytical skills and frameworks that you have previously learnt to a real business situation.

A case report is normally addressed to the company in question and should be written in such a way that the reader in the company will both understand its analysis and argument, and act on its recommendations or conclusions. A report should not be addressed to the course instructor. It must be in jargon-free business English, well argued, supported by sound analysis and have recommendations for action.

1. AUDIENCE

Knowing who is going to read a report will enable you to give the reader what he or she wants and needs. Before you put pen to paper be sure you can answer these questions:

—Who is my reader(s)?
—How much time will they have to read my report? (This indicates the maximum length of the report.)
—What is their relationship to me? (This will determine the tone of your writing—formal, authoritative, friendly or whatever.)
—How much do they know about the subject? (This will indicate what information can safely be omitted.)
—What to they want from this report? (This is the most important question of all, and you should bear it in mind constantly while you write, to be sure you are staying on the track.)

2. STRUCTURING THE REPORT

A report should logically argue a set of recommendations based on analysis, argument and justification. A report can be short, long, loose or highly structured depending on the writer and the context in which the report is written. No two reports will be alike. For case studies, whoever assigns the report will give you some guidelines as to what is needed, and with experience you will be able to rely more on your own judgement. The following is a model structure that can be used without major alteration for most reports, case study and business.

2.1 Model

—Title Page
   A cover page giving information on the title, origin etc.

—Summary
   A brief summary of the subject of the report and the recommendations. (On the title page is a case report.)

—Introduction
   A statement of the problems and purposes of the report. It may give background information and list the topics to be covered in the report, and/or a statement of the objectives of the company, departments etc.

—Analysis
   An analysis of the existing situation; identification of problems, causes and patterns; statement of assumptions.

—Statement and evaluation of alternatives
   In many instances some or all of the action that will be proposed will flow directly from the analysis. However often there are a number of distinct alternatives (including do nothing), which each have pros and cons. This section identifies and evaluates each of them.

—Recommendation and Implementation
   A statement and justification of each recommendation, with what steps that may be necessary to implement them. It will normally be completed with a concluding sentence or paragraph.

—Exhibits
   Much of the detailed figure analysis can be shown best in tabular or graph form as exhibits (usually placed at the end of the text in a case report).

A more detailed description of this model structure, together with examples is given in Appendix 1. This model is not intended as an outline for every report that you will write, you may choose to vary it, omit or emphasise particular elements. The chosen shape of the report will partly be determined by the audience and the content. Whatever structure that you use it is important to remember that the final recommendations must be argued, justified and supported by sound analysis. If much of your analysis is contained in exhibits then you must pay special care in referring to and drawing conclusion from them in the text. Exhibits are rarely self-explanatory.

A final word on structure is given by Eamonn Dunne (1):

'PRESENT IT BACK TO FRONT'

'Conclusions first, details last: that's the way to make your report more effective.

By arranging it so that the nuggets are on top, then the shale, and finally the sand, you allow the reader to decide for himself how much digging he needs to do to satisfy himself about the evidence which supports your conclusions. The less he needs to read, the more you should be pleased.

A business report is the raw material for a decision. The decision-maker does not want fine prose. He just hopes the writer has got his facts right; that he will spit them out without preamble; and that he can back them in detail, if necessary.

Report writing is not an art form. Don't build up to a dramatic climax, as in music or poetry. Start with the conclusion, and work down. Support it with the broad details. Then tuck in all the fine particles, so that they are there—and seen to be there—if they are needed.

As a rule, if your first page takes more than about a minute to read, it is not a conclusion. In ordinary business life, it is unusual to find a situation so complex that its essence cannot be distilled into five or six statements.

The reader may be ready to accept some of your conclusions instinctively. Others he may want to question. Almost certainly, he will consider some points more interesting, surprising or incredible than the rest. So your report should be set out and indexed, so that he can skip what he wants to skip, and go straight to the points which interest him most.

So you actually help him ignore most of what you have written.

The novelist hates the thought of a reader who skips pages or turns to the last one first "to see how it ends". But that is exactly what the serious report writer helps the reader to do: to read the last page first.

That is why he puts the last page first.'

3. WRITING THE REPORT

No matter how good the quality of the analysis, no report is of any use unless the reader both reads and understands it. The following steps will help you meet these objectives.

—Think

Analyse the problem thoroughly before you begin to write. Know what you are going to say and what your conclusions will be.

—Outline

Jot down the main ideas to be covered. A page or so of key words and phrases, arranged in logical order, will guide you in writing the body of the report.

—Write

Following your outline, write the body of the report. Write the introduction and conclusion last.

—Rest

Take a break for as long as you can. Give your a mind a rest. Then take a fresh look at what you have written.

—Revise

Rewrite awkward or obscure parts. Besides checking grammar and spelling, be on the lookout for unnecessary wordiness or repetition. Try to cut down your original draft to the most concise prose possible. Business reports are different from other academic writing, so stifle that impulse to embellish and "pad" what you have written: concentrate on paring it down (including exhibits).

—Proofread

Remember that you are responsible for errors in the final copy.

4. OTHER CONSIDERATIONS

—Avoid jargon

A good report should be easy to read. A lot of this comes down to good style and nothing ruins style as much as jargon and long words.

—Assumptions

The use of assumptions is a tricky decision in writing case study reports. On the one hand carefully selected simplifying assumptions can lead to a much clearer analysis. On the other hand cavalier use of assumptions to over-simplify the problems or alternatives will make a report meaningless. Assumptions should be reasonable and have a sound base.

—Argument and Justification

In any report, especially a case study report the reader will expect the conclusions or recommendations to follow directly and logically from the analysis. This requires that at a very minimum the conclusions and recommendations are connected to the analysis and not just stated in isolation. Normally there should be a proper, if brief, argument or justification. This may be contained in the recommendation section or it may be built into the analysis. It is particularly important to build in a proper argument or justification if conclusions are reached on recommendations made with the consideration of discreet alternatives.

—Collaboration

You will probably discuss case reports with your colleagues, but the report is expected to be your own work. You may use group exhibits, but be sure to include a footnote indicating that it is a group exhibit and naming the group members.

—Length

Reports are invariably much longer than they need to be to fulfil their objectives. Frequently case reports can be cut to half or even a third of.their length with a *gain* in clarity of argument. Ideas get lost in excessive verbiage. When writing, try to write concisely. Your instructor will usually give guidelines on length, please follow them.

—Repetition

Avoid repeating facts which are already well known to the reader and are not being used directly in your argument. Don't rewrite the case.

—Company Contacts

Do not contact companies or businessmen regarding cases without the specific consent of a faculty member.

—Use of the Library and References

In most case reports, you will not need to use outside information. Frequently, however, additional relevant material which will aid you in your work can be found in a business library. Of course, if you do use information from texts, journals, etc., the source must be credited. Use of such material and application of ideas and knowledge from other courses can provide perspective.

5. CONCLUSION

The ability to write reports that will be read and acted upon is a vital skill in Business. Considering the following can help you write good reports.

—Write for your audience
—Structure your report
—Know what you are going to say
—Say it clearly and concisely
—Argue and justify your conclusions and recommendations.

Appendix 1

STRUCTURE AND FORMAT OF A REPORT

1. Title Page

The title page is a cover sheet giving the following information:

TO: The Person IN THE CASE receiving the report (NOT the course instructor)

FROM: The writer of the report (YOU). (Even if the assignment says to write 'as Fred Smith', put *your* name on the title page so the instructor will know who wrote the report).

DATE: The date the report is submitted

SUBJECT: ⎰ These two items
⎱ comprise the
RECOMMENDATIONS: ⎱ Summary

2. Summary

In the model format, the summary appears on the title page. Here it is merely a brief statement of (1) the subject of the report and (2) its main recommendations. Exhibit 1 shows a sample title page, including summary.

On longer reports, the summary (often called the 'Executive Summary') will be a separate section, often highlighted by the use of a different coloured paper or a different typeface.

EXHIBIT 1

To:	Mr. Jonas, Managing Director, Excelsior Luggage Co. Ltd.
From:	Philip Fisher
Date:	February 2 1980
Subject:	Evaluation of accounting procedures and alternative investment proposals.
Recommendations:	1. That Excelsior change from full costing to direct costing accounting.
	2. That Excelsior purchase plastic shells from an extruder, for assembly into the new suitcase line.
	3. That Excelsior define clearly the problems with its customer service, and take steps to remedy them.

3. Introduction

Remember that your reader has just read your Summary, so he knows a bit about what you are going to cover.

A good introduction begins with a statement of the problem, perhaps with some background information, and states the purpose of the report. If you wish, you may then list the points to be covered in the report—for example, 'This report deals with the following topics: the consumer analysis, a statement of the alternatives, the chosen alternative and the plan of implementation'. You can use point form if the report is long. Make sure the titles you mention in your preview of the plan match those in the report.

Do not tell the reader how you went about writing the report. In some disciplines, such as Quantitative Methods, the tools used in analysis must be specified, but this specification should be presented in a separate section, not in the body of the report. Some report writers like to tell the reader what conclusion they reached in the introduction, but since the recommendation has been stated on the title page, mentioning it here is not necessary.

Please note that in the model format, the introduction is the only section without a heading. Exhibit 2 is an example of an introduction to a report.

EXHIBIT 2

In view of management's January decision to introduce slim line bottles into the off-trade lines, the company must make a decision regarding the particular crating methodology to be used as well as the best means to implement it.

The company is presently involved in a dual packing process: large plastic crates are now being used in the pub trade whereas off-trade lines are for the most part being packed in the traditional cardboard boxes. The savings involved in using plastic crates are substantial, and is is only recently that the competitive situation has changed sufficiently to allow plastic crates in off-trade orders as well. The crating activity itself takes place in the bottling department and consequently any and all changes will be confined to this department.

The first paragraph states the problem. Note that after reading the problem statement, you want to read on. After the introductory paragraph, the writer sets the limits of the report he is about to write by stating that all changes will be confined to the bottling department.

Another approach is to follow the statement of the problem with a description of the action necessary to remedy the situation. This approach is suitable if the action outlined is dealt with in the same order, in the report itself. In Exhibit 3, the author states the problem and the cause. He then outlines the process which must be followed to remedy the situation.

EXHIBIT 3

At present, Andrews Electronics Ltd. is being plagued by shortages in component parts, causing assembly delays and unacceptable increases in material and labour costs. With 18,000 parts required for its product lines, and a generally low demand for each, the company's manufacturing operations can be characterised as a job shop. Because of inefficient operations, the company is not as certain as it could be about the capabilities, economics, and requirements of its equipment and process technology. Before a decision to make or buy parts can be considered, the two alternatives should be compared. To do this, three general problem areas must first be improved. These areas are:

    (i) control over quality of production,
   (ii) control over inventory and
  (iii) scheduling.

3.1 Statement of the Company's Objectives

At the outset of a report, many writers like to state the company's objectives explicitly. Often a reader disagrees with the objectives you have set out, so it is better to let him know early. In stating the objectives of the company, gather the material ONLY from the case. Confine your discussion to only those objectives which will affect your decision.

You should be well aware of the fact that once you enter a business, it may not be necessary to state the company's objectives if you believe that the objectives are commonly known.

Exhibits 4 and 5 show ways of stating objectives. Note that the writer in Exhibit 5 decided to combine the company's background with its objectives.

4. Analysis

In the introduction, you have stated the main problem(s) and provided a plan of the report. In this section you should show the detailed analysis needed to identify the problems, their causes and possible solutions. In

EXHIBIT 4

Objectives

The objectives of J.K. Beverages are as follows:

(a) To remain competitive in the soft drink industry and maintain a high level of sales;
(b) To maintain its present steady rate of production despite seasonal sales fluctuations;
(c) To reduce labour and material costs of production in the Bottling Department; and
(d) To switch over the slim line bottles for all customers by June of this year.

EXHIBIT 5

Background and Objectives

Provincial Furniture Company Limited is a well-established, profitable, and stable operation.
The firm has responded to changing times by producing over half of its 12 suites with contemporary styling. Management has maintained that it wants to be known for making well designed merchandise of top quality, and definitely does not want to be known as a manufacturer of cheaper furniture. The firm has shown an aggressive sales policy. Eventually, management wishes to establish company distribution agents in place of the present agents.

many cases it will contain general analysis of the company's situation such as a financial ratio analysis, production process analysis, consumer and market analysis. This will provide a background for identifying and evaluating problems and solutions, together with any background information that the reader needs to understand your report.

In this section, you may wish to expand the statement of the problem so that every important item is mentioned. You may also wish to mention facts in the case which affect any of your alternative solutions to the problem. Certain assumptions may have been included in your analysis, and these can be explicitly stated in the analysis section.

In the introduction you may have mentioned a series of problems. In this section you could show how subordinate problems are interrelated. You could also discuss the causes of the problems at hand. Often a problem may be a symptom of a difficulty elsewhere in the organisation. This is the place to expose this type of information. Be sure to identify opinions, as opposed to facts, in the section (as in all others). In your analysis you may want to include information from readings or from previous cases. Include only information which affects this case directly.

As you write reports on cases you will notice that you must include some information which will not be needed as you write reports in industry. An instructor often wants to be sure that you have grasped the problem and can analyse the situation and apply specific methods of analysis or frameworks. As a result, case reports often include large analysis sections. A well written analysis will have an internal structure and logic that leads the leader from point to point and from analysis to conclusion.

4.1 Use of Exhibits

Much qualitative and quantitative analysis can best be presented as tables, graphs or lists in exhibits at the end of the report. This tends to make the report much easier to read and write, and arguments easier to structure. A vital skill is making the best use of the exhibits. Be sure to refer to each exhibit specifically; the reader will not normally read exhibits except when instructed to do so in the text. Explain carefully what the exhibits mean and what conclusions you are drawing from them. For example:

'Exhibit 7 shows that, on an average day, the Vickers packing machine will be a bottleneck. . . '

'The market for up-market cars, can be divided into a number of segments, (these are shown in Exhibit 2).'

4.2 Methods Used in Analysis

In many reports the method of analysis must be explicitly presented. This is necessary only when the plan of action is not obvious. For instance, do not say 'first I looked at Marketing, then I examined Finance, etc.' However, in a report dealing with quantitative data you may want to mention the computer program or statistical methods being used to analyse the problem.

4.3 Assumptions

You must decide whether it is important to state your assumptions in any given situation, so that your reader can better understand why you recommend a certain course of action. For instance, you might assume that no staff changes can be made; this assumption definitely limits your range of alternatives, and should probably be stated. Such assumptions should be reasonable given their context.

Be absolutely sure that the assumptions you are using are valid and are empirically supportable. If you are not sure of your assumptions reread the case to clarify your thinking.

Be careful to avoid unreasonable or cavalier assumptions, that assume away major parts of the problem or barriers to solutions.

5. Statement and Evaluation of the Alternatives

So far you have discussed the problem. You may have elected to present an analysis of the company's situation, the company's objectives, your objectives or your assumptions. Keep in mind what you have done, before beginning to write this section. If in your analysis you have progressed logically to a single solution or have already analysed the major alternatives you may choose to omit or not go into great detail in this section.

Often some action will be taken regardless of which alternative is chosen; some factors may influence the company regardless of the choice. State these points before you scrutinize each alternative for the reader.

Start by numbering alternatives (if there are more than two) and briefly stating each.

Give the reader all the information you have on each of the alternatives. Tell him their advantages and disadvantages. Tell him which facts in the case support which alternatives and why. Discuss the quantitative and qualitative aspects of each alternative. If you have a decision tree, discuss each branch briefly.

Now you can evaluate the alternatives. Discuss the monetary and non-monetary consequences of each of the alternatives. State clearly the criteria you are using to evaluate them. In this section, the discussion should be as neutral and objective as possible, leaving the final decision for the next sections, although some authors prefer to state which alternative they have chosen in their list of alternatives. In the latter case the chosen alternative is presented last, after the unusable alternatives had been rejected.

An 'Analysis of Alternatives' section is presented in Exhibit 6. In this case, the author had two alternatives. He decided to treat the first in detail since he was to reject it. Note that the second, and better alternative has very little information attached to it.

EXHIBIT 6

Analysis of the Alternatives

1. Introduce the New Cap
The present value of the earnings generated under the best sales and production conditions do not provide an adequate return (15 per cent) on funds invested. If the new cap does not sell as expected, the earnings provide almost no return on total net investment. The conclusions are generally the same, regardless of the model of equipment chosen. Exhibit 13 shows that increasing the selling price by £.005 lowers the level of return.
If the Roberts Company entered the market, SCC's earnings would be drastically reduced.
The effect of introducing the new cap on the company's 'book' income statement would be moderate under the best conditions. The profits illustrated in Exhibits 5 and 6 would be adjusted downward by the 'book' depreciation value. (Gordon—£27,100; Rogers—£37,300). The losses in the exhibits would be greater by the amount of 'book' depreciation.
At present the company is sufficiently liquid to cover current liabilities. The proposed investment of funds in machinery and working capital would require financing of £439,000 to £813,000. This would increase the company's debt to equity ratio, an effect which may not be desirable.
Introduction of the new cap would definitely enhance SCC's position as a leader in the beer bottling market. However, the cost to do this would not merit the potential return.
The expected monetary values for the equipment purchase decisions are very large negative amounts. This indicates that the company should not purchase either machine.
2. Do Nothing
This alternative allows the company or its holders to invest its funds in other projects which will earn a fifteen per cent return rate.

6. Recommendations and Plan of Implementation

The alternatives have been presented and evaluated. It is now your task to choose an alternative and recommend a course of action.

Remember that your main recommendation was stated on the title page. In this section you must specify each recommendation in detail and where necessary provide a detailed plan of implementation. Too many reports recommend and then end. Most reports should contain a section on how to implement the recommended changes. the 'Implementation of Recommendation' section in Exhibit 7 illustrates one method of handling this section. The author deals with personnel, the pay system and the phasing-out of employees.

EXHIBIT 7

Implementation of Recommendations

Mr. Jackson is being accepted be neither management nor the employees in his area (as indicated previously), and should be fired. Staff must be hired to replace those removed, possibly from within the cutting department. They must be capable of leading and training the operators. Training skills can be learned from the five existing people and from the engineer's training file.

Incorporate an incentive pay system with the base rate at standard production, phasing the system in as standard times are achieved. The 25% increase in work pace (see Exhibit VIII) in moving to the new system, can be reflected in the pay scale.

Twenty-three employees must be phased out of this department. The company employs 1,000 people. Assuming a low turnover rate of 10%, 20 jobs become available every two or three months. This programme of implementation has a six month deadline. Jobs in other sections of the plant can be offered to the women when they are no longer required in this department.

Management employee relations should not be strained if this method of inter-company movement is encouraged, and employees will strive for standard operations if they wish to stay in the department.

6.1 Conclusion

Most reports need a conclusion to sum up what has gone before or to make a forecast for the future (e.g., 'The adoption of these recommendations should result in an immediate increase in sales for the Gadget Division of QRS Company'.)

Do, however, avoid the fatuous. A report can only be weakened by a statement such as: 'I hope this attempt at consumer analysis will be of some assistance to the company, although I'm not too sure that all the findings are valid'.

7 Exhibits

Exhibits are normally placed at the end of the report as it is usually easier to assemble exhibits before writing and revising the text. In larger reports they are often placed in the text, when they are often referred to as tables or figures.

Exhibits are used to show data and analysis supporting the various sections of the text. Care in design and presentation of exhibits can greatly increase the impact of a report. Graphs and charts should be clear, with both axes properly labelled. Other visual forms of showing relationships between figures include histograms and pie charts. Raw data is often presented in table form. Ehrenberg (2) has suggested a number of guidelines for clear presentation of data in tables:

- —round to two effective digits
- —give row and column averages
- —put figures you want the reader to compare into columns, not rows
- —order the rows and columns by size (with the biggest number on top, where possible)
- —use single spacing between rows, and keep the columns close together too.
- —don't draw lines within the body of the table: they discourage the eye from sweeping down or across. If you want to separate off part of the table, leave an extra gap.
- —give a meaningful label to each row and column
- —give each table a one-sentence summary showing the main story.

References

1. Dunne, Eamonn. 'How to Make your Report more Acceptable. Present it "Back-to-front",' quoted in Madeiros, Lewis & Holmes, *Report Writing Handbook* (University of Western Ontario, 1975). Adapted by P. Barwise.
2. Ehrenberg, ASC, 'Some Rules of Data Presentation', Executive Office of the President: *Statistical Reporter*. May 1977, pp 306–310.